"Joel Williams's volume on Mark is a strong add
started by Murray Harris. Providing expert anal
Greek text, it also contains well-informed insigh
major themes of the Gospel, suggestions about ho
tions, and excellent bibliographies of classic older works as well as quite recent publications worth pursuing for further study. Highly recommended for those with only a little Greek, as well as for those with more advanced knowledge who want seasoned guidance on the text and message of Mark."

—Buist M. Fanning, senior professor emeritus of New Testament Studies, Dallas Theological Seminary

"Joel Williams's Exegetical Guide to the Greek text of Mark contains a wealth of information on this Gospel in an easily accessible format. It provides a tremendous entrée into the Greek text of Mark for beginning Greek students, and it is also a valuable resource for seasoned exegetes. It is rich with information on the style, grammar, discourse features, literary patterns, textual issues, and interpretive problems in the Greek text of Mark. The Bibliographies on various sections of the Greek text provide students with scholarly resources for further research, and the Homiletical Suggestions will help preachers convert their exegesis into sermons. This is a book for everyone who is serious about studying the Greek text of the Gospel of Mark!"

—W. Edward Glenny, professor of New Testament and Greek, University of Northwestern, St. Paul

"Williams's years of labor in the Greek text of Mark shine in this volume. He brings his familiarity with the best scholarship to bear on his patient examination of Mark's grammar and syntax. Alongside his judicious exegetical method, Williams offers numerous points of wise counsel for faithful exposition. There is no other work on the Greek text of Mark that equips readers to handle the second Gospel with such erudition and care."

—Daniel M. Gurtner, Ernest and Mildred Hogan Professor of New Testament Interpretation, The Southern Baptist Theological Seminary

"The EGGNT series is a great help to exegetes of the New Testament and to preachers seeking to be faithful proclaimers of the text of NT Scripture. With this volume on the Gospel of Mark, Joel Williams makes a contribution to the EGGNT series that is consistent with the purposes and format of the series. With proper attention to the secondary, scholarly literature on Mark, Williams seeks to attend primarily to the text of the Gospel of Mark as it has been laid it out by its Greek-speaking author. Bringing his years of experience in studying Mark and finding a faith-full confession in the Gospel's intentionally constructed narrative, Williams seeks to exegete the Gospel with the same faith orientation. With important insights for properly preaching the Gospels—and avoiding all-too-common errors in expositing them—Williams will be a significant friend to those studying the text of the Gospel of Mark for the purpose of proclaiming its message."

—Douglas S. Huffman, professor of New Testament, associate dean of biblical and theological studies, Talbot School of Theology, Biola University

"Joel Williams's commentary is a treasure trove for lay people, seminarians, and pastors who aim to study Mark in its original language but have mastered only the basics of Koine Greek. Williams supplies a thorough, accessible analysis of Mark's vocabulary and grammar along with insightful commentary on significant text-critical problems and exegetical quandaries. As he skillfully leads his readers through the Gospel's narrative structure, he highlights the growing conflict between the suffering Son of God and his fearful disciples. Especially helpful to preachers and teachers are Williams's homiletical suggestions, intended to invite congregations into the heart of Mark's teaching about Jesus' identity and mission as well as the demands and rewards of following him."

—Jocelyn McWhirter, Stanley S. Kresge Professor and Chair of Religious Studies, Albion College

"The EGGNT series provides valuable tools to students who have had several semesters of Greek but do not know how to apply that training in interpreting the Greek text. In the commentary on Mark's Gospel for this series, Joel Williams takes the reader through each verse of Mark and explains the grammatical issues in order to help the student better understand the text. He is thorough in his analysis along with ample references and citations, each of which is valuable to a student set to exegete and study Mark's Gospel. In addition, the *Introduction*—with its explanation of the author, the characteristics of Mark's Greek, the structure of the book, and principles for faithful exposition of Mark's Gospel—is valuable. In summary, this is a useful tool for students and teachers who are committed to studying God's Word in the Greek text."

—Andrew B. Spurgeon, professor of New Testament, Singapore Bible College, and general editor, Asia Bible Commentary

"The most common complaint I hear from my intermediate-level Greek students is that none of the commentaries, even the technical ones, deal comprehensively with the syntactical functions of Greek—things like the function of a genitive, a participle or a particular Greek tense. Finally, the EGGNT series is answering this need with in-depth analysis and exegesis of Greek forms. Joel Williams's commentary on Mark is a stellar addition to the series, a model of accuracy and clarity. This is an ideal textbook for exegetical courses on Mark's Gospel and an invaluable tool for pastors teaching through the Gospel."

—Mark L. Strauss, university professor of New Testament, Bethel Seminary

The Exegetical Guide to the Greek New Testament

Volumes Available

Matthew	Charles L. Quarles
Mark	Joel F. Williams
Luke	Alan J. Thompson
John	Murray J. Harris
Romans	John D. Harvey
2 Corinthians	Colin G. Kruse
Ephesians	Benjamin L. Merkle
Philippians	Joseph H. Hellerman
Colossians, Philemon	Murray J. Harris
Hebrews	Dana M. Harris
James	Chris A. Vlachos
1 Peter	Greg W. Forbes

Forthcoming Volumes

Acts	L. Scott Kellum
1 Corinthians	Jay E. Smith
Galatians	David A. Croteau
1–2 Thessalonians	David W. Chapman
1–2 Timothy, Titus	Ray Van Neste
2 Peter, Jude	Terry L. Wilder
1–3 John	Robert L. Plummer
Revelation	Alexander Stewart

EXEGETICAL GUIDE TO THE GREEK NEW TESTAMENT

MARK

Joel F. Williams

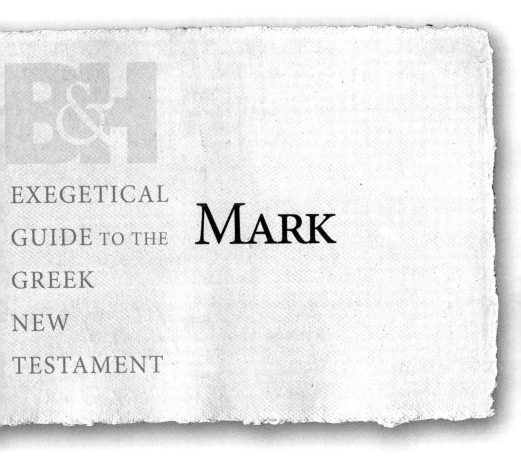

EXEGETICAL
GUIDE TO THE **MARK**
GREEK
NEW
TESTAMENT

Andreas J. Köstenberger
Robert W. Yarbrough
GENERAL EDITORS

ACADEMIC

Nashville, Tennessee

Printed in the United States of America

2 3 4 5 6 7 8 9 10 VP 26 25 24 23 22

To Becky for her love throughout life

Contents

Acknowledgments

At times, students ask me which class I enjoy teaching the most—a difficult question. I know that I love any class that involves teaching on the Gospel of Mark, most of all because I personally enjoy studying this particular book of the Bible so much. I find it constantly fascinating and absorbing. For me, the story of Mark's Gospel is overpowering, the story of God's messianic King, who came to serve, and I want to live my life within the context of this overarching narrative and in devotion to this King. However, I also love to teach New Testament Greek and to see firsthand the growth of students as they learn the language. They move from not knowing an *alpha* from a *beta* to, by the end of the second year, translating through New Testament texts and using Greek effectively in their study of the Bible. To see that kind of growth is rewarding for me as a teacher. These two sources of joy came together when I was offered the opportunity to work on this exegetical guide to the Greek text of Mark's Gospel. Therefore, I am grateful to Andreas Köstenberger for asking me to take on this project and for his encouragement to press on to the end.

Undoubtedly, it is appropriate for me to acknowledge my gratitude toward others as well. This project has led me to reflect frequently on the people who, through their kindness, have helped me along the way and who have shaped my thoughts on the Greek text of Mark. Over the years, debts accumulate. I am grateful to my own professors who took the time to teach me the details of Greek grammar and exegesis, most of all to Harold Hoehner and Buist Fanning, both of whom not only taught me at Dallas Theological Seminary but also went out of their way to take an interest in my ongoing ministry. My dissertation advisor at Marquette University, Richard Edwards, introduced me to the narrative study of Mark's Gospel and to the work of his own dissertation advisor, Norman Perrin. It was a privilege to learn about the Perrin school from inside the school itself. Elizabeth Struthers Malbon has significantly influenced my research on Mark's Gospel and has always been ready with a word of encouragement. She once told me that I seemed like one of her students even though I never took one of her classes. For me, that was an exceptionally kind compliment. I have also benefited from the annual SBL Mark Seminar, and I am grateful to the seminar leaders for their efforts in creating a culture of discussion and learning. My students, with their questions and insights, have pushed me to keep being a student myself, and I am thankful that I have been able to work with so many students who have been motivated to learn and who have motivated me to do the same.

Words cannot express all that my wife, Becky, has meant to me. She has loved me unconditionally and has joyfully walked through life with me, through all its opportunities and difficulties. She understands what it means to serve others. Her years of faithful work with refugees and immigrants provides one clear example; her willingness to move with me to the other side of the world to serve the growing church in Asia provides another. Together, we are grateful to Dr. Joseph Shao and to all the other kind people at the Biblical Seminary of the Philippines—faculty, staff, and students. They have made us feel welcome and right at home here in Manila. We are also grateful for our children, Anna, Matthew, and Luke, who have been a constant source of blessing. They were quick to encourage me to take on the task of writing this work, and they have maintained an interest in it throughout each step of the process. Part of the way they encourage and motivate us is through their own willingness to take on the challenges of life with a joyful spirit. I trust that as they go through life, they will grow to understand in a deeper way, as their parents have, that Jesus does all things well (Mark 7:37).

Publisher's Preface

It is with great excitement that we publish this volume of the Exegetical Guide to the Greek New Testament series. When the founding editor, Dr. Murray J. Harris, came to us seeking a new publishing partner, we gratefully accepted the offer. With the help of the coeditor, Andreas J. Köstenberger, we spent several years working together to acquire all of the authors we needed to complete the series. By God's grace we succeeded and contracted the last author in 2011. Originally working with another publishing house, Murray's efforts spanned more than twenty years. As God would have it, shortly after the final author was contracted, Murray decided God wanted him to withdraw as coeditor of the series. God made clear to him that he must devote his full attention to taking care of his wife, who faces the daily challenges caused by multiple sclerosis.

Over the course of many years, God has used Murray to teach his students how to properly exegete the Scriptures. He is an exceptional scholar and professor. But even more importantly, Murray is a man dedicated to serving Christ. His greatest joy is to respond in faithful obedience when his Master calls. "There can be no higher and more ennobling privilege than to have the Lord of the universe as one's Owner and Master and to be his accredited representative on earth."[1] Murray has once again heeded the call of his Master.

It is our privilege to dedicate the Exegetical Guide to the Greek New Testament series to Dr. Murray J. Harris. We pray that our readers will continue the work he started.

B&H Academic

---

1. Murray J. Harris, *Slave of Christ: A New Testament Metaphor for Total Devotion to Christ* (Downers Grove, IL: InterVarsity Press, 1999), 155.

General Introduction to the EGGNT Series

Studying the New Testament in the original Greek has become easier in recent years. Beginning students will work their way through an introductory grammar or other text, but then what? Grappling with difficult verb forms, rare vocabulary, and grammatical irregularities remains a formidable task for those who would advance beyond the initial stages of learning Greek to master the interpretive process. Intermediate grammars and grammatical analyses can help, but such tools, for all their value, still often operate at a distance from the Greek text itself, and analyses are often too brief to be genuinely helpful.

The Exegetical Guide to the Greek New Testament (EGGNT) aims to close the gap between the Greek text and the available tools. Each EGGNT volume aims to provide all the necessary information for understanding the Greek text and, in addition, includes homiletical helps and suggestions for further study. The EGGNT is not a full-scale commentary. Nevertheless, these guides will make interpreting a given New Testament book easier, in particular for those who are hard-pressed for time and yet want to preach or teach with accuracy and authority.

In terms of layout, each volume begins with a brief introduction to the particular book (including such matters as authorship, date, etc.), a basic outline, and a list of recommended commentaries. At the end of each volume, you will find a comprehensive exegetical outline of the book. The body of each volume is devoted to paragraph-by-paragraph exegesis of the text. The treatment of each paragraph includes:

1. The Greek text of the passage, phrase by phrase, from the fifth edition of the United Bible Societies' *Greek New Testament* (UBS[5]).
2. A structural analysis of the passage. Typically, verbal discussion of the structure of a given unit is followed by a diagram, whereby the verbal discussion serves to explain the diagram and the diagram serves to provide a visual aid illumining the structural discussion. While there is no one correct or standard way to diagram Greek sentences, the following format is typically followed in EGGNT volumes:
   a. The original Greek word order is maintained.

    b. When Greek words are omitted, this is indicated by ellipses (. . .).

    c. The diagramming method, moving from left to right, is predicated on the following. In clauses with a finite verb, the default order is typically verb-subject-object. In verbless clauses or clauses with nonfinite verb forms, the default order is typically subject-(verb)-object. Departures from these default orders are understood to be pragmatically motivated (e.g., contrast, emphasis, etc.).

    d. Indents are used to indicate subordination (e.g., in the case of dependent clauses).

    e. Retaining original word order, modifiers are centered above or below the word they modify (e.g., a prepositional phrase in relation to the verb).

    f. Where a given sentence or clause spans multiple lines of text, drawn lines are used, such as where a relative pronoun introduces a relative clause (often shifting emphasis).

    g. Underline is used to indicate imperatives; dotted underline is used to indicate repetition (the same word or cognate used multiple times in a given unit); the symbol ⋮ may be used where an article is separated from a noun or participle by interjected material (such as a prepositional phrase).

    h. In shorter letters diagrams are normally provided for every unit; in longer letters and Revelation, ellipses may be used to show less detail in diagramming (keeping larger blocks together on the same line) in order to focus primarily on the larger structure of a given unit; in the Gospels and Acts, detailed diagrams will usually not be provided, though less detailed diagrams may be used to illustrate important or more complex structural aspects of a given passage.

3. A discussion of each phrase of the passage with discussion of relevant vocabulary, significant textual variants, and detailed grammatical analysis, including parsing. When more than one solution is given for a particular exegetical issue, the author's own preference is indicated by an asterisk (*). When no preference is expressed, the options are judged to be evenly balanced, or it is assumed that the text is intentionally ambiguous. When a particular verb form may be parsed in more than one way, only the parsing appropriate in the specific context is supplied; but where there is difference of opinion among grammarians or commentators, both possibilities are given and the matter is discussed.

4. Various translations of significant words or phrases.

5. A list of suggested topics for further study with bibliography for each topic. An asterisk (*) in one of the "For Further Study" bibliographies draws attention to a discussion of the particular topic that is recommended as a useful introduction to the issues involved.

6. Homiletical suggestions designed to help the preacher or teacher move from the Greek text to a sermon outline that reflects careful exegesis. The first

suggestion for a particular paragraph of the text is always more exegetical than homiletical and consists of an outline of the entire paragraph. These detailed outlines of each paragraph build on the general outline proposed for the whole book and, if placed side by side, form a comprehensive exegetical outline of the book. All outlines are intended to serve as a basis for sermon preparation and should be adapted to the needs of a particular audience.[1]

The EGGNT volumes will serve a variety of readers. Those reading the Greek text for the first time may be content with the assistance with vocabulary, parsing, and translation. Readers with some experience in Greek may want to skip or skim these sections and focus attention on the discussions of grammar. More advanced students may choose to pursue the topics and references to technical works under "For Further Study," while pastors may be more interested in the movement from grammatical analysis to sermon outline. Teachers may appreciate having a resource that frees them to focus on exegetical details and theological matters.

The editors are pleased to present you with the individual installments of the EGGNT. We are grateful for each of the contributors who has labored long and hard over each phrase in the Greek New Testament. Together we share the conviction that "all Scripture is inspired by God and is profitable for teaching, for rebuking, for correcting, for training in righteousness" (2 Tim 3:16 CSB) and echo Paul's words to Timothy: "Be diligent to present yourself to God as one approved, a worker who doesn't need to be ashamed, correctly teaching the word of truth" (2 Tim 2:15).

Thanks to Michael Naylor, who served as assistant editor for this volume.

Andreas J. Köstenberger
Robert W. Yarbrough

---

1. As a Bible publisher, B&H Publishing follows the "Colorado Springs Guidelines for Translation of Gender-Related Language in Scripture." As an academic book publisher, B&H Academic asks that authors conform their manuscripts (including EGGNT exegetical outlines in English) to the B&H Academic style guide, which affirms the use of singular "he/his/him" as generic examples encompassing both genders. However, in their discussion of the Greek text, EGGNT authors have the freedom to analyze the text and reach their own conclusions regarding whether specific Greek words are gender specific or gender inclusive.

Abbreviations

For abbreviations used in discussion of text-critical matters, the reader should refer to the abbreviations listed in the Introduction to the United Bible Societies' *Greek New Testament*.

*	indicates the reading of the original hand of a manuscript as opposed to subsequent correctors of the manuscript, *or*
	indicates the writer's own preference when more than one solution is given for a particular exegetical problem, *or*
	in the "For Further Study" bibliographies, indicates a discussion of the particular topic that is recommended as a useful introduction to the issues involved
§, §§	paragraph, paragraphs

Books of the Old Testament

Gen	Genesis	Song	Song of Songs (Canticles)
Exod	Exodus	Isa	Isaiah
Lev	Leviticus	Jer	Jeremiah
Num	Numbers	Lam	Lamentations
Deut	Deuteronomy	Ezek	Ezekiel
Josh	Joshua	Dan	Daniel
Judg	Judges	Hos	Hosea
Ruth	Ruth	Joel	Joel
1–2 Sam	1–2 Samuel	Amos	Amos
1–2 Kgs	1–2 Kings	Obad	Obadiah
1–2 Chr	1–2 Chronicles	Jonah	Jonah
Ezra	Ezra	Mic	Micah
Neh	Nehemiah	Nah	Nahum
Esth	Esther	Hab	Habakkuk
Job	Job	Zeph	Zephaniah
Ps(s)	Psalm(s)	Hag	Haggai
Prov	Proverbs	Zech	Zechariah
Eccl	Ecclesiastes	Mal	Malachi

Books of the New Testament

Matt	Matthew	1–2 Thess	1–2 Thessalonians
Mark	Mark	1–2 Tim	1–2 Timothy
Luke	Luke	Titus	Titus
John	John	Phlm	Philemon
Acts	Acts	Heb	Hebrews
Rom	Romans	Jas	James
1–2 Cor	1–2 Corinthians	1–2 Pet	1–2 Peter
Gal	Galatians	1–3 John	1–3 John
Eph	Ephesians	Jude	Jude
Phil	Philippians	Rev	Revelation
Col	Colossians		

Dead Sea Scrolls

1QM	War Scroll
1QS	Rule of the Community
4QDeut	4Q Deuteronomy
4QFlor	4Q Florilegium
4QTest	4Q Testimonia
11QMelch	11Q Melchizedek
CD	Damascus Document

General Abbreviations

1 Clem.	1 Clement
1 En.	1 Enoch
AB	Anchor Bible
ABD	*The Anchor Bible Dictionary*, 6 vols., ed. D. N. Freedman (New York: Doubleday, 1992)
ABR	*Australian Biblical Review*
ABRL	Anchor Bible Reference Library
abs.	absolute(ly)
acc.	accusative
act.	active (voice)
adj.	adjective, adjectival(ly)
adv.	adverb(ial)(-ially)
anar.	anarthrous
AnBib	Analecta Biblica
Ant.	Josephus, *Jewish Antiquities*

aor.	aorist
apod.	apodosis
appos.	apposition, appositive, appositional
Aram.	Aramaic
art.	article, articular
AsJT	*Asia Journal of Theology*
AsTJ	*Asbury Theological Journal*
AThR	*Anglican Theological Review*
attrib.	attributive
aug.	augment/augmented
AUSS	*Andrews University Seminary Studies*
Barclay	W. Barclay, *The New Testament: A New Translation* (London: Collins, 1968–69)
BBR	*Bulletin for Biblical Research*
BDAG	*A Greek-English Lexicon of the New Testament and Other Early Christian Literature*, rev. and ed. F. W. Danker (Chicago/London: University of Chicago, 2000), based on W. Bauer's *Griechisch-Deutches Wörterbuch* (6th ed.) and on previous English ed. W. F. Arndt, F. W. Gingrich, and F. W. Danker. References to BDAG are by page number and quadrant on the page, *a* indicating the upper half and *b* the lower half of the left-hand column, and *c* and *d* the upper and lower halves of the right-hand column.
BDF	F. Blass and A. Debrunner, *A Greek Grammar of the New Testament and Other Early Christian Literature*, trans. and rev. by R. W. Funk (Chicago: University of Chicago, 1961)
Beale and Carson	G. K. Beale and D. A. Carson, eds., *Commentary on the New Testament Use of the Old Testament* (Grand Rapids: Baker, 2007)
BECNT	Baker Exegetical Commentary on the New Testament
BGk.	Biblical Greek (i.e., LXX and NT Greek)
BGk. hapax	Biblical Greek hapax
Bib	*Biblica*
BibInt	*Biblical Interpretation*
BibInt	Biblical Interpretation Series
BJRL	*Bulletin of the John Rylands University Library of Manchester*
BNTC	Black's New Testament Commentaries
BR	*Biblical Research*
BRev	*Bible Review*
Brooks	J. A. Brooks, *Mark,* New American Commentary (Nashville: Broadman, 1991)

Bruce	A. B. Bruce, "The Synoptic Gospels," vol. 1, pp. 1–651 in W. Robertson Nicoll, ed., *The Expositor's Greek Testament*, repr. ed. (Grand Rapids: Eerdmans, 1970)
BSac	*Bibliotheca Sacra*
BT	*The Bible Translator*
BTB	*Biblical Theology Bulletin*
Burton	E. de W. Burton, *Syntax of the Moods and Tenses in New Testament Greek,* 3rd ed. (Edinburgh: T&T Clark, 1898)
BZNW	Beihefte zur Zeitschrift für die neutestamentliche Wissenschaft
c.	circa (Lat.), about
Campbell, Basics	C. R. Campbell, *Basics of Verbal Aspect in Biblical Greek* (Grand Rapids: Zondervan, 2008)
Campbell, *VA*	C. R. Campbell, *Verbal Aspect, the Indicative Mood, and Narrative: Soundings in the Greek of the New Testament*, Studies in Biblical Greek 13 (New York: Peter Lang, 2007)
Campbell, *VANIV*	C. R. Campbell, *Verbal Aspect and Non-Indicative Verbs: Further Soundings in the Greek of the New Testament,* Studies in Biblical Greek 15 (New York: Lang, 2008)
Cassirer	H. W. Cassirer, *God's New Covenant: A New Testament Translation* (Grand Rapids: Eerdmans, 1989)
CBQ	*Catholic Biblical Quarterly*
CBQMS	Catholic Biblical Quarterly Monograph Series
CEV	Contemporary English Version (1995)
cf.	*confer* (Lat.), compare
CGk.	Classical Greek
CGTC	Cambridge Greek Testament Commentary
ch(s).	chapter(s)
circum.	circumstantial
CJT	*Canadian Journal of Theology*
comp.	comparative, comparison
ConBN	Coniectanea Biblica: New Testament Series
ConcC	Concordia Commentary
cond.	condition(al)
conj.	conjunctive, conjunction
consec.	consecutive
contemp.	contemporary/contemporaneous
correl.	correlative/correlation

Cranfield	C. E. B. Cranfield, *The Gospel According to Saint Mark,* Cambridge Greek Testament Commentary, repr. ed. with revised additional supplementary notes (Cambridge: Cambridge University Press, 1977)
CSB	Christian Standard Bible (2017)
cstr(s).	construction(s), construe(d)
CTJ	*Calvin Theological Journal*
CTM	*Concordia Theological Monthly*
CTQ	*Concordia Theological Quarterly*
CTR	*Criswell Theological Review*
CurBR	*Currents in Biblical Research*
CurBS	*Currents in Research: Biblical Studies*
CurTM	*Currents in Theology and Mission*
dat.	dative
DBIm	*Dictionary of Biblical Imagery,* ed. L. Ryken, J. C. Wilhoit, and T. Longman III (Downers Grove, IL: InterVarsity Press, 1998)
dbl.	double
Decker 1	R. J. Decker, *Mark 1–8: A Handbook on the Greek Text,* Baylor Handbook on the Greek New Testament (Waco, TX: Baylor University Press, 2014)
Decker 2	R. J. Decker, *Mark 9–16: A Handbook on the Greek Text,* Baylor Handbook on the Greek New Testament (Waco, TX: Baylor University Press, 2014)
decl.	declension, decline
def.	definite
delib.	deliberative
dem.	demonstrative
Did	*Didaskalia*
dimin.	diminutive
dir.	direct
DJG	*Dictionary of Jesus and the Gospels*, 2nd ed., ed. J. B. Green, J. K. Brown, and N. Perrin (Downers Grove, IL: InterVarsity Press, 2013)
DLNT	*Dictionary of the Later New Testament and Its Developments*, ed. R. P. Martin and P. H. Davids (Downers Grove, IL: InterVarsity Press, 1997)
DNTB	*Dictionary of New Testament Background*, ed. C. A. Evans and S. E. Porter (Downers Grove, IL: InterVarsity Press, 2000)

DPL	*Dictionary of Paul and His Letters*, ed. G. F. Hawthrone, R. P. Martin, and D. G. Reid (Downers Grove, IL: InterVarsity Press, 1993)
DSS	Dead Sea Scrolls
ed(s).	edited by, edition(s), editor(s)
EDNT	H. Balz and G. Schneider, eds., *Exegetical Dictionary of the New Testament*, 3 vols. (Grand Rapids: Eerdmans, 1990–93)
Edwards	J. R. Edwards, *The Gospel according to Mark,* Pillar New Testament Commentary (Grand Rapids: Eerdmans, 2002)
e.g.	*exempli gratia* (Lat.), for example
emph.	emphasis/emphatic
encl.	enclitic
Eng.	English
epex.	epexegetic(al), epexegetical(ly)
esp.	especially
ESV	English Standard Version (2001)
ET	English translation
et al.	*et alii* (Lat.), and others
ETL	*Ephemerides Theologicae Lovanienses*
etym.	etymology, etymologically
Evans	C. A. Evans, *Mark 8:27–16:20,* Word Biblical Commentary 34B (Nashville: Thomas Nelson, 2001)
EvQ	*Evangelical Quarterly*
EVV	English versions of the Bible
ExpTim	*Expository Times*
Fanning	B. Fanning, *Verbal Aspect in New Testament Greek* (Oxford: Oxford University Press, 1991)
fem.	feminine
f(f).	and the following (verse[s] or page[s])
fig.	figurative(ly)
fr.	from
France	R. T. France, *The Gospel of Mark*, New International Greek Testament Commentary (Grand Rapids: Eerdmans, 2002)
freq.	frequent(ly)
fut.	future
GBS	Guides to Biblical Scholarship
gen.	genitive
Gk.	Greek

GNB	Good News Bible (1976)
GNT	Good News Translation (1992)
GTJ	*Grace Theological Journal*
Guelich	R. A. Guelich, *Mark 1–8:26,* Word Biblical Commentary 34A (Dallas: Word, 1989)
Harris	M. J. Harris, *Prepositions and Theology in the Greek New Testament* (Grand Rapids: Zondervan, 2012)
Heb.	Hebrew, Hebraism
HeyJ	*Heythrop Journal*
HGk.	Hellenistic Greek
Hooker	M. D. Hooker, *The Gospel according to Saint Mark*, Black's New Testament Commentary, repr. ed. (Peabody, MA: Hendrickson, 2005)
hort.	hortatory
HTR	*Harvard Theological Review*
HTS	Harvard Theological Studies
HUT	Hermeneutische Untersuchungen zur Theologie
HvTSt	*Hervormde teologiese studies*
ibid.	*ibidem* (Lat.), in the same place
IBS	*Irish Biblical Studies*
IDBSup	*Interpreter's Dictionary of the Bible (Supplement Volume)*
i.e.	*id est* (Lat.), that is
impers.	impersonal(ly)
impf.	imperfect (tense)
impv.	imperative (mood), imperatival(ly)
incl.	including, inclusive
indecl.	indeclinable
indef.	indefinite
indic.	indicative (mood)
indir.	indirect
inf.	infinitive
ingr.	ingressive
instr.	instrument, instrumental(ly)
Int	*Interpretation*
interr.	interrogative
intrans.	intransitive(ly)
IRT	Issues in Religion and Theology

ISBE	G. W. Bromiley, et al., eds., *The International Standard Bible Encyclopedia*, 4 vols. (Grand Rapids: Eerdmans, 1979–88)
iter.	iterative
JB	Jerusalem Bible
JBL	*Journal of Biblical Literature*
JETS	*Journal of the Evangelical Theological Society*
JJS	*Journal of Jewish Studies*
Jos.	Josephus
Jos. Asen.	Joseph and Aseneth
JR	*Journal of Religion*
JSNT	*Journal for the Study of the New Testament*
JSNTSup	Journal for the Study of the New Testament Supplement Series
JTI	*Journal of Theological Interpretation*
JTS	*Journal of Theological Studies*
JTSA	*Journal of Theology for Southern Africa*
J.W.	Josephus, *Jewish War*
KJV	King James Version (= "Authorized Version," 1611)
KMP	A. J. Köstenberger, B. L. Merkle, and R. L. Plummer, *Going Deeper with New Testament Greek: An Intermediate Study of the Grammar and Syntax of the New Testament* (Nashville: B&H Academic, 2016)
Lane	W. L. Lane, *The Gospel of Mark*, New International Commentary on the New Testament (Grand Rapids: Eerdmans, 1974)
Lat.	Latin
LEB	Lexham English Bible
LEC	Library of Early Christianity
Let. Arist.	Letter of Aristeas
lit.	literal(ly)
LN	J. P. Louw and E. A. Nida, eds., *Introduction and Domains*, vol. 1 of *Greek-English Lexicon of the New Testament Based on Semantic Domains* (New York: United Bible Societies, 1988)
LNTS	Library of New Testament Studies
locat.	locative, locatival(ly)
LQ	*Lutheran Quarterly*
LSJ	H. G. Liddell and R. Scott, *Greek-English Lexicon* (Oxford: Clarendon, 1996)
LTJ	*Lutheran Theological Journal*
LXX	Septuagint (= Greek Old Testament)

Macc	Maccabees
Marcus 1	J. Marcus, *Mark 1–8*, Anchor Bible (New York: Doubleday, 2000)
Marcus 2	J. Marcus, *Mark 8–16*, Anchor Bible (New Haven: Yale University Press, 2009)
masc.	masculine
McKay	K. L. McKay, *A New Syntax of the Verb in New Testament Greek: An Aspectual Approach* (New York: Peter Lang, 1994)
Metzger	B. M. Metzger, *A Textual Commentary on the Greek New Testament* (Stuttgart: Deutsche Bibelgesellschaft; New York: United Bible Societies, 1994; original ed.,1971, based on UBS^3)
mg.	margin
MH	J. H. Moulton and W. F. Howard, *Accidence and Word-Formation*, vol. 2 of *A Grammar of New Testament Greek*, ed. J. H. Moulton (Edinburgh: T&T Clark, 1939)
mid.	middle
MM	J. H. Moulton and G. Milligan, *The Vocabulary of the Greek Testament Illustrated from the Papyri and Other Non-Literary Sources* (London: Hodder and Stoughton, 1929)
mng.	meaning
Moule	C. F. D. Moule, *An Idiom Book of New Testament Greek*, 2nd ed. (Cambridge: CUP, 1960)
Moulton	J. H. Moulton, *A Grammar of New Testament Greek,* vol. 1, *Prolegomena*, 3rd ed. (Edinburgh: T&T Clark, 1908)
MSG	*The Message*
MSJ	*The Master's Seminary Journal*
ms(s).	manuscript(s)
MT	Masoretic Text
n.	note
NA^{28}	*Novum Testamentum Graece*, 28th revised edition, Edited by Barbara Aland and others, © 2012 Deutsche Bibelgesellschaft, Stuttgart.
NAB	New American Bible
NAC	New American Commentary
NASB	New American Standard Bible (1995)
NDBT	*New Dictionary of Biblical Theology*, ed. T. D. Alexander and B. S. Rosner (Downers Grove, IL: InterVarsity Press, 2000)
NEB	New English Bible (1970)
neg.	negative, negation
Neot	*Neotestamentica*
NET	New English Translation Bible (2005)

NETS	New English Translations of the Septuagint (2007)
neut.	neuter
NICNT	New International Commentary on the New Testament
NIDB	*New Interpreter's Dictionary of the Bible*, ed. Katherine Doob Sakenfield, 5 vols. (Nashville: Abingdon, 2006–2009)
NIDNTT	*The New International Dictionary of New Testament Theology*, 3 vols., ed. C. Brown (Grand Rapids: Zondervan, 1975–78)
NIDNTTE	*New International Dictionary of New Testament Theology and Exegesis*, 5 vols., ed. M. Silva (Grand Rapids: Zondervan, 2014)
NIGTC	New International Greek Testament Commentary
NIV	New International Version (2011)
NIVAC	NIV Application Commentary
NJB	New Jerusalem Bible (1985)
NKJV	New King James Version
NLT	New Living Translation (2015)
nom.	nominative
NovT	*Novum Testamentum*
NovTSup	Novum Testamentum Supplements
NRSV	New Revised Standard Version (1990)
NSBT	New Studies in Biblical Theology
NT	New Testament
NT hapax	New Testament hapax legomenon
NTS	*New Testament Studies*
NTTS	New Testament Tools and Studies
obj.	object(ive)
Odes Sol.	Odes of Solomon
opt.	optative
orig.	origin, original(ly)
OT	Old Testament
p(p).	page(s)
pace	(from Lat. *pax*, peace) (in stating a contrary opinion) with all due respect to (the person named)
par(s).	parallel(s), parallelism
pass.	passive (voice)
periph.	periphrastic
pers.	person(al)
pf.	perfect(ive)

pl.	plural
pluperf.	pluperfect
PNTC	Pillar New Testament Commentary
Porter, *Idioms*	S. E. Porter, *Idioms of the Greek New Testament* (Sheffield: JSOT Press, 1992)
Porter, *VA*	S. E. Porter, *Verbal Aspect in the Greek of the New Testament, with Reference to Tense and Mood*, Studies in Biblical Greek 1 (New York: Peter Lang, 1989)
pos.	positive
poss.	possessive
postpos.	postpositive
pred.	predicate, predicative
pref.	prefix
prep.	preposition(al)
pres.	present
Presb	*Presbyterion*
prog.	progressive
pron.	pronoun, pronominal
prot.	protasis
PRSt	*Perspectives In Religious Studies*
Pss. Sol.	Psalms of Solomon
ptc.	participle, participial(ly)
ptcl.	particle
QR	*Quarterly Review*
qual.	qualitative
quan.	quantitative(ly)
R	A. T. Robertson, *A Grammar of the Greek New Testament in the Light of Historical Research*, 4th ed. (Nashville: Broadman, 1934)
RB	*Revue biblique*
RBS	Resources for Biblical Study
rdg(s).	(textual) reading(s)
REB	Revised English Bible (1990)
ref.	reference
refl.	reflexive
rel.	relative
rep.	repetition

ResQ	*Restoration Quarterly*
rev.	revise(d), reviser, revision
RevExp	*Review and Expositor*
RSV	Revised Standard Version (1952)
RTR	*Reformed Theological Review*
Runge	S. E. Runge, *Discourse Grammar of the Greek New Testament: A Practical Introduction for Teaching and Exegesis* (Peabody, MA: Hendrickson, 2010)
SBJT	*Southern Baptist Journal of Theology*
SBLDS	Society of Biblical Literature Dissertation Series
SBLGNT	Society of Biblical Literature Greek New Testament
SBLMS	Society of Biblical Literature Monograph Series
SBLSP	Society of Biblical Literature Seminar Papers
SBT	Studies in Biblical Theology
SE	*Studia Evangelica*
Sem.	Semitic, Semitism
sg.	single/singular
Sib. Or.	Sibylline Oracles
sim.	similar(ly)
Sir	Sirach/Ecclesiasticus
SJT	*Scottish Journal of Theology*
SNTSMS	Society for New Testament Studies Monograph Series
Spicq	C. Spicq, *Theological Lexicon of the New Testament*, translated and edited by J. D. Ernest, 3 vols. (Peabody, MA: Hendrickson, 1994)
SR	*Studies in Religion*
ST	*Studia Theologica*
Stein	R. H. Stein, *Mark*, Baker Exegetical Commentary on the New Testament (Grand Rapids: Baker Academic, 2008)
STL	Second Temple literature
Strauss	M. L. Strauss, *Mark*, Zondervan Exegetical Commentary on the New Testament (Grand Rapids: Zondervan, 2014)
subj.	subject(ive)
subjunc.	subjunctive
subord.	subordinate, subordination
subst.	substantive, substantival
suf.	suffix
superl.	superlative

Swete	H. B. Swete, *The Gospel according to St Mark*, 2nd ed. (London: Macmillan, 1908)
SwJT	*Southwestern Journal of Theology*
T	N. Turner, *A Grammar of New Testament Greek*, vol. 3, *Syntax* (Edinburgh: Clark, 1963)
Taylor	V. Taylor, *The Gospel according to St. Mark*, 2nd ed. (London: Macmillan, 1966)
TBT	*The Bible Today*
TCNT	Twentieth Century New Testament
TD	*Theology Digest*
TDNT	*Theological Dictionary of the New Testament*, 9 vols., ed. G. Kittel and G. Friedrich, trans. G. W. Bromiley (Grand Rapids: Eerdmans, 1964–74)
temp.	temporal(ly)
Them	*Themelios*
TD	*Theology Digest*
TJ	*Trinity Journal*
TLG	*Thesaurus Linguae Graecae*
TNIV	Today's New International Version
tr.	translate(d), translator, translation(s)
trans.	transitive
TS	*Theological Studies*
TTE	*The Theological Educator*
Turner, *Grammatical*	N. Turner, *Grammatical Insights into the New Testament* (Edinburgh: T&T Clark, 1965)
Turner, *Style*	N. Turner, *Style*, vol. 4 of *A Grammar of New Testament Greek*, ed. J. H. Moulton (Edinburgh: T&T Clark, 1976)
TynBul	*Tyndale Bulletin*
TZ	*Theologische Zeitschrift*
UBS[5]	*The Greek New Testament*, ed. B. Aland, K. Aland, J. Karavidopoulos, C. M. Martini, and B. M. Metzger, 5th rev. ed. (Stuttgart: Deutsche Bibelgesellschaft; New York: United Bible Societies, 2014)
USQR	*Union Seminary Quarterly Review*
untr.	untranslated
v., vv.	verse(s)
var(s).	variant (form[s] or reading[s])
vb(s).	verb(s)

VE	*Vox Evangelica*
viz.	*videlicet* (Lat.), namely
voc.	vocative
Voelz	J. W. Voelz, *Mark 1:1–8:26*, Concordia Commentary (St. Louis: Concordia, 2013)
vol(s).	volume(s)
vs.	versus
Wallace	D. B. Wallace, *Greek Grammar beyond the Basics: An Exegetical Syntax of the New Testament* (Grand Rapids: Zondervan, 1996)
WBC	Word Biblical Commentary
Wis	Wisdom of Solomon
WTJ	*Westminster Theological Journal*
WUNT	Wissenschaftliche Untersuchungen zum Neuen Testament
WW	*Word and World*
Yarbro Collins	A. Yarbro Collins, *Mark: A Commentary*, Hermeneia (Minneapolis: Fortress, 2007)
Z	M. Zerwick, *Biblical Greek Illustrated by Examples* (Rome: Pontifical Biblical Institute, 1963)
ZECNT	Zondervan Exegetical Commentary on the New Testament
ZG	M. Zerwick, *A Grammatical Analysis of the New Testament*, trans. M. Grosvenor (Rome: Pontifical Biblical Institute, 1988)
ZNW	*Zeitschrift für die neutestamentliche Wissenschaft und die Kunde der älteren Kirche*

MARK

Introduction

AUTHORSHIP

The text of Mark's Gospel lacks any direct self-reference by the author, but this fact does not mean, of course, that the author was unknown to the first recipients of the work. In Mark 15:21, the author refers to Simon of Cyrene as the father of Alexander and Rufus. Such a comment makes sense within the context of an early Christian community where people knew one another and had mutual friendships and relationships. The people who first received Mark's Gospel likely knew who Alexander and Rufus were, and their circle of relationships also therefore would have included the author, who knew them and was aware of their circumstances. In other words, at least among the earliest recipients, the authorship of this work was not a hidden mystery or obscure lost detail. Yet the fact remains that the author did not refer to himself and therefore did not consider his identity to be a crucial issue for the understanding of his gospel message concerning Jesus. As a result, the authorship of Mark's Gospel is more a matter of historical interest than a necessary first step in the interpretation of the book.

The practice of early Christian scribes, based on the uniform evidence of extant mss., was to provide the title εὐαγγέλιον κατὰ Μάρκον or the shortened form κατὰ Μάρκον at either the beginning or end of the text of Mark's Gospel. In this way, the title identified the book as providing the one message of the gospel—the story of the good news concerning Jesus—as narrated by Mark. This same use of titles occurred with copies of the other canonical Gospels as well, those of Matthew, Luke, and John. These titles function as notable witnesses to the authorship of the Gospels, since they likely came into use not long after the writing of the Gospels themselves, within the last decades of the first century. As soon as the Gospels began to be copied and circulated among various church communities, it would have been necessary to add titles to them, to distinguish them from one another and from other works used by believers. As a result, the name "Mark" came to be associated with this Gospel early in its circulation and reception (see Martin Hengel, *Studies in the Gospel of Mark* [Philadelphia: Fortress, 1985], 64–84).

In addition, the witness of Christian writers from the first centuries is both early and consistent with regard to the authorship of Mark's Gospel. The earliest and most important testimony comes from Papias, who was the bishop of Hierapolis, a city in Phrygia of Asia Minor, in the early part of the second century. Papias talked about the authorship of Mark's Gospel in a five-volume work known as *Interpretation of the Sayings of the Lord*, which was likely written around AD 95–110 (see Robert W. Yarbrough, "The Date of Papias: A Reassessment," *JETS* 26 [1983]: 181–91). Papias's work as a whole did not survive from ancient times, but fragments from it were preserved by Eusebius in the early part of the fourth century in his *Ecclesiastical History*, including Papias's comments on Mark (*Ecclesiastical History*, 3.39.15). According to this fragment, Papias stated (1) that Mark, although not a follower of the Lord during his earthly ministry, was a follower of Peter and served as his interpreter; (2) that Mark wrote down accurately the teaching of Peter concerning all that he remembered of the things said and done by the Lord; and (3) that Mark's Gospel lacked order and a systematic arrangement to the Lord's sayings, reflecting as it did the occasional nature of Peter's teaching. After Papias, other Christian sources from the second and third centuries make similar claims, indicating that Mark was the author of this Gospel and that his work reflected in some way the teaching of Peter (for a helpful gathering together of early traditions concerning Mark and his Gospel in the writings of Justin Martyr, Irenaeus, Hippolytus, the anti-Marcionite prologue, Tertullian, Clement of Alexandria, Origen, and others, see the work of C. Clifton Black, *Mark: Images of an Apostolic Interpreter* [Columbia, SC: University of South Carolina Press, 1994], who attempts to find a middle ground between maximalist and minimalist approaches to the evidence).

"Mark" was a common name in the Roman world at the time the NT books were being written, certainly one of the most common Lat. names in the Roman Empire. Yet the author of Mark's Gospel was a faithful adherent of a Jewish messianic movement, and likely was himself Jewish (cf. Marcus 1:19–21; Hengel, *Studies in the Gospel of Mark*, 29, 46). He recognized the need to explain Jewish traditions about ritual purity (7:3–5) and to translate Aram. words and phrases for the Gentiles in his audience (see the discussion at 7:34), and he apparently was in a position to do so because of his own ethnic background. Therefore, the more relevant point is that the use of the name "Mark" among Jews at the time of the NT was in fact extremely rare. By referring to "Mark" as one of the Gospel writers without any other further specification, early Christian writers assumed that this basic identification was sufficient. Their reference solely to "Mark" was apparently not confusing but rather easily understood as pointing to a well-known individual within the Christian community. John Mark, who is mentioned in Acts as working with Paul (12:12, 25; 13:5, 13; 15:37), fits that category. In addition, in light of the rarity of the name "Mark" within Jewish circles and perhaps therefore also among leaders and teachers within the early Christian missionary movement, it seems likely that the John Mark of Acts is the same Mark mentioned in the NT epistles (Col 4:10; Phlm 24; 2 Tim 4:11; 1 Pet 5:13). There are indications that point in this direction, such as the reference in Col 4:10 to Mark as a relative of Barnabas, a coworker with Paul, and the connection in 1 Pet 5:12–13 between Mark and Silvanus (or Silas), another coworker with Paul (on the name "Mark" and the identity of Mark the Gospel writer, see Richard Bauckham, *Jesus and the Eyewitnesses: The Gospels as Eyewitness Testimony*, 2nd ed. [Grand Rapids: Eerdmans, 2017], 538–42).

Mark, or as Acts 12:25 states it, John who was also called Mark, lived with his mother, named Mary, in Jerusalem during the early days of the church, and his mother's house served as a gathering place for believers (Acts 12:12). Mark departed from Jerusalem and accompanied Paul and Barnabas as their helper on their first missionary journey (12:25; 13:5), but in the middle of the journey, Mark—for reasons not explained in Acts—left them and returned to Jerusalem (13:13). When Paul and Barnabas were making plans for their second missionary endeavor, Barnabas wanted to take Mark along once again, but Paul would have nothing of it. Mark had already deserted them once, and once was enough. The disagreement between Paul and Barnabas on this matter became so sharp that Barnabas took Mark and headed in one direction while Paul chose Silas as a new missionary partner and headed in another (15:36–40). If the John Mark of Acts is the same Mark mentioned in the NT epistles, then some reconciliation between Paul and Mark must have taken place. In Col 4:10 and Phlm 24, Paul makes reference to Mark as one of his fellow workers in Rome during his imprisonment there, and in 2 Tim 4:11 Paul commends Mark as useful for service. Peter, also apparently writing from Rome, mentions the presence of Mark with him there, referring to him as his son, perhaps implying that Mark came to faith through his ministry (1 Pet 5:13). Mark's Gospel displays a keen sense of the potential for failure on the part of Jesus's followers but also an awareness of God's work through Jesus to bring about forgiveness and restoration. To some extent, those underlying themes may have grown out of Mark's own experience of failure and restoration to service.

OCCASION AND DATE

It is possible to gather some notable information about Mark's initial audience and its circumstances simply from a close reading of Mark's Gospel itself. For example, Mark must have assumed that his audience included Gk.-speaking Gentiles, that is, people who needed to have some Jewish traditions, groups, and terms explained (7:3–5; 12:18; 15:42) and Aram. words and phrases translated (see 7:34). Yet at the same time Mark felt no need to give details about significant people or basic concepts from the Jewish Scriptures. He could assume that most in his audience would know, for instance, who Isaiah or Elijah was and what it meant to be a prophet sent from God (1:2; 6:4, 15; 7:6; 8:28; 9:4–5, 11–13; 11:32; 15:35–36); who David was and what God had promised him concerning a coming kingdom (2:25; 10:47–48; 11:10; 12:35–37); and who Moses was and what it meant to live according to his commands (1:44; 7:9–10; 9:4–5; 10:3–9; 12:19, 26, 29–31). In addition, Mark must have thought that at least some in his audience were already devoted to Christ. In 9:41, Jesus is teaching his disciples about those who would give them a cup of water to drink. This act of kindness would take place "because you belong to Christ." If Mark recorded this saying of Jesus, like the other discipleship teaching in his Gospel, because he considered it particularly relevant to his audience, then he likely thought that some in his audience also belonged to Christ. Followers of Jesus in Mark's initial audience were listening in on Jesus's teaching as it moved past the disciples to reach their ears as well. In addition, Mark apparently believed that at least some in his audience knew what it meant to experience suffering and persecution because of their devotion to Jesus. In 13:13, Jesus states that his followers would be hated by all on account of his name, a situation that called for endurance. Mark seems to have written in a context where a statement like that would ring true, where believers felt the weight of hatred and recognized the need for endurance.

Mark wrote to help this audience understand more deeply the story concerning Jesus, who he was, what he came to accomplish, and what it means to follow him. At least part of Mark's purpose is clear from the first verse—he wanted to proclaim the good news about Jesus as the messianic King. The rest of the book fills out what it meant for Jesus to be the Messiah. As the Messiah, he lived his life with a unique authority from God and also suffered, died, and rose again to bring life and hope to his people. Yet this story concerning Jesus also has implications for those who follow him. Mark narrated his story in such a way that it calls on the followers of Jesus to live with faithfulness toward their Lord and to live according to the pattern of his life by taking the path of sacrifice and service toward those in need. Such a sacrificial life takes place within the context of this present difficult age, but even in this context God's kingdom mysteriously grows as believers share the message of Jesus and learn to live with a wholehearted love for God and others.

Interpreters have sometimes attempted to be more precise about the specific circumstances in which Mark wrote and therefore about his purpose for writing in light of them. The more traditional viewpoint has been that Mark's Gospel was written in Rome and reflected the difficulties faced by the church there, perhaps including those endured during the persecution under the emperor Nero in the 60s (see, e.g., Hengel, *Studies in the Gospel of Mark*, 1–30; on the suffering of the church in Rome under Nero, see esp. Tacitus, *Annals*, 15.44). Another proposal is that the writing of Mark took place in closer proximity to where the events recorded and prophesied in the Gospel actually happened, perhaps in Galilee or Syria and perhaps reflecting the suffering of Christians during the Jewish war against Rome that culminated with the destruction of the temple in AD 70 (see, e.g., Willi Marxsen, *Mark the Evangelist: Studies on the Redaction History of the Gospel* [Nashville: Abingdon, 1969]; Joel Marcus, "The Jewish War and the *Sitz im Leben* of Mark," *JBL* 111 [1992]: 441–62). Of these two options, the suggestion concerning Rome receives more support within early church tradition, which associates Mark's Gospel with the regions of Italy (anti-Marcionite prologue) or more specifically with Rome (Irenaeus, *Against Heresies,* 3.1.1.; Clement of Alexandria in his *Hypotypōseis* as recorded in Eusebius, *Ecclesiastical History,* 6.14.5–7). A Roman origin for Mark's Gospel may also help to explain the use of Latinisms in Mark, that is, Mark's use of Lat. loanwords and idiomatic phrases (for a list of examples, see Turner, *Style* 29–30). Early church tradition sometimes seems to place the writing of Mark's Gospel after the death of Peter (Irenaeus, *Against Heresies*, 3.1.1.; anti-Marcionite prologue) and sometimes before it (Clement of Alexandria in his *Hypotypōseis* as recorded in Eusebius, *Ecclesiastical*

History, 2.15.1–2; 6.14.5–7; Origen in his *Commentary on St. Matthew* as recorded in Eusebius, *Ecclesiastical History,* 6.25.3–6). If Mark was in Rome with Peter in the early 60s, as 1 Pet 5:13 seems to indicate, then a date for Mark's Gospel sometime in the 60s serves as a reasonable conjecture, likely not long before or not long after Peter's death, which took place in the midst of Nero's persecution.

Mark, of course, did not offer any concrete details about his own location or, for that matter, about the location and specific circumstances of his initial audience; he did not regard such information as a necessary background for interpreting his message. In fact, Mark may have been writing with more than just the needs of his initial audience in mind. Mark likely envisioned a broader audience as well, writing with the hope that his proclamation of the gospel would be circulated among a wider group of churches (see Richard Bauckham, ed., *The Gospel for All Christians: Rethinking the Gospel Audiences* [Grand Rapids: Eerdmans, 1998]). Mark did not write a narrowly defined, context-specific work, one containing hidden or coded language that might be badly misunderstood apart from the inside information available to the target audience. Instead, he wrote a proclamation of the gospel for a wide audience, a message that would stand open to all those who have ears to hear the good news about Jesus and the call to follow him.

FOR FURTHER STUDY

1. The Historical Circumstance behind Mark's Gospel

Bacon, Benjamin W. *Is Mark a Roman Gospel?* HTS 7. Cambridge, MA: Harvard University Press, 1919.

Bauckham, Richard. *Jesus and the Eyewitnesses: The Gospels as Eyewitness Testimony.* 2nd ed. Grand Rapids: Eerdmans, 2017.

Bauckham, Richard, ed. *The Gospels for All Christians: Rethinking the Gospel Audiences.* Grand Rapids: Eerdmans, 1998.

Black, C. Clifton. *Mark: Images of an Apostolic Interpreter.* Studies on Personalities of the New Testament. Columbia, SC: University of South Carolina Press, 1994.

Crossley, James G. *The Date of Mark's Gospel: Insight from the Law in Earliest Christianity.* JSNTSup 266. London: T&T Clark, 2004.

Donahue, John R. "Windows and Mirrors: The Setting of Mark's Gospel." *CBQ* 57 (1995): 1–26.

*Hengel, Martin. *Studies in the Gospel of Mark.* Philadelphia: Fortress, 1985.

Incigneri, Brian J. *The Gospel to the Romans: The Setting and Rhetoric of Mark's Gospel.* BibInt 65. Leiden: Brill, 2003.

Kee, Howard Clark, *Community of the New Age: Studies in Mark's Gospel.* Philadelphia: Westminster, 1977.

Marcus, Joel. "The Jewish War and the *Sitz im Leben* of Mark." *JBL* 111 (1992): 441–62.

Marxsen, Willi. *Mark the Evangelist: Studies on the Redaction History of the Gospel.* Nashville: Abingdon, 1969.

Peterson, Dwight N. *The Origins of Mark: The Markan Community in Current Debate.* BibInt 48. Leiden: Brill, 2000.

Roskam, H. N. *The Purpose of the Gospel of Mark in Its Historical and Social Context.* NovTSup 114. Leiden: Brill, 2004.

Winn, Adam. *The Purpose of Mark's Gospel: An Early Christian Response to Roman Imperial Propaganda.* WUNT 2/245. Tübingen: Mohr Siebeck, 2008.

OUTLINE

Mark's Gospel is a narrative. It is a historical narrative, but a narrative nonetheless, which has implications for the overall structure of the book. The outline presented in this exegetical guide seeks to take seriously the narrative shape of Mark's Gospel by paying close attention to significant narrative features, as well as to the patterned arrangement of the various episodes found in the story.

Like other narratives, Mark's Gospel presents a story with narrative features such as setting, plot, and characterization. A shift in setting or a turn in the plot or a change in characterization can mark out a new development in the narrative. One significant shift related to characterization takes place in 8:27–31, where Jesus begins to teach his disciples about his approaching suffering, death, and resurrection. This new emphasis in the characterization of Jesus divides the book into two halves. The first half of the book (1:1–8:26) highlights Jesus's miraculous power and his authoritative public teaching. This portrayal of Jesus prepares the way for Peter's confession of Jesus as the Christ at the midpoint of Mark's narrative (8:29). The second half of the book (8:27–16:8) moves Jesus on the path toward the cross, emphasizing his suffering, death, and resurrection. The second half shows Jesus more frequently teaching his disciples privately about his coming passion and the implications of his suffering for their own path as his followers. The second half also leads to a confession, this time by the centurion, who at the moment of Jesus's death declares Jesus to be the Son of God (15:39). In this way, the opening of Mark's Gospel, "the beginning of the gospel of Jesus Christ, the Son of God," finds its fulfillment in the confessions of Peter and the centurion.

Mark also uses changes in setting to identify different sections in his Gospel, and it is significant that these shifts in setting also correspond to important developments in the plot. Mark's plot is built around conflict between Jesus and the religious leaders and between Jesus and his disciples. The clashes between Jesus and the religious leaders revolve around the issue of authority, while the difficulties between Jesus and his disciples have to do with their inability to grasp the nature of Jesus's identity and mission. In both cases, the conflict moves the story forward to a resolution in the death and resurrection of Jesus. Careful attention to setting and plot divides the first half of Mark's Gospel into three sections: in the wilderness (1:1–13); in Galilee (1:14–3:35); and on and around the Sea of Galilee (4:1–8:26). The second half of Mark's Gospel also divides into three sections according to setting and plot: on the way (8:27–10:52); at the temple (11:1–13:37); and in and around Jerusalem (14:1–16:8).

Mark's Gospel is episodic. In other words, the story moves along through the narration of a series of episodes or events in the life of Jesus. Each episode presents a short scene depicting an incident in Jesus's ministry. Not only do shifts in the setting and plot define the different sections of Mark's Gospel, but these sections are also organized through literary patterns produced by the artful arrangement of episodes.

Mark sets out analogous or similar episodes into recognizable literary patterns to provide structure for the main sections in the book and to identify some of the primary concerns of the story. Even though Mark divided his material into episodes, it is worth remembering that the overall effect of his work is still a connected narrative, held together by developing plot lines and continuing themes. This is especially true in Mark's passion narrative (14:1–16:8), which is less episodic and more like a smoothly connected narrative.

Outlines struggle to display transitional passages, episodes that draw a major section to a close while at the same time they introduce a new one. For example, various outlines of Mark's Gospel differ on whether 1:14–15 is the close of the introduction or the beginning of a new section on Jesus's ministry in Galilee. The transitional character of these verses makes it difficult to know where to place them in the outline. The two miraculous healings of blind men in Mark—the blind man of Bethsaida (8:22–26) and Bartimaeus (10:46–52)—are often identified as transitional in nature. Indeed, they seem to frame the section in which Jesus teaches his disciples about the nature of discipleship while they are on the way to Jerusalem. The two major discourses in Mark's Gospel—the parables (4:1–34) and the eschatological discourse (13:1–37)— also appear to be transitional in nature. They stand at the break between major sections, summarizing important themes from the preceding narrative and introducing new developments in the following narrative. Because of the nature of outlines, these transitional passages will necessarily be included within one of the major sections, a decision based in this outline primarily on where the shift in setting takes place. However, some attempt will also be made to highlight their transitional nature.

The following summary outline seeks to reflect these basic narrative features of Mark's Gospel. A more complete outline appears at the end of the exegetical guide, and further explanations of the outline appear as each new section of Mark's Gospel is introduced in the exegetical guide.

I. Jesus as the Powerful Messiah (1:1–8:26)
   A. The Beginning of Jesus's Ministry: Preparation in the Wilderness (1:1–13)
      [Transition] Summary of Jesus's Preaching in Galilee (1:14–15)
   B. Jesus's Initial Ministry in Galilee (1:14–3:35)
      [Transition] Jesus's Ministry to the Crowd: The Parables Discourse (4:1–34)
   C. Jesus's Ministry on and around the Sea of Galilee (4:1–8:26)
      [Transition] Healing of the Blind Man of Bethsaida (8:22–26)

II. Jesus as the Suffering Son of God (8:27–16:8)
   A. Jesus's Ministry on the Way to Jerusalem (8:27–10:52)
      [Transition] Healing of Blind Bartimaeus (10:46–52)
   B. Jesus's Ministry at the Temple (11:1–13:37)

[Transition] Departure out of the Temple and Prediction of Its
Destruction: The Eschatological Discourse (13:1–37)
C. Jesus's Death on the Cross and Resurrection in Jerusalem (14:1–16:8)

FOR FURTHER STUDY

2. The Outline of Mark's Gospel

Dewey, Joanna. "The Literary Structure of the Controversy Stories in Mark 2:1–3:6." *JBL*
92 (1973): 394–401.
————. "Oral Methods of Structuring Narrative in Mark." *Int* 43 (1989): 32–44.
————. "Mark as Interwoven Tapestry: Forecasts and Echoes for a Listening Audience."
CBQ 53 (1991): 221–36.
————. "The Gospel of Mark as an Oral–Aural Event: Implications for Interpretation."
Pages 145–63 in *The New Literary Criticism and the New Testament*. Edited by Edgar V.
McKnight and Elizabeth Struthers Malbon. Valley Forge, PA: Trinity Press International,
1994.
Dodd, C. H. "The Framework of Gospel Narrative." Pages 1–11 in *New Testament Studies*.
Manchester: Manchester University Press, 1953.
Larsen, Kevin W. "The Structure of Mark's Gospel: Current Proposals." *CurBR* 3 (2004):
140–60.
Malbon, Elizabeth Struthers. "Echoes and Foreshadowings in Mark 4–8: Reading and
Rereading." *JBL* 112 (1993): 211–30.
————. "Enacted Christology: What Jesus Does." Pages 21–55 in *Mark's Jesus:
Characterization as Narrative Christology*. Waco: Baylor University Press, 2009.
Perrin, Norman. "Towards an Interpretation of the Gospel of Mark." Pages 1–78 in
Christology and a Modern Pilgrimage: A Discussion with Norman Perrin. Edited by
Hans Dieter Betz. Missoula, MT: Scholars Press, 1974.
Petersen, Norman R. "The Composition of Mark 4:1–8:26." *HTR* 73 (1980): 185–217.
Schweizer, Eduard. "Mark's Theological Achievement." Pages 42–63 in *The Interpretation
of Mark*. Edited by William Telford. IRT 7. Philadelphia: Fortress, 1985.
Smith, Stephen H. "The Literary Structure of Mark 11:1–12:40." *NovT* 31 (1989): 104–24.
*Williams, Joel. "Does Mark's Gospel Have an Outline?" *JETS* 49 (2006): 505–25.

3. The Study of Mark's Gospel as Narrative

Fowler, Robert M. *Let the Reader Understand: Reader-Response Criticism and the Gospel
of Mark*. Minneapolis: Fortress, 1991.
Frei, Hans W. *The Eclipse of Biblical Narrative: A Study in Eighteenth and Nineteenth
Century Hermeneutics*. New Haven, CT: Yale University Press, 1974.
Iverson, Kelly R., and Christopher W. Skinner, eds. *Mark as Story: Retrospect and
Prospect*. RBS 65. Atlanta: Society of Biblical Literature, 2011.
Kingsbury, Jack Dean. *Conflict in Mark: Jesus, Authorities, Disciples*. Minneapolis:
Fortress, 1989.
*Malbon, Elizabeth Struthers. "Narrative Criticism: How Does the Story Mean?" Pages
29–57 in *Mark and Method: New Approaches in Biblical Studies*. Edited by Janice Capel
Anderson and Stephen D. Moore. 2nd ed. Minneapolis: Fortress, 2008.

Moloney, Francis J. *Mark: Storyteller, Interpreter, Evangelist.* Peabody, MA: Hendrickson, 2004.

Moore, Stephen D. *Literary Criticism and the Gospels: The Theoretical Challenge.* New Haven: Yale University Press, 1989.

Powell, Mark Allan. *What Is Narrative Criticism?* GBS. Minneapolis: Fortress, 1990.

Rhoads, David, Joanna Dewey, and Donald Michie. *Mark as Story: An Introduction to the Narrative of a Gospel.* 3rd ed. Minneapolis: Fortress, 2012.

Smith, Stephen H. *A Lion with Wings: A Narrative-Critical Approach to Mark's Gospel.* Sheffield, UK: Sheffield Academic Press, 1996.

Tolbert, Mary Ann. *Sowing the Gospel: Mark's World in Literary-Historical Perspective.* Minneapolis: Fortress, 1989.

Wiarda, Timothy. *Interpreting Gospel Narratives: Scenes, People, and Theology.* Nashville: B&H Academic, 2010.

Williams, Joel F. "Listening to the Voice of the Storyteller in Mark's Gospel." *RevExp* 107 (2010): 309–21.

MARK'S GREEK STYLE

It is fair to say that Mark's grammatical style places him "toward the less literary end of the spectrum of New Testament writers" (Rodney J. Decker, "Markan Idiolect in the Study of the Greek of the New Testament," in *The Language of the New Testament: Context, History, and Development,* ed. Stanley E. Porter and Andrew W. Pitts [Leiden: Brill, 2013], 64) and that his Gk. is closer to "the everyday spoken Greek of the time" (Cranfield 20). However, it is also appropriate to add, as Cranfield does, that Mark's Gk. style serves his message well through "its simplicity and directness" (Cranfield 20). Still, Mark's Gospel displays a somewhat limited range of variation with regard to its use of different grammatical structures and syntactical features. In terms of Gk. style, Mark worked with a more limited linguistic palette in painting his portrait of Jesus.

As a result, Mark's Gk. style is fairly repetitive. In fact, some grammatical features appear in Mark's Gospel with sufficient frequency that they serve as characteristic traits of Mark's style. What follows is a list of some of these features. The verse or verses in parentheses after each item in the list indicate where a more detailed explanation can be found: (1) the freq. use of καί, with the conj. often appearing at the beginning of sentences and paragraphs (1:5); (2) the use of redundant participles with vbs. of saying, such as λέγων (1:7) and ἀποκριθείς (3:33); (3) the repeated use of the adv. εὐθύς (1:10); (4) the use of indef. 3rd pers. pl. vbs. to make general statements about what some unspecified group of people did or said (1:22; 3:21; 14:2); (5) the use of periph. participles, most often to express a periph. impf. (1:22), but also at times to express a periph. pres. (5:41), periph. fut. (13:13, 25), or periph. pluperf. (1:33); (6) the use of gen. abs. participles (1:32; 4:35), even at times when the subj. of the gen. abs. ptc. is actually mentioned in the main clause (5:2); (7) the use of multiple negatives to strengthen a statement or command (1:44; 9:1); (8) the common use of the art. as a pers. pron. when it occurs before the conj. δέ (1:45); (9) the use of ἄρχομαι as an auxiliary vb. with a complementary inf. (1:45); (10) the use of dim. nouns, often without necessarily conveying anything about the size of the person or object (3:9); (11) the use of the conj. ἵνα not only to introduce purpose clauses but also freq. to introduce subst. dir. obj. clauses that give the content of a request, a command, or a prayer (4:12; 5:10); and (12) the use of Aram. words, which Mark then translates into Gk. for his audience (7:34).

A significant amount of research in recent years concerning NT Gk. has investigated how tense conveys verbal aspect. Verbal aspect expresses how a speaker subjectively views an action, and by itself does not indicate the obj. nature of the action. So, e.g., the imperfective aspect of the pres. and impf. tenses views the action internally, as in progress, while the perfective aspect of the aor. tense views the action externally, as a whole (see Robert E. Picirilli, "The Meaning of the Tenses in New Testament Greek: Where Are We?" *JETS* 48 [2005]: 535–36). Scholarly discussions concerning aspect have the potential to provide insight into Mark's Gk. style, since verbal aspect, while central to the mng. of the Gk. vb., also interacts with other contextual factors to create common patterns of tense usage in Mark's Gospel (cf. Buist Fanning, "Greek Presents, Imperfects, and Aorists in the Synoptic Gospels: Their Contribution to Narrative Structuring," in *Discourse Studies and Biblical Interpretation: A Festschrift in Honor of Stephen H. Levinsohn*, ed. Steven E. Runge [Bellingham, WA: Logos Bible Software, 2011], 157–59). The following items, which concern Mark's use of vb. tenses in particular, can be added to the above list as further examples of common features in Mark's grammatical style: (1) the use of the historical pres. (1:12, 30); (2) the freq. use of the impf. to fill in background or explanatory information rather than to move the story line forward (1:21); (3) the use of aor. temp. adv. participles to express action antecedent to that of the main vb. (1:5); and (4) the repeated use of the pres. tense for general commands and prohibitions and the aor. tense for specific commands and prohibitions (1:15, 25; 2:11).

FOR FURTHER STUDY

4. Mark's Greek Style

*Decker, Rodney J. "Markan Idiolect in the Study of the Greek of the New Testament." Pages 43–66 in *The Language of the New Testament: Context, History, and Development*. Edited by Stanley E. Porter and Andrew W. Pitts. Linguistic Biblical Studies 6. Leiden: Brill, 2013.

Doudna, John Charles. *The Greek of the Gospel of Mark*. Journal of Biblical Literature Monograph Series 12. Philadelphia: Society of Biblical Literature, 1961.

Elliott, J. K., ed. *The Language and Style of the Gospel of Mark: An Edition of C. H. Turner's "Notes on Marcan Usage" Together with Other Comparable Studies*. NovTSup 71. Leiden: Brill, 1993.

Maloney, Elliott C. *Semitic Interference in Marcan Syntax*. SBLDS 51. Chico, CA: Scholars Press, 1981.

Neirynck, Frans. *Duality in Mark: Contributions to the Study of Markan Redaction*. Leuven: Leuven University Press, 1972.

Pryke, E. J. *Redactional Style in the Markan Gospel: A Study of Syntax and Vocabulary as Guides to Redaction in Mark*. SNTSMS 33. Cambridge: Cambridge University Press, 1978.

Turner, C. H. "Marcan Usage: Notes, Critical and Exegetical, on the Second Gospel." *JTS* 25 (1923–24): 377–86; 26 (1924–25): 12–20, 145–56, 225–40, 337–46; 27 (1925–26): 58–62; 28 (1926–27): 9–30, 349–62; 29 (1927–28): 275–89, 346–61.

Turner, Nigel. "The Style of Mark." Pages 11–30 in *Style*. Vol. 4 of *A Grammar of New Testament Greek*. Edinburgh: T&T Clark, 1976.

Voelz, James W. "The Greek of Codex Vaticanus in the Second Gospel and Marcan Greek." *NovT* 47 (2005): 209–49.

Vorster, W. S. "Bilingualism and the Greek of the New Testament: Semitic Interference in the Gospel of Mark." *Neot* 24 (1990): 215–28.

HOMILETICAL SUGGESTIONS FOR MARK'S GOSPEL

Scattered throughout this exegetical guide are "Homiletical Suggestions," brief outlines intended to point out possible directions for the exposition of Mark's Gospel. The goal is to move from careful exegetical work in the Gk. text to the faithful exposition of Mark's Gospel in preaching and teaching. The guiding principle for these "Homiletical Suggestions" is that the Gospel of Mark is about Jesus. That fact is, of course, an obvious truth, but an all too often neglected one with regard to each of the NT Gospels. Each Gospel is concerned with telling us about who Jesus is and what he came to accomplish. The evangelists also want to impress upon us the need to respond appropriately to Jesus by following him no matter what the cost might be. Therefore, an exposition that is faithful to Mark's Gospel must focus on Jesus and on what it means to follow him. When studying a passage or section in Mark's Gospel, two crucial questions deserve an answer: What is Mark seeking to communicate about Jesus? What is Mark seeking to communicate about an appropriate response to Jesus? Therefore, many of the suggested outlines for messages seek to address these questions directly, and all of them seek to focus on Jesus or on what it means to follow him. By concentrating on these two questions, it is possible to avoid three common pitfalls in the exposition of Gospel narrative (for a more detailed discussion, see Joel F. Williams, "Listening to the Voice of the Storyteller in Mark's Gospel," *RevExp* 107 [2010]: 309–21).

The first potential pitfall is allegorizing. The NT Gospels present a realistic narrative, a story that is true to life. They narrate a series of events that are presented as a realistic portrayal of the life, death, and resurrection of Jesus. The Gospels do not offer us an allegory or symbolic representation of a different, more significant story. In 2 Samuel 12, the prophet Nathan tells King David a story about a rich man who steals a poor man's lamb. Nathan's tale is an allegory, because beneath this surface story lies another one. The real mng. of Nathan's story concerns the actions by which David took the wife of Uriah the Hittite. The NT Gospels do not tell that kind of story. The story on the surface concerns the life, death, and resurrection of Jesus, and that story is what the Gospel narrative is about. Expositors sometimes fall into the trap of misusing the details of the Gospel narrative by treating them as symbols of our own present circumstances. Jesus calmed the storm on the Sea of Galilee by rebuking the wind and the waves (Mark 4:35–41). What are the storms of our lives that Jesus needs to calm today? Suddenly, a story about Jesus's power over nature becomes about us and our present problems. The great danger of allegorizing is that it can cause us to lose sight of what the Gospels say about Jesus in order to focus on ourselves and our own circumstances.

The second potential pitfall is over-harmonizing. Mark wrote a whole narrative, an overall story with connecting themes and plotlines that hold the story together. The mng. of any individual passage depends in significant ways on how that passage fits within Mark's narrative as a whole. Therefore, to understand what Mark wanted to emphasize about any particular episode in the life of Jesus, it is necessary to see how it fits within his Gospel story as a whole. This is why the "Homiletical Suggestions" in this exegetical guide cover not only individual passages but also larger sections in Mark's Gospel as a way to think about the Gospel more holistically. Sometimes in preaching and teaching, an expositor will take a passage out of its narrative context in Mark's Gospel as a whole, draw on information about that event from par. accounts in the other Gospels, and fill in some of the gaps in the story with historical background information and a fair amount of pious imagination. All of this material is then melted together to create a new harmonized whole. This new melted-together story becomes in essence a fifth Gospel account, different from that found in any of the four Gospels. Such over-harmonization has the potential to distract us from the specific contribution Mark wanted to make. What did *Mark* want to emphasize about Jesus and the appropriate way to respond to him?

The third potential pitfall is moralizing. Once again, the important principle to remember is that the Gospel of Mark is about Jesus. The various episodes in Mark's Gospel were not written to illustrate a moral. They do not offer lessons about life in general, lessons that can somehow be disconnected from Jesus, from who he is and what he came to accomplish. The NT Gospels do not give us morals to help us along whatever path we have chosen in life. Instead they tell us how God has so worked through Jesus that he demands what path we must take in life. The Gospel of Mark is a challenging book that calls on us to give our lives for Jesus and promises us that when we do so we find life as it is meant to be lived. It trivializes the message of Mark's Gospel, and the other NT Gospels as well, to use them for discovering general life principles about how to be successful or how to handle adversity or how to spend money wisely. The Gospels deserve to be treated more seriously than that, because Jesus himself, God's Messiah, deserves to be treated more seriously than that.

RECOMMENDED COMMENTARIES

The emph. in this exegetical guide in on issues related to the Gk. text of Mark's Gospel. The best commentaries in Eng. on Mark's Gospel for dealing with exegetical issues related to the Gk. text are those by Cranfield, France, Stein, and Voelz. They are consistently careful and reliable in their interpretation of the Gk. text.

Cranfield, C. E. B. *The Gospel according to Saint Mark*. CGTC. Reprinted with revised additional supplementary notes. Cambridge: Cambridge University Press, 1977.

France, R. T. *The Gospel of Mark*. NIGTC. Grand Rapids: Eerdmans, 2002.

Stein, Robert H. *Mark*. BECNT. Grand Rapids: Baker Academic, 2008.

Voelz, James W. *Mark 1:1–8:26*. ConcC. St. Louis: Concordia, 2013.

Voelz, James W., and Christopher W. Mitchell. *Mark 8:27–16:20*. ConC. St. Louis: Concordia, 2019.

Some older commentaries, such as those by Bruce, Swete, and Taylor, often include useful comments on details related to the Gk. text, although most of what may be found there appears in more recent commentaries as well.

Bruce, A. B. "The Synoptic Gospels." Vol. 1, pages 1–651 in *The Expositor's Greek Testament*. Edited by W. Robertson Nicoll. Reprint. Grand Rapids: Eerdmans, 1970.

Swete, Henry Barclay. *The Gospel according to St. Mark*. 2nd ed. London: Macmillan, 1908.

Taylor, Vincent. *The Gospel according to St. Mark*. 2nd ed. London: Macmillan, 1966.

Commentaries on Mark include more than simply exegetical guidance on the translation and grammar of the Gk. text. They cover matters related to tradition history, historical and literary backgrounds, and interpretive problems. In addition to those already mentioned, the following are some of the more helpful and detailed exegetical commentaries on Mark. Those by Marcus and by Yarbro Collins, in particular, provide a significant amount of information related to historical and literary backgrounds to Mark's Gospel.

Evans, Craig A. *Mark 8:27–16:20*. WBC. Nashville: Thomas Nelson, 2001.

Guelich, Robert A. *Mark 1–8:26*. WBC. Dallas: Word, 1989.

Lane, William L. *The Gospel of Mark*. NICNT. Grand Rapids: Eerdmans, 1974.

Marcus, Joel. *Mark 1–8*. AB. New York: Doubleday, 2000.

———. *Mark 8–16*. AB. New Haven, CT: Yale University Press, 2009.

Yarbro Collins, Adela. *Mark: A Commentary*. Hermeneia. Minneapolis: Fortress, 2007.

Some commentaries move more in the direction of exposition, providing guidance on how to present the message of Mark's Gospel to a broader audience, one that may include many who do not know the original language. The following are some of the better expositional commentaries, with the one by Strauss providing perhaps the best combination of careful exposition and helpful discussion concerning the contemp. relevance of Mark's Gospel.

Brooks, James A. *Mark*. NAC. Nashville: Broadman, 1991.

Edwards, James R. *The Gospel according to Mark*. PNTC. Grand Rapids: Eerdmans, 2002.

Garland, David E. *Mark*. NIVAC. Grand Rapids: Zondervan, 1996.

Hooker, Morna D. *The Gospel according to Saint Mark*. BNTC. Reprint. Peabody, MA: Hendrickson, 2005.

Strauss, Mark L. *Mark*. ZECNT. Grand Rapids: Zondervan, 2014.

I. Jesus as the Powerful
Messiah (1:1–8:26)

The first half of Mark's Gospel emphasizes the authority and miraculous power of Jesus. He calls disciples, and without question or delay they leave everything behind to follow him. He teaches throughout Galilee, eventually in open places to large crowds, and the people are struck with amazement over the authority of his teaching. He bests his opponents in debate, with the result that they are repeatedly left with nothing to say. He has control over unclean spirits, sickness and death, and even nature itself. This portrait of Jesus's power prepares the way for Peter's confession of Jesus as the Christ at the midpoint of Mark's narrative. Jesus has indeed shown himself to be God's Messiah. Most of the action in the first half of Mark takes place in or around Galilee. The story begins in the wilderness (1:1–13), then moves to Galilee, where Jesus begins his ministry (1:14–3:35), and then focuses on the Sea of Galilee, with Jesus crossing back and forth over the sea a number of times (4:1–8:26).

A. THE BEGINNING OF JESUS'S MINISTRY:
PREPARATION IN THE WILDERNESS (1:1–13)

All of the events within Mark's introduction take place in the wilderness (ἔρημος). At the start John the Baptist appears in the wilderness to prepare the way for the Lord (1:3–4), while at the end the Spirit moves Jesus out into the wilderness to be tempted by Satan (1:12–13). Therefore, Mark uses ἔρημος as a description of the setting at the beginning and end of the introduction, marking off the limits of the section. Elsewhere in his Gospel, Mark never uses ἔρημος as a noun to describe a setting but always as an adj. to modify τόπος, doing so at the times when Jesus seeks out deserted places for privacy, rest, and prayer (1:35, 45; 6:31, 32, 35).

The introduction sets up the plot of Mark's narrative and Jesus's subsequent dealings with the other people in the narrative by offering an initial insight into the identity of Jesus. He is the Christ, the beloved Son of God, the mightier one who will baptize with the Holy Spirit, and the one who overcomes the power of Satan. Of course, the introduction does not reveal every aspect of Jesus's identity and mission, since the purpose for the rest of the narrative is to explain what it means for Jesus to be the Christ, the Son of God.

Since the introduction is brief, the patterned arrangement of episodes is fairly simple. After the opening in v. 1, the introduction divides in half, with the first half focusing on John the Baptist (1:2–8) and the second half drawing attention to Jesus (1:9–13). There is some sense of symmetry between these two halves. The pattern of episodes progresses from John arriving in the wilderness (1:2–4) to John baptizing in the Jordan River (1:5–8) to Jesus being baptized in the Jordan (1:9–11) to Jesus being moved into the wilderness to be tempted by Satan (1:12–13).

1. Opening (1:1)

1:1 Ἀρχή, although anar., is translated as def., since, as the initial word in the opening title, it is sufficiently specific without the art. (R 781, 793; cf., e.g., Hos 1:2 LXX; Matt 1:1; Rev 1:1). The "beginning" seems to refer to the opening itself in 1:1, so that "the beginning of the gospel" (εὐαγγελίου, partitive gen.) simply indicates that Mark is starting his account of the gospel message (cf. Bruce 341). The word εὐαγγέλιον is used in the NT for the proclaimed message of "good news" concerning God's action in Jesus Christ (BDAG 402d). It appears most often in Paul's writings (sixty times out of seventy-six uses in the NT). For Paul, the gospel was the message about the life, death, and resurrection of Jesus, a message that brings salvation from sin and judgment to those who believe (Rom 1:1–6, 16–17; 1 Cor 15:1–11; 1 Thess 1:5–10). Paul proclaimed this message of good news to all those who would listen (e.g., Rom 15:19; 1 Cor 15:1; Gal 1:11; 2:2; 1 Thess 2:9). Mark's use of the term εὐαγγέλιον is similar to that of Paul, since for Mark the "good news" is the message about Jesus (1:1), one that is to be proclaimed in the whole world (13:10; 14:9).

The gen. Ἰησοῦ is an obj. gen. ("the good news about Jesus"), since the opening in 1:1 introduces Mark's Gospel as a whole, which is in fact a message about Jesus (ZG 100; T 211; Guelich 9; Lane 44–45; Stein 41). Mark clarifies the identity of Jesus with both Χριστοῦ and υἱοῦ θεοῦ. Since Mark immediately quotes from the Jewish Scriptures after his opening in 1:1, connecting the story of Jesus with them, it makes sense to understand these two designations within the context of their OT background. Χριστός, which means "anointed one" (i.e., "someone who has been ceremonially anointed for an office"), is the Gk. equivalent for the Heb. word mng. "Messiah" (*NIDNTT* 2:334; Brooks 38–39; cf. John 1:41; 4:25). In the OT, three categories of leaders were anointed with oil to indicate that they were chosen by God for his work: priests (e.g., Exod 29:7, 21; Num 3:3), prophets (e.g., 1 Kgs 19:16), and kings (e.g., 1 Sam 10:1; 16:12–13). With regard to these three categories, Jesus's kingly role stands out prominently in Mark's Gospel (e.g., Mark 15:32). Jesus is God's promised messianic King from the line of David (e.g., 10:47–48).

The absence of the phrase υἱοῦ θεοῦ in ℵ and Θ and several miniscule mss. is perhaps explainable as an accidental omission, given the sequence of six identical -ου endings in 1:1 (France 49; Metzger 62; on this text-critical problem, see Tommy Wasserman, "The 'Son of God' Was in the Beginning (Mark 1:1)," *JTS* 62 [2011]: 20–50). The prominence of the title "Son of God" in Mark makes its appearance at the beginning of this Gospel at least intrinsically probable (France 49). The result would be that the two great confessions in Mark—Peter's confession of Jesus as the Christ (8:29) and the centurion's confession of Jesus as the Son of God (15:39), the only two times in Mark that human characters declare the identity of Jesus—both reflect Mark's own initial identification of Jesus in the opening in 1:1. Like the title "Christ," "Son of God" is a messianic title. It has its roots in the OT, where the king, the descendant of David, is described as God's Son (2 Sam 7:8–16; Ps 2:1–12; 89:19–29; cf. also Isa 9:6–7; 4QFlor 1:10–13). However, "Son of God" also goes beyond being just a synonym for "Christ," because, as a title, it emphasizes the close relationship between the anointed king and God himself (*NIDNTT* 3:607).

FOR FURTHER STUDY

5. Mark's Christology

Boring, M. Eugene. "The Christology of Mark: Hermeneutical Issues for Systematic Theology." *Semeia* 30 (1984): 125–51.
———. "Markan Christology: God-Language for Jesus?" *NTS* 45 (1999): 451–71.
Broadhead, Edwin K. *Naming Jesus: Titular Christology in the Gospel of Mark.* JSNTSup 175. Sheffield, UK: Sheffield Academic Press, 1999.
Donahue, John R. "Jesus as the Parable of God in the Gospel of Mark." *Int* 32 (1978): 369–86.
Gathercole, Simon J. *The Pre-Existent Son: Recovering the Christologies of Matthew, Mark, and Luke.* Grand Rapids: Eerdmans, 2006.
Geddert, Timothy J. "The Implied YHWH Christology of Mark's Gospel: Mark's Challenge to the Reader to 'Connect the Dots.'" *BBR* 25 (2015): 325–40.
Henderson, Suzanne Watts. *Christology and Discipleship in the Gospel of Mark.* SNTSMS 135. Cambridge: Cambridge University Press, 2006.
*Johansson, Daniel. "The Identity of Jesus in the Gospel of Mark: Past and Present Proposals." *CurBR* 9 (2010–11): 364–93.
Kingsbury, Jack Dean. *The Christology of Mark's Gospel.* Philadelphia: Fortress, 1983.
Kirk, J. R. Daniel. *A Man Attested by God: The Human Jesus of the Synoptic Gospels.* Grand Rapids: Eerdmans, 2016.
Malbon, Elizabeth Struthers. *Mark's Jesus: Characterization as Narrative Christology.* Waco, TX: Baylor University Press, 2009.
Perrin, Norman. "The Christology of Mark: A Study in Methodology." *JR* 51 (1971): 171–87.
Tannehill, Robert C. "The Gospel of Mark as Narrative Christology." *Semeia* 16 (1979): 57–95.
Wrede, William. *The Messianic Secret.* Translated by J. C. C. Grieg. Cambridge: James Clarke, 1971.

6. The Genre of Mark's Gospel

Aune, David E. *The New Testament in Its Literary Environment.* LEC 8. Philadelphia: Westminster, 1987.
Burridge, Richard A. *What Are the Gospels? A Comparison with Graeco-Roman Biography.* 3rd ed. Waco, TX: Baylor University Press, 2018.

Diehl, Judith A. "What Is a 'Gospel'? Recent Studies in the Gospel Genre." *CurBR* 9 (2010–11): 171–99.

Guelich, Robert. "The Gospel Genre." Pages 183–219 in *Das Evangelium und die Evangelien*. Edited by Peter Stuhlmacher. WUNT 1/28. Tübingen: Mohr Siebeck, 1983.

Gundry, Robert H. "Recent Investigations into the Literary Genre 'Gospel.'" Pages 97–114 in *New Dimensions in New Testament Study*. Edited by Richard N. Longenecker and Merrill C. Tenney. Grand Rapids: Zondervan, 1974.

Keener, Craig S., and Edward T. Wright, eds. *Biographies and Jesus: What Does It Mean for the Gospels to Be Biographies?* Lexington, KY: Emeth, 2016.

Talbert, Charles H. *What Is a Gospel? The Genre of the Canonical Gospels*. Philadelphia: Fortress, 1977.

———. "Once Again: Gospel Genre." *Semeia* 43 (1988): 53–73.

Votaw, Clyde Weber. *The Gospels and Contemporary Biographies in the Greco-Roman World*. Philadelphia: Fortress, 1970.

*Yarbro Collins, Adela. "Genre." Pages 15–43 in *Mark*. Hermeneia. Minneapolis: Fortress, 2007.

2. John the Baptist's Preaching in the Wilderness (1:2–4)

1:2 A new sentence begins with the comp. conj. καθώς, which serves to associate the prophetic word in vv. 2–3 with John's ministry in v. 4 (NA[28]; UBS[5]; Bruce 341–42; Taylor 153; Cranfield 40). Just as prophesied in the Scriptures, John came to prepare the way. Some commentators reject this connection, arguing that Mark elsewhere always uses καθώς to support or explain a preceding statement (Guelich 6–7; France 50; Stein 42; cf. 4:33; 9:13; 11:6; 14:16, 21; 15:8; 16:7). However, καθώς as a subord. conj. precedes the main clause elsewhere in the NT (approximately 36 times out of 182 uses; e.g., Luke 1:2; John 20:21; Acts 7:17; Rom 1:28; 2 Cor 1:5; Phil 2:12; Heb 3:7), and the content of the prophetic quotation more clearly relates to the ministry of John than to the opening in 1:1. Γέγραπται, 3rd sg. pf. pass. indic. of γράφω, "write"; intensive pf. (emphasizing the present authority of what was written in the past [Wallace 57]; perhaps best translated with an Eng. pres. tense: "it is written"); ἰδού, "behold, look, see" (a particle used to draw attention to what follows, BDAG 468b; LN 91.13). Mark uses both ἰδού (seven times) and ἴδε (nine times). While properly impv. forms related to εἶδον (ἰδού, 2nd sg. aor. mid. impv.; ἴδε, 2nd sg. aor. act. impv.), both forms came to be stereotyped as particles so that they were used even when more than one person was addressed and when the object to be observed was in the nom. case (BDAG 466a, 468b; BDF §144; Wallace 60; on the accenting of ἰδού, see BDF §101). Ὅς introduces a rel. clause that conveys the idea of purpose (BDF §378; R 960); κατασκευάσει, 3rd sg. fut. act. indic. of κατασκευάζω, "make ready, prepare" (on the fut. tense, see 2:20).

1:3 Βοῶντος, gen. sg. masc. of the pres. act. ptc. of βοάω, "cry out, shout"; subst. ptc. even though anar. (BDF §413; T 151); ἑτοιμάσατε, 2nd pl. aor. act. impv. of ἑτοιμάζω, "prepare"; εὐθείας, acc. pl. fem. of εὐθύς, -εῖα, -ύ, "straight"; ποιεῖτε, 2nd pl. pres. act. impv. of ποιέω, "make"; τρίβους, acc. pl. fem. of τρίβος, -ου, ἡ, "path." The adj. εὐθείας modifies τρίβους in the sense that it functions as the complement in a dbl. acc. obj. complement cstr. (on an adj. used as a complement, see Wallace 182, 184).

1:4 Ἐγένετο, 3rd sg. aor. mid. indic. of dep. γίνομαι, "was there, came" (cf. BDAG 199c; Stein 44). The ptc. βαπτίζων (nom. sg. masc. of the pres. act. ptc. of βαπτίζω, "baptize") is either an adv. ptc. of manner ("John came baptizing") or an adj. ptc. ("John who baptizes"; with the ptc. functioning as a synonym for the noun ὁ βαπτιστής; cf. 6:24–25). On the one hand, the use of the art. ὁ with βαπτίζων points to an adj. ptc. On the other hand, the conj. καί connects βαπτίζων with κηρύσσων, and the coordination of the two participles seems to identify both as adv. The text-critical problem in v. 4 further complicates the decision. Some mss. do not include the art., while others do not include the καί. A few (most notably ‏א‎) include both the art. and καί. Perhaps the regular use of ὁ βαπτιστής as a title for John (Matt 3:1; 11:11, 12; 14:2, 8; 16:14; 17:13; Mark 6:25; 8:28; Luke 7:20, 33; 9:19) encouraged the addition of the art. with βαπτίζων, so that it would function similarly as a title (Stein 52–53; Metzger 62). Therefore, orig., βαπτίζων likely lacked the art. and functioned as an adv. ptc. of manner. Κηρύσσων, nom. sg. masc. of the pres. act. ptc. of κηρύσσω, "proclaim, preach" (also adv. ptc. of manner).

Βάπτισμα, acc. sg. neut. of βάπτισμα, -ατος, τό, "baptism"; μετανοίας, gen. sg. fem. of μετάνοια, -ας, ἡ, "repentance." Descriptive gen. is perhaps sufficient as a classification for μετανοίας (Wallace 80; KMP 90), since John's baptism, in a way not carefully defined by the gen., "symbolized or expressed repentance" (ZG 100; cf. Strauss 64). In the LXX, particularly in the prophets, the vb. related to μετάνοια (μετανοέω, "to repent") occurs in connection with vbs. mng. "to turn" (ἀποστρέφω, ἐπιστρέφω, cf. Isa 46:8; Jer 4:28; 18:8; 38:18–19 [31:18–19 Eng.]; Joel 2:13–14; Jonah 3:9–10). As a result, the two concepts, "to repent" and "to turn" became related in mng., and "repentance" became a common word for turning away from sin and turning toward God and his ways (*TDNT* 4:989–92; for more on important words in Mark, see Joel F. Williams, "Mark," in *The Bible Knowledge Key Word Study: The Gospels*, ed. Darrell L. Bock [Colorado Springs: Victor, 2002], 113–75). Εἰς, "for" (expressing purpose, BDAG 290d; ZG 100); ἄφεσιν, acc. sg. fem. of ἄφεσις, -εως, ἡ, "forgiveness"; ἁμαρτιῶν, obj. gen.

FOR FURTHER STUDY

7. The Use of the Old Testament in Mark's Gospel

Ahearne-Kroll, Stephen P. *The Psalms of Lament in Mark's Passion: Jesus' Davidic Suffering*. SNTSMS 142. Cambridge: Cambridge University Press, 2007.

Anderson, Hugh. "The Old Testament in Mark's Gospel." Pages 280–306 in *The Use of the Old Testament in the New and Other Essays*. Edited by James M. Efird. Durham, NC: Duke University Press, 1972.

France, R. T. *Jesus and the Old Testament: His Application of Old Testament Passages to Himself and His Mission*. London: Tyndale, 1971.

Hatina, Thomas R. *In Search of a Context: The Function of Scripture in Mark's Narrative*. JSNTSup 232. London: Sheffield Academic Press, 2002.

Hays, Richard B. *Echoes of Scripture in the Gospels*. Waco, TX: Baylor University Press, 2016.

Hooker, Morna D. "Mark." Pages 220–30 in *It Is Written: Scripture Citing Scripture*. Edited by D. A. Carson and H. G. M. Willamson. Cambridge: Cambridge University Press, 1988.

Juel, Donald. *Messianic Exegesis: Christological Interpretation of the Old Testament in Early Christianity*. Philadelphia: Fortress, 1988.

Kee, Howard Clark. "The Function of Scriptural Quotations and Allusions in Mark 11–16." Pages 165–88 in *Jesus und Paulus: Festschrift für Werner Georg Kümmel zum 70. Geburtstag*. Edited by E. Earle Ellis and Erich Grässer. Göttingen: Vandenhoeck & Ruprecht, 1975.

*Marcus, Joel. *The Way of the Lord: Christological Exegesis of the Old Testament in the Gospel of Mark*. Louisville: Westminster/John Knox, 1992.

Moo, Douglas J. *The Old Testament in the Gospel Passion Narratives*. Sheffield, UK: Almond, 1983.

Moyise, Steve. *Jesus and Scripture: Studying the New Testament Use of the Old Testament*. Grand Rapids: Baker Academic, 2010.

O'Brien, Kelli S. *The Use of Scripture in the Markan Passion Narrative*. LNTS 34. London: T&T Clark, 2010.

Watts, Rikki E. *Isaiah's New Exodus and Mark*. WUNT 2/88. Tübingen: Mohr Siebeck, 1997.

———. "Mark." Pages 111–249 in Beale and Carson.

Wiarda, Timothy. "Story-Sensitive Exegesis and Old Testament Allusions in Mark." *JETS* 49 (2006): 489–504.

3. John the Baptist's Baptizing Ministry in the Jordan (1:5–8)

1:5 In 1:5, for the first time, Mark begins a sentence with καί, a common feature of Mark's style. The conj. καί appears 1,091 times in Mark's Gospel, making it more freq. than any other word except the art. (1,510 times). The frequency with which Mark begins both sentences and paragraphs with καί has close pars. in the LXX, but it is unparalleled in orig. Gk. literature from ancient times. Therefore, this stylistic pattern almost certainly has a Sem. background (see Armin D. Baum, "Mark's Paratactic καί as a Secondary Syntactic Semitism," *NovT* 58 [2016]: 1–26). It would difficult to determine the reason for this or other Sem. features in Mark, whether they occur because Mark was a native speaker of a Sem. language such as Aram., because he used Sem. sources, or because he was stylistically influenced by the LXX (Baum, "Mark's Paratactic καί," 26).

Ἐξεπορεύετο, 3rd sg. impf. mid. indic. of dep. ἐκπορεύομαι, "go out" (sg. vb. with a compound subj. [see 12:33]; on the impf., see 1:21); ἐβαπτίζοντο, 3rd pl. impf. pass. indic. of βαπτίζω, "baptize"; ποταμῷ, dat. sg. masc. of ποταμός, -οῦ, ὁ, "river." Another common feature of Mark's style is the use of indef. pl. vbs. (i.e., a third person pl. vb. appearing without a stated subj. to indicate an action done by an undefined group of people [Z §§1, 3; see 1:22]). The use of ἐβαπτίζοντο may be the first example in Mark: "people were being baptized." Therefore, not all who came to see John may have responded with repentance through baptism. The picture of a more limited response fits better with Mark's later description of some from Judea who clearly knew about John's ministry but rejected it as being from God (11:27–33).

The ptc. ἐξομολογούμενοι (nom. pl. masc. of pres. mid. ptc. of ἐξομολογέω, "confess" [mng. with mid.]) is a temp. adv. ptc. expressing an action that is contemp. with the main vb. ("people were being baptized . . . as they were confessing their sins"). As a general rule, in Mark, the action of a temp. adv. ptc. in the pres. tense takes place at the same time as the action of the main vb., while the action of a temp. adv. ptc. in the aor. tense takes place before the action of the main vb. Nevertheless, the primary function of the pres. tense with a ptc. is to communicate verbal aspect (Fanning 406–9; cf. Voelz 1:32). The pres. tense offers an internal perspective, viewing the action as in process without regard to its beginning or end, watching it as it unfolds (Fanning 103; Wallace 514; Campbell, *VA* 13, 35–36). Likewise, the primary function of the aor. tense with a ptc. is to convey verbal aspect (Fanning 413–14), which for the aor. tense involves viewing the action as a whole from the outside, seeing the action in summary (Fanning 97; Wallace 554–55; Campbell, *VA* 103–4). Aor. temp. adv. participles are exceptionally common throughout Mark's Gospel. Of the 251 aor. participles in Mark, more than 75 percent of them are temp. adv. participles. The vast majority of these (roughly 97 percent) precede the main vb. in word order. Mark repeatedly uses aor. temp. adv. participles for antecedent action, not only when the ptc. precedes the main vb. in word order but also in the handful of cases when it follows (see, e.g., πλέξαντες in 15:17). Pres. temp. adv. participles are less freq. in Mark. Of the 247 pres. participles in Mark, about 15 percent of them are temp. adv. participles. Mark repeatedly uses pres. temp. adv. participles for contemp. action, whether the ptc. appears before the main vb. (see, e.g., παράγων in 1:16) or after it (see, e.g., διδάσκων in 12:35). Apparently, the summary aspect of the aor. tense made it conducive for expressing antecedent action with temp. adv. participles, while the imperfective aspect of the pres. tense contributed to its use for contemp. action with temp. adv. participles.

1:6 Ἦν, 3rd sg. impf. act. indic. of εἰμί, "be"; ἐνδεδυμένος, nom. sg. masc. of pf. mid. ptc. of ἐνδύω, "clothe oneself with, put on" (mng. with mid., BDAG 333d); periph. ptc. (on pluperf. periph. vb. forms, see 1:33). John's clothing of camel's hair (τρίχας, acc. pl. fem. of θρίξ, τριχός, ἡ, "hair"; καμήλου, gen. sg. masc. or fem. of κάμηλος, -ου, ὁ or ἡ, "camel") with a leather belt around his waist (ζώνην, acc. sg. fem. of ζώνη, -ης, ἡ, "belt"; δερματίνην, acc. sg. fem. of δερμάτινος, -η, -ον, "leather, made of leather"; ὀσφύν, acc. sg. fem. of ὀσφῦς, -ύος, ἡ, "waist") characterizes him as a prophet like Elijah (cf. 2 Kgs 1:8; Zech 13:4). Ἐσθίων, nom. sg. masc. of pres. act. ptc. of ἐσθίω, "eat"; periph. ptc. (probably emphasizing, in this context, the customary or habitual nature of John's diet; on impf. periph. vb. forms, see 1:22). His diet of locusts (ἀκρίδας, acc. pl. fem. of ἀκρίς, -ίδος, ἡ, "locust") and wild honey (μέλι, acc. sg. neut. of μέλι, -ιτος, τό, "honey"; ἄγριον, acc. sg. neut. of ἄγριος, -α, -ον, "wild") portrays him as a man of the wilderness, living off the land (Stein 49; France 69; Lane 51).

1:7 Ἐκήρυσσεν, 3rd sg. impf. act. indic. of κηρύσσω, "proclaim, preach"; λέγων, nom. sg. masc. of pres. act. ptc. of λέγω, "say." The ptc. λέγων is redundant, repeating what is already implied by the main vb. (Z §368; cf. Wallace 649–50), and is therefore often omitted in Eng. translations. The sg. form λέγων appears redundantly twelve times in Mark, while the pl. form λέγοντες is used in the same way another nine times (see also λέγοντας in 1:27; 2:12, and λέγουσα in 6:25). Ἔρχεται, 3rd sg. pres. mid. indic. of dep. ἔρχομαι, "come"; futuristic pres. (adding a sense of immediacy and certainty [Wallace 535; KMP 262]). The subst. adj. ἰσχυρότερος, the comp. form of ἰσχυρός, is followed by μου, a gen. of comp. ("the one who is stronger than me"). Κύψας, nom. sg. masc. of aor. act. ptc. of κύπτω, "bend down, stoop down"; temp. adv. ptc. antecedent (R 1126; see 1:5 on tense with participles); λῦσαι, aor. act. inf. of λύω, "loose, untie"; epex. inf. (related to the adj. ἱκανός to clarify the extent to which John feels himself unworthy [Burton §376; R 1052]); ἱμάντα, acc. sg. masc. of ἱμάς, -άντος, ὁ, "strap"; ὑποδημάτων, gen. pl. neut. of ὑπόδημα, -ατος, τό, "sandal"; partitive gen. The pers. pron. αὐτοῦ at the end of the clause is an unnecessary redundancy after the rel. pron. οὗ at the beginning of the clause (Z §201; T 325; R 722; Decker 1:10; on the Sem. influence behind this redundancy, see 7:25). Translations drop either the pers. pron. (e.g., ESV) or the rel. pron. (e.g., NET).

1:8 Ἐβάπτισα, 1st sg. aor. act. indic. of βαπτίζω, "baptize." The use of the aor. indic. with ἐβάπτισα seems to portray the event as having just happened ("I just now baptized you" [immediate past aor., see Fanning 280–81; Wallace 564–65; France 71]). Βαπτίσει, 3rd sg. fut. act. indic. of βαπτίζω, "baptize." The conj. δέ, used here in a context that shows contrast, occurs 155 times in Mark, although more freq. in the second half of the book than in the first half (forty-eight times in chs. 1–8 and 107 times in chs. 9–16; cf. Voelz 1:8). This conj. (along with its surrounding context) is used in Mark in several different ways: to show contrast within a saying (e.g., 1:8; 8:35; 13:31), to set off the beginning of a narrative unit or a shift in scene (e.g., 1:14; 7:24; 15:16), to introduce background information (e.g., 5:11; 7:26; 15:7), to show contrasting patterns of behavior (e.g., 4:34; 7:36; 11:8), to portray the continuation of the action or of someone's thoughts (e.g., 4:15; 12:16; 13:37), and—most freq. (about 40 percent of all uses)—to indicate a change of speaker in a conversation (e.g., 9:21, 23; 10:3–5, 36–39; on δέ, see also 10:31; on δέ as a developmental marker and the role of context in expressing contrast, see Runge 28–36). The contrast in John's statement is emphasized through the use of pers. pronouns. Since the ending of a vb. already indicates pers. and number, nom. forms of pers. pronouns are unnecessary. However, they can be included in order to heighten a contrast (BDF §277), as is the case with ἐγώ and αὐτός, thus drawing attention to the difference between John and the more powerful one.

4. Jesus's Baptism in the Jordan (1:9–11)

1:9 The pattern of "καὶ ἐγένετο + a time reference + another independent clause or an inf." sets up a sentence in which the independent clause or inf. actually functions as the subj. of ἐγένετο (Burton §§357, 359; Z §§388–89). "And it came about in those days that Jesus came" (ἐγένετο, 3rd sg. aor. mid. indic. of dep. γίνομαι, "come about, happen"; ἦλθεν, 3rd sg. aor. act. indic. of ἔρχομαι, "come"). The word "that" precedes "Jesus came," to indicate that the entire clause is functioning as a subst. (see 2:15, 23; 4:4 for a similar pattern). Most EVV simply omit any translation of καὶ ἐγένετο (e.g., ESV; NIV; NRSV). Ἐβαπτίσθη, 3rd sg. aor. pass. indic. of βαπτίζω, "baptize." Mark's use of the prep. εἰς in the phrase εἰς τὸν Ἰορδάνην is probably an example of εἰς used instead of ἐν for a local sense, a common tendency in Koine Gk. (BDF §205; Wallace 363; Harris 84–86, 230; Cranfield 52; cf. the use of ἐν in 1:5; on εἰς for ἐν, see 13:9).

1:10 In 1:10, one of Mark's favorite words, εὐθύς, appears for the first time. Mark's Gospel accounts for forty-one out of the fifty-one times the word occurs in the NT. English translations have made various attempts to express the mng. of the word. In the NIV, e.g., the following translations appear: "at once," "without delay," "just then," "quickly," "as soon as," "immediately," "then," "right," "at this," "just," "shortly," "very." Sometimes the NIV omits translating the word entirely (cf. 1:10, 21, 30; 2:12; 5:2; 8:10). By way of contrast, the NASB uses "immediately" for εὐθύς consistently throughout Mark, except in 1:23, where it translates the adv. as "just then." Sometimes εὐθύς has a temp. function, indicating that one action took place shortly after another event. Most often, however, the function of εὐθύς in Mark is simply to draw attention to a particularly dramatic event (France 76; Guelich 30; cf. Porter, *Idioms* 305), conveying something similar to "look at this!"

Ἀναβαίνων, nom. sg. masc. of pres. act. ptc. of ἀναβαίνω, "come up, go up"; temp. adv. ptc. contemp.; εἶδεν, 3rd sg. aor. act. indic. of ὁράω, "see"; σχιζομένους, acc. pl. masc. of pres. pass. ptc. of σχίζω, "tear apart"; περιστεράν, acc. sg. fem. of περιστερά, -ᾶς, ἡ, "dove"; καταβαῖνον, acc. sg. neut. of pres. act. ptc. of καταβαίνω, "come down." Both σχιζομένους and καταβαῖνον are supplementary (complementary) participles used with a main vb. that expresses perception (cf. BDF §416; Voelz 1:33). The two participles agree with the acc. dir. objects and complete the thought of what Jesus saw with regard to the heavens and the Spirit. Supplementary (complementary) participles are fairly common in Mark, occurring around twenty-three times with the pres. ptc. and five times with the pf. ptc. The vb. σχίζω is a striking term for the opening of the heavens, since it means to divide or tear something open by force (BDAG 981c). The only other use of σχίζω in Mark's Gospel is in 15:38, where it is used for the tearing of the temple's veil from top to bottom. After the tearing apart of the heavens, a heavenly voice identifies Jesus as the Son of God (1:11), and then later, after the tearing apart of the temple's veil, the centurion declares Jesus to be the Son of God (15:39).

1:11 Ἐγένετο, 3rd sg. aor. mid. indic. of dep. γίνομαι, "come to be, come"; εὐδόκησα, 1st sg. aor. act. indic. of εὐδοκέω, "be well pleased, take delight." The vb. εὐδόκησα has generated some discussion because, although it is an aor. indic., it does not appear to point back to a past event (for extended treatments, see Burton §55; Porter, *VA* 126–29). Instead, in this context, the vb. conveys a timeless action (Cranfield 56; Taylor 161–62), namely, God's constant attitude toward his Son. Therefore, it is best translated in Eng. with the pres. tense. Two suggestions for the use of a timeless aor. indic. in this verse are as follows:

1. The aor. tense by itself only conveys aspect, viewing the action as a whole, and does not express time even in the indic. mood. Instead, time is indicated by other contextual factors. Therefore, an aor. indic. vb. like εὐδόκησα can easily be timeless, since in this context there are no indicators of time (Porter, *Idioms* 39; cf. Campbell, *Basics* 36–37; Decker 1:xxix, 14).

2. The aor. tense does indeed convey aspect, viewing the action as a whole, but in the indic. mood it also expresses past time with some exceptions in certain well-defined contexts. What makes the use of εὐδόκησα exceptional is that Mark's rendering echoes the Heb. text of Isa 42:1. As a result, the aor. tense serves to translate the Heb. pf., which views an action as complete and can be used at times for a general state or a general truth. Therefore, εὐδόκησα is aor. because of Sem. interference (ZG 101; Turner, *Style* 16; Taylor 161–62; Matthew Black, *An Aramaic Approach to the Gospels and Acts*, 3rd ed. [Oxford: Clarendon, 1967], 128; Fanning 278).

5. Jesus's Temptation in the Wilderness (1:12–13)

1:12 Ἐκβάλλει, "drive out" (stronger than simply "send out"; cf. BDAG 299b–c); historical pres. (marking a new scene). The use of ἐκβάλλει in this verse provides the first example in Mark of the historical pres., i.e., a pres. indic. for an action that took place in the past. The historical pres. appears 151 times in Mark's Gospel. By way of comp., it occurs in Matthew at most ninety-three times and in Luke only eleven times, even though Matthew and Luke are both approximately 70 percent longer than Mark (Wallace 528). Two common patterns for the use of the historical pres. occur in Mark (Campbell, *VA* 68). First, more than 50 percent of the examples of the historical pres. involve vbs. of saying that introduce dir. or indir. discourse, with the vast majority of these being a form of λέγω (e.g., 1:30, 44; see 1:30 for further discussion). Second, a significant number of instances involve vbs. of motion. About half of the examples that follow this pattern make use of ἔρχομαι or συνέρχομαι. Typically, this second pattern appears (1) when a new scene begins (e.g., 1:21, 40; 3:31); (2) when there is a shift in focus to different participants within a scene (e.g., 2:3; 5:15); or (3) when participants change their location within a scene (e.g., 5:38, 40; 6:48; cf. Fanning 231–32). At times, an episode begins not just with a pres. tense vb. of motion but with a string of two or more historical presents initiated by the vb. of motion (cf. Fanning 235). So, e.g., in 5:22–23, one of the synagogue rulers "comes" (ἔρχεται) and "falls" (πίπτει) at Jesus's feet and "begs" (παρακαλεῖ) him to heal his daughter. The only exceptions to these two common patterns in Mark occur when a historical pres. vb. serves to describe a particularly dramatic event in a vivid way (e.g., 2:4; 11:4; 14:51; 16:4; see Fanning 233). There are some places in Mark where several dramatic historical pres. vbs. cluster together within a particular scene, the most notable instance occurring in the description of the crucifixion scene (15:21–27; cf. Campbell, *VA* 69–71, 74). In general, the use of the historical pres. serves to draw attention to an action (Porter, *Idioms* 31; Porter, *VA* 196). In addition—although this is sometimes debated—the use of the historical pres. also has the potential to narrate an event with vividness, portraying past events as though they were taking place in the present, right before our eyes (Fanning 226–31; Wallace 526–27; Burton §14; Voelz 1:15). Given the awkwardness of Mark's freq. use of the historical pres. for an Eng. translation, most versions translate such vbs. with the simple past. The NASB is unique in that it not only translates historical presents with the simple past but also marks them with an asterisk.

1:13 Ἦν, 3rd sg. impf. act. indic. of εἰμί, "be"; τεσσεράκοντα, indecl. number mng. "forty"; τεσσεράκοντα ἡμέρας, acc. for extent of time (cf. Wallace 202; ZG 101); πειραζόμενος, nom. sg. masc. of pres. pass. ptc. of πειράζω, "tempt." In light of the freq. use of periph. constructions in Mark, πειραζόμενος is probably a periph. ptc. rather than an adv. ptc. (cf. Stein 64; see 1:22). It is not unusual in Mark's Gospel for intervening words to appear between the form of εἰμί and the periph. ptc. Here in 1:13, there are five intervening words, but there are five or more words between the form of εἰμί and the periph. ptc. elsewhere in Mark (2:6, 18; 15:26, 40). Διηκόνουν, 3rd pl. impf. act. indic. of διακονέω, "serve" (on the impf., see 1:21).

FOR FURTHER STUDY

8. The Prologue of Mark's Gospel

Boring, M. Eugene. "Mark 1:1–15 and the Beginning of the Gospel." *Semeia* 52 (1990): 43–81.

Botner, Max. "Prophetic Script and Dramatic Enactment in Mark's Prologue." *BBR* 26 (2016): 369–80.

Garland, David E. "The Introduction to the Gospel and to Jesus as the Messiah and Son of God (Mark 1:1–13)." Pages 181–224 in *A Theology of Mark's Gospel: Good News about Jesus the Messiah, the Son of God*. Grand Rapids: Zondervan, 2015.

Guelich, Robert A. "'The Beginning of the Gospel': Mark 1:1–15." *BR* 27 (1982): 5–15.

Keck, Leander E. "The Introduction to Mark's Gospel." *NTS* 12 (1965–66): 352–70.

*Matera, Frank J. "The Prologue as the Interpretive Key to Mark's Gospel." *JSNT* 34 (1988): 3–20.

Mauser, Ulrich. *Christ in the Wilderness: The Wilderness Theme in the Second Gospel and Its Basis in the Biblical Tradition*. SBT 39. Naperville: Alec R. Allenson, 1963.

Ulansey, David. "The Heavenly Veil Torn: Mark's Cosmic *Inclusio*." *JBL* 110 (1991): 123–25.

HOMILETICAL SUGGESTIONS

Let Me Introduce You to Jesus (1:1–15)

1. What do we learn about Jesus? (1:1–13)
   a. Jesus is God's Messiah. (1:1)
   b. Jesus is the one promised by the prophets. (1:2–8)
   c. Jesus is the one loved by the Father and empowered by the Spirit. (1:9–11)
   d. Jesus is the one who overpowers Satan. (1:12–13)
2. What do we learn about responding to Jesus? (1:14–15)
   a. Repent: Reorient your life toward Jesus. (1:15)
   b. Believe: Risk your life on Jesus. (1:15)

Baptism and Identity (1:9–11)

1. Baptism and the identity of Jesus (1:9–11)
   a. The Son of God who is empowered by the Spirit (1:9–10)

     b. The Son of God who is loved by the Father (1:11)

2. Baptism and the identity of believers

     a. Disciples of Jesus (Matt 28:19–20)

     b. People with a new life in Christ (Rom 6:1–10)

     c. Members of the family of God (Gal 3:26–28; Eph 4:4–6)

Temptation: Jesus's and Ours (1:12–13; cf. Heb 4:15)

1. The reality of temptation for Jesus and for us

     a. A real problem for us (Jas 1:13–15)

     b. A real adversary for us (1 Pet 5:8)

2. The provision within temptation for Jesus and for us

     a. The provision of a new freedom for us (Rom 6:15–23)

     b. The provision of an escape for us (1 Cor 10:13)

     c. The provision of a battle plan for us (Eph 6:10–20)

B. JESUS'S INITIAL MINISTRY IN GALILEE (1:14–3:35)

Jesus comes into Galilee proclaiming the gospel of God (1:14). In this way, Mark shifts to a new setting, and Galilee becomes the general setting for Jesus's early ministry throughout 1:14–3:35. Other locations are mentioned—for example, by the Sea of Galilee (1:16; 2:13; 3:7), in Capernaum (1:21, 2:1), in deserted places (1:35, 45), at a mountain (3:13)—but all of these are within the more general setting of Galilee. Mark summarizes the setting for this portion of Jesus's ministry by stating that Jesus went into synagogues throughout Galilee, preaching and casting out demons (1:39).

Mark 1:14–3:35 portrays the authority of Jesus and introduces various groups and individuals, showing how they respond to Jesus and his authority. This section on Jesus's initial ministry in Galilee is particularly important for establishing the two main plotlines that connect the story as a whole, the conflict between Jesus and his disciples and that between Jesus and the religious leaders. In this section, Mark details Jesus's initial expectations of his disciples. He expects them to leave behind their routine pattern of life and to follow him (1:16–20; 2:13–14). He wants them to be with him, because his plan is eventually to send them out to further his work (3:13–14). By way of contrast, the religious leaders quickly come into conflict with Jesus and reject his authority. Early in the narrative, they take on themselves the task of seeking to destroy Jesus (3:6). The remainder of the narrative reveals whether or not the disciples will live up to Jesus's expectations and whether or not the religious leaders will achieve their goal of destroying Jesus.

Mark 1:14–3:35 breaks down into three subunits (1:14–45; 2:1–3:6; 3:7–35), with the middle one being the most obvious. In 2:1–3:6, Mark gathers together a series of controversy stories in which Jesus disputes with the religious leaders over issues such as the forgiveness of sin, fasting, and keeping the Sabbath. Before and after this series of controversies are subunits (1:14–45; 3:7–35) that follow a similar pattern. Both subunits begin with summary statements, one on the content of Jesus's preaching (1:14–15) and the other on the extent of Jesus's healing ministry (3:7–12). Each summary statement leads directly into an episode in which Jesus calls disciples, one on the call of the inner circle of disciples (1:16–20) and the other on the call of the twelve disciples (3:13–19). Mark follows up these call narratives with reports on the differing responses to the power and authority of Jesus (1:21–45; 3:20–35).

1. Summary and Initial Response (1:14–45)

Mark summarizes the message of Jesus as a proclamation concerning the kingdom of God (1:14–15). The kingdom is near, necessitating a response of repentance and belief in the gospel. After this summary of Jesus's message, Mark shows first the response of four disciples, who leave behind all they have to follow Jesus (1:16–20). The narrative continues with a representative day in the early ministry of Jesus in which he teaches in the synagogue, casts out demons, and heals many who are sick (1:21–39). The subunit concludes with a representative healing miracle, the cleansing of a leper (1:40–45). Initial responses to Jesus range from obedience to amazement to hopeful interest in his help to disobedience.

(a) [Transition] Summary of Jesus's Preaching in Galilee (1:14–15)

Mark 1:14–15 is a transitional passage, pointing back to the introduction (1:1–13) and pointing forward to Jesus's ministry in Galilee (1:14–3:35). Like the introduction, 1:14–15 makes reference to the gospel. The gospel is not only a message about Jesus (1:1), but it is also a message that Jesus himself proclaimed, one that declares the near-ness of the kingdom of God and the necessity of repentance and faith. Yet, 1:14–15 also turns attention to the next section. The ministry of John the Baptist comes to an end with his arrest, and Jesus arrives in Galilee to begin his public work.

1:14 Παραδοθῆναι, aor. pass. inf. of παραδίδωμι, "hand over, arrest." The prep. μετά with the acc. art. and the inf. expresses antecedent time ("after John was handed over"; R 1074; Wallace 594–95; Ἰωάννην, subj. of the inf.). In Mark, the aor. inf. is used when expressing antecedent time (with μετὰ τό; cf. 1:14; 14:28) and subsequent time (with πρίν or πρὶν ἤ; 14:30, 72), while the pres. inf. is used when expressing contemp. time (with ἐν τῷ; 4:4; 6:48; cf. Campbell, *VANIV* 105–6, 110–12; on μετὰ τό with the inf., see also 14:28). The vb. παραδίδωμι occurs twenty times in Mark, most often for handing someone over to the authorities or to judgment (*NIDNTTE* 3:624; MM 482–83). Through the repeated use of παραδίδωμι, Mark sets up a par. between the arrest of John the Baptist (1:14), the suffering of Jesus (e.g., 9:31; 10:33; 14:41), and the future persecution of Jesus's followers (13:9, 11–12). Ἦλθεν, 3rd sg. aor. act. indic. of ἔρχομαι, "come, go"; κηρύσσων, nom. sg. masc. of pres. act. ptc. of κηρύσσω, "proclaim, preach"; adv. ptc. of manner. In Mark's Gospel, the name Ἰησοῦς almost always occurs with an art. (which is not translated in Eng.). The only exceptions take place when Ἰησοῦς appears with a title or some other identifying description (1:1, 9; 10:47; 16:6) or when Ἰησοῦς is in the voc. case (1:24, 5:7; 10:47; cf. T 166–67).

1:15 Λέγων, nom. sg. masc. of pres. act. ptc. of λέγω, "say"; adv. ptc. of manner; ὅτι introduces dir. discourse (see 1:37); πεπλήρωται, 3rd sg. pf. pass. indic. of πληρόω, "fulfill, complete"; ἤγγικεν, 3rd sg. pf. act. indic. of ἐγγίζω, "come near, be near." About half of the uses of the pf. tense in the indic. mood in Mark occur with vbs. that either are in the pass. voice (as with πεπλήρωται; cf. e.g., 4:11; 11:21; 15:47; 16:4) or are both act. and intrans. (as with ἤγγικεν; cf. e.g., 7:29; 9:13; 14:4, 42). In such cases, the emph. of the pf. tense often falls on the present state of the subj. (cf. Fanning 160, 291–95; see also Wallace 574–76 on the intensive pf., which is often best translated with the Eng. pres. tense). In Mark's Gospel, the kingdom of God (θεοῦ; poss. gen. or subj. gen.) includes God's royal reign, his kingly authority or rule (cf. BDAG 168d), but also God's royal realm, in the sense that it is a place in which someone can even-tually live (14:25) or into which someone can enter (9:47; 10:15, 25; cf. *EDNT* 1:202). At times, Mark presents the kingdom of God as a future reality (14:25; 15:43), one that will come in power (9:1). However, Jesus also teaches his followers privately about a present form of the kingdom, a mystery form that is understood only by those on the inside (4:10–12). This hidden form begins in a small way like a seed but then grows, not by human effort but by God's work (4:22, 26–29, 30–32). Yet the mystery form of the kingdom is part of Jesus's private teaching. When Jesus publicly proclaims that the kingdom of God is near (1:15), he apparently means that the visible coming of God's kingdom in power is now imminent. The vb. ἐγγίζω can communicate "coming near" in either a spatial or a temporal sense (BDAG 270b–c; Decker 1:18). The description of the kingdom as coming, found later in Mark (9:1; cf. 11:10), points to a temporal sense for ἐγγίζω in 1:15. When ἐγγίζω appears in the NT in this temporal sense, it indicates not that an event has already arrived but that it is imminent, ready to take place at any moment (Matt 21:34; 26:45; Luke 21:20, 28; 22:1; Acts 7:17; Rom 13:12; Phil 2:30; Heb 10:25; Jas 5:8; 1 Pet 4:7). The same is true for the related adv. ἐγγύς when it is used in statements expressing nearness in time (Matt 24:32; 26:18; Mark 13:28; Luke 21:30; John 2:13; 6:4; 7:2; 11:55; Rom 13:11; Rev 1:3; 22:10). The coming of the Messiah is the pivotal moment in God's redemptive plan, after which the coming of the kingdom in power may happen at any time. Μετανοεῖτε, 2nd pl. pres. act. impv. of μετανοέω, "repent"; πιστεύετε, 2nd pl. pres. act. impv. of πιστεύω, "believe." General precepts normally occur in the pres. impv. (BDF §335; Fanning 325–35; Campbell, *VANIV* 81–84, 91–94), which is true for this context, since the impv. forms in 1:15 call on a broad audience in multiple contexts to respond with repentance and faith.

HOMILETICAL SUGGESTIONS

The Early Ministry in Galilee (1:14–3:35): Jesus's Authority and What to Do about It

1. Jesus's authority: Mark emphasizes Jesus's authority in 1:14–3:35.
    a. Jesus teaches with authority. (1:22; cf. 1:14–15)
    b. Jesus rescues people with authority. (1:27; cf. 1:34)
    c. Jesus forgives sin with authority. (2:10; cf. 2:7)
2. What to do about Jesus's authority: Mark highlights how various groups respond to Jesus's authority in 1:14–3:35.
    a. The disciples follow Jesus and prepare to carry on his mission. (1:16–20; 3:13–15)
    b. The crowds express amazement concerning Jesus and seek his help. (1:21–28; 3:7–10)
    c. The religious leaders object to Jesus and want to destroy him. (2:1–12; 3:1–6)
    d. The demons recognize Jesus and obey him. (1:23–27; 3:11–12)
    e. Jesus's new family listens to his teaching and does the will of God. (3:31–35)

(b) Calling of Disciples: The Inner Circle (1:16–20)

1:16 Παράγων, nom. sg. masc. of pres. act. ptc. of παράγω, "pass by"; temp. adv. ptc. contemp. (on παρά following a compound vb., see 1:21); εἶδεν, 3rd sg. aor. act. indic. of ὁράω, "see"; ἀδελφόν; acc. in simple appos.; ἀμφιβάλλοντας, acc. pl. masc. of pres. act. ptc. of ἀμφιβάλλω, "cast, cast a net"; supplementary (complementary) ptc. (Voelz 1:148; see 1:10). Since both Simon and Andrew were involved in the activity, the ptc. is pl., even though this leaves the ptc. without any specific word to agree with in

number. At times, Mark uses γάρ not to offer a reason for what precedes but to introduce an aside, i.e., a brief statement of clarification ("now, you see, for"; BDAG 189d;
Voelz 1:5, 36, 149; cf. 2:15; 5:42; 7:3; 16:4). Ἦσαν, 3rd pl. impf. act. indic. of εἰμί,
"be"; ἁλιεῖς, nom. pl. masc. of ἁλιεύς, -έως, ὁ, "fisherman, fisher."

1:17 Mark 1:17 presents the first instance of εἶπεν (3rd sg. aor. act. indic. of λέγω,
"say"), a form used approximately fifty-eight times in Mark (in light of its frequency,
it will not be parsed again). The word δεῦτε is an adv. functioning as an impv. particle
("Come!"; BDAG 220c), and like other imperatives it can also imply a cond. (R 1023;
Burton §269). If they come (and they should), they will no longer catch fish but rather
will eventually catch people. Ποιήσω, 1st sg. fut. act. indic. of ποιέω, "make"; γενέσθαι,
aor. mid. inf. of dep. γίνομαι, "become"; ἁλιεῖς, acc. pl. masc. of ἁλιεύς, -έως, ὁ, "fisherman, fisher"; ἀνθρώπων, obj. gen. The vb. ποιέω sometimes takes two accusatives in
a dbl. acc. obj.-complement cstr. (Wallace 183). In 1:17, the obj.-complement cstr.
is marked by the presence of the inf. γενέσθαι before the complement, although the
absence of the inf. would not have altered the mng. significantly (R 481; cf. the par. in
Matt 4:19, where the inf. is missing).

1:18 Ἀφέντες, nom. pl. masc. of aor. act. ptc. of ἀφίημι, "leave"; temp. adv. ptc.
antecedent; δίκτυα, acc. pl. neut. of δίκτυον, -ου, τό, "net"; ἠκολούθησαν, 3rd pl. aor.
act. indic. of ἀκολουθέω, "follow"; αὐτῷ, dat. dir. obj. In Mark's Gospel, those called
by Jesus inevitably leave something behind to follow him. In this instance, for Simon
and Andrew, it meant abandoning their nets, and therefore their old lives and liveli-
hood (cf. 1:20; 2:14; 10:28). Yet with the cost comes reward, indeed, an abundance in
the present age and eternal life in the age to come (10:29–30). While ἀκολουθέω sometimes means lit. to walk behind someone who is taking the lead (e.g., 3:7; 5:24; 14:13),
it often conveys in Mark the sense of accompanying Jesus as his disciple (e.g., 1:18;
2:14–15; 8:34; 10:21, 28, 52; 15:41; cf. *EDNT* 1:49). Following Jesus involves being
with him (3:13–14), participating in his ministry (1:17; 3:14–15), learning to think
the way he thinks (8:31–33), and accepting the pattern of his life as one's own (8:34).

1:19 Προβάς, nom. sg. masc. of aor. act. ptc. of προβαίνω, "go ahead, advance"; temp.
adv. ptc. antecedent. The neut. acc. form of the adj. ὀλίγος functions here as an adv. ("a
little farther"; cf. ZG 102; BDAG 703a; Porter, *Idioms* 121–22; see 14:25). Εἶδεν, 3rd
sg. aor. act. indic. of ὁράω, "see." In the phrase τὸν τοῦ Ζεβεδαίου, the noun modified
by the gen. is not stated (although the art. is), but in Eng. the noun must be supplied
("son"); this is a common omission with a gen. of relationship (Wallace 83, 235; R
767). Mark puts αὐτούς in the acc. case, so that it functions as a dir. obj. of εἶδεν,
even though εἶδεν is not repeated again after the καί (on καὶ αὐτούς and its possible
Aram. background, see Z §377). Sometimes Eng. translations simply omit the words
καὶ αὐτούς (e.g., NIV; NET; NLT). Καταρτίζοντας, acc. pl. masc. of pres. act. ptc. of
καταρτίζω, "put in order"; supplementary (complementary) ptc.; on δίκτυα, see 1:18.

1:20 Ἐκάλεσεν, 3rd sg. aor. act. indic. of καλέω, "call"; ἀφέντες, nom. pl. masc. of
aor. act. ptc. of ἀφίημι, "leave"; temp. adv. ptc. antecedent; μισθωτῶν, gen. pl. masc.
of μισθωτός, -οῦ, ὁ, "hired worker" (μισθωτός is an adj. but functions as a subst. in the

NT [BDAG 654a]); ἀπῆλθον, 3rd pl. aor. act. indic. of ἀπέρχομαι, "go after, follow." The beginning of the story of the disciples in Mark is entirely positive; they give up everything, following Jesus without hesitation. Perhaps as much as any book in the Bible, Mark's Gospel puts on display human frailty and failure, with the disciples as the prime examples. In light of the story of the disciples in Mark as a whole, it is important to remember that at the start their desire was to respond immediately and sacrificially to the call of Jesus and that in spite of all their weaknesses, Jesus never gives up on them.

FOR FURTHER STUDY

9. The Disciples in Mark's Gospel

Best, Ernest. *Following Jesus: Discipleship in the Gospel of Mark.* JSNTSup 4. Sheffield, UK: JSOT Press, 1981.

————. *Mark: The Gospel as Story.* Edinburgh: T. and T. Clark, 1983.

————. *Disciples and Discipleship: Studies in the Gospel according to Mark.* Edinburgh: T&T Clark, 1986.

Black, C. Clifton. *The Disciples according to Mark: Markan Redaction in Current Debate.* 2nd ed. Grand Rapids: Eerdmans, 2012.

Donahue, John R. *The Theology and Setting of Discipleship in the Gospel of Mark.* Milwaukee: Marquette University Press, 1983.

Garland, David E. "Mark's Theology of Discipleship." Pages 388–437 in *A Theology of Mark's Gospel: Good News about Jesus the Messiah, the Son of God.* Grand Rapids: Zondervan, 2015.

Henderson, Suzanne Watts. *Christology and Discipleship in the Gospel of Mark.* SNTSMS 135. Cambridge: Cambridge University Press, 2006.

Hurtado, Larry W. "Following Jesus in the Gospel of Mark—and Beyond." Pages 9–29 in *Patterns of Discipleship in the New Testament.* Edited by Richard N. Longenecker. Grand Rapids: Eerdmans, 1996.

Kingsbury, Jack Dean. "The Story of the Disciples." Pages 89–117 in *Conflict in Mark: Jesus, Authorities, Disciples.* Minneapolis: Fortress, 1989.

Malbon, Elizabeth Struthers. "Disciples/Crowds/Whoever: Markan Characters and Readers." *NovT* 28 (1986): 104–30.

————. "Text and Contexts: Interpreting the Disciples in Mark." *Semeia* 62 (1993): 81–102.

Matera, Frank J. "The Incomprehension of the Disciples and Peter's Confession (Mark 6,14–8,30)." *Bib* 70 (1989): 153–72.

Meye, Robert P. *Jesus and the Twelve: Discipleship and Revelation in Mark's Gospel.* Grand Rapids: Eerdmans, 1968.

*Tannehill, Robert C. "The Disciples in Mark: The Function of a Narrative Role." *JR* 57 (1977): 386–405.

HOMILETICAL SUGGESTIONS

Jesus and His Followers (1:14–20)

1. What do we learn about Jesus? (1:14–20)
   a. Jesus teaches the message of God. (1:14)
   b. Jesus arrives at the decisive moment in God's kingdom plan. (1:15)
   c. Jesus calls people to follow him. (1:16–20)
2. What do we learn about responding to Jesus? (1:18, 20)
   a. Leave: Disciples must leave something behind to follow Jesus. (1:18, 20)
   b. Follow: Disciples must follow Jesus immediately whenever he calls. (1:18, 20)

Following Jesus's Call on Your Life (1:16–20)

1. A look back: Jesus is worth following.
2. A look at this moment: Jesus calls us to follow him.
   a. A response that is swift: Disciples respond to Jesus's call immediately. (1:18, 20)
   b. A response that is sacrificial: Disciples respond to Jesus's call no matter the cost.
   c. A response that has a set goal: Disciples respond to Jesus's call to reach others for the kingdom. (1:17)
3. A look forward: Jesus can make something special out of failures.

(c) One Day in Capernaum (1:21–39)

1:21 To illustrate the nature of Jesus's early ministry in Galilee, Mark presents a collection of scenes that take place within the framework of a twenty-four-hour period. Within this representative day in Capernaum, the main features of Jesus's early ministry appear: teaching, exorcism, healing, and proclamation—all displaying Jesus's unique authority. Εἰσπορεύονται, 3rd pl. pres. mid. indic. of dep. εἰσπορεύομαι, "go into, enter"; historical pres. (see 1:12). The compound vb. εἰσπορεύονται serves as an example of how Mark often repeats the prep. from the beginning of a compound vb. in a prep. phrase after the vb. (cf. R 559–60). This repetition can happen in Mark with a variety of prepositions: ἀπό (e.g., ἀπέρχομαι in 1:42), διά (e.g., διέρχομαι in 10:25), εἰς (e.g., εἰσέρχομαι in 1:21), ἐκ (e.g., ἐκβάλλω in 7:26; ἐξέρχομαι in 1:25), ἐπί (e.g., ἐπιράπτω in 2:21), παρά (e.g., παράγω in 1:16), περί (e.g., περίκειται in 9:42), or πρός (e.g., προσπίπτω in 7:25; προσκολλάω in 10:7). Often in an Eng. translation, it is necessary to remove the repetition. The noun σάββατον follows the 2nd decl. pattern except in the dat. pl., which takes a 3rd decl. form (σάββασιν; BDAG 909b). The pl. can be used to refer to a single Sabbath day (BDAG 909d), a typical pattern for names of special days (T 26–27; R 408; BDF §141). Εἰσελθών, nom. sg. masc. of aor. act. ptc. of εἰσέρχομαι, "go into, enter"; temp. adv. ptc. antecedent; ἐδίδασκεν, 3rd sg. impf. act. indic. of διδάσκω, "teach."

As is often the case in the narrative sections of Mark, this passage includes a number of impf. vbs. (e.g., ἐδίδασκεν in 1:21, but see also 1:22, 23, 30, 31, 32, 33, 34, 35). The impf. tense appears in Mark's Gospel 292 times, with over 95 percent of those uses occurring in narrative rather than in discourse. The impf. tense provides an internal viewpoint of the action, without reference to the beginning or end, portraying the action as it unfolds (Wallace 541; cf. Fanning 27, 240). Mark's Gospel has a higher percentage of impf. vbs. than the other NT Gospels have (Fanning 254–55), and the specific use for most of them in Mark can probably be categorized simply as "descriptive impf." (cf. Fanning 247). In Mark's Gospel, the impf. tense regularly appears in certain types of contexts. One common pattern is that the impf. often records "off-line" information. In general, within Mark's narrative, aor. vbs. carry forward the main sequence of events, while impf. vbs. fill in background or explanatory information (Campbell, *VA* 91–96; cf. Fanning 19, 74–75, 191, 248–49; Rodney J. Decker, "The Function of the Imperfect Tense in Mark's Gospel," in *The Language of the New Testament: Context, History, and Development*, ed. Stanley E. Porter and Andrew W. Pitts [Leiden: Brill, 2013], 353–54, 356–60). The use of the impf. tense for "off-line" information may be one reason why Mark's Gospel freq. employs the impf. tense to relate the reactions of people to events in the narrative (with vbs. of amazement, see 1:22; with φοβέομαι, see 6:20). Nevertheless, while impf. vbs. often provide background information, they can also at times carry forward the main story line, as would be the case with ἐδίδασκεν in 1:21 (cf. Campbell, *VA* 96–98). In such cases, the use of the impf. portrays the action in a vivid way and draws the audience into the narrative to watch the action in progress as it unfolds (cf. Campbell, *VA* 93; Fanning 254–55). For example, Mark often uses an impf. vb. at the end of a healing miracle for a dramatic action that demonstrates the reality of the miracle (1:31; 5:13, 42; 6:35; 7:35; 8:25; 10:52). Another common pattern in Mark's Gospel is to use impf. vb. forms to introduce dir. or indir. discourse (Decker, "Function of the Imperfect," 353–56; cf. Fanning 282–90). This function is, of course, not the exclusive domain of the impf. tense in Mark, since the pres. and aor. tenses also freq. introduce dir. and indir. discourse. However, a significant number of impf. vb. forms in Mark introduce discourse and do so in a way that portrays the give-and-take of an ongoing conversation (cf. Fanning 286; on λέγω in the impf., see 2:16; on other impf. vbs. of saying, see 4:10; impf. vbs. of saying may also indicate repeated statements [see 6:14] or simultaneous speaking [see 5:28]). Finally, Mark sometimes uses the impf. in statements that portray repeated action (iter. impf.), which is most apparent when he includes a string of impf. tense vbs. within a summary section to present a series of actions that took place repeatedly (e.g., 3:11–12; 4:33–34; 6:13, 19–20, 56; 9:30–32; cf. Decker, "Function of the Imperfect," 358–60; Fanning 248).

1:22 Ἐξεπλήσσοντο, 3rd pl. impf. pass. indic. of ἐκπλήσσω, "be amazed, be overwhelmed" (mng. with pass.); ἐπί, "at, because of" (pointing to the basis for an emotion, BDAG 365a; Z §126). The vb. ἐξεπλήσσοντο provides the first obvious example of an indef. pl. vb. in Mark's Gospel, a common grammatical feature of Mark's style (see Taylor 47 for a list of possible examples; see also C. H. Turner, "Marcan Usage:

Notes, Critical and Exegetical, on the Second Gospel," *JTS* 25 [1924]: 377–86). Mark often uses pl. vbs. with no subj. expressed and no subj. implied beyond the general idea of "people" or "some people." Statements with indef. pl. vbs. make general claims about how an unspecified group of people acted or responded. The use of indef. pl. vbs. is less freq. in Matthew and Luke, where subjects are more clearly stated or are created through the use of the pass. voice (Taylor 47; Z §3). Mark uses four different vbs. for amazement, all of which seem to overlap in mng.: ἐκπλήσσω (e.g., 1:22; 5:20), ἐξίστημι (e.g., 2:12), θαμβέω (e.g., 1:27), and θαυμάζω (e.g., 5:20). In addition, these last two vbs. can take a prep. prefix that serves to intensify the vb. (ἐκθαμβέω in 9:15; 14:33; 16:5–6, and ἐκθαυμάζω in 12:17; on ἐκ as an intensifying prep. prefix, see 2 Cor 4:8), although even these intensive forms seem to overlap in mng. with the other vbs. of amazement. In general, Mark's preference is to use the impf. tense with such vbs. (e.g., when the six vbs. listed above occur for amazement in Mark, eleven out of the twenty total occurrences are impf., incl. eleven out of the sixteen uses in the indic.).

Another common grammatical feature of Mark's Gospel is the use of periph. participles (ἦν, 3rd sg. impf. act. indic. of εἰμί, "be"; διδάσκων, nom. sg. masc. of pres. act. ptc. of διδάσκω, "teach"). The impf. form of εἰμί and the pres. ptc. διδάσκων together produce an impf. verbal idea ("was teaching"; cf. Wallace 648; KMP 343). Of the different verbal periph. cstr(s). used in Mark, the periph. impf. appears the most often (cf. Taylor 45 for a list of eighteen examples). In Mark, the impf. periph. cstr. seems to be used in two types of contexts (cf. Fanning 314–15 for a similar point), in contexts that highlight a customary or repeated action (e.g., 1:6; 2:18; 5:5; 15:43) or in contexts that leave the impression that an action was continuing on for some time (e.g., 9:4; 10:32; 14:4, 40, 54; 15:40). Mark 1:22 seems to highlight the customary nature of Jesus's teaching, and, therefore, it provides a more general statement and not simply a statement about Jesus's teaching on this one occasion (Fanning 315). The ptc. ἔχων (nom. sg. masc. of pres. act. ptc. of ἔχω, "have") probably functions as a subst. ptc., even though it does not take an art., since in the comp. it stands par. to "the scribes."

1:23 The use of εὐθύς in 1:23 demonstrates that Mark does not always use this adv. as a temp. marker (either the man was there or not; he did not immediately appear in the synagogue out of nowhere). Instead, Mark uses εὐθύς in this context simply to point to a dramatic new development in the scene (see 1:10). ῏Ην, 3rd sg. impf. act. indic. of εἰμί, "be." The use of ἐν in the phrase ἄνθρωπος ἐν πνεύματι ἀκαθάρτῳ ("a man with an unclean spirit") indicates a close association (BDAG 328b; Z §§116–18); the man's association with an unclean spirit has left him under that spirit's influence or power. Mark uses "unclean spirit" and "demon" with equal frequency for hostile spirit beings, both eleven times, and he employs them interchangeably (cf. e.g., 6:7, 13; 7:25–26). Ἀνέκραξεν, 3rd sg. aor. act. indic. of ἀνακράζω, "cry out."

1:24 Λέγων, redundant ptc. (see 1:7). The mng. of the idiomatic expression τί ἡμῖν καὶ σοί can vary according to the context (Yarbro Collins 169). The use in 1:24 is similar to instances in the OT where the question communicates a rejection of any association with someone, esp. at a time when the speaker is seeking to maintain a safe distance from a potential aggressor (Judg 11:12; 2 Sam 16:10; 19:22; 1 Kgs 17:18; cf. France

103). The dat. pronouns ἡμῖν and σοί could therefore be categorized as examples of a dat. of association ("What [do you have to do] with us and [we have to do] with you?"). Both Ἰησοῦ (R 263; BDF §55) and Ναζαρηνέ (ZG 102) are voc.; ἦλθες, 2nd sg. aor. act. indic. of ἔρχομαι, "come, go"; ἀπολέσαι, aor. act. inf. of ἀπόλλυμι, "destroy"; inf. of purpose (which, in Mark, is almost always in the aor. tense [exceptions include 3:14–15; 13:22]). The pf. of οἶδα (1st sg. pf. act. indic. of οἶδα, "know") conveys a pres. mng. in the sense that it expresses a pres. state without any implication of a prior completed action that produced that state (Fanning 299; cf. Wallace 579–80). Forms of οἶδα, which occur twenty-one times in Mark, account for almost 20 percent of all pf. forms in Mark. Pluperfect forms of οἶδα (1:34; 9:6; 14:40; constituting three of the seven total pluperf. forms in Mark) convey a past state, once again without implying a prior action that produced the state (Fanning 308; cf. Wallace 586). The pron. σε in the demon's statement is acc. because, in anticipation of the indir. question introduced by τίς, the pron. has moved forward out of the dependent clause, where it would have been in the nom. case as the subj., and has moved into the main clause, where it now functions as the dir. obj. of οἶδα (R 488; T 325; Cranfield 76). In Eng., the pron. is best kept with the dependent clause (ESV: "I know who you are").

1:25 Ἐπετίμησεν, 3rd sg. aor. act. indic. of ἐπιτιμάω, "rebuke"; αὐτῷ, dat. dir. obj.; λέγων, redundant ptc.; φιμώθητι, 2nd sg. aor. pass. impv. of φιμόω, "silence, muzzle" (mng. with pass.: be silent, BDAG 1060b [on φιμόω, see 4:39]); ἔξελθε, 2nd sg. aor. act. impv. of ἐξέρχομαι, "come out"). Aor. impv. forms (such as φιμώθητι and ἔξελθε) typically appear in contexts that call for a specific command, an impv. to be obeyed in a concrete situation (in this case by the unclean spirit; cf. BDF §335; Fanning 325–35; Campbell, *VANIV* 81–86; although certain vbs. occur idiomatically in the pres. even in specific commands [e.g., ὑπάγω; Fanning 340–41, 343]; see also 2:11).

1:26 Σπαράξαν, nom. sg. neut. of aor. act. ptc. of σπαράσσω, "shake violently, shake to and fro"; temp. adv. ptc. antecedent. The vb. σπαράσσω occurs only three times in the NT (Mark 1:26; 9:26; Luke 9:39), always with reference to a demon doing harm to a human victim. Outside the NT, the word could be used for tearing or rending by an animal, such as a dog (LSJ 1624). In 2 Sam 22:8 LXX, the vb. is used with a mng. comparable to that found in Mark 1:26; there it refers to the forceful shaking of the foundations of heaven. The NIV rendering ("shook the man violently") appropriately conveys the sense of the vb. in Mark. Φωνῆσαν, nom. sg. neut. of aor. act. ptc. of φωνέω, "call out, cry out"; temp. adv. ptc. antecedent; φωνῇ, dat. of manner; ἐξῆλθεν, 3rd sg. aor. act. indic. of ἐξέρχομαι, "come out."

1:27 Ἐθαμβήθησαν, 3rd pl. aor. pass. indic. of θαμβέω, "be astonished, be amazed" (mng. with pass., BDAG 442c); συζητεῖν, pres. act. inf. of συζητέω, "discuss"; inf. of result (an inf. following ὥστε always takes the pres. tense in Mark); πρός, "with, among" (with a vb. of saying, cf. BDAG 874b). A pl. form of the refl. pron., such as ἑαυτούς, can have a reciprocal sense, equivalent to the mng. of ἀλλήλους (BDAG 269a; R 690; BDF §287). This use of the refl. pron. is fairly common in Mark, esp. when occurring with a vb. of saying (1:27; 9:10; 10:26; 11:31; 12:7; 14:4; 16:3). Λέγοντας,

acc. pl. masc. of pres. act. ptc. of λέγω, "say"; redundant ptc.; κατ', "with" (to introduce a characteristic, BDAG 513b); καί, ascensive; πνεύμασι, dat. dir. obj.; ἐπιτάσσει,
from ἐπιτάσσω, "command"; ὑπακούουσιν, from ὑπακούω, "obey"; αὐτῷ, dat. dir. obj.
(R 540). The prep. phrase κατ' ἐξουσίαν likely modifies the preceding phrase διδαχὴ
καινή ("a new teaching with authority") rather than the following vb. ἐπιτάσσει ("he
commands with authority"). Therefore, it reflects back on the similar reaction in 1:22,
which also connected Jesus's authority with his teaching.

1:28 Ἐξῆλθεν, 3rd sg. aor. act. indic. of ἐξέρχομαι, "go out"; ἀκοή, nom. sg. fem. of
ἀκοή, -ῆς, ἡ, "fame, report, news"; αὐτοῦ, obj. gen. (Taylor 177; Voelz 1:162); πανταχοῦ,
adv. mng. "everywhere." The adj. ὅλος appears in Mark's Gospel for the first time in
1:28 and eighteen times total. It is always in the pred. position in Mark but translated
as an attrib. adj. (R 774; BDF §275). Περίχωρον, acc. sg. fem. of περίχωρος, -ου, ἡ,
"surrounding region, neighborhood" (although technically περίχωρος is a two-terminal
adj. that functions as a fem. subst. in the NT [BDAG 808b]); Γαλιλαίας, gen. of appos.
(Stein 90).

1:29 Both ἐξελθόντες (nom. pl. masc. of aor. act. ptc. of ἐξέρχομαι, "go out, exit"; temp.
adv. ptc. antecedent) and ἦλθον (3rd pl. aor. act. indic. of ἔρχομαι, "come, go") are pl.
forms (on the text-critical problem, see Metzger 64 and Marcus 1:196 in support of pl.
rather than sg. forms). Presumably the pl. subj. includes Jesus along with Simon and
Andrew. James and John are listed as going with them and therefore are not included
in the subj. Since the limits of the pl. subj. are left ambiguous, others may have come
as well.

1:30 Πενθερά, nom. sg. fem. of πενθερά, -ᾶς, ἡ, "mother-in-law"; Σίμωνος, gen. of
relationship; κατέκειτο, 3rd sg. impf. mid. indic. of dep. κατάκειμαι, "lie down";
πυρέσσουσα, nom. sg. fem. of pres. act. ptc. of πυρέσσω, "suffer with a fever"; adv. ptc.
of cause; on λέγουσιν as "speak," see BDAG 590a. The use of λέγουσιν in 1:30 is the
first time that a form of λέγω appears as a historical pres. in Mark, a common grammatical pattern throughout Mark's Gospel as a whole (on the historical pres., see 1:12).
Mark uses various grammatical forms of λέγω to introduce dir. or indir. discourse,
incl.: pres. indic. (e.g., λέγει in 1:44); pres. ptc. (e.g., λέγων in 1:7); pres. inf. (e.g.,
λέγειν in 10:28); impf. indic. (e.g., ἔλεγον in 2:16); aor. indic. (e.g., εἶπεν in 1:17); aor.
ptc. (e.g., εἰπών in 14:39). Of the 288 uses of λέγω in Mark, about 73 are examples of
the historical pres. (approximately 25 percent of all uses). Other vbs., similar to λέγω,
that introduce dir. or indir. discourse with the historical pres. include: ἐπερωτάω (7:5),
παραγγέλλω (8:6), παρακαλέω (5:23; 7:32; 8:22), and φωνέω (10:49; see Fanning 233).
Mark regularly uses vbs. of saying with the historical pres. or with the impf. tense,
apparently to portray the ongoing nature of a conversation (Fanning 286–87; cf. e.g.,
5:7–10). In general, forms of λέγω are too freq. and easily recognizable to be parsed
in this guide.

1:31 Προσελθών, nom. sg. masc. of aor. act. ptc. of προσέρχομαι, "approach"; temp.
adv. ptc. antecedent; ἤγειρεν, 3rd sg. aor. act. indic. of ἐγείρω, "raise up"; κρατήσας,
nom. sg. masc. of aor. act. ptc. of κρατέω, "take hold of, grasp, seize"; temp. adv. ptc.

antecedent (Burton §134; R 860; Decker 1:32). The vb. κρατέω normally takes an acc. dir. obj. (e.g., 3:21; 7:3) but uses a gen. dir. obj. for taking hold of some part, like a hand, of a larger whole (e.g., 5:41; 9:27; cf. BDF §170). Ἀφῆκεν, 3rd sg. aor. act. indic. of ἀφίημι, "leave"; πυρετός, nom. sg. masc. of πυρετός, -οῦ, ὁ, "fever." The act of serving others (διηκόνει, 3rd sg. impf. act. indic. of διακονέω, "serve"; αὐτοῖς, dat. dir. obj.) demonstrates the reality of her healing (on the impf. at the end of healing miracles, see 1:21).

1:32 Ὀψίας, gen. sg. fem. of ὀψία, -ας, ἡ, "evening"; γενομένης, gen. sg. fem. of aor. mid. ptc. of dep. γίνομαι, "come to be, come" (cf. BDAG 197c); gen. abs.; temp. adv. ptc. antecedent. Gen. abs. constructions are fairly freq. in Mark's Gospel, appearing thirty-seven times. In Mark, the gen. abs. participles are almost evenly divided between pres. participles and aor. participles, and all of them function as temp. adv. participles, except for the gen. abs. ptc. in 11:11, which seems to be an adv. ptc. of cause (cf. e.g., NASB; NIV; CSB; Taylor 458). Aor. gen. abs. participles in Mark consistently express antecedent action in relation to the main vb., and pres. gen. abs. participles contemp. action. Ἔδυ, 3rd sg. aor. act. indic. of δύνω, "go down, set" ("when the sun set," i.e., when the Sabbath had come to an end); ἔφερον, 3rd pl. impf. act. indic. of φέρω, "bring, carry" (indef. pl. [see 1:22]); κακῶς, adv. mng. "badly," but used idiomatically with ἔχω to mean "be ill, be sick" (BDAG 502b); ἔχοντας, acc. pl. masc. of pres. act. ptc. of ἔχω, "have"; subst. ptc. The idiomatic cstr. involving ἔχω with the adv. κακῶς is difficult in Eng., since in Eng. the vb. "to have" works more naturally with an adj. ("those who have it bad"; R 546). The idiom refers to being sick with various diseases (see 1:34) and is best translated with that in mind ("those who were sick"). Δαιμονιζομένους, acc. pl. masc. of pres. mid. ptc. of dep. δαιμονίζομαι, "be possessed or tormented by a demon"; subst. ptc.

1:33 Ἦν, 3rd sg. impf. act. indic. of εἰμί, "be"; ἐπισυνηγμένη, nom. sg. fem. of pf. pass. ptc. of ἐπισυνάγω, "gather together"; periph. ptc.; πρός, "at, by" (indicating here a position near the door with the implication of facing toward it [LN 83.24]). The impf. form of εἰμί and the pf. ptc. ἐπισυνηγμένη create a pluperf. verbal idea (Wallace 648; cf. KMP 343–44; see Taylor 45 for the uses of the periph. pluperf. in Mark [1:6, 33; 6:52; 15:7, 26, 46]). Every pluperf. periph. cstr. in Mark uses ἦν, the 3rd sg. form of εἰμί, and a mid. or pass. ptc. form (there are no pluperf. mid. or pass. indic. forms in Mark). The emph. in each case is on certain results that existed in the past, which is often best expressed with the past tense in Eng. ("was gathered"). In each instance, the pluperf. periph. cstr. appears in a clause that provides background or "off-line" information for the continuing narrative (on the pluperf., see also 14:44).

1:34 Ἐθεράπευσεν, 3rd sg. aor. act. indic. of θεραπεύω, "heal"; on κακῶς ἔχοντας, see 1:32 (although in 1:34 ἔχοντας functions as an adj. ptc.); ποικίλαις, dat. pl. fem. of ποικίλος, -η, -ον, "various, many kinds of"; νόσοις, dat. pl. fem. of νόσος, -ου, ἡ, "disease, illness"; dat. of means (Voelz 1:170). Mark does not refer to the "many" that Jesus healed in 1:34 to set up a contrast with the "all" who were brought to him in 1:32, as though Jesus healed many but not all. Instead, Jesus healed them all, and the number of those healed was in fact many (on the incl. use of πολλοί, see *TDNT* 6:536–45). Ἐξέβαλεν, 3rd sg. aor. act. indic. of ἐκβάλλω, "cast out, drive out, send away"; ἤφιεν, 3rd sg. impf. act. indic. of ἀφίημι, "allow, permit"; λαλεῖν, pres. act. inf. of λαλέω, "speak"; complementary inf.; ὅτι, causal (Porter, *Idioms* 237); ἤδεισαν, 3rd pl. pluperf. act. indic. of οἶδα, "know" (on the pluperf. of οἶδα, see 1:24).

1:35 What takes place in the morning fills out the picture concerning Jesus's early ministry in Galilee according to this representative day in 1:21–39. Jesus's ministry is marked by prayer and a desire to proclaim his message throughout the whole of Galilee. Πρωΐ, adv. mng. "early, early in the morning"; ἔννυχα, acc. pl. neut. of the adj. ἔννυχος, -ον, "at night" (used here as an adv. [BDAG 338a; see 14:25]); λίαν, adv. indicating a high degree and with ἔννυχα mng.: "when it was still night" or "when it was still quite dark" (BDAG 594c); ἀναστάς, nom. sg. masc. of aor. act. ptc. of ἀνίστημι, "rise, set out"; temp. adv. ptc. antecedent; ἐξῆλθεν, 3rd sg. aor. act. indic. of ἐξέρχομαι, "go out"; ἀπῆλθεν, 3rd sg. aor. act. indic. of ἀπέρχομαι, "depart, go away"; ἔρημον, "isolated, desolate, deserted" (when used as an attrib. adj.); κἀκεῖ, "and there" (adv. formed through the combination of καί and ἐκεῖ [BDAG 499d]); προσηύχετο, 3rd sg. impf. mid. indic. of dep. προσεύχομαι, "pray." Mark's Gospel mentions Jesus spending time with God in prayer on three occasions: at the beginning (1:35), middle (6:46), and end (14:35–39) of his ministry, which leaves the impression that similar times alone in prayer were a regular practice for Jesus.

1:36 Κατεδίωξεν, 3rd sg. aor. act. indic. of καταδιώκω, "search for diligently" (sg. vb. with a compound subj. [see 12:33]). Mark's Gospel includes a number of compound vbs. with κατα- as the prep. prefix, at times to intensify the action and emphasize its completion (R 562–64, 606). In 1:36, the compound vb. καταδιώκω conveys that Simon and his companions searched diligently to make certain that they found Jesus (cf. R 562–63, who suggests "hunt down" for καταδιώκω). Other similar examples include: κατακλάω in 6:41; κατεσθίω in 4:4 and 12:40; and κατευλογέω in 10:16. At times, compound vbs. with κατα- as the prep. prefix are simply intensive: e.g., καταβαρύνω in 14:40; κατακόπτω in 5:5; and κατακυριεύω and κατεξουσιάζω in 10:42. Of course, sometimes the prep. prefix κατα- indicates direction (as with καταβαίνω), and sometimes it has no effect at all (R 562, 606). The use of the art. οἱ with μετ' αὐτοῦ causes the prep. phrase to function like a noun ("those with him"; R 766; Wallace 236). Similar uses of an art. with a prep. phrase include: τὰ πρὸς τὴν θύραν in 2:2 ("the [places] at the door"); οἱ μετ' αὐτοῦ in 2:25 ("those with him"); οἱ παρ' αὐτοῦ in 3:21 ("those from him"); οἱ περὶ αὐτόν in 4:10 ("those around him"); οἱ παρὰ τὴν ὁδόν in 4:15 ("those on the road"); τοὺς μετ' αὐτοῦ in 5:40 ("those with him"; cf. 2:25); οἱ ἐν τῇ Ἰουδαίᾳ in 13:14 ("those in Judea"); ὁ δὲ ἐπὶ τοῦ δώματος in 13:15 ("but the one on the housetop"); ὁ εἰς τὸν ἀγρόν in 13:16 ("the one in the field").

1:37 Εὗρον, 3rd pl. aor. act. indic. of εὑρίσκω, "find." In this context, ὅτι serves to introduce dir. discourse, since it follows a vb. of saying and the pron. σε would have necessarily changed to αὐτόν with indir. discourse (Porter, *Idioms* 269–70). Therefore, the ὅτι is omitted in translation. About one-third of the uses of ὅτι in Mark introduce dir.

discourse, while almost half introduce indir. discourse (on ὅτι with dir. discourse, see C. H. Turner, "Marcan Usage: Notes, Critical and Exegetical, on the Second Gospel," *JTS* 28 [1926–27]: 9–15).

1:38 Ἄγωμεν, 1st pl. pres. act. subjunc. of ἄγω, "go"; hort. subjunc. When used as a hort. subjunc., the vb. ἄγω becomes intrans. ("let us go"; ZG 103; BDAG 17a; cf. Matt 26:46; Mark 14:42; John 11:7, 15–16; 14:31; on the pres. tense, see 2:11). Ἀλλαχοῦ, adv. mng. "elsewhere, in another direction"; ἐχομένας, acc. pl. fem. of pres. mid. ptc. of ἔχω, "neighboring, surrounding" (mng. with mid. ptc. [BDAG 422d; LN 83.29]); adj. ptc.; κωμοπόλεις, acc. pl. fem. of κωμόπολις, -εως, ἡ, "country-town, market-town." The vb. ἔχω in the mid. indicates proximity, either spatial ("be next to") or temporal ("be next"); therefore, a mid. ptc. form of ἔχω used as an adj. ptc. to modify a place (such as κωμοπόλεις) means "the neighboring towns" or "the towns that are near-by" (ZG 104; BDAG 422d). Κηρύξω, 1st sg. aor. act. subjunc. of κηρύσσω, "preach, proclaim"; subjunc. in a purpose ἵνα clause; εἰς, "for" (expressing purpose [see BDAG 290d; R 595]); ἐξῆλθον, 1st sg. aor. act. indic. of ἐξέρχομαι, "come."

1:39 Ἦλθεν, 3rd sg. aor. act. indic. of ἔρχομαι, "come, go"; κηρύσσων, nom. sg. masc. of pres. act. ptc. of κηρύσσω, "preach, proclaim"; adv. ptc. of manner; on the use of εἰς for ἐν, see Harris 84–86; BDF §205 (see also 1:9; 13:9); ἐκβάλλων, nom. sg. masc. of pres. act. ptc. of ἐκβάλλω, "cast out, drive out, send away"; adv. ptc. of manner.

HOMILETICAL SUGGESTIONS

Authority and Mission (1:21–39)

1. What do we learn about Jesus's authority? (1:21–34)
   a. Jesus has the authority to teach the message of God. (1:21–22)
   b. Jesus has the authority to rescue people dominated by demonic oppression. (1:23–28)
   c. Jesus has the authority to heal people overtaken by the power of sickness. (1:29–34)
2. What do we learn about Jesus's mission? (1:35–39)
   a. Jesus maintained a focus on his mission through prayer. (1:35)
   b. Jesus was not distracted from his mission, even by other worthy tasks. (1:36–39)
3. What do we learn about responding to Jesus?
   a. Followers of Jesus live under his authority.
   b. Followers of Jesus live for his mission.

(d) Healing of the Leper (1:40–45)

1:40 After his summary of Jesus's ongoing ministry throughout Galilee (1:39), Mark offers one example of a healing miracle from this time and the type of response it produced, a response of overwhelming popularity that made it difficult for Jesus to continue his mission. Ἔρχεται, 3rd sg. pres. mid. indic. of dep. ἔρχομαι, "come, go";

historical pres. (see 1:12); λεπρός, nom. sg. masc. of λεπρός, -οῦ, ὁ, "leper, person with a disfiguring skin disease" (λεπρός is technically an adj. that normally functions as a subst. in the NT, BDAG 592c–d); παρακαλῶν, nom. sg. masc. of pres. act. ptc. of παρακαλέω, "implore, entreat, beg"; adv. ptc. of manner (the following two participles have the same function); γονυπετῶν, nom. sg. masc. of pres. act. ptc. of γονυπετέω, "kneel down"; λέγων, nom. sg. masc. of pres. act. ptc. of λέγω, "say"; ὅτι, introduces dir. discourse; θέλῃς, 2nd sg. pres. act. subjunc. of θέλω, "will, want, desire"; subjunc. in a 3rd class cond. clause; δύνασαι, 2nd sg. pres. mid. indic. of dep. δύναμαι, "be able to, can"; καθαρίσαι, aor. act. inf. of καθαρίζω, "make clean"; complementary inf. When 3rd class cond. clauses appear in Mark's Gospel (which happens approximately nineteen times), they set forth an action as a hypothetical possibility (see Porter, *Idioms* 262). Nevertheless, the leper's use of a 3rd class cond. clause is not an expression of doubt regarding Jesus's willingness to heal but rather an expression of humility, which is then followed by a statement of unquestioning confidence in Jesus's ability to heal (France 117; Cranfield 91).

1:41 Mark 1:41 begins with a complicated text-critical problem. The vast majority of NT mss. read σπλαγχνισθείς (nom. sg. masc. of aor. pass. ptc. of dep. σπλαγχνίζομαι, "have pity, have compassion"), while the Western ms. D and a few Lat. mss. read ὀργισθείς (nom. sg. masc. of aor. pass. ptc. of ὀργίζω, "be angry" [mng. with pass.]). Many commentators argue that ὀργισθείς, as the more difficult reading, is likely orig. (e.g., Taylor 187–88; Cranfield 92; Marcus 1: 206, 209; France 117–18; Edwards 70; Strauss 111–12). Yet the ms. support for σπλαγχνισθείς is early and widespread, and this reading is probably to be preferred (Metzger 65; Yarbro Collins 177). The reading ὀργισθείς may have arisen as a way to prepare for Jesus's stern treatment of the man in 1:43 or may have simply originated accidentally (on this last point, see Peter J. Williams "An Examination of Ehrman's Case for ὀργισθείς in Mark 1:41," *NovT* 54 [2012]: 1–12). Σπλαγχνισθείς, adv. ptc. of cause (on σπλαγχνίζομαι, see 6:34); ἐκτείνας, nom. sg. masc. of aor. act. ptc. of ἐκτείνω, "stretch out"; temp. adv. ptc. antecedent. The art. τήν probably functions as a poss. pron. ("stretching out his hand"; Wallace 216; cf. KMP 158), which leaves αὐτοῦ as the gen. dir. obj. of ἥψατο ("he touched him"; cf. BDAG 126b). Mark often uses the art. as a poss. pron. with χείρ (e.g., 1:31; 5:23; 7:3, 32) and often places the dir. obj. of ἅπτομαι before the vb. (e.g., 3:10; 5:31; 8:22; 10:13; cf. Voelz 1:178). Ἥψατο, 3rd sg. aor. mid. indic. of ἅπτω, "touch" (mng. with mid.); καθαρίσθητι, 2nd sg. aor. pass. impv. of καθαρίζω, "make clean"; pronouncement impv. (on the pass., see 10:40). At times (cf. also 7:34; 11:23), a pass. impv. does not express a command but rather a pronouncement, so that the impv. itself performs the deed (Wallace 492; cf. 440).

1:42 Ἀπῆλθεν, 3rd sg. aor. act. indic. of ἀπέρχομαι, "depart, go away, leave" (on ἀπ' after the compound vb., see 1:21); λέπρα, nom. sg. fem. of λέπρα, -ας, ἡ, "leprosy, disfiguring skin disease"; ἐκαθαρίσθη, 3rd sg. aor. pass. indic. of καθαρίζω, "make clean." In the Synoptic Gospels, the vb. καθαρίζω appears in connection with the healing of lepers but not with reference to other types of healings (Matt 8:2–3; 10:8; 11:5; Mark 1:40–42; Luke 4:27; 5:12–13; 7:22; 17:14, 17).

1:43 Ἐμβριμησάμενος, nom. sg. masc. of aor. mid. ptc. of dep. ἐμβριμάομαι, "warn sternly"; temp. adv. ptc. antecedent; αὐτῷ, dat. dir. obj. The vb. ἐμβριμάομαι is a surprisingly harsh word in this context, since it often implies an attitude of anger or displeasure (BDAG 322a; MM 206; cf. Dan 11:30 LXX; Mark 14:5). Later, the healed leper, in direct disobedience to Jesus's command, goes out and spreads the message concerning Jesus's miraculous power. Apparently, Jesus was able to foresee the likely disregard of his instructions by the healed man, and his stern warning was an attempt to impress upon the man the seriousness of his command (cf. Lane 87). Ἐξέβαλεν, 3rd sg. aor. act. indic. of ἐκβάλλω, "drive out, send away."

1:44 Ὅρα, 2nd sg. pres. act. impv. of ὁράω, "pay attention, see to it that" (mng. with an aor. subjunc. following; BDAG 720b). The impv. form of ὁράω can precede a prohibition expressed in the aor. subjunc. as a way to draw attention to the seriousness of that following command (cf. BDF §364; Matt 8:4; 18:10; 1 Thess 5:15). Εἴπῃς, 2nd sg. aor. act. subjunc. of λέγω, "say." The prohibitive subjunc. εἴπῃς occurs here with a combination of two negatives (μηδενί and μηδέν) to strengthen the prohibition (cf. BDF §431). In Eng., it is necessary to translate the negatives in such a way that they do not cancel each other out. The use of two or more negatives in a statement or command is a common feature of Mark's style (Taylor 46; Turner, *Style* 26; e.g., 5:3, which translated lit., states: "no one was no longer able to bind him not even with a chain"; other examples include 2:2; 3:20, 27; 5:37; 6:5; 7:12; 9:8; 11:2, 14; 12:14, 34; 14:25, 61; 15:5; 16:8). In addition, Mark's Gospel includes instances of οὐ μή with the aor. subjunc. (9:1, 41; 10:15; 13:2 [twice], 19, 30; 14:25) and with the fut. indic. (13:31; 14:31), all within sayings. Ὕπαγε, 2nd sg. pres. act. impv. of ὑπάγω, "go, depart" (on the pres. impv. of ὑπάγω, see 1:25, 2:11); δεῖξον, 2nd sg. aor. act. impv. of δείκνυμι, "show, make known"; προσένεγκε, 2nd sg. aor. act. impv. of προσφέρω, "offer, present"; καθαρισμοῦ, gen. sg. masc. of καθαρισμός, -οῦ, ὁ, "cleansing, purification." The rel. pron. ἅ appears here without an antecedent; either the antecedent must be supplied ("the things which") or the rel. pron. must be translated in a way that causes the rel. clause to function as the dir. obj. of προσένεγκε ("what"; cf. R 719–21). Προσέταξεν, 3rd sg. aor. act. indic. of προστάσσω, "command, order"; μαρτύριον, acc. sg. neut. of μαρτύριον, -ου, τό, "testimony"; αὐτοῖς, dat. of interest (disadvantage). This same phrase, εἰς μαρτύριον αὐτοῖς, appears elsewhere in Mark's Gospel in contexts where someone is giving a testimony against those who reject the message about Jesus (6:11; 13:9). The testimony mentioned in 1:44 likewise communicates the idea of incriminating evidence, a witness that exposes the guilt of others, apparently in this case, the religious leaders at the temple in Jerusalem (*TDNT* 4:502–3; Lane 87–88; cf. Jas 5:3).

1:45 The art. with ὁ δέ functions as a pers. pron. ("but he"; Wallace 211–12; cf. KMP 158). The idiomatic use of the art. as a pers. pron. before δέ appears approximately forty-six times in Mark's Gospel (used with ὁ δέ, οἱ δέ, and ἡ δέ [cf. 6:24; 7:28], but never in Mark with μέν). Often the next word following δέ is the main vb. of the clause (e.g., 3:4; 12:16; 16:6), although the next word can also be an adv. ptc. (e.g., 8:33; 10:50; 15:2) or an adv. (e.g., 6:50; 10:26; 14:70). It is possible that a ptc. following ὁ δέ or οἱ δέ might be a subst. ptc. (10:32; 13:13), in which case the art. is not a pers. pron., but goes with the ptc. However, a ptc. following ὁ δέ or οἱ δέ in Mark is normally an adv. ptc., as is true in 1:45 with ἐξελθών (nom. sg. masc. of aor. act. ptc. of ἐξέρχομαι, "go out"; temp. adv. ptc. antecedent). Ἤρξατο, 3rd sg. aor. mid. indic. of ἄρχω, "begin" (mng. with mid.); κηρύσσειν, pres. act. inf. of κηρύσσω, "proclaim, preach"; complementary inf. The use of ἄρχομαι with a complementary inf. appears twenty-six times in Mark, with the form of ἄρχομαι always in the aor. and the inf. always in the pres. This use of ἄρχομαι with an inf., in a sense, has a counterpart in the ingressive impf. (cf. Wallace 598; Campbell, VANIV 102–4), with the aor. form of ἄρχομαι emphasizing the beginning of the action and the pres. inf. showing its continuation. However, in Mark's Gospel it is often difficult to see in context how the use of ἄρχομαι with an inf. serves to highlight the beginning of an action rather than simply portraying an action in progress (cf. Taylor 48; BDF §392). One difference between Mark's use of an aor. form of ἄρχομαι with a pres. inf. and his use of the impf. tense is that, while the impf. often appears for background information, the use of the aor. form of ἄρχομαι with a pres. inf. normally serves to further the main story line. Πολλά, neut. acc. pl. of πολύς (used as an adv. to intensify the vb. [cf. ZG 104; BDAG 849d–50a]; πολλά as an intensifying adv. is common in Mark [see, e.g., 3:12; 5:10, 23, 38, 43; 6:20, 23; 9:26; 15:3]); διαφημίζειν, pres. act. inf. of διαφημίζω, "spread abroad"; complementary inf.; μηκέτι, adv. mng. "no longer"; αὐτόν, acc. subj. of the inf.; δύνασθαι, pres. mid. inf. of dep. δύναμαι, "be able to, can"; inf. of result; φανερῶς, adv. mng. "openly, publicly"; εἰσελθεῖν, aor. act. inf. of εἰσέρχομαι, "go into, enter"; complementary inf.; ἦν, 3rd sg. impf. act. indic. of εἰμί, "be, stay" (cf. BDAG 284c); ἤρχοντο, 3rd pl. impf. mid. indic. of dep. ἔρχομαι, "come, go" (indef. pl. vb. [see 1:22]); πάντοθεν, adv. mng. "from all directions, from everywhere."

FOR FURTHER STUDY

10. Miracles in Mark's Gospel

Achtemeier, Paul J. Jesus and the Miracle Tradition. Eugene, OR: Wipf and Stock, 2008.

Best, Ernest. "The Miracles in Mark." RevExp 75 (1978): 539–54.

Bolt, Peter G. Jesus' Defeat of Death: Persuading Mark's Early Readers. SNTSMS 125. Cambridge: Cambridge University Press, 2003.

Broadhead, Edwin K. Teaching with Authority: Miracles and Christology in the Gospel of Mark. JSNTSup 74. Sheffield, UK: JSOT Press, 1992.

Cotter, Wendy J. The Christ of the Miracle Stories: Portrait through Encounter. Grand Rapids: Baker Academic, 2010.

Dwyer, Timothy. The Motif of Wonder in the Gospel of Mark. JSNTSup 128. Sheffield, UK: Sheffield Academic Press, 1996.

Glasswell, M. E. "The Use of Miracles in the Markan Gospel." Pages 149–62 in Miracles: Cambridge Studies in Their Philosophy and History. Edited by C. F. D. Moule. London: Mowbray, 1965.

Keener, Craig S. Miracles: The Credibility of the New Testament Accounts. 2 vols. Grand Rapids: Baker Academic, 2011.

*Matera, Frank J. "'He Saved Others; He Cannot Save Himself': A Literary-Critical Perspective on the Markan Miracles." Int 47 (1993): 15–26.

Twelftree, Graham H. "The Miracles of Jesus in Mark." Pages 57–101 in *Jesus the Miracle Worker: A Historical and Theological Study.* Downers Grove, IL: InterVarsity, 1999.

Yarbro Collins, Adela. "Suffering and Healing in the Gospel of Mark." Pages 39–72 in *The Beginning of the Gospel: Probings of Mark in Context.* Minneapolis: Fortress, 1992.

HOMILETICAL SUGGESTIONS

Compassion and Mission (1:40–45)

1. What do we learn about Jesus? (1:40–45)
   a. Jesus cares: Jesus has the power and compassion to help those in need. (1:40–42)
   b. Jesus cares more: Jesus has a mission that goes beyond meeting the physical needs of people. (1:43–45)
2. What do we learn about responding to Jesus? (1:40, 44–45)
   a. Right recognition: Like the leper, believers should understand Jesus's willingness and power to meet their needs. (1:40)
   b. Wrong response: Unlike the healed leper, believers should be faithful to obey all of Jesus's commands. (1:44–45)

2. Controversy with Religious Leaders (2:1–3:6)

In 2:1–3:6, Mark brings together five controversy stories in which Jesus comes into conflict with the religious leaders. These controversies cover conflicts over Jesus's claim to forgive sin (2:1–12), Jesus's practice of eating with sinners (2:13–17), the failure of Jesus's disciples to fast (2:18–22), Jesus's attitude toward the Sabbath (2:23–28), and Jesus's healing on the Sabbath (3:1–6). Central to Jesus's criticism of the religious leaders is their failure to see that new wine does not belong in old wineskins (2:21–22). Holding fast to their traditions, they fail to account for the new work that God is doing through his Messiah, Jesus.

(a) Conflict over Healing and Forgiving Sin (2:1–12)

2:1 Mark 2:1–12 initiates a new development in the narrative by introducing Jesus's conflict with the religious leaders, in this instance over how his words and actions convey divine authority. Εἰσελθών, nom. sg. masc. of aor. act. ptc. of εἰσέρχομαι, "go into, enter"; temp. adv. ptc. antecedent (the ptc. details Jesus's movement, but the subj. of the main vb. [ἠκούσθη] is impers., so that the ptc. is left hanging [Taylor 192; Guelich 81]); δι᾽ ἡμερῶν, "several days later" (idiomatic expression indicating a point in time after an interval of several days [LN 67.59; BDAG 224b; Z §115; cf. NLT]); ἠκούσθη, 3rd sg. aor. pass. indic. of ἀκούω, "hear, learn" (cf. BDAG 38b: "it became known"). The pres. tense vb. ἐστίν should be translated as past in Eng. because of the differences in how Gk. and Eng. express indir. discourse, that is, reported speech. In Gk. the tense of the vb. in the orig. statement is generally retained, while in Eng. the tense of the vb. in indir. discourse is moved back to correspond with the time of speaking (Wallace 457; 537–38; Z §346; see also διαλογίζονται in 2:8).

2:2 Συνήχθησαν, 3rd pl. aor. pass. indic. of συνάγω, "gather, come together, assemble" (mng. with pass., which takes an act. intrans. force, BDAG 962d); μηκέτι, adv. mng. "no longer"; χωρεῖν, pres. act. inf. of χωρέω, "hold, contain, be room"; inf. of result; τὰ πρὸς τὴν θύραν, "the places at the door" (see 1:33, 36). The acc. case for the art. τά can be classified as either an acc. subj. of the inf. ("not even the space at the door contained [them] any longer"; cf. Taylor 193) or as an acc. of respect or reference with the inf. of χωρέω functioning as an impers. vb. ("there was no longer room even with respect to the space at the door"; Cranfield 96–97; cf. Moule 27; on dbl. negatives, see 1:44). The second option seems to fit better if μηδέ is pointing to an additional overcrowded space beyond the house itself. Ἐλάλει, 3rd sg. impf. act. indic. of λαλέω, "speak" (impf. for background information [see 1:21]).

2:3 Ἔρχονται, 3rd pl. pres. mid. indic. of dep. ἔρχομαι, "come, go"; historical pres. (see 2:4); indef. pl. vb. ("they came" [see 1:22]); φέροντες, nom. pl. masc. of pres. act. ptc. of φέρω, "bring, carry"; adv. ptc. of manner; παραλυτικόν, acc. sg. masc. of παραλυτικός, -οῦ, ὁ, "paralytic, lame person, disabled person" (παραλυτικός is technically an adj. that functions as a subst. in the NT [BDAG 768d]; παραλυτικός also appears in 2:4, 5, 9, 10). The term "paralytic" is simply a transliteration of the Gk. παραλυτικός. As a general term, the word refers to a person who is unable to walk without specifying the cause for the disability. However, it would be wrong to think of someone paralyzed from a spinal cord injury, since such an individual rarely, if ever, survived in antiquity (Dwight N. Peterson, "Translating παραλυτικός in Mark 2:1–12: A Proposal," *BBR* 16 [2006]: 261–72). Αἰρόμενον, acc. sg. masc. of pres. pass. ptc. of αἴρω, "take up"; adj. ptc. used without an art. to modify an anar. noun (cf. Voelz 1:190).

2:4 Δυνάμενοι, nom. pl. masc. of pres. mid. ptc. of dep. δύναμαι, "be able to, can"; adv. ptc. of cause; προσενέγκαι, aor. act. inf. of προσφέρω, "bring"; complementary inf.; αὐτῷ, indir. obj. (the dir. obj. must be supplied from the context [cf. BDAG 886b]); ἀπεστέγασαν, 3rd pl. aor. act. indic. of ἀποστεγάζω, "unroof, remove [a roof]"; στέγην, acc. sg. fem. of στέγη, -ης, ἡ, "roof"; ἦν, 3rd sg. impf. act. indic. of εἰμί, "be"; ἐξορύξαντες, nom. pl. masc. of aor. act. ptc. of ἐξορύσσω, "dig through"; temp. adv. ptc. antecedent; χαλῶσι, 3rd pl. pres. act. indic. of χαλάω, "let down, lower"; historical pres. The historical pres. vbs. in 2:1–12 for the most part follow typical patterns. The use of ἔρχονται in 2:3 marks a shift in focus to new participants in the scene (see 1:12), and λέγει in 2:5, 8, 10 introduces dir. discourse (see 1:12, 30). However, χαλῶσι in 2:4 does not fit the more typical patterns in Mark, and it appears to be used simply to draw attention to a particularly dramatic event, the lowering of the lame man through the hole in the roof (cf. Fanning 233). Κράβαττον, acc. sg. masc. of κράβαττος, -ου, ὁ, "mat, pallet, bed" (κράβαττος appears again in 2:9, 11–12).

2:5 Ἰδών, nom. sg. masc. of aor. act. ptc. of ὁράω, "see"; temp. adv. ptc. antecedent. By using the pl. gen. form αὐτῶν (subj. gen. [Wallace 116]), Mark shows that Jesus recognized the faith of the whole group. By addressing his words of forgiveness directly to the paralytic, Jesus clearly includes the paralytic among those who had faith. Τέκνον, voc.; ἀφίενται, 3rd pl. pres. pass. indic. of ἀφίημι, "forgive" (on the pass., see 10:40).

The pres. tense of ἀφίενται is an instantaneous pres. (Fanning 202–3; cf. Burton §13). A pres. indic. vb. can be used for an action that is accomplished by the act of speaking itself. The emph., therefore, is on the pres. time value of the vb. rather than on its perspective of viewing the action in progress. In accordance with Jesus's authoritative pronouncement, at that moment, the man's sins are forgiven.

2:6 Ἦσαν, 3rd pl. impf. act. indic. of εἰμί, "be"; γραμματέων, partitive gen.; καθήμενοι, nom. pl. masc. of pres. mid. ptc. of dep. κάθημαι, "sit"; διαλογιζόμενοι, nom. pl. masc. of pres. mid. ptc. of dep. διαλογίζομαι, "reason, ponder." Both καθήμενοι and διαλογιζόμενοι are functioning as periph. participles, which, when used along with the impf. form of εἰμί, serve to create an impf. verbal idea (see 1:22).

2:7 The neut. form of τίς can function adv. for "why?" (BDAG 1007d; R 738; Wallace 345; for other examples, see 2:8, 24; 4:40; 8:12; 10:18; 11:3; 12:15; 14:6, 63). The scribes simply state their accusation against Jesus as βλασφημεῖ, "he's blaspheming." Within a Jewish context in the 1st century AD, to blaspheme against God meant to speak or act with arrogant and insulting disrespect toward God or his work in the world (cf. Darrell L. Bock, *Blasphemy and Exaltation in Judaism: The Charge against Jesus in Mark 14:53–65*, repr. ed. [Grand Rapids: Baker, 2000], 30–112). This accusation from the scribes foreshadows Jesus's trial before the Sanhedrin, where he is condemned to death for blasphemy (14:63–64). Δύναται, 3rd sg. pres. mid. indic. of dep. δύναμαι, "be able to, can"; ἀφιέναι, pres. act. inf. of ἀφίημι, "forgive"; complementary inf.; εἰ μή, "except" (esp. without a vb. following [BDF §376; BDAG 278d]). The nom. ὁ θεός stands in appos. to εἷς to clarify who is the one, and the only one, who can forgive sins: God alone (cf. 10:18).

2:8 Ἐπιγνούς, nom. sg. masc. of aor. act. ptc. of ἐπιγινώσκω, "perceive, recognize"; temp. adv. ptc. antecedent; διαλογίζονται, 3rd pl. pres. mid. indic. of dep. διαλογίζομαι, "reason, ponder" (on the pres. tense in indir. discourse, see 2:1); διαλογίζεσθε, 2nd pl. pres. mid. indic. of dep. διαλογίζομαι, "reason, ponder."

2:9 Εὐκοπώτερον, nom. sg. neut. comp. adj. form of εὔκοπος, -ον, "easy"; εἰπεῖν, aor. act. inf. of λέγω, "say"; subst. inf. in appos. to τί; ἀφίενται, 3rd pl. pres. pass. indic. of ἀφίημι, "forgive"; ἔγειρε, 2nd sg. pres. act. impv. of ἐγείρω, "rise, arise, get up" (intrans. mng. with the impv. [BDAG 272b]); ἆρον, 2nd sg. aor. act. impv. of αἴρω, "take up"; περιπάτει, 2nd sg. pres. act. impv. of περιπατέω, "walk." The claim to forgive sins is easy to make in the sense that it is not verifiable. It would be more difficult for Jesus to command the paralytic to walk, since his words would be open to immediate verification (Guelich 88; Lane 96). Jesus's question in 2:9 includes three impv. forms, two in the pres. tense (ἔγειρε and περιπάτει) and one in the aor. tense (ἆρον). See 2:11 for more on the use of tense with impv. forms.

2:10 The new sentence starting in 2:10 begins with the subord. conj. ἵνα, while the main clause on which the ἵνα depends does not appear until 2:11. Between the subord. clause and the main clause, Mark inserts a parenthetical phrase ("he told the paralytic") to clarify that Jesus is no longer speaking to the scribes (France 129; cf. R 433–34). Εἰδῆτε, 2nd pl. pf. act. subjunc. of οἶδα, "know." The pf. tense appears in the subjunc. mood only ten times in the NT and always with a form of οἶδα. The use of the pf. with the subjunc., therefore, is apparently a lexically driven choice (cf. R 907). Ἀφιέναι, pres. act. inf. of ἀφίημι, "forgive"; epex. inf. (clarifying the nature of Jesus's authority).

In 2:10, the title "the Son of Man" occurs for the first time in Mark's Gospel. "The Son of Man" appears more freq. in Mark (fourteen times) than other messianic titles for Jesus, such as "Christ" (six times) or "Son of God" (seven times [when incl. 1:11; 9:7; and 14:61, but not 12:6 and 13:32]). In Mark, Jesus employs the title "the Son of Man" to emphasize certain aspects of his role and mission: his present authority on earth (2:10, 28); his suffering, death, and resurrection (see 8:31); and his future coming in power and glory (see 13:26). The statements in this last category allude to the Son of Man figure in Dan 7:13–14, so that the title identifies Jesus with the heavenly figure who appears before God to receive an everlasting dominion over all the nations as the representative of God's people (cf. Dan 7:27). This glorious power that Jesus will have as the Son of Man in the future presses back and creates implications for the present, so that he has a rightful claim to present authority.

2:11 Ἔγειρε, 2nd sg. pres. act. impv. of ἐγείρω, "rise, arise, get up" (act. intrans. mng. with the impv. [BDAG 272b]); ἆρον, 2nd sg. aor. act. impv. of αἴρω, "take up"; ὕπαγε, 2nd sg. pres. act. impv. of ὑπάγω, "go, depart." The sequence of tenses for the impv. forms in 2:11 is pres., aor., and pres. Normally, specific commands in concrete situations call for the use of aor. impv. forms (cf. BDF §335; Fanning 325–35). However, certain vbs., esp. vbs. of motion, came to be used idiomatically with the pres. tense in the impv. mood, even when used for specific commands (Fanning 340–54). The most common of such vbs. in Mark's Gospel is ὑπάγω (used as a pres. impv. twelve times, always in specific commands). Other vbs. in Mark that idiomatically use the pres. impv. in specific commands include: ἐγείρω (2:9, 11; 3:3; 5:41; 10:49; 14:42), περιπατέω (2:9), θαρσέω (6:50; 10:49), and φέρω (9:19; 11:2; 12:15). The pres. tense hort. subjunc. form ἄγωμεν (1:38; 14:42) also fits this pattern.

2:12 Ἠγέρθη, 3rd sg. aor. pass. indic. of ἐγείρω, "rise, get up" (act. intrans. mng. in pass. [BDAG 271d]); ἄρας, nom. sg. masc. of aor. act. ptc. of αἴρω, "take up"; temp. adv. ptc. antecedent; ἐξῆλθεν, 3rd sg. aor. act. indic. of ἐξέρχομαι, "go out"; ἐξίστασθαι, pres. mid. inf. of ἐξίστημι, "be amazed, be astonished" (mng. with mid.); inf. of result (on vbs. of amazement, see 1:22); πάντας, acc. subj. of the inf. Since Mark uses "all," he apparently intends to include the scribes among those who expressed amazement at Jesus's miraculous power and who glorified God (cf. 12:17; Stein 122; Lane 99). Δοξάζειν, pres. act. inf. of δοξάζω, "glorify, praise"; inf. of result; λέγοντας, acc. pl. masc. of pres. act. ptc. of λέγω, "say"; adv. ptc. of result (cf. 6:2; 7:37; 10:26); ὅτι, introduces dir. discourse; οὐδέποτε, adv. mng. "never"; εἴδομεν, 1st pl. aor. act. indic. of ὁράω, "see." The adv. οὕτως functions as a subst. in this context and serves as the dir. obj. of εἴδομεν ("anything like this"; cf. BDAG 742b; BDF §434; ZG 105).

FOR FURTHER STUDY

11. Jesus as the Son of Man in Mark's Gospel

Broadhead, Edwin K. "Son of Man." Pages 124–34 in *Naming Jesus: Titular Christology in the Gospel of Mark*. JSNTSup 175. Sheffield, UK: Sheffield Academic Press, 1999.

Burkett, Delbert. *The Son of Man Debate: A History and Evaluation*. SNTSMS 107. Cambridge: Cambridge University Press, 1999.

Caragounis, Chrys C. *The Son of Man: Vision and Interpretation*. WUNT 1/38. Tübingen: Mohr Siebeck, 1986.

Donahue, John R. "Recent Studies on the Origin of 'Son of Man' in the Gospels." *CBQ* 48 (1986): 484–98.

Hooker, Morna D. *The Son of Man in Mark: A Study of the Background of the Term 'Son of Man' and Its Use in St. Mark's Gospel*. Montreal: McGill University Press, 1967.

———. "Is the Son of Man Problem Really Insoluble?" Pages 155–68 in *Text and Interpretation: Studies in the New Testament Presented to Matthew Black*. Edited by Ernest Best and R. McL. Wilson. Cambridge: Cambridge University Press, 1979.

Hurtado, Larry W., and Paul L. Owen, eds. *"Who Is This Son of Man?" The Latest Scholarship on a Puzzling Expression of the Historical Jesus*. LNTS 390. London: T&T Clark, 2011.

Kingsbury, Jack Dean. "The Christology of Mark: The Son of Man." Pages 157–79 in *The Christology of Mark's Gospel*. Philadelphia: Fortress, 1983.

Malbon, Elizabeth Struthers. "Narrative Christology and the Son of Man: What the Markan Jesus Says Instead." *BibInt* 11 (2003): 373–85.

Marcus, Joel. "Son of Man as Son of Adam." *RB* 110 (2003): 38–61, 370–86.

*Marshall, I. Howard. "Who Is This Son of Man?" Pages 63–82 in *The Origins of New Testament Christology*. 2nd ed. Downers Grove, IL: InterVarsity, 1990.

———. "The Synoptic 'Son of Man' Sayings in the Light of Linguistic Study." Pages 72–94 in *To Tell the Mystery: Essays on New Testament Eschatology in Honor of Robert H. Gundry*. Edited by Thomas E. Schmidt and Moisés Silva. JSNTSup 100. Sheffield, UK: JSOT Press, 1994.

Moule, C. F. D. "'The Son of Man': Some of the Facts." *NTS* 41 (1995): 277–79.

Perrin, Norman. "The Creative Use of the Son of Man Traditions by Mark." *Union Seminary Quarterly Review* 23 (1967–68): 357–65.

Tödt, H. E. *The Son of Man in the Synoptic Tradition*. Philadelphia: Westminster, 1965.

HOMILETICAL SUGGESTIONS

What the Hole in the Roof Reveals (2:1–12)

1. What do we learn about Jesus? (2:1–12)
   a. Jesus acts with divine authority. (2:1–7)
   b. Jesus's power to meet physical needs reveals his power to meet spiritual needs. (2:8–12)
2. What do we learn about a life of faith? (2:3–5)
   a. People of faith will not be stopped from reaching out to Jesus for help. (2:3–4)
   b. People of faith receive forgiveness of sins. (2:5)

(b) Conflict over Eating with Sinners (2:13–17)

2:13 Jesus's conflict with the religious leaders continues in 2:13–17, this time over his association with sinners. Yet Jesus paid no heed to the objections and judgmental attitude of the scribes, because the very purpose for which he came was to bring hope to broken people who needed his help. Ἐξῆλθεν, 3rd sg. aor. act. indic. of ἐξέρχομαι, "go out"; ἤρχετο, 3rd sg. impf. mid. indic. of dep. ἔρχομαι, "come, go"; ἐδίδασκεν, 3rd sg. impf. act. indic. of διδάσκω, "teach." Through the use of two impf. vbs. (ἤρχετο and ἐδίδασκεν), Mark sets Jesus's teaching ministry as the background and context for his interaction with Levi and his association with sinners (on the impf., see 1:21).

2:14 Παράγων, nom. sg. masc. of pres. act. ptc. of παράγω, "pass by"; temp. adv. ptc. contemp.; εἶδεν, 3rd sg. aor. act. indic. of ὁράω, "see"; τόν, "the son" (on the art. followed by a gen. of relationship, see 1:19); καθήμενον, acc. sg. masc. of pres. mid. ptc. of dep. κάθημαι, "sit"; supplementary (complementary) ptc.; ἐπί, "at, by" (see BDAG 363c); τελώνιον, acc. sg. neut. of τελώνιον, -ου, τό, "tax office." A tax office was a toll collection booth, where tolls and customs on goods in transit were collected along major thoroughfares. The tax office at Capernaum probably collected customs on goods being transported into the territory of the tetrarch Herod Antipas either by boat or by road (*NIDNTTE* 4:480–84). Ἀκολούθει, 2nd sg. pres. act. impv. of ἀκολουθέω, "follow" (the pres. impv. portrays Jesus's command as a call to ongoing discipleship [cf. Fanning 345–46]); μοι, dat. dir. obj.; ἀναστάς, nom. sg. masc. of aor. act. ptc. of ἀνίστημι, "rise, stand up"; temp. adv. ptc. antecedent; ἠκολούθησεν, 3rd sg. aor. act. indic. of ἀκολουθέω, "follow"; αὐτῷ, dat. dir. obj.

2:15 Γίνεται, 3rd sg. pres. mid. indic. of dep. γίνομαι, "come about, happen"; κατακεῖσθαι, pres. mid. inf. of dep. κατάκειμαι, "recline for a meal, dine"; αὐτόν, acc. subj. of the inf. The inf. clause beginning with κατακεῖσθαι functions grammatically as the subj. of γίνεται, so that it is necessary to introduce the translation of the inf. with "that" in order to indicate in Eng. its use as a subst. ("and it came about that he was reclining for a meal"; see 1:9 for a similar cstr., but with the aor. ἐγένετο rather than the historical pres. γίνεται [R 1423: "the only example of γίνεται in this construction" in the NT]). Τελῶναι, nom. pl. masc. of τελώνης, -ου, ὁ, "tax-collector"; συνανέκειντο, 3rd pl. impf. mid. indic. of dep. συνανάκειμαι, "eat with, sit at table with"; τῷ Ἰησοῦ and τοῖς μαθηταῖς, dat. of association; ἦσαν, 3rd pl. impf. act. indic. of εἰμί, "be"; ἠκολούθουν, 3rd pl. impf. act. indic. of ἀκολουθέω, "follow"; αὐτῷ, dat. dir. obj. At this stage in the narrative, the exact number of Jesus's disciples is unclear—simply stated as "many"— but in 3:13–19 Jesus specifically appoints twelve men to be with him, and from that point on the "disciples" and the "twelve" seem to function as interchangeable terms.

2:16 Φαρισαίων, partitive gen. (Wallace 86; KMP 96); ἰδόντες, nom. pl. masc. of aor. act. ptc. of ὁράω, "see"; temp. adv. ptc. antecedent; ἐσθίει (1st use): pres. tense retained in indir. discourse but translated as past in Eng. (see 2:1); τελωνῶν, gen. pl. masc. of τελώνης, -ου, ὁ, "tax collector"; ἔλεγον, 3rd pl. impf. act. indic. of λέγω, "say" (impf. forms of λέγω will not be parsed again in light of their frequency). Impf. forms of λέγω appear repeatedly in Mark's Gospel, occurring approximately fifty times. Mark generally uses the impf. of λέγω to portray in a descriptive way the give-and-take of a conversation (cf. Fanning 286 [but see 5:28 and 6:14 for different uses]; for other vbs. that use the impf. to introduce dir. or indir. discourse, see 4:10). The question of the scribes begins with ὅτι, which in this case is the neut. sg. form of ὅστις. Forms of ὅστις normally function as rel. pronouns, but the neut. sg. form (often printed as ὅ τι) can introduce an indir. question (Acts 9:6), and in a way that is unique to Mark's Gospel within the NT, it can also be used to introduce a dir. question with the mng. "why?" (2:16; 9:11, 28; BDAG 730b; R 729–30; BDF §300; cf. Burton §349; Decker 1:57–58). What appears in ch. 2 of Mark is a series of events in which people question "why" (using τί, ὅτι, and διὰ τί) Jesus or his disciples act in the way that they do (2:7, 16, 18, 24; cf. Hooker 96).

2:17 Ἀκούσας, nom. sg. masc. of aor. act. ptc. of ἀκούω, "hear"; temp. adv. ptc. antecedent; ὅτι, introduces dir. discourse; ἰσχύοντες, nom. pl. masc. of pres. act. ptc. of ἰσχύω, "be in good health, be healthy" (BDAG 484c; LN 23.130); subst. ptc.; ἰατροῦ, gen. sg. masc. of ἰατρός, -οῦ, ὁ, "physician"; obj. gen.; ἔχοντες, nom. pl. masc. of pres. act. ptc. of ἔχω, "have"; subst. ptc.; κακῶς, adv. mng. "badly," but used idiomatically with ἔχω to mean "be ill, be sick," BDAG 502b (see 1:32); ἦλθον, 1st sg. aor. act. indic. of ἔρχομαι, "come, go"; καλέσαι, aor. act. inf. of καλέω, "call"; inf. of purpose.

HOMILETICAL SUGGESTIONS

Jesus and Hypocrites (2:13–17)

1. Jesus stands in contrast to hypocrites. (2:13–17)
   a. Jesus spent time with sinners. (2:15–16)
   b. Jesus came to call sinners to follow him. (2:13–14, 17)
2. Hypocrites stand in contrast to Jesus. (2:16–17)
   a. Hypocrites are judgmental toward anyone who is not as judgmental as they are. (2:16)
   b. Hypocrites do not recognize how much they need Jesus's help. (2:17)

(c) Conflict over Fasting (2:18–22)

2:18 The series of conflicts moves from a question about Jesus's pattern of eating with sinners to a question about his disciples' pattern of not fasting. Ἦσαν, 3rd pl. impf. act. indic. of εἰμί, "be"; νηστεύοντες, nom. pl. masc. of pres. act. ptc. of νηστεύω, "fast"; periph. ptc. (which conveys that this fasting was a customary practice [see 1:22]); ἔρχονται, 3rd pl. pres. mid. indic. of dep. ἔρχομαι, "come, go"; historical pres. (starting a new scene [see 1:12]). Both ἔρχονται and λέγουσιν are probably indef. pl. vbs., with the subj. for both being an undefined group of people (e.g., ESV; NRSV: "and people came and said to him" [see 1:22]). If it were the disciples of John and the Pharisees who came and spoke with Jesus, it would be difficult to understand why they would refer to themselves in their question in the third pers. (France 138). Διὰ τί, "why?"

(when introducing a question, BDAG 225d; 1007b); σοί, "your" (from the poss. adj. σός), is in the attrib. position and modifies μαθηταί (cf. BDAG 934b; Decker 1:59).

2:19 Μή, interr. particle used to introduce a question that expects a neg. answer ("they can't fast, can they?"; cf. BDF §427; R 1168, 1175); δύνανται, 3rd pl. pres. mid. indic. of dep. δύναμαι, "be able to, can." Οἱ υἱοὶ τοῦ νυμφῶνος lit. means "the sons of the wedding hall" (νυμφῶνος, gen. sg. masc. of νυμφών, -ῶνος, ὁ, "wedding hall"), a phrase that refers to the groom's attendants, the wedding guests who stood closest to the groom and played a part in the wedding ceremony (BDAG 681a; on the attrib. gen. following forms of υἱός, see Z §§40, 42–43; Moule 174–75). Ἐν ᾧ, "while, as long as" (BDAG 330a); νυμφίος (nom. sg. masc.) and νυμφίον (acc. sg. masc.) are both from νυμφίος, -ου, ὁ, "groom" (νυμφίος also appears in the following verse); νηστεύειν, pres. act. inf. of νηστεύω, "fast"; complementary inf.; ὅσον χρόνον, "as long as" (BDAG 729a; the acc. of ὅσον χρόνον is being used for extent of time [cf. R 528; Wallace 201–2; Voelz 1:213]).

2:20 Ἐλεύσονται, 3rd pl. fut. mid. indic. of dep. ἔρχομαι, "come"; ἀπαρθῇ, 3rd sg. aor. pass. subjunc. of ἀπαίρω, "take away"; subjunc. in indef. temp. clause; νηστεύσουσιν, 3rd pl. fut. act. indic. of νηστεύω, "fast." Mark 2:20 contains two fut. tense forms (ἐλεύσονται and νηστεύσουσιν). Mark's Gospel includes approximately 115 instances of the fut. tense, all of them in the indic. mood. The fut. almost always occurs in Mark within dir. discourse, although it can be used in indir. discourse as well (3:2; 11:13). In addition, the fut. appears in the narrator's opening quotation from the OT (1:2). The fut. is used in other OT quotations (e.g., 11:17; 14:27); however, after the opening quotation in 1:2, all other OT quotations in Mark appear within statements made by people in the narrative. Most uses of the fut. in Mark can be classified as "predictive futures," indicating an action that will take place at a time future to the time of the speaker (cf. Wallace 568; KMP 270).

2:21 The two brief parables in 2:21–22 stand at the center of the series of controversy stories in 2:1–3:6, and they are central to the overall message of this section. They emphasize the futility of trying to contain what is new within the constraints of the old structures. The presence of Jesus changes everything, including how sin and sinners are viewed and how religious practices such as fasting and Sabbath are kept. Ἐπίβλημα, acc. sg. neut. of ἐπίβλημα, -ατος, τό, "patch"; ῥάκους, gen. sg. neut. of ῥάκος, -ους, τό, "piece of cloth"; gen. of material (Wallace 91; KMP 94); ἀγνάφου, gen. sg. neut. of the adj. ἄγναφος, -ον, "new, unshrunk"; attrib. adj.; ἐπιράπτει, from ἐπιράπτω, "sew on"; παλαιόν, acc. sg. neut. of παλαιός, -ά, -όν, "old"; attrib. adj. Both the vb. ἐπιράπτει in 2:21 and the vb. βάλλει in 2:22 serve as examples of the gnomic pres., the use of the pres. tense for a timeless, universal truth (Wallace 523; Fanning 208–9). As a general principle, no one does something like this in light of the foreseeable consequences. Εἰ δὲ μή, "otherwise" (after a neg. clause [see BDAG 278d]); αἴρει, normally a trans. vb., which calls for a dir. obj. such as "something" to be supplied (BDAG 29a); πλήρωμα, nom. sg. neut. of πλήρωμα, -ατος, τό, "patch," that which makes something full or complete (BDAG 829c–d; used here as a synonym for ἐπίβλημα); παλαιοῦ, gen. sg.

neut. of παλαιός, -ά, -όν, "old"; subst. adj. and gen. of separation; χεῖρον, nom. sg. neut. of χείρων, -ον, "worse"; attrib. adj.; σχίσμα, nom. sg. neut. of σχίσμα, -ατος, τό, "tear"; γίνεται, 3rd sg. pres. mid. indic. of dep. γίνομαι, "come to be, develop" (BDAG 197b–c).

2:22 Βάλλει, "pour" (when used with liquids, BDAG 163d); νέον, acc. sg. masc. of νέος, -α, -ον, "new"; attrib. adj.; ἀσκούς (acc. pl. masc.) and ἀσκοί (nom. pl. masc.) are both from ἀσκός, -οῦ, ὁ, "wineskin"; παλαιούς, acc. pl. masc. of παλαιός, -ά, -όν, "old"; attrib. adj.; εἰ δὲ μή, "otherwise"; ῥήξει, 3rd sg. fut. act. indic. of ῥήγνυμι, "burst, break"; ἀπόλλυται, 3rd sg. pres. mid. indic. of ἀπόλλυμι, "perish, be ruined" (mng. with mid.). The acc. οἶνον is the dir. obj. of an implied βάλλει (cf. NASB; NRSV).

HOMILETICAL SUGGESTIONS

New Wineskins for New Wine (2:1–3:6)

1. The coming of Christ changes everything. (2:21–22)
2. Since the coming of Christ changes everything, our old ways must change.
   a. A change in attitude toward sin and sinners (2:1–17)
      (1) Christ forgives sin. (2:1–12)
      (2) Christ reaches out to sinners. (2:13–17)
   b. A change in attitude toward religious observances (2:18–3:6)
      (1) Christ gives us a new view of fasting. (2:18–20)
      (2) Christ gives us a new view of the Sabbath. (2:21–3:6)

(d) Conflict over Eating on the Sabbath (2:23–28)

2:23 In both 2:23–28 and 3:1–6, Jesus comes into conflict with the religious leaders over their traditions regarding the Sabbath. Ἐγένετο, 3rd sg. aor. mid. indic. of dep. γίνομαι, "come about, happen" (on the cstr. "ἐγένετο + time reference + an inf.," see 1:9 and 2:15); αὐτόν, acc. subj. of the inf. On the decl. pattern and use of the pl. for σάββατον, see 1:21. Παραπορεύεσθαι, pres. mid. inf. of dep. παραπορεύομαι, "go, go through"; subst. use of the inf., subj. of ἐγένετο ("that he was going"); σπορίμων, gen. pl. neut. of the adj. σπόριμος, -ον, "sown" (only used in the NT as a subst. in the neut. pl. for "grain-fields" [BDAG 939a]); ἤρξαντο, 3rd pl. aor. mid. indic. of ἄρχω, "begin" (mng. with mid.; on ἄρχομαι, see 1:45); ποιεῖν, pres. act. inf. of ποιέω, "make"; complementary inf.; τίλλοντες, nom. pl. masc. of pres. act. ptc. of τίλλω, "pluck, pick"; στάχυας, acc. pl. masc. of στάχυς, -υος, ὁ, "head of grain." The ptc. τίλλοντες is grammatically awkward in that the main action of the disciples—picking the grain—is expressed by the ptc., while the accompanying circumstance—making their way through the grainfield—appears in the complementary inf. (ποιεῖν) that depends on the main vb. (ἤρξαντο; cf. Z §376). Several translations handle the difficulty simply by switching the ptc. and the inf. (e.g., NET: "his disciples began to pick some heads of wheat as they made their way"; cf. ESV, NIV, NRSV). Perhaps another solution is to take the ptc. as expressing attendant circumstance, so that it is coordinate with the inf.: "his disciples began to make their way and to pick some heads of grain."

2:24 On ἴδε, see 1:2; τί, "why?" (see 2:7). The rel. pron. ὅ does not have an antecedent, with the result that it must either be supplied ("[that] which") or translated so that the rel. clause can function as the dir. obj. of ποιοῦσιν ("what"; cf. R 719–21; see 10:9; 13:37; 14:8; ὅ can also be translated as "what" when the rel. clause functions as the subj. of a vb.; see 4:25; 11:23; 14:9). Ἔξεστιν, 3rd sg. pres. act. indic. of ἔξεστιν, "it is lawful, it is permitted." The accusation made against the disciples was not that they were unlawfully picking grain from someone else's field, since the law allowed for plucking grain by hand to satisfy hunger (Deut 23:24–25). Rather, for the Pharisees, picking grain in order to eat the kernels was harvesting and therefore involved work on the Sabbath (Stein 145; Strauss 144–45).

2:25 Jesus responded to the Pharisees' complaint by drawing attention to the actions of David and his men at a time of great need and hunger (1 Sam 21:1–6). The underlying point from this example is that an action taken to meet a basic and immediate human need overrides the prohibition against work on the Sabbath (Yarbro Collins 202–3). Jesus answers the Pharisees' question with a question of his own, one that extends to the end of 2:26. Οὐδέποτε, adv. mng. "never"; ἀνέγνωτε, 2nd pl. aor. act. indic. of ἀναγινώσκω, "read"; τί, "what" (functioning here as a rel. pron. [cf. T 49]); ἐποίησεν, 3rd sg. aor. act. indic. of ποιέω, "do"; ἔσχεν, 3rd sg. aor. act. indic. of ἔχω, "have"; ἐπείνασεν, 3rd sg. aor. act. indic. of πεινάω, "hunger, be hungry" (sg. vb. with a compound subj. [see 12:33]); οἱ μετ᾽ αὐτοῦ, "those with him" (see 1:36).

2:26 David did what, under normal circumstances, would be unlawful—eating bread that was reserved for the priests alone—to meet the pressing need that faced him and his men. Εἰσῆλθεν, 3rd sg. aor. act. indic. of εἰσέρχομαι, "go into, enter"; προθέσεως, gen. sg. fem. of πρόθεσις, -εως, ἡ, "presentation"; attrib. gen.; ἔφαγεν, 3rd sg. aor. act. indic. of ἐσθίω, "eat"; ἔξεστιν, 3rd sg. pres. act. indic. of ἔξεστιν, "it is lawful, it is permitted"; φαγεῖν, aor. act. inf. of ἐσθίω, "eat"; subst. use of the inf., subj. of ἔξεστιν; εἰ μή, "except" (see 2:7); ἱερεῖς, acc. of respect or reference; ἔδωκεν, 3rd sg. aor. act. indic. of δίδωμι, "give"; καί (3rd use): adjunctive; οὖσιν, dat. pl. masc. of pres. act. ptc. of εἰμί, "be"; subst. ptc.

Jesus's summary of the OT story in vv. 25–26 seems purposefully shaped to highlight the relevance of the event in David's life to the present circumstances. However, this reshaping creates tensions between Jesus's summary and the account as it is recorded in 1 Sam 21:1–6. The most complicated of these tensions involves the prep. phrase ἐπὶ Ἀβιαθὰρ ἀρχιερέως, since the priest with whom David interacted at that time was Ahimelech, the father of Abiathar, not Abiathar himself. One possible explanation is to understand the prep. phrase ἐπὶ Ἀβιαθὰρ ἀρχιερέως as expressing a locat. idea for proximity within the scriptural text, "at" or "near the passage concerning Abiathar the high priest." This interpretation has the advantage of a par. example within Mark's Gospel. Mark 2:25–26 and 12:26 both record Jesus as asking similar questions: "Have you never read?" and "Haven't you read?" (2:25: οὐδέποτε ἀνέγνωτε; 12:26: οὐκ ἀνέγνωτε). Mark 12:26 continues on: "Haven't you read in the book of Moses, *in the passage about* [ἐπί] the bush . . . ?" Therefore, Mark can use ἐπί with the gen. to mean "in the passage about," indicating the section of Scripture where a particular event appears in the text. One problem with this interpretation of ἐπί in 2:25–26 is that Abiathar is not mentioned in the passage that Jesus is summarizing, but only for the first time in the following chapter. A reference to Abiathar would, therefore, only give a very general sense of the location of the event within the scriptural text. Perhaps Jesus wanted to mention Abiathar in particular because Abiathar was someone who served David and helped to protect his life, placing him in contrast to the religious leaders of Jesus's day, who opposed Jesus and who would shortly seek to destroy him.

2:27 Ἐγένετο, 3rd sg. aor. mid. indic. of dep. γίνομαι, "come to be, be established" (BDAG 197b); διά, "for the benefit of, for the sake of" (in this context; cf. LN 90.38; Harris 80; Moule 55). Jesus's argument can be understood at the level of God's intention for the law, that it must not be interpreted narrowly in a way that overlooks basic human need as though God cares only for his law and not for his people. However, the final verse in this present passage moves the argument to another level, since it lays claim to Jesus's authority over the Sabbath itself.

2:28 Ὥστε, "therefore" (when introducing an independent clause [BDAG 1107a; Burton §237]); κύριος, pred. nom.; καί, ascensive; σαββάτου, gen. of subordination. Within this passage, Jesus declares God's purpose for the Sabbath and defends his disciples' actions on the Sabbath. Therefore, to be Lord of the Sabbath at least includes revealing God's intentions for his law and setting the standards for what constitutes obedience to it.

(e) Conflict over Healing on the Sabbath (3:1–6)

3:1 As in 2:23–28, Jesus's view of the Sabbath becomes a point of contention in 3:1–6, this time as to whether or not it is appropriate to heal on the Sabbath. Εἰσῆλθεν, 3rd sg. aor. act. indic. of εἰσέρχομαι, "go into, enter"; ἦν, 3rd sg. impf. act. indic. of εἰμί, "be"; ἔχων, nom. sg. masc. of pres. act. ptc. of ἔχω, "have"; adj. ptc. without an art. to modify an anar. noun; ἐξηραμμένην, acc. sg. fem. of pf. pass. ptc. of ξηραίνω, "be paralyzed, be withered, be dried up" (mng. with pass.); adj. ptc. The use of ἐξηραμμένην as an adj. ptc. is somewhat unusual in that the art. appears with the noun (τὴν χεῖρα) but not the adj. ptc. The same cstr. occurs in 8:17, where the adj. ptc. πεπωρωμένην modifies τὴν καρδίαν. In both examples the noun is a dir. obj. of a form of ἔχω and the ptc. is pf. pass. (see R 789; cf. also Heb 5:14).

3:2 Παρετήρουν, 3rd pl. impf. act. indic. of παρατηρέω, "watch closely"; εἰ, "whether" (when introducing an indir. question [BDAG 278b; R 1045; see 10:2]); on the dat. pl. form σάββασιν, see 1:21; θεραπεύσει, 3rd sg. fut. act. indic. of θεραπεύω, "heal." The fut. tense of θεραπεύσει from the dir. question is retained in Gk. in the indir. question. In Eng., reported speech or thought from the past is expressed as past, which results in translating the fut. in indir. discourse with "would" rather than "will" (Z §346; cf. 11:13). Κατηγορήσωσιν, 3rd pl. aor. act. subjunc. of κατηγορέω, "bring charges against, accuse"; subjunc. in a purpose ἵνα clause; αὐτοῦ, gen. dir. obj. Since the man's cond. was not life-threatening (cf. m. Yoma 8.6), it was possible to wait for another day to heal him and so avoid work on the Sabbath (cf. Luke 13:14; CD 11:9–14; m. Shab. 14.3–4).

3:3 Λέγει, historical pres. (on the historical pres. with λέγω, which occurs in vv. 3, 4, and 5, see 1:12, 30); ξηράν, acc. sg. fem. of ξηρός, -ά, -όν, "withered, paralyzed"; attrib. adj.; ἔχοντι, dat. sg. masc. of pres. act. ptc. of ἔχω, "have"; adj. ptc.; ἔγειρε, 2nd sg. pres. act. impv. of ἐγείρω, "rise, get up" (intrans. mng. with the impv., BDAG 272b). The use of εἰς seems to imply motion in this context: "Arise and move into the midst of the gathering" (Moule 68; Harris 85; cf. 14:60; on the pres. tense for the impv. ἔγειρε, see 2:11).

3:4 Ἔξεστιν, 3rd sg. pres. act. indic. of ἔξεστιν, "it is lawful, it is permitted"; ποιῆσαι, aor. act. inf. of ποιέω, "do"; κακοποιῆσαι, aor. act. inf. of κακοποιέω, "do wrong"; σῶσαι, aor. act. inf. of σώζω, "save"; ἀποκτεῖναι, aor. act. inf. of ἀποκτείνω, "kill." The inf. forms are all functioning subst. to indicate the subj. of ἔξεστιν. On οἱ δέ, see 1:45; ἐσιώπων, 3rd pl. impf. act. indic. of σιωπάω, "keep silent." Mark uses σιωπάω three times in the impf., each time for a sustained silence in the presence of a questioner (3:4; 9:34; 14:61). Each of these three scenes is marked by tension, and the ongoing silence adds to that tension. In this scene, Jesus sets before his opponents two alternatives: to do good and save life or to do wrong and take life. Their silence, followed shortly by their plans to destroy Jesus, reveals which alternative they have chosen. The other path, taken by Jesus, recognizes that acts of mercy and kindness toward those in need are not prohibited on the Sabbath.

3:5 Περιβλεψάμενος, nom. sg. masc. of aor. mid. ptc. of περιβλέπω, "look around at" (mng. with mid.); temp. adv. ptc. antecedent; συλλυπούμενος, nom. sg. masc. of pres. pass. ptc. of συλλυπέω, "be grieved" (mng. with pass.); adv. ptc. of manner. The prep. prefix συν- in the compound vb. συλλυπέω does not indicate that Jesus was grieving together with others or for others; instead, the prefix simply intensifies the mng. of the vb. in this context (BDAG 956b; ZG 108). Ἐπί, "at" (indicating the basis for an emotion [Z §126]); πωρώσει, dat. sg. fem. of πώρωσις, -εως, ἡ, "hardness, dullness, stubbornness"; καρδίας, obj. gen. (on καρδίας as a distributive sg., see 6:52). The noun πώρωσις points to a cond. in which something has become hard or dull (BDAG 900d). The related vb. πωρόω can convey the mng. "to become hard, to petrify, to form a callous" (cf. LSJ 1561). In Mark's Gospel, the noun appears only here in 3:5, but the related vb. occurs twice, in 6:52 and 8:17, places where the disciples are acting with a lack of understanding because their hearts had been hardened. Consequently, hardness of heart in Mark reveals an intellectual dullness more than a lack of compassion. Ἔκτεινον, 2nd sg. aor. act. impv. of ἐκτείνω, "stretch out" (on aor. imperatives, see 1:25); ἐξέτεινεν, 3rd sg. aor. act. indic. of ἐκτείνω, "stretch out"; ἀπεκατεστάθη, 3rd sg. aor. pass. indic. of ἀποκαθίστημι, "restore." The vb. ἀπεκατεστάθη is unusual in that it not only has a dbl. prep. prefix, but it also takes a dbl. aug. in accordance with the two prefixes (R 368; cf. 8:25).

3:6 Ἐξελθόντες, nom. pl. masc. of aor. act. ptc. of ἐξέρχομαι, "go out, exit"; temp. adv. ptc. antecedent; συμβούλιον, acc. sg. neut. of συμβούλιον, -ου, τό, "plan"; ἐδίδουν, 3rd pl. impf. act. indic. of δίδωμι, "form, decide on" (mng. when used with συμβούλιον [BDAG 957b]); ἀπολέσωσιν, 3rd pl. aor. act. subjunc. of ἀπόλλυμι, "destroy." The conj. ὅπως after a vb. that conveys the idea of making a plan introduces not a purpose clause ("in order that") but rather an obj. clause, in this case, one that expresses an indir. question ("how, as to how"; cf. Matt 12:14; 22:15; note also the comparable use of πῶς in Mark 11:18; 14:1). The use of ὅπως and the subjunc. mood vb. ἀπολέσωσιν, therefore, approximates an indir. delib. question (Z §348; Burton §207; ZG 108).

FOR FURTHER STUDY

12. The Religious Leaders in Mark's Gospel

Cook, Michael J. *Mark's Treatment of the Jewish Leaders*. NovTSup 51. Leiden: Brill, 1978.

Dewey, Joanna. "The Literary Structure of the Controversy Stories in Mark 2:1–3:6." *JBL* 92 (1973): 394–401.

―――. *Markan Public Debate: Literary Technique, Concentric Structure, and Theology in Mark 2:1–3:6*. SBLDS 48. Chico, CA: Scholars Press, 1980.

Hanson, James S. *The Endangered Promises: Conflict in Mark*. SBLDS 171. Atlanta: Society of Biblical Literature, 2000.

Kingsbury, Jack Dean. "The Religious Authorities in the Gospel of Mark." *NTS* 36 (1990): 42–65.

*Malbon, Elizabeth Struthers. "The Jewish Leaders in the Gospel of Mark: A Literary Study of Marcan Characterization." *JBL* 108 (1989): 259–81.

Marcus, Joel. "The Scribes and the Pharisees." Pages 519–24 in *Mark 1–8*. AB. New York: Doubleday, 2000.

Neusner, Jacob, and Bruce D. Chilton, eds. *In Quest of the Historical Pharisees*. Waco, TX: Baylor University Press, 2007.

Saldarini, Anthony J. *Pharisees, Scribes and Sadducees in Palestinian Society: A Sociological Approach*. Reprint. Grand Rapids: Eerdmans, 2001.

Sanders, E. P. *Judaism: Practice and Belief, 63 BCE–66 CE*. Philadelphia: Trinity Press International, 1992.

Smith, Stephen H. "The Role of Jesus' Opponents in the Markan Drama." *NTS* 35 (1989): 161–82.

Stemberger, Günter. *Jewish Contemporaries of Jesus: Pharisees, Sadducees, Essenes*. Minneapolis: Fortress, 1995.

HOMILETICAL SUGGESTIONS

Jesus and God's Commands (2:23–3:6)

1. What do we learn about Jesus? (2:23–3:6)
   a. Jesus's authority: Jesus has the power to declare the purpose and standards of God's commands. (2:23–28)

    b. Jesus's anger: Jesus has a problem with people who use God's commands to keep others from God's mercy. (3:1–6)
2. What do we learn about obeying God's commands? (2:27–28; 3:4)
    a. A good purpose: God's commands are for our good. (2:27)
    b. A good prospect: God's commands give us the opportunity to do what is good. (3:4)
    c. A good Lord: God's commands are best understood by listening to Jesus. (2:28)

3. Summary and Initial Decision (3:7–35)

In a similar way to 1:14–45, Mark begins this subunit with a summary statement, this time concerning Jesus's extensive healing ministry (3:7–12). People from Galilee and the areas all around Galilee have heard about Jesus and come to him for help. Once again, Mark follows this summary statement with a description of Jesus's calling of disciples, this time the calling of the twelve (3:13–19). The narrative continues with other responses to Jesus and his authority. At this point, the responses are becoming more settled decisions: he has lost his mind (3:21); he is possessed by Satan (3:22); he teaches the way of God (3:34–35).

(a) Summary of Jesus's Healing in Galilee (3:7–12)

3:7 The story picks up in 3:7 with where it left off in 1:45, before the series of conflicts between Jesus and the religious leaders in 2:1–3:6. At the end of 1:45, people were coming to Jesus from everywhere because they heard of his power to heal. In 3:7–12, Mark summarizes how many people were seeking out help from Jesus, people from both Galilee and its surrounding regions. Ἀνεχώρησεν, 3rd sg. aor. act. indic. of ἀναχωρέω, "withdraw"; ἠκολούθησεν, 3rd sg. aor. act. indic. of ἀκολουθέω, "follow."

3:8 Πέραν, "the other side" (adv. functioning as an indecl. name for the territory on the eastern side of the Jordan river [BDAG 797a]). A collective sg. subj., such as πλῆθος, normally takes a sg. vb., with the group being viewed as a single whole (cf. 3:7). However, a collective sg. subj. can also take a pl. vb., with the recognition that a group is made up of a number of individuals (cf. Wallace 400–401; R 404). Therefore, in 3:8, πλῆθος is the subj. of the pl. vb. ἦλθον (see also the pl. ptc. ἀκούοντες). Ἀκούοντες, nom. pl. masc. of pres. act. ptc. of ἀκούω, "hear, hear about"; temp. adv. ptc. contemp. (cf. 6:2 for a similar use of ἀκούοντες); ἐποίει, 3rd sg. impf. act. indic. of ποιέω, "do." The impf. vb. ἐποίει, which appears in indir. discourse, retains the tense used in the orig. dir. discourse. In Eng., it is typical to push the tense back in time to reflect that it was said or heard in the past, so that the impf. in Gk. translates as a pluperf. in Eng. (e.g., NET: "when they heard about the things he had done"; cf. Wallace 552–53). Ἦλθον, 3rd pl. aor. act. indic. of ἔρχομαι, "come, go."

3:9 Πλοιάριον, nom. sg. neut. of πλοιάριον, -ου, τό, "small boat." A characteristic feature of Mark's style is the freq. use of diminutives, nouns that by their form indicate a small size (see Taylor 45 for a list of examples). Most diminutives are created by adding the suffix -ιον or -άριον to a noun (BDF §111). Diminutives were common in everyday, colloquial language, and Mark used them with greater frequency than any of the other NT writers (BDF §111). In 3:9, e.g., Mark uses the dim. noun πλοιάριον. Other diminutives that appear in Mark include: θυγάτριον ("little daughter"; 5:23; 7:25), ἰχθύδιον ("small fish"; 8:7), κοράσιον ("little girl"; 5:41, 42; 6:22, 28 [twice]), κυνάριον ("little dog"; 7:27, 28), παιδίον ("little child"; used twelve times in Mark), σανδάλιον ("sandal"; 6:9), ψιχίον ("small crumb"; 7:28), ὠτάριον ("ear"; 14:47), and παιδίσκη ("female slave"; 14:66, 69). Sometimes Mark may have made use of diminutives as a matter of routine, without any implication that the person or object was particularly small. The dim. ὠτάριον, e.g., became a common word for "ear," and it is unlikely that Mark was trying to make a point that the slave of the high priest had an unusually small ear (14:47). At other times, the use of a dim. may have been more intentional. Mark may have wanted to communicate that the few fish the disciples had before Jesus started to multiply them were indeed small (8:7). The boat prepared for Jesus in 3:9 should probably be thought of as a smaller boat, since Mark uses πλοιάριον only this one time in his Gospel, while he uses the non-dim. form πλοῖον seventeen times (on diminutives in Mark, see C. H. Turner, "Marcan Notes, Critical and Exegetical, on the Second Gospel," *JTS* 29 [1927–28]: 349–52). Προσκαρτερῇ, 3rd sg. pres. act. subjunc. of προσκαρτερέω, "stand ready"; subjunc. in dir. obj. ἵνα clause (cf. 5:10); αὐτῷ, dat. of interest (advantage); θλίβωσιν, 3rd pl. pres. act. subjunc. of θλίβω, "press upon, crowd"; subjunc. in purpose ἵνα clause.

3:10 Ἐθεράπευσεν, 3rd sg. aor. act. indic. of θεραπεύω, "heal." The use of the conj. γάρ with the aor. indic. vb. ἐθεράπευσεν points to an action that took place before Jesus asked his disciples to prepare a boat for him. Eng. is different from Gk. in that it calls for a pluperf. vb. to describe an action that took place before another past event (e.g., ESV: "for he had healed many"; cf. Z §290; see 5:8). Ἐπιπίπτειν, pres. act. inf. of ἐπιπίπτω, "fall on, press upon"; inf. of result; αὐτῷ, dat. dir. obj.; αὐτοῦ, gen. dir. obj.; ἅψωνται, 3rd pl. aor. mid. subjunc. of ἅπτω, "touch" (mng. with mid.); subjunc. in purpose ἵνα clause; εἶχον, 3rd pl. impf. act. indic. of ἔχω, "have"; μάστιγας, acc. pl. fem. of μάστιξ, -ιγος, ἡ, "scourge, torment, suffering" (on the mng. of μάστιξ, see 5:29).

3:11 In Mark, as a general rule, neut. pl. subjects take a sg. vb. (cf. Wallace 399–400; Porter, *Idioms* 73–74). However, Mark uses a pl. vb. when the neut. pl. subj. refers to pers. nouns, such as "unclean spirits" (3:11; 5:13) and "children" (13:12), or to nouns functioning as metaphors for people (7:28; 14:27; cf. 6:34; on neut. pl. subjects with a pers. sense, see T 313). Ἐθεώρουν, 3rd pl. impf. act. indic. of θεωρέω, "see, notice"; προσέπιπτον, 3rd pl. impf. act. indic. of προσπίπτω, "fall down before"; αὐτῷ, dat. dir. obj.; ἔκραζον, 3rd pl. impf. act. indic. of κράζω, "cry out"; λέγοντες, nom. pl. masc. of pres. act. ptc. of λέγω, "say"; redundant ptc.; ὅτι introduces dir. discourse. Perhaps the best way to explain the unusual use of the masc. ptc. λέγοντες rather than the neut. ptc. λέγοντα, which would agree with the neut. subj. πνεύματα, is by pointing to Mark's habit of using the masc. ptc. form of λέγω when expressing a redundant ptc. (cf. 5:12). Typically, in Mark, ὅταν introduces a clause with a vb. in the subjunc. mood, although there are exceptions where the vb. takes the indic. mood (3:11; 11:19; 11:25; cf. Voelz

1:6, 239). Mark uses ὅταν with the impf. indic. (ἐθεώρουν) in 3:11 to indicate multiple past occurrences of an event, while leaving as indef. the timing and number of the occurrences. Therefore, ἐθεώρουν is an iter. impf., expressing what happened repeatedly in the past, and the impf. vbs. in the main clause (προσέπιπτον, ἔκραζον) are also iter., expressing what happened again and again as a consequence (cf. LN 67.36; Z 358; ZG 108; on the impf. in summary statements, see 1:21).

3:12 Πολλά, acc. pl. of πολύς (used as an adv. to intensify the vb.: "sternly, strongly"; cf. ZG 108; BDAG 849d–850a); ἐπετίμα, 3rd sg. impf. act. indic. of ἐπιτιμάω, "rebuke" (iter. impf. in a summary statement [see 1:21]; αὐτοῖς, dat. dir. obj.; φανερόν, acc. sg. masc. of φανερός, -ά, -όν, "known, evident" (adj. functioning as an obj. complement in a dbl.-acc. cstr.); ποιήσωσιν, 3rd pl. aor. act. subjunc. of ποιέω, "make"; subjunc. in a ἵνα dir. obj. clause.

HOMILETICAL SUGGESTIONS

Coming to a Decision about Jesus (3:7–35)

1. The decision different groups come to about Jesus:
   a. The crowds: "Jesus can help us." (3:7–10)
   b. The unclean spirits: "Jesus has authority over us." (3:11–12)
   c. The disciples: "Jesus will prepare us for ministry." (3:13–19)
   d. The family of Jesus: "Jesus is an embarrassment to us." (3:20–21)
   e. The religious leaders: "Jesus is empowered by Satan." (3:22–30)
2. The decision we should come to about Jesus: We will do the will of God by listening to the teaching of Jesus. (3:31–35)

(b) Calling of Disciples: The Twelve (3:13–19)

3:13 Earlier in the narrative, Mark indicated that many disciples were following Jesus (2:15). Apparently, out of this larger group of followers, Jesus called twelve who would spend extended time with him (cf. Luke 6:13). Ἀναβαίνει, historical pres. (starting a new scene [see 1:12]); προσκαλεῖται, 3rd sg. pres. mid. indic. of προσκαλέω, "summon, call to oneself" (mng. with mid.); historical pres.; οὕς, "those whom" (rel. pron. without an antecedent, which should be supplied in Eng.; cf. 15:12; ZG 109); ἤθελεν, 3rd sg. impf. act. indic. of θέλω, "wish, want" (on the dbl. aug. with θέλω [ἠ-], see R 367–68); ἀπῆλθον, 3rd pl. aor. act. indic. of ἀπέρχομαι, "go" (see Z §132–33 on how ἀπό freq. loses any idea of separation when compounded with vbs.).

3:14 In 3:14–15, Mark clarifies why Jesus selected this smaller group of disciples, so that they might be with him and so that he might send them out to continue his work. In a sense, the first—spending time with Jesus—serves as an essential prerequisite for the second—going out on mission for Jesus. Ἐποίησεν, 3rd sg. aor. act. indic. of ποιέω, "make, appoint" (on the mng. of ποιέω, see *EDNT* 3:124; cf. Heb 3:2); καί, adjunctive; ἀποστόλους, obj. complement in a dbl.-acc. cstr.; ὠνόμασεν, 3rd sg. aor. act. indic. of ὀνομάζω, "name, call." The words οὕς καὶ ἀποστόλους ὠνόμασεν do not appear in the majority of mss., although they are included in a number of significant early witnesses (א, B, Θ, family 13). In agreement with some interpreters, who regard the words as a harmonization to Luke 6:13 (e.g., Cranfield 127; France 157), a few translations omit the words (e.g., NASB; NIV). Ὦσιν, 3rd pl. pres. act. subjunc. of εἰμί, "be"; ἀποστέλλῃ, 3rd sg. pres. act. subjunc. of ἀποστέλλω, "send"; ὦσιν and ἀποστέλλῃ, subjunc. in purpose ἵνα clause; κηρύσσειν, pres. act. inf. of κηρύσσω, "preach, proclaim"; inf. of purpose (cf. R 1088; Stein 170).

3:15 Ἔχειν, pres. act. inf. of ἔχω, "have"; inf. of purpose (cf. Stein 170–71); ἐκβάλλειν, pres. act. inf. of ἐκβάλλω, "cast out, drive out, send away"; epex. inf. The use of the pres. tense with inf. forms expressing purpose (κηρύσσειν in 3:14 and ἔχειν in 3:15) is somewhat unusual in Mark (see 1:24). Given the context of the appointment of the Twelve as those to be trained and sent out by Jesus, the inf. forms seem to be pointing to ongoing activities in the future mission of the twelve (prog. pres.). The mission of the Twelve is patterned after the work of Jesus, since he also came to proclaim the gospel of God and to have authority over demonic beings (cf. 1:14–15, 38–39).

3:16 The beginning of v. 16 essentially repeats the statement from the beginning of v. 14: "He appointed [ἐποίησεν, see 3:14] the Twelve." The one difference in the repeated clause is the addition of the art. before δώδεκα (an anaphoric art.). The words καὶ ἐποίησεν τοὺς δώδεκα are included in important early mss. (א B C Δ) but not in most mss. The clause may have dropped out since it is a somewhat unnecessary and awkward repetition (France 157; Yarbro Collins 214). If included, the words serve to resume Mark's introduction to the names of the Twelve, which are all in the acc. case since they stand in appos. to τοὺς δώδεκα, the dir. obj. of ἐποίησεν. The words καὶ ἐπέθηκεν ὄνομα τῷ Σίμωνι function as a parenthesis to clarify the name Peter (R 441, 433–34, 488), although it is difficult to translate them since the explanatory parenthesis comes before the word it clarifies. In Eng., it may be better to change the word order: "Peter (a name he gave to Simon)" (ἐπέθηκεν, 3rd sg. aor. act. indic. of ἐπιτίθημι, "place upon, give a name to" [LN 33.128]).

3:17 Τὸν τοῦ Ζεβεδαίου, "the son of Zebedee" (see 1:19); ἀδελφόν, acc. of simple appos.; Ἰακώβου, gen. of relationship. Mark includes a parenthetical explanation regarding the names of James and John. Jesus gave (ἐπέθηκεν, see 3:16) to them the name "Boanerges", that is, sons of thunder (βροντῆς, gen. sg. fem. of βροντή, -ῆς, ἡ, "thunder"; attrib. gen.). The pl. form ὀνόματα appears in most mss. (B D 28 have the sg.), but it is usually translated as a sg. since only one name is presented for the two brothers. The name Boanerges apparently is a combination of Heb. or Aram. words transliterated into Gk. letters, but the question of which words lie behind Boanerges has never received a satisfactory answer. Mark introduces his own translation of Boanerges with ὅ ἐστιν, a set expression that uses the neut. sg. rel. pron. ὅ without regard to the gender or number of the antecedent (R 411, 713–14; for other examples of the phrase following foreign words or concepts, see 7:11, 34; 12:42; 15:16, 42; cf. 5:41; 15:22, 34).

3:18 The rest of the Twelve are not singled out for attention by receiving special names from Jesus. Only the first three—Peter, James, and John—have that distinction, and they also function as Jesus's inner circle later in the narrative (5:37; 9:2; 14:33; cf. 13:3). Therefore, after the names of the first three, Mark moves more quickly through the rest of his list: Andrew, Philip, Bartholomew, Matthew, Thomas, James the son of Alphaeus, Thaddaeus, and Simon the Cananaean. "Cananaean" is a transliteration into Gk. letters of an Aram. word mng. "enthusiast, zealot" (BDAG 507c; cf. Luke's use of ζηλωτής in Luke 6:15; Acts 1:13).

3:19 Last on the list is Judas Iscariot. The orig. mng. of "Iscariot," though debated, was probably "man of Kerioth," a town in Judea (cf., e.g., France 163; Stein 174). Παρέδωκεν, 3rd sg. aor. act. indic. of παραδίδωμι, "hand over." The vb. παρέδωκεν is often translated in this context as "betrayed," and it is true that Judas's act of handing Jesus over to the authorities was a betrayal, a treacherous act done by a close follower (cf. Spicq 3:21–22). However, the translation "betrayed" obscures various pars. within Mark's Gospel, since the same vb. (παραδίδωμι) appears in connection with other similar events, such as the arrest of John the Baptist (1:14) and the persecution of believers (13:9, 11–12; cf. BDAG 762a). Moreover, Judas was not alone in this action, since the religious leaders handed Jesus over to Pilate (15:1, 10), who in turn handed him over to the soldiers for execution (15:15).

HOMILETICAL SUGGESTIONS

Discipleship Training (3:13–19)

1. A call from Jesus comes before our service for him. (3:13)
2. A relationship with Jesus comes before our service for him. (3:14a)
3. An example from Jesus comes before our service for him. (3:14b–15)

(c) Rejection by Jesus's Family and by the Scribes (3:20–30)

3:20 In Mark's Gospel, some observers come to decidedly negative opinions about Jesus early in his ministry, regarding him as either out of his mind or under the control of Satan. Ἔρχεται, 3rd sg. pres. mid. indic. of dep. ἔρχομαι, "come, go"; historical pres. (starting a new scene [see 1:12]); συνέρχεται, 3rd sg. pres. mid. indic. of dep. συνέρχομαι, "come together, assemble, gather"; δύνασθαι, pres. mid. inf. of dep. δύναμαι, "be able to, can"; inf. of result (Wallace 594; KMP 365); αὐτούς, acc. subj. of inf.; φαγεῖν, aor. act. inf. of ἐσθίω, "eat"; complementary inf.; on dbl. negatives, see 1:44.

3:21 Ἀκούσαντες, nom. pl. masc. of aor. act. ptc. of ἀκούω, "hear"; temp. adv. ptc. antecedent. Lit., οἱ παρ' αὐτοῦ means "those from him" (see 1:36 on a prep. phrase preceded by an art.), but the phrase also came to be used for those closely related to someone, i.e., one's family or relatives (BDAG 756d–57a; MM 479; R 614; Moulton 106–7). Ἐξῆλθον, 3rd pl. aor. act. indic. of ἐξέρχομαι, "come, go out"; κρατῆσαι, aor. act. inf. of κρατέω, "seize, take hold of"; inf. of purpose. The subj. of ἔλεγον is a matter of debate: who was insisting that Jesus had lost his mind (ἐξέστη, 3rd sg. aor. act. indic. of ἐξίστημι, "lose one's mind, be out of one's senses" [cf. *TDNT* 2:459–60])?

1. The vb. ἔλεγον points back in the immediate context to οἱ παρ' αὐτοῦ, so that Jesus's family was concerned about his mental stability (e.g., Wallace 403; Taylor 236–37).

*2. The vb. ἔλεγον is an indef. pl., so that this is a general reference to an unspecified group of people who were expressing their opinion about Jesus (e.g., Z §4; T 292; C. H. Turner, "Marcan Usage: Notes, Critical and Exegetical, on the Second Gospel," *JTS* 25 [1924]: 383–84).

Mark's common pattern of using indef. pl. vbs. makes the second view at least plausible (see 1:22). The second view also provides some explanation for what Jesus's family heard (ἀκούσαντες) that made them decide to take action. Jesus's family heard rumors of people saying that Jesus had lost his mind, and to protect the family from further embarrassment, they wanted to take him away.

3:22 Mark moves from his focus on Jesus's family (3:20–21) to a report concerning an accusation from certain scribes (3:22–30) and then eventually back to the account concerning Jesus's family (3:31–35). In this way, 3:20–35 is the first example of Mark's sandwich technique, a literary pattern in which he interrupts one story, inserts a second, and then returns to finish the first (cf. Edwards 11–12, 117–18). Other examples include 5:21–43; 6:7–30; 11:12–25; 14:1–11, 53–72. By bringing two stories together, Mark draws attention to the similarities and differences between the two events. Καταβάντες, nom. pl. masc. of aor. act. ptc. of καταβαίνω, "come down, go down"; adj. ptc (Porter, *Idioms* 186); ὅτι (1st and 2nd use): introduces dir. discourse. The term "Beelzebul" apparently originated as a name for the Canaanite god Baal and meant "lord of the household" (Marcus 1:272). In 3:22–23, the par. maintained between "Beelzebul" and "the ruler of the demons" and "Satan" indicates that Beelzebul is an alternative name for Satan. Ἔχει, "has, is possessed by" (cf. BDAG 421b–c); ἐν, "by" (expressing agency [cf. BDAG 329a; BDF §219]).

3:23 Jesus responded to the scribes' accusation that his authority comes from Satan by pointing out the lack of logic in their charge. Προσκαλεσάμενος, nom. sg. masc. of aor. mid. ptc. of προσκαλέω, "summon, call to oneself" (mng. with mid.); temp. adv. ptc. antecedent; ἐν, "by, by means of" (instr. use [Harris 119]); δύναται, 3rd sg. pres. mid. indic. of dep. δύναμαι, "be able to, can"; ἐκβάλλειν, pres. act. inf. of ἐκβάλλω, "cast out, drive out, send away"; complementary inf. If Satan is the ruler of the demons, then any act of driving away a demon is an attack on Satan's realm. The accusation of the scribes is irrational because it necessarily assumes that Satan is seeking to destroy his own power through Jesus.

3:24 The first two parables, one in v. 24 and the next in v. 25, present hypothetical examples that are then applied to Satan and his kingdom in v. 26. The first parable uses a 3rd class cond. clause to raise a hypothetical situation followed by a conclusion that offers a general principle of what happens in such a situation. If a kingdom is divided against itself, that kingdom is not able to stand. Μερισθῇ, 3rd sg. aor. pass. subjunc.

of μερίζω, "divide"; subjunc. in a 3rd class cond. clause; ἐπί, "against" (see BDAG 366a); δύναται, 3rd sg. pres. mid. indic. of dep. δύναμαι, "be able to, can"; σταθῆναι, aor. pass. inf. of ἵστημι, "stand, stand firm" (act. intrans. mng. with aor. pass. form); complementary inf. Since the aor. pass. of ἵστημι conveys an act. intrans. mng., there is no difference in mng. between the aor. pass. inf. form σταθῆναι in 3:24, 25, and the 2nd aor. act. inf. form στῆναι in 3:26, which is also intrans. (Z §231; BDAG 482c–d).

3:25 The second parable, which also uses a 3rd class cond. clause, is almost an exact repetition of the first with just a few differences in wording and word order (on μερισθῇ and σταθῆναι, see v. 24). Grammatically, the most significant difference is that the main vb. in the conclusion changes from the pres. to the fut. tense. Given the hypothetical situation of a divided house, that house will not be able to stand (δυνήσεται, 3rd sg. fut. mid. indic. of dep. δύναμαι, "be able to, can"). The conclusion is stated no longer as a pres. general principle but with more confidence as a def. fut. reality (e.g., cf. 1:40 with 5:28).

3:26 Verse 26 begins with a 1st class cond. clause. For the sake of argument, Jesus accepts the reasoning of the scribes as true within the cond. clause (cf. Wallace 690–94), to point out the necessary inference from their reasoning in his conclusion. However, the conclusion is so obviously false that it negates their perspective. Ἀνέστη, 3rd sg. aor. act. indic. of ἀνίστημι, "rise up"; ἐμερίσθη, 3rd sg. aor. pass. indic. of μερίζω, "divide"; δύναται, 3rd sg. pres. mid. indic. of dep. δύναμαι, "be able to, can"; στῆναι, aor. act. inf. of ἵστημι, "stand, stand firm" (intrans. mng. with 2nd aor. act. form [BDAG 482c–d]); complementary inf.; τέλος ἔχει, lit. "he has an end" (cf. BDAG 422a; 998b: "he is at an end"; NASB, CSB: he "is finished"). The conclusion in v. 26 is without question false, since Satan is clearly still powerful and has not come to an end. Therefore, Satan's kingdom is not divided, and Jesus is not casting out demons through the power of Satan.

3:27 On dbl. negatives, see 1:44; δύναται, 3rd sg. pres. mid. indic. of dep. δύναμαι, "be able to, can"; ἰσχυροῦ, subst. adj.; εἰσελθών, nom. sg. masc. of aor. act. ptc. of εἰσέρχομαι, "go into, enter"; temp. adv. ptc. antecedent; σκεύη, acc. pl. neut. of σκεῦος, -ους, τό, "thing, object" (a general term used in the pl. here for "property," BDAG 927c; or "possessions," ZG 110); διαρπάσαι, aor. act. inf. of διαρπάζω, "plunder thoroughly"; complementary inf.; ἐὰν μή, "unless" (see BDAG 267d–68a); πρῶτον, "first" (neut. acc. used as an adv. [BDAG 893b; see 14:25]); δήσῃ, 3rd sg. aor. act. subjunc. of δέω, "bind, tie"; subjunc. in a 3rd class cond. clause; διαρπάσει, 3rd sg. fut. act. indic. of διαρπάζω, "plunder thoroughly." The parables in 3:24–26, which picture Satan as powerful, and the parable in 3:27, which portrays him as bound, stand somewhat in tension with one another. However, that tension must be understood within the context of the story as a whole. Jesus came to bind Satan, but that will ultimately be accomplished through the entirety of his life, death, resurrection, and coming again in power and glory. Jesus's exorcisms were an expression of his opposition to the oppressive kingdom of Satan and a foretaste of its final demise. Therefore, Satan remains a powerful foe, but his doom is sure.

3:28 After refuting the scribes' accusation through parables, Jesus warns them directly about the potential consequences of their obstinate rejection in 3:28–29. Jesus prefaces his teaching with the introductory formula ἀμὴν λέγω ὑμῖν, the first of thirteen instances in Mark's Gospel. Normally, at that time, someone would say ἀμήν ("amen") to affirm the truth of another person's statement (e.g., Deut 27:15–26; 1 Chr 16:36; Jer 11:5; 1 Cor 14:16). Jesus, however, introduced his own statements with "amen," or as translated here, "Truly," affirming the truth of his words even before saying them (cf. *TDNT* 1:335–38). Ἀφεθήσεται, 3rd sg. fut. pass. indic. of ἀφίημι, "forgive" (sg. vb. with neut. pl. subj. [see 3:11]); υἱοῖς, dat. of reference or respect; ἀνθρώπων, gen. of relationship; ἁμαρτήματα, nom. pl. neut. of ἁμάρτημα, -τος, τό, "sin"; βλασφημίαι, nom. pl. fem. of βλασφημία, -ας, ἡ, "blasphemy, reviling" (ἁμαρτήματα and βλασφημίαι, nom. in simple appos. to πάντα); βλασφημήσωσιν, 3rd pl. aor. act. subjunc. of βλασφημέω, "blaspheme"; subjunc. in indef. rel. clause; ὅσα ἐάν, "as many as, whatever" (ZG 110; R 733). The neut. rel. pron. ὅσα is not in formal grammatical agreement with its fem. antecedent βλασφημίαι; instead the agreement is according to the sense of the antecedent (BDF §296).

3:29 Βλασφημήσῃ, 3rd sg. aor. act. subjunc. of βλασφημέω, "blaspheme"; subjunc. in indef. rel. clause; εἰς, "against" (see Harris 93–94); on ἔχει as a futuristic pres., see 14:7; ἄφεσιν, acc. sg. fem. of ἄφεσις, -εως, ἡ, "forgiveness"; ἔνοχος, nom. sg. masc. of ἔνοχος, -ον, "guilty," BDAG 338d; ἁμαρτήματος, gen. after certain adjectives (on ἁμάρτημα, see 3:28). The blasphemy against the Holy Spirit is best understood within the unique context of Jesus's controversy with the scribes (cf. Lane 146). His warning was for those who should have known better (the scribes from Jerusalem) and who had become so hardened in their rejection that they could look directly at the brightest light (the witness of the Holy Spirit in the miracles of Jesus) and call it darkness (the work of Satan). No one living today is in quite that same situation and therefore in quite that same danger. The balancing truth is that anyone who continually rejects the grace of God available through Jesus, while not beyond God's mercy, still runs the risk of finding it more and more difficult to repent and seek that grace.

3:30 Mark ends this controversy story with an explanation for why Jesus gave his warning to the scribes, because they claimed that Jesus was possessed by an unclean spirit. Mark uses ὅτι as a causal conj., but by doing so he creates a dependent clause without directly stating the main clause. A statement such as "Jesus spoke these words" is assumed.

FOR FURTHER STUDY

13. Satan and the Demons in Mark's Gospel

Best, Ernest. *The Temptation and the Passion: The Markan Soteriology.* 2nd ed. SNTSMS 2. Cambridge: Cambridge University Press, 1990.

Garrett, Susan R. *The Temptations of Jesus in Mark's Gospel.* Grand Rapids: Eerdmans, 1998.

Robinson, James M. *The Problem of History in Mark and Other Marcan Studies*. 2nd ed. Philadelphia: Fortress, 1982.

Shively, Elizabeth. "The Story Matters: Solving the Problem of the Parables in Mark 3.23–27." Pages 122–44 in *Between Author and Audience in Mark: Narration, Characterization, Interpretation*. Edited by Elizabeth Struthers Malbon. Sheffield, UK: Sheffield Phoenix, 2009.

———. *Apocalyptic Imagination in the Gospel of Mark: The Literary and Theological Role of Mark 3:22–30*. BZNW 189. Berlin: de Gruyter, 2012.

*———. "Characterizing the Non-Human: Satan in the Gospel of Mark." Pages 127–51 in *Character Studies and the Gospel of Mark*. Edited by Christopher W. Skinner and Matthew Ryan Hauge. LNTS 483. London: Bloomsbury T&T Clark, 2014.

Twelftree, Graham H. *Jesus the Exorcist: A Contribution to the Study of the Historical Jesus*. WUNT 2/54. Tübingen: Mohr Siebeck, 1993.

———. "Mark." Pages 101–28 in *In the Name of Jesus: Exorcism among Early Christians*. Grand Rapids: Baker Academic, 2007.

*Williams, Joel F. "The Characterization of the Demons in Mark's Gospel." Pages 103–17 in *Let the Reader Understand: Essays in Honor of Elizabeth Struthers Malbon*. Edited by Edwin K. Broadhead. LNTS 583. London: Bloomsbury T&T Clark, 2018.

HOMILETICAL SUGGESTIONS

Choosing Sides (3:20–30)

1. What do we learn about Jesus?
   a. Jesus cannot be easily dismissed as out of his mind or inherently evil.
   b. Jesus cannot be easily defeated by the power of Satan.
2. What do we learn about spiritual realities?
   a. Satan is a powerful enemy, who is ignored at our own risk.
   b. The Holy Spirit is a powerful witness, who is ignored at our own risk.
3. What do we learn about rejecting Jesus?
   a. An obstinate rejection of Jesus is exceptionally foolish.
   b. An obstinate rejection of Jesus is eternally dangerous.

(d) Jesus's True Family (3:31–35)

3:31 Throughout his narration of Jesus's early ministry in Galilee (1:14–3:35), Mark presents the varying responses to Jesus's authority. As a unit, 1:14–3:35 moves toward the response presented in the final passage of the unit (3:31–35), where Mark portrays a new community, Jesus's new family, eagerly listening to the teaching of Jesus and determined to do the will of God. Ἔρχεται, 3rd sg. pres. mid. indic. of dep. ἔρχομαι, "come, go"; historical pres. (starting a new scene [see 1:12]); sg. vb. with a compound subj. (see 12:33); στήκοντες, nom. pl. masc. of pres. act. ptc. of στήκω, "stand"; temp. adv. ptc. contemp. (on the formation of στήκω, see 13:35); ἀπέστειλαν, 3rd pl. aor. act. indic. of ἀποστέλλω, "send, send a message" (LN 17.1); καλοῦντες, nom. pl. masc. of pres. act. ptc. of καλέω, "call for, summon"; adv. ptc. of purpose (R 991, 1115; Voelz 1:266).

3:32 Ἐκάθητο, 3rd sg. impf. mid. indic. of dep. κάθημαι, "sit"; λέγουσιν, historical pres. (to introduce dir. discourse [see 1:12, 30; cf. λέγει in vv. 33–34]). A sg. collective subj. like ὄχλος normally takes a sg. vb., such as ἐκάθητο, viewing the crowd as a whole. However, a sg. collective subj. can also take a pl. vb., such as λέγουσιν, putting a greater emph. on the individuals within the group (Wallace 400–401; cf. R 404; see 3:8). Both ἰδού in v. 32 and ἴδε in v. 34 are particles that function like imperatives to draw attention to what follows ("behold, look"; see "See" in 1:2). The ms. evidence concerning the words καὶ αἱ ἀδελφαί σου is divided over their omission or inclusion. They may have been omitted by accident because of the confusion caused by their similarity to the immediately preceding words (καὶ οἱ ἀδελφοί σου), or they may have been added to prepare for Jesus's reference to his ἀδελφή in 3:35 (cf. Metzger 70; Yarbro Collins 225; concerning Jesus's sisters, see also 6:3).

3:33 Ἀποκριθείς, nom. sg. masc. of aor. pass. ptc. of dep. ἀποκρίνομαι, "answer." This is the first example in Mark of ἀποκριθείς used as a redundant ptc. in connection with a form of λέγω as the main vb. (with λέγει seven times, with εἶπεν five times, and with ἔλεγεν two times; in addition the pl. form ἀποκριθέντες appears with λέγουσιν in 11:33). As a redundant ptc., ἀποκριθείς overlaps in mng. with the main vb. and therefore is, by definition, contemp. with it. Typically, an aor. ptc. expresses antecedent time when used with a pres. tense main vb., with one common exception being a redundant aor. ptc. used with a historical pres. main vb. (such as ἀποκριθείς with λέγει; cf. Wallace 625; Burton §141). Since a redundant ptc. sounds unnecessarily repetitive in Eng., many translations omit it or render the ptc. as the main vb. and omit the form of λέγω (e.g., ESV: "and he answered them"). Jesus's reply in v. 33 is expressed as a rhetorical question, one that he will answer in the following two verses.

3:34 Περιβλεψάμενος, nom. sg. masc. of aor. mid. ptc. of περιβλέπω, "look around at" (mng. with mid.); temp. adv. ptc. antecedent; κύκλῳ, adv. mng. "in a circle, around" (the dat. of κύκλος "circle" became fixed as an adv.; cf. BDAG 574b; LN 83.19; καθημένους, acc. pl. masc. of pres. mid. ptc. of dep. κάθημαι, "sit"; subst. ptc. The people who were there with Jesus to listen to his teaching, these people belonged to Jesus's spiritual family as his true mother and brothers (on the nom. of exclamation after ἴδε, see Wallace 59–60 [cf. 13:1; 16:6]).

3:35 Whoever listens to the teaching of Jesus and responds to it by doing the will of God, this one belongs to Jesus's family and therefore the family of God. Ποιήσῃ, 3rd sg. aor. act. subjunc. of ποιέω, "do"; subjunc. in an indef. rel. clause; τοῦ θεοῦ, subj. gen.; οὗτος, nom. in simple appos. to ὅς. This passage by itself does little to define directly what it means to do the will of God. Since the phrase appears within the context of Jesus's teaching the crowd, doing the will of God certainly involves following the teaching of Jesus. The noun θέλημα occurs only once in Mark's Gospel as a whole, here in 3:35. The related vb. θέλω is used twenty-five times in Mark, but only once in connection with God's will, in Jesus's prayer in Gethsemane in 14:36. In that prayer, Jesus submits his own will to the Father's, obediently taking the path that leads to the cross. Belonging to Jesus's new community—though a privilege—is also demanding, since it involves following Jesus's example and accepting the path of sacrificial service.

HOMILETICAL SUGGESTIONS

A New Family (3:31–35)

1. Jesus's spiritual family stays near to Jesus to learn from him. (3:33–34)
2. Jesus's spiritual family learns from him to do God's will. (3:35)
3. (A look ahead): Jesus's spiritual family does the will of God no matter how difficult. (14:36)

C. JESUS'S MINISTRY ON AND AROUND
THE SEA OF GALILEE (4:1–8:26)

In Mark 4:1, while Jesus is teaching beside the Sea of Galilee, the size of the crowd becomes so large that he enters a boat in order to teach from it as it floats on the sea. Before 4:1, Mark shows Jesus alongside the sea (1:16; 2:13; 3:7) but never in a boat on the sea. From 4:1 until 8:26, Jesus is in and out of the boat traveling back and forth across the sea. In the final episode in this section (8:22–26), Jesus and his disciples exit the boat, and from that point on in the narrative the boat motif disappears entirely. Through the repeated mention of the boat and the continual crossing of the Sea of Galilee, Mark distinguishes the setting of 4:1–8:26 from the preceding and following sections of the narrative.

In 4:1–8:26, Mark demonstrates that Jesus has the power and compassion to be worthy of faith. Mark explains and commends a life of faith by showing the negative example of the disciples and the positive examples of minor characters, individuals who come out from the crowd to ask Jesus for healing. Therefore, the plot line concerning Jesus's relationship with his disciples takes a negative turn within this section. The disciples fail to understand Jesus's teaching in parables (4:10–13; 7:17–18; 8:15–16), lack sufficient faith in Jesus's miraculous power (4:40; 8:4, 15–16), and show confusion over his identity (4:41; 6:49).

One particularly prominent literary pattern in this section is a series of three boat scenes that present Jesus with his disciples: the stilling of the storm (4:35–41), the walking on the water (6:45–52), and the conversation concerning leaven (8:14–21). Jesus crosses the sea a number of times with his disciples in 4:1–8:26, but these three boat scenes are the only episodes that actually occur on the sea during a crossing. In each of them, either Jesus or Mark himself criticizes the disciples for their lack of faith or understanding (4:40; 6:52; 8:17–18). Through this literary pattern, Mark emphasizes the importance of a life of faith, a continuing trust in Jesus's ability and desire to care for his followers.

1. Cycle 1: Calming of the Sea (4:1–5:20)

The first boat scene portrays Jesus's miraculous power over nature, which provokes fear rather than faith from the disciples (4:35–41). The literary pattern of three boat scenes stands out more prominently in 4:1–8:26, because similar episodes come immediately before and after each boat scene. Before each one is a passage in which Jesus teaches a large crowd. After each one is a passage that describes Jesus's healing ministry. Before the first boat scene, Jesus ministers to the crowd through his teaching in parables (4:1–34), and after it Jesus heals the Gerasene demoniac (5:1–20). Therefore, 4:1–8:26 includes three cycles of episodes that portray in order: Jesus's ministry to the crowd, followed by a boat scene, followed by a report of Jesus's healing work.

(a) [Transition] Jesus's Ministry to the Crowd: The Parables Discourse (4:1–34)

The parables discourse (4:1–34) is a transitional passage, standing between Jesus's initial work in Galilee and his continuing ministry on and around the Sea of Galilee.

It looks back in that it serves to explain the varying initial responses to Jesus and his message about the kingdom, responses ranging from devotion to antagonism. The parables in this section, particularly the parable of the soils (4:1–20), help to make sense of these differing reactions. Jesus's explanation of the nature of the kingdom in these parables also looks back to the preceding section. In 1:14–15, Jesus comes into Galilee proclaiming that the kingdom of God is at hand. However, Mark's Gospel does not mention the kingdom of God again until the parables of ch. 4, which develop Jesus's understanding of the kingdom. At the same time, the parables discourse looks ahead to the following section. It introduces the theme of the incomprehension of the disciples (4:10–13), a theme that grows in importance in the following narrative. Also, this section introduces a shift in Jesus's interaction with the crowd. Before ch. 4, Mark typically portrays Jesus teaching indoors, in either a synagogue or a house. Beginning with this discourse and continuing on through this next section, Jesus teaches crowds so large that they can only meet outdoors.

(i) The Parable of the Soils (4:1–20)

4:1 Ἤρξατο, 3rd sg. aor. mid. indic. of ἄρχω, "begin" (mng. with mid.; on ἄρχομαι, see 1:45); διδάσκειν, pres. act. inf. of διδάσκω, "teach"; complementary inf.; παρά, "beside, by" (on παρά plus the acc. to modify a vb. that does not express movement, see Harris 171; R 615); συνάγεται, 3rd sg. pres. pass. indic. of συνάγω, "gather together, assemble" (mng. with pass. [BDAG 962d]); historical pres. (see 1:12). The attrib. adj. πλεῖστος is the superl. form of πολύς, although it occurs here with an elative sense, i.e., to show intensification rather than comp. ("a very large crowd" or "a huge crowd"; BDAG 849c–d; Wallace 300, 303; Moule 98). Αὐτόν, acc. subj. of the inf.; ἐμβάντα, acc. sg. masc. of aor. act. ptc. of ἐμβαίνω, "embark"; temp. adv. ptc. antecedent; καθῆσθαι, pres. mid. inf. of dep. κάθημαι, "sit"; inf. of result. The prep. phrase ἐν τῇ θαλάσσῃ refers back to the whole clause and therefore assumes Jesus's presence in the boat (cf. ZG 110; ESV: "he got into a boat and sat in it on the sea"). When the prep. πρός occurs with a spatial sense but without a vb. expressing movement, it can mean "by, near, facing" (R 624; Harris 189). Ἦσαν, 3rd pl. impf. act. indic. of εἰμί, "be" (pl. vb. with a collective sg. subj.; see 3:8).

4:2 Ἐδίδασκεν, 3rd sg. impf. act. indic. of διδάσκω, "teach." Two translations are possible for πολλά, "he was teaching them many things" (αὐτούς, dbl. acc. obj. of the person; πολλά, dbl. acc. obj. of the thing) or "he was teaching them at length" (with πολλά functioning as an adv. [see 6:34; cf. Voelz 1:272]). Ἐν (2nd use), "in the course of" (temp. use [see BDAG 330a; cf. ἐν τῇ διδαχῇ αὐτοῦ in 12:38]); αὐτοῦ, subj. gen.

4:3 Ἀκούετε, 2nd pl. pres. act. impv. of ἀκούω, hear, listen. The vb. ἀκούω shows up repeatedly in the parables discourse (thirteen times in 4:1–34). Such an emph. on hearing not only serves to draw attention to Jesus's teaching but also to clarify a major theme of the discourse, that the division between those inside and those outside the kingdom depends on how they hear and respond to the word (France 184–85). Although the parable in 4:3–9 begins with the sower who went out to sow (ἐξῆλθεν,

3rd sg. aor. act. indic. of ἐξέρχομαι, "go out"; σπείρων, nom. sg. masc. of pres. act. ptc. of σπείρω, "sow"; subst. ptc.; σπεῖραι, aor. act. inf. of σπείρω, "sow"; inf. of purpose [Decker 1:91; Cranfield 149]), the emph. in the rest of the parable falls esp. on the four types of soil that receive the seed.

4:4 The first three types of soil to receive seed fail to provide anything for the harvest. Ἐγένετο, 3rd sg. aor. mid. indic. of dep. γίνομαι, "come about, happen" (on καὶ ἐγένετο + time reference + independent clause, see 1:9; because of the complicated sentence structure, many EVV simply omit the translation of καὶ ἐγένετο). Σπείρειν, pres. act. inf. of σπείρω, sow; inf. of contemp. time ("while he was sowing" [Wallace 595; cf. KMP 366; on the common use of the pres. tense with the inf. following ἐν τῷ, see Campbell, *VANIV* 105–8]). The subj. (ὅ) of ἔπεσεν (3rd sg. aor. act. indic. of πίπτω, "fall"; see also same form in 4:5, 7, 8) functions in this context not as a rel. pron. but as a dem. pron., but since as a pron. it takes the place of the collective sg. noun "seed"— or a portion of that seed—it is perhaps best translated as "some" rather than "this one" (cf. BDAG 727d; Stein 197–98). The use of μέν sets ὅ in contrast with καὶ ἄλλο in 4:5, so that the seed that fell alongside the road stands in contrast to other seed that fell elsewhere. Most EVV omit the translation of μέν, since the context already implies a contrast. Ἦλθεν, 3rd sg. aor. act. indic. of ἔρχομαι, "come"; πετεινά, nom. pl. neut. of πετεινόν, -οῦ, τό, "bird" (neut. pl. subj. with a sg. vb.; see 3:11); κατέφαγεν, 3rd sg. aor. act. indic. of κατεσθίω, "eat up, devour" (on κατά as a prep. prefix for intensification and completion, see 1:36).

4:5 The use of ἄλλο (neut. sg. form of ἄλλος) serves to distinguish this particular portion of the seed from that mentioned earlier ("other seed"; cf. BDAG 46d). Ἔπεσεν, see 4:4; πετρῶδες, acc. sg. neut. of πετρώδης, -ες, "rocky" (with the adj. functioning here as a subst., "rocky ground," BDAG 810c); εἶχεν, 3rd sg. impf. act. indic. of ἔχω, "have"; ἐξανέτειλεν, 3rd sg. aor. act. indic. of ἐξανατέλλω, "spring up"; ἔχειν, pres. act. inf. of ἔχω, have; inf. of cause ("because it didn't have" [cf. Wallace 597; KMP 367; on the common use of the pres. tense with the inf. following διὰ τό, see Campbell, *VANIV* 108–9]); βάθος, acc. sg. neut. of βάθος, -ους, τό, "depth"; γῆς, attributed gen. (i.e., the soil was not deep).

4:6 Ἀνέτειλεν, 3rd sg. aor. act. indic. of ἀνατέλλω, "rise, spring up, dawn" (note the similarity in wording between the rising up of the plant [ἐξανέτειλεν] and that of the sun [ἀνέτειλεν]); ἐκαυματίσθη, 3rd sg. aor. pass. indic. of καυματίζω, "burn up, scorch"; ἔχειν, pres. act. inf. of ἔχω, have; inf. of cause; ῥίζαν, acc. sg. fem. of ῥίζα, -ης, ἡ, "[deep] root" (BDAG 905d); ἐξηράνθη, 3rd sg. aor. pass. indic. of ξηραίνω, "dry up."

4:7 Ἔπεσεν, see 4:4; ἀκάνθας (acc. pl. fem.) and ἄκανθαι (nom. pl. fem.) are both from ἄκανθα, -ης, ἡ, "thorn-plant"; ἀνέβησαν, 3rd pl. aor. act. indic. of ἀναβαίνω, "come up, grow up" (LN 23.196); συνέπνιξαν, 3rd pl. aor. act. indic. of συμπνίγω, "choke"; ἔδωκεν, 3rd sg. aor. act. indic. of δίδωμι, "give, produce" (BDAG 242d; LN 23.199).

4:8 Last of all, the good soil received the seed and produced an abundant harvest. At this point the parable switches from the sg. ἄλλο, "other seed," to the pl. ἄλλα, "other seeds" (neut. pl. of ἄλλος; with the neut. pl. subj. taking a sg. vb. [see 3:11]), perhaps as a way to prepare for the varying levels of crop yield mentioned at the end of the verse (Stein 200). Ἔπεσεν, see 4:4; ἐδίδου, 3rd sg. impf. act. indic. of δίδωμι, "give, produce"; ἀναβαίνοντα, nom. pl. neut. of pres. act. ptc. of ἀναβαίνω, "come up, grow up" (BDAG 58d); temp. adv. ptc. contemp.; αὐξανόμενα, nom. pl. neut. of pres. pass. ptc. of αὐξάνω, "grow, increase" (mng. with pass.); temp. adv. ptc. contemp.; ἔφερεν, 3rd sg. impf. act. indic. of φέρω, "bear, produce." The use of the impf. tense (ἐδίδου, ἔφερεν) to describe the fate of the seed in the good earth, along with the use of pres. ptc. forms (ἀναβαίνοντα, αὐξανόμενα), draws attention to the unfolding action and stands in contrast to the consistent use of the aor. tense to describe the fate of the seed in the previous three types of soil. The seed in the good earth is living, growing, and producing, while that in the other types of soil was devoured, scorched, and choked. The yield of the harvest is listed as one seed producing thirty (τριάκοντα), one sixty (ἑξήκοντα), and one a hundred (ἑκατόν) times, or in other words, thirtyfold, sixtyfold, and a hundredfold (cf. ZG 111; Z §158). The words τριάκοντα, ἑξήκοντα, and ἑκατόν are all indecl. numbers (BDAG 1015b; 298d; 349d).

4:9 The rel. pron. ὅς assumes an antecedent, which is not stated in Gk. but should be supplied in Eng. ("the one who"; BDAG 725d). Ὦτα, acc. pl. neut. of οὖς, ὠτός, τό, "ear"; ἀκούειν, pres. act. inf. of ἀκούω, "hear." The inf. ἀκούειν is epex., with the noun ὦτα functioning as a metaphor for a physical ability or capacity and the inf. explaining the nature of that ability ("ears [able] to hear"). The 3rd pers. impv. ἀκουέτω (3rd sg. pres. act. impv. of ἀκούω, "hear, listen") expresses a command, not simply a permission (Wallace 486; KMP 209). If a translation such as "let him hear" (cf. e.g., ESV) conveys the idea of permission, then it would be better to use a translation such as "should listen" (cf. e.g., NLT) to communicate the command more clearly.

4:10 With the change in scene beginning in 4:10, Mark interrupts the parables discourse and inserts a discussion between Jesus and his followers concerning the interpretation of the parable of the soils. As a result, Mark is not following a strict chronological sequence; rather, he includes at this point a conversation that took place at a later time (Stein 204, 206; Lane 155–56). Ἐγένετο, 3rd sg. aor. mid. indic. of dep. γίνομαι, "come to be, be there" (BDAG 199c); κατὰ μόνας, "alone, by himself," BDAG 512a (lit: "by only places"); ἠρώτων, 3rd pl. impf. act. indic. of ἐρωτάω, "ask about"; αὐτόν, dbl. acc. obj. of the person; παραβολάς, dbl. acc. obj. of the thing. Mark uses the vb. ἐρωτάω and more freq. the vb. ἐπερωτάω when introducing questions, either directly or indirectly. Mark's common pattern is to use both vbs. in the impf. tense, portraying the action as in progress, perhaps to picture the give-and-take of an ongoing dialogue (cf. Fanning 284, 286). Other vbs.—in addition to λέγω (see 2:16), ἐρωτάω, and ἐπερωτάω—that use the impf. to introduce dir. or indir. discourse in Mark include: κηρύσσω (1:7), κράζω (3:11; 10:48; 11:9), παρακαλέω (5:10, 18; 6:56), διαστέλλω (8:15), διαλογίζομαι (8:16; 11:31), διδάσκω (11:17), λαλέω (14:31), προσεύχομαι (14:35), ψευδομαρτυρέω (14:57), and βλασφημέω (15:29). The vb. φημί presents a special case, since ἔφη, by form, can be either impf. or aor. (9:12, 38; 10:20, 29; 12:24; 14:29). Approximately 30 percent of all impf. vb. forms in Mark's Gospel introduce dir. or indir. discourse.

Οἱ περὶ αὐτόν, "those around him" (on an art. with a prep. phrase, see 1:36). The immediately preceding context of Mark's Gospel serves to clarify the identity of οἱ περὶ αὐτόν. In 3:31–35, Mark refers to a crowd sitting around Jesus (3:32: περὶ αὐτόν) and to Jesus looking at those around him (3:34: τοὺς περὶ αὐτόν) as he is teaching. Jesus refers to these people as his true family because they are seeking to do the will of God. The same motif is present in 4:10. Those around Jesus are the people who hear Jesus's public teaching and who stay after the rest of the crowd has left because they are receptive to him and want to do God's will.

4:11 The term μυστήριον appears only this one time in Mark's Gospel. The more freq. use of the word in Paul's epistles serves to shed light on its use in Mark. In Paul's epistles, the term μυστήριον describes the wisdom of God that exceeds human understanding (Rom 11:25; 1 Cor 2:6–9) and the previously hidden thoughts of God that are now made known to his people (Rom 16:25–26; Eph 3:4–5, 9–10; Col 1:26–27). The "secret" or "mystery" is therefore divine truth that cannot be understood apart from divine revelation, truth that, although previously hidden, is now revealed to those who have ears to hear (cf. Cranfield 152–53; BDAG 662a). In Mark, the mystery concerns (or refers to; βασιλείας, gen. of reference [Stein 208]) the kingdom of God, or more specifically, the kingdom of God as it is described in the parables discourse, i.e., a present form of the kingdom that is a growing but hidden reality on earth until the final coming of the kingdom in power.

Δέδοται, 3rd sg. pf. pass. indic. of δίδωμι, "give"; γίνεται, 3rd sg. pres. mid. indic. of dep. γίνομαι, come to be, happen (sg. vb. with a neut. pl. subj.). "Those outside" (τοῖς ἔξω [adv. with art. functioning subst.]) stand in contrast to "those around Jesus" (οἱ περὶ αὐτόν). Since those around Jesus included his disciples and others who wanted to learn more from him, "those outside" must at least include the people who have just been left behind, the people in the crowd who have listened to Jesus but who have shown no further interest in what he has to say. Shortly before this passage, Jesus spoke in parables to scribes who had rejected him (3:22–23). By speaking to them in parables, Jesus treated them as outsiders. Therefore, "those outside" as a category also includes people hardened against the truth concerning Jesus.

4:12 The conj. ἵνα connects Jesus's words concerning outsiders to a quotation drawn from Isa 6:9–10, a passage on God's intention to hold some under judgment. A number of interpretations for the mng. of ἵνα in this context have been proposed, most of them seeking to avoid the idea that the purpose for Jesus's parables is to keep outsiders from understanding and therefore to keep them from finding forgiveness (see Porter, *VA* 325 for a helpful list of views). The most prominent views include:

1. Fulfillment ἵνα: The use of ἵνα in 4:12 serves as a citation formula to introduce a quotation of Scripture, and therefore it is shorthand for "in order that it might be fulfilled." In this view, the text in Isaiah simply demonstrates that the circumstances in Jesus's life fulfilled prophecy (e.g., ZG 111; Lane 159).
2. Causal ἵνα: Mark 4:12 is par. to Matt 13:13, which uses ὅτι instead of ἵνα. In this view, ἵνα in Mark conveys the same idea as ὅτι in Matthew—that

the incomprehension of people is not the goal toward which Jesus's use of
parables is aiming, but rather the reason why he must use parables (e.g., T
102–3).

3. Result ἵνα: The use of ἵνα in 4:12 indicates the result of Jesus's teaching in
parables but not his intended goal. The unintended consequence of parabolic
teaching is that some will hear the parables but not really understand and
therefore not repent or find forgiveness (e.g., Moule 142–43; Brooks 83).

*4. Purpose ἵνα: The use of ἵνα in 4:12 introduces the purpose for which Jesus
gives everything to those who are outside in parables. The goal is to keep
them in incomprehension and therefore on the path toward judgment (e.g.,
BDF §369; BDAG 477b; Cranfield 155–58; Marcus 1:299–300).

The conj. ἵνα appears freq. in Mark's Gospel (sixty-four times) and is commonly
used to introduce a purpose clause (e.g., 1:38; 2:10; 3:14; 7:9; 10:13; 12:2; 14:10;
16:1; with the other common use being to introduce a subst. dir. obj. clause [see 5:10]).
However, there are no examples of the use of ἵνα by itself in Mark, where it serves as a
shorthand for "in order that it might be fulfilled" or expresses a cause or communicates
an unintended result. In other words, other means were available that would more
easily convey such ideas than the use of ἵνα by itself (e.g., the use of ἵνα πληρωθῶσιν αἱ
γραφαί for a fulfillment formula [14:49]; the use of ὅτι for cause [4:29]; or the use of
ὥστε for result [1:45]). Perhaps it is helpful to remember that the judgment envisioned
in 4:12 is directed toward those who are outside, i.e., toward those who have already
come to their decision to reject Jesus and his authority.

Βλέποντες, nom. pl. masc. of pres. act. ptc. of βλέπω, "see"; adv. ptc. of concession
(cf. NET); βλέπωσιν, 3rd pl. pres. act. subjunc. of βλέπω, "see"; ἴδωσιν, 3rd pl. aor.
act. subjunc. of ὁράω, "see"; ἀκούοντες, nom. pl. masc. of pres. act. ptc. of ἀκούω,
"hear"; adv. ptc. of concession; ἀκούωσιν, 3rd pl. pres. act. subjunc. of ἀκούω, "hear";
συνιῶσιν, 3rd pl. pres. act. subjunc. of συνίημι, "understand." The conj. μήποτε
introduces a clause that indicates a negated purpose ("lest, in order that . . . not,"
BDAG 648c–d; cf. 14:2), a clause that explains why God keeps those who are outside
in their incomprehension and what he does not want to see happen. Ἐπιστρέψωσιν, 3rd
pl. aor. act. subjunc. of ἐπιστρέφω, "turn, return"; ἀφεθῇ, 3rd sg. aor. pass. subjunc. of
ἀφίημι, "forgive."

4:13 Mark 4:13 introduces a theme that grows in importance in the following narrative,
the lack of understanding on the part of the disciples and followers of Jesus. Οἴδατε,
2nd pl. pf. act. indic. of οἶδα, "know, understand." At times, a question beginning with
καί looks back to a preceding question or statement that implies a cond. idea. Based
on that cond., καί introduces a concluding question and is best translated as "then" (cf.
9:12; 10:26; cf. Z §459). Then how will you understand (γνώσεσθε, 2nd pl. fut. mid.
indic. of γινώσκω, "know, understand" [dep. in fut.]) any parables (on πᾶς as "any,"
see T 200; BDF §275)? In Mark, the relationship between outsiders and insiders is not
strictly antithetical. Just because outsiders do not see, hear, and understand, it does not
necessarily follow that insiders always will. In Mark's Gospel, insiders also struggle
to understand (cf. 8:17–21).

4:14 Σπείρων, nom. sg. masc. of pres. act. ptc. of σπείρω, "sow"; subst. ptc. Elsewhere, Mark uses "the word" without any other qualification to refer to the public message of Jesus (2:2; 4:33). In this way, "the word" is a similar expression to "the gospel of God," another phrase for Jesus's public message about the kingdom (1:14). Therefore, the parable of the soils is about the way different groups of people hear and respond to Jesus's proclamation concerning the kingdom.

4:15 Σπείρεται, 3rd sg. pres. pass. indic. of σπείρω, "sow"; ἀκούσωσιν, 3rd pl. aor. act. subjunc. of ἀκούω, "hear"; subjunc. in indef. temp. clause; ἔρχεται, 3rd sg. pres. mid. indic. of dep. ἔρχομαι, "come"; ἐσπαρμένον, acc. sg. masc. of pf. pass. ptc. of σπείρω, "sow"; adj. ptc. Mark 4:15 sets the pattern for how the interpretation relates to the parable. By referring to "the alongside-the-road ones" (οἱ παρὰ τὴν ὁδόν), the interpretation makes it clear that the comp. is between the different types of soil and different types of people. This comp. functions as a guide for the remainder of the interpretation. In 4:16, 18, 20, the grammatical structure shifts to subst. participles that describe people as though they were like seeds sown in different types of soil, but in spite of the awkwardness of the grammatical structure, the comp. ultimately is still between how the various types of soil receive the seed and how various kinds of people receive the word (France 203–5; Bruce 365–66). In 4:15, the soil alongside the road represents those who have hardened themselves against the truth and who therefore are easily blinded by Satan.

4:16 Πετρώδη, acc. pl. neut. of πετρώδης, -ες, "rocky" (the adj. is used subst. [as in 4:5], although now in the pl., "rocky places"); σπειρόμενοι, nom. pl. masc. of pres. pass. ptc. of σπείρω, "sow"; subst. ptc.; on ἀκούσωσιν, see 4:15. For the people represented by the rocky soil, what they hear and receive with joy is something less than the truth about the kingdom, because they somehow hear a message that contains no cost. Their quick acceptance, based as it is on their shallow understanding of the message, will turn to quick rejection when they begin to comprehend the actual truth about the kingdom and what it may cost them to be a part of it.

4:17 Ῥίζαν, acc. sg. fem. of ῥίζα, -ης, ἡ, "[firm] root," BDAG 905d; πρόσκαιροι, nom. pl. masc. of πρόσκαιρος, -ον, "temporary, transitory." The opposite of πρόσκαιρος, "temporary," is αἰώνιος, "eternal" (BDAG 881a). So, e.g., Paul contrasted the visible and temporary (πρόσκαιρα) with the invisible and eternal (αἰώνια; 2 Cor 4:18; cf. 4 Macc 15:2–3; Jos. Asen. 12:12). In a similar way, Mark's Gospel distinguishes between "this time" (τῷ καιρῷ τούτῳ) and "the coming age" (τῷ αἰῶνι τῷ ἐρχομένῳ) in which those who follow Jesus will receive "eternal life" (ζωὴν αἰώνιον; 10:30). Therefore, to be temporary involves not having eternal life or participating in the coming age. Εἶτα, adv. mng. "then, next"; γενομένης, gen. sg. fem. of aor. mid. ptc. of dep. γίνομαι, "come to be, arise" (BDAG 197b; fem. in agreement with θλίψεως); gen. abs.; temp. adv. ptc. antecedent; διωγμοῦ, gen. sg. masc. of διωγμός, -οῦ, ὁ, "persecution"; σκανδαλίζονται, 3rd pl. pres. pass. indic. of σκανδαλίζω, "cause to stumble" (on σκανδαλίζονται for falling away from the message of the kingdom in this context, see *TDNT* 7:349; on σκανδαλίζω, see 9:43).

4:18–19 On ἀκάνθας, see 4:7; on σπειρόμενοι, see 4:16; ἀκούσαντες, nom. pl. masc. of aor. act. ptc. of ἀκούω, "hear"; subst. ptc. The people portrayed as the ground over-grown with thorn plants underestimate the value of belonging to the kingdom and consequently allow the message of the kingdom to be choked out by lesser things: (1) the worries of the present age (μέριμναι, nom. pl. fem. of μέριμνα, -ης, ἡ, "anxiety, worry, care"; αἰῶνος, "of the present age" [BDAG 32c]), i.e., the kinds of things that people worry about when their lives are dominated by the values and standards of the present world (cf. LN 41.38; αἰῶνος, subj. gen.); (2) the deceitfulness of wealth (ἀπάτη, nom. sg. fem. of ἀπάτη, -ης, ἡ, "deceitfulness, deception"; πλούτου, gen. sg. masc. of πλοῦτος, -ου, ὁ, "wealth, riches"; subj. gen.), i.e., the pursuit of an abundance of pos-sessions, which is a deception because it cannot provide the fulfillment and happiness that it seems to promise (cf. LN 57.30); and (3) the desires for other things (cf. BDAG 372a, 602d), i.e., the constant craving for more and more, the pursuit of excess (cf. France 206). Εἰσπορευόμεναι, nom. pl. fem. of pres. mid. ptc. of dep. εἰσπορεύομαι, "enter"; temp. adv. ptc. contemp.; συμπνίγουσιν, from συμπνίγω, "choke"; γίνεται, 3rd sg. pres. mid. indic. of dep. γίνομαι, "become, prove to be" (BDAG 199b); ἄκαρπος, nom. sg. masc. of ἄκαρπος, -ον, "unfruitful, useless."

4:20 The fourth type of soil, the good earth, stands in contrast to the previous three types, since it represents the people who hear, truly understand, and receive the mes-sage of the kingdom. Σπαρέντες, nom. pl. masc. of aor. pass. ptc. of σπείρω, "sow"; subst. ptc.; οἵτινες, "who" (functioning in the same way as the def. rel. pron. in 4:16 [see R 957; cf. 9:1; 12:18; 15:7]); παραδέχονται, 3rd pl. pres. mid. indic. of dep. παραδέχομαι, "accept"; καρποφοροῦσιν, from καρποφορέω, "bear fruit." The parable ends not with the prospect of rejection or failure for those who bring the message of the kingdom, but with the hope of an abundant harvest (see 4:8 concerning thirtyfold, sixtyfold, and a hundredfold).

FOR FURTHER STUDY

14. The Kingdom of God in Mark's Gospel

Ambrozic, Aloysius M. *The Hidden Kingdom: A Redaction-Critical Study of the References to the Kingdom of God in Mark's Gospel*. CBQMS 2. Washington, DC: Catholic Biblical Association of America, 1972.

Beasley-Murray, G. R. *Jesus and the Kingdom of God*. Grand Rapids: Eerdmans, 1986.

Boring, M. Eugene. "The Kingdom of God in Mark." Pages 131–45 in *The Kingdom of God in 20th-Century Interpretation*. Edited by Wendell Willis. Peabody, MA: Hendrickson, 1987.

*Chilton, Bruce D., ed. *The Kingdom of God in the Teaching of Jesus*. IRT 5. Philadelphia: Fortress, 1984.

France, R. T. *Divine Government: God's Kingship in the Gospel of Mark*. London: SPCK, 1990.

Garland, David E. "The Kingdom of God in Mark." Pages 335–67 in *A Theology of Mark's Gospel: Good News about Jesus the Messiah, the Son of God*. Grand Rapids: Zondervan, 2015.

Kelber, Werner H. *The Kingdom in Mark: A New Place and a New Time.* Philadelphia: Fortress, 1974.

Ladd, George Eldon. *The Presence of the Future: The Eschatology of Biblical Realism.* 2nd ed. Grand Rapids: Eerdmans, 1974.

Malbon, Elizabeth Struthers. "Markan Narrative Christology and the Kingdom of God." Pages 177–93 in *Literary Encounters with the Reign of God.* Edited by Sharon H. Ringe and H. C. Paul Kim. London: T&T Clark, 2004.

Perrin, Norman. *The Kingdom of God in the Teaching of Jesus.* Philadelphia: Westminster, 1963.

———. *Jesus and the Language of the Kingdom: Symbol and Metaphor in New Testament Interpretation.* Philadelphia: Fortress, 1976.

HOMILETICAL SUGGESTIONS

How Different People Hear the Message of the Kingdom (4:13–20)

1. The soil by the path: Some people will not listen to the message of the kingdom because they have hardened themselves against it. (4:13–15)
2. The soil among the rocks: Some people will not listen to the message of the kingdom because they will only accept the promise of an easy life. (4:16–17)
3. The soil among the weeds: Some people will not listen to the message of the kingdom because they are distracted by lesser things. (4:18–19)
4. The good soil: Some people will listen to the message of the kingdom, welcome it, and have their lives changed by it. (4:20)

(ii) Encouragements to Listen (4:21–25)

4:21 Mark returns to Jesus's public teaching, having completed his account of Jesus's private explanation of the previous parable. Mark 4:21 contains two questions, both of which concern "a lamp" (λύχνος, nom. sg. masc. of ὁ λύχνος, -ου, ὁ, "lamp"). The art. used with λύχνος should be taken seriously as pointing to a def. object or individual (Stein 224). Since the lamp is said to come (ἔρχεται, 3rd sg. pres. mid. indic. of dep. ἔρχομαι, "come"), the metaphor of the lamp seems to be referring to a person who is able to move as opposed to an object that must be brought or carried in order to go from one place to another. Therefore, the lamp is probably best understood as a metaphor for Jesus himself (cf. Stein 224; Cranfield 164–65; Hooker 133–34; Lane 165–67), the one who has come (1:7, 14, 24, 38–39; 2:17; 10:45) and will come again (8:38; 13:26, 35–36; 14:62).

The first question begins with μήτι, an interr. particle that invites a neg. answer (BDAG 649c; BDF §§427, 440). The implied answer to the question is: no, the lamp is not coming in order to be hidden (τεθῇ, 3rd sg. aor. pass. subjunc. of τίθημι, "put, place"; subjunc. in a purpose ἵνα clause; μόδιον, acc. sg. masc. of μόδιος, -ου, ὁ, "peck measure, bushel basket"; κλίνην, acc. sg. fem. of κλίνη, -ης, ἡ, "bed"). The second question begins with οὐχ, indicating that an affirmative answer is expected (BDAG 734a; BDF §§427, 440; see also 4:38). The implied answer to the question is: yes, the lamp is coming to receive a place of prominence (λυχνίαν, acc. sg. fem. of λυχνία, -ας, ἥ, "lampstand"). The second question assumes but does not repeat the main clause from the first question (ἔρχεται ὁ λύχνος). The questions in 4:21 communicate that God's ultimate purpose is to reveal Jesus and the kingdom he brings. He is the lamp who will not finally be hidden.

4:22 The use of γάρ at the beginning of v. 22 indicates that this verse functions as an explanation in some way of v. 21. Yet, in contrast to the saying in v. 21, the saying in v. 22 assumes hiddenness. Although God's ultimate purpose is to bring the lamp into the open, at the present time it is hidden. Mark 4:22 explains that the time of hiddenness, however, is not forever, since present hiddenness serves the purpose of future revelation. Κρυπτόν, nom. sg. neut. of κρυπτός, -ή, -όν, hidden, secret (the neut. form of the pred. adj. makes clear that the subj. should be "nothing"; cf. ZG 113 [on this same point, see also the neut. pred. adj. ἀπόκρυφον in the next clause]); ἐὰν μή, "except, unless" (BDF §376); φανερωθῇ, 3rd sg. aor. pass. subjunc. of φανερόω, "reveal, make known"; subjunc. in a purpose ἵνα clause; ἐγένετο, 3rd sg. aor. mid. indic. of dep. γίνομαι, "come to be"; ἀπόκρυφον, nom. sg. neut. of ἀπόκρυφος, -ον, "hidden, concealed"; ἀλλά, used in the place of ἐὰν μή to mean "except" (Z §§469–70; Turner, *Style* 13); ἔλθῃ, 3rd sg. aor. act. subjunc. of ἔρχομαι, "come"; subjunc. in a purpose ἵνα clause; φανερόν, acc. sg. neut. of φανερός, -ά, -όν, "the open, public notice" (mng. with the subst. use of the adj., BDAG 1048a). The saying in 4:22 indicates that the time of vindication is coming when the hiddenness will be over and everyone will see the light. The larger narrative of Mark's Gospel points to the coming of the Son of Man in great power and glory as the time when everyone, including those who have rejected Jesus, will see the truth (13:26; 14:62).

4:23 The command to hear in 4:23 is worded in almost the same way as that in 4:9 (see 4:9 for the definition of ὦτα and the parsing of ἀκούειν and ἀκουέτω). The only difference in wording is that the command in 4:9 begins with "the one who" (ὅς), while the command in 4:23 starts with "if anyone" (εἴ τις; on the 1st class cond., see 9:35).

4:24 Mark 4:24 begins with yet another command to listen with care (βλέπετε, 2nd pl. pres. act. impv. of βλέπω, "consider, pay attention to" [cf. LN 27.58]; τί, "what, that which" [interr. pron. functioning as a rel. pron.; Z §221; France 210]). The following sayings in vv. 24–25 encourage obedience to this command by promising understanding to those who do so. Ἐν, "by" (instr. use); μέτρῳ, dat. sg. neut. of μέτρον, -ου, τό, "measure"; μετρεῖτε, from μετρέω, "measure, deal out, apportion"; μετρηθήσεται, 3rd sg. fut. pass. indic. of μετρέω, "measure, deal out, apportion"; προστεθήσεται, 3rd sg. fut. pass. indic. of προστίθημι, "add." To the same extent that you pay careful attention to the present veiled revelation of God concerning Jesus and the kingdom, understanding will be given to you, and indeed even more understanding will be offered to you.

4:25 The use of the conj. γάρ indicates that the saying in 4:25 serves as an explanation of the saying in 4:24. As a result, the continuing theme in 4:25 is the importance of careful attention to God's revelation in Jesus. The person who is able to hear and who diligently wants to make sense of God's revelation in Jesus, that one will receive understanding (ὅς, "the one who" [see 4:9]; δοθήσεται, 3rd sg. fut. pass. indic.

of δίδωμι, "give"). The person who has given up paying attention to God's revelation because of a rejection of Jesus or simply a disinterest in him and his message concerning the kingdom, that one will be left in blindness and will eventually lose the ability to recognize God's work in Jesus (καί, ascensive; ὅ, "what" [see 2:24]; ἀρθήσεται, 3rd sg. fut. pass. indic. of αἴρω, "take away").

HOMILETICAL SUGGESTIONS

Hiddenness and Revelation (4:21–25)

1. Present hiddenness, future revelation: The present time of hiddenness for Jesus and his kingdom will not last forever. (4:21–23)
2. Present hiddenness, present revelation: The present time of hiddenness for Jesus and his kingdom will not hinder those who seek understanding. (4:24–25)

(iii) The Parable of the Seed Growing by Itself (4:26–29)

4:26 The parables discourse in Mark 4 includes three parables concerning the present mystery form of the kingdom (the soils [4:1–20]; the seed growing by itself [4:26–29]; and the mustard seed [4:30–32]). The parable in 4:26–29, a passage unique to Mark's Gospel, teaches that the growth of the kingdom at the present time cannot be explained in terms of human effort or ingenuity. God's kingdom is God's work. The comp. conj. ὡς introduces a description of what the kingdom is like, comparing the kingdom to the depiction of the event as a whole rather than to only one part of the picture. The series of five subjunc. vbs. that follow the comp. conj. indicates that ὡς in this context stands for ὡς ἐάν, "as if" (ZG 113; BDF §380; cf. ESV; NRSV). Βάλῃ, 3rd sg. aor. act. subjunc. of βάλλω, "throw, scatter"; σπόρον, acc. sg. masc. of σπόρος, -ου, ὁ, "seed."

4:27 Καθεύδῃ, 3rd sg. pres. act. subjunc. of καθεύδω, "sleep"; ἐγείρηται, 3rd sg. pres. pass. subjunc. of ἐγείρω, "wake up, awaken" (act. intrans. mng. with pass; BDAG 271c). In this context, the pres. tense of καθεύδῃ and ἐγείρηται expresses an iter. action. He repeatedly goes to sleep night after night and gets up day after day. On σπόρος, see 4:26; βλαστᾷ, 3rd sg. pres. act. subjunc. of βλαστάνω, "sprout" (sometimes spelled βλαστάω [BDAG 177d]); μηκύνηται, 3rd sg. pres. mid. subjunc. of μηκύνω, "become long, grow long" (mng. with mid.); οἶδεν, 3rd sg. pf. act. indic. of οἶδα, "know"; ὡς οὐκ οἶδεν αὐτός, "(in such a way) as he himself does not know" (BDAG 1103d).

4:28 Αὐτομάτη, nom. sg. fem. of αὐτόματος, -η, -ον, "by itself, on its own"; καρποφορεῖ, from καρποφορέω, "bear fruit, bear crops." The adj. αὐτομάτη agrees grammatically with the noun γῆ, but it functions as an adv. modifying the vb. καρποφορεῖ, explaining how the earth bears fruit (R 549; ZG 113). Χόρτον, acc. sg. masc. of χόρτος, -ου, ὁ, "grass, stalk of grain," BDAG 1087c; εἶτα, adv. mng. "then, next"; στάχυν, acc. sg. masc. of στάχυς, -υος, ὁ, "head of grain." There is a text-critical problem related to the form of πλήρης; with the final -ς, it is an indecl. adj. (T 315–16; Z §11), and without the final -ς, it is an acc. sg. masc. of πλήρης, -ες, "complete, fully developed, fully ripened."

Σῖτον, acc. sg. masc. of σῖτος, -ου, ὁ, "wheat, grain"; στάχυϊ, dat. sg. masc. of στάχυς, -υος, ὁ, "head of grain."

4:29 Even though the man has contributed nothing beyond scattering the seed, the harvest arrives. In the same way, the growth of the present mystery form of the kingdom takes place apart from human strength and wisdom. Παραδοῖ, 3rd sg. aor. act. subjunc. of παραδίδωμι, "allow, permit" (BDAG 763b; LN 13.142); subjunc. in indef. temp. clause (on the formation of the subjunc. for δίδωμι and its compounds, see 8:37); δρέπανον, acc. sg. neut. of δρέπανον, -ου, τό, "sickle"; παρέστηκεν, 3rd sg. pf. act. indic. of παρίστημι, "be present, be here, have come" (with pres. intrans. mng. in pf.; cf. ZG 114); θερισμός, nom. sg. masc. of θερισμός, -οῦ, ὁ, "harvest."

(iv) The Parable of the Mustard Seed (4:30–32)

4:30 The last in the series of three parables concerning the present mystery form of the kingdom is the parable of the mustard seed, which illustrates the kingdom's remarkable growth. Ὁμοιώσωμεν, 1st pl. aor. act. subjunc. of ὁμοιόω, "compare"; ἐν, "with, by" (instr. use); θῶμεν, 1st pl. aor. act. subjunc. of τίθημι, "present, explain" (BDAG 1003c; LN 33.151). Both ὁμοιώσωμεν and θῶμεν function as delib. subjunctives (Cranfield 170), expressing a rhetorical question concerning the possibility of finding an appropriate means for illustrating the kingdom of God. By using the 1st pers. pl. with ὁμοιώσωμεν and θῶμεν, Jesus associates himself with his listeners and includes them in his search for an adequate picture of the kingdom (cf. BDF §280; R 678).

4:31 The parable compares the kingdom of God to a mustard seed, although not just to the seed but to the whole picture of the seed starting small and growing into a large plant. The dat. case of κόκκῳ (dat. sg. masc. of κόκκος, -ου, ὁ, seed, grain) assumes that ὡς is introducing the answer to the question raised by πῶς ὁμοιώσωμεν and therefore that ὡς is substituting for a word such as ὁμοιώσομεν ("we will compare it to a seed"; cf. Swete 86; Bruce 369). Σινάπεως, gen. sg. neut. of σίναπι, -εως, τό, "mustard plant"; attrib. gen. ("mustard seed"; cf. Stein 235). The rel. pron. ὅς begins a rel. clause that describes the mustard seed, but the vbs. in the clause for which ὅς is the subj. do not appear until the following verse (ἀναβαίνει, γίνεται, ποιεῖ). Inserted between ὅς and the main vbs. of the rel. clause is, first of all, an indef. temp. clause, "whenever it is sown on the ground" (σπαρῇ, 3rd sg. aor. pass. subjunc. of σπείρω, "sow"). Next comes an adv. ptc. clause of concession. The neut. ptc. ὄν (nom. sg. neut. of pres. act. ptc. of εἰμί, "be") should be masc.—according to strict grammar—in agreement with ὅς and κόκκῳ, but it takes the neut. apparently in connection with the following neut. noun σπερμάτων (Cranfield 170; France 215). As a result, the adj. μικρότερον as well as the adj. μεῖζον in the following verse are both neut. The comp. adj. μικρότερον is being used as a superl. adj., since the mustard seed is being compared to all of the other seeds (see Wallace 299–301). Likewise, the comp. adj. μεῖζον in the next verse is also functioning as a superl. adj.

4:32 The repetition of ὅταν σπαρῇ is resumptive (Cranfield 170; on σπαρῇ, see 4:31); i.e., the repetition serves to resume and recall the previous sentence structure after the interrupting ptc. clause. Some translations omit the resumptive clause, regarding it as unnecessarily repetitive (e.g., GNB; NLT). Γίνεται, 3rd sg. pres. mid. indic. of dep. γίνομαι, "become"; λαχάνων, gen. pl. neut. of λάχανον, -ου, τό, "garden herb, garden plant, vegetable"; κλάδους, acc. pl. masc. of κλάδος, -ου, ὁ, "branch"; δύνασθαι, pres. mid. inf. of dep. δύναμαι, "be able to, can"; inf. of result; σκιάν, acc. sg. fem. of σκιά, -ᾶς, ἡ, "shade"; πετεινά, acc. pl. neut. of πετεινόν, -οῦ, τό, "bird"; acc. subj. of the inf.; κατασκηνοῦν, pres. act. inf. of κατασκηνόω, "live, settle, nest"; complementary inf. The contrast between the size of the mustard seed and the full-grown mustard plant is in fact dramatic, since it can grow to the height of ten to twelve feet (*TDNT* 7:228). The eventual size of the kingdom of God will stand in dramatic contrast to the seemingly small start within Jesus's ministry among his followers.

HOMILETICAL SUGGESTIONS

Parables about the Kingdom (4:1–34)

1. An inevitable kingdom (parable of the soils): The message of the kingdom will spread in ways that go beyond all human rejection. (4:1–20)
2. A supernatural kingdom (parable of the seed growing by itself): The message of the kingdom will spread in ways that go beyond all human effort. (4:26–29)
3. A growing kingdom (parable of the mustard seed): The message of the kingdom will spread in ways that go beyond all human expectation. (4:30–32)

(v) Summary of Jesus's Teaching through Parables (4:33–34)

4:33 Mark brings the parables discourse to a close by summarizing the general pattern of Jesus's teaching ministry in vv. 33–34. Mark's use of impf. vbs. throughout the summary seems to indicate that teaching with parables was Jesus's customary practice and that such teaching took place on repeated occasions (France 217, 246–47). Παραβολαῖς, dat. of means or instr.; ἐλάλει, 3rd sg. impf. act. indic. of λαλέω, "speak" (see also the same form in 4:34); on λόγον, see 4:14. The conj. καθώς in this context means "to the extent that" (BDAG 493d; cf. Guelich 256–57), indicating that Jesus was able to communicate the word only insofar as people had the ability to hear and understand it (ἠδύναντο, 3rd pl. impf. mid. indic. of dep. δύναμαι, "be able to"; ἀκούειν, pres. act. inf. of ἀκούω, hear; complementary inf.). The vb. δύναμαι can take either a dbl. aug. as in ἠδύναντο (cf. 4:33; 6:19; 7:24; 9:28; 14:5) or a single aug. as in ἐδύνατο (cf. 5:3; 6:5; see R 367–68).

4:34 Jesus also made it his practice to explain (ἐπέλυεν, 3rd sg. impf. act. indic. of ἐπιλύω, "explain, interpret") all aspects of his teaching to his own disciples privately (κατ᾽ ἰδίαν, stereotyped phrase mng. "by himself, privately"; BDAG 467c; T 18). However, in his public ministry, Jesus made it his practice to speak only in parables, that is, in a manner that was consistently indirect and veiled (Cranfield 172).

FOR FURTHER STUDY

15. The Parables Discourse

Beavis, Mary Ann. *Mark's Audience: The Literary and Social History of Mark 4.11–12.* JSNTSup 33. Sheffield, UK: Sheffield Academic Press, 1989.

*Blomberg, Craig L. *Interpreting the Parables.* 2nd ed. Downers Grove, IL: InterVarsity, 2012.

Dodd, C. H. *The Parables of the Kingdom.* New York: Charles Scribner's Sons, 1961.

Fay, Greg. "Introduction to Incomprehension: The Literary Structure of Mark 4:1–34." *CBQ* 51 (1989): 65–81.

Jeremias, Joachim. *The Parables of Jesus.* 2nd rev. ed. New York: Charles Scribner's Sons, 1972.

Marcus, Joel. "Mark 4:10–12 and Marcan Epistemology." *JBL* 103 (1984): 557–74.

———. *The Mystery of the Kingdom of God.* SBLDS 90. Atlanta: Scholars Press, 1986.

Payne, Philip Barton. "The Authenticity of the Parable of the Sower and Its Interpretation." Pages 163–207 in *Studies of History and Tradition in the Four Gospels.* Vol. 1 of *Gospel Perspectives.* Edited by R. T. France and David Wenham. Sheffield, UK: JSOT Press, 1980.

Räisänen, Heikki. "The Parable Theory." Pages 76–143 in *The "Messianic Secret" in Mark.* Edinburgh: T&T Clark, 1990.

Snodgrass, Klyne R. *Stories with Intent: A Comprehensive Guide to the Parables of Jesus.* Grand Rapids: Eerdmans, 2008.

Sweat, Laura C. *The Theological Role of Paradox in the Gospel of Mark.* LNTS 492. London: Bloomsbury T&T Clark, 2013.

(b) First Boat Scene: Stilling of the Storm (4:35–41)

4:35 In this first boat scene in Mark, the disciples, having experienced the power of Jesus and his care for them, begin to reflect on his identity. Λέγει is historical pres. Several instances of the historical pres. cluster together in this passage, incl. also παραλαμβάνουσιν in v. 36, γίνεται in v. 37, and ἐγείρουσιν and λέγουσιν in v. 38. In this way, they serve to highlight the dramatic nature of the event and draw the audience into the experience of the narrative (cf. Campbell, *VA* 74–76; on the historical pres., see 1:12; the additional use of the impf. with ἐπέβαλλεν in 4:37 and ἔλεγον in 4:41 apparently has the same purpose). Ὀψίας, gen. sg. fem. of ὀψία, -ας, ἡ, "evening"; γενομένης, gen. sg. fem. of aor. mid. ptc. of γίνομαι, "become, come to be"; temp. adv. ptc. antecedent. Most often, gen. absolutes in Mark's Gospel precede rather than follow the main vb., with the only two exceptions being here in 4:35 and in 16:2 (cf. BDF §423; T 322). Διέλθωμεν, 1st pl. aor. act. subjunc. of διέρχομαι, "cross over, go through"; hort. subjunc.; τὸ πέραν, "the other side" (an adv. with an art. used as a subst. to indicate the shore or land on the other side of the Sea of Galilee [BDAG 796d]).

4:36 Ἀφέντες, nom. pl. masc. of aor. act. ptc. of ἀφίημι, "send away, leave"; temp. adv. ptc. antecedent; ἦν, 3rd sg. impf. act. indic. of εἰμί, "be" (used twice in v. 36). Since the "other boats" (ἄλλα, nom. pl. neut. of the adj. ἄλλος; πλοῖα, neut. pl. subj. with a sg. vb. [see 3:11]) mentioned here do not appear again in the episode, they should probably be treated as part of the crowd that Jesus and the disciples left behind. Perhaps the crowd listening to Jesus's parables became so large that some abandoned their place along the shore and entered boats in order to come closer to the teacher (cf. Bruce 370).

4:37 "And a great windstorm arose" (ESV; γίνεται, 3rd sg. pres. mid. indic. of dep. γίνομαι, "come to be, arise" (BDAG 197b); λαῖλαψ, nom. sg. fem. of λαῖλαψ, -απος, ἡ, "storm, whirlwind," cf. BDAG 581d; μεγάλη, attrib. adj.; ἀνέμου, attrib. gen.). The neut. pl. subj. τὰ κύματα (nom. pl. neut. of κῦμα, -ατος, τό, "wave") takes the sg. vb. ἐπέβαλλεν (3rd sg. impf. act. indic. of ἐπιβάλλω "throw oneself, beat upon"). When forms of βάλλω and its compounds (such as ἐπιβάλλω) are used intrans., they may express a reflexive idea as a substitute for a dir. obj. (T 51–52; "the waves were throwing themselves into the boat"). Γεμίζεσθαι, pres. pass. inf. of γεμίζω, "fill"; inf. of result; τὸ πλοῖον, acc. subj. of the inf.

4:38 Ἦν, 3rd sg. impf. act. indic. of εἰμί, "be"; πρύμνῃ, dat. sg. fem. of πρύμνα, -ης, ἡ, "stern, back of the boat"; προσκεφάλαιον, acc. sg. neut. of προσκεφάλαιον, -ου, τό, "cushion, pillow, place to lay one's head"; καθεύδων, nom. sg. masc. of pres. act. ptc. of καθεύδω, "sleep"; periph. ptc. (Cranfield 178; Decker 1:112–13). Although Jesus was undoubtedly tired, his sleep also revealed a trust in God's will (cf. Jesus's teaching on God's will in 3:35 and his subsequent rebuke of the disciples for their lack of faith in 4:40). Jesus knew that he and the disciples were doing God's will and therefore could depend on God's care for them. Later in Mark's narrative, by way of contrast, Jesus struggles to submit to the Father's will in Gethsemane (14:32–42). Jesus could both rest in the Father's will and wrestle with it. Ἐγείρουσιν from ἐγείρω "wake, rouse"; διδάσκαλε, voc. Questions beginning with οὐ (and related forms, such as οὐκ [6:3; 12:26; 14:37, 60], οὐχ [4:21; 6:3], or οὐδέ [12:10]) are expressed in such a way as to indicate that an affirmative answer is expected (BDAG 734a; BDF §§427, 440; see also 4:21). Therefore, the disciples' question assumes Jesus's care for them, although in this context it also implies a request for help. The ὅτι clause (ὅτι ἀπολλύμεθα) functions as the subj. of μέλει (R 453; μέλει, 3rd sg. pres. act. indic. of μέλει, "be a care, be a concern"). "The fact that we are perishing [ἀπολλύμεθα, 1st pl. pres. mid. indic. of ἀπόλλυμι, 'perish' (mng. with mid.), BDAG 116a] is a concern to you, isn't it?"

4:39 Διεγερθείς, nom. sg. masc. of aor. pass. ptc. of διεγείρω, "wake up, awaken"; temp. adv. ptc. antecedent; ἐπετίμησεν, 3rd sg. aor. act. indic. of ἐπιτιμάω, "rebuke"; τῷ ἀνέμῳ, dat. dir. obj.; σιώπα, 2nd sg. pres. act. impv. of σιωπάω, "be quiet." Normally, specific commands in concrete situations call for the use of an aor. impv. form (see 1:25; 2:11), but it is possible to supersede that typical pattern when the imperfective aspect of the pres. impv. combines with other contextual factors to convey a command that calls for a prog. action (cf. Fanning 364–65). The great calm of the wind and the sea at the end of v. 39 shows that the pres. impv. form σιώπα expresses a demand for ongoing quietness. Πεφίμωσο, 2nd sg. pf. pass. impv. of φιμόω, "muzzle, silence, put to silence." Outside of this use of πεφίμωσο, the pf. impv. appears only rarely in the NT (ἔρρωσθε in Acts 15:29 and possibly ἴστε in Eph 5:5; Heb 12:17; and Jas 1:19 [R 330, 360, 908; Wallace 485, 718]). Literally, the vb. φιμόω means "to shut a mouth with a muzzle" (cf. Deut 25:4 LXX; 1 Tim 5:18), but it can also be used fig. to mean "to silence" (BDAG 1060b; cf. Matt 22:12, 34; Luke 4:35; 1 Pet 2:15). As a pf. impv. form, πεφίμωσο emphasizes the demand for a continuing state ("be silent and remain so"; cf. Cranfield 174). Ἐκόπασεν, 3rd sg. aor. act. indic. of κοπάζω, "stop, rest, cease"; ἐγένετο, 3rd sg. aor. mid. indic. of γίνομαι, "come to be, come about" (BDAG 197b). Notice the repeated use of μεγάλη, contrasting the great storm in v. 37 with the great calm in v. 39 (γαλήνη, nom. sg. fem. of γαλήνη, -ης, ἡ, calm).

4:40 Having spoken to the sea with two commands, Jesus now asks the disciples two questions. The first is "Why are you cowardly?" (τί, "why?" [see 2:7]; δειλοί, nom. pl. masc. of δειλός, -ή, -όν, "cowardly, timid"; pred. adj.). Jesus's second question ("Do you still have no faith?") assumes that by this point the disciples should have reached a greater level of trust in God and his ways.

4:41 After Jesus turned the great storm (4:37) into a great calm (4:39), the disciples, lit., "feared a great fear" (4:41; ἐφοβήθησαν, 3rd pl. aor. pass. indic. of φοβέομαι, "fear, be afraid of"). That this fear is now directed toward Jesus is clear from the disciples' question: "Who then is this, that even the wind and the sea obey him?" (ESV). The wording of this question raises three grammatical issues, the first being the most complex. First, the use of ὅτι may be explained as:

1. being almost equal in force to ὥστε "with the result that" (R 699; T 318);
2. expressing the reason why the question is asked "(we ask) because" (BDF §456; Z §420);
3. taking the place of a rel. pron. "whom" (Z §424); or
*4. functioning as an ellipsis for "(in consideration of the fact) that" (BDAG 732a).

With the fourth option, ὅτι introduces an explanatory clause that serves to identify what event or fact necessitates that such a question be asked. A similar grammatical pattern appears in John 2:18: "What sign are you showing us, (in consideration of the fact) that you are doing these things?" Second, the two uses of καί may be translated as either "both the wind and the sea" (taking them as correl. conjunctions; T 335) or "even the wind and the sea" (taking the first καί as ascensive; BDF §444). Third, the compound subj. ("wind and sea") uses the sg. vb. ὑπακούει (from ὑπακούω, "obey, follow, be subject to"; with a dat. dir. obj. [αὐτῷ]), emphasizing the totality of the subj. (R 405; concerning a sg. vb. with a compound subj., see 12:33). All of the natural forces that caused the storm—all of them together—obey Jesus.

FOR FURTHER STUDY

16. The Three Boat Scenes in Mark (4:35–41; 6:45–52; 8:14–21)

Achtemeier, Paul J. "Toward the Isolation of Pre-Markan Miracle Catenae." *JBL* 89 (1970): 265–91.

———. "The Origin and Function of the Pre-Markan Miracle Catenae." *JBL* 91 (1972): 198–221.

Gibson, Jeffrey B. "The Rebuke of the Disciples in Mark 8:14–21." *JSNT* 27 (1986): 31–47.

Heil, John Paul. *Jesus Walking on the Sea: Meaning and Gospel Functions of Matt. 14:22–33, Mark 6:45–52, and John 6:15b–21*. AnBib 87. Rome: Biblical Institute Press, 1981.

Henderson, Suzanne Watts. "'Concerning the Loaves': Comprehending Incomprehension in Mark 6.45–52." *JSNT* 83 (2001): 3–26.

Malbon, Elizabeth Struthers. "Echoes and Foreshadowings in Mark 4–8: Reading and Rereading." *JBL* 112 (1993): 211–30.

McPhee, Brian D. "Walk, Don't Run: Jesus's Water Walking Is Unparalleled in Greco-Roman Mythology." *JBL* 135 (2016): 763–77.

*Petersen, Norman R. "The Composition of Mark 4:1–8:26." *HTR* 73 (1980): 185–217.

Quesnell, Quentin. *The Mind of Mark: Interpretation and Method through the Exegesis of Mark 6,52*. AnBib 38. Rome: Pontifical Biblical Institute, 1969.

Yarbro Collins, Adela. "Rulers, Divine Men, and Walking on the Water (Mark 6:45–52)." Pages 207–27 in *Religious Propaganda and Missionary Competition in the New Testament World: Essays Honoring Dieter Georgi*. Edited by Lukas Bormann, Kelly Del Tredici, and Angela Standhartinger. NovTSup 74. Leiden: Brill, 1994.

17. Divine Man Christology in Mark

Betz, Hans Dieter. "Jesus as Divine Man." Pages 114–33 in *Jesus and the Historian: Written in Honor of Ernest Cadman Colwell*. Edited by F. Thomas Trotter. Philadelphia: Westminster, 1968.

Betz, Otto. "The Concept of the So-called 'Divine Man' in Mark's Christology." Pages 229–40 in *Studies in New Testament and Early Christian Literature: Essays in Honor of Allen P. Wikgren*. Edited by David Edward Aune. NovTSup 33. Leiden: Brill, 1972.

Blackburn, Barry. *Theios Anēr and the Markan Miracle Traditions: A Critique of the Theios Anēr Concept as an Interpretative Background of the Miracle Traditions Used by Mark*. WUNT 2/40. Tübingen: Mohr Siebeck, 1991.

Hadas, Moses, and Morton Smith. *Heroes and Gods: Spiritual Biographies in Antiquity*. New York: Harper & Row, 1965.

Holladay, Carl R. *Theios Aner in Hellenistic Judaism: A Critique of the Use of This Category in New Testament Christology*. SBLDS 40. Missoula, MT: Scholars Press, 1977.

Keck, Leander E. "Mark 3:7–12 and Mark's Christology." *JBL* 84 (1965): 341–58.

Kee, Howard C. "Aretalogy and Gospel." *JBL* 92 (1973): 402–22.

*Kingsbury, Jack Dean. "The 'Divine Man' as the Key to Mark's Christology—The End of an Era?" *Int* 35 (1981): 243–57.

Koskenniemi, Erkki. "Apollonius of Tyana: A Typical ΘΕΙΟΣ ΑΝΗΡ?" *JBL* 117 (1998): 455–67.

Lane, William L. "*Theios Anēr* Christology and the Gospel of Mark." Pages 144–61 in *New Dimensions in New Testament Study*. Edited by Richard N. Longenecker and Merrill C. Tenney. Grand Rapids: Zondervan, 1974.

Smith, Morton. "Prolegomena to a Discussion of Aretalogies, Divine Men, the Gospels and Jesus." *JBL* 90 (1971): 174–99.

Tiede, David Lenz. *The Charismatic Figure as Miracle Worker*. SBLDS 1. Missoula, MT: Society of Biblical Literature, 1972.

Weeden, Theodore J. "The Heresy That Necessitated Mark's Gospel." *ZNW* 59 (1968): 145–58.

_____. *Mark—Traditions in Conflict.* Philadelphia: Fortress, 1971.

HOMILETICAL SUGGESTIONS

The Power of Jesus and People of Faith (4:35–41)

1. What do we learn about Jesus?
   a. Jesus has confidence in the Father's plan. (4:35–38)
   b. Jesus has control over nature. (4:39)
   c. Jesus has a concern for the faith of his people. (4:40–41)
2. What do we learn about becoming people of faith?
   a. People of faith rest in Jesus's care. (4:35–38)
   b. People of faith recognize Jesus's power. (4:39)
   c. People of faith reflect on Jesus's identity. (4:40–41)

Three Boat Scenes and a Life of Faith (Mark 4–8)

1. Stilling the storm: A life of faith involves recognizing Jesus's power and care. (4:35–41)
2. Walking on the water: A life of faith involves rejecting fear in light of Jesus's presence. (6:45–52)
3. Warning about leaven: A life of faith involves remembering Jesus's previous provisions. (8:14–21)

(c) Healing of the Gerasene Demoniac (5:1–20)

5:1 Chapter 5 of Mark's Gospel presents three examples of people with overwhelming needs, but Mark shows that none of them are beyond hope because of Jesus. The chapter begins with the deliverance of a demon-possessed man, a broken and tormented man deeply in need of Jesus's compassion and power. ῏Ηλθον, 3rd pl. aor. act. indic. of ἔρχομαι, "come, go"; πέραν, an adv. with the art. functioning as a subst., "the shore/land on the other side," BDAG 796d. For a discussion of the text-critical issues related to the region of the Gerasenes and the problem of its location, see Cranfield 176; Brooks 89–90.

5:2 Ἐξελθόντος, gen. sg. masc. of aor. act. ptc. of ἐξέρχομαι, "come out, exit, step out"; gen. abs., temp. adv. ptc. antecedent (on the repetition of a prep. following a compound vb., see 1:21); on the use of εὐθύς to draw attention to a dramatic event, see 1:10; ὑπήντησεν, 3rd sg. aor. act. indic. of ὑπαντάω, "meet"; αὐτῷ, dat. dir. obj.; ἐν, "with" (association; see 1:23). As a gen. abs., ἐξελθόντος αὐτοῦ should be grammatically unconnected to the main clause, but in actuality the subj. of the gen. abs. (αὐτοῦ, referring to Jesus) is mentioned again in the dat. dir. obj. (αὐτῷ, once again referring to Jesus). The par. passage in Luke's Gospel more correctly places the ptc. in the dat. case (ἐξελθόντι; Luke 8:27). Other examples of the use of the gen. abs. when the subj. of the ptc. is mentioned again later in the main clause appear in Mark 5:18, 21; 6:22; 9:9, 28; 10:17; 11:27; 13:1, 3 (on gen. abs. participles, see 1:32; on the overlap between the subj. of a gen. abs. ptc. with a noun in the main clause, see BDF §423; T 322–23; Z §49).

5:3 As is often the case, Mark uses impf. tense vbs. in 5:3–5 to provide background information. In fact, 5:1–20 offers a helpful picture of the common ways Mark uses tenses in his narration. Aor. tense vbs. carry forward the story line by expressing the main sequence of events (e.g., 5:1–2, 6, 12–17, 20), while impf. tense vbs. fill in background information (e.g., 5:3–5, 11; see 1:21; cf. Fanning 191, 248). According to another common pattern, impf. vbs. and historical pres. vbs. introduce dialogue in ways that portray the give-and-take of an ongoing conversation (e.g., 5:7–10, 18–19; see 1:12, 30; 4:10). In addition, the impf. can be used to draw attention to an action in the main storyline in a particularly vivid way (e.g., 5:13, 20; see 1:21), and the historical pres. can be used to introduce new participants within a scene (e.g., 5:15; see 1:12).

Κατοίκησιν, acc. sg. fem. of κατοίκησις, -εως, ἡ, "home, dwelling"; εἶχεν, 3rd sg. impf. act. indic. of ἔχω, "have"; μνήμασιν, dat. pl. neut. of μνῆμα, -ατος, τό, "tomb, grave"; ἁλύσει, dat. sg. fem. of ἅλυσις, -εως, ἡ, "chain"; dat. of means or instr.; ἐδύνατο, 3rd sg. impf. mid. indic. of dep. δύναμαι, "be able to, can"; δῆσαι, aor. act. inf. of δέω, "bind, tie"; complementary inf. In ways that are difficult to express in Eng., the Gk. in 5:3 uses redundant negatives to strengthen the statement and to convey how impossible it was to restrain the man (see 1:44; cf. Porter, *Idioms* 283–84). Lit., Mark writes, "No one was able to bind him, not any longer, not even with a chain."

5:4 This verse follows up διὰ τό with three pf. inf. forms to express cause, although not to explain the reason why the demon-possessed man could not be subdued but to set forth the evidence for why this was known to be true (Burton §408; T 143). Αὐτόν, acc. subj. of inf. (the acc. forms ἁλύσεις and πέδας later in the verse also function as the subj. of an inf.); πολλάκις, adv. mng. "many times"; πέδαις (dat. pl. fem.; dat. of means or instr.) and later in the verse πέδας (acc. pl. fem.) are both from πέδη, -ης, ἡ, "shackle, fetter"; ἁλύσεσιν (dat. pl. fem.) and later in the verse ἁλύσεις (acc. pl. fem.) are both from ἅλυσις, -εως, ἡ, "chain"; δεδέσθαι, pf. pass. inf. of δέω, "bind, tie"; διεσπάσθαι, pf. pass. inf. of διασπάω, "tear apart"; συντετρῖφθαι, pf. pass. inf. of συντρίβω, "shatter, break"; ἴσχυεν, 3rd sg. impf. act. indic. of ἰσχύω, "be able to, have power to"; δαμάσαι, aor. act. inf. of δαμάζω, "subdue, tame, control"; complementary inf. The three pf. inf. forms (δεδέσθαι, διεσπάσθαι, συντετρῖφθαι), the only pf. inf. forms in Mark, portray a state of affairs based on past actions, with the state of affairs existing in reference to the time of the main vb. (i.e., ἐδύνατο in v. 3; cf. Burton §108; infinitives with διὰ τό normally take the pres., not pf. tense [e.g., 4:5–6]; Campbell, *VANIV* 108).

5:5 Διὰ παντός, idiomatic phrase mng. "constantly" or "continually" (BDAG 224b; MM 146); both νυκτός and ἡμέρας, gen. of time expressing the time within which an action takes place (ZG 115); μνήμασιν, dat. pl. neut. of μνῆμα, -ατος, τό, "tomb, grave"; ἦν, 3rd sg. impf. act. indic. of εἰμί, "be"; κράζων, nom. sg. masc. of pres. act. ptc. of κράζω, "cry out"; periph. ptc.; κατακόπτων, nom. sg. masc. of pres. act. ptc. of κατακόπτω, "cut, gash" (on κατα- as an intensifying prep. prefix, see 1:36); periph. ptc.; λίθοις, dat. of means or instr. The impf. form of εἰμί is used with both pres. ptc. forms (κράζων and κατακόπτων) to create impf. periph. constructions (Wallace 648; KMP 343), which Mark often uses to express customary or repeated action (see 1:22). The demon-possessed man's isolation, painful wails, and self-destructive behavior were the regular patterns of his existence.

5:6 Ἰδών, nom. sg. masc. of aor. act. ptc. of ὁράω, "see"; temp. adv. ptc. anteced- ent; μακρόθεν, adv. used with the prep. ἀπό for "from far away, from a distance"; ἔδραμεν, 3rd sg. aor. act. indic. of τρέχω, "run"; προσεκύνησεν, 3rd sg. aor. act. indic. of προσκυνέω, "fall down before, prostrate oneself before"; αὐτῷ, dat. dir. obj. Adverbs with the suffix -θεν normally answer the question, "From where?"; however, with μακρόθεν the mng. of the suffix became so weakened that it came to be used freq. with ἀπό to communicate clearly the mng. of the adv. as "from far away" (R 300; BDAG 612c; BDF §104; see also 8:3; 11:13; 14:54; 15:40; cf. ἐκ παιδιόθεν in 9:21 and ἀπ' ἄνωθεν in 15:38).

5:7 Κράξας, nom. sg. masc. of aor. act. ptc. of κράζω, "cry out"; redundant ptc.; φωνῇ, dat. of means or instr.; ἐμοί and σοί, dat. of association, i.e., "What (do you have to do) with me and (do I have to do) with you?" (see the discussion on the similar phrase in 1:24); Ἰησοῦ and υἱέ, both voc. (see 10:47); ὑψίστου, gen. sg. masc. of ὕψιστος, -η, -ον, "the Most High" (superl. adj. used of God to distinguish him from lesser deities and other objects of devotion, BDAG 1045b); ὁρκίζω, "adjure, implore"; βασανίσῃς, 2nd sg. aor. act. subjunc. of βασανίζω, "torment"; prohibitive subjunc. The pres. indic. vb. ὁρκίζω is an instantaneous pres. (Wallace 518; cf. Fanning 202–3; see 2:5), indicating an action that is accomplished in the very act of speaking. The acc. θεόν ("by God") is an example of an acc. used in an oath (Wallace 205; ZG 116); i.e., the unclean spirit is calling on Jesus—strangely invoking the authority of God in the process—to swear an oath that he would fulfill the following request not to bring torment.

5:8 Τὸ πνεῦμα, nom. for voc. (Wallace 58; cf. Z §34); ἔξελθε, 2nd sg. aor. act. impv. of ἐξέρχομαι, "come out" (on the aor. impv., see 1:25; 2:11). The use of the impf. with ἔλεγεν ("he had been saying") calls for some explanation. The pluperf. in Eng. indi- cates an action that took place before another past event. In Gk., prior past action can simply be expressed by an aor. or impf. vb. with the context showing that the action preceded another event that has already happened (Z §290). Therefore, in translating ἔλεγεν into Eng., it is necessary to use the pluperf. to communicate that Jesus's words in v. 8 took place before the demon's resistance to his authority in v. 7 (cf. e.g., 6:18).

5:9 Ἐπηρώτα, 3rd sg. impf. act. indic. of ἐπερωτάω, "ask"; σοι and μοι, dat. of poss.; λεγιών, nom. sg. of λεγιών, -ῶνος, ἡ, "legion" (probably masc. in this context, since it is functioning as a name; cf. the masc. form in 5:15; BDAG 588a); πολλοί, pred. adj. (R 656). The name offered by the unclean spirit, Legion, was a military term for the largest unit of troops in the Roman army. In the first century AD, a legion at full strength consisted of approximately 6,000 soldiers, and 25 legions formed the core of the Roman army as a whole (*EDNT* 2:345–46; BDAG 588a).

5:10 Mark 5:10 reflects the grammatical difficulty of narrating consistently the speech of one man possessed by many demons (Hooker 143). The subj. of the sg. vb. παρεκάλει appears to be the one speaking voice that serves as the spokesperson for the many demons who are mentioned later in the verse with the neut. pl. pron. αὐτά. Παρεκάλει, 3rd sg. impf. act. indic. of παρακαλέω, "implore, entreat, beg"; πολλά, "earnestly" (neut. acc. pl. of πολύς functioning as an adv. to intensify the vb.; see 1:45); ἀποστείλῃ, 3rd sg. aor. act. subjunc. of ἀποστέλλω, send; subjunc. in dir. obj. ἵνα clause. In Mark's Gospel, ἔξω can function as an adv., answering the question "where?" (e.g., 1:45; 3:31–32; 11:4), but ἔξω can also serve as a prep. that takes a gen. obj. (e.g., 5:10; 8:23; 11:19; 12:8). When used as a prep. in Mark, ἔξω answers the question "from where?" and is translated "out of," so that it overlaps in mng. with ἐκ (cf. BDAG 354b–c; Z §84). A common use for the conj. ἵνα in Mark is to introduce a dir. obj. clause (see Wallace 475; Burton §§200–204; Z §§406–7; Voelz 1:4, 35). In Mark's Gospel, dir. obj. ἵνα clauses generally express the content of a request (e.g., 5:18; 6:25; 7:26), a command (e.g., 3:12; 5:43; 6:8), or a prayer (e.g., 13:18; 14:35; for more on ἵνα in Mark, see C. H. Turner, "Marcan Usage: Notes, Critical and Exegetical, on the Second Gospel," *JTS* 29 [1927–28]: 356–59). Since this use of ἵνα overlaps in function with the use of the inf. for indir. discourse, it is sometimes possible to translate the ἵνα clause with an inf. in Eng. ("he was begging him earnestly not to send them out of the region").

5:11 The conj. δέ in 5:11 functions as an explanatory conj. used to indicate that Mark is providing additional background information. Ἦν, 3rd sg. impf. act. indic. of εἰμί, "be"; ἀγέλη, nom. sg. fem. of ἀγέλη, -ης, ἡ, "herd"; χοίρων, gen. pl. masc. of χοῖρος, -ου, ὁ, "pig, swine"; βοσκομένη, nom. sg. fem. of pres. pass. ptc. of βόσκω, "graze, feed" (mng. with pass.); periph. ptc. (on the impf. periph. cstr. to highlight a customary action, see 1:22). The prep. πρός only rarely is followed by the dat. rather than the acc. in the NT, only seven times (Mark 5:11; Luke 19:37; John 18:16; 20:11, 12 [twice], Rev 1:13), always with a spatial sense (Harris 189; πρὸς τῷ ὄρει, "on the hillside," further specifying what is meant by the adv. ἐκεῖ ["there"]).

5:12 Παρεκάλεσαν, 3rd pl. aor. act. indic. of παρακαλέω, "implore, entreat, beg"; λέγοντες, nom. pl. masc. of pres. act. ptc. of λέγω, "say"; redundant ptc.; πέμψον, 2nd sg. aor. act. impv. of πέμπω, "send"; χοίρους, acc. pl. masc. of χοῖρος, -ου, ὁ, "pig, swine"; εἰσέλθωμεν, 1st pl. aor. act. subjunc. of εἰσέρχομαι, "go into, enter"; subjunc. in purpose ἵνα clause (cf. NASB, CSB, Cranfield 179). One difference between the request in 5:12 as compared with that in 5:10 is that it comes no longer from a single voice but from many voices (note the difference between the sg. vb. παρεκάλει in 5:10 and the pl. vb. παρεκάλεσαν in 5:12). The demons speak on their own behalf apart from the man, apparently recognizing that their control over him is soon coming to an end (Swete 96). The use of the masc. ptc. λέγοντες when the implied subj. of παρεκάλεσαν is "the unclean spirits" (a neut. noun) can perhaps be best explained as a reflection of Mark's habit of using the masc. ptc. form of λέγω when expressing a redundant ptc. (cf. 3:11). Mark correctly uses the neut. pl. ptc. ἐξελθόντα to agree with "unclean spirits" in the following verse.

5:13 Ἐπέτρεψεν, 3rd sg. aor. act. indic. of ἐπιτρέπω, "allow, permit"; αὐτοῖς, dat. dir. obj.; ἐξελθόντα, nom. pl. neut. of aor. act. ptc. of ἐξέρχομαι, "come out"; temp. adv. ptc. antecedent; εἰσῆλθον, 3rd pl. aor. act. indic. of εἰσέρχομαι, "go into, enter" (on a neut. pl. subj. with a pl. vb., see 3:11); χοίρους, see 5:12; ὥρμησεν, 3rd sg. aor. act. indic. of ὁρμάω, "rush"; ἀγέλη, nom. sg. fem. of ἀγέλη, -ης, ἡ, "herd"; κρημνοῦ, gen. sg. masc. of κρημνός, -οῦ, ὁ, "steep slope, steep bank, cliff"; ὡς, "about, approximately, nearly" (when used with numbers; BDAG 1105d; R 968); δισχίλιοι, nom. pl. masc. of δισχίλιοι, -αι, -α, "two thousand"; ἐπνίγοντο, 3rd pl. impf. pass. indic. πνίγω, "be choked, drown" (mng. with pass.). The final disaster for the pigs, and by way of representation for the demons, who will now likely face the punishment they feared (5:7), is portrayed dramatically through the use of the impf. tense (ἐπνίγοντο; cf. Voelz 1:348 [see 1:21]).

5:14 Βόσκοντες, nom. pl. masc. of pres. act. ptc. of βόσκω, "herd, tend"; subst. ptc.; ἔφυγον, 3rd pl. aor. act. indic. of φεύγω, "flee"; ἀπήγγειλαν, 3rd pl. aor. act. indic. of ἀπαγγέλλω, "report, announce" (a dir. obj. of ἀπήγγειλαν, such as "the news," is implied but not stated); εἰς, "in" (on εἰς for ἐν, see 13:9; cf. Harris 84–86); ἀγρούς, "countryside" (see LN 1.87); ἦλθον, 3rd pl. aor. act. indic. of ἔρχομαι, "come" (on indef. pl. vbs., see 1:22); ἰδεῖν, aor. act. inf. of ὁράω, "see"; inf. of purpose; γεγονός, nom. sg. neut. of pf. act. ptc. of γίνομαι, "come to be, take place, happen" (BDAG 197c); subst. ptc. The interr. pron. τί is introducing an indir. question (Porter, *Idioms* 274–75), and in Gk. with reported speech or thought, the tense of the vb. in the orig. question is retained in the indir. discourse (in Eng., "what it was that had happened"; see 2:1).

5:15 Ἔρχονται, 3rd pl. pres. mid. indic. of dep. ἔρχομαι, "come"; θεωροῦσιν from θεωρέω (on the historical pres. in this context, see 5:3; cf. Fanning 232); δαιμονιζόμενον, acc. sg. masc. of pres. mid. ptc. of dep. δαιμονίζομαι, "be possessed by a demon"; subst. ptc. The three supplementary (complementary) participles that follow complete the thought of what the people saw when they looked at the man (cf. 1:10; BDF §416; Voelz 1:349; καθήμενον, acc. sg. masc. of pres. mid. ptc. of dep. κάθημαι, "sit"; ἱματισμένον, acc. sg. masc. of pf. pass. ptc. of ἱματίζω, "clothe"; σωφρονοῦντα, acc. sg. masc. of pres. act. ptc. of σωφρονέω, "be of sound mind, be in one's right mind"). Ἐσχηκότα, acc. sg. masc. of pf. act. ptc. of ἔχω, "have"; subst. ptc. in simple appos. to τὸν δαιμονιζόμενον (in this context the pf. ptc. ἐσχηκότα expresses an existing state that is antecedent to the main vb. ["the one who had had"; cf. Fanning 416–17; R 1117; Burton §156]); λεγιῶνα, acc. sg. masc. of λεγιών, -ῶνος, ἡ, "legion"; ἐφοβήθησαν, 3rd pl. aor. pass. indic. of φοβέομαι, "be afraid." The pres. ptc. τὸν δαιμονιζόμενον (contemp. in relation to the main vb.) describes the man from the perspective of the people from that region, as he was known to them—the demon-possessed man—even though he was no longer under demonic control (cf. the similar use of the pres. ptc. in 5:16). Later, in 5:18, the use of the aor. ptc. ὁ δαιμονισθείς (antecedent in relation to the main vb.) describes the man from the perspective of Jesus, the correct viewpoint since the time of his possession was now past (cf. France 231–32; Strauss 220). Although most EVV translate τὸν λεγιῶνα as though it were simply a reference to the demons as a group (e.g., ESV: "the one who had had the legion"), it is better to translate it as a proper name ("the one who had had Legion"). Mark generally uses the art. with names (see, e.g., the discussion on 1:14), and λεγιών, normally a fem. noun, appears here with a masc. art. (τὸν λεγιῶνα) because it is functioning as a name (T 21; the Gk. text should probably capitalize Λεγιῶνα).

5:16 Διηγήσαντο, 3rd pl. aor. mid. indic. of dep. διηγέομαι, "tell, relate, describe"; ἰδόντες, nom. pl. masc. of aor. act. ptc. of ὁράω, "see"; subst. ptc.; ἐγένετο, 3rd sg. aor. mid. indic. of dep. γίνομαι, "come to be, happen" (BDAG 198a); δαιμονιζομένῳ, dat. sg. masc. of pres. mid. ptc. of dep. δαιμονίζομαι, "be possessed by a demon"; subst. ptc. and dat. of interest (advantage); χοίρων, see 5:11. The aor. vb. ἐγένετο, which appears in indir. discourse in this verse, retains the tense used in the orig. statement. In Eng., it is necessary to push the tense back in time to clarify that the event happened before the report. As a result, the aor. in Gk. translates as a pluperf. in Eng. (cf. Wallace 456–57).

5:17 Ἤρξαντο, 3rd pl. aor. mid. indic. of ἄρχω, "begin" (mng. with mid.; on ἄρχομαι, see 1:45); παρακαλεῖν, pres. act. inf. of παρακαλέω, "implore, entreat, beg"; complementary inf.; ἀπελθεῖν, aor. act. inf. of ἀπέρχομαι, "depart, go away"; inf. of indir. discourse; ὁρίων, gen. pl. neut. of ὅριον, -ου, τό, "region, district" (mng. with pl. [BDAG 723b]).

5:18 Ἐμβαίνοντος, gen. sg. masc. of pres. act. ptc. of ἐμβαίνω, "embark"; gen. abs. (see 1:32; 5:2), temp. adv. ptc. contemp.; παρεκάλει, 3rd sg. impf. act. indic. of παρακαλέω, "implore, entreat, beg"; δαιμονισθείς, nom. sg. masc. of aor. pass. ptc. dep. δαιμονίζομαι, "be possessed by a demon"; subst. ptc.; ᾖ, 3rd sg. pres. act. subjunc. of εἰμί, "be"; subjunc. in dir. obj. ἵνα clause (see 5:10). The wording of the man's request echoes the phrase used to describe the unique calling of the Twelve in 3:14 (ἵνα ὦσιν μετ' αὐτοῦ) and should be interpreted in that light (Stein 258–59; France 232). The man was asking to join the small group of disciples who traveled with Jesus and who were being prepared to continue Jesus's ministry.

5:19 Ἀφῆκεν, 3rd sg. aor. act. indic. of ἀφίημι, "let, allow"; ὕπαγε, 2nd sg. pres. act. impv. of ὑπάγω, "go, depart"; σούς, acc. pl. masc. of σός, σή, σόν, "your" (used here with the art. as a subst., "your people" [cf. BDAG 934b] or "your household" [cf. MM 581] or "your family" [cf. ZG 117]); ἀπάγγειλον, 2nd sg. aor. act. impv. of ἀπαγγέλλω, "report, announce"; πεποίηκεν, 3rd sg. pf. act. indic. of ποιέω, "do"; σοι, dat. of interest (advantage); ἠλέησεν, 3rd sg. aor. act. indic. of ἐλεέω, "have mercy on." The proximity of the poss. adj. σούς to the poss. pron. σου indicates that the man's people bear some relationship with his house. In other words, the man should talk with his family, the people who are at his house (NLT: "go home to your family"). As is typical, an aor. impv. (ἀπάγγειλον) is used to express a specific command, one to be obeyed in a concrete situation (see 1:25). Other impv. forms in this passage follow this same pattern (ἔξελθε in 5:8 and πέμψον in 5:12; cf. the aor. prohibitive subjunc. βασανίσῃς in 5:7). The one exception in the passage is ὕπαγε, an impv. form Mark idiomatically uses in the pres. tense for specific commands (see 2:11).

5:20 Ἀπῆλθεν, 3rd sg. aor. act. indic. of ἀπέρχομαι, "depart, go away"; ἤρξατο, 3rd sg. aor. mid. indic. of ἄρχω, "begin" (mng. with mid.; cf. 5:17); κηρύσσειν, pres. act. inf.

of κηρύσσω, "proclaim"; complementary inf.; ἐποίησεν, 3rd sg. aor. act. indic. of ποιέω, "do" (on the aor. tense in indir. discourse, see 5:16); αὐτῷ, dat. of interest (advantage); ἐθαύμαζον, 3rd pl. impf. act. indic. of θαυμάζω, "marvel, be astonished" (on vbs. for amazement, see 1:22).

HOMILETICAL SUGGESTIONS

Life outside the Tombs (5:1–20)

1. What do we learn about spiritual realities?
   a. Demonic beings seek to create human pain and destruction. (5:4–5)
   b. Demonic beings seek to create human isolation. (5:2–3)
2. What do we learn about Jesus?
   a. Jesus seeks to restore broken people to human well-being.
   b. Jesus seeks to restore isolated people to human community.
   c. Jesus has the authority to restore such people no matter how strong the demonic power.

2. Interval: Faith and Unbelief (5:21–6:29)

The threefold pattern of teaching the crowd, the boat scene, and the healing miracle appears in three cycles within Mark 4–8. Between the first and second is an interval of three passages that highlight the themes of faith and unbelief. The intertwined stories of Jairus and the hemorrhaging woman portray people of faith (5:21–43), while people of unbelief appear in Jesus's rejection in Nazareth (6:1–6) and in the intertwined stories of the mission of the disciples and Herod's execution of John the Baptist (6:7–29).

(a) The Faith of the Hemorrhaging Woman and Jairus (5:21–43)

5:21 Mark 5:21–43 presents two people from different backgrounds (Jairus and the hemorrhaging woman), who both respond with faith toward Jesus in the midst of their desperate circumstances (on the sandwich literary pattern, see 3:22). Jesus takes time for both and proves himself worthy of their faith, even though their situations seemed beyond hope. Διαπεράσαντος, gen. sg. masc. of aor. act. ptc. of διαπεράω, "cross over"; gen. abs. (see 1:32; 5:2), temp. adv. ptc. antecedent; πέραν, see 5:1; συνήχθη, 3rd sg. aor. pass. indic. of συνάγω, "gather, come together, assemble" (mng. with pass., BDAG 962d); ἐπ': "to, around" (see BDAG 364c, 962d); ἦν, 3rd sg. impf. act. indic. of εἰμί, "be."

5:22 A common pattern in Mark is the use of the historical pres. with a vb. of motion at the beginning of a scene (ἔρχεται, 3rd sg. pres. mid. indic. of dep. ἔρχομαι, "come"; on the historical pres., see 1:12, 30), sometimes followed, as in 5:22–23, by related, subsequent actions also expressed with historical pres. vbs. (πίπτει, παρακαλεῖ). Ἀρχισυναγώγων, gen. pl. masc. of ἀρχισυνάγωγος, -ου, ὁ, "synagogue leader"; partitive gen. (cf. Wallace 85); ὀνόματι, dat. of reference or respect (ZG 117). The number εἷς can serve as an equivalent to the indef. pron. τις, so that εἷς followed by a partitive gen.

(e.g., 12:28; 13:1; 14:66) functions in a similar way to an indef. art. ("one of the syna-gogue leaders" means "a certain synagogue leader" or simply "a synagogue leader"; cf. BDAG 292d; Z §155). A synagogue leader was an elected official whose primary responsibilities involved the supervision of the synagogue building and the organiza-tion of the synagogue worship services (*TDNT* 7:844–47). Ἰδών, nom. sg. masc. of aor. act. ptc. of ὁράω, "see"; temp. adv. ptc. antecedent.

5:23 Πολλά, "earnestly" (see 5:10); λέγων, nom. sg. masc. of pres. act. ptc. of λέγω, "say"; redundant ptc.; ὅτι, introduces dir. discourse; θυγάτριον, nom. sg. neut. of θυγάτριον, -ου, τό, "little daughter"; ἐσχάτως, adv. mng. "finally," but used idiomati-cally with ἔχειν to mean "to be at the point of death," BDAG 398b (more lit.: "she has it terminally" [cf. Marcus 1:356] or "she has it in the last stages" [cf. R 299]; on the difficulty for Eng. of Gk. idioms that use ἔχω with an adv., see R 546; cf. 1:32); ἐλθών, nom. sg. masc. of aor. act. ptc. of ἔρχομαι, "come"; ptc. of attendant circumstance; ἐπιθῇς, 2nd sg. aor. act. subjunc. of ἐπιτίθημι, "lay on"; σωθῇ, 3rd sg. aor. pass. subjunc. of σῴζω, "save, restore to health" (on σῴζω, see 5:34); ζήσῃ, 3rd sg. aor. act. subjunc. of ζάω, "live"; both σωθῇ and ζήσῃ, subjunc. in purpose ἵνα clause. This passage uses several diminutives for Jairus's daughter: "little daughter" (θυγάτριον [5:23]), "little child" (παιδίον [5:39, 40, 41]), and "little girl" (κοράσιον [5:41, 42]; on diminutives, see 3:9). Such nouns may serve to draw attention to the girl's young age, although on the lips of Jairus "little daughter" may also be a term of affection (Stein 266; Taylor 288). The first use of ἵνα in the verse calls for attention. On occasion (e.g., 2 Cor 8:7; Eph 5:33), the subjunc. appears after ἵνα with the force of a command or request and therefore functions as a main vb. in an independent rather than subord. clause (Z §415; Wallace 476–77; Turner, *Style* 23; R 943, 994). As a result, the ἵνα should not be trans-lated. As a ptc. of attendant circumstance, ἐλθών takes on a similar force to the mood of the vb. it modifies (ἐπιθῇς), thereby indicating the prior action that must take place in order to fulfill the request ("come and lay your hands"; cf. Wallace 640–44; KMP 336–37).

5:24 Ἀπῆλθεν, 3rd sg. aor. act. indic. of ἀπέρχομαι, "depart, go away"; ἠκολούθει, 3rd sg. impf. act. indic. of ἀκολουθέω, "follow, accompany"; συνέθλιβον, 3rd pl. impf. act. indic. of συνθλίβω, "press together on, press around" (on the impf. for background information, here to set the scene for the woman's actions in the following verses, see 1:21). A collective sg. subj. (such as ὄχλος) normally takes a sg. vb. (such as ἠκολούθει), since the group is viewed as a single whole. However, a collective sg. subj. can also take a pl. vb. (such as συνέθλιβον), since a crowd is made up of many individuals (cf. Wallace 400–401; R 404).

5:25 Mark uses a series of adj. participles in 5:25–26 (οὖσα, παθοῦσα, δαπανήσασα, ὠφεληθεῖσα, ἐλθοῦσα), all of them without the art. to modify the anar. noun γυνή (cf. R 1105; T 152), to describe a desperately needy woman and her condition. This unusual use—for Mark—of a whole series of adj. participles seems to convey a compounding description of the overwhelming problems faced by the woman (cf. France 236). Mark begins his depiction of the woman's difficulties by saying, literally, that she was (οὖσα, nom. sg. fem. of pres. act. ptc. of εἰμί, "be") with a flow of blood for twelve years (ἐν, "with" [expressing close association, Z §116–17; Moule 78]; ῥύσει, dat. sg. fem. of ῥύσις, -εως, ἡ, "flow"; αἵματος, subj. gen.; ἔτη, acc. for extent of time [cf. Decker 1:131]). The woman's ailment was a chronic condition of vaginal bleeding, a condition that would render her ceremonially unclean (cf. "flow of blood" in 5:25 with Lev 15:25 LXX and "fountain of her blood" in 5:29 with Lev 12:7 LXX).

5:26 Παθοῦσα, nom. sg. fem. of aor. act. ptc. of πάσχω, "suffer, endure"; ἰατρῶν, gen. pl. masc. of ἰατρός, -οῦ, ὁ, "physician." The prep. ὑπό with the gen. ("by"), although normally used with a pass. vb., appears here with an act. vb. form (παθοῦσα) to highlight the pass. sense of her suffering—she suffered at the hands of many physicians (ZG 118; cf. BDAG 1036a). Δαπανήσασα, nom. sg. fem. of aor. act. ptc. of δαπανάω, "spend, spend freely"; τὰ παρ' αὐτῆς πάντα, "all that she had" (lit., "all the things from her"); ὠφεληθεῖσα, nom. sg. fem. of aor. pass. ptc. of ὠφελέω, "help, benefit"; μηδέν, adv. acc. "not at all, in no way" (BDAG 647c, Voelz 1:364). The use of ἔρχομαι (ἐλθοῦσα, nom. sg. fem. of aor. act. ptc. of ἔρχομαι, "come") with the prep. phrase εἰς τὸ χεῖρον (χεῖρον, acc. sg. neut. of χείρων, -ον, "worse") is an idiomatic expression mng. "to become worse, to grow worse" (LN 13.50, 23.150; ZG 118).

5:27 Before Mark reaches the main vb. of the sentence, he includes two more participles (ἀκούσασα; ἐλθοῦσα), both of which function not as adj. participles but as temp. adv. participles (cf. R 1105; Stein 268; both expressing antecedent time). As a result, Mark includes a total of seven participles between the subj. of the sentence (γυνή) at the beginning of 5:25 and the main vb. (ἥψατο) in 5:27. Ἀκούσασα, nom. sg. fem. of aor. act. ptc. of ἀκούω, "hear"; ἐλθοῦσα, nom. sg. fem. of aor. act. ptc. of ἔρχομαι, "come"; ὄπισθεν, adv. mng. "from behind"; ἥψατο, 3rd sg. aor. mid. indic. of ἅπτω, "touch" (mng. with mid.); ἱματίου, gen. dir. obj. Mark's Gospel does not use the prep. ἐν with the vb. ἔρχομαι to convey the idea of movement from one place into another (e.g., from outside the crowd into it) but uses ἐν in such contexts for movement within a sphere or area (Turner, *Style* 22; T 257; cf. the use of ἐν and εἰς in 13:14; 15:41). The woman was within the crowd, trying to position herself in such a way that she could touch Jesus's cloak.

5:28 Ὅτι, introduces dir. discourse; ἅψωμαι, 1st sg. aor. mid. subjunc. of ἅπτω, "touch" (mng. with mid.); subjunc. in 3rd class cond. clause; κἄν, particle formed through the combination of καί and ἐάν mng. "even if only, at least, even just" (BDAG 507b; ZG 118); ἱματίων, gen. dir. obj.; σωθήσομαι, 1st sg. fut. pass. indic. of σῴζω, "save; restore to health" (on σῴζω, see 5:34). An impf. tense vb. (e.g., ἔλεγεν in v. 28) can introduce simultaneous action, that is, an action taking place at the same time as a previously mentioned event expressed in the aor. tense (ἥψατο in v. 27; see Fanning 288–89). The impf. vb. points back to what was going through the woman's mind when she decided to touch Jesus's clothes.

5:29 Πηγή, nom. sg. fem. of πηγή, -ῆς, ἡ, "fountain, spring"; ἐξηράνθη, 3rd sg. aor. pass. indic. of ξηραίνω, "dry up"; ἔγνω, 3rd sg. aor. act. indic. of γινώσκω, "perceive, realize" (BDAG 200b–c); ἴαται, 3rd sg. pf. pass. indic. of ἰάομαι, "heal, cure"; μάστιγος, gen.

sg. fem. of μάστιξ, -ιγος, ἡ, "scourge, suffering, affliction." In Gk., reported speech or thought generally retains the tense of the vb. from the original (see 2:1). Therefore, what the woman orig. realized was: "I have been healed" or perhaps better "I am healed," as a way of conveying the use of the pf. in this context to emphasize her present state (with the vb., since it is in indir. discourse, being moved back in time in Eng.: "that she was healed"). The word used for the woman's affliction (μάστιξ) lit. refers to a whip or the lash from a whip (BDAG 620d; Spicq 2:453–56; cf. Acts 22:24; Heb 11:36). Mark uses the related vb. μαστιγόω for the scourging that Jesus would receive before his death on the cross (10:34). In addition to the lit. sense, the word can have a fig. one, as in Mark 3:10; 5:29, 34, where it refers to a severe and painful affliction (BDAG 620d–621a; TDNT 4:518–19). The Eng. word "scourge" is similar in that it can be used lit. for a whip or fig. for a harsh affliction.

5:30 Ἐπιγνούς, nom. sg. masc. of aor. act. ptc. of ἐπιγινώσκω, "perceive, recognize"; temp. adv. ptc. antecedent; ἐξελθοῦσαν, acc. sg. fem. of aor. act. ptc. of ἐξέρχομαι, "go out," The position of the prep. phrase (ἐξ αὐτοῦ) between the art. τήν and the related noun δύναμιν indicates that the prep. phrase is adj. modifying δύναμιν, rather than adv. modifying ἐξελθοῦσαν (e.g., NASB: "that the power proceeding from Him had gone forth"; cf. Taylor 291). The ptc. ἐξελθοῦσαν, as a ptc. of indir. discourse (R 1123; Voelz 1:34, 365; cf. Wallace 645–46), is in the acc. case and follows a vb. of perception (ἐπιγνούς) as a way of giving the content of what Jesus recognized. In Eng., it is helpful to insert the word "that" to introduce the indir. discourse. Ἐπιστραφείς, nom. sg. masc. of aor. pass. ptc. of ἐπιστρέφω, "turn around" (mng. with pass.); temp. adv. ptc. antecedent; ἥψατο, 3rd sg. aor. mid. indic. of ἅπτω, "touch" (mng. with mid.); ἱματίων, gen. dir. obj.; μου, gen. of poss.

5:31 Συνθλίβοντα, acc. sg. masc. of pres. act. ptc. of συνθλίβω, "press together on, press around"; supplementary (complementary) ptc. (see 1:10); ἥψατο, see 5:30; μου, gen. dir. obj. With regard to vbs. of saying in this passage, Mark uses the impf. to convey the ongoing nature of a conversation (see ἔλεγεν in 5:30 and ἔλεγον in 5:31) and then uses the aor. tense to portray the conversation as coming to a close (see εἶπεν in 5:33, 34; cf. Fanning 286, 290).

5:32 Περιεβλέπετο, 3rd sg. impf. mid. indic. of περιβλέπω, "look around" (mng. with mid.); ἰδεῖν, aor. act. inf. of ὁράω, "see"; inf. of purpose; ποιήσασαν, acc. sg. fem. of aor. act. ptc. of ποιέω, "do"; subst. ptc. The impf. with a vb. of activity such as περιεβλέπετο provides a vivid portrayal of the action. The impf. presents Jesus's activity of looking around as it unfolds with some part the action stretching before and after the point at which it is portrayed. As a result, the impf. conveys an ongoing search on the part of Jesus (NIV: "Jesus kept looking around"; cf. Fanning 145–46). The subst. ptc. ποιήσασαν is fem., leaving the impression that Jesus's unique knowledge extended beyond a recognition that a miraculous healing had taken place to a realization that the one who had been healed was a woman (Stein 270; Marcus 1:359; Voelz 1:365). At least, it would be difficult to argue that Mark believed somehow that Jesus could know the one detail but not the other.

5:33 Φοβηθεῖσα, nom. sg. fem. of aor. pass. ptc. of φοβέομαι, "fear, be afraid"; adv. ptc. of manner; τρέμουσα, nom. sg. fem. of pres. act ptc. of τρέμω, "tremble, quiver"; adv. ptc. of manner; εἰδυῖα, nom. sg. fem. of pf. act. ptc. of οἶδα, "know"; adv. ptc. of cause (on the pf. ptc. with οἶδα, see 1:24); γέγονεν, 3rd sg. pf. act. indic. of γίνομαι, "come to be, happen" (on the use of the pf. tense in indir. discourse, see 5:29). The rel. pron. ὅ functions like an interr. pron. in that it is introducing an indir. question ("what?"; R 726). Ἦλθεν, 3rd sg. aor. act. indic. of ἔρχομαι, "come, go"; προσέπεσεν, 3rd sg. aor. act. indic. of προσπίπτω, "fall down before"; αὐτῷ, dat. dir. obj.

5:34 On ὁ δέ, see 1:45; θυγάτηρ, nom. for voc. (R 264, 462); σου, subj. gen. (Wallace 116); σέσωκεν, 3rd sg. pf. act. indic. of σῴζω, "save." The vb. σῴζω can refer to deliverance from physical danger and affliction or deliverance from eternal judgment (BDAG 982b–83b). The use of σῴζω for eternal salvation appears in 10:26, where "being saved" is par. to "inheriting or receiving eternal life" (10:17, 30) and "entering the kingdom of God" (10:23–25). The primary mng. of σῴζω in this passage (5:23, 28, 34), however, relates to deliverance from physical difficulty, since "being saved" is par. to "being healed from affliction" (5:34; cf. Guelich 299). Yet even in this passage, σῴζω seems to point beyond a mere physical healing from a particular affliction to a greater sense of wholeness and well-being, since the woman's deliverance allows her to live in peace (cf. Guelich 299–300). Ὕπαγε, 2nd sg. pres. act. impv. of ὑπάγω, "go, depart" (on the pres. impv. with ὑπάγω, see 2:11); on the use of εἰς for ἐν in this farewell expression, see Harris 85; BDF §206; ZG 119 [see also 13:9]; ἴσθι, 2nd sg. pres. act. impv. of εἰμί, "be"; ὑγιής, nom. sg. fem. of ὑγιής, -ές, "healed", BDAG 1023b; μάστιγος, gen. sg. fem. of μάστιξ, -ιγος, ἡ, "scourge, suffering, affliction" (on the mng. of μάστιξ, see 5:29).

5:35 Λαλοῦντος, gen. sg. masc. of pres. act ptc. of λαλέω, "speak"; gen. abs., temp. adv. ptc. contemp.; ἔρχονται, 3rd pl. pres. mid. indic. of dep. ἔρχομαι, "come"; ἀρχισυναγώγου, gen. sg. masc. of ἀρχισυνάγωγος, -ου, ὁ, "synagogue leader"; λέγοντες, nom. pl. masc. of pres. act. ptc. of λέγω, "say"; adv. ptc. of manner (cf. 1:40; 13:6); ὅτι, introduces dir. discourse; ἀπέθανεν, 3rd sg. aor. act. indic. of ἀποθνῄσκω, "die"; τί, "why?" (see 2:7); σκύλλεις, from σκύλλω, "trouble, bother, annoy." The vb. ἔρχονται is an example of an indef. pl. vb., since no subj. is expressed and no subj. is implied beyond the general idea of "some people" (see 1:22). It is also an example of a historical pres. (see 1:12, 30), one of several in 5:35–43, all of which follow common patterns for the use of the historical pres. in Mark (ἔρχονται [5:35]: a vb. of motion to draw attention to new participants in a scene; λέγει [5:36, 39, 41]: a vb. of saying to introduce dir. discourse; ἔρχονται, θεωρεῖ, παραλαμβάνει, εἰσπορεύεται [5:38, 40]: vbs. of motion to show participants within a scene moving and changing their location). The prep. phrase ἀπὸ τοῦ ἀρχισυναγώγου (lit.: "from the synagogue leader") assumes but does not state directly that the people came from the house of the synagogue leader (R 502). The missing reference to the house should be supplied in translation to avoid giving the impression that the synagogue leader somehow sent a message to himself.

5:36 Παρακούσας, nom. sg. masc. of aor. act. ptc. of παρακούω, "overhear"; temp. adv. ptc. antecedent; λόγον, "report" (BDAG 599b); λαλούμενον, acc. sg. masc. of pres. pass. ptc. of λαλέω, "speak"; temp. adv. ptc. contemp.; ἀρχισυναγώγῳ, dat. sg. masc. of ἀρχισυνάγωγος, -ου, ὁ, "synagogue leader"; φοβοῦ, 2nd sg. pres. pass. impv. of φοβέομαι, "fear, be afraid"; μόνον, adv. use of neut. sg. form, "only" (BDAG 659a); πίστευε, 2nd sg. pres. act impv. of πιστεύω, "believe." When the pres. impv. form of φοβέομαι occurs in a specific prohibition, the command is normally directed toward someone who is already afraid (NASB: "do not be afraid any longer"; see 6:50). The pres. impv. form πίστευε in this context also calls for attention. Most often, pres. impv. forms serve to convey general precepts rather than specific commands directed toward an individual in a concrete situation (cf. BDF §335; Fanning 325–35). In contrast to the normal pattern, the pres. impv. form πίστευε functions as a specific command directed toward Jairus in 5:36. Since Jesus is asking Jairus not to give up hope but to continue on to his home with confidence, the pres. tense appears to be used for a specific command in this context, to emphasize the ongoing nature of the expected action: keep on believing (cf. Fanning 364–65).

5:37 Ἀφῆκεν, 3rd sg. aor. act. indic. of ἀφίημι, "let, allow"; οὐκ . . . οὐδένα, on dbl. negatives to strengthen a statement, see 1:44; συνακολουθῆσαι, aor. act. inf. of συνακολουθέω, "follow"; complementary inf.; εἰ μή, "except" (see 2:7). Although not mentioned, Jairus was undoubtedly also included among those who went with Jesus (as implied by 5:40).

5:38 Ἔρχονται, 3rd pl. pres. mid. indic. of dep. ἔρχομαι, "come"; ἀρχισυναγώγου, see 5:35; θόρυβον, acc. sg. masc. of θόρυβος, -ου, ὁ, "turmoil, uproar, commotion"; κλαίοντας, acc. pl. masc. of pres. act. ptc. of κλαίω, "weep, cry"; ἀλαλάζοντας, acc. pl. masc. of pres. act. ptc. of ἀλαλάζω, "wail"; πολλά, "loudly" (used as an adv. to intensify the ptc.; see 5:10). In 5:38, the prep. εἰς means "to" (like πρός) rather than "into," since Jesus came to the house but did not enter it until the next verse (on εἰς and the overlap of prepositions, see Harris 34–35; Z §97). Both κλαίοντας and ἀλαλάζοντας function as subst. participles but without the art. (Voelz 1:368; Decker 1:139), with the result that the actions of weeping and wailing are attributed to an indef. group of people.

5:39 Εἰσελθών, nom. sg. masc. of aor. act. ptc. of εἰσέρχομαι, "go into, enter"; temp. adv. ptc. antecedent; τί, "why?" (see 2:7); θορυβεῖσθε, 2nd pl. pres. pass. indic. of θορυβέω, "disturb, agitate"; ἀπέθανεν, 3rd sg. aor. act. indic. of ἀποθνήσκω, "die"; καθεύδει, from καθεύδω, "sleep." The NT uses two different vbs. for sleep, καθεύδω and κοιμάω (cf. *NIDNTTE* 2:575, 705–6). The vb. καθεύδω is used twenty-two times in the NT (eight of those instances in Mark), most often as a reference to physical sleep. The vb. κοιμάω (used eighteen times in the NT) appears most often as a euphemism for death (e.g., Matt 27:52; Acts 7:60; 1 Cor. 15:20; 1 Thess 4:13) and much less freq. as a reference to physical sleep (e.g., Matt 28:13; Acts 12:6). Although in the Bible "sleep" serves as a freq. metaphor for death, Mark 5:39 uses καθεύδω not κοιμάω and therefore expresses Jesus's statement in a way that could be easily misinterpreted as indicating that the girl was literally asleep. Jesus's parabolic language has the potential to be heard but misunderstood (cf. 4:11–12).

5:40 Κατεγέλων, 3rd pl. impf. act. indic. of καταγελάω, "laugh at, ridicule"; αὐτοῦ, gen. dir. obj.; ἐκβαλών, nom. sg. masc. of aor. act. ptc. of ἐκβάλλω, "drive out"; temp. adv. ptc. antecedent; παιδίου, gen. of relationship; τούς μετ' αὐτοῦ, "those with him" (on the art. with a prep. phrase, see 1:36); εἰσπορεύεται, 3rd sg. pres. mid. indic. of dep. εἰσπορεύομαι, "go into, enter"; ἦν, 3rd sg. impf. act. indic. of εἰμί, "be." The use of the impf. with κατεγέλων portrays vividly the ridicule directed at Jesus, showing the action as it unfolds (cf. the impf. vb. in 5:32).

5:41 Κρατήσας, nom. sg. masc. of aor. act. ptc. of κρατέω, "take hold of, grasp, seize"; temp. adv. ptc. antecedent; χειρός, gen. dir. obj. (see 1:31); ταλιθα κουμ, on Aram. words or phrases in Mark, see 7:34; μεθερμηνευόμενον, nom. sg. neut. pres. pass. ptc. of μεθερμηνεύω, "translate"; κοράσιον, nom. sg. neut. of κοράσιον, -ου, τό, "little girl"; nom. with an art. for voc. (T 34; Z §34; BDF §147); ἔγειρε, 2nd sg. pres. act. impv. of ἐγείρω, "arise, get up" (intrans. mng. with the impv. [BDAG 272b]; on the use of the pres. tense, see 2:11). The whole Aram. phrase (ταλιθα κουμ) serves as the antecedent for the neut. sg. rel. pron. ὅ (cf. R 713–14), which is then followed by ἐστιν μεθερμηνευόμενον. The ptc. μεθερμηνευόμενον may be either a temp. adv. ptc. ("which, when being translated, is"; cf. ZG 119; Moule 17) or a periph. ptc. ("which is being translated"; cf. Burton §20; R 881; Porter, *VA* 455–56; Fanning 312). Perhaps μεθερμηνευόμενον as a periph. ptc. is more likely given Mark's freq. use of periph. participles (see 1:22, 33), although the use of pres. periph. constructions in Mark's Gospel would be limited to this one set explanatory phrase, ὅ ἐστιν μεθερμηνευόμενον (see also 15:22, 34). Another argument in favor of taking μεθερμηνευόμενον as periph. is that John's Gospel uses the same explanatory phrase (ὅ ἐστιν μεθερμηνευόμενον) in John 1:41 and then uses the simple pres. indic. (ὅ ἑρμηνεύεται) in the following v., 1:42, to express the same idea.

5:42 Κοράσιον, see 5:41; ἀνέστη, 3rd sg. aor. act. indic. of ἀνίστημι, "rise, stand up"; περιεπάτει, 3rd sg. impf. act. indic. of περιπατέω, "walk around" (another example of the impf. moving the narrative forward and drawing attention to a particularly dramatic event [cf. 5:32, 40]; on the impf., see 1:21); γάρ, "now, for" (introducing a brief clarification, BDAG 189d; see 1:16 on γάρ); ἦν, 3rd sg. impf. act. indic. of εἰμί, "be"; ἐτῶν, attrib. gen. (cf. ZG 120); ἐξέστησαν, 3rd pl. aor. act. indic. of ἐξίστημι, "be amazed, be astonished" (on vbs. for amazement, see 1:22); ἐκστάσει, dat. sg. fem. of ἔκστασις, -εως, ἡ, "amazement, astonishment"; cognate dat. as a subcategory of a dat. of manner. A cognate dat., such as ἐκστάσει, serves to emphasize the action of the vb. and therefore can often be translated as an adv. (Wallace 168–69; KMP 135; e.g., NIV: "they were completely astonished").

5:43 Διεστείλατο, 3rd sg. aor. mid. indic. of διαστέλλω, "order, give orders" (mng. with mid.); πολλά, "strictly" (used as an adv. to intensify the vb.; see 5:10); γνοῖ, 3rd sg. aor. act. subjunc. of γινώσκω, "know"; subjunc. in a dir. obj. ἵνα clause (on the subjunc. form γνοῖ instead of γνῷ, see R 308; BDF §95; cf. 9:30); on εἶπεν for "command, tell, order," see BDAG 287a; δοθῆναι, aor. pass. inf. of δίδωμι, "give"; inf. of indir. discourse; φαγεῖν, aor. act. inf. of ἐσθίω, "eat"; epex. inf. to the implied subj. of δοθῆναι. In Mark's Gospel, a healing that takes place in a private setting often leads to a command to secrecy from Jesus (e.g., 1:45). Mark gives no indication that Jesus's command to secrecy was disobeyed in this case, leaving the impression that the girl's parents did not talk about what had happened—at least not until Jesus was able to leave and carry on his teaching ministry.

FOR FURTHER STUDY

18. Women in Mark's Gospel

Aernie, Jeffrey W. "Cruciform Discipleship: The Narrative Function of the Women in Mark 15–16." *JBL* 135 (2016): 779–97.

Anderson, Janice Capel. "Feminist Criticism: The Dancing Daughter." Pages 111–43 in *Mark and Method: New Approaches in Biblical Studies*. 2nd ed. Edited by Janice Capel Anderson and Stephen D. Moore. Minneapolis: Fortress, 2008.

Bauckham, Richard. *Gospel Women: Studies in the Named Women in the Gospels*. Grand Rapids: Eerdmans, 2002.

Beavis, Mary Ann. "Women as Models of Faith in Mark." *BTB* 18 (1988): 3–9.

Betsworth, Sharon. *The Reign of God Is Such as These: A Socio-Literary Analysis of Daughters in the Gospel of Mark*. LNTS 422. London: T&T Clark, 2010.

Levine, Amy-Jill, ed. *A Feminist Companion to Mark*. Sheffield, UK: Sheffield Academic Press, 2001.

*Malbon, Elizabeth Struthers. "Fallible Followers: Women and Men in the Gospel of Mark." *Semeia* 28 (1983): 29–48.

Miller, Susan. *Women in Mark's Gospel*. JSNTSup 259. London: T&T Clark, 2004.

_____. "Women Characters in Mark." Pages 174–93 in *Character Studies and the Gospel of Mark*. Edited by Christopher W. Skinner and Matthew Ryan Hauge. LNTS 483. London: Bloomsbury T&T Clark, 2014.

Munro, Winsome. "Women Disciples in Mark?" *CBQ* 44 (1982): 225–41.

Swartley, Willard M. "The Role of Women in Mark's Gospel: A Narrative Analysis." *BTB* 27 (1997): 16–22.

19. Minor Characters in Mark's Gospel

Bolt, Peter G. *Jesus' Defeat of Death: Persuading Mark's Early Readers*. SNTSMS 125. Cambridge: Cambridge University Press, 2003.

Malbon, Elizabeth Struthers. "The Poor Widow in Mark and Her Poor Rich Readers." *CBQ* 53 (1991): 589–604.

*_____. "The Major Importance of the Minor Characters in Mark." Pages 58–86 in *The New Literary Criticism and the New Testament*. Edited by Edgar V. McKnight and Elizabeth Struthers Malbon. Valley Forge, PA: Trinity Press International, 1994.

_____. "'Reflected Christology': An Aspect of Narrative 'Christology' in the Gospel of Mark." *PRSt* 26 (1999): 127–45.

Rhoads, David, Joanna Dewey, and Donald Michie. "The Minor Characters." Pages 130–35 in *Mark as Story: An Introduction to the Narrative of a Gospel*. 3rd ed. Minneapolis: Fortress, 2012.

Smith, Stephen H. "Minor Characters." Pages 76–80 in *A Lion with Wings: A Narrative-Critical Approach to Mark's Gospel*. Sheffield, UK: Sheffield Academic Press, 1996.

Williams, Joel F. *Other Followers of Jesus: Minor Characters as Major Figures in Mark's Gospel*. JSNTSup 102. Sheffield, UK: Sheffield Academic Press, 1994.

———. "Discipleship and Minor Characters in Mark's Gospel." *BSac* 153 (1996): 332–43.

———. "Jesus' Love for the Rich Man (Mark 10:21): A Disputed Response toward a Disputed Character." Pages 145–61 in *Between Author and Audience in Mark: Narration, Characterization, Interpretation*. Edited by Elizabeth Struthers Malbon. Sheffield, UK: Sheffield Phoenix, 2009.

HOMILETICAL SUGGESTIONS

Examples of Faith (5:21–43)

1. What do we learn about Jesus?
   a. Jesus has authority over sickness and death.
   b. Jesus will stop and make time for a person of faith.
2. What do we learn about a life of faith?
   a. Faith recognizes that Jesus can be trusted even when circumstances look hopeless.
   b. Faith recognizes that Jesus can be trusted even when it is necessary to wait.

(b) Unbelief at Nazareth (6:1–6)

6:1 After presenting examples of faith in the previous section, Mark in this passage offers as an opposite example the people in Jesus's hometown who struggled with unbelief, at least in part, because of their familiarity with Jesus. Ἐξῆλθεν, 3rd sg. aor. act. indic. of ἐξέρχομαι, "go out"; ἔρχεται, 3rd sg. pres. mid. indic. of dep. ἔρχομαι, "come, go"; πατρίδα, acc. sg. fem. of πατρίς, -ίδος, ἡ, "hometown"; αὐτῷ, dat. dir. obj. Mark often uses the historical pres. with vbs. of motion, such as ἔρχεται and ἀκολουθοῦσιν, when opening up a new scene (see 1:12). That Jesus's hometown was Nazareth is clear from 1:9, where Jesus was described as coming from Nazareth of Galilee (see also the references to Jesus as a Nazarene: 1:24; 10:47; 14:67; 16:6; cf. Luke 4:16).

6:2 Γενομένου, gen. sg. neut. of aor. mid. ptc. of dep. γίνομαι, "come, take place, happen"; gen. abs., temp. adv. ptc. antecedent; ἤρξατο, 3rd sg. aor. mid. indic. of ἄρχω, "begin" (mng. with mid.; on ἄρχομαι, see 1:45); διδάσκειν, pres. act. inf. of διδάσκω, "teach"; complementary inf.; ἀκούοντες, nom. pl. masc. of pres. act. ptc. of ἀκούω, "hear"; temp. adv. ptc. contemp.; ἐξεπλήσσοντο, 3rd pl. impf. pass. indic. of ἐκπλήσσω, "be amazed, be overwhelmed" (mng. with pass.). The impf. tense of the vb. (ἐξεπλήσσοντο) for the amazement of the townspeople matches the impf. tense of the vb. in 6:6 (ἐθαύμαζεν) for Jesus's amazement concerning their unbelief (see 1:22 on vbs. of amazement). Λέγοντες, nom. pl. masc. of pres. act. ptc. of λέγω, "say"; adv. ptc. of result (cf. 7:37; 10:26); δοθεῖσα, nom. sg. fem. of aor. pass. ptc. of δίδωμι, "give"; adj. ptc.; δυνάμεις, "works of power, miracles, wonders," (BDAG 263b); γινόμεναι, nom. pl. fem. of pres. mid. ptc. of dep. γίνομαι, "come to be, take place, be performed" (BDAG 197a); adj. ptc. The translation of the last clause in 6:2 is complicated by text-critical issues. The more difficult and therefore more likely orig. reading (found in א, B, 33, 892; cf. Metzger 75) does not have an art. before the adj. τοιαῦται or the ptc. γινόμεναι, even though in context τοιαῦται is probably an attrib. adj. and γινόμεναι is probably an adj. ptc. (which explains the use of an art. before both the adj. and the ptc. by א2 and Δ). This grammatical interpretation—as well as the absence of any interr. words—seems to indicate that the clause is more likely an exclamation than another question ("And such works of power that are being performed by his hands!" [cf. NRSV]).

6:3 The questions in 6:3, which begin with οὐχ and οὐκ, expect an affirmative answer (see 4:21, 38). These questions cast a negative light on the amazement toward Jesus in the previous verse, since they convey that Jesus and his family were well-known but not highly regarded in the community. Τέκτων, nom. sg. masc. of τέκτων, -ονος, ὁ, "builder." Although τέκτων is often translated as "carpenter," the term was broader than that and referred to someone who worked with stone, wood, and sometimes metal in various construction and building projects (Ken M. Campbell, "What Was Jesus's Occupation?" *JETS* 48 [2005]: 501–19). Πρός, "with" (used here in connection with εἶναι to convey not motion but a position with others [Harris 191; Moule 52; cf. Wallace 359]); ἐσκανδαλίζοντο, 3rd pl. impf. pass. indic. of σκανδαλίζω, "cause to stumble" (on σκανδαλίζω, see 9:43); on the causal use of ἐν, see Z §119. The designation of Jesus by his mother's name is unusual, and, in the context of the disregard that the people of Nazareth expressed toward him, the designation may have been a way to cast doubt on Jesus's legitimacy (cf. Marcus 1:374–75).

6:4 Ὅτι, introduces dir. discourse; ἄτιμος, nom. sg. masc. of ἄτιμος, -ον, "dishonored, without honor"; εἰ μή, "except," see 2:7; πατρίδι, dat. sg. fem. of πατρίς, -ίδος, ἡ, "hometown"; συγγενεῦσιν, dat. pl. masc. of συγγενής, -ές, related (although the adj. is used subst. in the NT for "relatives," BDAG 950c); οἰκία, "household" or "family" (see BDAG 695c; LN 10.8). On a minor point, the placement of the accent on ἔστιν does not follow the normal pattern for an encl. whenever it is immediately preceded by οὐκ (6:4; 9:40; 10:40; 12:27, 31, 32; 16:6), τοῦτ' (7:2), or καί (12:11; see D. A. Carson, *Greek Accents: A Student's Manual* [Grand Rapids: Baker, 1985], 50–51).

6:5 Ἐδύνατο, 3rd sg. impf. mid. indic. of dep. δύναμαι, "be able to, can"; ποιῆσαι, aor. act. inf. of ποιέω, "do"; complementary inf.; on dbl. negatives to emphasize a point, see 1:44; ἀρρώστοις, dat. pl. masc. of ἄρρωστος, -ον, "sick, ill"; ἐπιθείς, nom. sg. masc. of aor. act. ptc. of ἐπιτίθημι, "lay on"; adv. ptc. of means; ἐθεράπευσεν, 3rd sg. aor. act. indic. of θεραπεύω, "heal" (the implied dir. obj. of ἐθεράπευσεν, which is left unstated in this context, should be supplied in Eng.). Most often the words εἰ μή (together mng. "except") do not occur with a finite vb. following (BDF §376; BDAG 278d; cf. e.g., 2:7; 5:37; 6:4, 8; 9:29; 11:13), but when they do, as in 6:5, the phrase means "except that" (BDF §376). The compound vb. ἐπιτίθημι sometimes repeats the prep. ἐπί after the vb. (e.g., 8:25), but in Mark's Gospel the normal pattern is to use the dat. case with ἐπιτίθημι instead (e.g., ἀρρώστοις in 6:5 or αὐτῷ in 7:32; cf. BDF §202).

6:6 While Mark's Gospel refers repeatedly to people's amazement at Jesus, it only mentions Jesus's amazement this one time. Unbelief astonished him. Ἐθαύμαζεν, 3rd sg. impf. act. indic. of θαυμάζω, "wonder, marvel, be astonished"; ἀπιστίαν, acc. sg. fem. of ἀπιστία, -ας, ἡ, "unbelief"; περιῆγεν, 3rd sg. impf. act. indic. of περιάγω, "go around"; κύκλῳ, adv. mng. "all around"; διδάσκων, nom. sg. masc. of pres. act. ptc. of διδάσκω, "teach"; adv. ptc. of manner.

FOR FURTHER STUDY

20. Faith and Unbelief in Mark's Gospel

Beavis, Mary Ann. "Mark's Teaching on Faith." *BTB* 16 (1986): 139–42.

Dowd, Sharyn Echols. *Prayer, Power and the Problem of Suffering: Mark 11:22–25 in the Context of Markan Theology.* SBLDS 105. Atlanta: Scholars Press, 1988.

*Marshall, Christopher D. *Faith as a Theme in Mark's Narrative.* SNTSMS 64. Cambridge: Cambridge University Press, 1989.

Schweizer, Eduard. "The Portrayal of the Life of Faith in the Gospel of Mark." *Int* 32 (1978): 387–99.

Thompson, Mary R. *The Role of Disbelief in Mark: A New Approach to the Second Gospel.* New York: Paulist, 1989.

Yeung, Maureen W. *Faith in Jesus and Paul: A Comparison with Special Reference to "Faith that Can Remove Mountains" and "Your Faith Has Healed/Saved You."* WUNT 2/147. Tübingen: Mohr Siebeck, 2002.

HOMILETICAL SUGGESTIONS

The Wonder of Unbelief (6:1–6)

1. Too familiar with Jesus to listen to his wisdom.
2. Too familiar with Jesus to live under his power.
3. Too familiar with Jesus to look for his compassion.

(c) Mission of the Disciples and the Unbelief of Herod (6:7–29)

6:7 Using a sandwich technique (see 3:22 on this literary pattern), Mark places his description of the death of John the Baptist at the hands of Herod (6:14–29) within his presentation of the disciples' mission (6:7–13, 30). In this way, the seemingly successful mission of the disciples stands in contrast to the foolish unbelief of Herod and the costly obedience of the faithful prophet. Προσκαλεῖται, 3rd sg. pres. mid. indic. of προσκαλέω, "summon, call to oneself" (mng. with mid.); historical pres. (starting a new scene [see 1:12]); ἤρξατο, 3rd sg. aor. mid. indic. of ἄρχω, "begin" (mng. with mid.; on ἄρχομαι, see 1:45); ἀποστέλλειν, pres. act. inf. of ἀποστέλλω, "send"; complementary inf.; δύο δύο, an idiomatic way in Gk. to express a distributive sense, "two by two" (R 284; Z §157; BDAG 264d; Decker 1:147–48); ἐδίδου, 3rd sg. impf. act. indic. of δίδωμι, "give"; πνευμάτων, gen. of subordination. Mark employs a series of impf. vbs. to describe Jesus's preparation of the disciples for their mission, providing background information for the mission itself (ἐδίδου in 6:7; παρήγγειλεν in 6:8; ἔλεγεν in 6:10; on the impf., see 1:21).

6:8 In 6:8–9, Jesus instructs his disciples before their mission concerning the acceptable provisions for their journey, provisions that, since they were so minimal, highlight the urgency of the task and the necessity of depending on God. Παρήγγειλεν, 3rd sg. aor. act. indic. of παραγγέλλω, "give orders, command"; αἴρωσιν, 3rd pl. pres. act. subjunc. of αἴρω, "take"; subjunc. in a dir. obj. ἵνα clause for an indir. command; εἰ μή, "except" (see 2:7); ῥάβδον, acc. sg. fem. of ῥάβδος, -ου, ἡ, "staff, walking stick"; μόνον, neut. sg. form used as an adv., which often happens in connection with negatives (BDAG 659a–b; cf. Matt 21:19); πήραν, acc. sg. fem. of πήρα, -ας, ἡ, "knapsack, traveler's bag"; εἰς (2nd use): "in" (on εἰς for ἐν, see 13:9; cf. Z §99; Harris 84); ζώνην, acc. sg. fem. of ζώνη, -ης, ἡ, "belt"; χαλκόν, acc. sg. masc. of χαλκός, -οῦ, ὁ, "money." Included among the prohibited items was money, or more specifically, "copper coins" (χαλκόν; cf. BDAG 1076d), which were commonly carried in a belt and were less valuable than gold or silver coins (cf. Matt 10:9; i.e., Jesus did not allow them to take even small change).

6:9 Mark 6:9 continues Jesus's instructions, but in ways that shift the grammatical structure. The ptc. ὑποδεδεμένους (acc. pl. masc. of pf. mid. ptc. of ὑποδέω, "tie beneath, put on" [mng. with mid.]; temp. adv. ptc. antecedent) apparently assumes an inf., such as ἐκπορεύεσθαι (cf. R 441; BDF §470; Bruce 379). In this way, Jesus commanded them to go after having put on sandals (σανδάλια, acc. pl. neut. of σανδάλιον, -ου, τό, "sandal"; dir. obj. of ὑποδεδεμένους). The ptc. ὑποδεδεμένους is not modifying σανδάλια (since they do not agree in gender); rather, it relates back to the disciples (that is, back to αὐτοῖς in v. 8; see R 413 for the common lack of agreement in case with participles, using 6:9 as an example). The grammatical structure shifts again, moving from indir. discourse to dir. discourse, with the use of ἐνδύσησθε, a prohibitive subjunc. (see BDF §470 on the lack of extended indir. discourse in the NT and the common shift to dir. discourse). Ἐνδύσησθε, 2nd pl. aor. mid. subjunc. of ἐνδύω, "clothe oneself, put on, wear" (mng. with mid.); χιτῶνας, acc. pl. masc. of χιτών, -ῶνος, ὁ, "tunic, shirt").

6:10 Jesus instructs the disciples both on how to respond to those who welcome them (6:10) and to those who reject their message (6:11). Ὅπου ἐάν, "wherever" or "whenever" depending on the context (see 9:18); εἰσέλθητε, 2nd pl. aor. act. subjunc. of εἰσέρχομαι, "go into, enter"; subjunc. in an indef. rel. clause; μένετε, 2nd pl. pres. act. impv. of μένω, "remain, stay"; ἐξέλθητε, 2nd pl. aor. act. subjunc. of ἐξέρχομαι, "go out"; subjunc. in an indef. temp. clause. Ἕως is normally used with ἄν when it is functioning as a conj. and is normally followed by an aor. subjunc. vb. (as in 6:10; 9:1; 12:36), but see ἕως followed by an aor. subjunc. vb. without ἄν at 14:32 (cf. BDAG 422d–23a). In 6:10, Jesus's point is that the disciples should accept whatever hospitality is offered to them rather than moving from one house to another, looking for better accommodations.

6:11 Ὅς ἂν τόπος, "whatever place"; δέξηται, 3rd sg. aor. mid. subjunc. of dep. δέχομαι, "receive, welcome"; subjunc. in an indef. rel. clause; ἀκούσωσιν, 3rd pl. aor. act. subjunc. of ἀκούω, "hear, listen to"; subjunc. in an indef. rel. clause. In this context, the noun τόπος does not simply indicate a "place" but represents "the inhabitants in a place" (LN 11.59), which explains the shift from the sg. form δέξηται (the place does not receive them) to the pl. form ἀκούσωσιν (the people in that place do not listen to them). Ἐκπορευόμενοι, nom. pl. masc. of pres. mid. ptc. of dep. ἐκπορεύομαι, go out; attendant circumstance ptc. (cf. NIV); ἐκτινάξατε, 2nd pl. aor. act. impv. of ἐκτινάσσω, "shake off"; χοῦν, acc. sg. masc. of χοῦς, χοός, ὁ, "dust"; ὑποκάτω, adv. functioning as a prep. with a gen. obj., "under, beneath," BDAG 1038a; the 2nd use of the art. τόν indicates that the prep. phrase is functioning adj. to modify χοῦν (see the similar use of the art. in 11:2, 25; 13:25; 15:43); εἰς, "for" (purpose); μαρτύριον, acc. sg. neut. of μαρτύριον, -ου, τό, "testimony"; αὐτοῖς, dat. of interest (disadvantage), ZG 121; *TDNT* 4:503 (see 1:44). The action of shaking dust off one's feet or clothes symbolizes a decision to discontinue all association with those who have refused God's message and who, because of this rejection, are heading toward God's judgment (Matt 10:14; Luke 10:10–11; Acts 13:51; 18:6; cf. Marcus 1:384).

6:12 In 6:12–13, Mark reports on the success of the disciples' mission—they proclaim Jesus's message, cast out demons, and heal the sick. Ἐξελθόντες, nom. pl. masc. of aor. act. ptc. of ἐξέρχομαι, "go out"; temp. adv. ptc. antecedent; ἐκήρυξαν, 3rd pl. aor. act. indic. of κηρύσσω, proclaim, preach; μετανοῶσιν, 3rd pl. pres. act. subjunc. of μετανοέω, "repent"; subjunc. in a dir. obj. ἵνα clause for an indir. command (on indef. pl. vbs., see 1:22).

6:13 Ἐξέβαλλον, 3rd pl. impf. act. indic. of ἐκβάλλω, "cast out, drive out, send away"; ἤλειφον, 3rd pl. impf. act. indic. of ἀλείφω, "anoint"; ἐλαίῳ, dat. sg. neut. of ἔλαιον, -ου, τό, "olive oil"; ἀρρώστους, acc. pl. masc. of ἄρρωστος, -ον, "sick, ill"; ἐθεράπευον, 3rd pl. impf. act. indic. of θεραπεύω, "heal." The impf. vbs. in this verse along with the use of πολλά and πολλούς mark out the actions as iter.—they repeatedly delivered those oppressed by demons and repeatedly healed those who were sick (cf. Voelz 1:392).

6:14–15 Mark shifts his focus away from the mission of the disciples to Herod and his concern that Jesus might be John the Baptist raised from the dead. Mark then takes this opportunity to fill in information concerning what happened to John after his arrest. Ἤκουσεν, 3rd sg. aor. act. indic. of ἀκούω, "hear"; φανερόν, nom. sg. neut. of φανερός, -ά, -όν, "known, well known, widely known" (LN 28.28); ἐγένετο, 3rd sg. aor. mid. indic. of dep. γίνομαι, "become, come to be" (on translating the aor. as a pluperf., see 3:10); βαπτίζων, nom. sg. masc. of pres. act. ptc. of βαπτίζω, "baptize"; subst. ptc. in appos. to Ἰωάννης (Decker 1:153); ἐγήγερται, 3rd sg. pf. pass. indic. of ἐγείρω, "raise"; ἐνεργοῦσιν, from ἐνεργέω, "be at work, be active" (mng. when used as an intrans. vb.); δυνάμεις, "miraculous powers" (i.e., power expressed through a variety of miraculous deeds; cf. France 253).

The 3rd pl. form ἔλεγον, read by B, W, and a few other mss., and supported by D (which has ἐλέγοσαν), is probably orig. in 6:14. The 3rd sg. form ἔλεγεν, read by most mss., was likely a change, making this vb. agree in person and number with ἤκουσεν at the beginning of the verse (Metzger 76; cf. Yarbro Collins 294; France 251). Therefore, instead of reporting what Herod was saying, καὶ ἔλεγον begins a digression that offers in 6:14–15 a series of three common opinions concerning what people were saying about Jesus (cf. 8:28; on indef. pl. vbs. as a common grammatical feature in Mark, see 1:22). Most often, Mark uses the impf. of λέγω to portray in a descriptive way the give-and-take of an ongoing conversation (cf. Fanning 286; e.g., 3:22, 23; 7:27; 15:12, 14). Yet Mark uses the impf. of λέγω in other ways as well (e.g., 5:8, 28), as Mark's account concerning Herod and John the Baptist confirms. The impf. of λέγω can introduce a statement that has been made repeatedly by an individual (6:16, 18; see perhaps also 16:3) or a statement that has been expressed on a number of occasions by a number of people (6:14–15; see also e.g., 3:21; 14:31; cf. Fanning 287).

6:16 Ἀκούσας, nom. sg. masc. of aor. act. ptc. of ἀκούω, "hear"; temp. adv. ptc. antecedent; ἀπεκεφάλισα, 1st sg. aor. act. indic. of ἀποκεφαλίζω, "behead"; ἠγέρθη, 3rd sg. aor. pass. indic. of ἐγείρω, "raise." The acc. Ἰωάννην is the antecedent of the rel. pron. ὅν, but instead of preceding the rel. pron. it is actually incorporated into the rel. clause (R 718–19; Porter, *Idioms* 253; Robertson counts fifty-four examples of incorporation in the NT). In addition, the case of Ἰωάννην has been drawn to the case of the rel. pron. by reverse attraction, so that it has changed from nom. to acc. (R 719; T 324). The dem. pron. οὗτος is resumptive, repeating the subj. and reverting back to the nom. case (R 719). The end result of the complicated grammar is that the rel. clause ὅν ἐγὼ ἀπεκεφάλισα comes first in Herod's statement, a place for greater prominence and emph. In addition, the nom. pers. pron. ἐγώ also seems to be included for emph. The somewhat awkward grammar and word order serves to heighten Herod's guilty sense of responsibility for John's beheading.

6:17 In 6:16, Herod emphasized his responsibility for John's death, and in 6:17 Mark uses the intensive pron. αὐτός to emphasize his agreement with that assessment (αὐτός in the pred. position with ὁ Ἡρῴδης as intensive pron., "Herod himself," cf. Porter, *Idioms* 120; France 256). Ἀποστείλας, nom. sg. masc. of aor. act. ptc. of ἀποστέλλω, "send"; temp. adv. ptc. antecedent; ἐκράτησεν, 3rd sg. aor. act. indic. of κρατέω, "seize, arrest, apprehend"; ἔδησεν, 3rd sg. aor. act. indic. of δέω, "bind." Herod's motivation for the arrest and imprisonment of John came from his marriage (ἐγάμησεν, 3rd sg. aor. act. indic. of γαμέω, "marry") to Herodias, who had been the wife of his brother, and from John's subsequent condemnation of that marriage (on Herodias's first husband, see Harold W. Hoehner, *Herod Antipas* [Cambridge: Cambridge University Press, 1972] 131–36; cf. Jos., *Ant.* 18.5.1 §109).

6:18 In Eng., the pluperf. is used to express the idea of an action that took place before another past event (i.e., "John had been saying" before his arrest). Greek simply uses the aor. or impf., allowing the context to communicate the time relationship to other events (Z §290; T 67; Moule 10; Wallace 549). Ὅτι, introduces dir. discourse; ἔξεστιν,

3rd sg. pres. act. indic. of ἔξεστιν, "it is lawful, it is permitted"; σοι, dat. of reference or respect; ἔχειν, pres. act. inf. of ἔχω, "have"; subst. use of the inf., subj. of ἔξεστιν. The vb. ἔξεστιν along with a neg. regularly occurs in the Gospels to point to what is forbidden in the law of Moses (e.g., Matt 27:6; Mark 2:24, 26; Luke 6:2, 4; John 5:10; cf. EDNT 2:5). The Mosaic law prohibited a man from marrying his brother's wife (Lev 18:16; 20:21), except when that brother died without leaving any children (Deut 25:5–10; Mark 12:19). The exception obviously did not apply in Herod's case.

6:19 Ἐνεῖχεν, 3rd sg. impf. act. indic. of ἐνέχω, "bear ill will, be resentful, hold a grudge." The vb. ἐνέχω, an intrans. vb. that takes a dat. of interest expressing disadvantage (αὐτῷ, "against him"; R 539, 800), is similar to the Eng. colloq. expression "to have it in for someone" (BDAG 336a). Ἤθελεν, 3rd sg. impf. act. indic. of θέλω, "want, wish"; ἀποκτεῖναι, aor. act. inf. of ἀποκτείνω, "kill"; complementary inf.; καί (2nd use): contrastive, "and yet"; ἠδύνατο, 3rd sg. impf. mid. indic. of dep. δύναμαι, "be able to, can." The series of impf. vbs. in 6:19–20 function to provide background information for the main sequence of events that are carried forward using the aor. tense in 6:21–29 (see 1:21 on the impf.).

6:20 Ἐφοβεῖτο, 3rd sg. impf. pass. indic. of φοβέομαι, "be afraid of, fear"; εἰδώς, nom. sg. masc. of pf. act. ptc. of οἶδα, "know"; adv. ptc. of cause (on the pf. ptc. with οἶδα, see 1:24); αὐτόν, acc. subj. of an implied indir. discourse inf. εἶναι; συνετήρει, 3rd sg. impf. act. indic. of συντηρέω, "protect, defend." Mark seems to prefer to use the vb. φοβέομαι in the impf. tense in the indic. mood (six times in the impf. indic. vs. three times in the aor. indic.). The impf. provides a more vivid description of the fear but does not seem to make a distinctive claim about the nature or duration of that fear (cf. the impf. in 11:32 with the aor. in 12:12). Ἀκούσας, nom. sg. masc. of aor. act. ptc. of ἀκούω, "hear, listen to"; temp. adv. ptc. antecedent; αὐτοῦ, gen. dir. obj.; ἠπόρει, 3rd sg. impf. act. indic. of ἀπορέω, "be at a loss, be perplexed, be in doubt" (lit. "to be without a way" [πόρος, "way"], cf. BDAG 119b; ZG 122). The neut. acc. pl. form πολλά (from πολύς) functions as an adv. to intensify the vb. ("he was greatly perplexed," BDAG 849d–850a). Καί (3rd use): contrastive, "and yet"; ἡδέως, adv. mng. "gladly, with delight"; αὐτοῦ, gen. dir. obj.; ἤκουεν, 3rd sg. impf. act. indic. of ἀκούω, "hear, listen to."

6:21 Γενομένης, gen. sg. fem. of aor. mid. ptc. of dep. γίνομαι, "come to be, arrive" (BDAG 197c); gen. abs. ptc., temp. adv. ptc. antecedent; εὐκαίρου, gen. sg. fem. of the two-terminal adj. εὔκαιρος, -ον, "opportune, favorable, well timed." The gen. abs. ptc. γενομένης is dependent on the main vb. ἤρεσεν, which does not appear until the next verse—when Herodias's opportunity came, her daughter pleased Herod with a dance. That sounds like the daughter's dance was part of Herodias's scheme from the beginning. Most EVV translate the gen. abs. ptc. as a main vb., since the ptc. is at such a distance from the actual main vb. Γενεσίοις, dat. pl. neut. of γενέσια, -ίων, τά, "birthday celebration" (only used in the pl., BDAG 192c); dat. of time (R 523; Moule 43; Wallace 157); names of feasts and other days of celebration were often in the pl. (R 408; T 26–27; see also 14:1); δεῖπνον, acc. sg. neut. of δεῖπνον, -ου, τό, "dinner, feast" (when used with ποιεῖν the phrase means "to give a dinner," BDAG 215d); ἐποίησεν, 3rd sg. aor. act. indic. of ποιέω, "make, give"; μεγιστᾶσιν, dat. pl. masc. of μεγιστάν, -ᾶνος, ὁ, "high-ranking man, great man" (i.e., the leading men in Herod's court, cf. MM 393; BDAG 625a; Dan 5:23 LXX); χιλιάρχοις, dat. pl. masc. of χιλίαρχος, -ου, ὁ, "military commander" (lit., "those who lead a thousand soldiers"); πρώτοις, adj. used here subst. for "the leading men, the most prominent men," BDAG 894a (lit. "the first ones," i.e., the local aristocracy rather than governmental or military leaders [Marcus 1:396]).

6:22 A difficult text-critical problem presents itself in 6:22. Several significant early mss. read τῆς θυγατρὸς αὐτοῦ Ἡρῳδιάδος ("his daughter Herodias" [cf. NRSV; NET; NLT]; ℵ, B, D, L, Δ, 565), while most mss. incl. other important early witnesses support the reading τῆς θυγατρὸς αὐτῆς τῆς Ἡρῳδιάδος ("the daughter of Herodias herself" [NASB; cf. NIV; ESV]; A, C, K, N, W [except without the art. after αὐτῆς], Γ, Θ, family 13, and the majority of Gk. mss.; with αὐτῆς in the pred. position and functioning in this reading as an intensive pron., which in this context can almost take on a dem. sense, "the daughter of this very Herodias" [see BDAG 153a]). The first reading, which identifies the daughter as Herod's and gives her the name "Herodias," seems impossible within the flow of the narrative. Indeed, the narrative itself instead identifies the girl elsewhere as Herodias's daughter (6:24, 28; cf. also Matt 14:6). The second reading should probably be preferred as necessary to the logic of the story (see Hoehner, *Herod Antipas* 151–54; Cranfield 211–12; Brooks 105–6; France 254–55, 258). Perhaps a scribe, puzzled by the unnecessary intensive pron. αὐτῆς, mechanically changed it to αὐτοῦ without reflecting on the difficulty that the change created for the narrative context.

Mark 6:22 adds two more gen. abs. participles to the series of three such participles that began in 6:21. Both εἰσελθούσης (gen. sg. fem. of aor. act. ptc. of εἰσέρχομαι, "go in, enter"; temp. adv. ptc. antecedent) and ὀρχησαμένης (gen. sg. fem. of aor. mid. ptc. of dep. ὀρχέομαι, "dance"; temp. adv. ptc. antecedent) have τῆς θυγατρός as their gen. subj., which is grammatically unusual in that the subj. of the gen. abs. participles is the same as the implied subj. of the main vb. (cf. Z §49; T 322). Ἤρεσεν, 3rd sg. aor. act. indic. of ἀρέσκω, "please"; Ἡρῴδῃ, dat. dir. obj.; συνανακειμένοις, dat. pl. masc. of pres. mid. ptc. of dep. συνανάκειμαι, "eat with, dine with"; subst. ptc. In certain passages in the LXX, the vb. ἀρέσκω takes on connotations of arousing or satisfying sexual interest (Gen 19:8; Esth 2:4, 9; Job 31:10 LXX; cf. Jdt 12:14). A similar mng. is suggested here because of the apparently all-male audience and the king's excessive promise (Marcus 1:396). Κορασίῳ, dat. sg. neut. of κοράσιον, -ου, τό, "girl"; αἴτησον, 2nd sg. aor. act. impv. of αἰτέω, "ask, ask for"; με, dbl. acc., obj. of the person; ὃ ἐάν, dbl. acc., obj. of the thing (Moule 33; Wallace 182; see the similar use of the dbl. acc. in 6:23; 10:35); θέλῃς, 2nd sg. pres. act. subjunc. of θέλω, "wish, want, desire"; subjunc. in indef. rel. clause; δώσω, 1st sg. fut. act. indic. of δίδωμι, "give."

6:23 Ὤμοσεν, 3rd sg. aor. act indic. of ὀμνύω, "swear, take an oath." The use of the neut. acc. pl. form of πολύς (i.e. πολλά) as an adv. to intensify the vb. (BDAG 849d–850a) is characteristic of Mark's style (1:45; 3:12; 5:10, 23, 38, 43; 6:20; 9:26) and is likely original (included in D, Θ, 28, 565, 700, and apparently 𝔓⁴⁵; Metzger 77). Αἰτήσῃς, 2nd sg. aor. act. subjunc. of αἰτέω, "ask, ask for"; subjunc. in indef. rel. clause; δώσω, 1st sg. fut. act. indic. of δίδωμι, "give"; ἕως, used as a prep. taking a gen. obj., "until, up to"; ἡμίσους, gen. sg. neut. of ἥμισυς, -εια, -υ, "half"; τῆς βασιλείας, partitive gen. (R 502). The rel. pron. ὅστις appears in the acc. case—as in Mark 6:23—only in the neut.; otherwise it only occurs in the nom. (R 729; BDAG 729d; the neut. sg. form of ὅστις is printed as ὅ τι to distinguish it from the conj. ὅτι; in 6:23 ὅ τι is used with ἐάν to create an indef. rel. pron.: "whatever").

6:24 Ἐξελθοῦσα, nom. sg. fem. of aor. act. ptc. of ἐξέρχομαι, "go out"; temp. adv. ptc. antecedent; αἰτήσωμαι, 1st sg. aor. mid. subjunc. of αἰτέω, "ask, ask for" (mng. with mid.), delib. subjunc. A subtle distinction sometimes exists between the use of αἰτέω in the act. voice (such as by the king in 6:22–23) and the use of that same vb. in the mid. voice (such as by the girl in 6:24–25). While αἰτέω in the act. voice appears to be a general term for making a request, the mid. form of αἰτέω is often preferred in commercial or business contexts (BDF §316; R 805; Z §234; cf. *TDNT* 1:192). The shift to the mid. form of αἰτέω in 6:24–25 seems to communicate that the girl views the king's offer more narrowly as a contractual or legal obligation and her request as part of a business transaction. On the art. as a pers. pron. before δέ, see 1:45; κεφαλήν, acc. as the dir. obj. of an implied impv. (such as αἴτησαι); βαπτίζοντος, gen. sg. masc. of pres. act. ptc. of βαπτίζω, "baptize"; subst. ptc. in appos. to Ἰωάννου.

6:25 Εἰσελθοῦσα, nom. sg. fem. of aor. act. ptc. of εἰσέρχομαι, "go in, enter"; temp. adv. ptc. antecedent; σπουδῆς, gen. sg. fem. of σπουδή, -ῆς, ἡ, "haste, speed"; ᾐτήσατο, 3rd sg. aor. mid. indic. of αἰτέω, "ask, ask for" (mng. with mid.); λέγουσα, nom. sg. fem. of pres. act. ptc. of λέγω, "say"; redundant ptc.; ἐξαυτῆς, adv. mng. "at once, immediately, right now"; δῷς, 2nd sg. aor. act. subjunc. of δίδωμι, "give"; subjunc. in a dir. obj. ἵνα clause; πίνακι, dat. sg. masc. of πίναξ, -ακος, ὁ, "platter"; βαπτιστοῦ, gen. sg. masc. of βαπτιστής, -οῦ, ὁ, "Baptist, Baptizer." The use of θέλω with ἵνα is essentially equivalent to an impv. (Moule 145; BDF §387; BDAG 476d–477a). In fact, the par. account in Matthew uses the impv. δός (Matt 14:8).

6:26 Περίλυπος, nom. sg. masc. of περίλυπος, -ον, "deeply grieved"; γενόμενος, nom. sg. masc. of aor. mid. ptc. of dep. γίνομαι, "come to be, become"; adv. ptc. of concession (cf. Bruce 382; Stein 306; Voelz 1:407); ὅρκους, acc. pl. masc. of ὅρκος, -ου, ὁ, "oath"; ἀνακειμένους, acc. pl. masc. of pres. mid. ptc. of dep. ἀνάκειμαι, "dine, recline for dinner, be a dinner guest"; subst. ptc.; ἠθέλησεν, 3rd sg. aor. act. indic. of θέλω, "want, wish"; ἀθετῆσαι, aor. act. inf. of ἀθετέω, "reject"; complementary inf. Mark's use of διὰ τοὺς ὅρκους καὶ τοὺς ἀνακειμένους may be an example of hendiadys, a figure of speech in which the conj. καί coordinates two ideas even though one is a further clarification of the other and dependent on it ("on account of his oaths in the presence of his dinner guests," cf. BDF §442; T 335–36; Z §460).

6:27 Ἀποστείλας, nom. sg. masc. of aor. act. ptc. of ἀποστέλλω, "send"; temp. adv. ptc. antecedent; σπεκουλάτορα, acc. sg. masc. of σπεκουλάτωρ, -ορος, ὁ, "bodyguard, executioner"; ἐπέταξεν, 3rd sg. aor. act. indic. of ἐπιτάσσω, "order, command"; ἐνέγκαι, aor. act. inf. of φέρω, "bring"; indir. discourse inf.; ἀπελθών, nom. sg. masc. of aor. act. ptc. of ἀπέρχομαι, "depart, go away"; temp. adv. ptc. antecedent; ἀπεκεφάλισεν, 3rd sg. aor. act. indic. of ἀποκεφαλίζω, "behead." The term σπεκουλάτωρ (a Lat. loanword) does not refer specifically to an official executioner but rather to a member of a group of bodyguards who could be called on to do all sorts of "dirty business" for the ruler, including executions (Marcus 1:397; Spicq 3:157–59; cf. Tacitus, *Histories* 1:24–25, 2.11; Suetonius, *Claudius* 35; Seneca, *On Anger* 1.18.4).

6:28 Ἤνεγκεν, 3rd sg. aor. act. indic. of φέρω, "bring"; πίνακι, dat. sg. masc. of πίναξ, -ακος, ὁ, "platter"; ἔδωκεν, 3rd sg. aor. act. indic. of δίδωμι, "give"; both κορασίῳ (dat. sg. neut.) and κοράσιον (nom. sg. neut.) are from κοράσιον, -ου, τό, "girl." Although Herodias was the one who manipulated the circumstances to bring about John the Baptist's execution, Herod was the one who bore the sense of guilt (6:16). Indeed, he was the ruler, although one who could not control himself and would not protect the righteous.

6:29 Ἀκούσαντες, nom. pl. masc. of aor. act. ptc. of ἀκούω, "hear, receive news" (cf. LN 33.212); temp. adv. ptc. antecedent; ἦλθον, 3rd pl. aor. act. indic. of ἔρχομαι, "come, go"; ἦραν, 3rd pl. aor. act. indic. of αἴρω, "take, take away"; πτῶμα, acc. sg. neut. of πτῶμα, -ατος, τό, "corpse, dead body"; ἔθηκαν, 3rd pl. aor. act. indic. of τίθημι, "lay, place." The vocabulary used for John the Baptist's burial is strikingly similar to the wording used for Jesus's burial by Joseph of Arimathea, with one major difference being that Jesus is not buried by his disciples. Other than that one difference, both scenes involve the receiving of a dead body (πτῶμα in 6:29; 15:45), which is then placed (ἔθηκαν/ἔθηκεν in 6:29; 15:46) in a tomb (ἐν μνημείῳ in 6:29; 15:46). In fact, the whole story of John's fate serves as a foreshadowing of what would happen to Jesus.

HOMILETICAL SUGGESTIONS

The Master and the Mission (6:7–29)

1. What do we learn about Jesus?
   a. Jesus wants to extend his ministry through his followers. (6:7–13)
   b. Jesus takes the path of sacrifice like his forerunner. (6:14–29)
2. What do we learn about the mission?
   a. The mission continues the work of Jesus. (6:7, 12–13)
   b. The mission demands an attitude of urgent obedience. (6:8–10)
   c. The mission faces opposition.
      (1) Some will not listen. (6:11)
      (2) Some will violently oppose. (6:14–29)

Herod's Recipe for a Disastrous Life (6:14–29)

1. A king who can't control himself
2. A protector who can't watch over the righteous
3. A guilt-ridden man who can't identify his Savior

3. Cycle 2: Walking on the Sea (6:30–56)

In the second boat scene, Jesus walks on the water (6:45–52). Once again, the disciples respond to the miraculous power of Jesus with a lack of understanding and fear. According to Mark, they have hardened hearts. As with the previous boat scene, this second one is preceded by Jesus's ministry toward the crowd—his teaching and feeding of a crowd of five thousand (6:30–44). In addition, like the previous pattern, the second boat scene is followed by Jesus's healing ministry, this time in a summary of Jesus's healing work at Gennesaret (6:53–56).

(a) Jesus's Ministry to the Crowd: Feeding of the 5,000 (6:30–44)

6:30 The return of the disciples from their mission closes out the previous section, wrapping the account concerning the mission of the Twelve around the story about Herod and John the Baptist (see 6:7). However, Mark 6:30 also opens up the next scene, since the return of the Twelve causes Jesus to seek a time of rest for them, which in turn leads to Jesus's unplanned ministry to the crowd. Therefore, as often happens in Mark, a historical pres. vb. indicates the beginning of a new scene (συνάγονται; see also λέγει in 6:31; on the historical pres., see 1:12). One result of the smooth transition between the previous passage and this account of Jesus's feeding of the 5,000 is that the banquet of the foolish and violent King Herod stands more starkly in contrast with the banquet of Jesus, the compassionate Shepherd who cares for his people and who expects his disciples to reflect this same care. Συνάγονται, 3rd pl. pres. pass. indic. of συνάγω, "gather together, assemble" (the pass. of συνάγω can express an act. intrans. sense: "come together, gather" [BDAG 962d; Voelz 1:414]); ἀπήγγειλαν, 3rd pl. aor. act. indic. of ἀπαγγέλλω, "report, announce"; ὅσα, see 11:24; ἐποίησαν, 3rd pl. aor. act. indic. of ποιέω, "do"; ἐδίδαξαν, 3rd pl. aor. act. indic. of διδάσκω, "teach" (on translating the aor. in indir. discourse with an Eng. pluperf., see 5:16).

6:31 Δεῦτε, adv. functioning as an impv. particle, "come!" (BDAG 220c); ἀναπαύσασθε, 2nd pl. aor. mid. impv. of ἀναπαύω, "rest" (mng. with mid.). The intensive pron. αὐτοί modifies the subj. ὑμεῖς in order to highlight that the commands are for the disciples alone (ὑμεῖς αὐτοί, "you by yourselves"; BDAG 152d; cf. Z §198), a point that is emphasized again by the idiom κατ' ἰδίαν ("privately, alone"; BDAG 467c; ZG 123; the same phrase appears again in 6:32). The command to rest is modified by ὀλίγον, a neut. acc. form of the adj. ὀλίγος that is functioning as an adv. ("for a little while"; BDAG 703a; Porter, Idioms 121–22; R 487–88). Ἐρχόμενοι, nom. pl. masc. of pres. mid. ptc. of dep. ἔρχομαι, "come"; subst. ptc.; ὑπάγοντες, nom. pl. masc. of pres. act. ptc. of ὑπάγω, "go, depart"; subst. ptc.; ἦσαν, 3rd pl. impf. act. indic. of εἰμί, "be"; εὐκαίρουν, 3rd pl. impf. act. indic. of εὐκαιρέω, "have time, have opportunity"; φαγεῖν, aor. act. inf. of ἐσθίω, "eat"; inf. of purpose.

6:32 Ἀπῆλθον, 3rd pl. aor. act. indic. of ἀπέρχομαι, "depart, go away." Mark's reference to the boat (τῷ πλοίῳ) picks up an important motif that runs throughout Mark 4:1–8:26, a section that shows Jesus and his disciples traveling back and forth across the Sea of Galilee in a boat. In light of this continuing motif, the use of the art. with "the boat" is probably anaphoric; it points back to the boat that has already appeared repeatedly in the narrative.

6:33 Εἶδον, 3rd pl. aor. act. indic. of ὁράω, "see"; ὑπάγοντας, acc. pl. masc. of pres. act. ptc. of ὑπάγω, "go, depart"; supplementary (complementary) ptc. (see 1:10). The subj. of εἶδον is probably indef. in light of the freq. use of indef. 3rd pl vbs. in Mark ("people saw"; see 1:22). As a result, πολλοί is the subj. of just ἐπέγνωσαν (Cranfield 215; Taylor 320), and the following vbs.—συνέδραμον and προῆλθον—are likely also indef. pl. vbs. ("many recognized . . . and people ran together . . . and arrived before"). Ἐπέγνωσαν, 3rd pl. aor. act. indic. of ἐπιγινώσκω, "recognize"; πεζῇ, adv. mng. "by land, on foot"; συνέδραμον, 3rd pl. aor. act. indic. of συντρέχω, "run together"; προῆλθον, 3rd pl. aor. act. indic. of προέρχομαι, "go on ahead of, arrive before."

6:34 Ἐξελθών, nom. sg. masc. of aor. act. ptc. of ἐξέρχομαι, "come out, disembark"; temp. adv. ptc. antecedent; εἶδεν, 3rd sg. aor. act. indic. of ὁράω, "see." The adj. πολύν is attrib. modifying the anar. noun ὄχλον (πολύς can mean "large, great" when used with a noun like ὄχλος that denotes a plurality [BDAG 848c]; that ὄχλος is a collective sg. noun also explains how it serves as the antecedent to the pl. pron. αὐτούς). Ἐσπλαγχνίσθη, 3rd sg. aor. pass. indic. of dep. σπλαγχνίζομαι, "have pity, have compassion." The vb. σπλαγχνίζομαι occurs twelve times in the NT, with all of these uses appearing in the Synoptic Gospels. The related noun σπλάγχνον occurs eleven times in the NT, with only one of the uses appearing in the Synoptic Gospels (Luke 1:78). The pl. form of the noun, σπλάγχνα, when used lit., means "entrails, inward parts" (e.g., Acts 1:18). However, such inner body parts came to be viewed as the source and seat of human emotions, and therefore σπλάγχνα came to be used metaphorically for compassion or affection (BDAG 938c–d; *NIDNTTE* 4:351–52). In Mark's Gospel, the vb. σπλαγχνίζομαι refers exclusively to the deep sense of compassion that Jesus had for needy people, an emotional response that caused him to act on their behalf (1:41; 6:34; 8:2; 9:22). Ἦσαν, 3rd pl. impf. act. indic. of εἰμί, "be"; ἔχοντα, nom. pl. neut. of pres. act. ptc. of ἔχω, "have"; adj. ptc. without an art. modifying an anar. noun (cf. Voelz 1:419); ποιμένα, acc. sg. masc. of ποιμήν, -ένος, ὁ, "shepherd"; ἤρξατο, 3rd sg. aor. mid. indic. of ἄρχω, "begin" (mng. with mid.; on ἄρχομαι, see 1:45); διδάσκειν, pres. act. inf. of διδάσκω, "teach"; complementary inf. The adj. πολλά may be functioning either subst. as the obj. of the thing in a dbl. acc. cstr. ("he began to teach them many things"; BDAG 848a) or adv. to intensify the action ("he began to teach them earnestly" or "he began to teach them at length"; BDF §155; cf. Cranfield 217; Voelz 1:419).

6:35 Γενομένης, gen. sg. fem. of aor. mid. ptc. of dep. γίνομαι, "become, come to be"; gen. abs.; temp. adv. ptc. antecedent; προσελθόντες, nom. pl. masc. of aor. act. ptc. of προσέρχομαι, "approach, come to"; temp. adv. ptc. antecedent; αὐτῷ, dat. dir. obj. of προσελθόντες; on the impf. of λέγω, see 2:16 (in addition, on the historical pres. of λέγω, such as in 6:37, 38, see 1:30); ὅτι, introduces dir. discourse; ἔρημός, pred. adj.; ὁ τόπος, "this place" (when the art. points to something that is present at the time of speaking, it can function like a dem. pron. [Wallace 221]). The idiomatic phrase ὥρας πολλῆς (lit. "much hour") points to a time that is "very late," given the circumstances (LN 67.77). It was considerably past the time when these people should have eaten.

6:36 Ἀπόλυσον, 2nd sg. aor. act. impv. of ἀπολύω, "let go, send away, dismiss." The use of the aor. tense for the impv. ἀπόλυσον fits the pattern for how Mark uses impv. forms elsewhere (see 2:11). Aor. impv. forms appear for specific commands in concrete situations (see also δότε in 6:37, ἴδετε in 6:38, and the use of the inf. ἀνακλῖναι for an indir. command in 6:39 [on the inf., cf. Fanning 384]; the pres. impv. of ὑπάγω, such as ὑπάγετε in 6:38, serves as a common exception [see 2:11]). Ἀπελθόντες, nom. pl. masc. of aor. act. ptc. of ἀπέρχομαι, "depart, go away"; attendant circumstance ptc.; κύκλῳ, dat. of κύκλος ("circle"), which became fixed in form as an adv., although it functions in this context as an adj. mng. "nearby, surrounding" (BDAG 574b–c; Harris 247); ἀγοράσωσιν, 3rd pl. aor. act. subjunc. of ἀγοράζω, "buy, purchase"; subjunc. in a purpose ἵνα clause. The subjunc. mood in an indir. question retains the mood that was used in the dir. question (R 1043–44; BDF §368; T 116–17; Wallace 478). Therefore τί φάγωσιν (3rd pl. aor. act. subjunc. of ἐσθίω, "eat") represents an indir. delib. question (the dir. delib. question would have been: "What should we eat?"). An indir. delib. question creates a somewhat awkward sentence structure in Eng. ("in order that they might buy for themselves what they should eat") and may need to be smoothed out in translation ("in order that they might buy for themselves something to eat"; cf. Wallace 478).

6:37 On ὁ δέ, see 1:45 (the same use of the art is in 6:38); ἀποκριθείς, nom. sg. masc. of aor. pass. ptc. of dep. ἀποκρίνομαι, "answer"; redundant ptc.; δότε, 2nd pl. aor. act. impv. of δίδωμι, "give." The nom. pers. pron. ὑμεῖς, which, in light of the ending of the impv. vb., is grammatically unnecessary, seems to be included in this context for the sake of emph. (T 37; Marcus 1:407; cf. Wallace 321–23; see also the discussion at 13:9). The focus is on the disciples; the task belongs to them. The inf. φαγεῖν (aor. act. inf. of ἐσθίω, "eat"), which appears twice in the verse, is an epex. inf., i.e., an inf. that serves to clarify, explain, or qualify a noun (cf. Wallace 607; KMP 372). However, in 6:37, the noun is only implied and must be supplied when translating into Eng. ("something to eat" or "food to eat"). Ἀπελθόντες, nom. pl. masc. of aor. act. ptc. of ἀπέρχομαι, "depart, go away"; attendant circumstance ptc. (Wallace 644); ἀγοράσωμεν, 1st pl. aor. act. subjunc. of ἀγοράζω, "buy, purchase"; delib. subjunc. (T 98); δηναρίων, gen. pl. neut. of δηνάριον, -ου, τό, "denarius"; διακοσίων, gen. pl. neut. of διακόσιοι, -αι, -α, "two hundred"; gen. of price (Wallace 122; KMP 103; Cranfield 217; Voelz 1:421); δώσομεν, 1st pl. fut. act. indic. of δίδωμι, "give"). The vb. δώσομεν is a delib. fut., expressing not a question of fact but a question about what should be done. The extent to which the delib. aor. subjunc. and the delib. fut. indic. overlap in mng. is made clear by the way Mark coordinates ἀγοράσωμεν and δώσομεν with καί (R 875–76, 934; Wallace 465–66, 570). A denarius was the standard silver coin during Jesus's time, and, according to Matt 20:2, it was an acceptable daily wage for a common laborer (cf. LN 6.75; *EDNT* 1:296).

6:38 The disciples only had meager provisions for such a large crowd, but when they put what they had in Jesus's hands, it became sufficient. Ὑπάγετε, 2nd pl. pres. act. impv. of ὑπάγω, "go, depart"; ἴδετε, 2nd pl. aor. act. impv. of ὁράω, "see"; γνόντες, nom. pl. masc. of aor. act. ptc. of γινώσκω, "find out" (LN 27.2); temp. adv. ptc. antecedent; ἰχθύας, acc. pl. masc. of ἰχθύς, -ύος, ὁ, "fish."

6:39 Ἐπέταξεν, 3rd sg. aor. act. indic. of ἐπιτάσσω, "order, command"; αὐτοῖς, dat. dir. obj., with the pron. referring to the disciples; ἀνακλῖναι, aor. act. inf. of ἀνακλίνω, "cause to recline for a meal, place as guest" (BDAG 65b); inf. of indir. discourse (R 1084); πάντας, dir. obj. of ἀνακλῖναι (since ἀνακλίνω is trans.). Jesus's instructions included having the people sit in groups (συμπόσια, nom. pl. neut. of συμπόσιον, -ου, τό, "group sharing a meal, group of people eating together"). The repetition of συμπόσια συμπόσια has a distributive force, indicating a number of groups distributed over a particular area ("in groups" or "group by group"; cf. BDF §493; BDAG 959d; LN11.5, n. 3). According to the form, the case of συμπόσια could be either nom. or acc., but in context, nom. is the more likely. In the next verse (6:40), Mark uses a similar distributive expression, πρασιαὶ πρασιαί, which is clearly nom. The nom. case of συμπόσια, as well as that of πρασιαί in the following verse, is perhaps best explained as a parenthetic nom. (R 460, cf. also 487), i.e., a nom. in a parenthetical clause or phrase that appears within a sentence that has a different nom. subj. (cf. Wallace 53–54). Χλωρῷ, dat. sg. masc. of χλωρός, -ά, -ό, "green"; χόρτῳ, dat. sg. masc. of χόρτος, -ου, ὁ, "grass."

6:40 Ἀνέπεσαν, 3rd pl. aor. act. indic. of ἀναπίπτω, "recline at a meal, sit down to eat." To describe the scene of the crowd sitting down to eat, Mark uses πρασιαί (nom. pl. fem. of πρασιά, -ᾶς, ἡ), which lit. means "garden plot, garden bed" (BDAG 860b; MM 533). The picture is of the crowd sitting down arranged in regular patterns in such a way that the whole scene looked like garden plots (cf. MM 533; on the distributive sense for the repetition of πρασιαί and on the use of the nom., see 6:39). The use of κατά with numbers can express a distributive sense, dividing the whole into parts (BDAG 512b–c suggests "in hundreds and in fifties"; both ἑκατόν ["one hundred"] and πεντήκοντα ["fifty"] are indecl. numbers; on the distributive use of κατά, see also BDF §248; R 673; Porter, *Idioms* 164).

6:41 Λαβών, nom. sg. masc. of aor. act. ptc. of λαμβάνω, "take, receive"; temp. adv. ptc. antecedent; ἰχθύας, acc. pl. masc. of ἰχθύς, -ύος, ὁ, "fish" (ἰχθύας appears twice in 6:41); ἀναβλέψας, nom. sg. masc. of aor. act. ptc. of ἀναβλέπω, "look up"; temp. adv. ptc. antecedent; εὐλόγησεν, 3rd sg. aor. act indic. of εὐλογέω, "bless, offer a blessing, give thanks." Since Jesus looked up to heaven before the blessing, the blessing was apparently directed toward God (i.e., that Jesus expressed thanks to God for the bread, rather than that Jesus blessed or consecrated the bread; for both options, see BDAG 408a–b; on Jesus's blessing as directed toward God, see Cranfield 219). Κατέκλασεν, 3rd sg. aor. act. indic. of κατακλάω, "break in pieces, break thoroughly" (see 1:36 on the use of κατά as a prep. prefix to create a compound vb. that expresses intensive and completed action); ἐδίδου, 3rd sg. impf. act. indic. of δίδωμι, "give." The switch in tense to the impf. with ἐδίδου, esp. in a context in which a large crowd is being served, expresses a repeated action, that Jesus went on giving bread to the disciples over and over again (iter. impf.; cf. T 67; ZG 124; Stein 317). Παρατιθῶσιν, 3rd pl. pres. act. subjunc. of παρατίθημι, "set before, serve"; subjunc. in a purpose ἵνα clause; ἐμέρισεν, 3rd sg. aor. act. indic. of μερίζω, "divide, distribute."

6:42 Ἔφαγον, 3rd pl. aor. act. indic. of ἐσθίω, "eat"; ἐχορτάσθησαν, 3rd pl. aor. pass. indic. of χορτάζω, "feed, fill, satisfy." The vb. χορτάζω is used in contexts in which people (or animals) eat to the point of being full or satisfied (MM 690; *EDNT* 3:470). To hunger (using the act. of πεινάω) sometimes stands as the opposite of what it means to be satisfied (using the pass. of χορτάζω; e.g., Luke 6:21; Phil 4:12). For Mark to say that the crowd was filled means that no one left hungry or wanting more.

6:43 Ἦραν, 3rd pl. aor. act. indic. of αἴρω, "take up, pick up"; κλάσματα, acc. pl. neut. of κλάσμα, -ατος, τό, "fragment, piece"; κοφίνων, gen. pl. masc. of κόφινος, -ου, ὁ, "basket" (δώδεκα, which modifies κοφίνων, is indecl.); πληρώματα, acc. pl. neut. of πλήρωμα, -ατος, τό, "that which is enough to fill," BDAG 829c. Mark's somewhat awkward syntax is best explained as follows: πληρώματα is acc. because it stands in appos. to the dir. obj. κλάσματα, and the gen. κοφίνων is syntactically related to πληρώματα as an obj. gen. (cf. Rom 13:10; 1 Cor 10:26 for a similar use of the gen. after πλήρωμα). "They took up fragments, enough to fill twelve baskets." Ἰχθύων, gen. pl. masc. of ἰχθύς, -ύος, ὁ, "fish." The prep. ἀπό expresses a partitive idea and creates a subst. phrase by assuming an indef. pron. such as τινας ("some of the fish"; cf. T 208–9). The type of basket mentioned by Mark in 6:43 (κόφινος) was distinguishable from other baskets not by its size—it could be of various sizes—but by its association with the Jewish people (LSJ 988; MM 357; Marcus 1:411; cf. Juvenal, *Satires* 3.14; 6.542). Mark's mention of Jewish baskets fits the context of this miraculous feeding, since it apparently took place on the side of the Sea of Galilee with a predominantly Jewish population in contrast to the feeding of the 4,000 (8:1–10), which took place on the side of the Sea of Galilee with a predominantly Gentile population.

6:44 Φαγόντες, nom. pl. masc. of aor. act. ptc. of ἐσθίω, "eat"; subst. ptc. (cf. ESV; CSB); ἦσαν, 3rd pl. impf. act. indic. of εἰμί, "be"; πεντακισχίλιοι, nom. pl. masc. of πεντακισχίλιοι, -αι, -α, "five thousand." In pointing out the extent of the crowd, Mark does not use a term for people in general (e.g., ἄνθρωποι; cf. BDAG 81a–b) but rather, one for adult males more specifically (ἄνδρες; cf. BDAG 79b–c). The presence of women and children at the scene undoubtedly would have made the size of the crowd considerably larger (cf. Matt 14:21).

FOR FURTHER STUDY

21. The Feeding Miracles

Bammel, E. "The Feeding of the Multitude." Pages 211–40 in *Jesus and the Politics of His Day*. Edited by Ernst Bammel and C. F. D. Moule. Cambridge: Cambridge University Press, 1984.

*Bassler, Jouette M. "The Parable of the Loaves." *JR* 66 (1986): 157–72.

Boobyer, G. H. "The Eucharistic Interpretation of the Miracles of the Loaves in St. Mark's Gospel." *JTS* 3 (1952): 161–71.

———. "The Miracles of the Loaves and the Gentiles in St. Mark's Gospel." *SJT* 6 (1953): 77–87.

Donfried, Karl Paul. "The Feeding Narratives and the Marcan Community: Mark 6,30–45 and 8,1–10." Pages 95–103 in *Kirche: Festschrift für Günther Bornkamm zum 75. Geburtstag*. Edited by Dieter Lührmann and Georg Strecker. Tübingen: Mohr Siebeck, 1980.

Fowler, Robert M. *Loaves and Fishes: The Function of the Feeding Stories in the Gospel of Mark*. SBLDS 54. Chico, CA: Scholars Press, 1981.

Henderson, Suzanne Watts. "'Concerning the Loaves': Comprehending Incomprehension in Mark 6.45–52." *JSNT* 83 (2001): 3–26.

Masuda, Sanae. "The Good News of the Miracle of the Bread: The Tradition and Its Markan Redaction." *NTS* 28 (1982): 191–219.

Montefiore, Hugh. "Revolt in the Desert? (Mark vi. 30ff.)." *NTS* 8 (1961–62): 135–41.

HOMILETICAL SUGGESTIONS

The Good Shepherd (6:30–44)

1. What do we learn about Jesus?
   a. Jesus viewed people as sheep without a shepherd, requiring his leadership and care.
   b. Jesus viewed his disciples as co-shepherds, extending his compassion to others.
2. What do we learn about serving Jesus?
   a. We must view people as Jesus does—they need his care.
   b. We must view our inadequacies as Jesus does—we need his empowerment.

(b) Second Boat Scene: Walking on the Water (6:45–52)

6:45 The second boat scene in Mark's Gospel, like the first (4:35–41), highlights Jesus's miraculous authority and the disciples' inability to comprehend the extent of Jesus's power and care for them. Ἠνάγκασεν, 3rd sg. aor. act. indic. of ἀναγκάζω, "urge, press" (BDAG 60c); ἐμβῆναι, aor. act. inf. of ἐμβαίνω, "embark"; indir. discourse inf.; προάγειν, pres. act. inf. of προάγω, "go before, go ahead, precede"; indir. discourse inf.; εἰς, "to" (used in place of πρός [Z §97]); πέραν, an adv. with the art. functioning as a subst., "the shore/land on the other side" (BDAG 796d). The clause ἕως αὐτὸς ἀπολύει τὸν ὄχλον continues the indir. discourse that started with the preceding two infinitives (cf. Burton §328; Voelz 1:433–34): "while he dismissed the crowd" (on ἕως as "while," see BDAG 423c; LN 67.139). The vb. ἀπολύει is in the pres. tense because in Gk. reported speech retains the tense of the vb. in the dir. statement (ZG 125; cf. Wallace 457, 537–38; on translating reported speech, see 2:1).

6:46 Ἀποταξάμενος, nom. sg. masc. of aor. mid. ptc. of ἀποτάσσω, "say good-bye to, take leave of" (mng. with mid.); temp. adv. ptc. antecedent; αὐτοῖς, dat. dir. obj.; ἀπῆλθεν, 3rd sg. aor. act. indic. of ἀπέρχομαι, "depart, go away"; προσεύξασθαι, aor.

mid. inf. of dep. προσεύχομαι, "pray"; purpose inf. Since the previous verse ends with Jesus planning to dismiss the crowd, the pron. αὐτοῖς probably refers to the crowd rather than to the disciples. Therefore, the antecedent of the pl. pron. αὐτοῖς is the collective sg. noun ὄχλον, so that the agreement is according to sense rather than strict grammatical number (R 684; T 40).

6:47 Mark uses the gen. abs. const. ὀψίας γενομένης "when evening came" (ὀψίας, gen. sg. fem. of ὀψία, -ας, ἡ, "evening"; γενομένης, gen. sg. fem. of aor. mid. ptc. of dep. γίνομαι, "come to be, come" [BDAG 197c]; gen. abs. ptc.; temp. adv. ptc. antecedent) five times in his Gospel (1:32; 4:35; 6:47; 14:17; 15:42). Mark employs this expression as a general time reference, which—if necessary for the story—he will then clarify with more specific time references in the context (cf. the reference to "around the fourth watch of the night" in 6:48). Ἦν, 3rd sg. impf. act. indic. of εἰμί, "be."

6:48 Ἰδών, nom. sg. masc. of aor. act. ptc. of ὁράω, "see"; temp. adv. ptc. antecedent; βασανιζομένους, acc. pl. masc. of pres. pass. ptc. of βασανίζω, "torment, harass"; supplementary (complementary) ptc. (see 1:10); ἐλαύνειν, pres. act. inf. of ἐλαύνω, "drive, row, row a boat"; inf. of contemp. time ("as they were rowing the boat"); ἦν, 3rd sg. impf. act. indic. of εἰμί, "be"; ἐναντίος, nom. sg. masc. of ἐναντίος, -α, -ον, "against, contrary"; αὐτοῖς, use of dat. after certain adj. (cf. R 537; Wallace 174); τετάρτην, acc. sg. fem. of τέταρτος, -η, -ον, "fourth"; νυκτός, gen. of time (Wallace 124; KMP 99); ἔρχεται, 3rd sg. pres. mid. indic. of dep. ἔρχομαι, "come, go"; historical pres. (used with vb. of motion to show someone changing location in a scene [see 1:12]); περιπατῶν, nom. sg. masc. of pres. act. ptc. of περιπατέω, "walk"; adv. ptc. of means. The time reference, "the fourth watch of the night," follows the Roman custom of dividing the time between 6:00 p.m. and 6:00 a.m. into four equal periods or "watches," so-called because those responsible for security were divided into four groups and assigned the task of standing guard during one of the four time periods (BDAG 1067d; cf. 13:35). Since the fourth watch was from 3:00 to 6:00 a.m., translations such as "shortly before dawn" (NIV) or "as the night was ending" (NET) seek to communicate the time frame in Eng.

The OT provides an important background for understanding Jesus's action of walking on the water (cf. Marcus 1:431–32; Edwards 198). Jesus is acting with divine power (cf. 2:7), because it is God alone who walks on the waves of the sea (Job 9:8; cf. Job 38:16; Hab 3:15), who makes his way through the sea and his path through mighty waters (Isa 43:16). The OT also helps to make sense of the otherwise puzzling note that Jesus wanted to pass by his disciples (ἤθελεν, 3rd sg. impf. act. indic. of θέλω, "want, wish"; παρελθεῖν, aor. act. inf. of παρέρχομαι, "pass by"; complementary inf.). The language is similar to that used for God's revelation of his glory to Moses (Exod 33:17–34:8; cf. Marcus 1:426; Yarbro Collins 334). In response to Moses's request to see God's glory, the Lord places him in the cleft of a rock and covers him with his hand, while his glory passes by (Exod 33:19, 22; 34:6; cf. 1 Kgs 19:11–13; Job 9:11). For Jesus to want to pass by his disciples, therefore, means that he desired to reveal his glory to them.

6:49 On οἱ δέ, see 1:45 (the same use for the art. appears with ὁ δέ in 6:50). Ἰδόντες, nom. pl. masc. of aor. act. ptc. of ὁράω, "see"; temp. adv. ptc. antecedent; περιπατοῦντα, acc. sg. masc. of pres. act. ptc. of περιπατέω, "walk"; supplementary (complementary) ptc.; ἔδοξαν, 3rd pl. aor. act. indic. of δοκέω, "think, suppose"; φάντασμα, nom. sg. neut. of φάντασμα, -ατος, τό, ghost; ἀνέκραξαν, 3rd pl. aor. act. indic. of ἀνακράζω, "cry out." The conj. ὅτι introduces indir. discourse, and the pres. tense vb. in the clause (ἐστιν) retains the tense of the orig. thought (Wallace 539; cf. R 1029; on translating reported speech, see 2:1).

6:50 Εἶδον, 3rd pl. aor. act. indic. of ὁράω, "see"; ἐταράχθησαν, 3rd pl. aor. pass. indic. of ταράσσω, "be troubled, frightened, terrified" (mng. with pass.); ἐλάλησεν, 3rd sg. aor. act. indic. of λαλέω, "speak"; λέγει, historical pres. (with λέγω; see 1:12, 30); θαρσεῖτε, 2nd pl. pres. act. impv. of θαρσέω, "have courage, take courage"; φοβεῖσθε, 2nd pl. pres. pass. impv. of φοβέομαι, "fear, be afraid." The vb. θαρσέω, when used as an impv., appears consistently in the pres. tense, apparently as a fixed idiom (Fanning 348–50). The vb. φοβέομαι, when used in a prohibition, appears with both the pres. impv. (e.g., Matt 28:10; Acts 18:9; Rev 1:17) and the aor. subjunc. (e.g., Matt 1:20; 10:26; 1 Pet 3:14). When used with the pres. impv. for a specific command in a given situation, the prohibition is directed toward those who are clearly already afraid (e.g., Matt 17:7; Luke 1:13; 2:10; Rev 1:17) or who at least have good reason to be afraid (Mark 5:36; Acts 27:24; Rev 2:10). In this way, the use of the pres. impv. with φοβέομαι in specific prohibitions functions as a command to stop being afraid (cf. Fanning 337).

At times, the phrase ἐγώ εἰμι can express simple identification (e.g., John 9:9). Nevertheless, by using ἐγώ εἰμι, Mark has Jesus express himself in a way that can potentially communicate more than just mere identification ("It is I."). Given the significant number of OT allusions in this passage, it is possible that Mark's quotation of Jesus's words as ἐγώ εἰμι conveys a deeper significance, calling to mind God's revelation of his name as "I am" to Moses (Exod 3:14; cf. Lane 237; Marcus 1:427; Stein 326).

6:51 Ἀνέβη, 3rd sg. aor. act. indic. of ἀναβαίνω, "go up, climb up"; ἐκόπασεν, 3rd sg. aor. act. indic. of κοπάζω, "rest, cease." In order to communicate the extent of the disciples' amazement, Mark modifies the main vb. ἐξίσταντο (3rd pl. impf. mid. indic. of ἐξίστημι, "be amazed, be astonished" [mng. with mid.]; on vbs. of amazement, see 1:22) with two adv. expressions: λίαν (adv. indicating a high degree, "exceedingly") and ἐκ περισσοῦ (περισσοῦ is the gen. sg. neut. of περισσός, -ή, -όν, "abundant," used idiomatically as the obj. of ἐκ in an adv. phrase mng. "extremely," BDAG, 298b; cf. LN 78.20). The 1st adv. expression λίαν is strengthened by the 2nd adv. expression ἐκ περισσοῦ, so that the entire phrase can mean "altogether" (BDAG 594b).

6:52 Συνῆκαν, 3rd pl. aor. act. indic. of συνίημι, "understand, comprehend." The prep. ἐπί with the dat. points here to the basis on which the disciples should have been able to come to an understanding (BDAG 364d; for similar uses of ἐπί with the dat., see 1:22; 3:5; 10:22, 24). The point is not that the disciples failed to make sense of the loaves but that they failed to understand Jesus and the nature of his authority based on what he did with the loaves. Ἦν, 3rd sg. impf. act. indic. of εἰμί, "be"; πεπωρωμένη, nom. sg. fem. of pf. pass. ptc. of πωρόω, "harden"; periph. ptc. (on hardness of heart, see 3:5). Mark uses a pluperf. periph. cstr. several times to emphasize certain results or a certain state that existed in the past (perhaps best expressed with the past tense in Eng.; see 1:33). The sg. noun καρδία has a distributive sense in 6:52, the heart that belongs to each one of the disciples (T 23; cf. R 409). Most EVV communicate this distributive sense by translating the sg. καρδία with the pl. "hearts" (NKJV and NASB keep the sg.).

HOMILETICAL SUGGESTIONS

Tripping over Jesus's Walk on the Water (6:45–52)

1. What do we learn about Jesus?
   a. Jesus went out of his way to be alone with God.
   b. Yet Jesus also acts in a way that God alone can act.
   c. And Jesus also speaks in a way that God alone can speak.
2. What do we learn about a life of faith?
   a. Don't underestimate what Jesus can do for you.
   b. Don't underestimate what Jesus has already done for you in the past.

(c) Healing at Gennesaret (6:53–56)

6:53 Just as earlier in the narrative (6:33), people recognize Jesus, causing a crowd to gather. Jesus's response is the same, to serve those who come to him with compassion (6:34), esp. this time with his healing ministry. Διαπεράσαντες, nom. pl. masc. of aor. act. ptc. of διαπεράω, "cross over"; temp. adv. ptc. antecedent; ἦλθον, 3rd pl. aor. act. indic. of ἔρχομαι, "come, go"; προσωρμίσθησαν, 3rd pl. aor. pass. indic. of προσορμίζω, "come into harbor, anchor, tie up a boat" (mng. with pass.).

6:54 Mark 6:54 includes two adv. participles, the first of which is a gen. abs. ptc. Both are syntactically related to the main vb. that does not appear until the following verse (περιέδραμον). Ἐξελθόντων, gen. pl. masc. of aor. act. ptc. of ἐξέρχομαι, "come out, disembark"; gen. abs.; temp. adv. ptc. antecedent; ἐπιγνόντες, nom. pl. masc. of aor. act. ptc. of ἐπιγινώσκω, "recognize"; temp. adv. ptc. antecedent.

6:55 Περιέδραμον, 3rd pl. aor. act. indic. of περιτρέχω, "run about, run throughout" (on indef. pl. vbs., see 1:22); ἤρξαντο, 3rd pl. aor. mid. indic. of ἄρχω, "begin" (mng. with mid.; on ἄρχομαι, see 1:45); κραβάττοις, dat. pl. masc. of κράβαττος, -ου, ὁ, "mattress, pallet, bed, mat"; κακῶς, adv. mng. "badly," but used idiomatically with ἔχω to mean "be ill, be sick," BDAG 502b (see the discussion at 1:32); ἔχοντας, acc. pl. masc. of pres. act. ptc. of ἔχω, "have"; subst. ptc.; περιφέρειν, pres. act. inf. of περιφέρω, "carry about, carry here and there"; complementary inf.; ἤκουον, 3rd pl. impf. act. indic. of ἀκούω, "hear"; ἐστίν, on the retained pres. in indir. discourse, see 2:1. In this context, the impf. tense of ἤκουον seems to indicate simultaneous action (for a similar use of the impf., see 5:28). The impf. vb. points back to the conversation that was going on at the same time that people were rushing around and gathering the sick, that is, a conversation about where Jesus might be (cf. Fanning 288–89).

6:56 Mark uses the indef. rel. adv. ὅπου ἄν ("wherever"; see 9:18), which, when followed by an impf. indic., introduces a repeated action in the past (BDAG 717b; R 969; T 92–93; Voelz 1:6, 446; cf. the impf. indic. with ὅταν in 3:11). The other impf. vbs. in the verse are also iter., since they point to actions that happened in various places (on the impf. for repeated action, see 1:21). Εἰσεπορεύετο, 3rd sg. impf. mid. indic. of dep. εἰσπορεύομαι, "go into, enter"; ἀγρούς, "farm settlements" (see LN 1.93); ἀγοραῖς, dat. pl. fem. of ἀγορά, -ᾶς, ἡ, "marketplace"; ἐτίθεσαν, 3rd pl. impf. act. indic. of τίθημι, "lay, place"; ἀσθενοῦντας, acc. pl. masc. of pres. act. ptc. of ἀσθενέω, "be sick"; subst. ptc.; παρεκάλουν, 3rd pl. impf. act. indic. of παρακαλέω, "implore, entreat, beg"; κἄν, particle formed through the combination of καί and ἐάν mng. "even if only, at least, even just" when used without a vb. (BDAG 507b; R 208, 1025; ZG 126); κρασπέδου, gen. sg. neut. of κράσπεδον, -ου, ὁ, "hem, tassel"; gen. dir. obj. The noun κράσπεδον appears in the pl. in the LXX (Num 15:38–39; Deut 22:12) and in the NT (Matt 23:5) for the tassels worn by Jewish men at the four corners of their garments (*TDNT* 3:904; Marcus 1:437; Stein 332), which were intended to remind them to obey God's commands and to be set apart as holy to God (Num 15:40). Ἱματίου, partitive gen.; ἅψωνται, 3rd pl. aor. mid. subjunc. of ἅπτω, "touch" (mng. with mid.); subjunc. in a dir. obj. ἵνα clause (cf. Stein 332; see 5:10). The addition of ἄν after ὅσοι makes the expression more general: "all those who, whoever, as many as ever," BDAG 729b). Ἥψαντο, 3rd pl. aor. mid. indic. of ἅπτω, "touch" (mng. with mid.); αὐτοῦ, gen. dir. obj. (probably neut. here ["it"] rather than masc. ["him"], so that what they wanted to touch and what they actually touched correspond); ἐσῴζοντο, 3rd pl. impf. pass. indic. of σῴζω, "save" (on σῴζω, see 5:34).

4. Interval: Matters of the Heart (7:1–37)

Chapter 7 of Mark's Gospel stands between the second and third boat scenes. This interval includes three passages that emphasize the importance of the heart over against external factors. Jesus's dispute with the scribes and Pharisees over tradition demonstrates that impurity and defilement come from within (7:1–23). Jesus's healing of a Gentile woman's daughter (7:24–30) and his healing of a Gentile deaf mute (7:31–37) reveal that God's favor extends to people of faith outside of Israel.

(a) Dispute over Tradition (7:1–23)

7:1 After a long absence from the narrative, the religious leaders reappear in this passage to voice their objection to Jesus about the way his disciples neglect their tradition. Jesus uses this objection as an opportunity to point out their hypocrisy and to explain what it means to obey God from the heart. Συνάγονται, 3rd pl. pres. pass. indic. of συνάγω, "gather, come together, assemble" (act. intrans. mng. with pass. form [BDAG 962d]; historical pres. (starting a new scene [see 1:12; cf. Porter, *Idioms* 301–2]; ἐπερωτῶσιν in 7:5 is also a historical pres.); ἐλθόντες, nom. pl. masc. of aor. act. ptc. of ἔρχομαι, "come." The ptc. ἐλθόντες seems to be adj. even though it is anar. (ZG

126); ἐλθόντες apparently lacks the art. because it modifies the indef. pron. τινες (for a similar cstr., see 15:21). Therefore, only the scribes came from Jerusalem, not the Pharisees (cf. ESV, which uses word order to clarify this point).

7:2 The sentence structure of 7:2 is complicated by the fact that 7:3–4 is a long parenthesis explaining the traditions related to ceremonial cleansings. The adv. ptc. ἰδόντες (nom. pl. masc. of aor. act. ptc. of ὁράω, "see"; temp. adv. ptc. antecedent) is syntactically related to the main vb. ἐπερωτῶσιν, which does not appear until 7:5. However, when Mark returns in 7:5 to the sentence that he began in 7:2, he starts again with the conj. καί as though he were beginning a new sentence (cf. Bruce 38; Cranfield 231; Lane 242). Most EVV translate ἰδόντες as a main vb., to simplify Mark's complicated sentence structure (e.g., NET: "they saw").

Κοιναῖς, dat. pl. fem. of κοινός, -ή, -όν, "common, defiled, ceremonially unclean"; χερσίν, dat. of means; ἀνίπτοις, dat. pl. fem. of the two-terminal adj. ἄνιπτος, -ον, "unwashed"; ἐσθίουσιν, on the use of the retained pres. in indir. discourse, see 2:1; ἄρτους, used here for food more generally (BDAG 136d). Although the acc. pron. τινάς in the phrase τινὰς τῶν μαθητῶν αὐτοῦ functions as the dir. obj. of ἰδόντες, it also points ahead to what the subj. will be in the following subord. clause (cf. Turner, *Style* 16: on this cstr. ["prolepsis"], see 11:32). Once again, most EVV simplify Mark's sentence structure by placing the phrase "some of his disciples" within the subord. clause as the subject of ἐσθίουσιν (e.g., ESV: "they saw that some of his disciples ate").

7:3 Γάρ, "now, for" (introducing a clarification [see 1:16]); ἐὰν μή, "unless" (see BDAG 267d–268a [ἐὰν μή also appears in 7:4]); νίψωνται, 3rd pl. aor. mid. subjunc. of νίπτω, "wash"; subjunc. in a 3rd class cond. clause. The mid. voice of νίπτω is typically used for washing oneself or some part of oneself (e.g., "wash one's own hands," [BDAG 674b]; therefore, the mid. of νίπτω can be both trans. and intrans. [R 806]). Literally, Mark states that the washing of the hands was done "in a fist" (πυγμῇ, dat. sg. fem. of πυγμή, -ῆς, ἡ, "fist"), but what such a qualification means is difficult to understand. The proper practice for ceremonial washing may have involved pouring a small amount of water on each hand with the fingers cupped, so that they were neither tightly clenched nor spread wide. This method would have allowed the entire hand to be washed with a minimal and economical amount of water (Stephen M. Reynolds, "ΠΥΓΜΗΙ [Mark 7:3] as 'Cupped Hand,'" *JBL* 85 [1966]: 87–88; James G. Crossley, "Halakah and Mark 7.3: 'with the hand in the shape of a fist,'" *NTS* 58 [2012]: 57–68). The translation "in the proper way" (CEV; cf. LN 8.35) is an attempt to convey the probable underlying significance for Mark's use of πυγμῇ. Κρατοῦντες, nom. pl. masc. of pres. act. ptc. of κρατέω, "hold, hold fast to" (BDAG 565a); adv. ptc. of cause; παράδοσιν, acc. sg. fem. of παράδοσις, -εως, ἡ, "tradition."

7:4 The prep. phrase ἀπ' ἀγορᾶς (gen. sg. fem. of ἀγορά, -ᾶς, ἡ, "marketplace") requires something to be supplied in order to clarify its syntactical relationship to the rest of the clause. Since the following vb. is in the mid. voice (βαπτίσωνται, 3rd pl. aor. mid. subjunc. of βαπτίζω, "wash, purify, immerse"; subjunc. in a 3rd class cond. clause; "they wash themselves"), the prep. phrase ἀπ' ἀγορᾶς seems to be necessarily referring to the people who are returning from the marketplace rather than to the things brought back from the marketplace (BDAG 14b–c; on βαπτίσωνται as a dir. mid., see R 806–7). Therefore, the prep. phrase ἀπ' ἀγορᾶς should be clarified as mng. "when they return from the marketplace," not "the things from the marketplace" (BDAG 14b; cf. BDF §209; T 259). Since the marketplace exposed people to a variety of possible sources of ritual impurity, ceremonial washing before eating was a practical response for those who wanted to maintain their purification (cf. France 282; Stein 340).

Ἄλλα, nom. pl. neut. of ἄλλος, -η, -ο; the sg. vb. ἐστιν can be translated as "there are" [ZG 127], since ἄλλα, as a neut. pl. pred. nom., would imply a neut. pl. subj. when ἐστιν functions as an impers. vb. (see 3:11 on neut. pl. subjects with a sg. vb.); παρέλαβον, 3rd pl. aor. act. indic. of παραλαμβάνω, "receive"; κρατεῖν, pres. act. inf. of κρατέω, "hold, hold fast to"; inf. of result; βαπτισμούς, acc. pl. masc. of βαπτισμός, -οῦ, ὁ, "ritual washing, ceremonial washing" (acc. in simple appos. to ἅ); ποτηρίων, obj. gen.; ξεστῶν, gen. pl. masc. of ξέστης, -ου, ὁ, "pitcher, jug"; χαλκίων, gen. pl. neut. of χαλκίον, -ου, τό, "bronze vessel"; κλινῶν, gen. pl. fem. of κλίνη, -ης, ἡ, "dining couch," BDAG 549d. When Mark refers to the purification of dining couches that had become ceremonially unclean, he is apparently reporting accurately certain early Jewish traditions (cf. *m. Miq.* 7.7; *m. Kel.* 19.1; see James G. Crossley, "Halakah and Mark 7.4: '... and beds,'" *JSNT* 25 [2003]: 433–47). The omission of καὶ κλινῶν from some early mss. (𝔓⁴⁵ ℵ B L Δ 28) may reflect confusion concerning Jewish traditions on the part of Gentile copyists, since they may have found washing or immersing a dining couch difficult to imagine.

7:5 In 7:5, Mark returns to complete the sentence that he began in 7:2, although awkwardly because he unnecessarily begins again with καί. Ἐπερωτῶσιν, 3rd pl. pres. act. indic. of ἐπερωτάω, "ask"; διὰ τί, "on account of what, for what reason, why?" (BDAG 225d; 1007b; ZG 127); περιπατοῦσιν, used fig. for "living" or "conducting one's life" as a matter of consistent pattern or lifestyle (cf. BDAG 803c–d); παράδοσιν, acc. sg. fem. of παράδοσις, -εως, ἡ, "tradition"; κοιναῖς, dat. pl. fem. of κοινός, -ή, -όν, "common, defiled, ceremonially unclean"; ἄρτον, "food," see 7:2 (there is probably no significant difference between the sg. ἄρτον in 7:5 and the pl. ἄρτους in 7:2 [cf. France 281]).

7:6 Jesus's answer (on ὁ δέ, see 1:45) to the Pharisees and scribes begins with an attack on their hypocrisy, a judgment that he will base first on the way they use their tradition to set aside obedience to the commands of God (7:6–13) and second on the way they neglect internal matters of the heart (7:14–23). Ἐπροφήτευσεν, 3rd sg. aor. act. indic. of προφητεύω, "prophesy, foretell"; καλῶς, "rightly, appropriately" (BDAG 506a; ZG 127); ὑποκριτῶν, gen. pl. masc. of ὑποκριτής, -οῦ, ὁ, "pretender, hypocrite"; gen in simple appos. to ὑμῶν. In 7:6–7, Jesus clarifies his characterization of the Pharisees and scribes as hypocrites by quoting from Isa 29:13, with 7:8–13 developing the second half of the verse and 7:14–23 developing the first half. Γέγραπται, 3rd sg. pf. pass. indic. of γράφω, "write" (on the pf. with γέγραπται, see 1:2); ὅτι, introduces dir. discourse; χείλεσιν, dat. pl. neut. of χεῖλος, -ους, τό, "lips" (mng. with pl., BDAG 1081d); τιμᾷ, 3rd sg. pres. act. indic. of τιμάω, "honor"; on the distributive use of the sg. καρδία, see 6:52; ἀπέχει, from ἀπέχω, "be distant, be far" (which is strengthened by πόρρω, an adv. mng. "far away").

7:7 Μάτην, adv. mng. "in vain, to no end"; σέβονται, 3rd pl. pres. mid. indic. of σέβω, "worship" (mng. with mid.); διδάσκοντες, nom. pl. masc. of pres. act. ptc. of διδάσκω, "teach"; adv. ptc. of cause; διδασκαλίας, acc. pl. fem. of διδασκαλία, -ας, ἡ, "teaching, instruction, doctrine"; ἐντάλματα, acc. pl. neut. of ἔνταλμα, -ατος, τό, "commandment"; ἀνθρώπων, subj. gen. The noun διδασκαλίας is the complement in a dbl. acc. obj. complement cstr., while ἐντάλματα is the obj. Normally, in a dbl. acc. obj. complement cstr., the obj. comes first, but not always (cf. Wallace 184, who estimates that the complement comes first about 20 percent of the time). Since ἐντάλματα is furthered clarified by the gen. ἀνθρώπων, it is the more def. of the two accusatives and therefore the obj. In Eng., the word "as" can precede the complement in order to identify it as such.

7:8 Ἀφέντες, nom. pl. masc. of aor. act. ptc. of ἀφίημι, "leave, abandon"; θεοῦ, subj. gen.; παράδοσιν, acc. sg. fem. of παράδοσις, -εως, ἡ, "tradition" (see also the same form in 7:9); ἀνθρώπων, subj. gen. The action in the ptc. ἀφέντες, although not identical, is coordinate with that of the main vb. κρατεῖτε (attendant circumstance ptc.). The two actions are sufficiently interrelated that to do the one will necessarily involve doing the other.

7:9 The tone of sarcasm in Jesus's use of καλῶς (NAB: "How well you have set aside the commandment of God"; cf. Strauss 301) emphasizes the charge of hypocrisy, because it commends them for the cleverness with which they disobey God and yet still portray themselves as righteous. Ἀθετεῖτε, from ἀθετέω, "reject, declare invalid, nullify, ignore"; ἵνα, purpose (i.e., they set aside God's commandment with a goal in mind). The nature of the goal is complicated by a text-critical problem. The religious leaders are seeking either to "establish" their tradition (στήσητε, 2nd pl. aor. act. subjunc of ἵστημι, "establish, maintain," cf. BDAG 482b; supported by D, W, Θ, family 1, 28, 565, 2542) or to "keep" their tradition (τηρήσητε, 2nd pl. aor. act. subjunc. of τηρέω, "keep, observe"; supported by most other mss.). Of the two readings, στήσητε may be the more difficult and therefore the more likely to be orig., since τηρήσητε fits more naturally within a passage on tradition (France 276). "To establish" the tradition means that the goal for these hypocrites was not only to follow the tradition themselves but to impose it on others.

7:10 Τίμα, 2nd sg. pres. act. impv. of τιμάω, "honor"; κακολογῶν, nom. sg. masc. of pres. act. ptc. of κακολογέω, "speak evil of, revile"; subst. ptc.; τελευτάτω, 3rd sg. pres. act. impv. of τελευτάω, "die." A cognate dat. (such as θανάτῳ, which is cognate conceptually) serves to emphasize the action of the vb. it modifies (in this case, τελευτάτω) and is often best translated as an adv. (e.g., "surely, certainly"; cf. Wallace 168–69; on the use of the cognate dat. to replicate in Gk. the use in Heb. of the inf. abs. with a main vb. of the same root for emphasis, see Moule 177–78; Z §§60–62).

7:11 Ὑμεῖς, emph. (both because it is placed at the beginning of the clause and because it is grammatically unnecessary [Stein 342]; creates a sharp contrast between what they say as opposed to what God said through Moses). Εἴπῃ, 3rd sg. aor. act. subjunc. of λέγω, "say"; subjunc. in a 3rd class cond. clause. A grammatically complicated quotation expresses what a man might say to his parents to withhold finances or property from them. The indef. rel. clause ὃ ἐὰν ἐξ ἐμοῦ ὠφεληθῇς as a whole functions as the subj. of this statement, with an understood ἐστίν (Decker 1:188). The indef. rel. pron. itself ὃ ἐάν is an acc. of respect/reference related to ὠφεληθῇς (Moule 131; ZG 128). Whatever (support) from me with respect to which you might have received help (ὠφεληθῇς, 2nd sg. aor. pass. subjunc. of ὠφελέω, "receive help, be benefited" [mng. with pass.], [BDAG 1107d]; subjunc. in indef. rel. clause) is Corban (κορβᾶν, indecl. word ["Corban"] transliterated from Heb., mng. "gift to God," [BDAG 559c; R 279]). In a parenthesis (cf. BDF §465), Mark defines the Heb. word Corban as "gift" (δῶρον, nom. sg. neut. of δῶρον, -ου, τό, "gift"), with the assumption that the gift is offered to God (on the nature of Corban and the situation Jesus envisions, see esp. Cranfield 237–38).

7:12 Ἀφίετε, from ἀφίημι, "permit, allow"; ποιῆσαι, aor. act. inf. of ποιέω, "do"; complementary inf.; πατρί, dat. of interest (advantage). In Gk., the combination of two negatives, such as the use of οὐκέτι with οὐδέν, serves to strengthen the negation (see 1:44). In Eng., it is necessary to translate οὐδέν as "anything" to keep the two negatives from canceling out one another. Normally μηδέν would be used with an inf., but οὐδέν can appear with the inf. when the main vb. is also negated with a form related to οὐ (R 1162; Burton §482).

7:13 Ἀκυροῦντες, nom. pl. masc. of pres. act. ptc. of ἀκυρόω, "make void, nullify"; adv. ptc. of result (ESV: "thus making void"; cf. Wallace 639; KMP 335); παραδόσει, dat. sg. fem. of παράδοσις, -εως, ἡ, "tradition"; dat. of means; παρεδώκατε, 2nd pl. aor. act. indic. of παραδίδωμι, "hand down, pass on." The case of the rel. pron. ᾗ (which normally would have been acc. since ᾗ is the dir. obj. of παρεδώκατε) has attracted to the dat. case of the antecedent παραδόσει (Wallace 339; ZG 128). This is the only example of the attraction of a rel. pron. to the case of its antecedent in Mark's Gospel (R 715; Z §16). Παρόμοια, acc. pl. neut. of παρόμοιος, -α, -ον, similar, like.

7:14 Προσκαλεσάμενος, nom. sg. masc. of aor. mid. ptc. of προσκαλέω, summon, call to oneself (mng. with mid.); temp. adv. ptc. antecedent; ἀκούσατε, 2nd pl. aor. act. impv. of ἀκούω, "hear, listen to"; μου, gen. dir. obj.; πάντες, modifies the unexpressed subj. of ἀκούσατε; σύνετε, 2nd pl. aor. act. impv. of συνίημι, "understand, comprehend." Normally, impv. forms take the aor. tense to express specific commands to be obeyed in a concrete situation (see 1:25) and the pres. tense to express general precepts (see 1:15). Elsewhere in Mark, the impv. forms of ἀκούω always appear in the pres. tense (4:3, 9, 23; 9:7; 12:29). By way of contrast, 7:14 uses the aor. impv. form ἀκούσατε, along with the aor. impv. σύνετε, portraying these commands as specific to the occasion (cf. Fanning 333, 365).

7:15 Most often, ἔξωθεν ("from outside") functions as an adv. (ten of the thirteen times it appears in the NT; e.g., 7:18), but it can also be used as a prep. with a gen. obj. (as in Mark 7:15; Rev 11:2; 14:20; cf. R 642; Moule 84; Harris 246). The art. τοῦ with ἀνθρώπου is a generic art. and therefore distinguishes humanity as a class (cf. Wallace 227–28; KMP 157). To express this idea in Eng., τοῦ ἀνθρώπου is best translated as an indef. noun ("a man"), referring to humanity as a whole by pointing to one representative (the generic art. with ἄνθρωπος appears three times in 7:15; cf. also 7:18, 20, 21, 23). Although periph. participles are freq. in Mark (see 1:22), the periph. pres.—a pres. tense form of εἰμί with a pres. tense ptc.—is not (see 5:41). The periph. pres. seems confined in Mark to the set phrase ὅ ἐστιν μεθερμηνευόμενον (5:41; 15:22, 34). Therefore, εἰσπορευόμενον (nom. sg. neut. of pres. mid. ptc. of dep. εἰσπορεύομαι, "go into, enter") is probably not a periph. ptc. but rather an adj. ptc. (cf. Voelz 1:462; NKJV; CSB; it is anar. because οὐδέν, the word it modifies, never takes an art.). The prep. from the beginning of a compound vb. is often repeated in a prep. phrase after the vb. (e.g., with the use of both εἰς and ἐκ after compound vbs. in this passage [see 1:21]). Δύναται, 3rd sg. pres. mid. indic. of dep. δύναμαι, "be able to, can"; κοινῶσαι, aor. act. inf. of κοινόω, "make common, make impure, defile"; complementary inf.; ἐκπορευόμενα, nom. pl. neut. of pres. mid. ptc. of dep. ἐκπορεύομαι, "come out, go out, proceed"; subst. ptc.; ἐστιν, sg. vb. with a neut. pl. subj. (see 3:11); κοινοῦντα, nom. pl. neut. of pres. act. ptc. of κοινόω, "make common, make impure, defile"; subst. ptc.

Although the words of Mark 7:16 (εἴ τις ἔχει ὦτα ἀκούειν ἀκουέτω, "if anyone has ears to hear, he should hear"; cf. 4:23 for the same statement) appear in the majority of Gk. mss. of Mark's Gospel, they are not found in important early mss., incl. the oldest mss. of Mark's Gospel (א, B, L, Δ, 0274, and others; see Metzger 94–95). Therefore, many recent EVV do not include them and skip from 7:15 to 7:17 (exceptions include NKJV and NASB, although NASB puts v. 16 in brackets to indicate that it is not in the earliest mss.).

7:17 Εἰσῆλθεν, 3rd sg. aor. act. indic. of εἰσέρχομαι, go into, enter (on the use of the aor. for a prior past action, see 5:8); ἐπηρώτων, 3rd pl. impf. act. indic. of ἐπερωτάω, "ask about" (on the impf., see 4:10). The term "parable" in this context seems to be used for an enigmatic saying (Yarbro Collins 355). By using the term "parable" in 7:17, Mark connects this passage with the pattern found earlier in 4:10, 33–34, in which the disciples privately seek out further instruction from Jesus concerning his parabolic teaching.

7:18 Οὕτως, translated "so" when used to introduce a question, or to paraphrase further "so am I to conclude that, do you mean to tell me that" (cf. BDAG 742a; Matt 26:40; 1 Cor 6:5); καί, adjunctive use; ἀσύνετοι, nom. pl. masc. of ἀσύνετος, -ον, "without understanding, senseless"; νοεῖτε, from νοέω, "perceive, understand"; εἰσπορευόμενον, nom. sg. neut. of pres. mid. ptc. of dep. εἰσπορεύομαι, "go into, enter"; adj. ptc.; ἔξωθεν, adv. mng. "from outside"; δύναται, 3rd sg. pres. mid. indic. of dep. δύναμαι, "be able to, can"; κοινῶσαι, aor. act. inf. of κοινόω, "make common, make impure, defile"; complementary inf.

7:19 Εἰσπορεύεται, 3rd sg. pres. mid. indic. of dep. εἰσπορεύομαι, "go into, enter"; κοιλίαν, acc. sg. fem. of κοιλία, -ας, ἡ, "stomach"; ἀφεδρῶνα, acc. sg. masc. of ἀφεδρών, -ῶνος, ὁ, "toilet, latrine"; ἐκπορεύεται, 3rd sg. pres. mid. indic. of dep. ἐκπορεύομαι, "come out, go out"; καθαρίζων, nom. sg. masc. of pres. act. ptc. of καθαρίζω, "make clean, cleanse, declare clean"; adv. ptc. of result; βρώματα, acc. pl. neut. of βρῶμα, -ατος, τό, "food" (mng. with pl.). The ptc. καθαρίζων is nom. sg. masc., agreeing with the implied subj. of λέγει (i.e., Jesus) at the beginning of 7:18 (cf. Z §15; Cranfield 241). Jesus's words in 7:18–19 do not include any nouns, stated or implied, that are nom. sg. masc. Therefore, the ptc. is not part of Jesus's words but is part of Mark's words about Jesus and about the significance of what he said. Mark's conclusion is that Jesus's teaching led to the setting aside of the OT food laws, laws concerning clean and unclean food, what could and could not be eaten (cf. Leviticus 11).

7:20 The repetition of an introductory formula to start Jesus's teaching once again (ἔλεγεν δὲ ὅτι; with ὅτι here introducing dir. discourse) seems to confirm that the preceding clause (καθαρίζων πάντα τὰ βρώματα) was a parenthetical statement from Mark (France 292; Bruce 389). Ἐκπορευόμενον, nom. sg. neut. of pres. mid. ptc. of dep. ἐκπορεύομαι, "come out, go out, proceed"; subst. ptc.; κοινοῖ, 3rd sg. pres. act. indic. of κοινόω, "make common, make impure, defile." The subst. ptc. τὸ ἐκπορευόμενον, as a pendent nom., is the logical subj. of the sentence. However, it is replaced by the dem. pron. ἐκεῖνο, which functions grammatically as the actual subj. of the sentence (Turner, *Style* 21; cf. Z §25; Wallace 51–52; NKJV: "What comes out of a man, that defiles a man").

7:21 Ἔσωθεν, adv. mng. "from within"; καρδίας, on the use of the sg., see 6:52; διαλογισμοί, nom. pl. masc. of διαλογισμός, -οῦ, ὁ, "thought, reasoning"; ἐκπορεύονται, 3rd pl. pres. mid. indic. of dep. ἐκπορεύομαι, "come out, go out, proceed." Mark 7:21–22 includes a list of defiling sins, but the reference to evil thoughts (οἱ διαλογισμοὶ οἱ κακοί) comes first and is separated from the rest of the list by coming before rather than after the main vb. Therefore, the reference to evil thoughts seems to serve as an overarching category for the list of sins to follow (Stein 346), all of which stand in appos. to διαλογισμοί and all of which grow out of corrupt thinking. In the following list of twelve kinds of evil, the first six are in the pl. and the last six are in the sg. Abstract nouns appear in the pl. in Gk. in ways that do not sound completely natural in Eng., which generally uses the sg. with abstract nouns (R 408; T 27–28). In Gk., when the pl. is used with an abstract noun for a general category of sin, the use of the pl. may lay stress on the individual acts within the overall category (R 408; ZG 128). However, in Eng., it may still be best to translate the abstract nouns with the sg. in order to be clear that the whole category is in view (e.g., ESV; NET; NIV; NRSV). Πορνεῖαι, nom. pl. fem. of πορνεία, -ας, ἡ, "sexual immorality"; κλοπαί, nom. pl. fem. of κλοπή, -ῆς, ἡ, "theft, stealing"; φόνοι, nom. pl. masc. of φόνος, -ου, ὁ, "murder, killing."

7:22 Μοιχεῖαι, nom. pl. fem. of μοιχεία, -ας, ἡ, "adultery"; πλεονεξίαι, nom. pl. fem. of πλεονεξία, -ας, ἡ, "greed, covetousness"; πονηρίαι, nom. pl. fem. of πονηρία, -ας, ἡ, "wickedness, evil"; δόλος, nom. sg. masc. of δόλος, -ου, ὁ, "deceit"; ἀσέλγεια, nom. sg. fem. of ἀσέλγεια, -ας, ἡ, "sensuality, licentiousness"; βλασφημία, nom. sg. fem. of βλασφημία, -ας, ἡ, "reviling, slander, blasphemy"; ὑπερηφανία, nom. sg. fem. of ὑπερηφανία, -ας, ἡ, "arrogance, haughtiness, pride"; ἀφροσύνη, nom. sg. fem. of ἀφροσύνη, -ης, ἡ, "foolishness, lack of sense." Perhaps the item in the list that calls for the most attention is "an evil eye" (NKJV). Eng. translations often use "envy" to express the mng. of "an evil eye" as a metaphor for tight-fisted selfishness (e.g., ESV; NET; NIV). A person with an evil eye refuses to give to those in need (Deut 15:9; cf. Sir 35:8–10), chases after wealth (Prov 28:22), wants what others have (Sir 14:8–10), and responds with jealousy when others receive generous gifts (Matt 20:15). The metaphor of an evil eye portrays the attitude of someone who carefully keeps an eye on personal possessions out of stinginess and an eye on what belongs to others out of greed.

7:23 Mark 7:23 serves as a summary of 7:20–22. All these evil things in the above list proceed from within (ἐκπορεύεται, 3rd sg. pres. mid. indic. of dep. ἐκπορεύομαι, "come out, go out, proceed"; sg. vb. with a neut. pl. subj. [see 3:11]; ἔσωθεν, adv. mng. "from within") and defile a man (κοινοῖ, 3rd sg. pres. act. indic. of κοινόω, "make common, make impure, defile").

FOR FURTHER STUDY

22. Jesus and the Law in Mark

Banks, Robert. *Jesus and the Law in the Synoptic Tradition.* SNTSMS 28. Cambridge: Cambridge University Press, 1975.

Booth, Roger P. *Jesus and the Laws of Purity: Tradition History and Legal History in Mark 7.* JSNTSup 13. Sheffield, UK: JSOT Press, 1986.

Crossley, James G. *The Date of Mark's Gospel: Insight from the Law in Earliest Christianity.* JSNTSup 266. London: T&T Clark, 2004.

Dunn, James D. G. *Jesus, Paul and the Law: Studies in Mark and Galatians.* Louisville: Westminster/John Knox, 1990.

Loader, William R. G. *Jesus' Attitude towards the Law: A Study of the Gospels.* WUNT 2/97. Tübingen: Mohr Siebeck, 1997.

Meier, John P. *Law and Love.* Vol. 4 of *A Marginal Jew: Rethinking the Historical Jesus.* Anchor Yale Bible Reference Library. New Haven, CT: Yale University Press, 2009.

*Moo, Douglas J. "Jesus and the Authority of the Mosaic Law." *JSNT* 20 (1984): 3–49.

Sanders, E. P. "The Law." Pages 245–69 in *Jesus and Judaism.* Philadelphia: Fortress, 1985.

———. "The Synoptic Jesus and the Law." Pages 1–96 in *Jewish Law from Jesus to the Mishnah: Five Studies.* Philadelphia: Trinity Press International, 1990.

HOMILETICAL SUGGESTIONS

How to Be a Hypocrite (7:1–23)

1. Make every effort to force your rules on others (for best results, communicate how much more righteous you are than everyone else). (7:1–5)
2. Make up lots of rules (for best results, create rules that are unrelated to what God cares about). (7:6–13)

3. Make up rules esp. about external behavior (for best results, care as little as possible about matters of the heart). (7:14–23)

(b) Healing of a Gentile Woman's Daughter (7:24–30)

7:24 In Mark 7:24–30, Jesus once again encounters a person of faith, although this time a Gentile woman. Her ethnicity does not exclude her from Jesus's help, because—as she herself recognizes—God's grace is sufficiently abundant to meet the needs of anyone who comes to Jesus with humility and faith. Ἀναστάς, nom. sg. masc. of aor. act. ptc. of ἀνίστημι, "rise, set out"; temp. adv. ptc. antecedent; ἀπῆλθεν, 3rd sg. aor. act. indic. of ἀπέρχομαι, "depart, go away"; ὅρια, acc. pl. neut. of ὅριον, -ου, τό, "region, district" (mng. with pl., BDAG 723b); εἰσελθών, nom. sg. masc. of aor. act. ptc. of εἰσέρχομαι, "go into, enter"; temp. adv. ptc. antecedent; οὐδένα, used instead of μηδένα, perhaps because the neg. relates more to the indic. ἤθελεν than to the inf. γνῶναι (see BDF §429); ἤθελεν, 3rd sg. impf. act. indic. of θέλω, "want, wish"; γνῶναι, aor. act. inf. of γινώσκω, "know, find out"; complementary inf.; καί (2nd use): contrastive, "and yet" (Cranfield 246); ἠδυνήθη, 3rd sg. aor. pass. indic. of dep. δύναμαι, "be able to, can"; λαθεῖν, aor. act. inf. of λανθάνω, "escape notice, be hidden"; complementary inf.

7:25 Ἀκούσασα, nom. sg. fem. of aor. act. ptc. of ἀκούω, "hear"; temp. adv. ptc. anteced-ent; εἶχεν, 3rd sg. impf. act. indic. of ἔχω, "have" (impf. for background information [see 1:21]); θυγάτριον, nom. sg. neut. of θυγάτριον, -ου, τό, "little daughter." This pas-sage has several other diminutives besides θυγάτριον, incl. κυνάριον, "little dog" (7:27, 28), ψιχίον, "little crumb" (7:28), and παιδίον, "little child" (7:28, 30; on diminutives, see 3:9). The pers. pron. αὐτῆς in the rel. clause is redundant after the rel. pron. ἧς, and it is unnecessary to translate the pers. pron. in Eng. The presence of αὐτῆς is probably due to Sem. influence, since in Heb. and Aram. the rel. pron. is indecl. and without gender. Therefore, an added pers. pron. serves to indicate the case, number, and gen-der of the rel. pron. (R 683; BDF §297; T 21; Moule 176; Z §201; cf. 1:7; 13:19). Ἐλθοῦσα, nom. sg. fem. of aor. act. ptc. of ἔρχομαι, "come"; temp. adv. ptc. antecedent; προσέπεσεν, 3rd sg. aor. act. indic. of προσπίπτω, "fall down."

7:26 Mark stresses the woman's status as a Gentile by saying that she was Greek (ἦν, 3rd sg. impf. act. indic. of εἰμί, "be"; Ἑλληνίς, nom. sg. fem. of Ἑλληνίς, -ίδος, ἡ, "Greek woman"), i.e., Greek in terms of language and culture (cf. Cranfield 247; Brooks 121). With respect to her specific ethnic background (γένει, dat. of reference or respect; ZG 129), she was Syrophoenician (Συροφοινίκισσα, nom. sg. fem. of Συροφοινίκισσα, -ης, ἡ, "Syrophoenician woman"), i.e., her place of orig. was in Phoenicia, the southern part of Syria along the Mediterranean coast (cf. Yarbro Collins 366; Voelz 1:478). Ἠρώτα, 3rd sg. impf. act. indic. of ἐρωτάω, "ask, request" (on the impf. with ἐρωτάω, see 4:10); ἐκβάλῃ, 3rd sg. aor. act. subjunc. of ἐκβάλλω, "cast out, drive out, send away"; subjunc. in a dir. obj. ἵνα clause to express a request (see 5:10).

7:27 Ἄφες, 2nd sg. aor. act. impv. of ἀφίημι, "allow, let, permit"; χορτασθῆναι, aor. pass. inf. of χορτάζω, "feed, fill, satisfy"; complementary inf.; λαβεῖν, aor. act. inf. of λαμβάνω, "take"; epex. inf.; κυναρίοις, dat. pl. neut. of κυνάριον, -ου, τό, "little dog";

βαλεῖν, aor. act. inf. of βάλλω, "throw"; epex. inf. Jesus's answer sounds like a rejection based on the woman's status as a Gentile, a rejection offered in fairly harsh terms. Jesus's refusal to help the woman is difficult to understand in the context of Mark's narrative as a whole, since Jesus has already healed people from the area around Tyre (3:7–12) and delivered a Gentile from demon possession (5:1–20). Interpreters have suggested several possible solutions to this problem (see Joel F. Williams, "Mark 7:27: Jesus's Puzzling Statement," in *Interpreting the New Testament Text: Introduction to the Art and Science of Exegesis*, ed. Darrell L. Bock and Buist M. Fanning [Wheaton, IL: Crossway, 2006], pp. 341–49, for an extended discussion of these solutions).

1. Jesus's response was a refusal based not on the woman's status as a Gentile but on her interruption of his time with the disciples. The time Jesus devoted to his disciples should not be taken away and given instead to the woman's daughter.

2. Jesus's response was a hesitant affirmation on his part that his ministry ought to be limited to the people of Israel. The woman's answer caused Jesus to change his mind and to see that he also had a responsibility to minister to the Gentiles.

*3. Jesus's response was a test of the woman's faith, an obstacle put in her path to see if she had the type of faith that Jesus honored. The woman's answer showed that she passed the test, since she displayed both humility and trust in the abundance of God's mercy in Jesus, an abundance that could spill over to the Gentiles.

7:28 On the art. ἡ as a pers. pron., see 1:45; ἀπεκρίθη, 3rd sg. aor. pass. indic. of dep. ἀποκρίνομαι, "answer"; κύριε, voc.; καί, ascensive; κυνάρια, nom. pl. neut. of κυνάριον, -ου, τό, "little dog"; ὑποκάτω, adv. functioning as a prep. with a gen. obj., "under, beneath" (BDAG 1038a); τραπέζης, gen. sg. fem. of τράπεζα, -ης, ἡ, "table"; ἐσθίουσιν, on a neut. pl. subj. with a pl. vb., see 3:11; ψιχίων, gen. pl. neut. of ψιχίον, -ου, τό, "crumb." The woman negotiates the obstacle put in her path by humbly acknowledging her need as a Gentile for mercy and by trusting that only a crumb of help from Jesus would be enough.

7:29 Λόγον, "statement" (BDAG 600b); ὕπαγε, 2nd sg. pres. act. impv. of ὑπάγω, "go, depart" (on the pres. impv. form of ὑπάγω, see 2:11); ἐξελήλυθεν, 3rd sg. pf. act. indic. of ἐξέρχομαι, "come out, go out." When a vb. such as ἐξέρχομαι, one that conveys the accomplishment of an action, uses the pf. tense, the emph. is on the completion of the action, although the pf. still implies a resulting state (cf. Fanning 297–98; see also ἐξεληλυθός in 7:30 and ἐλήλυθεν in 9:13). Therefore, the pf. tense form ἐξελήλυθεν puts the stress on the departure of the demon as a completed act.

7:30 Ἀπελθοῦσα, nom. sg. fem. of aor. act. ptc. of ἀπέρχομαι, "depart, go away"; temp. adv. ptc. antecedent; εὗρεν, 3rd sg. aor. act. indic. of εὑρίσκω, "find"; βεβλημένον, acc. sg. neut. of pf. pass. ptc. of βάλλω, "lay" (possible mng. of the pass. in contexts of sickness, disability, or rest [cf. BDAG 163c; ZG 129]); supplementary (complementary) ptc. (cf. Voelz 1:479); κλίνην, acc. sg. fem. of κλίνη, -ης, ἡ, "bed"; ἐξεληλυθός, acc. sg.

neut. of pf. act. ptc. of ἐξέρχομαι, "come out, go out"; supplementary (complementary) ptc.

HOMILETICAL SUGGESTIONS

Jesus and Gentiles (7:24–30)

1. What do we learn about Jesus?
   a. The forefront of Jesus's mission: Jesus gave priority in his ministry to the people of Israel as God's promised Messiah. (7:27)
   b. The foresight of Jesus's mission: Jesus looked ahead to a time when God's kingdom blessings would reach the Gentiles. (7:27)
   c. The foretaste of Jesus's mission: Jesus showed mercy to Gentiles who came to him in faith as a taste of what was to come. (7:29–30)
2. What do we learn about a life of faith?
   a. People of faith believe that God's grace through Jesus is abundant enough to reach anyone.
   b. People of faith believe that God's grace through Jesus is sufficient enough to meet any need.

(c) Healing of a Gentile Who Is Deaf (7:31–37)

7:31 Of all Mark's healing stories, the two that are the most similar are the healing of the deaf man in 7:31–37 and the healing of the blind man of Bethsaida in 8:22–26. Interestingly, in between these two miracles, Jesus questions the disciples concerning their lack of spiritual insight, their inability to see and hear as they should (8:14–21; cf. the homiletical suggestion after 8:26). The adv. πάλιν ("again") likely points to Jesus's arrival again in the Decapolis, which is on the Gentile side of the Sea of Galilee, where he previously encountered the Gerasene demoniac (in which case πάλιν modifies the main vb. ἦλθεν rather than the ptc. ἐξελθών; cf. 14:39, 40). Ἐξελθών, nom. sg. masc. of aor. act. ptc. of ἐξέρχομαι, "come out, go out"; temp. adv. ptc. antecedent; ὁρίων, gen. pl. neut. of ὅριον, -ου, τό, "region, district" (mng. with pl., BDAG 723b); ἦλθεν, 3rd sg. aor. act. indic. of ἔρχομαι, "come, go"; εἰς, "to" (εἰς used for πρός [BDF §207; Z §97]). When the prep. ἀνά takes μέσον (acc. sg. neut. of μέσος) as its obj., the prep. phrase as a whole means "in the midst of" and takes another obj. in the gen. case (BDAG 57d, 635c; Taylor 353).

7:32 Both main vbs. (φέρουσιν and παρακαλοῦσιν) are indef. pl. and historical pres. vbs. (see 1:22 on indef. pl. vbs.; see 1:12 on historical pres. vbs. at the beginning of a new scene). Κωφόν, acc. sg. masc. of κωφός, -ή, -όν, "deaf"; μογιλάλον, acc. sg. masc. of μογιλάλος, -ον, "speaking with difficulty, having an impediment in one's speech." The word μογιλάλος (which combines μόγις ["with difficulty"] and λαλέω ["I speak"], BDAG 656a) seems to indicate that the man was not completely mute. Mark's description of the man's healing—that he was able to speak correctly (7:35)—supports this same conclusion. Ἐπιθῇ, 3rd sg. aor. act. subjunc. of ἐπιτίθημι, "lay on"; subjunc. in a dir. obj. ἵνα clause to express a request (see 5:10); αὐτῷ, dat. dir. obj.; τήν, art. used as poss. pron. (R 769–70; Wallace 216).

7:33 Ἀπολαβόμενος, nom. sg. masc. of aor. mid. ptc. of ἀπολαμβάνω, "take away, take aside" (mng. with mid.); temp. adv. ptc. antecedent; κατ᾽ ἰδίαν, "privately, by himself" (BDAG 467c; ZG 130); ἔβαλεν, 3rd sg. aor. act. indic. of βάλλω, "put," BDAG 163d; δακτύλους, acc. pl. masc. of δάκτυλος, -ου, ὁ, "finger"; ὦτα, acc. pl. neut. of οὖς, ὠτός, τό, "ear"; πτύσας, nom. sg. masc. of aor. act ptc. of πτύω, "spit"; temp. adv. ptc. antecedent; ἥψατο, 3rd sg. aor. mid. indic. of ἅπτω, "touch" (mng. with mid.); γλώσσης, gen. dir. obj. (Wallace 132). Jesus's activity in healing the deaf man extends beyond what he normally did in healing others earlier in Mark's Gospel. Perhaps one factor to be considered is that in this instance Jesus was seeking to communicate through physical contact with a man who could not hear (cf. France 303).

7:34 Ἀναβλέψας, nom. sg. masc. of aor. act. ptc. of ἀναβλέπω, "look up"; temp. adv. ptc. antecedent; ἐστέναξεν, 3rd sg. aor. act. indic. of στενάζω, "sigh, groan." The actual healing takes place at the moment of Jesus's authoritative word, which Mark reports as "ephphatha," an Aram. word that means (on ὅ ἐστιν, see 3:17) "be opened" (διανοίχθητι, 2nd sg. aor. pass. impv. of διανοίγω, "open"; pronouncement impv. [see 1:41]; on the pass., see 10:40). Aram. words or phrases appear at various places within Mark's Gospel: "Boanerges" in 3:17, "talitha koum" in 5:41, "ephphatha" in 7:34, "hosanna" in 11:9–10, "abba" in 14:36, "Golgotha" in 15:22, and "Eloi, Eloi lemá sabachtháni" in 15:34. Each time, they seem to depict an event, statement, or place as particularly memorable. Mark translates all these Aram. words or phrases into Gk. for the benefit of his audience, with the exception of "hosanna." Although διανοίχθητι is impv. in form, it does not give a command to be obeyed but rather makes a pronouncement. The pass. impv. pronounces what should happen and by so doing causes the action to take place at that moment (Wallace 440, 492–93; cf. 1:41; 11:23).

7:35 Ἠνοίγησαν, 3rd pl. aor. pass. indic. of ἀνοίγω, "open"; ἀκοαί, nom. pl. fem. of ἀκοή, -ῆς, ἡ, "ear"; ἐλύθη, 3rd sg. aor. pass. indic. of λύω, "loose, release, untie"; δεσμός, nom. sg. masc. of δεσμός, -οῦ, ὁ, "bond, fetter"; ἐλάλει, 3rd sg. impf. act. indic. of λαλέω, "speak" (on the impf. for portraying the reality of a miracle in a dramatic way, see 1:21); ὀρθῶς, adv. mng. "correctly, normally." English versions struggle with how to translate Mark's metaphorical language concerning a "bond" or "fetter" on the man's tongue. Many simply do not offer any Eng. equivalent for δεσμός (e.g., ESV: "his tongue was released"; cf. NRSV; NIV, NET). Other versions take away the metaphor and offer a more literal portrayal of the healing (e.g., NASB: "the impediment of his tongue was removed"; cf. NKJV). Possible translations that seek to retain something of Mark's imagery include "his tongue was unshackled" (Marcus 1:475) or "his imprisoned tongue was set free" (with γλώσσης as an attributed gen.).

7:36 Διεστείλατο, 3rd sg. aor. mid. indic. of διαστέλλω, "order, give orders" (mng. with mid.); αὐτοῖς, dat. dir. obj.; λέγωσιν, 3rd pl. pres. act. subjunc. of λέγω, "speak, report" (BDAG 590a); subjunc. in a dir. obj. ἵνα clause to express a command (see 5:10). The use of ὅσον with μᾶλλον περισσότερον causes them to function together as correl. (i.e., paired) adverbs ("as much as . . . so much the more"; BDAG 729b). Therefore, the acc. sg. neut. form ὅσον is functioning as an adv. rather than as an adj. or a pron. (ZG 130; Voelz 1:487). Likewise, the acc. sg. neut. form περισσότερον (from περισσότερος, -α, -ον) is functioning not as a comp. adj. but as an adv. (mng. "even more"), and it is used here in combination with the adv. μᾶλλον to heighten the contrast ("so much the more"; BDAG 614a, 806a; BDF §246; T 29). The effect of these correl. adverbs is to create a more general summary of what took place frequently when Jesus commanded people to remain silent. The use of impf. tense vbs. (διεστέλλετο, 3rd sg. impf. mid. indic. of διαστέλλω, "order, give orders" [mng. with mid.]; ἐκήρυσσον, 3rd pl. impf. act. indic. of κηρύσσω, "proclaim") in such a context causes them to portray actions that took place repeatedly (iter. impf.; cf. Taylor 356).

7:37 The compound adv. ὑπερπερισσῶς ("to an extraordinary degree, beyond all measure, completely"), which has the prep. prefix ὑπέρ added to the adv. περισσῶς, points to an excess above and beyond the abundant amazement that could have already been expected (cf. LN 78.34; on compound adverbs, see R 296–97, 546). Ἐξεπλήσσοντο, 3rd pl. impf. pass. indic. of ἐκπλήσσω, "be amazed, be overwhelmed" (mng. with pass.; on vbs. for amazement, see 1:22); ἐξεπλήσσοντο is likely an indef. 3rd pl. vb. (i.e., the subj. is an unspecified group of people responding to the proclamation of 7:36 [see 1:22]); λέγοντες, nom. pl. masc. of pres. act. ptc. of λέγω, "say"; adv. ptc. of result (see 6:2; 10:26); πεποίηκεν, 3rd sg. pf. act. indic. of ποιέω, "do"; καί, ascensive; κωφούς, acc. pl. masc. of κωφός, -ή, -όν, "deaf"; ἀκούειν, pres. act. inf. of ἀκούω, "hear"; complementary inf.; ἀλάλους, acc. pl. masc. of ἄλαλος, -ον, "mute, unable to speak"; λαλεῖν, pres. act. inf. of λαλέω, "speak"; complementary inf. (on ποιέω as a helper vb. that can take a complementary inf., see James L. Boyer, "The Classification of Infinitives: A Statistical Study," *GTJ* 6 [1985]: 7).

5. Cycle 3: Conversation on the Sea (8:1–26)

In the third boat scene (8:14–21), Jesus warns his disciples about the leaven of the Pharisees and Herod, but they completely misunderstand the true significance of his teaching. For them, it is an opportunity to worry about their lack of food, even after Jesus's feeding miracles. Like the second boat scene, this third one is preceded by Jesus's ministry of teaching and feeding the crowd, this time a crowd of four thousand (8:1–9). In addition, Mark sets up Jesus's conversation with his disciples in the boat through a brief encounter between Jesus and the unbelieving Pharisees (8:10–13). Like the other boat scenes, this third instance is followed by a report of Jesus's healing ministry, the restoration of sight for a blind man at Bethsaida (8:22–26).

(a) Jesus's Ministry to the Crowd: Feeding of the Four Thousand (8:1–9)

8:1 The two feeding miracles in Mark's Gospel, although showing variation in certain details, are still two very similar scenes. Through this repetition, Mark confirms the compassion of Jesus toward hungry people and emphasizes the inability of the disciples to comprehend Jesus's power and their own role in extending his work. Ἐν ἐκείναις ταῖς ἡμέραις points to the time period in which Jesus was in the Decapolis near the Sea of Galilee (7:31), i.e., in a predominantly Gentile territory (Cranfield 255; Strauss 330–31); ὄχλου, a collective sg. noun, which therefore can take a sg. ptc. (such as ὄντος) and a pl. ptc. (such as ἐχόντων; [R 407; cf. the similar pattern in 3:7–8, 32]); ὄντος, gen. sg. masc. of pres. act. ptc. of εἰμί, "be present" (BDAG 283b); gen. abs. ptc.; temp. adv ptc. contemp.; ἐχόντων, gen. pl. masc. of pres. act. ptc. of ἔχω, "have"; gen. abs. ptc.; temp. adv. ptc. contemp.; φάγωσιν, 3rd pl. aor. act. subjunc. of ἐσθίω, "eat." In Gk., an indir. question will retain the subjunc. mood of the orig. dir. question (see 6:36), which for τί φάγωσιν would be a delib. question: "What should we eat?" Since an indir. delib. question creates an awkward sentence structure in Eng. (lit.: "when they did not have what they should eat"), it must be smoothed out in translation ("when they did not have anything to eat" [cf. Wallace 478; Burton §346]). Προσκαλεσάμενος, nom. sg. masc. of aor. mid. ptc. of προσκαλέω, summon, call to oneself (mng. with mid.); temp. adv. ptc. antecedent; λέγει, historical pres. (see 1:12, 30).

8:2 Σπλαγχνίζομαι, 1st sg. pres. mid. indic. of dep. σπλαγχνίζομαι, "have pity, have compassion" (on σπλαγχνίζομαι, see 6:34); προσμένουσιν, from προσμένω, "remain with, stay with"; μοι, dat. dir. obj.; φάγωσιν, 3rd pl. aor. act. subjunc. of ἐσθίω, "eat" (on τί φάγωσιν, see 8:1). The use of the nom. case to express the extent of time (as with ἡμέραι τρεῖς ["for three days"]) is rare, since the acc. case is normally used instead (R 460; Porter, *Idioms* 87; ZG 130). Because ἡμέραι τρεῖς expresses extent of time, it is necessary to translate the pres. indic. προσμένουσιν as "they have remained," since in Eng. the pf. is used to convey a past action that is still continuing (Voelz 1:497).

8:3 Ἀπολύσω, 1st sg. aor. act. subjunc. of ἀπολύω, "let go, send away, dismiss"; subjunc. in a 3rd class cond. clause; νήστεις, acc. pl. masc. of νῆστις, -ιος or -ιδος, ὁ or ἡ, "hungry"; complement in a dbl. acc. obj. complement cstr.; ἐκλυθήσονται, 3rd pl. fut. pass. indic. of ἐκλύω, "become weary, give out, collapse" (mng. with pass.). The last clause in 8:3 highlights the acute nature of the problem for those in the crowd who have come from far away (μακρόθεν, adv. used in combination with the prep. ἀπό so that the whole phrase means "from far away, from a distance" [see 5:6]; ἥκασιν, 3rd pl. pf. act. indic. of ἥκω, "have come" [mng. with pf.]).

8:4 Ἀπεκρίθησαν, 3rd pl. aor. pass. indic. of dep. ἀποκρίνομαι, "answer"; ὅτι, introduces dir. discourse; πόθεν, "how?" in this context (ZG 131); δυνήσεται, 3rd sg. fut. mid. indic. of dep. δύναμαι, "be able to, can"; χορτάσαι, aor. act. inf. of χορτάζω, "feed, fill, satisfy"; complementary inf.; ἄρτων, gen. of content (cf. Wallace 92–94); ἐρημίας, gen. sg. fem. of ἐρημία, -ας, ἡ, "desert." At this point in the narrative, esp. after the previous feeding of the 5,000, the disciples' question in 8:4 reveals an almost inexplicable lack of faith in Jesus's power to care for hungry people. A more appropriate response from the disciples would have been: "You have proven that you have the power to feed a multitude with very little. What do we have—no matter how apparently inadequate— that you might be able to use to care for these people who need our help?"

8:5 Ἠρώτα, 3rd sg. impf. act. indic. of ἐρωτάω, "ask" (on the impf. with ἐρωτάω, see 4:10); on οἱ δέ, see 1:45; εἶπαν, 3rd pl. aor. act. indic. of λέγω, "say." Mark's Gospel consistently uses the 1st aor. ending (without the -σ-) on the 2nd aor. stem for 3rd pl.

aor. indic. forms of λέγω (i.e., εἶπαν; on such forms, see R 346; cf. 8:5, 28; 10:4, 37, 39; 11:6; 12:7, 16; 16:8). In addition, he uses 1st aor. endings with the 1st sg. indic. form (εἶπα in 9:18), the 2nd sg. impv. form (εἰπόν in 13:4), and the 2nd pl. impv. form (εἴπατε in 11:3; 14:14; 16:7).

8:6 Παραγγέλλει, historical pres. (introducing indir. discourse [see 1:12, 30; cf. Fanning 233]); ὄχλῳ, dat. dir. obj.; ἀναπεσεῖν, aor. act. inf. of ἀναπίπτω, "recline for a meal, sit down to eat"; inf. of indir. discourse; λαβών, nom. sg. masc. of aor. act. ptc. of λαμβάνω, "take, receive"; temp. adv. ptc. antecedent; εὐχαριστήσας, nom. sg. masc. of aor. act. ptc. of εὐχαριστέω, "give thanks"; temp. adv. ptc. antecedent; ἔκλασεν, 3rd sg. aor. act. indic. of κλάω, "break"; ἐδίδου, 3rd sg. impf. act. indic. of δίδωμι, "give." As in 6:41, the switch in tense to the impf. with ἐδίδου, esp. within a context where the disciples were receiving the bread in order to serve it to a large crowd, communicates that Jesus repeatedly gave bread to the disciples (iter. impf.; see the discussion at 6:41). Παρατιθῶσιν, 3rd pl. pres. act. subjunc. of παρατίθημι, "set before, serve"; subjunc. in a purpose ἵνα clause; παρέθηκαν, 3rd pl. aor. act. indic. of παρατίθημι, "set before, serve."

8:7 Εἶχον, 3rd pl. impf. act. indic. of ἔχω, "have" (impf. for background information [see 1:21]); ἰχθύδια, acc. pl. neut. of ἰχθύδιον, -ου, τό, "little fish, small fish" (on diminutives, incl. ἰχθύδια in particular, see 3:9). Εὐλογήσας, nom. sg. masc. of aor. act. ptc. εὐλογέω, "bless, give thanks, praise"; temp. adv. ptc. antecedent. The ms. evidence is divided concerning the acc. pron. αὐτά, with the oldest mss. placing αὐτά after εὐλογήσας, other mss. incl. αὐτά before εὐλογήσας, and some mss. omitting αὐτά altogether. Earlier in a similar scene, in 6:41, εὐλόγησεν did not take an acc., and in that context the blessing seems to be directed toward God, since Jesus expresses his blessing after looking up to heaven. If αὐτά is orig. in 8:7, it should probably be understood as an acc. of respect or reference ("after he blessed [God] for them"; Cranfield 256–57; cf. *TDNT* 2:762; Brooks 126; NIV; GNB). By taking αὐτά as an acc. of respect or reverence in 8:7, there seems to be a consistent pattern in Mark's Gospel of Jesus blessing (i.e., praising) God for food before he gives it to others (cf. 6:41; 14:22). Εἶπεν, "tell, order" (BDAG 287a; the indir. obj. αὐτοῖς is understood from the context [ZG 131]); καί (last used in the verse): adjunctive; παρατιθέναι, pres. act. inf. of παρατίθημι, set before, serve; inf. of indir. discourse expressing a command (R 1046–47).

8:8 Ἔφαγον, 3rd pl. aor. act. indic. of ἐσθίω, "eat"; ἐχορτάσθησαν, 3rd pl. aor. pass. indic. of χορτάζω, "feed, fill, satisfy" (on χορτάζω, see 6:42); ἦραν, 3rd pl. aor. act. indic. of αἴρω, "take up, pick up"; περισσεύματα, acc. pl. neut. of περίσσευμα, -ατος, τό, "piece left over, what remains"; dir. obj. of ἦραν; κλασμάτων, gen. pl. neut. of κλάσμα, -ατος, τό, "fragment" (perhaps partitive gen. modifying περισσεύματα, or more likely gen. of content, modifying σπυρίδας); σπυρίδας, acc. pl. fem. of σπυρίς, -ίδος, ἡ, "basket"; acc. in simple appos. to περισσεύματα (cf. NIV: "seven basketfuls of broken pieces that were left over"). The term used for "basket" (σπυρίς) in 8:8 is different from the term used for "basket" (κόφινος) in 6:43 in the previous feeding miracle. Unlike the baskets referred to earlier, the ones mentioned in 8:8 did not have any special association with the Jewish people (Marcus 1:489; France 309), which would be fitting for a predominantly Gentile crowd. Both types of baskets could come in a variety of sizes (MM 357; Spicq 3:230). A σπυρίς could be large enough to hold Saul during his escape out of Damascus (Acts 9:25) or small enough to serve as a lunch pail (Athenaeus, *Deipnosophistae* 8.365a). Therefore, it would be difficult to determine which contained more leftovers, the twelve baskets in 6:43 or the seven baskets in 8:8.

8:9 ῏Ησαν, 3rd pl. impf. act. indic. of εἰμί, "be"; ὡς, "about, approximately" (when used with numbers [BDAG 1105d; R 968]); τετρακισχίλιοι, nom. pl. masc. of τετρακισχίλιοι, -αι, -α, "four thousand"; ἀπέλυσεν, 3rd sg. aor. act. indic. of ἀπολύω, "let go, send away, dismiss." Mark ends his account of this feeding miracle with a summary of the number of people fed, this time about four thousand people. The earlier feeding miracle for the 5,000 also ended in this way. The overall similarity between the two scenes heightens the disciples' failure, but in spite of their failure, Jesus did not give up on them. Instead, he persisted in including them in the task of serving needy people.

HOMILETICAL SUGGESTIONS

The Two Feeding Miracles: What the Disciples Should Have Said (6:30–44; 8:1–9)

1. What the disciples should have said about the crowd (6:35–36)
   a. What they said: "The people should take care of themselves."
   b. What they should have said: "The people need compassion and care. What can we do to help?"
2. What the disciples should have said about themselves (6:37)
   a. What they said: "It is unreasonable to think we have anything to offer."
   b. What they should have said: "We are inadequate in ourselves. Will you help us?"
3. What the disciples should have said about Jesus (8:4)
   a. What they said: "The problem is too big even for you."
   b. What they should have said: "You have proven yourself repeatedly. Will you help us again?"

(b) Test from the Pharisees (8:10–13)

8:10 The brief controversy with the Pharisees in 8:10–13 helps to set the context for the boat scene that follows (8:14–21), a scene in which Jesus warns the disciples about the potentially negative influence of the Pharisees. Ἐμβάς, nom. sg. masc. of aor. act. ptc. of ἐμβαίνω, "embark"; temp. adv. ptc. antecedent; ἦλθεν, 3rd sg. aor. act. indic. of ἔρχομαι, "come, go"; μέρη, pl. of μέρος means "region, district" when referring to a geographical area (BDAG 633b).

8:11 Ἐξῆλθον, 3rd pl. aor. act. indic. of ἐξέρχομαι, "come, go out"; ἤρξαντο, 3rd pl. aor. mid. indic. of ἄρχω, "begin" (mng. with mid.; on ἄρχομαι, see 1:45); συζητεῖν, pres. act. inf. of συζητέω, "dispute, debate, argue"; complementary inf.; αὐτῷ, dat. of association (cf. R 528–29); ζητοῦντες, nom. pl. masc. of pres. act. ptc. of ζητέω, "seek, demand"

(BDAG 428d; LN 33.167); attendant circumstance ptc. (cf. Voelz 1:503). Mark's Gospel uses "sign" (σημεῖον) for "an outward compelling proof of divine authority" (Cranfield 257). The word σημεῖον appears less freq. in Mark (8:11, 12; 13:4, 22) than in the other NT Gospels (thirteen times in Matthew; eleven times in Luke; seventeen times in John). In Mark, the desire for a sign consistently has negative connotations, since it reveals a stubborn refusal to believe (8:11–12; cf. 1 Cor 1:20–23) or a dangerous openness to deception (13:4–5, 22; cf. 2 Thess 2:9–10). Πειράζοντες, nom. pl. masc. of pres. act. ptc. of πειράζω, "test"; adv. ptc. of purpose (on πειράζω, see 10:2).

8:12 Ἀναστενάξας, nom. sg. masc. of aor. act. ptc. of ἀναστενάζω, "sigh deeply"; temp. adv. ptc. antecedent (the prep. prefix ἀνα- on the compound vb. ἀναστενάζω intensifies the action; cf. Cranfield 258; Moule 87–88); πνεύματι, dat. of sphere; τί, "why?" (see 2:7). The primary background for Jesus's reference to ἡ γενεὰ αὕτη ("this generation") is in the OT, in descriptions of the unbelieving and rebellious generation during the time of the wilderness wanderings (Num 32:13; Deut 1:35; 2:14; 32:5, 20; Ps 12:7; 78:8; 95:10). Therefore, "this generation" is a pejorative label, referring to a sinful and unbelieving class of people who are destined for the judgment of God (cf. *NIDNTT* 2:36). Later in Mark's Gospel, Jesus describes "this generation" as "adulterous and sinful" (8:38) and "unbelieving" (9:19). In the eschatological discourse, Jesus predicts that "this generation" will be present at the end and will not pass away before the coming of the Son of Man (13:30). Unbelieving people who rebel against God with hardened hearts will be present right up to the end of the age but will then finally meet their judgment.

Ἀμὴν λέγω ὑμῖν, affirms the truth of the following words. What appears next is a cond. clause without an expressed conclusion, which is an idiomatic way of communicating a strongly negative assertion or an oath (R 1024; BDF §§372, 454; T 333; Burton §272; Z §400). A statement recorded in 2 Kgs 6:31 provides an example of the full form of such an expression; it may be briefly paraphrased as: "May God do so to me and more, if he remains alive today." The point is to communicate an emph. neg. ("he will certainly not remain alive today") or a solemn oath ("I swear to God that he will not remain alive today"). Yet often with such an expression the cond. clause stands alone, and the conclusion ("may such and such happen") is left unexpressed (e.g., in the LXX in Gen 14:23; Num 32:11; Deut 1:35; 1 Sam 3:14; 14:45; Ps 94:11 [Eng. Ps 95:11, which is quoted in Heb 3:11; 4:3, 5]). Therefore, Jesus's statement in 8:12 ("if a sign will be given [δοθήσεται, 3rd sg. fut. pass. indic. of δίδωμι, give] to this generation") conveys a strongly worded negative assertion ("a sign will not be given to this generation") or an oath ("I swear that a sign will not be given to this generation").

8:13 In 8:13, Jesus leaves the Pharisees abruptly in order to teach his disciples in the following boat scene. Ἀφείς, nom. sg. masc. of aor. act. ptc. of ἀφίημι, "leave, depart from"; temp. adv. ptc. antecedent; ἐμβάς, nom. sg. masc. of aor. act. ptc. of ἐμβαίνω, "embark, step into a boat"; temp. adv. ptc. antecedent; ἀπῆλθεν, 3rd sg. aor. act. indic. of ἀπέρχομαι, "depart, go away"; πέραν, an adv. with the art. functioning as a subst., "the shore/land on the other side" (BDAG 796d).

(c) Third Boat Scene: Warning about Leaven (8:14–21)

8:14 The three boat scenes in Mark's Gospel (4:35–41; 6:45–52; 8:14–21) are somewhat repetitive, since in each one the disciples display a lack of understanding and inadequate faith. Yet they are more than just repetitive, because as the narrative is progressing, the disciples have more and more reason to trust Jesus, and therefore their inadequate response is more and more blameworthy. Ἐπελάθοντο, 3rd pl. aor. mid. indic. of dep. ἐπιλανθάνομαι, "forget." Most EVV translate the aor. form ἐπελάθοντο with a pluperf. ("they had forgotten") in order to show that this action took place before they were in the boat with only one loaf (cf. R 840–41; Burton §§48, 53; Moule 16; Z §290; see 3:10). Λαβεῖν, aor. act. inf. of λαμβάνω, "take"; dir. obj. inf.; εἰ μή, "except" (see 2:7); εἶχον, 3rd pl. impf. act. indic. of ἔχω, "have"; μεθ᾽ ἑαυτῶν, Eng. normally uses a pers. pron. rather than a refl. pron. as the obj. of "with" ("with them" rather than "with themselves"; see translations of the refl. pron. after μετά in Matt 12:45; 15:30; 25:3; 26:11; Mark 8:14; 9:8; 14:7; John 12:8; 2 Tim 4:11).

8:15 In 8:14–21, Mark uses a series of impf. and pres. tense vbs. to introduce dir. and indir. discourse (impf. in 8:15, 16, 21; pres. in 8:17, 19, 20). In this way, the impf. and pres. vbs. portray the ongoing give-and-take of a conversation (see 1:12, 30; 2:16; 4:10). Διεστέλλετο, 3rd sg. impf. mid. indic. of διαστέλλω, "order, give orders" (mng. with mid.); αὐτοῖς, dat. dir. obj. of διεστέλλετο (R 541); λέγων, nom. sg. masc. of pres. act. ptc. of λέγω, "say"; redundant ptc.; ὁρᾶτε, 2nd pl. pres. act. impv. of ὁράω, "look out" (BDAG 720b); βλέπετε, 2nd pl. pres. act. impv. of βλέπω, "beware of, watch out for" (mng. when used with ἀπό [see BDAG 179c; Decker 1:212; cf. 12:38]); ζύμης, gen. sg. fem. of ζύμη, -ης, ἡ, "leaven." The word for leaven (ζύμη) is not synonymous with "yeast," even though some versions translate it that way (NIV; NET; NLT; NRSV). Leaven refers to old fermented dough, which was thoroughly mixed into a new batch of dough to make the bread rise (*NIDNTTE* 2:362; BDAG 429c).

8:16 Διελογίζοντο, 3rd pl. impf. mid. indic. of dep. διαλογίζομαι, "discuss, argue"; πρός, "with, among" (after vbs. of speaking [BDAG 874b; cf. ZG 132]); ὅτι, introduces indir. discourse (France 316–17). In Gk. the tense of the vb. in the orig. dir. discourse will be retained in indir. discourse (see 2:1). Therefore, ἔχουσιν is in the pres. tense in the reported discussion of the disciples but it must be translated as a past tense in Eng., because the discussion took place in the past (cf. T 64).

8:17 Γνούς, nom. sg. masc. of aor. act. ptc. of γινώσκω, "perceive, realize, become aware of" (cf. BDAG 200b); temp. adv. ptc. antecedent; τί, "why?" (see 2:7); διαλογίζεσθε, 2nd pl. pres. mid. indic. of dep. διαλογίζομαι, "discuss, argue"; νοεῖτε, from νοέω, "perceive, understand"; συνίετε, from συνίημι, "understand, comprehend"; πεπωρωμένην, acc. sg. fem. of pf. pass. ptc. of πωρόω, "harden"; adj. ptc.; complement in a dbl. acc. obj. complement cstr. (on the use of the distributive sg. καρδίαν, see 6:52). In Mark's Gospel, a hard heart is primarily an intellectual problem, a dullness in thinking that causes people to lack insight into Jesus's identity and teaching (see 3:5).

8:18 Ἔχοντες, nom. pl. masc. of pres. act. ptc. of ἔχω, "have"; adv. ptc. of concession (Wallace 634; KMP 333); ὦτα, acc. pl. neut. of οὖς, ὠτός, τό, "ear"; μνημονεύετε, from μνημονεύω, "remember." Mark 8:18 recalls the language used earlier in the narrative to describe those who were outside and who therefore could not understand his parables and had not received the mystery of the kingdom of God (4:11–12).

8:19 Jesus's appeal to remember at the end of the previous verse introduces the questions in 8:19–20, questions that force the disciples to recall what took place at the feeding of the five thousand and the feeding of the four thousand. Ἔκλασα, 1st sg. aor. act. indic. of κλάω, "break"; εἰς, "for" (used with the acc. to express the same idea as a dat. of advantage [BDAG 290d; cf. R 535; Moule 69; see also εἰς in 8:20]); πεντακισχιλίους, acc. pl. masc. of πεντακισχίλιοι, -αι, -α, "five thousand"; κοφίνους, acc. pl. masc. of κόφινος, -ου, ὁ, "basket"; κλασμάτων, gen. pl. neut. of κλάσμα, -ατος, τό, "fragment"; gen. of content; πλήρεις, acc. pl. masc. of πλήρης, -ες, "full, filled"; ἤρατε, 2nd pl. aor. act. indic. of αἴρω, "take up, pick up."

8:20 In the adv. clause beginning with the conj. ὅτε, the question assumes but does not restate the vb. ἔκλασα that appeared following ὅτε in the similarly structured question in the preceding verse. In addition, the question assumes but does not restate the noun ἄρτους after the adj. ἑπτά. Τετρακισχιλίους, acc. pl. masc. of τετρακισχίλιοι, -αι, -α, "four thousand"; σπυρίδων, gen. pl. fem. of σπυρίς, -ίδος, ἡ, "basket"; πληρώματα, acc. pl. neut. of πλήρωμα, -ατος, τό, "that which is enough to fill" (BDAG 829c); κλασμάτων, gen. pl. neut. of κλάσμα, -ατος, τό, "fragment"; ἤρατε, 2nd pl. aor. act. indic. of αἴρω, "take up, pick up." With the use of πληρώματα, the complicated syntactical structure in 8:20 is similar to that found in 6:43. The vb. ἤρατε takes the acc. πληρώματα as a dir. obj. The gen. noun σπυρίδων, which is syntactically related to πληρώματα as an obj. gen., is modified by the interr. adj. πόσων. Finally, κλασμάτων is a gen. of content modifying σπυρίδων ("You picked up enough to fill how many baskets of fragments?"; on κλασμάτων as a gen. of content, see Cranfield 262).

8:21 Jesus ends with one last question: "Don't you understand (συνίετε, from συνίημι, understand, comprehend) yet?" What exactly the disciples should understand based on the number of baskets that they picked up after each miraculous feeding is left open-ended. At the most basic level, they should understand that Jesus is able to take a few loaves of bread and multiply them in such a way that he could feed a large crowd and still have more left over. The point is not that the disciples can always expect a miraculous provision of food. However, the reality of Jesus's power and compassion means that they need not be so anxiously preoccupied with their material provision that they miss out on Jesus's teaching or fail to think deeply about it (cf. Cranfield 262). Still, Jesus's teaching and questions in 8:14–21 are sufficiently enigmatic to cause confusion, and it is difficult to be overly critical of the disciples. It is possible both to see and not see when trying to understand Jesus.

HOMILETICAL SUGGESTIONS

Forgetful Followers (8:14–21)

1. Why we should not be too similar to the disciples:

    a. Because they do not remember all that Jesus has done for them in the past

    b. Because they do not trust Jesus to care for them in the present

2. Why we should not be too critical of the disciples:

    a. Because Jesus can often be difficult to understand

    b. Because we can often respond just like them

(d) [Transition] Healing of the Blind Man of Bethsaida (8:22–26)

This healing story functions as a transitional passage, coming at the end of Jesus's ministry by the Sea of Galilee and opening up the next section on discipleship teaching. Mark 8:22–26 illustrates again that Jesus helps those who come to him in faith, a prominent theme throughout chs. 4–8 (note the close similarities between the healing in 8:22–26 and that in 7:31–37). What is unique about 8:22–26 is that Jesus heals the blind man in two stages. In the immediately preceding passage, Jesus has just criticized the disciples for their spiritual blindness. They are in need of further help to understand as they should. In this way, the healing of the blind man in two stages prepares the way for the next section. It creates the expectation and hope that the disciples can be healed of their spiritual blindness through a second touch of additional teaching from Jesus.

8:22 According to a common pattern in Mark's Gospel, the shift into a new scene begins with a series of historical pres. vbs. (ἔρχονται, φέρουσιν, παρακαλοῦσιν), the first of which is a vb. of motion (see 1:12). Ἔρχονται, 3rd pl. pres. mid. indic. of dep. ἔρχομαι, "come"; φέρουσιν and παρακαλοῦσιν, indef. pl. vbs. with an unspecified group of "people" as the subj. (see 1:22); ἅψηται, 3rd sg. aor. mid. subjunc. of ἅπτω, "touch" (mng. with mid.); subjunc. in a dir. obj. ἵνα clause to express a request (see 5:10); αὐτοῦ, gen. dir. obj.

8:23 Ἐπιλαβόμενος, nom. sg. masc. of aor. mid. ptc. of dep. ἐπιλαμβάνομαι, "take hold of, grasp"; temp. adv. ptc. antecedent; χειρός, gen. dir. obj. (R 507–8); ἐξήνεγκεν, 3rd sg. aor. act. indic. of ἐκφέρω, "bring out, lead out"; ἔξω, functioning as a prep. (see 5:10); πτύσας, nom. sg. masc. of aor. act ptc. of πτύω, "spit"; temp. adv. ptc. antecedent; εἰς, "on" (when the action is directed toward a body part (see T 256; cf. BDAG 289a); ὄμματα, acc. pl. neut. of ὄμμα, -ατος, τό, "eye"; ἐπιθείς, nom. sg. masc. of aor. act. ptc. of ἐπιτίθημι, "lay on"; temp. adv. ptc. antecedent; τάς, art. expressing a poss. pron. (cf. Wallace 215; KMP 158; see also the same use of τάς in 8:25); ἐπηρώτα, 3rd sg. impf. act. indic. of ἐπερωτάω, "ask" (on the impf. of ἐπερωτάω, see 4:10). In this context, εἰ introduces a dir. question and therefore functions like ὅτι when it introduces dir. discourse (R 916; BDF §440; Moule 151, 158; Z §401; cf. Voelz 1:517). It is not necessary to translate εἰ, since Eng. uses quotation marks to indicate a dir. question. Τι, neut. indef. pron.

8:24 Ἀναβλέψας, nom. sg. masc. of aor. act. ptc. of ἀναβλέπω, "receive sight, look up"; temp. adv. ptc. antecedent. In the NT, the vb. ἀναβλέπω conveys two distinct meanings: (1) to look up; or (2) to regain or receive sight (BDAG 59b). When the vb. means "to look up," the context involves people with sight directing their eyes toward something (e.g., 6:41; 7:34; 16:4). However, the vb. normally indicates regaining or receiving sight in passages that describe the healing of someone who is blind (e.g., Matt 1:5; Mark 10:51–52; Luke 18:41–43; John 9:11; Acts 9:17–18). Given that kind of context in Mark 8:24, ἀναβλέψας is probably best translated to indicate that the man did in fact receive his sight (NET: "regaining his sight"; cf. Guelich 433; Stein 391; Voelz 1:517).

The man's words themselves are jumbled and difficult to decipher. One syntactical clue for making sense of the sentence structure is found in the ptc. περιπατοῦντας (acc. pl. masc. of pres. act. ptc. of περιπατέω, "walk, walk around"). Mark often uses a vb. of seeing with both an acc. dir. obj. and an acc. supplementary (complementary) ptc. (e.g., 13:26: ὄψονται τὸν υἱὸν τοῦ ἀνθρώπου ἐρχόμενον ["they will see the Son of Man coming"]; cf. 1:10, 16, 19; 2:14; 5:15, 31; 6:33, 48–49; 9:1, 14, 38; 11:20; 13:14, 29; 14:62, 67; 16:5). Consequently, since the ὅτι clause has a vb. of seeing (ὁρῶ, 1st sg. pres. act. indic. of ὁράω, "see") and also what appears to be an acc. pl. masc. supplementary (complementary) ptc. (περιπατοῦντας), the context seems to demand an acc. pl. masc. noun to function as the dir. obj. of ὁρῶ. One possibility is that τοὺς ἀνθρώπους is the acc. dir. obj. that the context demands, even though it precedes rather than follows ὅτι. The result would be a sentence in which the main clause—consisting solely of βλέπω—expresses the reality of the man's new sight, while the subord. clause communicates the inadequacy of that new sight (Voelz 1:518): "I do see, because [ὅτι, causal] I see men walking as trees" (δένδρα, acc. pl. neut. of δένδρον, -ου, τό, tree). Perhaps the awkward word order serves to convey the man's confusion and excitement.

8:25 In a way that does not fit the pattern of other healing miracles in Mark, this one demanded a second touch from Jesus. Εἶτα, adv. mng. "then, next"; ἐπέθηκεν, 3rd sg. aor. act. indic. of ἐπιτίθημι, "lay on"; διέβλεψεν, 3rd sg. aor. act. indic. of διαβλέπω, "look intently" (BDAG 226c; cf. LN 24.36); ἀπεκατέστη, 3rd sg. aor. act. indic. of ἀποκαθίστημι, "be restored, be cured" (intrans. mng. with act. [BDAG 111d]; concerning the dbl. aug. on ἀπεκατέστη, see 3:5); ἐνέβλεπεν, 3rd sg. impf. act. indic. of ἐμβλέπω, "be able to see" (for a similar use of ἐμβλέπω, see Acts 22:11; cf. NLT; on the impf. to portray the reality of a healing miracle, see 1:21); τηλαυγῶς, adv. mng. "clearly, plainly."

8:26 Ἀπέστειλεν, 3rd sg. aor. act. indic. of ἀποστέλλω, "send"; λέγων, nom. sg. masc. of pres. act. ptc. of λέγω, "say"; attendant circumstance ptc. (cf. 12:6 for a similar use of λέγων); εἰσέλθῃς, 2nd sg. aor. act. subjunc. of εἰσέρχομαι, "go into, enter"; prohibitive subjunc. (on the aor. tense for specific commands, see 1:25; 2:11). This scene concludes in a way that is similar to earlier episodes in which Jesus healed someone in a private setting, with a command to silence (1:45; 5:20, 43; 7:36). By going to his home and by staying away from the village, the man would not have an opportunity to spread the news about Jesus's miraculous power to heal.

HOMILETICAL SUGGESTIONS

Three Difficult Healings (7:31–8:26)

1. Jesus does all things well, even with difficult cases. (7:31–37)
2. Difficult cases sometimes involve a second touch from Jesus. (8:22–26)
3. Disciples can be difficult cases. (8:14–21)
   a. They may need a second touch from Jesus.
   b. They may need hope from Jesus that he can do well even with them.

II. Jesus as the Suffering Son of God (8:27–16:8)

The most obvious structural marker in Mark's Gospel is the statement in 8:31 that Jesus began to teach his disciples that the Son of Man must suffer many things. A new phase in Mark's characterization of Jesus begins at this pivot point in the story, one that emphasizes Jesus's suffering more than his power. Jesus's destiny in the cross has implications as well for his disciples, who must learn to deny self, take up the cross, and follow their Lord. In contrast to the first half of Mark's Gospel, which takes place in and around Galilee, the second half takes place on the way to Jerusalem (8:27–10:52), in the temple area at Jerusalem (11:1–13:37), and in and around Jerusalem in a more general way (14:1–16:8).

A. JESUS'S MINISTRY ON THE WAY TO JERUSALEM (8:27–10:52)

In Mark 8:27, Jesus—while he is on the way—asks the disciples a question about his identity. Peter makes his confession that Jesus is the Christ (8:29), after which Jesus begins to teach his disciples about the coming suffering of the Son of Man (8:31). The setting of this episode as "on the way" marks off the beginning of a new section in the narrative. Throughout this section, Mark provides continuing reminders that Jesus is on the way (8:27; 9:33, 34; 10:17, 32, 46, 52), and 10:32–34 makes it clear that he is traveling to Jerusalem, where he will suffer, die, and rise again. Although Mark uses the word "way" (ὁδός) elsewhere in his Gospel, he makes the term function as a description for a setting only in 8:27–10:52. This section ends with Bartimaeus, a blind beggar healed by Jesus, following him on the way (10:52). In the next episode, Jesus enters Jerusalem and its temple (11:1–11). At that point, with the shift in setting, the focus of Jesus's ministry changes.

The point of Mark 8:27–10:52 is to look ahead to Jesus's coming death and resurrection and to explain the implications of his suffering for his followers. The focus of this section is clearly on the plotline of Jesus's relationship with the disciples. Even when he casts out a demon or disputes with the Pharisees or talks with a rich man about eternal life, Jesus takes time with his disciples at the end of the event to teach them privately about the significance of what just happened (9:28–29; 10:10–12, 23–31). The negative picture of the disciples only increases in this section. Earlier, they did not show insight into Jesus's power and care for them. Now, they fail to grasp the mission of the Messiah and what that mission means for their own lives.

In 8:27–10:52, Mark arranges his material around three passion predictions by Jesus. In each, Jesus points forward to the suffering, death, and resurrection of the Son of Man (8:31; 9:31; 10:32–34). After each prediction, the disciples put on display their lack of understanding concerning Jesus's mission and what it means for them as his followers (8:32; 9:33–34; 10:35–41). After each instance of misunderstanding, Jesus responds by teaching his disciples about the nature of true discipleship (8:34–38; 9:35–50; 10:42–45). This repeated pattern of prediction followed by misunderstanding followed by teaching on discipleship provides the basic structure for Mark 8:27–10:52.

FOR FURTHER STUDY

23. Mark's Central Section (8:27–10:52)

*Best, Ernest. "Discipleship in Mark: Mark 8.22–10.52." *SJT* 23 (1970): 323–37.

———. *Following Jesus: Discipleship in the Gospel of Mark*. JSNTSup 4. Sheffield, UK: JSOT Press, 1981.

Fleddermann, Harry. "The Discipleship Discourse (Mark 9:33–40)." *CBQ* 43 (1981): 57–75.

Kaminouchi, Alberto de Mingo. *"But It Is Not So Among You": Echoes of Power in Mark 10.32–45*. JSNTSup 249. London: T&T Clark, 2003.

Perrin, Norman. "Towards an Interpretation of the Gospel of Mark." Pages 1–78 in *Christology and a Modern Pilgrimage: A Discussion with Norman Perrin*. Edited by Hans Dieter Betz. Missoula, MT: Scholars Press, 1974.

Robbins, Vernon K. "Summons and Outline in Mark: The Three-Step Progression." *NovT* 23 (1981): 97–114.

Santos, Narry F. "Jesus' Paradoxical Teaching in Mark 8:35; 9:35; and 10:43–44." *BSac* 157 (2000): 15–25.

———. *Slave of All: The Paradox of Authority and Servanthood in the Gospel of Mark*. JSNTSup 237. London: Sheffield Academic Press, 2003.

Schweizer, Eduard. "Mark's Theological Achievement." Pages 42–63 in *The Interpretation of Mark*. Edited by William Telford. IRT 7. Philadelphia: Fortress, 1985.

1. Cycle 1: Prediction and Response (8:27–38)

After Peter's confession of Jesus as the Christ, Jesus predicts for the first time that as the Son of Man he will suffer, be rejected and killed, and after three days rise again. Peter, apparently unwilling to accept the idea of a suffering Messiah, rebukes Jesus. The disciples are setting their minds on human ways of thinking rather than God's way of thinking. Jesus calls together the crowd along with the disciples, making it clear that his teaching on discipleship is for "anyone" and "whoever." What it takes to be a follower of Jesus is self-denial, a willingness to give one's life, and a determination to take Jesus's way as the pattern for one's own life. Therefore, 8:27–38 provides the first example of the threefold pattern of (1) prediction; (2) misunderstanding; and (3) teaching on discipleship.

(a) First Passion Prediction (8:27–31)

8:27 Ἐξῆλθεν, 3rd sg. aor. act. indic. of ἐξέρχομαι, "come, go out" (on a sg. vb. with a compound subj., see 12:33). According to Mark, Jesus's conversation with the disciples took place "on the way" (ἐν τῇ ὁδῷ). In Mark's Gospel, the noun ὁδός functions both lit. and metaphorically. The word can refer to a literal path or road (4:4, 15) or to the way of God in a metaphorical sense, i.e., to the manner of life God expects (12:14). Yet it is often difficult to separate lit. and fig. uses of ὁδός, since they can overlap (*EDNT* 2:491–92). The references to the "way" clustered in Mark 8–10 do not sort themselves out neatly into lit. or metaphorical uses, since, although Jesus may be walking on an actual road, he is also on the path that God has prepared for him, obediently following God's plan for his life. Ἐπηρώτα, 3rd sg. impf. act. indic. of ἐπερωτάω, "ask" (on ἐπερωτάω, see 4:10; the same impf. form appears in 8:29); λέγων, nom. sg. masc. of pres. act. ptc. of λέγω, "say"; redundant ptc.; οἱ ἄνθρωποι, used for "people" in general (ZG 133; cf. T 293; Moule 28); εἶναι, pres. act. inf. of εἰμί, "be"; inf. of indir. discourse. Two accusatives can occur in connection with an equative vb. inf. such as εἶναι, with one being the acc. subj. of the inf. and the other the pred. acc. In this instance, the pers. pron. με is the acc. subj. of the inf., since it is the "known entity," leaving the interr. pron. τίνα as the pred. acc. (Wallace 42–43, 194–95; see esp. n. 71 on p. 195).

8:28 On οἱ δέ, see 1:45; on the ending for εἶπαν, see 8:5; λέγοντες, nom. pl. masc. of pres. act. ptc. of λέγω, "say"; redundant ptc.; βαπτιστήν, acc. sg. masc. of βαπτιστής, -οῦ, ὁ, "Baptist, Baptizer"; προφητῶν, partitive gen. The acc. case of Ἰωάννην assumes a sentence structure similar to that found in Jesus's question, implying but not stating the words λέγουσιν οἱ ἄνθρωποί σε εἶναι (Bruce 397; Cranfield 268; i.e., Ἰωάννην is a pred. acc. following the implied indir. discourse inf. εἶναι). The second name on the list, Ἠλίαν, is also in the acc. case and assumes a similar sentence structure. Then the grammatical pattern changes. After the second ἄλλοι, the vb. λέγουσιν is still assumed, but ὅτι introduces an indir. discourse clause, one that implies the words σὺ εἶ (Cranfield 268; cf. R 1028). Therefore, εἷς is functioning as a pred. nom. in the clause. Popular opinion concerning Jesus focused on his role as a prophet, but such an assessment fell short of the truth. Mark's Gospel does present Jesus as a prophet (e.g., 6:4; 14:65), but also as more than a prophet.

8:29 Ἐπηρώτα, 3rd sg. impf. act. indic. of ἐπερωτάω, "ask." The nom. pers. pron. ὑμεῖς—grammatically unnecessary given the ending of the vb. λέγετε—puts the emph. on the disciples, on what their understanding of Jesus is in contrast to the perspectives just mentioned (cf. ZG 133; Taylor 376; Marcus 2:603). Jesus's questions in 8:27 and 8:29 follow a similar grammatical pattern, both using forms of λέγω as the main vb. and εἶναι (pres. act. inf. of εἰμί, "be") as an inf. of indir. discourse (on the acc. forms τίνα and με, see 8:27). In Peter's answer (ἀποκριθείς, nom. sg. masc. of aor. pass. ptc. of dep. ἀποκρίνομαι, "answer"; redundant ptc.), the nom. pron. σύ—also grammatically unnecessary because of the form of the vb. εἶ—starts the reply in the same way that ὑμεῖς stood at the beginning of Jesus's question (σύ is the subj., since it is a pron., and the art. noun ὁ Χριστός is the pred. nom.; cf. Wallace 44–45; KMP 54–55). In contrast to the prophetic figures mentioned by people, Jesus is the Messiah. From the very beginning of his Gospel, Mark presents Jesus as the Christ (i.e., the Messiah, the promised king from the line of David [see 1:1]). Therefore, Peter was correct to identify Jesus as the Christ, but as the following verses demonstrate, Peter and Jesus had different ideas about what that meant.

8:30 Ἐπετίμησεν, 3rd sg. aor. act. indic. of ἐπιτιμάω, "sternly warn, rebuke"; αὐτοῖς, dat. dir. obj. Normally in Mark, the vb. ἐπιτιμάω is used for rebuke, i.e., for an expression of strong disapproval given in order to put a stop to an action that was taking place (cf. BDAG 384d; on ἐπιτιμάω, see 8:32). In 8:30, the vb. ἐπιτιμάω is used for a strongly worded warning, i.e., for an attempt to prevent an action from happening, an action that would meet with disapproval. Λέγωσιν, 3rd pl. pres. act. subjunc. of λέγω, "speak, report" (BDAG 590a); subjunc. in a dir. obj. ἵνα clause to express a command (see 5:10). Jesus's command to the disciples to remain silent is somewhat different from the previous commands to silence that Jesus directed toward those who received healing (1:45; 5:20, 43; 7:36–37; 8:26). Earlier Jesus sought to limit information about his miraculous power when he healed people in private, apparently because the increasing fame brought about by his miracles made it difficult for him to focus on other important aspects of his ministry. By way of contrast, in 8:30, Jesus warns his disciples not to speak about his messianic identity. Why? As the following narrative shows, at this point the disciples did not have a clear picture of what it meant for Jesus to be the Messiah (cf. 8:32). Therefore, it was not the time for them to tell others about his messianic identity; rather, it was the time for them to learn.

8:31 Ἤρξατο, 3rd sg. aor. mid. indic. of ἄρχω, "begin" (mng. with mid.; on ἄρχομαι, see 1:45); διδάσκειν, pres. act. inf. of διδάσκω, "teach"; complementary inf.; δεῖ, 3rd sg. pres. act. indic. of δεῖ, "it is necessary, one must." At times in Mark's Gospel, the vb. δεῖ points to events that must happen because they are part of God's plan as it has been announced in the Scriptures (cf. Lane 294; Stein 401; *EDNT* 1:279–80). In this way, "it is necessary" (δεῖ) can correspond to "just as it is written" (καθὼς γέγραπται; cf. 8:31 with 14:21). Υἱόν, acc. of respect or reference; on πολλά, see 9:12; παθεῖν, aor. act. inf. of πάσχω, "suffer"; subst. use of the inf., subj. of δεῖ (cf. Wallace 601; KMP 369; the same use of the inf. applies to all four inf. forms that follow δεῖ in 8:31); ἀποδοκιμασθῆναι, aor. pass. inf. of ἀποδοκιμάζω, "reject"; ἀποκτανθῆναι, aor. pass. inf. of ἀποκτείνω, "kill." In standard Jewish usage, "after three days" meant "the day after tomorrow" and therefore was equivalent to "on the third day" (cf. Matt 16:21; Luke 9:22). The last part of the first day and the first part of the third day were both counted as days (France 336–37; LN 67.48; cf. Harold W. Hoehner, *Chronological Aspects of the Life of Christ* [Grand Rapids: Zondervan, 1977], 71–74). Ἀναστῆναι, aor. act. inf. of ἀνίστημι, "rise."

Jesus uses the title "the Son of Man" to refer to himself in his messianic role, preferring this title to "Christ" since it allows him to emphasize the aspects of his messianic identity that are most important to him (see also 2:10; 13:26). Central to Jesus's role as the Son of Man is his suffering, death, and resurrection as the representative for

God's people, and in Mark's Gospel Jesus repeatedly uses the title "the Son of Man" with reference to that part of his mission (8:31; 9:9, 12, 31; 10:33, 45; 14:21, 41). If Jesus's reference to the Son of Man alludes to the heavenly figure in Dan 7:13–14, who represents God's people (cf. Dan 7:27), then it is understandable why Jesus would say that the Son of Man must suffer (cf. Marcus 2:613). As the representative for God's people, he must fully experience their suffering (Dan 7:19, 21, 23–25), a suffering that necessarily precedes the coming of the kingdom of God (Dan 7:17–18, 22, 26–27).

FOR FURTHER STUDY

24. The Messianic Secret in Mark

Aune, David E. "The Problem of the Messianic Secret." *NovT* 11 (1969): 1–31.

Blevins, James L. *The Messianic Secret in Markan Research, 1901–1976.* Washington, DC: University Press of America, 1981.

Burkill, T. A. *Mysterious Revelation: An Examination of the Philosophy of St. Mark's Gospel.* Ithaca, NY: Cornell University Press, 1963.

Iverson, Kelly R. "'Wherever the Gospel is Preached': The Paradox of Secrecy in the Gospel of Mark." Pages 181–209 in *Mark as Story: Retrospect and Prospect.* Edited by Kelly R. Iverson and Christopher W. Skinner. RBS 65. Atlanta: Society of Biblical Literature, 2011.

Kingsbury, Jack Dean. "The Shape of the Problem: The Secret of Jesus' Identity in Mark." Pages 1–23 in *The Christology of Mark's Gospel.* Philadelphia: Fortress, 1983.

Malbon, Elizabeth Struthers. "History, Theology, Story: Re-Contextualizing Mark's 'Messianic Secret' as Characterization." Pages 35–56 in *Character Studies and the Gospel of Mark.* Edited by Christopher W. Skinner and Matthew Ryan Hauge. LNTS 483. London: Bloomsbury T&T Clark, 2014.

Moule, Charles Francis Digby. "On Defining the Messianic Secret in Mark." Pages 239–52 in *Jesus und Paulus: Festschrift für Werner Georg Kümmel zum 70. Geburtstag.* Edited by E. Earle Ellis and Erich Grässer. Göttingen: Vandenhoeck & Ruprecht, 1975.

Perrin, Norman. "The Wredestrasse Becomes the Hauptstrasse: Reflections on the Reprinting of the Dodd Festschrift." *JR* 46 (1966): 296–300.

Räisänen, Heikki. *The "Messianic Secret" in Mark.* Edinburgh: T&T Clark, 1990.

*Tuckett, Christopher, ed. *The Messianic Secret.* IRT 1. Philadelphia: Fortress, 1983.

Watson, David F. *Honor among Christians: The Cultural Key to the Messianic Secret.* Minneapolis: Fortress, 2010.

Watson, Francis. "The Social Function of Mark's Secrecy Motif." *JSNT* 24 (1985): 49–69.

Wrede, William. *The Messianic Secret.* Translated by J. C. C. Grieg. Cambridge: James Clarke, 1971.

Yarbro Collins, Adela. "Messianic Secret and the Gospel of Mark: Secrecy in Jewish Apocalypticism, the Hellenistic Mystery Religions, and Magic." Pages 11–30 in *Rending the Veil: Concealment and Secrecy in the History of Religions.* Edited by Elliot R. Wolfson. New York: Seven Bridges, 1999.

(b) Misunderstanding by the Disciples: Rebuke of Peter (8:32–33)

8:32 Παρρησίᾳ, "plainly, openly," (BDAG 781c); dat. of manner; ἐλάλει, 3rd sg. impf. act. indic. of λαλέω, "speak"; προσλαβόμενος, nom. sg. masc. of aor. mid. ptc.

of προσλαμβάνω, "take aside" (mng. with mid.); temp. adv. ptc. antecedent; ἤρξατο, 3rd sg. aor. mid. indic. of ἄρχω, "begin" (mng. with mid.; on ἄρχομαι, see 1:45); ἐπιτιμᾶν, pres. act. inf. of ἐπιτιμάω, "rebuke"; complementary inf.; αὐτῷ, dat. dir. obj. "To rebuke" means to express strong disapproval for the purpose of putting a stop to some undesired action (BDAG 384d). In Mark's Gospel, Jesus effectively rebukes unclean spirits (1:25; 3:12; 9:25), a threatening storm (4:39), and his own disciples (8:33). However, whenever anyone other than Jesus takes up the task of rebuking, it is always a misguided attempt to hinder a fitting action: a prediction of messianic suffering (8:32), a request for Jesus's blessing (10:13), and a cry to Jesus for mercy (10:48). Although Peter's objection is not spelled out directly, his problem seems to be related directly to what Jesus just taught, that the messianic role necessarily entailed suffering. Peter may have regarded the Messiah as only an earthly ruler who would restore righteousness, freedom, and prosperity to Israel, a nation under the oppression of wicked foreign rulers (cf. Pss. Sol. 17–18).

8:33 On ὁ δέ, see 1:45; ἐπιστραφείς, nom. sg. masc. of aor. pass. ptc. of ἐπιστρέφω, "turn around" (mng. with pass.); temp. adv. ptc. antecedent; ἰδών, nom. sg. masc. of aor. act. ptc. of ὁράω, "see, look at"; temp. adv. ptc. antecedent; ἐπετίμησεν, 3rd sg. aor. act. indic. of ἐπιτιμάω, "rebuke"; Πέτρῳ, dat. dir. obj.; ὕπαγε, 2nd sg. pres. act. impv. of ὑπάγω, "go, depart"; Σατανᾶ, voc. of simple address from Σατανᾶς (cf. ZG 133; Wallace 68). When a neut. pl. art., such as τά, stands before a gen. noun or phrase, it implies but does not state "things" (Wallace 235–36; R 767; i.e., τὰ τοῦ θεοῦ can be translated "the things of God," and τὰ τῶν ἀνθρώπων "the things of men" [for a similar use of the neut. pl. art., see 12:17]). In Mark's Gospel, Jesus's path of sacrificial service stands at the center of God's plan. Any opposition to this path comes from a limited human perspective, which ultimately has its source in the work of Satan.

(c) Jesus's Instructions on Discipleship: Taking Up the Cross (8:34–38)

8:34 After he summoned the crowd together with the disciples (προσκαλεσάμενος, nom. sg. masc. of aor. mid. ptc. of προσκαλέω, "summon, call to oneself" [mng. with mid.]; temp. adv. ptc. antecedent), Jesus placed three demands on anyone who wants to follow after him (on the 1st class cond., see the discussion concerning the similar use in 9:35; ἀκολουθεῖν, pres. act. inf. of ἀκολουθέω, follow [on ἀκολουθέω, see 1:18]; complementary inf.). Each of these demands is expressed through a 3rd pers. impv. English versions have traditionally translated 3rd pers. impv. forms in a way that can easily be misunderstood as expressing a permissive idea, as allowing an action to take place (e.g., ESV: "let him deny himself"). However, a 3rd pers. impv. is a command, a statement about what must happen, and is best translated in a way that makes that clear (e.g., NET: "he must deny himself"; see Wallace 486; KMP 209).

The first demand for a follower of Jesus is self-denial (ἀπαρνησάσθω, 3rd sg. aor. mid. impv. of dep. ἀπαρνέομαι, "deny"). To deny self means to say no to self-centered concerns (Cranfield 281–82), to refuse to make personal desires and self-interest the focus of one's life (Hooker 208), and to reject self as the determining factor for one's goals, aspirations, and desires in life (Stein 407).

The second demand on the follower of Jesus calls for taking up one's cross (ἀράτω, 3rd sg. aor. act. impv. of αἴρω, "take up"). As part of the punishment of crucifixion, the condemned prisoner took up the crossbeam and carried it out to the place of execution. There the outstretched arms of the prisoner were tied or nailed to the crossbeam, which was then raised up along with the prisoner's body in order to fasten it to an upright post already implanted in the ground (*TDNT* 7:573–74). For Jesus to call on his followers to take up their cross meant to accept the position of a condemned prisoner and therefore to be prepared at any moment to give up their lives for his sake.

The third demand for discipleship is to keep on following Jesus (ἀκολουθείτω, 3rd sg. pres. act. impv. of ἀκολουθέω, "follow"; μοι, dat. dir. obj.). Jesus called for a sustained devotion to him and to the pattern of his life, a pattern characterized by a willingness to suffer and by a determination to live with sacrificial service toward others. The shift to the pres. tense with ἀκολουθείτω, after the use of the aor. tense with the previous two impv. forms, seems designed in this context to stress the continuous nature of the command and the importance of a persistent faithfulness to Jesus (Taylor 381; Stein 407).

Most often, general precepts use pres. impv. forms, while specific commands call for aor. impv. forms (see 1:15, 25; 2:11). Since the three commands in Mark 8:34 are addressed to "anyone [who] wants to follow," they are all general commands, incl. the first two that are expressed with an aor. impv. Different attempts have been made to account for aor. impv. forms being used for general commands in this context, and some attempt to explain the anomaly seems necessary, since Mark otherwise fairly consistently follows the pattern of using aor. impv. forms for specific commands (see 13:28 for one other exception). For the most part, the discussion has centered on the par. in Luke 9:23, which uses the same three commands with the same sequence of tenses. Three possible explanations for the use of the aor. tense with the first two commands are:

1. The aor. impv. forms express distributive commands. The summary aspect of the aor. tense is appropriate for a context in which general commands must be obeyed by each individual who wants to follow Jesus (Fanning 367).

2. The aor. impv. forms express prerequisite commands. The summary aspect of the aor. tense is well suited for a context in which general commands must be obeyed before another command. One must deny self and take up the cross before being able to follow Jesus (Campbell, *VANIV* 89; cf. Marcus 2:617).

3. The aor. impv. forms simply express summary commands, treating the action as a whole, and the first two commands are in the aor. tense mainly to show that they are less heavily marked. The third impv., using the more heavily marked pres. tense, draws attention to the process of following Jesus (Porter, *VA* 351, 355). The use of the aor. tense with the first two commands does make the shift to the pres. tense with the third stand out more clearly and therefore does highlight the continuous nature of the pres. impv. The follower of Jesus must keep on following.

8:35 Mark 8:35 explains the first reason why the demands of following Jesus are worth accepting (γάρ, causal; for the second reason, see 8:38). Θέλῃ, 3rd sg. pres. act. subjunc. of θέλω, "want, wish"; subjunc. in indef. rel. clause; σῶσαι, aor. act. inf. of σῴζω, "save"; complementary inf.; ἀπολέσει, 3rd sg. fut. act. indic. of ἀπόλλυμι, "lose" (form appears twice in v. 35). The fut. indic. is sometimes used in places where the aor. subjunc. more commonly appears, e.g., in a delib. question as in 6:37, in an indef. rel. clause as in 8:35, in emph. neg. as in 13:31; 14:31, or in a purpose clause following μήποτε as in 14:2 (cf. Wallace 571). Σώσει, 3rd sg. fut. act. indic. of σῴζω, "save." The noun ψυχή has a dbl. mng. in 8:35, for life in this present age and for life in the age to come (cf. Cranfield 282; Lane 308–9). The people who cling to the life of this present age will find out that they have lost out on the more valuable life of the age to come. The people who willingly give up their tight grip on life at the present time for the sake of Jesus and the gospel, these are the ones who will preserve for themselves the unending life of the age to come. Moreover, these eternal realities impose themselves on present existence (cf. 10:28–30). Living a self-focused life results in losing out on life even as it is meant to be lived at the present time. Self-denial and devotion to Jesus lead not only to life in the age to come but also to true life in the present, a life of meaning and significance.

8:36 Both 8:36 and 8:37 present rhetorical questions. Both verses use the conj. γάρ as a way of indicating that these questions explain why life in the age to come is so valuable and why it would be worth giving up life in the present age to gain it. Τί, dbl. acc. obj. of the thing; ὠφελεῖ, from ὠφελέω, "help, benefit, profit" (sg. vb. with compound subj.); ἄνθρωπον, dbl. acc. obj. of the person; κερδῆσαι, aor. act. inf. of κερδαίνω, "gain"; subst. use of the inf., subj. of ὠφελεῖ; ζημιωθῆναι, aor. pass. inf. of ζημιόω, "suffer loss of, forfeit" (mng. with pass.); subst. use of the inf., subj. of ὠφελεῖ. Even if it were possible to gain everything in this present age that anyone could want by holding tightly to a self-focused life, such a gain would finally be worthless because it would only lead to the loss of the more valuable life in the age to come (cf. 10:17–22).

8:37 Τί, obj. in a dbl. acc. obj. complement cstr.; δοῖ, 3rd sg. aor. act. subjunc. of δίδωμι, "give"; delib. subjunc. (R 935; Wallace 467; on the formation of the subjunc. for δίδωμι and its compounds, see R 308–9; BDF §95; cf. 4:29; 14:10–11); ἀντάλλαγμα, acc. sg. neut. of ἀντάλλαγμα, -ατος, τό, "something given in exchange"; complement in a dbl. acc. obj. complement cstr.; ψυχῆς, gen. of price (cf. Wallace 122; KMP 102–3). The implied answer to the question in 8:27 is that nothing in this present age would be sufficiently valuable to lose one's life in the age to come for it. Therefore, giving one's life or anything in this present age for Jesus is worth the cost, since it all becomes insignificant in comp. to gaining life in the age to come.

8:38 Mark 8:38 offers a second reason for why following Jesus is worth the cost (γάρ, causal; cf. Stein 409; see 8:35 for the first reason). Devotion to Jesus leads to honor rather than shame at the future judgment when the Son of Man comes in glory and power. Ἐπαισχυνθῇ, 3rd sg. aor. pass. subjunc. of dep. ἐπαισχύνομαι, "be ashamed of"; subjunc. in an indef. rel. clause; on γενεά, see 8:12; μοιχαλίδι, dat. sg. fem. of μοιχαλίς,

-ίδος, ἡ, "adulterous, unfaithful" (used as an adj. in this context, although actually a noun mng. "adulteress" [BDAG 656c]); καί, adjunctive; ἐπαισχυνθήσεται, 3rd sg. fut. pass. indic. of dep. ἐπαισχύνομαι, "be ashamed of"; ἔλθῃ, 3rd sg. aor. act. subjunc. of ἔρχομαι, come; subjunc. in an indef. temp. clause (on ἐν with a form of ἔρχομαι, see 5:27). Matt 10:32–33 records a similar saying of Jesus in which he declares that he will confess before his Father in heaven whoever confesses him before others and that he will deny before his Father in heaven whoever denies him before others (cf. Luke 12:8–9). The use of the vb. ἐπαισχύνομαι in Mark 8:38 is similar to the language of confession and denial in Matt 10:32–33 (cf. *EDNT* 1:42; Stein 410). Those who are ashamed of Jesus will renounce or deny him. They will refuse to confess or publicly declare any loyalty to him. In response, Jesus will repudiate them; he will refuse to acknowledge their place in his kingdom when he comes again.

HOMILETICAL SUGGESTIONS

The Demands and Delights of Discipleship (8:34–38)

1. What are the costs in following Jesus?
   a. Self-denial (8:34a)
   b. Willingness to give one's life (8:34b)
   c. Determination to follow the pattern of Jesus's life (8:34c)
2. What are the rewards in following Jesus?
   a. Life in the coming kingdom (8:35–37)
   b. Honor in the coming judgment (8:38)

2. Interval: What Followers of Jesus Can Expect (9:1–29)

Between the first and second passion predictions, Mark includes three episodes that clarify what followers of Jesus can expect from the path they have chosen. The transfiguration (9:1–8) looks ahead to the glory that Jesus will have when the time of hiddenness is over, when he comes in the glory of his Father with the holy angels. This foretaste of future kingdom glory is important for the disciples. Present sacrifice is not the end; future vindication lies ahead. Yet Jesus's teaching on Elijah (9:9–13) highlights that the promise of future glory does not negate present suffering. In addition, Jesus's deliverance of the possessed boy (9:14–29) functions as a reminder to his followers that they can expect to be continually dependent on God's help through prayer.

(a) The Transfiguration (9:1–8)

9:1 Jesus's saying in 9:1 serves as a connecting link between the description of his teaching in 8:34–38 and the account of his transfiguration in 9:2–8, and therefore between the glory of the Son of Man as it will be revealed to all when the kingdom fully arrives and the glory of Jesus as it was revealed to a few at the transfiguration as a foretaste of that kingdom. On ἀμήν, see 3:28; ἑστηκότων, gen. pl. masc. of pf. act. ptc. of ἵστημι, "stand" (pres. tense intrans. mng. with pf. [BDAG 482d; ZG 134]); subst.

ptc. (the pf. form of ἵστημι only appears with ptc. forms in Mark [9:1; 11:5; 13:14], T 82); οἵτινες, used as a def. rel. pron. (R 957; cf. 4:20; 12:18; 15:7). Mark's Gospel uses οὐ μή to express a statement of emph. neg. ten times, most often with an aor. subjunc. vb. (9:1, 41; 10:15; 13:2 [twice], 19, 30; 14:25) but also with a fut. indic. vb. (13:31; 14:31). Such emph. neg. statements rule out even the possibility of a particular action taking place in the future (cf. Wallace 468–69; KMP 205). Emphatic neg. appears almost exclusively in Jesus's sayings in Mark (cf. Wallace 468; T 96); the only exception is Peter's emph. neg. statement in which he insists that he will not deny Jesus (14:31). Clearly, the reliability of the speaker determines the reliability of the emph. neg. statement. Γεύσωνται, 3rd pl. aor. mid. subjunc. of dep. γεύομαι, "taste, come to know" (cf. BDAG 195c); θανάτου, gen. dir. obj.; ἕως ἄν, "until" (with an aor. subjunc. vb. following [see 6:10]); ἴδωσιν, 3rd pl. aor. act. subjunc. of ὁράω, "see"; subjunc. in an indef. temp. clause; ἐληλυθυῖαν, acc. sg. fem. of pf. act. ptc. of ἔρχομαι, "come"; supplementary (complementary) ptc.; ἐν, "with" (expressing manner [BDAG 330a]).

9:2 Mark carefully ties his account of the transfiguration to Jesus's prediction in 9:1 by indicating the time interval between Jesus's words and their fulfillment, i.e., after six days (ἕξ, "six" [indecl. number]). Παραλαμβάνει, historical pres. (starting a new scene [see 1:12; cf. Fanning 232; Porter, *Idioms* 31]); ἀναφέρει, from ἀναφέρω, "take up, lead up, bring up"; historical pres.; ὑψηλόν, acc. sg. neut. of ὑψηλός, -ή, -όν, high; κατ' ἰδίαν, "by oneself, privately" (BDAG 467c); μόνους, redundant after κατ' ἰδίαν but used to emphasize the private nature of the setting (cf. Evans 35; many EVV leave μόνους untr.); μετεμορφώθη, 3rd sg. aor. pass. indic. of μεταμορφόω, "be transfigured, be transformed" (mng. with pass.).

9:3 Ἐγένετο, 3rd sg. aor. mid. indic. of dep. γίνομαι, "come to be"; neut. pl. subj. with sg. vb. (see 3:11). The ptc. στίλβοντα (nom. pl. neut. of pres. act. ptc. of στίλβω, "shine, be radiant") is functioning as an adj. ptc. in a pred. position (see Burton §429–32; Wallace 618–19; for similar examples, see Matt 7:14; 21:9; Mark 11:9–10; Gal 1:22; Heb 4:12; 7:3; Jas 2:15) and is therefore grammatically par. to the following pred. adj. λευκά (nom. pl. neut. of λευκός, -ή, -όν, "white"; modified by λίαν [adv. indicating a high degree, "exceedingly, intensely, very"]). In Eng., it may be best to translate the ptc. στίλβοντα as an adj. to clarify its function and to show its par. relationship with the adj. λευκά ("radiant, intensely white"; cf. ESV). Οἷα, acc. pl. neut. of οἷος, -α, -ον, "such as" (because of Sem. influence, οὕτως is used redundantly with οἷα and need not be translated [R 722–23; Z §§201–2]); γναφεύς, nom. sg. masc. of γναφεύς, -έως, ὁ, "cloth refiner, launderer"; δύναται, 3rd sg. pres. mid. indic. of dep. δύναμαι, "be able to, can"; λευκᾶναι, aor. act. inf. of λευκαίνω, "make white, whiten"; complementary inf. The noun γναφεύς, which appears only here in the NT, refers to a person involved in the trade of preparing, cleaning, and bleaching woolen cloth (Lane 315; Marcus 2:632). One difficulty with translating the word is that in many present-day cultures those who want to whiten cloth often turn to a product rather than to a person in a profession. Perhaps another way to communicate Mark's idea is to say that Jesus's clothes became intensely white, "far whiter than any earthly bleach could ever make them" (NLT).

9:4 Ὤφθη, 3rd sg. aor. pass. indic. of ὁράω, "become visible, appear" (mng. with pass., BDAG 719d). In the NT, the aor. pass. of ὁράω is used at times for the sudden and unexpected appearance of someone in a supernatural event (e.g., Luke 1:11; 24:34; Acts 7:2, 30, 35; 9:17; 13:31; 1 Cor 15:5–8; cf. Cranfield 290; Wallace 165). Mark uses an impf. periph. cstr. to show that Elijah and Moses were speaking with Jesus (ἦσαν, 3rd pl. impf. act. indic. of εἰμί, "be"; συλλαλοῦντες, nom. pl. masc. of pres. act. ptc. of συλλαλέω, "speak with, talk with"; τῷ Ἰησοῦ, dat. of association [cf. Wallace 160; R 528–29]). By portraying the action in progress, the impf. periph. cstr. seems to imply that the conversation went on for some time (see the discussion at 1:22).

9:5 Ἀποκριθείς, nom. sg. masc. of aor. pass. ptc. of dep. ἀποκρίνομαι, "answer"; redundant ptc. (see 3:33). The use of ἀποκριθείς as a redundant ptc. is sufficiently formulaic that it appears even when there is no statement or question in the immediate context to be answered (cf. 10:24; 11:14; 12:35; 14:48 [Z §366]). Λέγει, historical pres. (see 1:12, 30); ῥαββί, "rabbi, teacher" (an honorary form of address). The Gk. word ῥαββί is a transliteration of the Heb. word that lit. means "my great one" (also used in 11:21; 14:45; cf. the heightened form ῥαββουνί in 10:51). Eventually, "Rabbi" became a technical title within Jewish sources for an ordained teacher of the law, but at the time of Jesus it was used as an expression of honor toward any influential person, although often toward a teacher. As a result, even at the time of Jesus, there was a common connection between the title "Rabbi" and the title "Teacher" (Matt 23:7–8; John 1:38; 3:2; cf. *EDNT* 3:205–6; Marcus 2:633; Evans 37, 50, 134). Ἡμᾶς, acc. of respect or reference; εἶναι, pres. act. inf. of εἰμί, "be"; subst. use of the inf., subj. of ἐστιν (Wallace 600; KMP 370); ποιήσωμεν, 1st pl. aor. act. subjunc. of ποιέω, make; hort. subjunc.; σκηνάς, acc. pl. fem. of σκηνή, -ῆς, ἡ, "tabernacle, booth, temporary shelter."

9:6 In 9:6, Mark explains why Peter offered such an odd and puzzling suggestion in the previous verse (γάρ, explanatory); his words were an expression of his fear and lack of understanding (ᾔδει, 3rd sg. pluperf. act. indic. of οἶδα, "know"; pluperf. with past stative mng. [see 1:24]; ἀποκριθῇ, 3rd sg. aor. pass. subjunc. of dep. ἀποκρίνομαι, "answer"; ἔκφοβοι, nom. pl. masc. of ἔκφοβος, -ον, "terrified, very much afraid"; ἐγένοντο, 3rd pl. aor. mid. indic. of dep. γίνομαι, "be, become"). The interr. pron. τί introduces an indir. question. Since in Gk. indir. speech retains the mood of the dir. speech, the subjunc. vb. ἀποκριθῇ in the indir. question implies a delib. use of the subjunc. in the dir. question: "What should I answer?" (Z §348; R 738, 1031; T 116–17).

9:7 Ἐγένετο, 3rd sg. aor. mid. indic. of dep. γίνομαι, "come, come to be" (ἐγένετο appears twice in 9:7); both νεφέλη (nom. sg. fem.) and later in the verse νεφέλης (gen. sg. fem.) are from νεφέλη, -ης, ἡ, "cloud"; ἐπισκιάζουσα, nom. sg. fem. of pres. act. ptc. of ἐπισκιάζω, "overshadow, cover"; adv. ptc. of result (Wallace 638; KMP 335); αὐτοῖς, dat. dir. obj.; ἀκούετε, 2nd pl. pres. act. impv. of ἀκούω, "hear, listen to"; αὐτοῦ, gen. dir. obj. Since the impv. ἀκούετε is in the pres. tense, it is presented to the disciples as a general command, what they should make it their habit to do (Fanning 332–33; see also 1:15). In context, the command to listen to Jesus points back to the previous passage, where he predicted his coming suffering and called on his followers to deny themselves and be willing to suffer for him.

9:8 Ἐξάπινα, adv. mng. "suddenly, all at once"; περιβλεψάμενοι, nom. pl. masc. of aor. mid. ptc. of περιβλέπω, "look around" (mng. with mid.); temp. adv. ptc. antecedent; οὐκέτι οὐδένα, on two negatives to strengthen a statement, see 1:44; εἶδον, 3rd pl. aor. act. indic. of ὁράω, "see." In a way that is similar to its use in 4:22, ἀλλά functions as an equivalent to εἰ μή and means "except" (Z §469–70; BDF §448; a number of mss. actually have εἰ μή instead of ἀλλά). On the translation of the refl. pron. with μετά, see 8:14.

HOMILETICAL SUGGESTIONS

What Can Followers of Jesus Expect Out of Life (9:1–29)?

1. The transfiguration: Followers of Jesus can expect future glory. (9:1–8)
2. The conversation about Elijah: Followers of Jesus can expect present suffering. (9:9–13)
3. The deliverance of the possessed son: Followers of Jesus can expect the need for continual dependence. (9:14–29)

The Glory of Jesus (9:1–8)

1. What does the passage teach about Jesus?
   a. The transfiguration is a promise of future glory for Jesus.
   b. The transfiguration is a proof of the present authority of Jesus.
2. What does the passage teach about following Jesus?
   a. Jesus's glory demonstrates the value of living for Jesus with self-denial.
   b. God's voice demonstrates the wisdom of listening to Jesus with care.

(b) Teaching on Elijah (9:9–13)

9:9 After the transfiguration, Jesus and his three disciples carry on a conversation about Elijah and the necessary suffering of the Son of Man, a conversation sparked by Jesus's reference to his coming resurrection. The exchange reveals that the disciples are still struggling to make sense of the suffering of the Messiah. Καταβαινόντων, gen. pl. masc. of pres. act. ptc. of καταβαίνω, "come down, go down"; gen. abs. ptc. (on the gen. abs., see 1:32; 5:2); temp. adv. ptc. contemp.; διεστείλατο, 3rd sg. aor. mid. indic. of διαστέλλω, "order, give orders to" (mng. with mid.); αὐτοῖς, dat. dir. obj.; ἅ, "what" (neut. pl. rel. pron. without an antecedent [see 1:44]); εἶδον, 3rd pl. aor. act. indic. of ὁράω, "see" (on translating the aor. with the Eng. pluperf. for prior past action, see 3:10; 5:8; cf. Z §290); διηγήσωνται, 3rd pl. aor. mid. subjunc. of dep. διηγέομαι, "tell, relate, describe"; subjunc. in a dir. obj. ἵνα clause to express a command (see 5:10). The words εἰ μή, when occurring together, mean "except" (see 2:7). Therefore, the phrase εἰ μὴ ὅταν lit. means "except whenever," but normally it is translated as a whole phrase with "until" (cf. ZG 135; LN 67.119). Ἀναστῇ, 3rd sg. aor. act. subjunc.

of ἀνίστημι, rise (in Eng. ἀναστῇ should be translated as a pluperf., since it points to a prior past action [cf. ZG 135]).

9:10 The NASB serves as a useful guide for the translation of this verse: "They seized upon that statement, discussing with one another what rising from the dead meant" (cf. Marcus 2:643). In this translation, λόγον is taken to refer to Jesus's statement or command to the disciples in the preceding verse (cf. ZG 135). In addition, this translation correctly regards the prep. phrase πρὸς ἑαυτούς as modifying the ptc. συζητοῦντες (nom. pl. masc. of pres. act. ptc. of συζητέω, "discuss") rather than the vb. ἐκράτησαν (3rd pl. aor. act. indic. of κρατέω, "seize upon, hold fast to"). The vb. συζητέω occurs ten times in the NT, six of those times in Mark (with the other four in Luke-Acts). Out of those six uses in Mark, the form of συζητέω is clearly modified by a prep. phrase beginning with πρός in 1:27; 9:14, 16 (see also Luke 22:23; Acts 9:29; on πρός as "with, among" and on ἑαυτούς as "one another" with vbs. of speaking, see 1:27). The vb. κρατέω occurs forty-seven times in the NT, fifteen of which are in Mark. A prep. phrase beginning with πρός never modifies a form of κρατέω in any other NT use of the vb. The ptc. συζητοῦντες is likely an adv. ptc. of result (cf. Wallace 638 for the common pattern of an adv. ptc. of result following the vb.)—the disciples latched on to Jesus's statement, particularly the part about the resurrection, and as a result they were discussing with one another what this rising (ἀναστῆναι, aor. act. inf. of ἀνίστημι, rise; subst. use of the inf., subj. of ἐστιν, Burton §393; T 140) from the dead meant (on ἐστιν as "means" when used in explanations, see BDAG 284a; *EDNT* 1:392). The art. with the inf. ἀναστῆναι is anaphoric, referring back to the resurrection of the Son of Man from the dead mentioned in the previous verse rather than to the resurrection in general (BDF §399; cf. Stein 424; Decker 2:8).

9:11 Ἐπηρώτων, 3rd pl. impf. act. indic. of ἐπερωτάω, "ask" (on the impf. with ἐπερωτάω, see 4:10); λέγοντες, nom. pl. masc. of pres. act. ptc. of λέγω, "say"; redundant ptc. The disciples' question begins with ὅτι, which in this instance is not the conj. ὅτι but the neut. sg. form of ὅστις (see the discussion at 2:16). At times in Mark, the neut. sg. form of ὅστις introduces a dir. question with the mng. "why?" (2:16; 9:11, 28). Ἡλίαν, acc. of respect or reference; δεῖ, 3rd sg. pres. act. indic. of δεῖ, "it is necessary, one must" (on δεῖ, see 8:31); ἐλθεῖν, aor. act. inf. of ἔρχομαι, "come"; subst. use of the inf., subj. of δεῖ (Wallace 601; KMP 370); πρῶτον, neut. acc. form functioning as an adv. [see the same use in v. 12]). Within the context of a discussion about the resurrection of the Son of Man, the logic behind the disciples' question seems to be as follows: if Elijah is indeed coming before the Messiah to prepare the way and bring restoration—as the scribes say (cf. Mal 3:1; 4:5–6)—why would the Messiah need to die and then rise again? Therefore, are the scribes correct in saying that Elijah comes first?

9:12 Jesus agrees with the teaching of the scribes concerning the coming of Elijah insofar as it goes (on ὁ δέ, see 1:45; ἔφη, 3rd sg. impf. or aor. act. indic. of φημί, "say"; ἐλθών, nom. sg. masc. of aor. act. ptc. of ἔρχομαι, "come"; temp. adv. ptc. antecedent; ἀποκαθιστάνει, from ἀποκαθιστάνω, "restore, reestablish"). However, the presence of μέν signals that Jesus will also offer a contrasting qualification to their teaching. That contrasting qualification appears in 9:13 (on μέν in correl. with ἀλλά in Mark 9:12–13, see BDF §447; BDAG 630a; cf. Acts 4:16–17; Rom 14:20; 1 Cor 14:17). The grammatical point is significant in that it shows how Jesus is not contrasting Elijah and the Son of Man, but rather is contrasting two different views on Elijah: the view of the scribes, which is accurate only to a point, and his own view, which fully takes into consideration the scriptural teaching on the Son of Man. To prepare for his qualification to the teaching of the scribes, Jesus challenges the disciples with a question related to the scriptural teaching on the suffering of the Son of Man. Γέγραπται, 3rd sg. pf. pass. indic. of γράφω, "write" (on the pf. with γέγραπται, see 1:2); on ἐπί with the acc. to mean "about, concerning," see BDF §233; BDAG 366b (cf. 14:21, which uses περί with γέγραπται); πολλά, acc. dir. obj. (CSB: "must suffer many things") or acc. pl. of πολύς used as an adv. to intensify the vb. (see 1:45; NLT: "must suffer greatly"); πάθῃ, 3rd sg. aor. act. subjunc. of πάσχω, "suffer"; subjunc. used in a subst. ἵνα clause, subj. of γέγραπται (cf. Porter, *Idioms* 238); ἐξουδενηθῇ, 3rd sg. aor. pass. subjunc. of ἐξουδενέω, "treat with contempt, despise." The vb. ἐξουδενέω contains within it the word οὐδέν ("nothing"), so that it could be translated lit. as "make someone out to be nothing" (BDAG 352a; Lane 322). The vb. communicates a contemptuous attitude toward the Son of Man that despises him as insignificant. Yet such messianic suffering and rejection seem to stand in conflict with the restorative work of Elijah. How should this apparent conflict be resolved?

9:13 According to Jesus, Elijah (in the person of John the Baptist; see the connection between Mal 3:1 and John the Baptist in Mark 1:2–4 and Mark's description of John in a way that recalls Elijah in 1:6) has come but was also rejected. Ἐλήλυθεν, 3rd sg. pf. act. indic. of ἔρχομαι, "come"; ἐποίησαν, 3rd pl. aor. act. indic. of ποιέω, "do" (on indef. 3rd pl. vbs., see 1:22); ἤθελον, 3rd pl. impf. act. indic. of θέλω, "want, wish." The use of καί . . . καί in this context serves to connect two clauses, so that καί . . . καί can be translated "both . . . and" or "not only . . . but also" (BDAG 495d). For Jesus, John the Baptist fulfilled the prophecy concerning the coming Elijah, but instead of finishing his promised work of restoration, he faced rejection and suffering, which took place in accordance with the scriptural teaching concerning the Son of Man (γέγραπται, 3rd sg. pf. pass. indic. of γράφω, "write"). In this way, καθὼς γέγραπται ἐπ' αὐτόν in 9:13 stands par. to γέγραπται ἐπὶ τὸν υἱὸν τοῦ ἀνθρώπου in 9:12, so that the antecedent of the pron. αὐτόν in 9:13 is not Ἡλίας but τὸν υἱὸν τοῦ ἀνθρώπου (cf. also 14:21). The prophesied suffering and rejection of the Son of Man determines the course of his forerunner. The restoration of all things will indeed happen, but the path to that restoration will be much more difficult than the scribes had imagined.

(c) Healing of the Possessed Boy (9:14–29)

9:14 The healing miracle in 9:14–29 highlights the need for faith. The father of the boy with an unclean spirit needs to overcome his doubts, while the disciples need to show their trust in God through a faithful devotion to prayer. Ἐλθόντες, nom. pl. masc. of aor. act. ptc. of ἔρχομαι, "come, go"; temp. adv. ptc. antecedent; εἶδον, 3rd pl. aor. act.

indic. of ὁράω, "see"; συζητοῦντας, acc. pl. masc. of pres. act ptc. of συζητέω, "dispute, debate, argue"; supplementary (complementary) ptc.; πρός, "with, among" (after vbs. of speaking [see BDAG 874b; see also the same use for πρός in 9:16]).

9:15 Ἰδόντες, nom. pl. masc. of aor. act. ptc. of ὁράω, "see"; temp. adv. ptc. antecedent; ἐξεθαμβήθησαν, 3rd pl. aor. pass. indic. of ἐκθαμβέω, "be excited, be amazed" (mng. with pass.). A collective sg. subj., such as ὄχλος, can take a pl. vb. and be modified by a pl. ptc., since a crowd is composed of a number of individuals (see 3:8; Wallace 401; R 404, 407). Προστρέχοντες, nom. pl. masc. of pres. act. ptc. of προστρέχω, "run up to"; temp. adv. ptc. contemp.; ἠσπάζοντο, 3rd pl. impf. mid. indic. of dep. ἀσπάζομαι, "greet, welcome." This passage uses the impf. tense in ways that are typical for Mark's Gospel as a whole (see 1:21; 2:16; 4:10): to provide background information and set the scene (ἠσπάζοντο in 9:15; cf. Decker 2:13); to portray a dramatic event in a vivid way by showing the action in progress (ἐκυλίετο in 9:20; cf. Fanning 145–46); and to express the give-and-take of an ongoing conversation (ἔλεγεν in 9:24 and ἐπηρώτων in 9:28).

9:16 Ἐπηρώτησεν, 3rd sg. aor. act. indic. of ἐπερωτάω, "ask." The referent of αὐτούς apparently includes the crowd, since that was the group coming to Jesus and welcoming him. However, Jesus may have also directed his question toward the scribes, who by this point would have joined the group of people gathering around Jesus. At least, Jesus's question is more directly related to the activity of the scribes, i.e., their dispute with the disciples. Συζητεῖτε, from συζητέω, "dispute about, argue about, debate"; πρός, see 9:14.

9:17 The answer to Jesus's question (ἀπεκρίθη, 3rd sg. aor. pass. indic. of dep. ἀποκρίνομαι, "answer") comes not from the scribes but from an individual out of the crowd (ἐκ τοῦ ὄχλου, partitive [see Z §80]), a father whose son was oppressed by a demon. Διδάσκαλε, voc.; ἤνεγκα, 1st sg. aor. act. indic. of φέρω, "bring"; ἔχοντα, acc. sg. masc. of pres. act. ptc. of ἔχω, "have"; adv. ptc. of cause (cf. ESV); ἄλαλον, acc. sg. neut. of ἄλαλος, -ον, "mute, unable to speak." The adj. ἄλαλον describes not the spirit itself but rather one difficulty that the spirit inflicted upon the boy (cf. BDAG 41b).

9:18 The rel. adv. ὅπου appears with ἐάν or ἄν five times in Mark, once followed by the indic. mood and four times by the subjunc. mood. When used with ἐάν or ἄν, ὅπου can mean either "wherever" or "whenever" (BDAG 717b; for "wherever" in 9:18, see RSV, NKJV; for "whenever" in 9:18, see NIV, NRSV, NET, ESV). Since later in the passage, in 9:22, the father emphasizes the dangerous places where the spirit attacks the boy, perhaps "wherever" fits the context better. Καταλάβῃ, 3rd sg. aor. act. subjunc. of καταλαμβάνω, "seize, overtake, come upon"; subjunc. in indef. rel. clause; ῥήσσει, from ῥήσσω, "throw down" (BDAG 905c); ἀφρίζει, from ἀφρίζω, "foam at the mouth"; τρίζει, from τρίζω, "grind, gnash"; ὀδόντας, acc. pl. masc. of ὀδούς, -όντος, ὁ, "tooth"; ξηραίνεται, 3rd sg. pres. pass. indic. of ξηραίνω, "become stiff, be paralyzed" (mng. with pass., BDAG 684d–685a). At the end of his answer, the father explains what was causing the dispute, the inability of the disciples to drive away the demon. Εἶπα, 1st sg. aor. act. indic. of λέγω, "tell, order" (BDAG 287a); ἐκβάλωσιν, 3rd pl. aor. act.

subjunc. of ἐκβάλλω, "cast out, drive out, send away"; subjunc. in a dir. obj. ἵνα clause to express a request or command (see 5:10; on the overlap in usage between ἵνα with the subjunc. and the inf., see Z §407); ἴσχυσαν, 3rd pl. aor. act. indic. of ἰσχύω, "be able to, have power to."

9:19 On ὁ δέ in both 9:19 and 9:21, see 1:45; ἀποκριθείς, nom. sg. masc. of aor. pass. ptc. of dep. ἀποκρίνομαι, "answer"; redundant ptc. Jesus prefaces his address to the unbelieving generation with Ὦ (γενεά, nom. for voc. [R 264; Wallace 57; on γενεά, see 8:12]; ἄπιστος, nom. sg. fem. of the two-terminal adj. ἄπιστος, -ον, "unbelieving"). Ὦ is sometimes translated as "O" (cf. BDAG 1101a) but may also be left untr. since it can sound archaic in Eng. (cf. Strauss 397). When this interjection appears in the NT before a voc., or a nom. used as a voc., it expresses deep emotion on the part of the speaker (Z §35; T 33; BDF §146; Wallace 69; although the use of Ὦ in Acts is an exception to this general principle). Πότε, interr. pron. mng. "when?" (the phrase ἕως πότε can mean "how long" as well as "until when," [BDAG 423c, 856c]); πρός, "with" (expresses pers. relationship with someone rather than motion toward something when used with a form of εἰμί [Harris 191–92]); ἔσομαι, 1st sg. fut. mid. indic. of εἰμί, "be" (dep. in fut.); ἀνέξομαι, 1st sg. fut. mid. indic. of ἀνέχω, "endure, bear with, put up with" (dep. in fut.); ὑμῶν, gen. dir. obj.; φέρετε, 2nd pl. pres. act. impv. of φέρω, "bring." The impv. of φέρω is idiomatically used in the pres., incl. in contexts that call for a specific command in a concrete situation, which would normally take the aor. tense (Fanning 347–48; BDF §336; on pres. and aor. impv. forms, see 1:15; 2:11).

9:20 Ἤνεγκαν, 3rd pl. aor. act. indic. of φέρω, "bring" (on indef. pl. vbs., see 1:22); ἰδών, nom. sg. masc. of aor. act. ptc. of ὁράω, "see"; temp. adv. ptc. antecedent (a masc. ptc. may modify a neut. noun that refers to a personal being [BDF §134; T 311–12]); συνεσπάραξεν, 3rd sg. aor. act. indic. of συσπαράσσω, "shake violently, agitate violently" (the compound form συσπαράσσω is similar in mng. to the simple form σπαράσσω [cf. Decker 2:17; see 1:26 on σπαράσσω]); πεσών, nom. sg. masc. of aor. act. ptc. of πίπτω, "fall"; temp. adv. ptc. antecedent; ἐκυλίετο, 3rd sg. impf. pass. indic. of κυλίω, "roll oneself" (mng. with pass.); ἀφρίζων, nom. sg. masc. of pres. act. ptc. of ἀφρίζω, "foam at the mouth"; adv. ptc. of manner.

9:21 Ἐπηρώτησεν, 3rd sg. aor. act. indic. of ἐπερωτάω, "ask"; πόσος χρόνος, "how much time, how long" (ZG 136; BDAG 855d); ὡς, used as temp. conj., "since" (R 974; BDAG 1106a); γέγονεν, 3rd sg. pf. act. indic. of γίνομαι, "come to be, take place, happen" (BDAG 198a); αὐτῷ, dat. of interest (disadvantage). The prep. ἐκ expresses a temp. idea in this context ("from," BDAG 298a), but the adv. παιδιόθεν already means "from childhood," with the result that the suffix -θεν (also mng. "from") has a weakened sense and becomes redundant (R 300; Moule 73; Taylor 399 [cf. ἀπὸ μακρόθεν in 5:6]).

9:22 Πολλάκις, adv. mng. "many times, often"; ἔβαλεν, 3rd sg. aor. act. indic. of βάλλω, "throw, put" (an aor. tense vb., such as ἔβαλεν, can summarize a series of repeated events, looking at the many occurrences as a whole [constative aor.; cf. Z §253; Fanning 161–62, 173, 258–59]); καί, ascensive (ZG 136). The repeated nature of the demon's attacks may explain the use of the pl. form ὕδατα; the spirit threw the boy into water on a number of occasions (Stein 437). Ἀπολέσῃ, 3rd sg. aor. act. subjunc. of ἀπόλλυμι, "destroy"; subjunc. in a purpose ἵνα clause. The father introduces his plea for help with a 1st class cond. clause, "if you can do anything" (δύνῃ, 2nd sg. pres. mid. indic. of dep. δύναμαι, "be able to, can"; δύναμαι normally takes a complementary inf. in Mark [twenty-nine times with an inf. in Mark and four times without: 6:19; 9:22–23; 10:39]; the use of δύναμαι in 9:22 leaves ποιεῖν to be supplied [cf. BDAG 262b]). Given the father's struggle with faith, the use of the 1st class cond. clause seems less like an expression of confidence in Jesus's ability and more like an expression of desperate hope (Decker 2:18). Βοήθησον, 2nd sg. aor. act. impv. of βοηθέω, "help, come to the aid of"; ἡμῖν, dat. dir. obj.; σπλαγχνισθείς, nom. sg. masc. of aor. pass. ptc. of dep. σπλαγχνίζομαι, "have pity, have compassion"; adv. ptc. of means (on σπλαγχνίζομαι, see 6:34).

9:23 The neut. sg. art. τό can be used before quoted words, statements, or sentence fragments, to mark the quotation (BDF §267; R 766; T 182; Wallace 237–38). One possible way to translate the neut. art. is simply to put quotation marks around the quoted words: "'If you can'" (on δύνῃ, see 9:22). A longer paraphrase of 9:23 designed to communicate the function of τό would be "With regard to your words 'if you can,' everything is possible to the one who believes" (πιστεύοντι, dat. sg. masc. of pres. act. ptc. of πιστεύω, "believe"; subst. ptc.; dat. of interest [advantage]).

9:24 Κράξας, nom. sg. masc. of aor. act. ptc. of κράζω, "cry out"; redundant ptc.; βοήθει, 2nd sg. pres. act. impv. of βοηθέω, "help, come to the aid of"; ἀπιστίᾳ, dat. sg. fem. of ἀπιστία, -ας, ἡ, "unbelief"; dat. dir. obj. The request for help shifts from the aor. impv. βοήθησον in 9:22 (in keeping with the use of the aor. impv. for specific commands; see 2:11) to the pres. impv. βοήθει, which in the context appears to be a plea for ongoing help in the struggle with unbelief (cf. Fanning 326, 364 on the potential for the pres. impv. to express a durative action). The father's cry in 9:24 demonstrates that faith and unbelief are not mutually exclusive categories in Mark's Gospel, since the same individual can experience both at the same time.

9:25 Ἰδών, nom. sg. masc. of aor. act. ptc. of ὁράω, "see"; temp. adv. ptc. antecedent or adv. ptc. of cause (cf. Decker 2:21); ἐπισυντρέχει, from ἐπισυντρέχω, "run together, come together hurriedly, rush together" (on translating the pres. tense in indir. discourse, see 2:1); ἐπετίμησεν, 3rd sg. aor. act. indic. of ἐπιτιμάω, "rebuke"; πνεύματι, dat. dir. obj.; λέγων, nom. sg. masc. of pres. act. ptc. of λέγω, "say"; redundant ptc.; ἄλαλον, nom. sg. neut. of ἄλαλος, -ον, "mute, unable to speak"; κωφόν, nom. sg. neut. of κωφός, -ή, -όν, "deaf"; πνεῦμα, nom. for voc. (since used with nom. art. [Z §34; R 769]); Jesus's expression of command (ἐπιτάσσω, "order, command") to the demon includes the nom. pers. pron. ἐγώ, which is grammatically unnecessary since the ending of the vb. already identifies the subj. The use of ἐγώ highlights the authority of Jesus, pointing to him as the one who is able to demand obedience from the demon (France 368–69; Stein 435). Ἔξελθε, 2nd sg. aor. act. impv. of ἐξέρχομαι, "come out of" (on compound vbs. with a following prep., see 1:21); μηκέτι, adv. mng. "no longer, never again"; εἰσέλθῃς, 2nd sg. aor. act. subjunc. of εἰσέρχομαι, "go into, enter"; prohibitive subjunc. (on the aor. with specific prohibitions, see 2:11).

9:26 Κράξας, nom. sg. masc. of aor. act. ptc. of κράζω, "cry out"; temp. adv. ptc. antecedent (masc. ptc. with an implied neut. subj. [πνεῦμα]; see 9:20); πολλά, "all the more" (neut. acc. pl. of πολύς used as an adv. to intensify the vb. [cf. BDAG 849d–850a; LN 78.3]); σπαράξας, nom. sg. masc. of aor. act. ptc. of σπαράσσω, "shake violently, shake to and fro"; temp. adv. ptc. antecedent (on the mng. of σπαράσσω, see 1:26); ἐξῆλθεν, 3rd sg. aor. act. indic. of ἐξέρχομαι, "come out"; ἐγένετο, 3rd sg. aor. mid. indic. of dep. γίνομαι, "became, come to be"; ὡσεί, "as, like" (lit. "as if"; cf. BDAG 1106c); νεκρός, subst. adj., "a dead body, a corpse" (cf. Strauss 399–400); πολλούς, acc. subj. of the inf. (perhaps mng. "all who were there [and there were many there]"; on the incl. use of πολλοί, see 1:34); λέγειν, pres. act. inf. of λέγω, "say"; inf. of result; ἀπέθανεν, 3rd sg. aor. act. indic. of ἀποθνήσκω, "die" (on the aor. in indir. discourse, see 5:16).

9:27 The exact condition of the boy—whether he had actually died or only appeared to have died—is never completely clarified. However, the language that Mark uses for Jesus's miraculous work par(s). that found in his earlier account of the raising of Jairus's daughter in 5:41–42, which at least suggests that the boy had died. Κρατήσας, nom. sg. masc. of aor. act. ptc. of κρατέω, "take hold of, grasp, seize"; temp. adv. ptc. antecedent (cf. κρατήσας in 5:41); χειρός, gen. dir. obj. (cf. χειρός in 5:41); ἤγειρεν, 3rd sg. aor. act. indic. of ἐγείρω, "raise up" (cf. ἔγειρε in 5:41); ἀνέστη, 3rd sg. aor. act. indic. of ἀνίστημι, "rise, stand up" (cf. ἀνέστη in 5:42).

9:28 Mark concludes this miracle story with a private conversation between the disciples and Jesus, in this way continuing the emph. found in the broader section of 8:27–10:52 on Jesus's discipleship teaching. Εἰσελθόντος, gen. sg. masc. of aor. act. ptc. of εἰσέρχομαι, "go into, enter"; temp. adv. ptc. antecedent (on the use and misuse of the gen. abs., see 1:32; 5:2); κατ' ἰδίαν, "privately" (BDAG 467c); ἐπηρώτων, 3rd pl. impf. act. indic. of ἐπερωτάω, "ask." The disciples' question begins with ὅτι, not the conj. ὅτι but the neut. sg. form of ὅστις, which in Mark's Gospel can function to introduce a dir. question with the mng. "why?" (see the discussion at 2:16; cf. 9:11). Ἠδυνήθημεν, 1st pl. aor. pass. indic. of dep. δύναμαι, "be able to, can"; ἐκβαλεῖν, aor. act. inf. of ἐκβάλλω, "cast out, drive out, send away"; complementary inf.

9:29 Γένος, nom. sg. neut. of γένος, -ους, τό, "class, kind" (BDAG 194d–195a); ἐν, "by" (instr.); δύναται, 3rd sg. pres. mid. indic. of dep. δύναμαι, "be able to, can"; ἐξελθεῖν, aor. act. inf. of ἐξέρχομαι, "come out"; complementary inf.; εἰ μή, "except" (see 2:7). Although the majority of mss. include καὶ νηστείᾳ ("and fasting") after προσευχῇ, it is easier to explain the addition of these words than their omission if they were orig., esp. since references to fasting were also apparently added to the ms. tradition at other places in the NT (Acts 10:30; 1 Cor 7:5). The shorter reading without the reference to fasting (supported by ℵ, B, 0274, and the Itala ms. k) is therefore likely the original (cf. Metzger 85; Cranfield 304–5; cf. also Mark 2:19, where Jesus teaches that the disciples need not fast while he is present with them). Thus prayer is the answer for the disciples, but this answer points beyond itself to the kind of faith and dependence upon

God that a whole life pattern of prayer represents (cf. the close relationship between prayer and faith in 11:22–24).

HOMILETICAL SUGGESTIONS

Help for the Unbelief of Believers (9:14–29)

1. What do we learn about Jesus?
   a. Jesus understands the power of God toward those who believe. (9:22–23)
   b. Jesus understands the power of prayer. (9:28–29)
2. What do we learn about a life of faith?
   a. What we learn from the father: faith can falter. (9:22–24)
   b. What we learn from the disciples: faith can fail. (9:18, 28)
   c. What we learn from Jesus: faith can grow. (9:23–27, 29)
      (1) Jesus helps the faltering.
      (2) Jesus encourages the failing.

3. Cycle 2: Prediction and Response (9:30–50)

The second passion prediction cycle follows the same threefold pattern as the first. Jesus predicts that as the Son of Man he will be handed over and killed but will rise again (9:30–32). The disciples reflect their lack of understanding by arguing with one another about which of them is the greatest (9:33–34). Jesus responds with teaching on what it means to follow him, a willingness to be last and the servant of all, even of the least (9:35–37). What is unique about this passage in comparison with the other passion prediction sections is that, after Jesus's teaching on service, Mark includes an extended group of sayings from Jesus on discipleship (9:38–50).

(a) Second Passion Prediction (9:30–32)

9:30 Κἀκεῖθεν, "and from there" (an adv. formed through the combination of καί and ἐκεῖθεν [BDAG 499d]); ἐξελθόντες, nom. pl. masc. of aor. act. ptc. of ἐξέρχομαι, "go out"; temp. adv. ptc. antecedent; παρεπορεύοντο, 3rd pl. impf. mid. indic. of dep. παραπορεύομαι, "go, go through, pass through"; ἤθελεν, 3rd sg. impf. act. indic. of θέλω, "want, wish"; γνοῖ, 3rd sg. aor. act. subjunc. of γινώσκω, "know"; subunc. in a complementary ἵνα clause (on the subjunc. form γνοῖ instead of γνῷ, see R 308; BDF §95; cf. 5:43). When the conj. ἵνα follows a form of θέλω, the ἵνα cstr. can function like a complementary inf. (a similar phrase using the inf., οὐδένα ἤθελεν γνῶναι, appears in 7:24 [see Wallace 476; BDAG 476b; cf. 10:35]). In 9:30–32, Mark strings together a series of six impf. vbs. (παρεπορεύοντο and ἤθελεν in 9:30; ἐδίδασκεν and ἔλεγεν in 9:31; ἠγνόουν and ἐφοβοῦντο in 9:32). Elsewhere in Mark's Gospel, impf. vbs. cluster together in sections that summarize repeated events (see the discussion at 1:21). Therefore, the cluster of impf. vbs. in 9:30–32 leaves the impression that Mark is describing an ongoing journey and summarizing what Jesus taught and how the disciples reacted on a number of occasions during that time.

9:31 Ἐδίδασκεν, 3rd sg. impf. act. indic. of διδάσκω, "teach"; ὅτι, introduces dir. discourse; παραδίδοται, 3rd sg. pres. pass. indic. of παραδίδωμι, "hand over, deliver." By form, παραδίδοται is a pres. indic., but it describes a future event (futuristic pres.). As a result, its temp. reference is the same as that expressed in the following two fut. tense vbs. (ἀποκτενοῦσιν and ἀναστήσεται). Within a prophetic prediction, a futuristic pres. describes a future event as though it were already occurring and therefore vividly portrays the certainty of that coming event (Fanning 225). Ἀποκτενοῦσιν, 3rd pl. fut. act. indic. of ἀποκτείνω, "kill"; ἀποκτανθείς, nom. sg. masc. of aor. pass. ptc. of ἀποκτείνω, "kill"; temp. adv. ptc. antecedent; ἀναστήσεται, 3rd sg. fut. mid. indic. of ἀνίστημι, "rise" (act. intrans. mng. with fut. mid.).

9:32 Ἠγνόουν, 3rd pl. impf. act. indic. of ἀγνοέω, "fail to understand"; ἐφοβοῦντο, 3rd pl. impf. pass. indic. of φοβέομαι, "fear, be afraid"; ἐπερωτῆσαι, aor. act. inf. of ἐπερωτάω, "ask"; complementary inf. (cf. BDF §392). In Mark's narrative, the disciples are not normally reluctant to ask Jesus for clarification about his teaching (4:10; 7:17; 9:11; 10:10; 13:3). Perhaps their fear shows that by this point they understood just enough to know that they really did not want to know more (cf. France 372).

(b) Misunderstanding by the Disciples: Debate about the Greatest (9:33–34)

9:33 The misunderstanding of the disciples is once again put on display through their ill-timed argument about personal status. Ἦλθον, 3rd pl. aor. act. indic. of ἔρχομαι, "come, go"; γενόμενος, nom. sg. masc. of aor. mid. ptc. of dep. γίνομαι, "come to be, be there" (BDAG 199c); temp. adv. ptc. antecedent; ἐπηρώτα, 3rd sg. impf. act. indic. of ἐπερωτάω, "ask" (on the impf. with ἐπερωτάω, see 4:10); διελογίζεσθε, 2nd pl. impf. mid. indic. of dep. διαλογίζομαι, "discuss, argue about."

9:34 On οἱ δέ, see 1:45; ἐσιώπων, 3rd pl. impf. act. indic. of σιωπάω, "keep silent" (on the use of the impf. with σιωπάω in Mark, see 3:4); πρός, "with, among" (expressing association [BDAG 874b; R 529]); διελέχθησαν, 3rd pl. aor. pass. indic. of dep. διαλέγομαι, "discuss, argue about." In light of the use of γάρ, which in this context points to an action before the silence of the disciples, Eng. calls for the use of a pluperf. vb. to translate the aor. vb. διελέχθησαν (see 3:10). The words διαλογίζομαι (9:33) and διαλέγομαι (9:34) are used interchangeably in this context, with both words being able to indicate a discussion or, in a controversy setting, an argument (Decker 2:26; BDAG 232; cf. TDNT 2:96). In Gk. there is a general tendency to use a comp. adj. in contexts where Eng. would typically use a superl. adj. (Z §147; Moule 97). Since the argument on the way involved all the disciples, the comp. adj. μείζων (comp. form of μέγας, [BDAG 623c]) is functioning as a superl. adj. and should be translated in Eng. as "greatest."

(c) Jesus's Instructions on Discipleship: Learning to Be Last (9:35–50)

9:35 Καθίσας, nom. sg. masc. of aor. act. ptc. of καθίζω, "sit down"; temp. adv. ptc. antecedent; ἐφώνησεν, 3rd sg. aor. act. indic. of φωνέω, "call, summon"; λέγει, historical pres. (see 1:30); εἶναι, pres. act. inf. of εἰμί, "be"; complementary inf.; ἔσται, 3rd sg. fut. mid. indic. of εἰμί, "be" (dep. in fut.). Four times in Mark, Jesus uses a 1st class cond. clause that includes a form of the indef. pron. τις (4:23: "if anyone has ears to hear"; 8:34: "if anyone wants to follow after me"; 9:35: "if anyone wants to be first"; 11:25: "if you have anything against anyone"). In each case, the indication from the context seems to be that the cond. is stating a true hypothesis (e.g., there are in fact some who want to be first, since, after all, the disciples have been arguing about who was the greatest [on 1st class cond. clauses, see Porter, *Idioms* 256–59]). In addition, in each of these four instances, the conclusion drawn from the cond. has an imperatival force. Mark 9:35 uses an imperatival fut., i.e., the use of a fut. indic. vb. to express a command in an emphatic or solemn way (ἔσται, "must be"; see Wallace 452–53, 569–70, 718–19; KMP 271–72). Jesus's solemn command to his followers is to be last of all and servant of all.

9:36 Λαβών, nom. sg. masc. of aor. act. ptc. of λαμβάνω, "take, receive"; temp. adv. ptc. antecedent; ἔστησεν, 3rd sg. aor. act. indic. of ἵστημι, "set, place" (trans. mng. with 1st aor. act.; BDAG 482a). The pers. pron. αὐτό is neut. because it refers back to the neut. noun παιδίον. The complicating factor for an Eng. translation is that a pers. pron. referring back to a single child would normally need to be either masc. or fem. However, the use of the Gk. neut. pron. offers no guidance; the child may have been either a girl or a boy. Most versions solve the translational problem by opting for the masc. pron. "him" for αὐτό. The NIV and NLT rephrase the verse to avoid any use of a pers. pron. for the child, while the NRSV retains the neut. pron., referring to the child as "it." Ἐναγκαλισάμενος, nom. sg. masc. of aor. mid. ptc. of dep. ἐναγκαλίζομαι, "wrap one's arms around, take into one's arms"; temp. adv. ptc. antecedent.

9:37 Παιδίων, partitive gen.; δέξηται, 3rd sg. aor. mid. subjunc. of dep. δέχομαι, "receive, welcome"; subjunc. in indef. rel. clause. The prep. ἐπί with the dat. in this context indicates the grounds or basis for an action, and the reference to "name" in the prep. phrase stands for the person himself. As a result, "in my name" conveys the idea of "on the basis of devotion to Christ" (cf. ZG 138; Z §126; Hooker 228). Δέχεται, 3rd sg. pres. mid. indic. of dep. δέχομαι, "receive, welcome." In the first century, children had no social status, no claim to power or influence. To accept them, i.e., to treat them as significant and as deserving of attention and honor (cf. France 374), would have involved taking a position below the lowest in society. Δέχηται, 3rd sg. pres. mid. subjunc. of dep. δέχομαι, "receive, welcome"; subjunc. in indef. rel. clause; οὐκ . . . ἀλλά, "not so much . . . as" (see T 329–30; Z §445); ἀποστείλαντα, acc. sg. masc. of aor. act. ptc. of ἀποστέλλω, "send"; subst. ptc.

9:38 Mark 9:38–50 expands the section on Jesus's teaching by adding a series of mostly independent sayings connected together by a catchword pattern (cf. Cranfield 312; France 375, 370–80; Stein 441; see, e.g., how the catchword ὀνόματι hooks together the sayings in 9:37–41). This organizational pattern makes it necessary to interpret 9:38–50 as a collection of generally separate sayings rather than as a sustained, step-by-step argument (cf. Stein 446). Ἔφη, 3rd sg. impf. or aor. act. indic. of φημί, "say"; διδάσκαλε, voc.; εἴδομεν, 1st pl. aor. act. indic. of ὁράω, "see"; ἐκβάλλοντα, acc. sg. masc. of pres. act. ptc. of ἐκβάλλω, "cast out, drive out, send away"; supplementary (complementary) ptc.; ἐκωλύομεν, 1st pl. impf. act. indic. of κωλύω, "hinder, prevent, forbid"; ἠκολούθει, 3rd sg. impf. act. indic. of ἀκολουθέω, "follow"; ἡμῖν, dat. dir. obj. Since vbs. in the impf. tense only rarely appear in discourse as opposed to narrative in Mark's Gospel (see 1:21), the impf. ἐκωλύομεν and the impf. ἠκολούθει in John's statement both call for some explanation. The use of the impf. with a vb. like κωλύω, a vb. whose lexical mng. conveys an accomplishment, portrays the action as an incomplete process, continuing on without reaching its end point. If the context implies some resistance to the action (as 9:39 does), then the impf. can be categorized as a conative impf., an action attempted but not completed (Fanning 152; on ἐκωλύομεν as a conative impf., see BDF §326; T 65; Moule 9; Lane 341). Mark regularly uses the vb. ἀκολουθέω to communicate the idea of discipleship, being a follower of Jesus (see 1:18 on the mng. of ἀκολουθέω) and often in the pres. or impf. tense to portray the ongoing nature of discipleship (cf. 2:14–15; 8:34; 10:21, 32, 52; 15:41). However, the use of ἠκολούθει as a term for ongoing discipleship (prog. impf.) makes the pl. dir. obj. "us" appear all the more out of place. John seems to include himself and others among the Twelve on the same level as Jesus and as equal recipients of devotion.

9:39–40 Κωλύετε, 2nd pl. pres. act. impv. of κωλύω, "hinder, prevent, forbid." Normally, the aor. tense is used for a specific prohibition (see 2:11), but here, within this concrete set of circumstances, the pres. impv. appears. One possible reason for this use of the pres. tense for a specific command is that it is capable of expressing a conative sense, so that Jesus is rejecting even the attempt to hinder the miracle worker (Fanning 366; cf. the conative impf. in 9:38). Jesus offers two reasons for his command not to hinder by using two γάρ clauses (in 9:39 and 9:40). The first reason encourages a welcoming openness toward all who serve in the name of Christ, while the second encourages the same toward all who are not actively opposing the followers of Jesus. Ποιήσει, 3rd sg. fut. act. indic. of ποιέω, "do, perform"; gnomic fut.; δύναμιν, "miracle, mighty work, deed of power"; ἐπί, idiom of authorization, "by the authority received through calling on Jesus's name" (cf. BDAG 366d); δυνήσεται, 3rd sg. fut. mid. indic. of dep. δύναμαι, "be able to, can"; gnomic fut.; ταχύ, neut. sg. form of ταχύς functioning here not as an adj. but as an adv. mng. "soon afterward" (BDAG 993a–b); κακολογῆσαι, aor. act. inf. of κακολογέω, "speak evil of, revile"; complementary inf.; on ὅς without an antecedent, see 4:9 ("the one who"); καθ': "against" (expressing opposition [see Harris 154, 165–66]); ὑπέρ, "for" (expressing advantage, benefit [see Harris 209]).

9:41 Ποτίσῃ, 3rd sg. aor. act. subjunc. of ποτίζω, "give to drink"; subjunc. in indef. rel. clause (used with a dbl. acc. of the person [ὑμᾶς] and thing [ποτήριον]); ὕδατος, gen. of content. This gift of a cup of water is offered because of the name, because the recipient of this gift belongs to Christ (Χριστοῦ, gen. of possession). Since the ὅτι clause stands in appos. to the prep. phrase ἐν ὀνόματι (R 1033–34; Decker 2:31), the prep. ἐν is functioning in a causal sense. There are thirteen times in Mark's Gospel where Jesus prefaces a statement with ἀμὴν λέγω ὑμῖν to affirm the truth of his own words before he actually says them (see 3:28 on ἀμήν). The truth according to Jesus is that all who act with kindness toward his followers will be rewarded (ἀπολέσῃ, 3rd sg. aor. act. subjunc. of ἀπόλλυμι, "lose"; emph. neg. subjunc. [see 9:1]).

9:42 The indef. rel. pron. ὃς ἄν is a pendent nom.; although it is the logical subj. of the sentence, it is grammatically independent and is replaced later by the pron. αὐτῷ as required by the grammatical structure of the sentence itself (see Wallace 51–53; KMP 59–61). Σκανδαλίσῃ, 3rd sg. aor. act. subjunc. of σκανδαλίζω, "cause to stumble"; subjunc. in indef. rel. clause; μικρῶν, partitive gen.; πιστευόντων, gen. pl. masc. of pres. act. ptc. of πιστεύω, "believe"; adj. ptc. (on εἰς after πιστεύω to indicate the object of faith, see Harris 236–37). The cond. sentence in 9:42 is probably best understood as a contrary-to-fact cond. with pres. reference (BDAG 277c–d; see also see Z §311; Taylor 410), and it is probably best translated that way (cf. e.g., ESV: "would be . . . were hung . . . were thrown"). When μᾶλλον appears with the positive adj. καλόν, it causes καλόν to function as a comp. adj. ("better" [R 663]; for καλόν as a comp. adj., see also 9:43, 45, 47; 14:21). Αὐτῷ, dat. of interest (advantage); περίκειται, 3rd sg. pres. mid. indic. of dep. περίκειμαι, be placed around (on the repetition of a prep. after a compound vb., see 1:21); μύλος, nom. sg. masc. of μύλος, -ου, ὁ, "millstone"; ὀνικός, nom. sg. masc. of ὀνικός, -ή, -όν, "pertaining to a donkey" (when used with μύλος it indicates a "heavy millstone" designed to be moved by a donkey; cf. BDAG 661a, 711b [Evans 70: "a donkey-driven millstone"]); τράχηλον, acc. sg. masc. of τράχηλος, -ου, ὁ, "neck"; βέβληται, 3rd sg. pf. pass. indic. of βάλλω, "throw."

9:43 Each of the three par. sayings in 9:43–48 begins with a 3rd class cond. clause that points to a possible source of temptation that may turn someone away from devotion to Jesus (on 3rd class cond. clauses, see 1:40). Following the cond. clause, each saying includes an impv. that uses hyperbolic language to call for drastic action in turning away from temptation. Finally, each saying ends with a comp. statement that shows the overriding value of entering into life in God's kingdom. Σκανδαλίζῃ, 3rd sg. pres. act. subjunc. of σκανδαλίζω, "cause to stumble"; subjunc. in a 3rd class cond. clause. The vb. σκανδαλίζω appears eight times in Mark's Gospel, typically in contexts where it is clear that "cause to stumble" involves a falling away from faith or from devotion to Jesus and the pursuit of the kingdom (cf. *EDNT* 3:248; see, e.g., 4:17; 6:3; 14:27). Therefore, Jesus's call for drastic measures in 9:43–47 is more targeted than simply seeking to avoid sin in general. Ἀπόκοψον, 2nd sg. aor. act. impv. of ἀποκόπτω, "cut off." The positive adj. καλόν is once again functioning as a comp. adj. (as in 9:42), although this time it is the comp. word ἤ that necessitates understanding καλόν as a comp. adj. (R 661; BDF §245). Σε, acc. of respect or reference; κυλλόν, acc. sg. masc. of κυλλός, -ή, -όν, "crippled, maimed"; εἰσελθεῖν, aor. act. inf. of εἰσέρχομαι, "go into, enter"; subst. use of the inf., subj. of ἐστίν; ἔχοντα, acc. sg. masc. of pres. act. ptc. of ἔχω, "have"; adv. ptc. of manner; ἀπελθεῖν, aor. act. inf. of ἀπέρχομαι, "depart, go away"; subst. use of the inf., subj. of implied ἐστίν; γέενναν, acc. sg. fem. of γέεννα, -ης, ἡ, "Gehenna, hell"; ἄσβεστον, acc. sg. neut. of ἄσβεστος, -ον, "inextinguishable, unquenchable."

The words in vv. 44 and 46 repeat exactly the same clause found in v. 48: "where their worm does not die, and the fire is not quenched." However, unlike v. 48, the words in vv. 44 and 46 are lacking in a number of important early mss. (א, B, C, L, W, Δ, Ψ, family 1, and others). It is much more likely that the words were added to the ms. tradition to make the three sayings in 9:43–48 as par. as possible than that an orig. threefold repetition was eliminated (Metzger 86–87; France 379; Strauss 414). As a result, most recent translations do not include vv. 44 and 46, skipping directly from v. 43 to v. 45 and from v. 45 to v. 47 (exceptions are NKJV, which includes both verses, and NASB, which includes both verses but in brackets, to indicate that they are not in the earliest mss.).

9:45 Σκανδαλίζῃ, 3rd sg. pres. act. subjunc. of σκανδαλίζω, "cause to stumble"; subjunc. in a 3rd class cond. clause; ἀπόκοψον, 2nd sg. aor. act. impv. of ἀποκόπτω, "cut off"; σε, acc. of respect or reference; εἰσελθεῖν, aor. act. inf. of εἰσέρχομαι, "go into, enter"; subst. use of the inf., subj. of ἐστίν; χωλόν, acc. sg. masc. of χωλός, -ή, -όν, "lame"; ἔχοντα, acc. sg. masc. of pres. act. ptc. of ἔχω, "have"; adv. ptc. of manner; βληθῆναι, aor. pass. inf. of βάλλω, "throw"; subst. use of the inf., subj. of implied ἐστίν; γέενναν, acc. sg. fem. of γέεννα, -ης, ἡ, "Gehenna, hell." One difference between 9:43 and 9:45 involves the change in how the stumbling person arrives at the place of judgment, departing into hell in 9:43 but being thrown into hell in 9:45. In this way, the judgment appears more forceful—more out of the stumbling person's control and more as a result of divine punishment.

9:47 Σκανδαλίζῃ, 3rd sg. pres. act. subjunc. of σκανδαλίζω, "cause to stumble"; subjunc. in a 3rd class cond. clause; ἔκβαλε, 2nd sg. aor. act. impv. of ἐκβάλλω, "gouge out, tear out and throw away" (BDAG 299d); σε, acc. of respect or reference; μονόφθαλμον, acc. sg. masc. of μονόφθαλμος, -ον, "one-eyed, with one eye"; εἰσελθεῖν, aor. act. inf. of εἰσέρχομαι, "go into, enter"; subst. use of the inf., subj. of ἐστίν. Instead of using the phrase "to enter into life" as in vv. 43, 45, the saying in v. 47 has "to enter into the kingdom of God," identifying them as par. and overlapping expressions. Ἔχοντα, acc. sg. masc. of pres. act. ptc. of ἔχω, "have"; adv. ptc. of manner; βληθῆναι, aor. pass. inf. of βάλλω, "throw"; subst. use of the inf., subj. of implied ἐστίν; γέενναν, acc. sg. fem. of γέεννα, -ης, ἡ, "Gehenna, hell."

9:48 The word used for "hell" in 9:43–47, γέεννα ("Gehenna"), came from the Heb. name for Ben Hinnom Valley, a ravine outside of Jerusalem. The reforming king Josiah desecrated the place (2 Kgs 23:10) because it had previously served as a location for offering child sacrifices to the god Molech (2 Kgs 16:3; 21:6; Jer 7:31; 32:35). As a place of evil and defilement outside the city of God's holy temple, Gehenna became a metaphor for the place of final judgment away from the presence of God. Mark 9:48 continues the picture of final judgment with words drawn from Isa 66:24. Those who have rebelled against God will endure a disturbing fate, like that of corpses suffering unending destruction from maggots and fire (σκώληξ, nom. sg. of σκώληξ, -ηκος, ὁ, "worm, maggot"; τελευτᾷ, 3rd sg. pres. act. indic. of τελευτάω, "die"; σβέννυται, 3rd sg. pres. pass. indic. of σβέννυμι, "quench, extinguish, put out").

9:49 What does it mean that everyone will be salted with fire (πυρί, dat. of means/instr.; ἁλισθήσεται, 3rd sg. fut. pass. indic. of ἁλίζω, "salt")? This brief saying makes the most sense within the context of the OT sacrificial system, in which certain sacrifices were salted before being burnt on the altar as an offering to God (Lev 2:13; cf. Ezek 43:24; cf. Cranfield 315–16). Even followers of Jesus will face fiery trials and persecutions (cf. 1 Pet 1:6–7; 4:12–13; Mark 10:29–30), so that they might be like sacrifices seasoned by suffering and then offered to God.

9:50 Καλόν, pred. adj.; ἅλας, nom. sg. neut. of ἅλας, -ατος, τό, "salt"; ἄναλον, nom. sg. neut. of ἄναλος -ον, "saltless, without salt, deprived of its salt content" (LN 5.27; BDAG 67c); γένηται, 3rd sg. aor. mid. subjunc. of dep. γίνομαι, "become, prove to be, turn out to be" (BDAG 199b); subjunc. in a 3rd class cond. clause; ἐν, "with, by" (expressing instr.); ἀρτύσετε, 2nd pl. fut. act. indic. of ἀρτύω, "season." What was sold as salt was often far less than pure, a mixture of salt and other impurities. In the humid weather, the actual salt could leach out, leaving behind a worthless residue (France 385; LN 5.25; cf. *NIDNTTE* 1:217). Followers of Jesus are useful to those around them, but if they fail to live according to the ways of Jesus, what makes them valuable to others suddenly disappears. Ἔχετε, 2nd pl. pres. act. impv. of ἔχω, "have"; ἅλα, acc. sg. neut., of ἅλα, an alternative spelling of ἅλας, -ατος, τό, "salt" (BDAG 41b) (on the form of ἅλα, see R 269; on ἑαυτοῖς as the 2nd pers. pl. refl. pron., see 13:9); εἰρηνεύετε, 2nd pl. pres. act. impv. of εἰρηνεύω, "live in peace, keep the peace"; ἐν, "with" (expressing association).

HOMILETICAL SUGGESTIONS

The Way Up Is Down (9:33–37)

1. Discipleship problem: I want to be first. (9:33–34)
2. Discipleship teaching: Jesus wants me to be last. (9:35)
3. Discipleship illustration: Jesus wants me to serve the least. (9:36–37)

But They Are Not in Our Group (9:38–40)

How should believers respond to others outside their own specific group who serve in the name of Jesus?

1. Be an encouragement, not a hindrance. (9:38–39)
2. Make allies, not enemies. (9:40)

4. Interval: What Jesus Expects of His Followers (10:1–31)

Between the second and third passion prediction, Mark includes three events, each of which ends with Jesus teaching his disciples about what he expects from them as his followers. These passages cover the topics of divorce (10:1–12), children and the kingdom (10:13–16), and wealth (10:17–31). Jesus expects his followers to live with faithfulness and a wholehearted obedience, with humble service toward those regarded as unimportant, and with sacrifice for his sake and for the sake of the gospel.

(a) Teaching on Divorce (10:1–12)

10:1 Ἀναστάς, nom. sg. masc. of aor. act. ptc. of ἀνίστημι, "rise, set out"; temp. adv. ptc. antecedent; ἔρχεται, 3rd sg. pres. mid. indic. of dep. ἔρχομαι, "come, go"; ὅρια, acc. pl. neut. of ὅριον, -ου, τό, "region, district" (mng. with pl., BDAG 723b); πέραν τοῦ Ἰορδάνου, the adv. πέραν functions as an indecl. name for the territory on the other (eastern) side of the river Jordan (BDAG 797a); συμπορεύονται, 3rd pl. pres. mid. indic. of dep. συμπορεύομαι, "come together, gather"; εἰώθει, 3rd sg. pluperf. act. indic. of εἴωθα, "be accustomed to do, be one's custom" (the pluperf. of εἴωθα conveys a past stative mng.; for the similar use of the pluperf. with οἶδα, see 1:24); ἐδίδασκεν, 3rd sg. impf. act. indic. of διδάσκω, "teach." Mark's use of the historical pres. in 10:1 (ἔρχεται and συμπορεύονται) fits with his common pattern of employing such vbs. at the beginning of a new scene, often with the first being a vb. of motion (see 1:12). The use of the impf. ἐδίδασκεν also follows a common pattern in that Mark freq. uses impf. vbs. for background information when setting the scene (see 1:21).

10:2 Προσελθόντες, nom. pl. masc. of aor. act. ptc. of προσέρχομαι, "approach, come to"; temp. adv. ptc. antecedent; ἐπηρώτων, 3rd pl. impf. act. indic. of ἐπερωτάω, "ask" (on the impf. of ἐπερωτάω, see 4:10). When used as an interr. particle, εἰ introduces a question, but it can be a question in either dir. discourse or, more freq., indir. discourse (BDF §440). Mark uses it both ways (with dir. discourse: 8:23; with indir. discourse: 3:2; 11:13; 15:36, 44). In 10:2, εἰ is probably introducing indir. discourse ("whether"; BDAG 278b; R 916; an adv. ptc. like πειράζοντες would more likely precede rather than follow dir. discourse). Ἔξεστιν, 3rd sg. pres. act. indic. of ἔξεστιν, "it is lawful" (on the pres. retained in indir. discourse, see 2:1); ἀνδρί, dat. of reference or respect; ἀπολῦσαι, aor. act. inf. of ἀπολύω, "divorce"; subst. use of the inf., subj. of ἔξεστιν; πειράζοντες, nom. pl. masc. of pres. act. ptc. of πειράζω, "test"; adv. ptc. of purpose. The vb. πειράζω occurs in the pres. tense as an adv. ptc. eleven times in the NT (if John 8:6 is included). Of those eleven times, πειράζω is functioning as an adv. ptc. of purpose nine times, incl. both examples in Mark (cf. Wallace 636; KMP 334; see Matt 16:1; 19:3; 22:35; Mark 8:11; 10:2; Luke 4:2; 11:16; John 6:6; 8:6; the two examples not fitting this pattern are in Heb 11:7; Jas 1:13).

10:3 On the surface, the focus of the conversation between Jesus and the Pharisees is on the subject of divorce, but just below the surface is a debate on what it means to be "lawful." On ὁ δέ in 10:3, 5 and οἱ δέ in 10:4, see 1:45; ἀποκριθείς, nom. sg. masc. of aor. pass. ptc. of dep. ἀποκρίνομαι, "answer"; redundant ptc.; ἐνετείλατο, 3rd sg. aor. mid. indic. of dep. ἐντέλλομαι, "command."

10:4 Jesus asked the Pharisees about what Moses commanded, and they answer by talking about what Moses permitted. For Mark, that answer sheds light on the differing attitudes between Jesus and the Pharisees concerning what it means to obey God and his law. On the ending of εἶπαν, see 8:5; ἐπέτρεψεν, 3rd sg. aor. act. indic. of ἐπιτρέπω, "allow, permit"; ἀποστασίου, gen. sg. neut. of ἀποστάσιον, -ου, ὁ, "written notice of divorce" (although βιβλίον ἀποστασίου as a whole phrase means "certificate of divorce"; cf. BDAG 120c); γράψαι, aor. act. inf. of γράφω, "write"; subst. use of the inf., dir. obj. of ἐπέτρεψεν; ἀπολῦσαι, aor. act. inf. of ἀπολύω, "divorce" (same use of inf. as with γράψαι; the one doing the action in both infinitives is implied in the preceding context [ἀνδρί in 10:2]; cf. Decker 2:41). The Pharisees' answer makes reference to Deut 24:1–4, a passage that assumes the practice of divorce and regulates it in a way that provides some measure of protection for the wife. Apparently, for the Pharisees this passage meant that God permitted divorce in the sense that it had his approval and would not come under his judgment (Cranfield 319). Jesus's response would be to direct them back to God's design for marriage, to what the law details concerning God's ultimate desire for marriage.

10:5 The prep. πρός can convey the idea of reference (e.g., 12:12) in such a way that it is equivalent to the idea of cause ("because of, on account of"; BDAG 875a; cf. BDF §239; Z §98). Σκληροκαρδίαν, acc. sg. fem. of σκληροκαρδία, -ας, ἡ, "hardness of heart, stubbornness"; ἔγραψεν, 3rd sg. aor. act. indic. of γράφω, "write." God's regulation of divorce is a concession, necessitated by human sinfulness, and therefore an attempt to limit its destructiveness. In this way, Jesus makes a distinction between commands that set forth God's will for his people, i.e., God's ultimate desires, and commands that take into account human sinfulness and seek to minimize its consequences (Cranfield 319).

10:6 Jesus points to God's plan for marriage by directing the Pharisees' attention to the creation account, in particular to Gen 1:27 (in v. 6) and to Gen 2:24 (in vv. 7–8). Κτίσεως, gen. sg. fem. of κτίσις, -εως, ἡ, "creation, world"; gen. of appos.; ἄρσεν, acc. sg. neut. of ἄρσην, -εν, "male"; θῆλυ, acc. sg. neut. of θῆλυς, -εια, -υ, "female" (both adjectives are complements in a dbl. acc. obj. complement cstr.). The use of the neut. form of the adj. for "male" and "female" may seem usual for words referring to people, but the neut. is sometimes used with reference to people if the emph. is not on any particular individual but rather on a general quality (BDF §138; Decker 2:42). Ἐποίησεν, 3rd sg. aor. act. indic. of ποιέω, "make." God's created design for marriage is from the beginning and therefore from before the fall and the entrance of sin and brokenness into the world. That design expresses God's will for marriage, and—for those who follow Jesus—it takes priority over any subsequent concessions made necessary by human sinfulness (France 392).

10:7 Καταλείψει, 3rd sg. fut. act indic. of καταλείπω, "leave, leave behind"; προσκολληθήσεται, 3rd sg. fut. pass. indic. of προσκολλάω, "join." The words καὶ προσκολληθήσεται πρὸς τὴν γυναῖκα αὐτοῦ do not appear in a few of the earliest Gk. mss. (ℵ, B, Ψ, 892). However, the words seem necessary for the sense of Mark's text, since otherwise the reference to the two who become one flesh in 10:8 goes back to the father and mother, not the husband and wife. The clause could very well have dropped out accidentally, with the eye of the scribe skipping from one καί to the next (Metzger 88–89; France 387; Yarbro Collins 457). The vb. προσκολλάω, which is related to the Gk. word for "glue" (κόλλα), can be used with a lit. sense of "stick to," but it can also be used in the pass. in the context of human relationships with a metaphorical sense of "be joined to, be faithfully devoted to" (BDAG 881d; *NIDNTTE* 2:718–20).

10:8 Ἔσονται, 3rd pl. fut. mid. indic. of εἰμί, "be" (dep. in fut.). The prep. εἰς with the acc. appears at times in the NT as a replacement for the pred. nom. (Z §32; Wallace 47; KMP 54). This idiom happens most often in OT quotations, where it serves as a lit. translation of the Heb. (see BDB 225–26 for הָיָה followed by the prep. לְ to mean "become"). The inference drawn by Jesus (ὥστε, inferential conj.; cf. Taylor 419) based on the teaching from Gen 1:27 and 2:24 is that the husband and wife are no longer two but instead one flesh. This inference concerning the oneness of marriage prepares the way for Jesus's final conclusion in the following verse.

10:9 The conj. οὖν appears only five times in Mark, always as an inferential conj. and always in dialogue. Of those five times, the conclusion introduced by οὖν appears in the form of a command two times (10:9; 13:35) and in the form of a question three times (11:31; 12:9; 15:12). On ὅ as "what," see 2:24; συνέζευξεν, 3rd sg. aor. act. indic. of συζεύγνυμι, "join together, pair." The vb. συζεύγνυμι means lit. "yoke together" (e.g., for yoking horses together [Herodotus, *Histories* 4.189; Xenophon, *Cyropaedia* 2.2.26]), but it can also be used more generally for the joining together of any two items (e.g., for two wings being joined together [Ezek 1:11, 23 LXX]; for the uniting of a husband and wife in marriage [e.g., Jos., *Ant.* 6.13.8 §309; see LSJ 1669; BDAG 954b]). Χωριζέτω, 3rd sg. pres. act. impv. of χωρίζω, "separate, divide." Jesus's concluding command in 10:9 is an important reminder to those who want to obey God wholeheartedly—they should preserve the oneness that God intended and created for marriage.

10:10 On εἰς for ἐν, see BDF §205; Z §99; Harris 84–86 (see also 13:9); ἐπηρώτων, 3rd pl. impf. act. indic. of ἐπερωτάω, "ask"; on the impf. of ἐπερωτάω, see 4:10. In 10:10, the scene changes but the conversation concerning divorce continues. In this way, Jesus's teaching in the following verses becomes part of his overall teaching on discipleship in 8:27–10:52.

10:11 Ἀπολύσῃ, 3rd sg. aor. act. subjunc. of ἀπολύω, "divorce"; subjunc. in indef. rel. clause; γαμήσῃ, 3rd sg. aor. act. subjunc. of γαμέω, "marry"; subjunc. in indef. rel. clause; μοιχᾶται, 3rd sg. pres. pass. indic. of μοιχάω, "commit adultery" (mng. with pass.). The act of adultery is "against her," i.e., against the man's first wife. The prep. ἐπί with the acc. can be used to convey that the action is hostile toward someone or something ("against," BDAG 366c–d; cf. ἐπί with the acc. in 3:24–26; 13:8, 12). For a man to divorce his wife and thus free himself to marry another, is an act of sin against his wife and, based on the context, an act incompatible with following Jesus as a disciple.

10:12 Mark's Gospel includes a balancing statement from Jesus, one that views divorce and remarriage from the perspective of the wife. The need to live out the implications of discipleship within the marriage relationship falls equally upon both the husband and the wife. Ἀπολύσασα, nom. sg. fem. of aor. act. ptc. of ἀπολύω, "divorce," temp. adv. ptc. antecedent; γαμήσῃ, 3rd sg. aor. act. subjunc. of γαμέω, "marry"; subjunc. in a 3rd class cond. clause; μοιχᾶται, 3rd sg. pres. pass. indic. of μοιχάω, "commit adultery" (mng. with pass.).

FOR FURTHER STUDY

25. Jesus and Divorce

Collins, John J. "Marriage, Divorce, and Family in Second Temple Judaism." Pages 104–62 in *Families in Ancient Israel*. Edited by Leo G. Perdue, Joseph Blenkinsopp, John J. Collins, and Carol Meyers. Louisville: Westminster John Knox, 1997.

Collins, Raymond F. *Divorce in the New Testament*. Collegeville, MN: Liturgical Press, 1992.

Instone-Brewer, David. *Divorce and Remarriage in the Bible: The Social and Literary Context*. Grand Rapids: Eerdmans, 2002.

Keener, Craig S. *And Marries Another: Divorce and Remarriage in the Teaching of the New Testament*. Peabody, MA: Hendrickson, 1991.

Köstenberger, Andreas J. with David W. Jones. Pages 225–32, 275–85 in *God, Marriage, and Family: Rebuilding the Biblical Foundation*. 2nd ed. Wheaton, IL: Crossway, 2010.

Meier, John P. "Jesus' Teaching on Divorce." Pages 74–181 in *Law and Love*. Vol. 4 of *A Marginal Jesus: Rethinking the Historical Jesus*. Anchor Yale Bible Reference Library. New Haven, CT: Yale University Press, 2009.

*Stein, Robert H. "'Is It Lawful for a Man to Divorce His Wife?'" *JETS* 22 (1979): 115–21.

Strauss, Mark L., ed. *Remarriage after Divorce in Today's Church: 3 Views*. Grand Rapids: Zondervan, 2006.

Wenham, Gordon J., and William E. Heth. *Jesus and Divorce*. 2nd ed. Eugene, OR: Wipf and Stock, 2002.

(b) Children and the Kingdom (10:13–16)

10:13 This passage once again emphasizes Jesus's teaching of his disciples, this time concerning the need to recognize their helplessness and to respond with humble faith. Προσέφερον, 3rd pl. impf. act. indic. of προσφέρω, "bring" (impf. for background information [see 1:21]). The vb. προσέφερον is an indef. pl. vb., so that the implied subj. is a general reference to "some people" (see 1:22). Ἅψηται, 3rd sg. aor. mid. subjunc. of ἅπτω, "touch, place one's hands on" (mng. with mid.); subjunc. in a purpose ἵνα clause; αὐτῶν, gen. dir. obj. The purpose for bringing the children was presumably that Jesus might bless them, as he does in v. 16. Ἐπετίμησαν, 3rd pl. aor. act. indic. of ἐπιτιμάω, "rebuke"; αὐτοῖς, dat. dir. obj.

10:14 Ἰδών, nom. sg. masc. of aor. act. ptc. of ὁράω, "see"; temp. adv. ptc. antecedent; ἠγανάκτησεν, 3rd sg. aor. act. indic. of ἀγανακτέω, "be indignant, be angry." The vb. ἀγανακτέω is an emotional word that conveys a sense of indignation, even anger, at a perceived wrong (BDAG 5a; Spicq 1:5–7), all of which adds weight to the following commands of Jesus. Ἄφετε, 2nd pl. aor. act. impv. of ἀφίημι, "allow, let, permit"; ἔρχεσθαι, pres. mid. inf. of dep. ἔρχομαι, "come, go"; complementary inf.; κωλύετε, 2nd pl. pres. act. impv. of κωλύω, "hinder, prevent, forbid." The basis or reason (γάρ) for these commands is that the kingdom of God belongs to such as these. The poss. gen. τοιούτων is similar to the poss. gen. αὐτῶν in Matt 5:3, 10, where Jesus says that "the kingdom of heaven is theirs" (αὐτῶν ἐστιν ἡ βασιλεία τῶν οὐρανῶν). The kingdom does not belong to such ones in the sense that they have exclusive ownership over it, since after all, it is God's kingdom. Instead the kingdom belongs to these children who are coming to Jesus in the sense that they have a rightful share in it (France 396).

10:15 On ἀμήν, see 3:28; δέξηται, 3rd sg. aor. mid. subjunc. of dep. δέχομαι, "receive, be open to, accept"; subjunc. in indef. rel. clause; παιδίον, probably nom. ("as a child receives it") rather than acc. ("as he receives a child"); εἰσέλθῃ, 3rd sg. aor. act. subjunc. of εἰσέρχομαι, "go into, enter"; emph. neg. subjunc. (see 9:1); on the repetition of εἰς after a compound vb., see 1:21. The noun παιδίον appears twelve times in Mark's Gospel, always in a lit. sense with reference to children of a young age. Earlier in Mark, Jesus presented a child (παιδίον) as an object lesson for his status-seeking disciples to teach them about the importance of lowly service (9:36–37). Followers of Jesus must be willing to welcome children, those who have no claim to power or status or influence. In a similar way, to receive the kingdom as a παιδίον means to set aside the pursuit for significance according to the world's standards and to come to God with humility and faith in recognition of one's own helplessness (cf. Cranfield 323–24; Brooks 160).

10:16 Ἐναγκαλισάμενος, nom. sg. masc. of aor. mid. ptc. of dep. ἐναγκαλίζομαι, "wrap one's arms around"; temp. adv. ptc. antecedent; κατευλόγει, 3rd sg. impf. act. indic. of κατευλογέω, "bless" (on the impf. for a dramatic event at the end of a passage, see 1:21); τιθείς, nom. sg. masc. of pres. act. ptc. of τίθημι, "lay, place"; temp. adv. ptc. contemp. The compound vb. κατευλογέω appears only this one time in the NT, while εὐλογέω without the prep. prefix occurs forty-one times in the NT, incl. five times in Mark. In Mark's Gospel, several compound vbs. with κατα- as the prep. prefix emphasize the intensity and completion of an action (see the discussion at 1:36). That same function is certainly possible for κατευλογέω in 10:16. By using κατευλογέω instead of the more common εὐλογέω, Mark was likely indicating that Jesus made certain that he fully finished the task of blessing the children.

(c) The Rich Man (10:17–31)

10:17 Jesus's conversation with a rich man stands as the third in a series of three events in 10:1–31 in which Jesus takes time to teach his disciples, this time with regard to wealth and entrance into the kingdom. Ἐκπορευομένου, gen. sg. masc. of pres. mid. ptc. of dep. ἐκπορεύομαι, "go out, set out"; gen. abs. ptc.; temp. adv. ptc. contemp. (on the use and misuse of the gen. abs. in Mark, see 1:32; 5:2); προσδραμών, nom. sg. masc. of aor. act. ptc. of προστρέχω, "run up to"; temp. adv. ptc. antecedent; εἷς, "someone, a certain one" (functioning as an indef. pron., i.e., an equivalent of τις; R 675; BDF §247; Z §155); γονυπετήσας, nom. sg. masc. of aor. act. ptc. of γονυπετέω, "kneel down before"; temp. adv. ptc. antecedent; ἐπηρώτα, 3rd sg. impf. act. indic. of ἐπερωτάω, "ask" (on the impf. of ἐπερωτάω, see 4:10); διδάσκαλε ἀγαθέ, both the noun and adj. are voc.; ποιήσω, 1st sg. aor. act. subjunc. of ποιέω, "do"; delib. subjunc.; κληρονομήσω, 1st sg. aor. act. subjunc. of κληρονομέω, "inherit, obtain, receive"; subjunc. in a purpose ἵνα clause. Most often, the NT uses the vb. κληρονομέω in contexts related to inheriting or receiving the promises and gifts of God (*TDNT* 3:781). This instance in 10:17 is the only use of κληρονομέω in

Mark, although κληρονομία ("inheritance") and κληρονόμος ("heir") appear in the parable of the vineyard (12:7). In Mark's Gospel, "inheriting eternal life," "entering life," "entering the kingdom of God," and "being saved" are all par. expressions (note the similar use of these phrases in 9:43, 45, 47; 10:17, 23–25, 26; cf. Stein 468).

10:18 Τί, "why?" (see 2:7); λέγεις, "call, identify someone as" (when used with a dbl. acc.; see BDAG 590b; cf. 12:37; 15:12); ἀγαθόν, complement in a dbl. acc. obj. complement cstr.; ἀγαθός, pred. adj.; εἰ μή, "except" (see 2:7); θεός, nom. in appos. to εἷς ("one, namely, God"; cf. 2:7). Jesus's response in 10:18 is not a confession of his own sinfulness but rather a challenge to the man's notion of goodness. For Jesus, true goodness belongs to God, who is good in an unlimited way, not by achievement or effort but by his eternal character. Even a modest attempt to reflect on this point should have caused the man to recognize that God's perfect goodness complicated his quest for life in God's kingdom. However, that does not seem to have happened, since at the next opportunity the man simply drops the offending word and addresses Jesus as "teacher" (10:20) rather than "good teacher" (10:17).

10:19 Οἶδας, 2nd sg. pf. act. indic. of οἶδα, "know" (on the pf. with οἶδα, see 1:24). In 10:19, Jesus offers the man a rough summary of the second half of the Ten Commandments, the part that governs behavior toward other people. Almost every commandment in the list is expressed by a prohibitive subjunc. (μή with the aor. subjunc.). The one that does not fit this grammatical pattern is the positive command about honoring parents (which is expressed instead with a pres. impv.). Φονεύσῃς, 2nd sg. aor. act. subjunc. of φονεύω, "murder, kill"; μοιχεύσῃς, 2nd sg. aor. act. subjunc. of μοιχεύω, "commit adultery"; κλέψῃς, 2nd sg. aor. act. subjunc. of κλέπτω, "steal"; ψευδομαρτυρήσῃς, 2nd sg. aor. act. subjunc. of ψευδομαρτυρέω, "bear false witness, give false testimony"; ἀποστερήσῃς, 2nd sg. aor. act. subjunc. of ἀποστερέω, "defraud"; τίμα, 2nd sg. pres. act. impv. of τιμάω, "honor." One unusual feature of this list is that Jesus omits the commandment against coveting, replacing it with one against defrauding, apparently as an expansion of the prohibition against stealing (cf. Stein 469).

10:20 On ὁ δέ, see 1:45 (cf. 10:22, 26); ἔφη, 3rd sg. impf. or aor. act. indic. of φημί, "say"; διδάσκαλε, voc.; ἐφυλαξάμην, 1st sg. aor. mid. indic. of φυλάσσω, "keep, observe" (mng. with mid.); νεότητος, gen. sg. fem. of νεότης, -τητος, ἡ, "youth." The use the mid. voice with ἐφυλαξάμην can perhaps be best explained by the influence of the LXX (BDAG 1068d). The vb. φυλάσσω is common in the LXX (appearing more than 450 times), with the act. and mid. used interchangeably, often for keeping (i.e., obeying) the commandments of the divine covenant (*TDNT* 9:237; cf. Taylor 428). So, e.g., φυλάσσω appears seventeen times in Exodus, nine times in the mid. and eight times in the act., with no clear distinction in mng. (cf. the mid. in Exod 31:14 with the act. in Exod 31:16). The vb. φυλάσσω occurs fifty-five times in Deuteronomy, thirty-eight times in the mid. and seventeen times in the act., once again with an overlap in mng. (cf. the mid. in Deut 26:17 with the act. in Deut 26:18). Therefore, the significance of the man's claim in Mark 10:20 is not found so much in the use of the mid.

voice in ἐφυλαξάμην as it is in the complete self-confidence that he expresses in his claim to have fulfilled all of his obligations as set forth in God's commands.

10:21 In the previous passage (10:13–16), Jesus commended the example of children, who in their helplessness were ready to enter into the kingdom of God. This man must be forced into recognizing how helpless his situation is before he is prepared to find eternal life. Ἐμβλέψας, nom. sg. masc. of aor. act. ptc. of ἐμβλέπω, "look at"; temp. adv. ptc. antecedent; ἠγάπησεν, 3rd sg. aor. act. indic. of ἀγαπάω, "love." The use of ὑστερεῖ (from ὑστερέω, "lack, be in need of") is unusual. Normally, the person with the need functions as the subj. of ὑστερέω, while what is lacking appears in the gen. (Decker 2:52; e.g., Luke 22:35). With ἕν σε ὑστερεῖ in Mark 10:21, what is lacking functions as the subj., while the person with the need appears in the acc. case (cf. Ps 22:1 LXX). Most Eng. translations find it necessary to reverse the order (e.g., ESV: "You lack one thing"). Ὕπαγε, 2nd sg. pres. act. impv. of ὑπάγω, "go, depart" (on the pres. impv. with ὑπάγω, see 2:11); πώλησον, 2nd sg. aor. act. impv. of πωλέω, "sell" (on the aor. with specific commands, see 2:11); δός, 2nd sg. aor. act. impv. of δίδωμι, "give"; ἕξεις, 2nd sg. fut. act. indic. of ἔχω, "have"; θησαυρόν, acc. sg. masc. of θησαυρός, -οῦ, ὁ, "treasure"; δεῦρο, adv. functioning as an impv. particle, almost like a vb., "come!" (cf. BDAG 220b; R 302); ἀκολούθει, 2nd sg. pres. act. impv. of ἀκολουθέω, "follow" (on the pres. impv. of ἀκολουθέω for ongoing discipleship, see 2:14); μοι, dat. dir. obj.

10:22 Στυγνάσας, nom. sg. masc. of aor. act. ptc. of στυγνάζω, "be shocked, be appalled"; temp. adv. ptc. antecedent. The ptc. στυγνάσας seems to be similar to the following ptc. λυπούμενος in that it describes the man's intense emotional reaction to Jesus's demands. Therefore, it is better to translate it in a way that emphasizes the man's internal response (e.g., NRSV: "he was shocked"; see the first suggested translation in BDAG 949c; cf. Ezek 27:35; 28:19; 32:10 LXX) than in a way that simply portrays his outward appearance (e.g., NIV: "the man's face fell"; cf. NET; NLT). Ἐπί with the dat.: "at" (when expressing the grounds for an emotional reaction, see Z §126 [same mng. for ἐπί in 10:24]); λόγῳ, "statement" (see BDAG 600b); ἀπῆλθεν, 3rd sg. aor. act. indic. of ἀπέρχομαι, "depart, go away"; λυπούμενος, nom. sg. masc. of pres. pass. ptc. of λυπέω, "grieve, be sad, be distressed" (mng. with pass.); adv. ptc. of manner (cf. Wallace 628; KMP 330); ἦν, 3rd sg. impf. act. indic. of εἰμί, "be"; ἔχων, nom. sg. masc. of pres. act. ptc. of ἔχω, "have"; periph. ptc.; κτήματα, acc. pl. neut. of κτῆμα, -ατος, τό, "possessions, things acquired" (mng. with pl., BDAG 572b; related to the vb. κτάομαι, "acquire, buy for oneself"). The use of a periph. impf. cstr. in this context seems to communicate that the man's position of wealth was characteristic of his circumstances for a broad period of time (cf. Fanning 315; on the periph. impf. cstr., see 1:22).

10:23 Περιβλεψάμενος, nom. sg. masc. of aor. mid. ptc. of περιβλέπω, "look around" (mng. with mid.); temp. adv. ptc. antecedent. On the historical pres. with λέγω in 10:23, 24, 27, see 1:12, 30. The interr. particle πῶς introduces not only questions but also at times exclamations (BDAG 901c; R 302; Moule 207), which happens in both

10:23 and 10:24. The use of πῶς and δυσκόλως (adv. mng. "with difficulty") together at the beginning of this exclamation can be translated as "how with difficulty" or "with what difficulty" (ZG 141). Χρήματα, acc. pl. neut. of χρῆμα, -ατος, τό, "wealth, means" (mng. with pl., BDAG 1089a; related to the vb. χράομαι, "use, make use of"). The pl. form χρήματα can be used for economic resources, usually with the implication that a person has an abundance of such resources ready to be used (LN 57.31). Ἔχοντες, nom. pl. masc. of pres. act. ptc. of ἔχω, "have"; subst. ptc.; εἰσελεύσονται, 3rd pl. fut. mid. indic. of dep. εἰσέρχομαι, "go into, enter."

10:24 Ἐθαμβοῦντο, 3rd pl. impf. pass. indic. of θαμβέω, "be astonished, be amazed" (mng. with pass., BDAG 442c; on the impf. with vbs. for amazement, see 1:22); ἀποκριθείς, nom. sg. masc. of aor. pass. ptc. of dep. ἀποκρίνομαι, "answer"; redundant ptc.; τέκνα, nom. for voc. (on the classification of pl. forms as nom. instead of voc., see Wallace 67, n. 6); δύσκολον, nom. sg. neut. of δύσκολος, -ον, "difficult, hard" (used together with πῶς for an exclamation: "how difficult"); εἰσελθεῖν, aor. act. inf. of εἰσέρχομαι, "go into, enter"; subst. use of the inf., subj. of ἐστιν.

10:25 Εὐκοπώτερον, nom. sg. neut. comp. adj. form of εὔκοπος, -ον, "easy"; κάμηλον, acc. sg. masc. or fem. of κάμηλος, -ου, ὁ or ἡ, "camel"; acc. of reference or respect; τρυμαλιᾶς, gen. sg. fem. of τρυμαλιά, -ᾶς, ἡ, "eye, hole"; ῥαφίδος, gen. sg. fem. of ῥαφίς, -ίδος, ἡ, "needle"; partitive gen.; διελθεῖν, aor. act. inf. of διέρχομαι, "pass through"; subst. use of the inf., subj. of ἐστιν (on a compound vb. with a prep. phrase following, see 1:21); πλούσιον, acc. of reference or respect; εἰσελθεῖν, aor. act. inf. of εἰσέρχομαι, "go into, enter"; subst. use of the inf., subj. of implied ἐστιν. There is no reason to reduce the severity of this statement. Just as it is impossible for a large camel to squeeze through the tiny eye of a needle, so also it is impossible to fit a rich person through the entrance to the kingdom of God. The only hope for the wealthy lies with the God who can accomplish the impossible (10:27).

10:26 Περισσῶς, adv. mng. "even more, exceedingly"; ἐξεπλήσσοντο, 3rd pl. impf. pass. indic. of ἐκπλήσσω, "be amazed, be overwhelmed" (mng. with pass.); λέγοντες, nom. pl. masc. of pres. act. ptc. of λέγω, "say"; adv. ptc. of result (see 6:2; 7:37); ἑαυτούς, "one another" (see 1:27). When καί introduces a question that expresses surprise at a previous and unexpected statement, it can be translated as "then" (LN 91.12; BDAG 495b; cf. Z §459; BDF §442). Δύναται, 3rd sg. pres. mid. indic. of dep. δύναμαι, "be able to, can"; σωθῆναι, aor. pass. inf. of σῴζω, "save"; complementary inf. The pass. form of σῴζω conveys the idea of eternal salvation in this context, since "being saved" stands as a par. expression to "inheriting or receiving eternal life" (10:17, 30) and "entering the kingdom of God" (10:23–25; on σῴζω, see 5:34).

10:27 Ἐμβλέψας, nom. sg. masc. of aor. act. ptc. of ἐμβλέπω, "look at"; temp. adv. ptc. antecedent; αὐτοῖς, dat. dir. obj.; παρά with the dat.: "with, with regard to" (expressing pers. reference; see BDAG 757b–c; Harris 172); ἀδύνατον, nom. sg. neut. of ἀδύνατος, -ον, impossible; pred. adj.; δυνατά, pred. adj. The saying in 10:27 is key for understanding Jesus's conversation with both the rich man and the disciples (Cranfield 332; Brooks 165). Entering the kingdom, inheriting eternal life, finding salvation—these things are beyond human capabilities, for rich and poor alike. Therefore, it is necessary to recognize one's helplessness before God and to receive mercy from the one who is able to do what is humanly impossible.

10:28 Ἤρξατο, 3rd sg. aor. mid. indic. of ἄρχω, "begin" (mng. with mid.; on ἄρχομαι, see 1:45); λέγειν, pres. act. inf. of λέγω, "say"; complementary inf.; on ἰδού, see 1:2. The nom. pers. pron. ἡμεῖς, which is not necessary since the ending of the vb. already indicates the subj., seems to be included in order to emphasize the contrast between the disciples and the rich man (Wallace 322; BDF §277). Peter points out that the disciples did what the rich man refused to do; they abandoned their previous life and became followers of Jesus. Ἀφήκαμεν, 1st pl. aor. act. indic. of ἀφίημι, "leave"; ἠκολουθήκαμεν, 1st pl. pf. act. indic. of ἀκολουθέω, "follow"; σοι, dat. dir. obj.

10:29 Jesus's response to Peter is both an affirmation (vv. 29–30) and a correction (v. 31). Mark 10:29 includes only the first half of the sentence that functions as Jesus's encouragement to the disciples, with the second half coming in 10:30. The first half of the sentence in 10:29 identifies the people who will receive the promises found in the second half in 10:30. Ἔφη, 3rd sg. impf. or aor. act. indic. of φημί, "say"; on ἀμήν, see 3:28; ἀφῆκεν, 3rd sg. aor. act. indic. of ἀφίημι, "leave."

10:30 Mark 10:30 begins with ἐὰν μὴ λάβῃ ("if he does not receive"), a grammatically awkward 3rd class cond. cstr., where one would more naturally expect ὃς οὐ λήμψεται ("who will not receive"; R 1020; ZG 141), and many EVV choose to translate it that way (e.g., CSB; ESV; NET; NRSV). Λάβῃ, 3rd sg. aor. act. subjunc. of λαμβάνω, "receive"; subjunc. in a 3rd class cond. clause; ἑκατονταπλασίονα, acc. pl. neut. of ἑκατονταπλασίων, -ον, "a hundred times as much, a hundredfold." The list of what is gained in v. 30 is similar to the list of what is lost in v. 29, although with a few variations. One minor variation is that the conj. connecting the items shifts from ἤ in v. 29 to καί in v. 30, which has the effect of emphasizing the magnitude of the reward (Cranfield 333). Διωγμῶν, gen. pl. masc. of διωγμός, -οῦ, ὁ, "persecution"; ἐρχομένῳ, dat. sg. masc. of pres. mid. ptc. of dep. ἔρχομαι, "come"; adj. ptc.

10:31 Ἔσονται, 3rd pl. fut. mid. indic. of εἰμί, "be" (dep. in fut.). Mark 10:31 has been interpreted in two different ways, based in part on two different interpretations of the conj. δέ in this verse (for more on δέ in Mark, see 1:8):

1. The conj. δέ has a connective function in 10:31. The teaching in v. 31 is a continuation of Jesus's words of encouragement found in vv. 29–30. The first, those who are rich and powerful in the present time, will find themselves to be the last in the age to come. Those who are last now in the estimation of this present age, such as the disciples who have left everything to follow Jesus, will find themselves to be first in the age to come (Hooker 243; Yarbro Collins 483; Strauss 446).

*2. The conj. δέ has a contrastive function in 10:31. In vv. 29–30 Jesus encourages his disciples with promised rewards in light of their sacrifices, but in contrast to that in v. 31 Jesus warns his disciples against an attitude that desires recognition and a higher rank based on that sacrifice. Being first in

God's kingdom is not nearly so predictable, and a preoccupation with being first may result in finding oneself finally among the last (Swete 233; Cranfield 333–34; France 408–9).

The conj. δέ does appear in contexts in Mark's Gospel where it can express either a connective or a contrastive idea, both within narrative (for connective, see, e.g., 12:16; for contrastive, see, e.g., 7:36) and within dialogue (for connective, see, e.g., 4:15; for contrastive, see, e.g., 10:43). However, to be more specific concerning dialogue, when δέ appears in Jesus's teaching it does so in a contrastive context at least 80 percent of the time, which would seem to lend support to the view that 10:31 is a contrastive warning to the disciples.

HOMILETICAL SUGGESTIONS

What Does Jesus Expect from His Followers (10:1–31)?

1. On marriage and divorce: Jesus expects wholehearted obedience. (10:1–12)
2. On children: Jesus expects childlike faith. (10:13–16)
3. On wealth: Jesus expects self-denying sacrifice. (10:17–31)

Finding Your Way through the Eye of the Needle (10:17–31)

1. What do we learn about Jesus?
   a. Jesus loves us enough to expose our need. (10:21)
   b. Jesus loves us enough to repay our every sacrifice. (10:29–30)
   c. Jesus loves us enough to give us eternal life. (10:30)
2. What do we learn about eternal life?
   a. Receiving eternal life is impossible apart from following Jesus. (10:27)
   b. Anything that stands in the way of following Jesus must go. (10:23–25)
   c. All of this—following Jesus, leaving what stands in the way—is impossible apart from the gracious work of God. (10:27)

5. Cycle 3: Prediction and Response (10:32–45)

The threefold pattern of prediction/misunderstanding/teaching on discipleship appears again in Mark 10:32–45. Of the three passion predictions, the third is the most extensive, with Jesus explaining in more detail the nature of the suffering that awaits him in Jerusalem (10:32–34). James and John respond by asking Jesus for the places of highest honor in his kingdom, which only offends the other disciples because they wanted those places (10:35–41). In response, Jesus teaches the disciples that they must be willing to live as servants, as slaves of all. Jesus himself did not come to be served but to serve and give his life (10:42–45).

(a) Third Passion Prediction (10:32–34)

10:32 Ἦσαν, 3rd pl. impf. act. indic. of εἰμί, "be"; ἀναβαίνοντες, nom. pl. masc. of pres. act. ptc. of ἀναβαίνω, "go up"; periph. ptc. (R 888; Wallace 648; on the impf.

periph. cstr., see 1:22); ἦν, 3rd sg. impf. act. indic. of εἰμί, "be"; προάγων, nom. sg. masc. of pres. act. ptc. of προάγω, "go before"; periph. ptc. (Burton §34; Wallace 648); ἐθαμβοῦντο, 3rd pl. impf. pass. indic. of θαμβέω, "be astonished, be amazed" (mng. with pass., BDAG 442c; on vbs. of amazement, see 1:22); ἀκολουθοῦντες, nom. pl. masc. of pres. act. ptc. of ἀκολουθέω, "follow"; subst. ptc.; ἐφοβοῦντο, 3rd pl. impf. pass. indic. of φοβέομαι, "fear, be afraid" (on φοβέομαι in the impf., see 6:20); παραλαβών, nom. sg. masc. of aor. act. ptc. of παραλαμβάνω, "take aside"; temp. adv. ptc. antecedent; ἤρξατο, 3rd sg. aor. mid. indic. of ἄρχω, "begin" (mng. with mid.; on ἄρχομαι, see 1:45); λέγειν, pres. act. inf. of λέγω, "say, tell"; complementary inf.; μέλλοντα, acc. pl. neut. of pres. act. ptc. of μέλλω, "be about to, be destined to"; subst. ptc.; συμβαίνειν, pres. act. inf. of συμβαίνω, "happen"; complementary inf.; αὐτῷ, dat. of reference or respect.

10:33 Ὅτι, introduces dir. discourse; on ἰδού, see 1:2. The vb. ἀναβαίνομεν is a futuristic pres. in that it describes a process that is already going on in the present but that will not reach its point of termination until sometime in the future (Fanning 221–23; Wallace 537; cf. 14:21; 16:7). Παραδοθήσεται, 3rd sg. fut. pass. indic. of παραδίδωμι, "hand over" (on παραδίδωμι, see 3:19); κατακρινοῦσιν, 3rd pl. fut. act. indic. of κατακρίνω, "condemn, pronounce a sentence on"; παραδώσουσιν, 3rd pl. fut. act. indic. of παραδίδωμι, "hand over."

10:34 Ἐμπαίξουσιν, 3rd pl. fut. act. indic. of ἐμπαίζω, "mock, ridicule"; αὐτῷ, dat. dir. obj. (twice in 10:34); ἐμπτύσουσιν, 3rd pl. fut. act. indic. of ἐμπτύω, "spit on"; μαστιγώσουσιν, 3rd pl. fut. act. indic. of μαστιγόω, "scourge, whip, flog"; ἀποκτενοῦσιν, 3rd pl. fut. act. indic. of ἀποκτείνω, "kill"; on "after three days," see 8:31; ἀναστήσεται, 3rd sg. fut. mid. indic. of ἀνίστημι, "rise" (act. intrans. mng. with fut. mid.).

(b) Misunderstanding by the Disciples: Request of James and John (10:35–41)

10:35 Προσπορεύονται, 3rd pl. pres. mid. indic. of dep. προσπορεύομαι, "approach, come up to" (on a pl. vb. with a compound subj., see 12:33); historical present (starting a new scene [see 1:12]); αὐτῷ, dat. dir. obj.; Ζεβεδαίου, gen. of relationship (R 501); λέγοντες, nom. pl. masc. of pres. act. ptc. of λέγω, "say"; attendant circumstance ptc.; διδάσκαλε, voc.; αἰτήσωμεν, 1st pl. aor. act. subjunc. of αἰτέω, "ask"; subjunc. in indef. rel. clause; ποιήσῃς, 2nd sg. aor. act. subjunc. of ποιέω, "do"; subjunc. in a complementary ἵνα clause; ἡμῖν, dat. of interest (advantage). The conj. ἵνα, when following the helping vb. θέλομεν, introduces a complementary clause that functions as an equivalent to a complementary inf., and it is probably best translated that way ("we want you to do"; Z §§406–7; Wallace 476). The vb. αἰτήσωμεν takes a dbl. acc., with both an obj. of the person (σε) and an obj. of the thing (ὃ ἐάν; cf. 6:22–23).

10:36 On ὁ δέ, see 1:45; ποιήσω, 1st sg. aor. act. subjunc. of ποιέω, "do"; ὑμῖν, dat. of interest (advantage). The text-critical problem in 10:36 calls for attention. The rdg. that best explains the rise of the other variants and therefore is probably the earliest is τί θέλετε ποιήσω ὑμῖν, found in C, Θ, family 1, family 13, 565, 1424 (France 414; Yarbro Collins 493). The reading is typical of Mark's style elsewhere (10:51; 14:12;

15:9, 12), and moreover fits a general pattern of Gk. usage in which, when the 2nd pers. form of θέλω is followed by a 1st pers. subjunc. vb. in a question, the conj. ἵνα is omitted but understood from the context. The pattern is consistent elsewhere in the NT (along with the verses just listed in Mark, see Matt 13:28; 20:32; 26:17; 27:17, 21; Luke 9:54; 18:41; 22:9; in the LXX, see Exod 2:7). The entire cstr. is similar to a question expressed by a delib. subjunc., since it asks for someone's opinion about what should be done (cf. Burton §171; Decker 2:241). The rdgs. τί θέλετέ με ποιῆσαι ὑμῖν and τί θέλετε ποιῆσαι με ὑμῖν both appear to be attempted improvements, replacing the subjunc. with an inf., while the rdg. τί θέλετέ [με] ποιήσω ὑμῖν seems to be a conflation, incl. as it does both the με and the subjunc. ποιήσω. If what Mark wrote was τί θέλετε ποιήσω ὑμῖν, then the subjunc. form ποιήσω also needs some explanation. The presence of the subjunc. ποιήσω after θέλετε implies that a complementary ἵνα has been omitted. As a result, the subjunc. is functionally equivalent to a complementary inf. and can be translated that way (e.g., ESV: "What do you want me to do for you?"; note also that, when the subjunc. ποιήσω is translated as an inf., it becomes necessary in Eng. to shift the subj. of ποιήσω ["I"] to the dir. obj. of θέλετε ["me"]).

10:37 On οἱ δέ in 10:37, 39, see 1:45; on the ending of εἶπαν in 10:37, 39, see 8:5; δός, 2nd sg. aor. act. impv. of δίδωμι, "give, grant" (on δός with ἵνα as "grant that," see BDAG 243c); εἷς . . . καὶ εἷς, nom. in simple appos. to the implied subj. of καθίσωμεν; ἀριστερῶν, gen. pl. neut. of ἀριστερός, -ά, -όν, "left" (on the pl. with δεξιῶν, ἀριστερῶν, and εὐωνύμων [in 10:40] where Eng. uses the sg., see R 408; BDF §141). The use of the prep. ἐκ to express a position next to someone ("at, on") is not common outside of the stereotyped pair of phrases "at the right" and "at the left" (Harris 107; cf. BDAG 296b). According to the custom of the day, the place of highest honor was at the right, while the place next in honor was at the left (Lane 379; Yarbro Collins 495–96; cf. 2 Sam 16:6; 1 Kgs 2:19; Ps 45:9; 110:1; 1 Esd 4:29; Sir 12:12; Mark 12:36; 14:62; Jos. *Ant.* 6.11.9 §235). Καθίσωμεν, 1st pl. aor. act. subjunc. of καθίζω, "sit, sit down"; subjunc. in a dir. obj. ἵνα clause introducing a request (see 5:10).

10:38 Οἴδατε, 2nd pl. pf. act. indic. of οἶδα, "know, understand" (on οἶδα, see 1:24); τί, "what, that which" (interr. pron. used as a rel. pron., cf. 2:25; 4:24; 14:36); αἰτεῖσθε, 2nd pl. pres. mid. indic. of αἰτέω, "ask, ask for, request" (mng. with mid.). Later in the narrative, Mark uses a phrase that matches almost exactly the wording of the request from James and John (15:27: "one on his right and one on his left" [ἕνα ἐκ δεξιῶν καὶ ἕνα ἐξ εὐωνύμων αὐτοῦ]; using εὐώνυμος, a synonym for ἀριστερός; cf. 10:40), but this time the phrase refers to the two thieves being crucified on either side of Jesus. The irony of this par. shows that James and John indeed did not know what they were asking for when they requested these places (cf. France 418; Evans 118). The mid. form of αἰτέω overlaps in mng. with the act. form, but the mid. form often appears in the context of commercial or business transactions (see the discussion at 6:24). The voice changes from the act. form αἰτήσωμεν in the initial request from James and John (10:35) to the mid. form αἰτεῖσθε in Jesus's response (10:38). The shift in voice may be noteworthy (Porter, *Idioms* 69–70) and may indicate that Jesus is portraying their request more like a negotiated contract, one that involves some cost on their part.

Δύνασθε, 2nd pl. pres. mid. indic. of dep. δύναμαι, "be able to, can"; πιεῖν, aor. act. inf. of πίνω, "drink"; complementary inf.; βάπτισμα, acc. sg. neut. of βάπτισμα, -ατος, τό, "baptism"; βαπτίζομαι, 1st sg. pres. pass. indic. of βαπτίζω, "baptize"; βαπτισθῆναι, aor. pass. inf. of βαπτίζω, "baptize"; complementary inf. The vb. βαπτίζω can take a dbl. acc. with an obj. of the person and an obj. of the thing. In addition, for βαπτίζω, the obj. of the thing can be a cognate acc. (see R 482; Wallace 189), in which case it should be prefaced in Eng. by the prep. "with." Therefore, the noun βάπτισμα and the rel. pron. ὅ should be prefaced by "with" in Eng., since they both function as a cognate acc. (cf. R. 478, 717) and as an acc. of the retained obj. of the thing with a pass. vb. (see R 484–85; Wallace 197; cf. also βάπτισμα and ὅ in 10:39).

10:39 Δυνάμεθα, 1st pl. pres. mid. indic. of dep. δύναμαι, "be able to, can." Jesus does not object to what—in light of the rest of the narrative—appears to be a superficial overconfidence on the part of James and John. Instead, he affirms that they will indeed suffer in the future according to the pattern of his own life (on the future faithfulness of the disciples, see also 13:9–13). Πίεσθε, 2nd pl. fut. mid. indic. of πίνω, "drink" (dep. in fut.); on βάπτισμα and βαπτίζομαι, see 10:38; βαπτισθήσεσθε, 2nd pl. fut. pass. indic. of βαπτίζω, "baptize."

10:40 Καθίσαι, aor. act. inf. of καθίζω, "sit, sit down"; subst. use of the inf., subj. of ἔστιν (cf. Wallace 234; KMP 369); on ἐκ, see 10:37; εὐωνύμων, gen. pl. neut. of εὐώνυμος, -ον, "left"; δοῦναι, aor. act. inf. of δίδωμι, "give, grant"; epex. inf. to the adj. ἐμόν (cf. R 1076); οἷς, dat. of interest (advantage); ἡτοίμασται, 3rd sg. pf. pass. indic. of ἑτοιμάζω, "prepare." The use of the rel. clause οἷς ἡτοίμασται after the conj. ἀλλ' creates a compressed expression that assumes but does not state a main vb. (such as ἔστιν) and an antecedent for the rel. pron. (such as ἐκείνοις; cf. T 324; France 417). The pass. voice with ἡτοίμασται is an example of the so-called divine passive, a pass. in which the agent is left unexpressed but in which God is the obvious agent in context (see Wallace 437–38). Interpreters have sometimes exaggerated the frequency with which divine passives appear in Mark's Gospel (see Beniamin Pascut, "The So-Called Passivum Divinum in Mark's Gospel," *NovT* 54 [2012]: 313–33). At times, the pass. voice appears when the focus of the passage is on the subj. of the pass. vb., and an explicit reference to the agent would unnecessarily detract from that focus (e.g., 6:16; 8:12; 9:31; 10:33; 14:27). At times, Jesus uses the pres. pass. to make an authoritative pronouncement, so that the action takes place by the act of speaking itself (e.g., 2:5; "your sins are forgiven"; cf. 1:41; 7:34). Since Jesus is the one giving the pronouncement, he is the agent of the action. Sometimes interpreters have wrongly labeled these authoritative pronouncements by Jesus as divine passives, leaving the impression that Jesus was not the one who accomplished the action (see, e.g., Joachim Jeremias, *New Testament Theology: The Proclamation of Jesus* [New York: Charles Scribner's Sons, 1971], 9–14, esp. 11). At times, Mark uses the pass. to report that Jesus's words or actions were indeed effective in bringing about healing for a needy person (e.g., 1:42; 3:5; 5:29; 6:56; 7:35). Examples such as these should also not be categorized as "divine passives," since that would detract from Mark's emphasis on the healing power of Jesus.

10:41 Ἀκούσαντες, nom. pl. masc. of aor. act. ptc. of ἀκούω, "hear"; temp. adv. ptc. antecedent; δέκα, indecl. number, "ten" (on the art. with a number to indicate a portion of a larger group, see T 178; cf. BDF §480); ἤρξαντο, 3rd pl. aor. mid. indic. of ἄρχω, "begin" (mng. with mid.; on ἄρχομαι, see 1:45); ἀγανακτεῖν, pres. act. inf. of ἀγανακτέω, "be indignant, be angry"; complementary inf. Apparently, the other ten disciples were angry because James and John were cutting in ahead of them to gain an unfair advantage in the competition for the places of highest rank (France 418). All of this—the request of James and John and the angry response of the other disciples—demonstrates the continuing need for instruction on what it means to be great in the context of the kingdom of God.

(c) Jesus's Instructions on Discipleship: Learning to Be a Servant (10:42–45)

10:42 Προσκαλεσάμενος, nom. sg. masc. of aor. mid. ptc. of προσκαλέω, "summon, call to oneself" (mng. with mid.); temp. adv. ptc. antecedent; λέγει, historical pres. (see 1:30); οἴδατε, 2nd pl. pf. act. indic. of οἶδα, "know, understand" (on οἶδα, see 1:24); δοκοῦντες, nom. pl. masc. of pres. act. ptc. of δοκέω, "seem"; subst. ptc.; ἄρχειν, pres. act. inf. of ἄρχω, "rule, govern"; complementary inf. (Decker 2:70); ἐθνῶν, gen. dir. obj. (see R 510 for vbs. of ruling commonly taking a gen. dir. obj. [three examples in 10:42]); κατακυριεύουσιν, from κατακυριεύω, "lord it over, be master over, rule"; κατεξουσιάζουσιν, from κατεξουσιάζω, "exercise authority over, tyrannize." The compound vbs. κατακυριεύουσιν and κατεξουσιάζουσιν both use the prep. κατά as a prefix to intensify the action of the vb. (on compound vbs. with κατά as a prefix, see 1:36). The rulers of this world want to dominate others with controlling force and to impose their will on them.

10:43 What Jesus wants for his followers—a life of service—stands in contrast (δέ) to what is so easily observed among the rulers in this world. Θέλῃ, 3rd sg. pres. act. subjunc. of θέλω, "want, wish"; subjunc. in an indef. rel. clause; γενέσθαι, aor. mid. inf. of dep. γίνομαι, "become"; complementary inf.; ἔσται, 3rd sg. fut. mid. indic. of εἰμί, "be" (dep. in fut.); command indic. At the time of the NT, a common, concrete mng. for the word διάκονος was "one who waits on tables, one who serves a meal to others." This more limited reference appears in the NT with regard to the noun διάκονος (John 2:5, 9; cf. Matt 22:13), the related noun διακονία (Luke 10:40; Acts 6:1), and the related vb. διακονέω (Mark 1:31; Luke 10:40; 12:37; 17:8; 22:27; John 12:2; Acts 6:2). This concrete sense for διάκονος still echoes in the more general and comprehensive uses of the word. A servant, like someone who waits on tables and serves food to guests, takes an inferior position in order to meet the needs of others (*TDNT* 2:82–85, 88; cf. Luke 22:26–27).

10:44 Θέλῃ, 3rd sg. pres. act. subjunc. of θέλω, "want, wish"; subjunc. in an indef. rel. clause; εἶναι, pres. act. inf. of εἰμί, "be"; complementary inf.; ἔσται, 3rd sg. fut. mid. indic. of εἰμί, "be" (dep. in fut.); command indic. The saying in 10:44 strengthens the point already made in 10:43. Being first is higher than being great, and being a slave of all is lower than being a servant (Yarbro Collins 499; Strauss 458). Outside of 10:44, all the other uses of δοῦλος in Mark's Gospel refer lit. to workers who are the property of an owner (12:2, 4; 13:34; 14:47). However, the word δοῦλος also has an extended mng., one that portrays a δοῦλος as someone who gives allegiance to another and who therefore is under obligation to this "master" (BDAG 260b; cf. Rom 6:17–20). The notion of obligation or compulsion distinguishes the mng. of "slave" from that of "servant" (*TDNT* 2:261). Slaves do not serve as a matter of choice, since they are not free and do not belong to themselves.

10:45 The reason (γάρ) why followers of Jesus live with humble and self-sacrificial service toward others is because that is the pattern set before them by Jesus's life. Καί, ascensive; ἦλθεν, 3rd sg. aor. act. indic. of ἔρχομαι, "come"; διακονηθῆναι, aor. pass. inf. of διακονέω, "serve"; purpose inf.; διακονῆσαι, aor. act. inf. of διακονέω, "serve"; purpose inf.; δοῦναι, aor. act. inf. of δίδωμι, "give"; purpose inf.; λύτρον, acc. sg. neut. of λύτρον, -ου, τό, "ransom, price of release" (often introduced in Eng. with "as" because it is a complement in a dbl. acc. obj.-complement cstr.). Outside of the NT, the noun λύτρον is commonly used for a ransom, i.e., for a payment made to bring about release and to buy freedom for those held in bondage, including prisoners of war, slaves, and debtors (MM 382–83; *TDNT* 4:340; *EDNT* 2:365; Spicq 425–28). In the NT, λύτρον only appears in Mark 10:45 and the par. passage in Matt 20:28, although 1 Tim 2:6 contains the related compound word ἀντίλυτρον. These NT passages picture Jesus's death as a payment given to buy freedom for those held in bondage. The prevailing sense for ἀντί (prep. taking a gen. obj.) is "instead of, in place of," conveying the idea of substitution (see the extended discussion on ἀντί esp. as it applies to Mark 10:45 in Harris 49–54; see also *TDNT* 1:372–73; *EDNT* 1:108–9; Wallace 365–67). Examples of such a mng. are easy to find. Abraham offered up a ram as a burnt offering "instead of" (ἀντί) his son Isaac (Gen 22:13 LXX). David lamented for Absalom, wishing that he had died "in place of" (ἀντί) his son (2 Kgdms 18:33 LXX). According to Jesus, if a son asks for a fish, his father would never think to give him a snake "instead of" (ἀντί) a fish (Luke 11:11). The use of ἀντί to express substitution also fits in the context of Mark 10:45, since the prep. phrase beginning with ἀντί is adj. (Decker 2:72) and modifies λύτρον, another word that conveys the idea of substitution. A ransom is a payment that is received as a substitute in exchange for those who had forfeited their freedom (cf. Jos., *Ant.* 14.7.1 §107). The use of "many" (πολλῶν) to indicate the people who benefit from Jesus's ransom is probably intended to communicate that Jesus gave his life for all, not just for some (on the incl. use of πολλοί, see *TDNT* 6:536–45, esp. pp. 543–45; Cranfield 343; cf. Mark 1:34; 6:2; 14:24 for a similar use of πολλοί; cf. also the ransom saying in 1 Tim 2:6 which refers to Jesus's ransom as given for "all" [πάντων]). The point of using "many" is not to say that Jesus gave his life for many but still less than all; instead the point is to say that Jesus gave his life for all who are, in fact, many.

FOR FURTHER STUDY

26. The Meaning of Jesus's Death in Mark

Bolt, Peter G. *The Cross from a Distance: Atonement in Mark's Gospel*. NSBT. Downers Grove, IL: InterVarsity, 2004.

Carroll, John T., and Joel B. Green. *The Death of Jesus in Early Christianity*. Peabody, MA: Hendrickson, 1995.

Dowd, Sharon, and Elizabeth Struthers Malbon. "The Significance of Jesus' Death in Mark: Narrative Context and Authorial Audience." *JBL* 125 (2006): 271–97.

Hooker, Morna D. "Mark." Pages 47–67 in *Not Ashamed of the Gospel: New Testament Interpretations of the Death of Christ*. Grand Rapids: Eerdmans, 1994.

Marcus, Joel. "Crucifixion as Parodic Exaltation." *JBL* 125 (2006): 73–87.

Stuhlmacher, Peter. "Vicariously Giving His Life for Many, Mark 10:45 (Matt. 20:28)." Pages 16–29 in *Reconciliation, Law, and Righteousness: Essays in Biblical Theology*. Philadelphia: Fortress, 1986.

*Watts, Rikki E. "Jesus' Death, Isaiah 53, and Mark 10:45: A Crux Revisited." Pages 125–51 in *Jesus and the Suffering Servant: Isaiah 53 and Christian Origins*. Edited by William H. Bellinger Jr. and William R. Farmer. Harrisburg, PA: Trinity Press International, 1998.

Yarbro Collins, Adela. "The Signification of Mark 10:45 among Gentile Christians." *HTR* 90 (1997): 371–82.

———. "Finding Meaning in the Death of Jesus." *JR* 78 (1998): 175–96.

———. "Mark's Interpretation of the Death of Jesus." *JBL* 128 (2009): 545–54.

HOMILETICAL SUGGESTIONS

Disciples of a Perfect Master (10:35–45)

1. Disciples of Jesus do not live to serve themselves. (10:35–41)
2. Disciples of Jesus live to serve the least. (10:42–44)
   a. As servants, we must put the needs of others above our own.
   b. As slaves, we have no choice but to serve others, since we do not belong to ourselves.
3. Why do disciples of Jesus live this way? Because our Lord lived his life as a sacrificial service for us. (10:45)

(d) [Transition] Healing of Blind Bartimaeus (10:46–52)

This section (8:27–10:52) ends with the healing of blind Bartimaeus, which serves as another transitional passage. As the conclusion to this section, the renewed sight of Bartimaeus, a man who recognizes the identity of Jesus and follows him in the way, stands in contrast to the ongoing difficulty of the disciples, who struggle to see clearly what it means to follow. This episode also points forward to the following narrative, since Bartimaeus cries out to Jesus using the title "Son of David" (10:47–48). The next section opens with the triumphal entry, in which the crowd takes up the perspective of

Bartimaeus, calling out their blessings toward Jesus and the coming kingdom of David (11:9–10). In a way, Bartimaeus starts the triumphal entry of Jesus into Jerusalem.

10:46 Ἔρχονται, 3rd pl. pres. mid. indic. of dep. ἔρχομαι, "come"; historical pres. (starting a new scene, see 1:12); ἐκπορευομένου, gen. sg. masc. of pres. mid. ptc. of dep. ἐκπορεύομαι, "go out"; gen. abs.; temp. adv. ptc. contemp. (sg. ptc. in agreement with the first-named individual [αὐτοῦ] in the compound subj.); ἱκανός, "sufficient enough, large, considerable" (perhaps implying in the context that the crowd was as large as could be expected under the circumstances [see LN 59.12]); Τιμαίου, gen. of relationship (since the Aram. word *bar* conveys the idea "son of," Βαρτιμαῖος actually means "son of Timaeus" [Marcus 2:759]); προσαίτης, nom. sg. masc. of προσαίτης, -ου, ὁ, "beggar"; ἐκάθητο, 3rd sg. impf. mid. indic. of dep. κάθημαι, "sit" (on the impf. for background information, see 1:21); παρά with the acc.: "at the side of" (when used to modify a vb. not conveying motion [see Harris 171]).

10:47 Ἀκούσας, nom. sg. masc. of aor. act. ptc. of ἀκούω, "hear"; temp. adv. ptc. antecedent; ἐστιν, on the translation of the pres. tense in indir. discourse as past in Eng., see 2:1; ἤρξατο, 3rd sg. aor. mid. indic. of ἄρχω, "begin" (mng. with mid.; on ἄρχομαι, see 1:45); κράζειν, pres. act. inf. of κράζω, "cry out, shout"; complementary inf.; λέγειν, pres. act. inf. of λέγω, "say"; complementary inf.; ἐλέησον, 2nd sg. aor. act. impv. of ἐλεέω, "have mercy." Both υἱέ and Ἰησοῦ are voc. forms (Ἰησοῦ serves as the gen., dat., and voc. form; on the decl. of Ἰησοῦς, see BDF §55; R 263), and Δαυίδ, which is indecl. (BDAG 212d; BDF §53), functions in this context as a gen. of relationship to υἱέ. "Son of David" is a messianic title that highlights the Messiah's status as a descendant of David who inherits God's promises to David (*TDNT* 8:480–82; see 2 Sam 7:12–16, where God promises to establish David's royal line so that his house, throne, and kingdom would endure forever).

10:48 Ἐπετίμων, 3rd pl. impf. act. indic. of ἐπιτιμάω, "rebuke, sternly order"; αὐτῷ, dat. dir. obj.; σιωπήσῃ, 3rd sg. aor. act. subjunc. of σιωπάω, "be quiet"; subjunc. in a dir. obj. ἵνα clause (when introducing the content of a command, ἵνα can be translated into Eng. with an inf. of indir. discourse [see 5:10]); on ὁ δέ in v. 48 and v. 50, see 1:45; ἔκραζεν, 3rd sg. impf. act. indic. of κράζω, "cry out, shout." To show the heightened determination by the blind man, Mark uses πολλῷ before the comp. adv. μᾶλλον to indicate the extent to which his effort had increased (lit. "more by much"; πολλῷ, dat. of measure; see Wallace 166–67). In light of the qualification that the action expressed by ἔκραζεν was taking place "all the more," the impf. with ἔκραζεν portrays the action as repeated (iter. impf.). The preceding impf. ἐπετίμων matches that same action (also iter. impf.), so that repeated attempts to silence the blind man only met with repeated cries for help. Ἐλέησον, 2nd sg. aor. act. impv. of ἐλεέω, "have mercy."

10:49 Στάς, nom. sg. masc. of aor. act. ptc. of ἵστημι, "stand still, stop" (BDAG 482c); temp. adv. ptc. antecedent; φωνήσατε, 2nd pl. aor. act. impv. of φωνέω, "call, summon"; φωνοῦσιν, historical pres. (used with vbs. that introduce dir. and indir. discourse [see 1:12, 30]); λέγοντες, nom. pl. masc. of pres. act. ptc. of λέγω, "say"; redundant ptc.; θάρσει, 2nd sg. pres. act. impv. of θαρσέω, "have courage, take heart"; ἔγειρε, 2nd sg. pres. act. impv. of ἐγείρω, "rise, get up, come" (BDAG 272b). The normal pattern in Mark's Gospel is to express specific commands in concrete situations in the aor. tense. For the most part, the commands—and requests—in this passage follow that pattern (see the aor. impv. forms in 10:47, 48, 49 and the aor. subjunc. form used in indir. discourse in 10:48). However, certain vbs. idiomatically appear in the pres. tense in the impv. mood even when used for specific commands, incl. θάρσει and ἔγειρε in 10:49 and ὕπαγε in 10:52 (see the discussion at 2:11).

10:50 Ἀποβαλών, nom. sg. masc. of aor. act. ptc. of ἀποβάλλω, "throw aside, throw off"; temp. adv. ptc. antecedent; ἀναπηδήσας, nom. sg. masc. of aor. act. ptc. of ἀναπηδάω, "jump up"; temp. adv. ptc. antecedent; ἦλθεν, 3rd sg. aor. act. indic. of ἔρχομαι, "come." In contrast to Matthew and Luke (cf. Matt 20:32; Luke 18:40), Mark records that the blind man threw aside his cloak. The noun ἱμάτιον may refer to clothing in general, but it points more specifically to an outer garment, a cloak, in contexts where it is laid aside in order to pursue some activity (*EDNT* 2:187; cf. John 13:4; Acts 7:58). It may have been the custom of the day for beggars to spread out a cloak on the ground in front of themselves in order to receive alms (Taylor 449; Hooker 253), so that Mark was portraying Bartimaeus as leaving behind a valuable possession or even his means of income in order to come to Jesus.

10:51 Ἀποκριθείς, nom. sg. masc. of aor. pass. ptc. of dep. ἀποκρίνομαι, "answer"; redundant ptc.; ποιήσω, 1st sg. aor. act. subjunc. of ποιέω, "do"; subjunc. after an implied complementary ἵνα; σοι, dat. of interest (advantage). Whenever Mark uses a 2nd pers. form of θέλω in a question and follows it with a 1st pers. subjunc. vb., he omits the conj. ἵνα before the subjunc. form (10:36, 51; 14:12; 15:9, 12; see the discussion at 10:36). As a result, ποιήσω assumes an implied complementary ἵνα and therefore is equivalent to a complementary inf. ("to do"). Ραββουνι, an indecl. Aram. loanword with a 1st pers. suffix, used here as a voc., mng. "my master, my teacher" (Decker 2:77). Although ραββουνι is a more emph. form of ῥαββί (BDAG 902b; ZG 143), in the NT ραββουνι and ῥαββί are roughly equivalent in mng., with both being used most often by students as a title of respect for their teacher (*TDNT* 6:961–65; on ῥαββί, see 9:5). Ἀναβλέψω; 1st sg. aor. act. subjunc. of ἀναβλέπω, "regain sight, see again, receive sight" (on the mng. of ἀναβλέπω, see 8:24). The subord. conj. ἵνα implies an assumed main vb. (θέλω), so that it is functioning as a complementary ἵνα, which in turn is probably best translated as a complementary inf. (Decker 2:77; Cranfield 346; see, e.g., GNB: "I want to see again"). In this way, the underlying grammatical structure of Bartimaeus's answer corresponds to that of Jesus's question (except that Jesus's question omits the ἵνα and Bartimaeus's answer omits the form of the helping vb. θέλω).

10:52 Ὕπαγε, 2nd sg. pres. act. impv. of ὑπάγω, "go, depart"; σου, subj. gen.; σέσωκεν, 3rd sg. pf. act. indic. of σῴζω, "save" (on σῴζω, see 5:34); ἀνέβλεψεν, 3rd sg. aor. act. indic. of ἀναβλέπω, "regain sight, see again, receive sight"; ἠκολούθει, 3rd sg. impf. act. indic. of ἀκολουθέω, "follow" (on the impf. for a dramatic event at the end of a miracle story, see 1:21); αὐτῷ, dat. dir. obj. Mark undoubtedly portrays the healed blind man in a lit. sense as walking behind Jesus and heading with him toward Jerusalem. However, the vb. ἀκολουθέω can also have a metaphorical sense in Mark to indicate someone's personal allegiance to Jesus and his teaching. This metaphorical mng. for ἀκολουθέω occurs whenever Mark refers to individuals following Jesus (1:18; 2:14; 8:34; 10:21, 28; 10:52; 14:54; 15:41; on ἀκολουθέω, see 1:18). Therefore, Mark's point seems to be that Bartimaeus became a follower of Jesus (the noun ὁδός can also have metaphorical overtones for a path in life prepared for by God [see 8:27]).

FOR FURTHER STUDY

27. Jesus as "Son of David" in Mark

Ahearne-Kroll, Stephen P. *The Psalms of Lament in Mark's Passion: Jesus' Davidic Suffering*. SNTSMS 142. Cambridge: Cambridge University Press, 2007.

Botner, Max. "What Has Mark's Christ to Do with David's Son? A History of Interpretation." *CurBR* 16 (2017–18): 50–70.

Broadhead, Edwin K. "Son of David." Pages 109–15 in *Naming Jesus: Titular Christology in the Gospel of Mark*. JSNTSup 175. Sheffield, UK: Sheffield Academic Press, 1999.

Chilton, Bruce. "Jesus *ben David*: Reflections on the *Davidssohnfrage*." *JSNT* 14 (1982): 88–112.

Hahn, Ferdinand. "Son of David." Pages 240–78 in *The Titles of Jesus in Christology: Their History in Early Christianity*. New York: World Publishing, 1969.

*Kingsbury, Jack Dean. "The Christology of Mark: The Davidic Messiah-King, the Son of God." Pages 47–155 in *The Christology of Mark's Gospel*. Philadelphia: Fortress, 1983.

Malbon, Elizabeth Struthers. "The Jesus of Mark and the 'Son of David.'" Pages 162–85 in *Between Author and Audience in Mark: Narration, Characterization, Interpretation*. Edited by Elizabeth Struthers Malbon. Sheffield, UK: Sheffield Phoenix, 2009.

Marcus, Joel. "Mark 12:35–37: David's Son and David's Lord." Pages 130–52 in *The Way of the Lord: Christological Exegesis of the Old Testament in the Gospel of Mark*. Louisville: Westminster John Knox, 1992.

Matera, Frank J. *The Kingship of Jesus: Composition and Theology in Mark 15*. SBLDS 66. Chico, CA: Scholars Press, 1982.

Smith, Stephen H. "The Function of the Son of David Tradition in Mark's Gospel." *NTS* 42 (1996): 523–39.

HOMILETICAL SUGGESTIONS

The King and the Beggar (10:46–52)

1. What do we learn about Jesus?
   a. The king who hears: Jesus is a messianic king who hears the cries of the poor. (10:49)
   b. The king who sees: Jesus is a messianic king who sees the faith of the needy. (10:51)
2. What do we learn about a life of faith?
   a. The beggar's right hope: People of faith set their hope on Jesus, our king and teacher. (10:47–48, 50)

    b. The beggar's right request: People of faith call on Jesus to meet their needs. (10:51)

    c. The beggar's right response: People of faith follow Jesus out of gratitude for his grace. (10:52)

B. JESUS'S MINISTRY AT THE TEMPLE (11:1–13:37)

All the events in 11:1–13:37 take place either on the way to the temple, in the temple, or on the way out of the temple. The section begins with the triumphal entry, in which Jesus comes to the city of Jerusalem and immediately enters the temple (11:1–11). At the end of the section, as he is exiting the temple for the last time, Jesus predicts its destruction (13:1–4). After traveling to the Mount of Olives, Jesus sits down opposite the temple and gives his eschatological discourse to his closest disciples (13:5–37). The temple never functions as a setting outside of chs. 11–13 in Mark's Gospel. The term used for the whole temple precinct (ἱερόν) appears repeatedly in chs. 11–13 (11:11, 15, 16, 27; 12:35; 13:1, 3), but otherwise only at the arrest of Jesus in Mark 14:49, when Jesus refers back to his time of teaching in the temple.

Mark 11–13 explains the nature of the controversy between Jesus and the religious leaders. In this section, the plotline related to the escalating conflict between Jesus and the religious leaders moves to the forefront, a conflict that revolves around Jesus's God-given authority and refusal of the religious leaders to accept it (11:27–33). They are like wicked tenant farmers who refuse to give the owner what rightfully belongs to him and who kill the owner's servants and even his son (12:1–12). The end for them will be a greater condemnation (12:9, 40). Yet Mark's inclusion of the story of the wise scribe holds open another possibility: that thoughtful scribes might recognize the truth of Jesus's words and be open to the kingdom of God (12:28–34). Although the disciples move into the background in chs. 11–13, one segment of their story line is more prominent in this section than in the others. In the eschatological discourse in ch. 13, Jesus predicts that the disciples will testify concerning him in the midst of persecution as they spread the gospel message to the nations (13:9–13). Through this prediction of Jesus, we know that the end of the story for the disciples is that, in spite of their misunderstandings and failures, they will become fishers of people.

Mark structures his narrative in this section around three journeys by Jesus to the temple on three successive days (11:1–11; 11:12–19; 11:20–13:37). The description of what takes place at the temple grows in length with each successive day. The final day in the temple contains by far the most content. On that day, Jesus answers the questions of the religious leaders and criticizes their teaching and behavior. As he leaves the temple, he predicts its destruction and he teaches a select group of his disciples about the future in the eschatological discourse.

1. First Trip to the Temple (11:1–11)

The first trip to the temple begins with the triumphal entry of Jesus into Jerusalem in which many offer praise to God for the one who comes in the name of the Lord and for the coming kingdom of David (11:1–10). All Jesus does when he arrives in the temple is look around, and then he leaves the temple and the city of Jerusalem to stay the night in Bethany, a short distance from Jerusalem (11:11).

(a) Travel to the Temple: The Triumphal Entry (11:1–10)

11:1 Ἐγγίζουσιν, historical pres. (at the beginning of a new scene [see 1:12; cf. also ἀποστέλλει in v. 1 and λέγει in v. 2]); ἐλαιῶν, gen. pl. fem. of ἐλαία, -ας, ἡ, "olive" (τὸ ὄρος τῶν ἐλαιῶν, "the Mount of Olives"). Each prep. in the opening temp. clause is challenging to translate (the first εἰς corresponds to the mng. of πρός [see Z §97]; the second εἰς means "in the vicinity of" [see BDAG 288d–289a]; πρός in this context means "near" [see Harris 189; BDAG 875b–c; cf. e.g., Mark 4:1]).

11:2 Ὑπάγετε, 2nd pl. pres. act. impv. of ὑπάγω, "go, depart" (on the impv. of ὑπάγω, see 2:11); κατέναντι, adv. used as a prep. with a gen. obj., "opposite, ahead of" (the 2nd use of the art. τήν indicates that the prep. phrase is functioning adj. to modify κώμην [cf. 6:11; 11:25; 13:25; 15:43]); εἰσπορευόμενοι, nom. pl. masc. of pres. mid. ptc. of dep. εἰσπορεύομαι, "go into, enter"; temp. adv. ptc. contemp. (on the prep. after a compound vb., see 1:21); εὑρήσετε, 2nd pl. fut. act. indic. of εὑρίσκω, "find"; πῶλον, acc. sg. masc. of πῶλος, -ου, ὁ, "colt, horse" (the same form occurs in vv. 4, 5, 7). Although the noun πῶλος commonly refers to the colt of a horse, it may also indicate the young offspring of other kinds of animals, incl. often the colt of a donkey (*TDNT* 6:959–61; MM 561; cf. Justin, *1 Apol.* 54.7). Mark's decision to use πῶλος may be due to the appearance of the word in the LXX in Zech 9:9. In that verse, Israel's king, one who is righteous and humble and able to bring salvation, comes to Jerusalem riding on a donkey (LXX: ὑποζύγιον, "pack animal, donkey," BDAG 1037d), that is, on a young colt (LXX: πῶλον; see also Matt 21:1–7; John 12:14–15). Δεδεμένον, acc. sg. masc. of pf. pass. ptc. of δέω, tie; adj. ptc.; οὐδεὶς οὔπω, "no one ever," (BDAG 737b) (on a dbl. neg. to strengthen a statement, see 1:44; the partitive gen. ἀνθρώπων [normally left untr.] also adds emph. by highlighting the all-encompassing scope of the statement); ἐκάθισεν, 3rd sg. aor. act. indic. of καθίζω, "sit down"; λύσατε, 2nd pl. aor. act. impv. of λύω, "untie, loose"; φέρετε, 2nd pl. pres. act. impv. of φέρω, bring. The shift from the aor. λύσατε to the pres. φέρετε is probably not significant, since φέρετε almost always occurs in the pres. tense with impv. forms (Fanning 347–48; BDF §336; cf. 9:19; 12:15).

11:3 Εἴπῃ, 3rd sg. aor. act. subjunc. of λέγω, "say"; subjunc. in a 3rd class cond. clause; τί, "why" (see 2:7); εἴπατε, 2nd pl. aor. act. impv. of λέγω, "say" (on the ending of εἴπατε, see 8:5; cf. εἶπαν in 11:6); αὐτοῦ, obj. gen. to χρείαν; πάλιν, "back" (with vbs. of sending, going, turning, calling [BDAG 752b–c]). The vb. ἀποστέλλει in this context functions as a futuristic pres. in the sense that, while the pledge to act occurs in the pres., the actual carrying out of the deed will only take place in the fut. (cf. Fanning 223–24; Wallace 536). The purpose for this type of futuristic pres. is to emphasize the immediacy of the action, the intention to accomplish it in the near future.

11:4 Ἀπῆλθον, 3rd pl. aor. act. indic. of ἀπέρχομαι, "depart, go away"; εὗρον, 3rd pl. aor. act. indic. of εὑρίσκω, "find"; on πῶλον, see 11:2; δεδεμένον, acc. sg. masc. of pf. pass. ptc. of δέω, "tie"; adj. ptc.; πρός, "at, by, near" (BDAG 875b–c); ἀμφόδου, gen. sg. neut. of ἄμφοδον, -ου, τό, "street, thoroughfare." Mark uses a historical pres. vb. (λύουσιν) to describe the disciples' obedient action of untying the colt. This instance of the pres. tense does not fit the most common patterns for the use of the historical pres. in Mark (see 1:12, 30). Instead, the purpose for the historical pres. with λύουσιν seems to be solely to draw attention to a particularly dramatic event in the passage as a whole (Fanning 233). The disciples untie a colt that does not belong to them, not knowing what will happen next but fully prepared by Jesus with the words to say if someone challenges them.

11:5 Just as Jesus anticipated, some of the bystanders at the scene object when the disciples untie the colt. Ἑστηκότων, gen. pl. masc. of pf. act. ptc. of ἵστημι, "stand" (pres. intrans. mng. with pf., BDAG 482d–483a); subst. ptc. and partitive gen.; λύοντες, nom. pl. masc. of pres. act. ptc. of λύω, "untie, loose"; adv. ptc. of means (T 154; Decker 2:82); on πῶλον, see 11:2.

11:6 On οἱ δέ, see 1:45. In this context καθώς introduces an action that took place before the conversation of the disciples with the bystanders; in Eng., it is necessary to use a pluperf. vb. to express prior past action for εἶπεν (see 3:10; cf. ZG 144; Z §290). Ἀφῆκαν, 3rd pl. aor. act. indic. of ἀφίημι, "allow, permit, give permission."

11:7 Φέρουσιν, historical present (for participants changing their location within a scene [see 1:12; cf. also ἐπιβάλλουσιν]). On πῶλον, see 11:2; ἐπιβάλλουσιν, from ἐπιβάλλω, "put on, throw on"; αὐτῷ, dat. dir. obj. After the colt was prepared by placing cloaks on it as a makeshift saddle (Stein 505), Jesus sat (ἐκάθισεν, 3rd sg. aor. act. indic. of καθίζω, "sit") on it in order to ride into the city of Jerusalem as the messianic king in fulfillment of Zech 9:9.

11:8 Ἔστρωσαν, 3rd pl. aor. act. indic. of στρωννύω, "spread out"; ἄλλοι, nom. subj. of implied ἔστρωσαν; στιβάδας, acc. pl. fem. of στιβάς, -άδος, ἡ, "bed of grass and leaves"; κόψαντες, nom. pl. masc. of aor. act. ptc. of κόπτω, "cut"; temp. adv. ptc. antecedent. The noun στιβάς occurs only this one time in the NT. In extrabiblical lit., the word is used with reference to grass, straw, and leaves that could be stuffed into a mattress to create a soft place to lie down (see LSJ 1645; MM 589–90). Mark creates a picture of people cutting down tall grass and leaves from the surrounding fields and gathering all of it together in the road to create a comfortable, "bed-like" path for Jesus and the colt.

11:9 Προάγοντες, nom. pl. masc. of pres. act. ptc. of προάγω, "go before"; subst. ptc.; ἀκολουθοῦντες, nom. pl. masc. of pres. act. ptc. of ἀκολουθέω, "follow"; subst. ptc. Given the presence of many people who are crying out in the midst of a procession, the use of the impf. vb. ἔκραζον (3rd pl. impf. act. indic. of κράζω, "cry out") conveys the idea of repeated action (iter. impf.), likely indicating both that many people pick up and repeat the acclamation and that individuals in the crowd cry out repeatedly. The word ὡσαννά is a Gk. transliteration that derives from an Aram. form of the Heb. phrase found at the beginning of Ps 118:25, a phrase that expresses a cry to God for help: "save now" (*EDNT* 3:509; Joseph A. Fitzmyer, "Aramaic Evidence Affecting the Interpretation of Hosanna in the New Testament," in *Tradition and Interpretation in the New Testament: Essays in Honor of E. Earle Ellis*, ed. Gerald W. Hawthorne and Otto Betz [Grand Rapids: Eerdmans, 1987], 110–18). The word appears six times in the NT, always in connection with Jesus's entry into Jerusalem (Matt 21:9 [twice], 15;

Mark 11:9, 10; John 12:13). These uses in the NT indicate that ὡσαννά had shifted in mng., so that it no longer functions as a cry to God for help but as an expression of joyful celebration. The exact nature of that shift in mng. is difficult to sort out, since the Gospels themselves are the earliest evidence available for a new mng. At least in Mark's Gospel, the word ὡσαννά does not seem to function as a cry of greeting, since those who have been traveling along with Jesus to Jerusalem appear to comprise the majority of the crowd that is shouting "Hosanna." Instead, ὡσαννά seems to be an exclamation of praise to the God who now saves (cf. Matt 21:16 where Jesus compares the cry "Hosanna to the Son of David" to a statement of praise; see also Did. 10:6). Εὐλογημένος, nom. sg. masc. of pf. pass. ptc. of εὐλογέω, "bless"; pred. adj. ptc. (on pred. adj. participles, see 11:10); ἐρχόμενος, nom. sg. masc. of pres. mid. ptc. of dep. ἔρχομαι, "come"; subst. ptc.

11:10 Εὐλογημένη, nom. sg. fem. of pf. pass. ptc. of εὐλογέω, "bless"; ἐρχομένη, nom. sg. fem. of pres. mid. ptc. of dep. ἔρχομαι, "come." An adj. ptc. can function in two different ways, as an attrib. adj. or as a pred. adj. (for a discussion, see Burton §§420–33; Wallace 617–19; KMP 325). Mark 11:10 provides an example of both. Like any other adj., an adj. ptc. that modifies a noun or noun substitute is attrib., while an adj. ptc. that asserts something about a noun or noun substitute is pred. (Wallace 306–14; KMP 163–69). Often, a pred. adj. is used in connection with an equative vb., but the equative vb. may be implied rather than stated. In 11:10, εὐλογημένη is a pred. adj. ptc.; it is used in a sentence with an implied equative vb., and it asserts something about the coming kingdom (that it is "blessed"). In 11:10, ἐρχομένη is an adj. ptc. in the first attrib. position, and so is modifying βασιλεία, "the coming kingdom" (in light of the much greater frequency in Mark's Gospel of attrib. adj. participles in comp. to pred. adj. participles, attrib. adj. participles are simply given the label "adj. ptc."). The concluding cry of "hosanna" adds the prep. phrase "in the highest places" (ὑψίστοις, dat. pl. neut. of ὕψιστος, -η, -ον, highest; superl. adj.), i.e., in the heights of heaven, where God dwells.

(b) Observation of the Temple and Departure to Bethany (11:11)

11:11 Εἰσῆλθεν, 3rd sg. aor. act. indic. of εἰσέρχομαι, "go into, enter." The noun ἱερόν, which appears for the first time in Mark in 11:11, refers to the entire temple complex, with its courts, porticoes, and buildings (BDAG 470a). When Mark wanted to refer to the actual temple sanctuary, with the holy place and the holy of holies, he used the word ναός (e.g., 15:38). Περιβλεψάμενος, nom. sg. masc. of aor. mid. ptc. of περιβλέπω, "look around at" (mng. with mid.); temp. adv. ptc. antecedent; ὀψίας, gen. sg. fem. of ὄψιος, -α, -ον, "late"; οὔσης, gen. sg. fem. of pres. act. ptc. of εἰμί, "be"; gen. abs. ptc.; adv. ptc. of cause (cf. Taylor 458; except for this one example, the gen. abs. is always a temp. adv. ptc. in Mark [see 1:32]); ἐξῆλθεν, 3rd sg. aor. act. indic. of ἐξέρχομαι, "go out." In 11:1–11, Jesus enters into Jerusalem as the messianic king. Although many celebrate with shouts of praise in hope that the kingdom may now soon arrive, it is doubtful that they fully understand the path of suffering that the king must take to bring in that kingdom. When the Messiah arrives at the temple complex, he is met with indifference. The king has arrived, and apparently no one at the temple is paying attention.

HOMILETICAL SUGGESTIONS

Jesus as the Messianic King (11:1–11)

1. The arrival of the king: Jesus intentionally presents himself as the messianic king in fulfillment of prophecy. (11:1–7)
2. The celebration of the king: Some people welcome the king but need to learn more about him and his kingdom. (11:8–10)
3. The indifference toward the king: Some people—even religious ones—pay no attention to the king. (11:11)

2. Second Trip to the Temple (11:12–19)

In general, Mark organizes his material in chs. 11–13 around three trips to the temple on three successive days. The main event on the second day takes place when Jesus puts a stop to the distracting activities in the temple area that are keeping it from functioning as a house of prayer for all the nations. However, Mark also uses another literary pattern at this point in the narrative: a sandwich pattern (see the discussion at 3:22)—the temple cleansing scene (11:15–19) is inserted within the account of the cursing of the fig tree (11:12–14, 20–25). In this way, the incident concerning the fig tree serves as an interpretive guide for understanding Jesus's actions in the temple cleansing. These two literary patterns are overlapping, with the result that the first two parts of the sandwich pattern take place on the second day at Jerusalem, while the last part of the sandwich pattern occurs on the third day.

(a) Travel to the Temple: Cursing of the Fig Tree (11:12–14)

11:12 The adv. ἐπαύριον (mng. "tomorrow" [BDAG 360a]) occurs only this one time in Mark's Gospel. It appears seventeen times total in the NT, always preceded by a fem. dat. art. and always implying but not stating the fem. dat. noun ἡμέρᾳ. In the fully stated phrase, τῇ ἐπαύριον ἡμέρᾳ, the adv. ἐπαύριον would function as an adj., so that the entire phrase means "on the next day" or "on the following day," and it carries this same mng. even when ἡμέρᾳ is omitted (cf. Wallace 232; Decker 2:87). Ἐξελθόντων, gen. pl. masc. of aor. act. ptc. of ἐξέρχομαι, come out, go out; gen. abs. ptc.; temp. adv. ptc. antecedent; ἐπείνασεν, 3rd sg. aor. act. indic. of πεινάω, "hunger, be hungry."

11:13 Ἰδών, nom. sg. masc. of aor. act. ptc. of ὁράω, "see"; temp. adv. ptc. antecedent; συκῆν, acc. sg. fem. of συκῆ, -ῆς, ἡ, "fig tree"; ἀπὸ μακρόθεν, "from far away, from a distance" (see 5:6); ἔχουσαν, acc. sg. fem. of pres. act. ptc. of ἔχω, "have"; adj. ptc. (cf. T 161; Decker 2:87; anar. adj. ptc. modifying the anar. noun συκῆν); φύλλα, acc. pl. neut. of φύλλον, -ου, τό, "leaf"; ἦλθεν, 3rd sg. aor. act. indic. of ἔρχομαι, "come." The words εἰ ἄρα introduce a tentative indir. question ("whether perhaps, if perhaps"; BDAG 127c). Every other time that Mark uses εἰ to introduce an indir. question (3:2;

10:2; 15:36, 44), he always employs a vb. of speaking (e.g., "they asked" [ἐπηρώτων]; 10:2) or a vb. of perception (e.g., "let us see" [ἴδωμεν]; 15:36) before εἰ to prepare for the indir. question. In 11:13, a vb. of perception before εἰ, although not stated, is implied and should be supplied in an Eng. translation ("to see"). Εὑρήσει, 3rd sg. fut. act. indic. of εὑρίσκω, "find" (on the translation of the fut. tense in indir. discourse, see 3:2); ἐλθών, nom. sg. masc. of aor. act. ptc. of ἔρχομαι, "come"; temp. adv. ptc. antecedent; εὗρεν, 3rd sg. aor. act. indic. of εὑρίσκω, "find"; εἰ μή, "except" (see 2:7); ἦν, 3rd sg. impf. act. indic. of εἰμί, "be"; σύκων, gen. pl. neut of σῦκον, -ου, τό, "fig" (on καιρὸς . . . σύκων as an idiomatic expression for "time when figs are ripe," see BDAG 498a). The reason (γάρ) why Jesus only found leaves on the tree was because it was the wrong time of year to expect ripe figs. Mark seems to have included this γάρ clause at the end of 11:13 to show that Jesus intentionally came to the fig tree not for food but for the tree's symbolic value (Brooks 182; France 441; Stein 513). The temple had become like this fig tree, with an appearance of life and fruitfulness, but it was all just leaves and no actual fruit.

11:14 Ἀποκριθείς, nom. sg. masc. of aor. pass. ptc. of dep. ἀποκρίνομαι, "answer"; redundant ptc.; μηκέτι, adv. mng. "no longer" (on dbl. negatives, see 1:44; μή and forms with μή are used to negate an opt. vb. that expresses a wish [Burton §47]); φάγοι, 3rd sg. aor. act. opt. of ἐσθίω, "eat." The vb. form φάγοι, the only use of the opt. mood in Mark, fits within the category of voluntative opt. (Wallace 481–83; Porter, *Idioms* 60; R 939), i.e., an opt. used in an independent clause to express a wish or prayer ("may no one eat"). Since the opt. in 11:14 communicates a desire for evil or judgment to come upon the fig tree, the wish is also a curse or imprecation (Wallace 482; Burton §176; T 122; Fanning 406; cf. 11:21 where Peter refers to the fig tree as cursed by Jesus [for the only other examples of the opt. for a curse or imprecation in the NT, see Acts 8:20 and Jude 9]). Ἤκουον, 3rd pl. impf. act. indic. of ἀκούω, "hear, listen to" (the impf. provides background information for the later conversation about the fig tree in 11:20–22 [see 1:21; cf. Bruce 417; Decker 2:89]).

(b) Cleansing of the Temple (11:15–18)

11:15 Ἔρχονται, 3rd pl. pres. mid. indic. of dep. ἔρχομαι, "come"; historical pres. (starting a new scene [see 1:12]); εἰσελθών, nom. sg. masc. of aor. act. ptc. of εἰσέρχομαι, "go into, enter"; temp. adv. ptc. antecedent; ἤρξατο, 3rd sg. aor. mid. indic. of ἄρχω, "begin" (mng. with mid.; on ἄρχομαι, see 1:45); ἐκβάλλειν, pres. act. inf. of ἐκβάλλω, "cast out, drive out"; complementary inf.; πωλοῦντας, acc. pl. masc. of pres. act. ptc. of πωλέω, "sell"; subst. ptc.; ἀγοράζοντας, acc. pl. masc. of pres. act. ptc. of ἀγοράζω, "buy"; subst. ptc. The selling and buying related to the sacrificial system. To assist worshipers in offering blemish-free sacrifices, animals officially approved for sacrifice were sold in the temple area (Stein 515). Τραπέζας, acc. pl. fem. of τράπεζα, -ης, ἡ, "table"; κολλυβιστῶν, gen. pl. masc. of κολλυβιστής, -οῦ, ὁ, "moneychanger." Moneychangers were necessary because of the requirements surrounding the annual temple tax (Exod 30:13–16; cf. Matt 17:24–27; m. Sheq. 1:1–2:5). Since the tax was to be paid in the currency "the sanctuary" (Exod 30:13), money changers were necessary in order to exchange the more common Roman coins for Tyrian shekels, the closest available equivalent to the old Heb. shekel (Lane 405; Stein 515–16). Καθέδρας, acc. pl. fem. of καθέδρα, -ας, ἡ, "chair, seat"; πωλούντων, gen. pl. masc. of pres. act. ptc. of πωλέω, "sell"; subst. ptc.; περιστεράς, acc. pl. fem. of περιστερά, -ᾶς, ἡ, "dove, pigeon." People who sold doves were also on the scene, because doves were an acceptable and more affordable sacrifice for the poor for certain types of offerings (Lev 12:6–8; 14:21–22; cf. Luke 2:22–24). Κατέστρεψεν, 3rd sg. aor. act. indic. of καταστρέφω, "overturn."

11:16 Ἤφιεν, 3rd sg. impf. act. indic. of ἀφίημι, "allow, permit"; διενέγκῃ, 3rd sg. aor. act. subjunc. of διαφέρω, "carry through"; subjunc. in a complementary ἵνα clause (on the prep. after a compound vb., see 1:21); σκεῦος, acc. sg. neut. of σκεῦος, -ους, τό, "thing, object." At times, Mark uses an impf. vb. within the main sequence of events to draw attention to a dramatic action as it unfolds (see 1:21). The impf. vb. ἤφιεν adds one more vivid action on the part of Jesus in the temple; he shuts down business as usual. When ἀφίημι functions as a helper vb., it normally uses a complementary inf. (1:34; 5:37; 7:12, 27; 10:14). Only this one time in the NT does ἀφίημι take a complementary ἵνα with the subjunc. (Burton §210; Decker 2:90), which even here is best translated into Eng. as a complementary inf. ("and would not permit anyone to carry"; cf. 10:35). The noun σκεῦος often refers in a very general way to some object useful for some purpose, although the context can clarify more specifically the nature of that object and its purpose (BDAG 927c–d; LN 6.1; Decker 2:90). The use of "merchandise" for σκεῦος in a few EVV is an attempt to specify the mng. of σκεῦος in light of the business context within the temple (e.g., NIV; NASB; NET). At least for as long as it took him to make his point, Jesus stopped the movement of anything that might make the temple more like a market and less like a place of worship.

11:17 Ἐδίδασκεν, 3rd sg. impf. act. indic. of διδάσκω, "teach" (impf. to introduce dir. discourse [see 1:21; 2:16; 4:10]). Jesus's words in 11:17 are framed as a question, one that expects an affirmative answer (on οὐ at the beginning of a question, see 4:21, 38). The implied answer is: yes, this is written (γέγραπται, 3rd sg. pf. pass. indic. of γράφω, "write" [on γέγραπται, see 1:2]). Ὅτι, introduces dir. discourse; οἶκος (2nd use): pred. nom. (on the pass. of καλέω as an equative vb., see Wallace 40); προσευχῆς, gen. of purpose; κληθήσεται, 3rd sg. fut. pass. indic. of καλέω, "call"; ἔθνεσιν, dat. of interest (advantage). For Jesus, the commerce in the temple had crowded out the temple's true purpose, as it was expressed in the eschatological hope of Isa 56:7, that the temple should be a place for prayer and worship for all the nations. Jesus continued by contrasting (δέ) God's intention for the temple with what it had become, a place of financial exploitation. The emph. use of the nom. pron. ὑμεῖς (see Wallace 321–22), which is grammatically unnecessary since the subj. is already implied in the ending of πεποιήκατε, highlights the contrast between God and those who are using the temple to enrich themselves. Πεποιήκατε, 2nd pl. pf. act. indic. of ποιέω, "make"; σπήλαιον, acc. sg. neut. of σπήλαιον, -ου, τό, "den, cave, hideout"; complement in a dbl. acc. obj.-complement cstr.; λῃστῶν, gen. pl. masc. of λῃστής, -οῦ, ὁ, "robber, violent criminal." The word for "robber" (λῃστής) is a strong word that differs from the word for "thief" (κλέπτης); thieves steal secretly through cunning, while robbers steal openly through threats or acts of violence (*NIDNTT* 3:377; Spicq 389–90).

11:18 Ἤκουσαν, 3rd pl. aor. act. indic. of ἀκούω, "hear"; ἐζήτουν, 3rd pl. impf. act. indic. of ζητέω, "consider" (BDAG 428c); ἀπολέσωσιν, 3rd pl. aor. act. subjunc. of ἀπόλλυμι, "destroy"; delib. subjunc. The conj. πῶς introduces an indir. question, in this instance an indir. delib. question (BDAG 901b–c; Taylor 464; Lane 403). The mood of the dir. speech is retained in the indir. speech, so that the use of the subjunc. in indir. discourse necessarily corresponds to one of the uses for the subjunc. mood in independent clauses (Z §348). The question for the religious leaders was not whether they might be able to find a way to kill Jesus (as seems to be implied by some translations; e.g., NRSV: "they kept looking for a way to kill him"). Instead they were asking a delib. question about how it should best be done in light of Jesus's popularity with the crowd. Ἐφοβοῦντο, 3rd pl. impf. pass. indic. of φοβέομαι, "fear, be afraid of"; ἐξεπλήσσετο, 3rd sg. impf. pass. indic. of ἐκπλήσσω, "be amazed, be overwhelmed" (mng. with pass.); ἐπί, "at" (when indicating the grounds for an emotional response; Z §126). Vbs. used to show the reaction of people to important events tend to appear in the impf. tense in Mark (see 1:21, 22; 6:20), since the impf. is often used for information that is "off-line" (i.e., off the main story line or sequence of events).

(c) Departure out of the City (11:19)

11:19 Although the conj. ὅταν normally introduces a clause with a subjunc. mood vb., Mark also uses it with an indic. mood vb. (3:11; 11:19, 25; cf. 6:56). Mark 11:19 is the one place in this Gospel where ὅταν occurs with an aor. indic. vb. The conj. ὅταν with either the impf. or aor. indic. normally expresses a repeated past action that is left indef. with regard to its exact timing or number (cf. BDF §§367, 382; T 92–93; cf. Voelz 1:6). Therefore, 11:19 offers a summary of Jesus's normal routine (BDF §367; T 93) rather than just a description of the specific event of Jesus's departure at the end of his second day in Jerusalem. Ὀψέ, adv. mng. "late," but used here like an indecl. subst. mng. "evening" (BDAG 746b); ἐγένετο, 3rd sg. aor. mid. indic. of dep. γίνομαι, "come, come to be"; ἐξεπορεύοντο, 3rd pl. impf. mid. indic. of dep. ἐκπορεύομαι, "go out, go"; iter. impf. (used within a summary statement; see 1:21).

3. Third Trip to the Temple (11:20–13:37)

During the third trip to the temple, Jesus uses the withering of the fig tree as an opportunity to call on his disciples to trust God, which leads to a collection of sayings concerning faith and prayer (11:20–26). In the temple on the third day, Jesus engages in a series of controversies with the religious leaders (11:27–12:44). The conflict revolves around authority—Jesus speaks and acts with divine authority, but for the most part, the religious leaders reject that authority. Yet the opposition to Jesus among the religious leaders is not complete, since there is at least one wise scribe who is open to Jesus's teaching and therefore open to the kingdom of God (12:28–34). On the way out of the temple, Jesus predicts its destruction (13:1–4) and, while sitting opposite the temple, he teaches about the future in his eschatological discourse (13:5–37).

(a) Travel to the Temple: Cursed Fig Tree and the Prayer of Faith (11:20–26)

11:20 Παραπορευόμενοι, nom. pl. masc. of pres. mid. ptc. of dep. παραπορεύομαι, "pass by, go along"; temp. adv. ptc. contemp.; πρωΐ, adv. mng. "early, early in the morning"; εἶδον, 3rd pl. aor. act. indic. of ὁράω, "see"; συκῆν, acc. sg. fem. of συκῆ, -ῆς, ἡ, "fig tree"; ἐξηραμμένην, acc. sg. fem. of pf. pass. ptc. of ξηραίνω, "be withered, be dried up" (mng. with pass.); supplementary (complementary) ptc.; ῥιζῶν, gen. pl. fem. of ῥίζα, -ης, ἡ, "root." For the tree to be withered from the roots (ἐκ ῥιζῶν) means that the entire tree was dead, incl. the roots (LN 3.47).

11:21 Ἀναμνησθείς, nom. sg. masc. of aor. pass. ptc. of ἀναμιμνήσκω, "be reminded, remember" (mng. with pass.); temp. adv. ptc. antecedent; on ῥαββί, see 9:5; ἴδε, "look" (see 1:2); συκῆ, nom. sg. fem. of συκῆ, -ῆς, ἡ, "fig tree"; κατηράσω, 2nd sg. aor. mid. indic. of dep. καταράομαι, "curse"; ἐξήρανται, 3rd sg. pf. pass. indic. ξηραίνω, "be withered, be dried up" (mng. with pass.); intensive pf. (often best translated with the Eng. pres. tense [see 1:15]. Although it is difficult to measure the extent of Peter's understanding, in the context of the broader narrative, the cursing of the fig tree can scarcely represent anything other than judgment on the temple and its leadership. Therefore, Jesus's response in the next verse expresses his message to the disciples in light of the coming destruction of the temple as symbolized by the withered tree.

11:22 Ἀποκριθείς, nom. sg. masc. of aor. pass. ptc. of dep. ἀποκρίνομαι, "answer"; redundant ptc.; ἔχετε, 2nd pl. pres. act. impv. of ἔχω, "have" (pres. impv. for general precept [see 1:15] cf. πιστεύετε in 11:24 and ἀφίετε in 11:25); θεοῦ, obj. gen. (R 500; Wallace 116, 119; KMP 98). As an obj. gen., θεοῦ functions like a dir. obj. of the verbal idea implicit in πίστιν ("to believe in"), and therefore the entire phrase πίστιν θεοῦ can be translated into Eng. as "faith in God." The tragic destruction of the temple will test the faith of God's people, but they must always trust him that his ways are righteous and his will is perfect (cf. Jesus's call for endurance in 13:13 in light of coming difficulties).

11:23 The organizational structure for Jesus's sayings in 11:22–25 is similar to the catchword pattern found in 9:35–50 (see 9:38). The sayings in vv. 23 and 24 link back to v. 22 through references to "faith/believe" (πίστιν [11:22]; πιστεύῃ [11:23]; πιστεύετε [11:24]). The saying in 11:25 links back to 11:24 through the catchword "pray" (προσεύχεσθε [11:24]; προσευχόμενοι [11:25]). The implication of this organizational pattern is that vv. 23–25 should be interpreted as added independent sayings and not as continuing steps in an overall argument that speaks directly to the immediate context concerning the fig tree. On ἀμὴν λέγω ὑμῖν, see 3:28; εἴπῃ, 3rd sg. aor. act. subjunc. of λέγω, "say"; subjunc. in an indef. rel. clause (same use for the following two subjunc. vbs.); ἄρθητι, 2nd sg. aor. pass. impv. of αἴρω, "take up, lift up"; βλήθητι, 2nd sg. aor. pass. impv. of βάλλω, "throw"; διακριθῇ, 3rd sg. aor. pass. subjunc. of διακρίνω, "doubt, waver" (mng. with pass. [cf. BDAG 231d; BDF §78]); πιστεύῃ, 3rd sg. pres. act. subjunc. of πιστεύω, "believe"; ὅ, "what" (see 2:24); γίνεται, 3rd sg. pres. mid. indic. of dep. γίνομαι, "come to be, happen, take place." The vb. γίνεται functions as a futuristic pres., since it describes a fut. event using a pres. indic. form (cf. Wallace

536; KMP 262–63). The purpose for this futuristic pres. is to emphasize the certainty in the believer's mind that this fut. event will indeed take place. Ἔσται, 3rd sg. fut. mid. indic. of εἰμί, "happen, be granted" (BDAG 285b; dep. in fut.). What is normally impossible for any human is possible for God and therefore also for the one who has faith in God, since God is responsive to faith (cf. 9:23; 10:27).

11:24 The use of ὅσος with an antecedent is not common, except when it takes a form of πᾶς or ἅπας as the antecedent (e.g., πάντες ὅσοι "all who"; πάντα ὅσα "all that"; cf. R 732; BDAG 729b). In 11:24, the antecedent πάντα functions as the dir. obj. of ἐλάβετε, while ὅσα functions as a rel. pron. and the dir. obj. of προσεύχεσθε and αἰτεῖσθε. Προσεύχεσθε, 2nd pl. pres. mid. indic. of dep. προσεύχομαι, "pray for"; αἰτεῖσθε, 2nd pl. pres. mid. indic. of αἰτέω, "ask for" (mng. with mid.); πιστεύετε, 2nd pl. pres. act. impv. of πιστεύω, "believe"; ἐλάβετε, 2nd pl. aor. act. indic. of λαμβάνω, "receive"; ἔσται, 3rd sg. fut. mid. indic. of εἰμί, "happen, be granted" (BDAG 285b; dep. in fut.). In the cstr. "impv. + καί + fut. indic.," the impv. form functions as a cond. impv., while the fut. indic. gives the conclusion of what will happen if the cond. is met (Wallace 489–90; cf. R 1022–23; Burton §269). However, with a cond. impv., the impv. still retains the force of a command (if you believe—and you should—it will be granted to you). The vb. ἐλάβετε is an example of a proleptic aor., the use of the aor. indic. to portray a fut. event as if it were already accomplished in order to emphasize the certainty of the event (Wallace 563–64; see also Fanning 270–74).

11:25 The saying in 11:25 begins with ὅταν followed by a pres. indic. vb. (the only example in Mark; on ὅταν with the indic., see 11:19). The cstr. conveys repeated action in this context, so that the following command applies to every time that someone prays. Στήκετε, 2nd pl. pres. act. indic. of στήκω, "stand"; customary pres. (on the formation of στήκω, see 13:35); προσευχόμενοι, nom. pl. masc. of pres. mid. ptc. of dep. προσεύχομαι, "pray"; adv. ptc. of purpose; ἀφίετε, 2nd pl. pres. act. impv. of ἀφίημι, "forgive." Four times in Mark's Gospel, a saying of Jesus uses a 1st class cond. clause that includes a form of the indef. pron. τις (4:23; 8:34; 9:35; 11:25; see the discussion at 9:35), and each time the cond. is portrayed as a true hypothesis. The 1st class cond. clause "if you have anything against anyone" assumes that this is indeed the case. The art. ὁ before the prep. phrase ἐν τοῖς οὐρανοῖς means that it is functioning adj. to modify πατήρ (see 6:11; 11:2; 13:25; 15:43). Ἀφῇ, 3rd sg. aor. act. subjunc. of ἀφίημι, "forgive"; παραπτώματα, acc. pl. neut. of παράπτωμα, -ατος, τό, "offense, wrongdoing." The conj. ἵνα introduces a purpose clause: we forgive in order that we might be forgiven by God (cf. Matt 6:12, 14; Luke 6:37). Yet this necessity for forgiveness takes place in the context of prayer. It makes little sense to stand before God in prayer, recognizing the extent to which we have wronged him, and refuse to forgive others for their offenses against us (cf. Matt 18:21–35).

The words in 11:26 (εἰ δὲ ὑμεῖς οὐκ ἀφίετε, οὐδὲ ὁ πατὴρ ὑμῶν ὁ ἐν τοῖς οὐρανοῖς ἀφήσει τὰ παραπτώματα ὑμῶν, "but if you do not forgive, neither will your Father in heaven forgive your sins") do not appear in important early mss. of Mark's Gospel (ℵ, B, L, W, Δ, Ψ, and others). The most likely possibility is that the words were copied from Matt 6:15, which in Matthew's Gospel comes right after the saying that is par. to the one found in Mark 11:25 (Metzger 93). As a result, most recent translations do not include 11:26 and skip right from v. 25 to v. 27 (exceptions include NKJV and NASB, although NASB puts v. 26 in brackets to indicate that it is not in the earliest mss.).

FOR FURTHER STUDY

28. Jesus and the Temple

Donahue, John R. "Temple, Trial, and Royal Christology (Mark 14:53–65)." Pages 61–79 in *The Passion in Mark: Studies on Mark 14–16*. Edited by Werner H. Kelber. Philadelphia: Fortress, 1976.

Driggers, Ira Brent. "The Politics of Divine Presence: Temple as Locus of Conflict in the Gospel of Mark." *BibInt* 15 (2007): 227–47.

*Evans, Craig. "Jesus' Action in the Temple: Cleansing or Portent of Destruction?" *CBQ* 51 (1989): 237–70.

Gaston, Lloyd. *No Stone on Another: Studies in the Significance of the Fall of Jerusalem in the Synoptic Gospels*. NovTSup 23. Leiden: Brill, 1970.

Gray, Timothy C. *The Temple in the Gospel of Mark: A Study in Its Narrative Role*. WUNT 2/242. Tübingen: Mohr Siebeck, 2008.

Juel, Donald. *Messiah and Temple: The Trial of Jesus in the Gospel of Mark*. SBLDS 31. Missoula, MT: Scholars Press, 1977.

Malbon, Elizabeth Struthers. "Architectural Space." Pages 106–40 in *Narrative Space and Mythic Meaning in Mark*. San Francisco: Harper & Row, 1986.

Perrin, Nicholas. *Jesus the Temple*. Grand Rapids: Baker Academic, 2010.

Sanders, E. P. "Jesus and the Temple." Pages 61–76 in *Jesus and Judaism*. Philadelphia: Fortress, 1985.

Telford, William R. *The Barren Temple and the Withered Tree: A Redaction-Critical Analysis of the Cursing of the Fig-Tree Pericope in Mark's Gospel and Its Relation to the Cleansing of the Temple Tradition*. JSNTSup 1. Sheffield, UK: JSOT Press, 1980.

Wardle, Timothy. *The Jerusalem Temple and Early Christian Identity*. WUNT 2/291. Tübingen: Mohr Siebeck, 2010.

Watts, Rikk E. "The Lord's House and David's Lord: The Psalms and Mark's Perspective on Jesus and the Temple." *BibInt* 15 (2007): 307–22.

HOMILETICAL SUGGESTIONS

The Temple and the Fig Tree (11:12–25)

1. What do we learn about Jesus?
   a. Jesus zealously cares about the true worship of God among all the nations. (11:17a)
   b. Jesus zealously stands opposed to those who use the worship of God to enrich themselves. (11:17b)
2. What do we learn about a life of faith?
   a. People of faith express their trust in God through hope—even when hope seems humanly impossible. (11:22–23)

b. People of faith express their trust in God through prayer. (11:24)

c. People of faith express their trust in God through forgiveness. (11:25)

(b) Teaching in the Temple (11:27–12:44)

In the temple on the third day, Jesus engages in a series of controversies with the religious leaders (11:27–12:44). The controversies begin with Jesus's refusal to respond to the demands of the chief priests and scribes that he offer some justification for his authoritative actions (11:27–33). Instead, Jesus offers a parable and scriptural teaching that challenge the legitimacy of their authority (12:1–12). The rest of Jesus's teaching in the temple appears in two sets of three encounters. In the first set of three passages (12:13–17, 18–27, 28–34), Jesus answers questions brought to him by religious leaders, with the third passage portraying the positive example of the wise scribe. In the second set of three passages (12:35–37, 38–40, 41–44), Jesus takes the initiative to state his own perspective as it stands in opposition to the teaching and behavior of the scribes, with the third passage portraying the positive example of the poor widow. The wise scribe and the poor widow reveal how different the circumstances might be if the religious leaders as a group lived with a wholehearted love toward God and others and with a sacrificial devotion to the work of God.

(i) Question and Parable about Jesus's Authority (11:27–12:12)

11:27 Ἔρχονται, 3rd pl. pres. mid. indic. of dep. ἔρχομαι, "come"; historical pres. (starting a new scene [see 1:12]); περιπατοῦντος, gen. sg. masc. of pres. act. ptc. of περιπατέω, "walk"; gen. abs. ptc.; temp. adv. ptc. contemp. (on the use and misuse of the gen. abs. in Mark, see 1:32; 5:2). The second use of ἔρχονται in the verse, which is also a historical pres. vb., serves to introduce new participants in the scene (see 1:12).

11:28 When used as a qualitative interr. word in connection with a noun, ποῖος asks the question "what kind of?" Although it sometimes simply means "what?" (cf. 12:28), it seems to retain its qualitative sense in the phrase ἐν ποίᾳ ἐξουσίᾳ ("by what kind of authority?" [R 740; Wallace 346]; see also vv. 29, 33). In his response to their question, Jesus sets out two possible kinds of authority, divine authority and human authority, so that at least that part of Jesus's answer assumes that ποῖος retains its qualitative sense. The conj. ἤ often introduces a question, sometimes to show that the question is par. to a preceding one and supplements it in some way (BDAG 432d). If translating the conj. ἤ as "or" suggests that the religious leaders were giving Jesus two alternative questions, either of which he could answer, then it is probably best simply to omit translating ἤ (cf. e.g., NLT; NRSV; CSB). Ἔδωκεν, 3rd sg. aor. act. indic. of δίδωμι, "give"; ποιῇς, 2nd sg. pres. act. subjunc. of ποιέω, "do"; subjunc. in an epex. ἵνα clause. The ἵνα clause is epex. to the noun ἐξουσίαν and so clarifies or explains the authority that Jesus has. The grammatical function of an epex. ἵνα clause is par. to that of an epex. inf., and it is probably best to translate it into Eng. with an inf. ("authority to do these things").

11:29 Ἐπερωτήσω, 1st sg. fut. act. indic. of ἐπερωτάω, "ask"; ὑμᾶς, dbl. acc. obj. of the person; λόγον, dbl. acc. obj. of the thing (on λόγος as "question" in this context, see

BDAG 599b); ἀποκρίθητε, 2nd pl. aor. pass. impv. of dep. ἀποκρίνομαι, "answer"; ἐρῶ, 1st sg. fut. act. indic. of λέγω, "say, tell." As a cond. impv. (cf. Cranfield 363; Taylor 470; Marcus 2:796), ἀποκρίθητε gives a cond. to be met before Jesus will answer any question about the nature of his authority. However, a cond. impv. still retains the force of a command (on the cond. impv. cstr., see 11:24). If the religious leaders answer Jesus's question—and they should—he will tell them the source of his authority.

11:30 Βάπτισμα, nom. sg. neut. of βάπτισμα, -ατος, τό, "baptism." The 2nd art. τό before the gen. Ἰωάννου places that gen. in the 2nd attrib. position, clarifying that Ἰωάννου modifies βάπτισμα. The mng. would not be essentially any different if the 2nd art. τό were absent (Wallace 214). Ἦν, 3rd sg. impf. act. indic. of εἰμί, "be"; ἀποκρίθητε, 2nd pl. aor. pass. impv. of dep. ἀποκρίνομαι, "answer."

11:31 Jesus's question in 11:30 created a dilemma for the religious leaders, one not easily avoided, since whatever answer they might give would expose their refusal to recognize or accept divine authority. Διελογίζοντο, 3rd pl. impf. mid. indic. of dep. διαλογίζομαι, "discuss, argue" (on the impf., see 4:10); πρός, "with, among" (when used with a vb. of saying [BDAG 874b]); ἑαυτούς, "one another" (see 1:27); λέγοντες, nom. pl. masc. of pres. act. ptc. of λέγω, "say"; redundant ptc.; εἴπωμεν, 1st pl. aor. act. subjunc. of λέγω, "say"; subjunc. in a 3rd class cond. clause; ἐρεῖ, 3rd sg. fut. act. indic. of λέγω, "say"; διὰ τί, "why?" (when introducing a question [BDAG 225d; 1007b]); ἐπιστεύσατε, 2nd pl. aor. act. indic. of πιστεύω, "believe"; αὐτῷ, dat. dir. obj.

11:32 There are two possible ways to translate εἴπωμεν (1st pl. aor. act. subjunc. of λέγω, "say"):

1. "if we say": With this translation, εἴπωμεν in v. 32 is par. to εἴπωμεν in v. 31. Both use the subjunc. within a 3rd class cond. clause, but the cond. conj. ἐάν only appears in v. 31 (e.g., NIV; NKJV; NET; CSB).
2. "should we say?": With this translation, εἴπωμεν in v. 32 functions as a delib. subjunc. The use of εἴπωμεν in v. 32 is not grammatically par. to the use of εἴπωμεν in v. 31, which explains why ἐάν does not appear in v. 32 (e.g., NASB; NRSV; NLT; ESV).

With both translation possibilities, the discussion of the religious leaders ends abruptly with Mark stepping in to explain the nature of their dilemma. Ἐφοβοῦντο, 3rd pl. impf. pass. indic. of φοβέομαι, "fear, be afraid of" (on the impf. for background information, see 1:21; 6:20); εἶχον, 3rd pl. impf. act. indic. of ἔχω, "hold, consider"; ὄντως, adv. mng. "really, certainly, in truth"; ἦν, 3rd sg. impf. act. indic. of εἰμί, "be." The use of the acc. case with Ἰωάννην is an example of prolepsis, i.e., an anticipation of the subj. in a following subord. clause by making it the dir. obj. of the vb. in the main clause (BDF §§408, 476; T 148–49; Turner, *Style* 16; for similar examples, see 7:2; 12:34). One way to simplify the grammatical structure in an Eng. translation is to move Ἰωάννην to the subord. clause, where it can function as the subj. of ἦν (with ὄντως, the adv. that comes after Ἰωάννην, also probably anticipating the subord. clause: "that John really was a prophet" [Bruce 420; Cranfield 363]).

11:33 Ἀποκριθέντες, nom. pl. masc. of aor. pass. ptc. of dep. ἀποκρίνομαι, "answer"; redundant ptc.; λέγουσιν, historical pres. (see 1:12, 30; cf. also λέγει later in the 11:33); οἴδαμεν, 1st pl. pf. act. indic. of οἶδα, "know" (on οἶδα, see 1:24). Since the religious leaders do not answer his question, Jesus refuses to respond to their questions about the nature of his authority. The message conveyed by this refusal is that, like John, Jesus has authority from God and that, just as they did with John, the religious leaders would reject Jesus's authority as well. For Jesus, the religious leaders have forfeited any right to demand answers to their questions.

12:1 Jesus refuses to answer directly the questions of the religious leaders about his authority, but that does not mean he is finished talking with them. Instead he uses a parable and Scripture to challenge the legitimacy of their own claim to have authority over God's people. Ἤρξατο, 3rd sg. aor. mid. indic. of ἄρχω, "begin" (mng. with mid.; on ἄρχομαι, see 1:45); λαλεῖν, pres. act. inf. of λαλέω, "speak"; complementary inf.; ἀμπελῶνα, acc. sg. masc. of ἀμπελών, -ῶνος, ὁ, "vineyard"; ἐφύτευσεν, 3rd sg. aor. act. indic. of φυτεύω, "plant"; περιέθηκεν, 3rd sg. aor. act. indic. of περιτίθημι, "put around, place around"; φραγμόν, acc. sg. masc. of φραγμός, -οῦ, ὁ, "fence, hedge, wall"; ὤρυξεν, 3rd sg. aor. act. indic. of ὀρύσσω, "dig out"; ὑπολήνιον, acc. sg. neut. of ὑπολήνιον, -ου, τό, "trough (vat) under a wine press" (to collect the grape juice pressed out) (LN 7.67; BDF §123; cf. ὑπό [under] and ληνός [wine press]); ᾠκοδόμησεν, 3rd sg. aor. act. indic. of οἰκοδομέω, "build"; πύργον, acc. sg. masc. of πύργος, -ου, ὁ, "watchtower, tower"; ἐξέδετο, 3rd sg. aor. mid. indic. of ἐκδίδωμι, "lease, rent" (mng. with mid.; on the formation of ἐξέδετο, see BDF §94); γεωργοῖς, dat. pl. masc. of γεωργός, -οῦ, ὁ, "tenant farmer"; ἀπεδήμησεν, 3rd sg. aor. act. indic. of ἀποδημέω, "go on a journey." Jesus's parable assumes the social and economic background of the time in which large estates often belonged to absentee owners who leased out the property to tenant farmers, who actually worked the land. The lease agreement would normally stipulate that a portion of the produce went to the owner for the rent payment (see C. H. Dodd, *The Parables of the Kingdom*, 2nd ed. [New York: Charles Scribner's Sons, 1961], 96–98; Joachim Jeremias, *The Parables of Jesus*, 2nd ed. [New York: Charles Scribner's Sons, 1972], 74–76; France 459).

12:2 Ἀπέστειλεν, 3rd sg. aor. act. indic. of ἀποστέλλω, "send." Both γεωργούς [acc. pl. masc.] and later in v. 2 γεωργῶν [gen. pl. masc.] are from γεωργός, -οῦ, ὁ, "tenant farmer." Καιρῷ, "at the proper time" (BDAG 497d); dat. of time (Wallace 157; KMP 130); λάβῃ, 3rd sg. aor. act. subjunc. of λαμβάνω, "collect" (BDAG 584a); subjunc. in a purpose ἵνα clause; ἀμπελῶνος, gen. sg. masc. of ἀμπελών, -ῶνος, ὁ, "vineyard." The prep. phrase beginning with ἀπό functions as a partitive expression, marking out a part of the whole harvest. Such a partitive expression can be used as a subst., so that the entire prep. phrase functions like a noun and as the dir. obj. of λάβῃ ("part of the produce" [LN 63.20; T 208–9; Turner, *Style* 15]).

12:3 Λαβόντες, nom. pl. masc. of aor. act. ptc. of λαμβάνω, "seize, lay hands on" (BDAG 583d); temp. adv. ptc. antecedent; αὐτόν, dir. obj. of λαβόντες and the implied dir. obj. of the following two vbs.; ἔδειραν, 3rd pl. aor. act. indic. of δέρω, "beat";

ἀπέστειλαν, 3rd pl. aor. act. indic. of ἀποστέλλω, "send away"; κενόν, acc. sg. masc. of κενός, -ή, -όν, "empty-handed, empty, without anything" (LN 57.42); complement in a dbl. acc. obj. complement cstr.

12:4 Ἀπέστειλεν, 3rd sg. aor. act. indic. of ἀποστέλλω, "send"; κἀκεῖνον, acc. sg. masc. of κἀκεῖνος, -η, -ο, and that one (formed through the combination of καί and ἐκεῖνος [BDAG 500a]); ἐκεφαλίωσαν, 3rd pl. aor. act. indic. of κεφαλιόω, "strike on the head"; ἠτίμασαν, 3rd pl. aor. act. indic. of ἀτιμάζω, "dishonor, treat shamefully." The word ἐκεφαλίωσαν is unusual in its spelling (from κεφαλιόω rather than the more common κεφαλαιόω; in fact, this use in 12:4 is the only known example of a form of κεφαλιόω in extant Gk. literature [Swete 268; MM 342; cf. Yarbro Collins 540]). As far as mng. is concerned, κεφαλιόω should probably mean "sum up, complete," since that is what κεφαλαιόω means (cf. also κεφάλαιον, "sum, summary, main point"). However, the context of 12:4 demands a definition for κεφαλιόω such as "strike on the head" (BDAG 541d; 542c; MM 342; LSJ 945). Perhaps κεφαλιόω is analogous to a vb. like γναθόω, a word that means "hit on the cheek" (related to the noun γνάθος, "cheek" [LSJ 353]). In a similar way, κεφαλιόω would convey hitting someone on the head (related to κεφάλιον, a dim. form of the noun κεφαλή, "head" [Swete 268; cf. MH 395]). It is unlikely that κεφαλιόω means "behead," since the vb. κεφαλίζω (or the compound vb. ἀποκεφαλίζω as in 6:27) conveys that mng. (LSJ 945). The word formation for κεφαλίζω follows the same pattern as vbs. such as λαιμίζω, "cut the throat" (related to the noun λαιμός, "throat" [LSJ 1024]) and ῥαχίζω, "cut through the spine" (related to the noun ῥάχις, "spine" [LSJ 1566; cf. MH 395]).

12:5 Ἀπέστειλεν, 3rd sg. aor. act. indic. of ἀποστέλλω, "send"; κἀκεῖνον, see 12:4; ἀπέκτειναν, 3rd pl. aor. act. indic. of ἀποκτείνω, "kill." The acc. with πολλοὺς ἄλλους indicates that ἄλλους is functioning as the dir. obj. of an implied vb. or, perhaps better, vbs. The context implies both that the landowner sent many others and that the tenant farmers mistreated them all (cf. Bruce 421). The rel. pron. οὕς, which appears twice in v. 5, is serving as a dem. pron. and can be translated as "some" or "others" (BDAG 727d; BDF §250). Δέροντες, nom. pl. masc. of pres. act. ptc. of δέρω, "beat"; adv. ptc. of means (how the tenant farmers mistreated the many messengers sent to them); ἀποκτέννοντες, nom. pl. masc. of pres. act. ptc. of ἀποκτέννω (alternate spelling of ἀποκτείνω, [BDAG 114b]), "kill"; adv. ptc. of means (in the NT, forms of ἀποκτέννω appear only in Matt 10:28; Mark 12:5; 2 Cor 3:6; and Rev 6:11, all without any distinction in mng. from forms of ἀποκτείνω).

12:6 Εἶχεν, 3rd sg. impf. act. indic. of ἔχω, "have" (impf. for background information [see 1:21]); υἱόν, acc. in simple appos. to ἕνα; ἀπέστειλεν, 3rd sg. aor. act. indic. of ἀποστέλλω, "send"; ἔσχατον, neut. acc. form functions as an adv., "finally, last of all" (when describing the last in a series of actions [BDAG 398a; Decker 2:110–11; cf. 12:22]); λέγων, nom. sg. masc. of pres. act. ptc. of λέγω, "say"; attendant circumstance ptc. (cf. 8:26 for a similar use of λέγων); ὅτι, introduces dir. discourse; ἐντραπήσονται, 3rd pl. fut. pass. indic. of ἐντρέπω, "respect, show deference to" (mng. with pass.).

12:7 Γεωργοί, nom. pl. masc. of γεωργός, -οῦ, ὁ, "tenant farmer"; ἑαυτούς, "one another" (see 1:27); on the ending of εἶπαν, see 8:5; ὅτι, introduces dir. discourse; κληρονόμος, nom. sg. masc. of κληρονόμος, -ου, ὁ, "heir"; pred. nom.; δεῦτε, adv. functioning as an impv. particle, "come!" (BDAG 220c); ἀποκτείνωμεν, 1st pl. pres. or aor. act. subjunc. of ἀποκτείνω, "kill"; hort. subjunc.; ἡμῶν, poss. gen.; ἔσται, 3rd sg. fut. mid. indic. of εἰμί, "be" (dep. in fut.); κληρονομία, nom. sg. fem. of κληρονομία, -ας, ἡ, "inheritance." The use of the hort. subjunc. with ἀποκτείνωμεν in this context is similar to that of a cond. impv. followed by a fut. indic. (see 11:24). The fut. indic. expresses what will take place if the cond. expressed in the hort. subjunc. is met. However, the hort. subjunc. still retains the force of a command. If they kill the heir—and this is something they think they should do—the inheritance will belong to them.

12:8 Λαβόντες, nom. pl. masc. of aor. act. ptc. of λαμβάνω, "seize, lay hands on" (BDAG 583d); temp. adv. ptc. antecedent; ἀπέκτειναν, 3rd pl. aor. act. indic. of ἀποκτείνω, "kill"; ἐξέβαλον, 3rd pl. aor. act. indic. of ἐκβάλλω, "throw out"; on ἔξω, see 5:10; ἀμπελῶνος, gen. sg. masc. of ἀμπελών, -ῶνος, ὁ, "vineyard."

12:9 Ποιήσει, 3rd sg. fut. act. indic. of ποιέω, "do"; on κύριος as "owner" in the context of the parable, see BDAG 577a; ἀμπελῶνος, gen. sg. masc. of ἀμπελών, -ῶνος, ὁ, "vineyard"; ἐλεύσεται, 3rd sg. fut. mid. indic. of dep. ἔρχομαι, "come"; ἀπολέσει, 3rd sg. fut. act. indic. of ἀπόλλυμι, "destroy"; γεωργούς, acc. pl. masc. of γεωργός, -οῦ, ὁ, "tenant farmer"; δώσει, 3rd sg. fut. act. indic. of δίδωμι, "give"; ἀμπελῶνα, acc. sg. masc. of ἀμπελών, -ῶνος, ὁ, "vineyard." Jesus does not specify the identity of the "others" (ἄλλοις) who receive the vineyard, and in fact there is no necessity to do so, since they may simply be part of the logic of the parable without corresponding directly to some other def. group outside of the parable.

12:10 Jesus's question (which spans vv. 10–11) begins with οὐδέ, indicating that the expected answer is affirmative ("You have read, haven't you?" [see 4:21, 38]; ἀνέγνωτε, 2nd pl. aor. act. indic. of ἀναγινώσκω, "read"; a constative aor. vb. referring to an indef. past occurrence is translated with the Eng. pf. tense [Fanning 260–61]). Although framed as a question, Jesus's words carry the force of a rebuke (Decker 2:113), implying that the religious leaders should have already read and understood the relevance of the Scripture he is about to cite (Ps 118:22–23). The acc. case with λίθον is an example of inverse attraction, where the antecedent (λίθον) assimilates to the case of the rel. pron. (ὅν) that is modifying it (R 717–18; BDF §295; T 324; Z §19; Wallace 339; Porter, *Idioms* 252). Since λίθον, as the subj. of ἐγενήθη, does not use the expected nom. case, the dem. pron. οὗτος restates the subj. immediately before ἐγενήθη (Decker 2:113; cf. Turner, *Style* 21). Ἀπεδοκίμασαν, 3rd pl. aor. act. indic. of ἀποδοκιμάζω, "reject"; οἰκοδομοῦντες, nom. pl. masc. of pres. act. ptc. of οἰκοδομέω, "build"; subst. ptc.; ἐγενήθη, 3rd sg. aor. pass. indic. of dep. γίνομαι, "become"; γωνίας, gen. sg. fem. of γωνία, -ας, ἡ, "corner" (with the phrase κεφαλὴν γωνίας being translated as "cornerstone" [BDAG 209d, 542b–c]). At times, but esp. in OT quotations, the prep. εἰς with the acc. substitutes for the pred. nom. (see 10:8; since the function of the prep. εἰς is to mark out its object as the pred. noun, it can be omitted in translation).

12:11 Ἐγένετο, 3rd sg. aor. mid. indic. of dep. γίνομαι, "come to be, come about." Normally in Gk., a neut. dem. pron. is used to refer back to an entire concept, such as the whole idea of the rejected stone becoming the Lord's chosen cornerstone. The use of the unexpected fem. dem. pron. αὕτη is the result of a close formal translation of the Heb. text, which, absent any Heb. neut. forms, employed a fem. dem. pron. in this context (R 254, 704; BDF §138; Moule 182; T 21; cf. Decker 2:114). Θαυμαστή, nom. sg. fem. of θαυμαστός, -ή, -όν, remarkable, "awe inspiring, wonder producing." The adj. θαυμαστή (fem. in agreement with αὕτη) is related to the vb. θαυμάζω, one of several vbs. that Mark uses for a response of amazement toward God's work through Jesus (see, e.g., 5:20; cf. ἐκθαυμάζω in 12:17). In a similar way, the adj. θαυμαστός describes something that causes a response of wonder or amazement in observers (BDAG 445b).

12:12 Ἐζήτουν, 3rd pl. impf. act. indic. of ζητέω, "strive, want, seek"; κρατῆσαι, aor. act. inf. of κρατέω, "seize, arrest"; subst. inf., dir. obj. of ἐζήτουν (R 1060; Burton §387); καί (2nd use): "and yet, but" (indicating a contrast; BDF §442; Z §455); ἐφοβήθησαν, 3rd pl. aor. pass. indic. of φοβέομαι, "fear, be afraid of." The γάρ clause gives the reason why they wanted to arrest Jesus (modifying ἐζήτουν rather than ἐφοβήθησαν; Cranfield 369). Ἔγνωσαν, 3rd pl. aor. act. indic. of γινώσκω, "know, understand, realize"; εἶπεν, on the aor. in indir. discourse, see 5:16 (cf. BDF §324). The prep. πρός can indicate the content of parable ("about them"; cf. LN 90.25) or can express opposition, how the parable was hostile to the religious leaders ("against them"; cf. LN 90.33). Ἀφέντες, nom. pl. masc. of aor. act. ptc. of ἀφίημι, "leave"; temp. adv. ptc. antecedent; ἀπῆλθον, 3rd pl. aor. act. indic. of ἀπέρχομαι, "depart, go away."

HOMILETICAL SUGGESTIONS

Does Jesus Have Authority from God (11:27–12:12)?

1. An answer through a refusal: Jesus has divine authority as the prophet of God. (11:27–33)
2. An answer through a parable: Jesus has divine authority as the Son of God. (12:1–9)
3. An answer through a quotation: Jesus has divine authority as the chosen cornerstone of God. (12:10–12)

(ii) Question about Taxes (12:13–17)

12:13 Mark 12:13–17 begins a series of three passages in which people associated with the religious leaders approach Jesus with a question: the first from the Pharisees and the Herodians (12:13–17), the second from the Sadducees (12:18–27), and the third from an individual scribe (12:28–34). Ἀποστέλλουσιν, historical pres. (starting a new scene [see 1:12]); τῶν Φαρισαίων καὶ τῶν Ἡρῳδιανῶν, partitive gen. (the art. is repeated to distinguish the two groups [R 786]); ἀγρεύσωσιν, 3rd pl. aor. act. subjunc. of ἀγρεύω, "catch off guard, trap"; subjunc. in a purpose ἵνα clause. The vb. ἀγρεύω can mean in a lit. sense "to catch or trap an animal, to hunt, to track a prey" (cf. MM 6; LSJ

14; see, e.g., Xenophon, *On Hunting* 12.6; Job 10:16 LXX), or it can take a fig. mng. such as "to catch someone in an unguarded moment for the purpose of causing harm" (cf. BDAG 15b; LSJ 14; see, e.g., Prov 5:22; 6:26 LXX). Λόγῳ, dat. of means or instr. (Stein 543; on λόγος as "statement," see BDAG 600b).

12:14 Ἐλθόντες, nom. pl. masc. of aor. act. ptc. of ἔρχομαι, "come, go"; temp. adv. ptc. antecedent; λέγουσιν, historical pres. (with a form of λέγω [see 1:12, 30]; cf. 12:16); διδάσκαλε, voc.; οἴδαμεν, 1st pl. pf. act. indic. of οἶδα, "know" (on οἶδα, see 1:24); ἀληθής, "truthful, honest" (BDAG 43b); pred. adj.; μέλει, 3rd sg. pres. act. indic. of μέλει, "it is a care, it is a concern." In this context, μέλει functions as an impers. vb., i.e., a vb. in which a subj. is not specified, not even implicitly, so that in a formal Eng. translation, a vague reference to "it" must function as the subj. (on impers. vbs., see Moule 27–29; Porter, *Idioms* 77–78; contrast the other use of μέλει in 4:38 [a subst. ὅτι clause serves as the subj.]). Σοι, ethical dat. (a subset of the dat. of reference or respect [see Wallace 146–47; KMP 126]); on dbl. negatives, see 1:44. The NT uses several par. expressions for acting with partiality, incl. "to look into a face" (βλέπειν εἰς πρόσωπον; Matt 22:16; Mark 12:14), "to esteem a face" (θαυμάζειν πρόσωπον; Jude 16), and "to receive a face" (λαμβάνειν πρόσωπον; Luke 20:21; Gal 2:6; cf. the related words προσωπολημπτέω [Jas 2:9]; προσωπολήμπτης [Acts 10:34]; προσωπολημψία [Rom 2:11; Eph 6:9; Col 3:25; Jas 2:1]; and ἀπροσωπολήμπτως [1 Pet 1:17]; see *TDNT* 6:779–80). Each one of these expressions conveys the idea of looking at someone first before deciding how to act or speak based on that person's economic level (cf. Jas 2:1–9), social status (cf. Eph 6:5–9), or ethnic background (cf. Acts 10:34–35; Rom 2:9–12). Ἐπί with the gen.: "in accordance with, based on" (BDAG 365c); ἔξεστιν, 3rd sg. pres. act. indic. of ἔξεστιν, "it is right, it is lawful"; δοῦναι, aor. act. inf. of δίδωμι, "give, pay" (on δίδωμι for paying with reference to a financial transaction, see BDAG 242c); subst. inf., subj. of ἔξεστιν; κῆνσον, acc. sg. masc. of κῆνσος, -ου, ὁ, "tax, poll tax, imperial tax"; δῶμεν, 1st pl. aor. act. subjunc. of δίδωμι, "give, pay"; delib. subjunc.

12:15 On ὁ δέ, see 1:45 (cf. οἱ δέ in v. 16); εἰδώς, nom. sg. masc. of pf. act. ptc. of οἶδα, "know"; adv. ptc. of cause (on the pf. ptc. with οἶδα, see 1:24); ὑπόκρισιν, acc. sg. fem. of ὑπόκρισις, -εως, ἡ, "pretense, hypocrisy"; τί, "why" (see 2:7); φέρετε, 2nd pl. pres. act. impv. of φέρω, "bring" (on the pres. impv. of φέρετε, see 11:2); δηνάριον, acc. sg. neut. of δηνάριον, -ου, τό, "denarius." At the time of Jesus, a denarius was the standard Roman silver coin in circulation (BDAG 223c; *EDNT* 1:296; according to Matt 20:2, it was an acceptable daily wage for a common laborer). Ἴδω, 1st sg. aor. act. subjunc. of ὁράω, see; subjunc. in a purpose ἵνα clause.

12:16 Ἤνεγκαν, 3rd pl. aor. act. indic. of φέρω, "bring"; εἰκών, nom. sg. fem. of εἰκών, -όνος, ἡ, "image, likeness." The image on the coin was likely that of Tiberius, the reigning emperor or "Caesar" at the time of Jesus, since he ruled from AD 14 to AD 37. Ἐπιγραφή, nom. sg. fem. of ἐπιγραφή, -ῆς, ἡ, "inscription." The inscription surrounding the image of Tiberius on the coin uses abbreviations, but a translation of the full inscription would be "Tiberius Caesar, son of the divine Augustus, (himself) Augustus." On the reverse side of the coin, the inscription, also abbreviated, reads "high priest" (see Strauss 525; Marcus 2:824; H. St J. Hart, "The Coin of 'Render unto Caesar . . .' [A Note on Some Aspects of Mark 12:13–17; Matt 22:15–22; Luke 20:20–26]," in *Jesus and the Politics of His Day* [ed. Ernst Bammel and C. F. D. Moule; Cambridge: Cambridge University Press, 1984], 241–48). On the ending for εἶπαν, see 8:5; Καίσαρος, poss. gen.

12:17 When the neut. pl. art. τά stands before a gen. noun, such as Καίσαρος or θεοῦ, the art. implies but does not state "things" (see 8:33). Since both Καίσαρος and θεοῦ function as a poss. gen., τὰ Καίσαρος is equivalent to "the things belonging to Caesar," and τὰ τοῦ θεοῦ corresponds to "the things belonging to God." When the Pharisees and the Herodians ask their questions about paying taxes, they do so using forms of the vb. δίδωμι (δοῦναι and δῶμεν in v. 14). Jesus answers them using a form of the compound vb. ἀποδίδωμι (ἀπόδοτε, 2nd pl. aor. act. impv. of ἀποδίδωμι, "pay, render"; for two different views on the aor. tense with this impv., see Fanning 354–55 and Campbell, *VANIV* 90–91; the aor. seems in part to be lexically driven, since almost 90 percent of all impv. forms of δίδωμι and its compounds in the NT use the aor.). It is true that δίδωμι and ἀποδίδωμι overlap in mng., since both can be used for payment of taxes and other financial transactions (BDAG 109d–110a; 242c). However, in contexts related to finances, the vb. ἀποδίδωμι normally conveys making a payment that is owed (cf. e.g., Rom 13:7). Elsewhere in the NT, ἀποδίδωμι occurs for fulfilling contractual obligations, such as paying a debt (Matt 5:26; 18:25–26, 28–30, 34; Luke 7:42; 12:59), a wage (Matt 20:8), or rent bill (Matt 21:41; Luke 10:35). Jesus's answer, expressed as it is using ἀποδίδωμι, portrays people as under obligation, both to the government to pay tax but more important to God to fulfill all that he commands (cf. *EDNT* 1:128; Swete 276; Cranfield 372). Ἐξεθαύμαζον, 3rd pl. impf. act. indic. of ἐκθαυμάζω, "be amazed" (on vbs. of amazement, see 1:22).

(iii) Question about the Resurrection (12:18–27)

12:18 The Sadducees make their first and only appearance in Mark when they come to Jesus with a question about the resurrection. Ἔρχονται, 3rd pl. pres. mid. indic. of dep. ἔρχομαι, "come"; historical pres. (starting a new scene [see 1:12]). The use of Σαδδουκαῖοι without an art. in this context marks the noun as indef. (see, e.g., NRSV: "some Sadducees"). Οἵτινες, used here as a def. rel. pron. (see R 957; cf. 4:20; 9:1; 15:7); λέγουσιν, customary pres.; εἶναι, pres. act. inf. of εἰμί, "be"; inf. of indir. discourse (Burton §390; Wallace 603–4; KMP 371). Mark introduces the question from the Sadducees in v. 18 (ἐπηρώτων, 3rd pl. impf. act. indic. of ἐπερωτάω, "ask" [on the impf. with ἐπερωτάω, see 4:10]; λέγοντες, nom. pl. masc. of pres. act. ptc. of λέγω, "say"; redundant ptc.), but the rather convoluted question takes all of vv. 19–23 to explain.

12:19 Διδάσκαλε, voc.; ἔγραψεν, 3rd sg. aor. act. indic. of γράφω, "write"; τινος, gen. of relationship; ἀποθάνῃ, 3rd sg. aor. act. subjunc. of ἀποθνῄσκω, "die"; subjunc. in a 3rd class cond. clause (cf. also the following two subjunc. vbs.); καταλίπῃ, 3rd sg. aor. act. subjunc. of καταλείπω, "leave behind"; καί, "and yet" (contrastive); ἀφῇ, 3rd sg. aor. act. subjunc. of ἀφίημι, "leave." There are two possible ways to classify the conj. ἵνα in 12:19. If this is an example of an impv. ἵνα (Z §415; cf. 5:23), then the following subjunc. vbs. are functioning like main vbs. in an independent clause and have the force of 3rd pers. commands ("his brother must take the wife and raise up offspring"). If this is an example of ἵνα introducing a dir. obj. clause (which is the more likely option in light of Mark's usage elsewhere [see the discussion at 5:10; cf. BDAG 476c; Cranfield 374]), then the presence of ἵνα implies a preceding but unstated independent clause, such as a repetition of Μωϋσῆς ἔγραψεν ("Moses also wrote that his brother should take the wife and raise up offspring"). Λάβῃ, 3rd sg. aor. act. subjunc. of λαμβάνω, "take, receive"; ἐξαναστήσῃ, 3rd sg. aor. act. subjunc. of ἐξανίστημι, "raise up, produce"; ἀδελφῷ, dat. of interest (advantage).

12:20 Based on the commandment from Moses, the Sadducees construct a hypothetical test case in vv. 20–22 to demonstrate, at least to their satisfaction, that careful obedience to Moses's command would make nonsense of a future resurrection. Ἦσαν, 3rd pl. impf. act. indic. of εἰμί, "be"; ἔλαβεν, 3rd sg. aor. act. indic. of λαμβάνω, "take, receive"; ἀποθνῄσκων, nom. sg. masc. of pres. act. ptc. of ἀποθνῄσκω, "die"; temp. adv. ptc. contemp.; ἀφῆκεν, 3rd sg. aor. act. indic. of ἀφίημι, "leave."

12:21 Ἔλαβεν, 3rd sg. aor. act. indic. of λαμβάνω, "take, receive"; ἀπέθανεν, 3rd sg. aor. act. indic. of ἀποθνῄσκω, "die"; καταλιπών, nom. sg. masc. of aor. act. ptc. of καταλείπω, "leave behind"; attendant circumstance ptc. (in this passage, καταλείπω [vv. 19, 21] and ἀφίημι [vv. 19, 20, 22] function as synonyms). The use of ὁ τρίτος as a nom. subj. implies a series of unstated vbs. that would portray the par. experience of the third brother (i.e., ἔλαβεν, ἀπέθανεν, οὐκ ἀφῆκεν). Ὡσαύτως, adv. mng. "likewise, in the same way, similarly."

12:22 Ἀφῆκαν, 3rd pl. aor. act. indic. of ἀφίημι, "leave." The neut. acc. form of the adj. ἔσχατον can function as an adv., as it does in this context in modifying ἀπέθανεν (BDAG 398a; Decker 2:123). A gen., such as πάντων can follow an adv., esp. when it conveys a partitive idea ("last of all"; see Wallace 134). Καί, adjunctive; ἀπέθανεν, 3rd sg. aor. act. indic. of ἀποθνῄσκω, "die."

12:23 Finally, the Sadducees come to their actual question. Ἀναστῶσιν, 3rd pl. aor. act. subjunc. of ἀνίστημι, "rise, rise again"; subjunc. in an indef. temp. clause (indef. in terms of when it will happen, not how many times it will happen). The use of two genitives in the question τίνος αὐτῶν ἔσται γυνή; makes for an awkward Eng. translation (lit: "she will be the wife of which of them?"; τίνος, gen. of relationship; αὐτῶν, partitive gen., [BDF §164]), and many EVV simply omit any translation of αὐτῶν (e.g., ESV: "whose wife will she be?"). Ἔσται, 3rd sg. fut. mid. indic. of εἰμί, "be" (dep. in fut.); ἔσχον, 3rd pl. aor. act. indic. of ἔχω, "have" (on the aor. for a summary or composite of repeated events, see Fanning 258–59, 262); γυναῖκα, "as a wife" (complement in a dbl. acc. obj. complement cstr. [Wallace 187]).

12:24 Ἔφη, 3rd sg. impf. or aor. act. indic. of φημί, "say." Questions beginning with οὐ expect an affirmative answer ("You are mistaken, aren't you?"; see 4:21, 28). Πλανᾶσθε, 2nd pl. pres. pass. indic. of πλανάω, "be mistaken" (mng. with pass.; BDAG

822a). Although the prep. phrase διὰ τοῦτο often refers back to a previous statement or argument, in this context it points forward, anticipating the participial clause beginning with μὴ εἰδότες (in other words, the participial clause stands in appos. to διὰ τοῦτο [cf. Wallace 333; Bruce 423; France 474]). Εἰδότες, nom. pl. masc. of pf. act. ptc. of οἶδα, "know"; adv. ptc. of cause (on οἶδα as a ptc., see 1:24).

12:25 The use of the pl. vb. γαμίζονται—since it refers to the general practice of women being given in marriage—signals that Jesus is no longer speaking about the one woman and her marriage relationship to seven brothers. Therefore, the vb. ἀναστῶσιν is an indef. pl. vb. ("when people rise again"; on indef. pl. vbs., see 1:22), and the pres. indic. vbs. in v. 25 (γαμοῦσιν, γαμίζονται, εἰσίν; cf. also the pres. indic. ἐγείρονται in v. 26) function as gnomic pres. tense vbs. to create a statement of general truth (on the gnomic pres., see Fanning 208–11; Wallace 523–24; KMP 258–59). Νεκρῶν, subst. adj.; ἀναστῶσιν, 3rd pl. aor. act. subjunc. of ἀνίστημι, "rise, rise again"; subjunc. in an indef. temp. clause (as in v. 23, indef. in terms of when it will happen, not how many times it will happen); γαμίζονται, 3rd pl. pres. pass. indic. of γαμίζω, "give [a woman] in marriage" (BDAG 188b). The nom. case noun ἄγγελοι serves as the subj. of an implied vb. (εἰσίν) in the comp. clause, and the prep. phrase ἐν τοῖς οὐρανοῖς is adj., modifying ἄγγελοι (ZG 148; "as the angels in heaven are"; cf. Cranfield 375).

12:26 The ὅτι clause is epex. to τῶν νεκρῶν; i.e., it explains what specifically Jesus intends to discuss with regard to the dead (on the epex. ὅτι, see Wallace 459–60). Eng. might more naturally use a ptc. ([Decker 2:126; cf. e.g., NET: "now as for the dead being raised"]; ἐγείρονται, 3rd pl. pres. pass. indic. of of ἐγείρω, raise). Jesus frames his quotation of Exod 3:6 as a rhetorical question, one that begins with οὐκ and therefore expects an affirmative answer ("you have read, haven't you?" [see 4:21, 38; cf. the similar question in 12:10]; ἀνέγνωτε, 2nd pl. aor. act. indic. of ἀναγινώσκω, "read"). Βίβλῳ, dat. sg. fem. of βίβλος, -ου, ἡ, "book"; βάτου, gen. sg. masc. of βάτος, -ου, ὁ, "bush" (the prep. phrase ἐπὶ τοῦ βάτου [lit: "at the bush"] is short for "in the passage about the bush" [cf. BDAG 171d, 363d; R 603]); λέγων, nom. sg. masc. of pres. act. ptc. of λέγω, "say"; redundant ptc.

12:27 Νεκρῶν, subst. adj.; ζώντων, gen. pl. masc. of pres. act. ptc. of ζάω, "live"; subst. ptc.; πολύ, "greatly, very much, badly" (neut. acc. form used as an adv. [BDAG 850a; Wallace 293]); πλανᾶσθε, 2nd pl. pres. pass. indic. of πλανάω, "be mistaken" (mng. with pass.; BDAG 822b). Jesus's argument from Exod 3:6 seems to focus on the covenant faithfulness of God (cf. France 471–72, 475). He spoke to Moses as the God who made a covenant with his forefathers, with Abraham, Isaac, and Jacob, and this covenant-making and covenant-keeping God would be true to all of his promises—not just to the descendants of these forefathers but to Abraham, Isaac, and Jacob themselves. The resurrection is necessary because God will fulfill his promises to Abraham, Isaac, and Jacob when they are fully alive. He is not the kind of God who fulfills his promises to the dead but to the living, and if necessary to those who are living because he has raised them up to life again.

(iv) Question about the Greatest Commandment (12:28–34)

12:28 Since Jesus's teaching in 12:28–34 is on God's foremost commands, it is broadly relevant to all who want to obey God. Yet given the context in which this passage appears, i.e., in a series of conflicts with the religious leaders, it is particularly relevant in that setting. For Mark, Jesus came into conflict with the religious establishment because its leaders did not strive to obey God's most important commands. The positive response of this one scribe offers a glimpse into another path, one not chosen by the religious leaders as a whole. Προσελθών, nom. sg. masc. of aor. act. ptc. of προσέρχομαι, "approach, come near"; temp. adv. ptc. antecedent (on the complicated series of participles in 12:28, see esp. Swete 283); on εἷς as an equivalent to the indef. pron. τις, see 5:22; ἀκούσας, nom. sg. masc. of aor. act. ptc. of ἀκούω, "hear"; adv. ptc. of cause (giving the reason why the scribe approached); αὐτῶν, gen. dir. obj.; συζητούντων, gen. pl. masc. of pres. act. ptc. of συζητέω, "dispute, debate"; supplementary (complementary) ptc.; ἰδών, nom. sg. masc. of aor. act. ptc. of ὁράω, "see"; adv. ptc. of cause (giving the reason why the scribe asked his question); ἀπεκρίθη, 3rd sg. aor. pass. indic. of dep. ἀποκρίνομαι, "answer" (on an aor. in indir. discourse, see 5:16); ἐπηρώτησεν, 3rd sg. aor. act. indic. of ἐπερωτάω, "ask." The scribe's question begins with ποία, functioning as an interr. adj. and modifying ἐντολή ("which commandment?" [BDAG 843d]; at times, ποῖος loses its qualitative sense ["what sort of?"] and overlaps in mng. with τίς [BDAG 843d–844a; R 740]; on ποῖος, see also 11:28). Πρώτη, "foremost, most important" (BDAG 893d; LN 65.52); pred. adj.; πάντων, on a partitive gen. after an adj., see Wallace 134. Sometimes forms of πᾶς do not follow expected patterns. The idiomatic use of the neut. form πάντων occurs here to intensify a superlative adj. (πρώτη), where the fem. form πασῶν would normally be expected in order to match the gender of ἐντολή (Z §12; BDF §164; Cranfield 377).

12:29 Jesus answers the question about the most important commandment in vv. 29–30 by quoting from Deut 6:4–5. He also adds a second commandment in v. 31, one that flows out of the first, by quoting from Lev 19:18. Ἀπεκρίθη, 3rd sg. aor. pass. indic. of dep. ἀποκρίνομαι, "answer"; ὅτι, introduces dir. discourse; πρώτη, pred. adj. (the quotation serves as the subj. of ἐστίν); ἄκουε, 2nd sg. pres. act. impv. of ἀκούω, "hear, listen"; Ἰσραήλ, an indecl. proper noun functioning as a voc. The second use of the nom. case noun κύριος in v. 29 stands in appos. to θεός, which in turn stands in appos. to the first use of κύριος in the verse. Εἷς, pred. adj.

12:30 The command to love God is expressed with an impv. fut. (ἀγαπήσεις, 2nd sg. fut. act. indic. of ἀγαπάω, "love"), a use that appears in the NT primarily in OT quotes (Wallace 569; KMP 271). Some Eng. translations seek to retain the impv. fut. (e.g., NASB, ESV: "you shall love"), while others just use an impv. (e.g., NIV, NET: "love"). On ὅλος, see 1:28; διανοίας, gen. sg. fem. of διάνοια, -ας, ἡ, "mind." The noun διάνοια is used for the inner life of humans, but with a special emphasis on the capacity for thinking or reasoning (BDAG 234b). The inclusion of the prep. phrase "with all your mind" serves to highlight other words in the passage related to thinking, such as σύνεσις ("understanding") in v. 33 and νουνεχῶς ("thoughtfully") in v. 34 (NET), thereby making the love of God with one's mind an emphasis in the passage as a whole. Ἰσχύος, gen. sg. fem. of ἰσχύς, -ύος, ἡ, "strength."

12:31 The scribe asked only about the foremost command, but Jesus adds a second that is subordinate to the first but grows out it. A wholehearted love for God leads to a faithful love for one's neighbor. Δευτέρα, pred. adj.; ἀγαπήσεις, 2nd sg. fut. act. indic. of ἀγαπάω, "love"; impv. fut.; πλησίον, "neighbor" (adv. used with the art. as a subst. [BDAG 830b]); σεαυτόν, dir. obj. of an implied ἀγαπᾷς ("you love"); μείζων, comp. form of μέγας; pred. adj.; τούτων, gen. of comp.

12:32 Καλῶς, "well said!" (used as an exclamation expressing a positive reaction to someone else's statement [BDAG 506a; ZG 149; NIV; NLT]; on καλῶς as an exclamation in this context, see Taylor 488); διδάσκαλε, voc.; ἐπί with the gen.: "in accordance with, based on" (see BDAG 365c; cf. 12:14); εἶπες, 2nd sg. aor. act. indic. of λέγω, "say, speak." In v. 32, the scribe summarizes briefly Deut 6:4: "he is one" (εἷς, pred. adj.); and he expands on it with words drawn from Deut 4:35 and Isa 45:21 (cf. Yarbro Collins 575): "and there is no other except him." While πλήν is an adv., in the NT it is used most often as a conj. but also at times—such as in Mark 12:32—as a prep. with a gen. obj. to denote an exception (BDAG 826c–d; R 1187).

12:33 Ἀγαπᾶν (twice in verse): pres. act. inf. of ἀγαπάω, "love"; subst. inf., subj. of ἐστιν; συνέσεως, gen. sg. fem. of σύνεσις, -εως, ἡ, "understanding, intelligence"; ἰσχύος, "strength" (see 12:30); πλησίον, "neighbor" (see 12:31); περισσότερον, nom. sg. neut. of περισσότερος, -α, -ον, "greater, more important"; comp. form of περισσός; pred. adj.; ὁλοκαυτωμάτων, gen. pl. neut. of ὁλοκαύτωμα, -ατος, τό, "whole burnt offering"; gen. of comp.; θυσιῶν, gen. of comp. The two infinitives create a compound subj. that takes a sg. vb. (ἐστιν, which in 12:33 follows the compound subj.). When the vb. precedes a compound subj., it normally agrees with the first noun in the compound subj. and therefore is often sg. (BDF §135 [1a]; cf. e.g., Mark 1:5, 36; 3:31, 33; 8:27, 36 [where the subj. involves two subst. infinitives]; 13:3; 14:1, 43; 16:8). When the vb. follows a compound subj., it is normally pl. (BDF §135 [1b]; cf. e.g., Mark 13:31; 15:47; 16:1). Variations from these patterns occur, but usually for a reason. In 10:35, a pl. vb. precedes the compound subj. "James and John, the sons of Zebedee," which seems to indicate that each brother was actively involved in approaching Jesus to ask for the best places in the coming kingdom. In 4:41, a sg. vb. follows the compound subj. "the wind and the sea," which seems to stress the totality of the subj., that all of nature, incl. the wind and the sea, was obedient to Jesus's command (R 405; for other examples, see Matt 6:19; 1 Cor 15:50; Jas 5:3). In a similar way, in 12:33, the use of the sg. vb. ἐστιν with the compound subj. seems to stress the totality of Jesus's teaching on love. Of course, these are still two commands, with loving God as the foremost and loving one's neighbor as second in importance, just as the wind and the sea are still two aspects of nature. However, Jesus's call for love when viewed as whole, incl. both love for God and love for one's neighbor, all of that together points to something that is far more significant to God than offering sacrifices.

12:34 Ἰδών, nom. sg. masc. of aor. act. ptc. of ὁράω, "see"; temp. adv. ptc. antecedent. The use of αὐτόν after ἰδών is an example of prolepsis (see 11:32). The acc. pron. αὐτόν serves as the dir. obj. of ἰδών but also as an anticipation of the subj. of ἀπεκρίθη in the following ὅτι clause. Most EVV simplify the grammatical structure by translating αὐτόν only as the subj. of ἀπεκρίθη (3rd sg. aor. pass. indic. of dep. ἀποκρίνομαι, "answer" [on the aor. in indir. discourse, see 5:16]). Νουνεχῶς, adv. mng. "thoughtfully, wisely." In light of the scribe's wise response, Jesus declares that he is not far (μακράν, adv. mng. "far") from the kingdom of God. Jesus's intentionally understated assessment should be taken as a positive description of the scribe's spiritual cond. and as an encouragement to the scribe to continue thinking deeply (cf. Yarbro Collins 577). On dbl. negatives to strengthen a statement, see 1:44; ἐτόλμα, 3rd sg. impf. act. indic. of τολμάω, "dare"; ἐπερωτῆσαι, aor. act. inf. of ἐπερωτάω, "question, ask a question"; complementary inf.

HOMILETICAL SUGGESTIONS

What Does God Care About (12:28–34)?

1. God cares most of all that we love him completely. (12:29–30, 33)
    a. With all our hearts and souls
    b. With all our minds and understanding
    c. With all our strength
2. God cares almost as much that we love those around us. (12:31, 33)
    a. Giving priority to others over self
    b. Giving priority to people over religious activities

(v) Critique of the Teaching of the Scribes (12:35–37)

12:35 Mark 12:35–37 is the first in a series of three passages in which Jesus takes the initiative to communicate his views on the scribes, including on their teaching and actions. In this passage, Jesus begins by contesting the adequacy of the scribes' teaching on the Messiah as the Son of David. Ἀποκριθείς, nom. sg. masc. of aor. pass. ptc. of dep. ἀποκρίνομαι, "answer"; redundant ptc.; on the impf. with ἔλεγεν, see 1:21; 2:16; διδάσκων, nom. sg. masc. of pres. act. ptc. of διδάσκω, "teach"; temp. adv. ptc. contemp.; πῶς, "how?" in the sense of "with what right?" or "with what evidence?" (see BDAG 901a); λέγουσιν, "say" in the sense of "maintain, declare, proclaim as teaching" (see BDAG 590a); υἱός, pred. nom.; Δαυίδ, indecl. noun functioning as a gen. of relationship.

12:36 Jesus quotes from Ps 110:1 to cast doubt on the sufficiency of the scribes' understanding of the Messiah. In Ps 110:1, David spoke in a way that complicates what it means for the Messiah to be the Son of David, since David himself assigned to the Messiah a superior title and position. Αὐτός, "himself" (intensive pron. [see Wallace 348–49; KMP 392; BDAG 152c; LN 92.37]; cf. the same use for αὐτός in 12:37); ἐν with the dat.: expresses close association and influence (see BDAG 328b; Z §116);

κάθου, 2nd sg. pres. mid. impv. of dep. κάθημαι, "sit"; ἐκ δεξιῶν, see 10:37; ἕως ἄν, "until" (used as a conj. [see 6:10]); θῶ, 1st sg. aor. act. subjunc. of τίθημι, "put, place"; subjunc. in an indef. temp. clause; ὑποκάτω, "under, beneath" (adv. functioning as a prep. with a gen. obj. [BDAG 1038a]).

12:37 Λέγει, "call, identify someone as" (when used with a dbl. acc. [see BDAG 590b]; cf. 10:18; 15:12); κύριον, complement in a dbl. acc. obj. complement cstr. The conj. καί is best translated as "then," when it introduces a question provoked by an unexpected or surprising statement (see 10:26). Πόθεν, interr. adv. mng. "how, in what way, how is it that?" (when used in a question concerning the manner in which something can be true [cf. LN 89.86; BDAG 838d]). The appropriate response to Jesus's otherwise unanswered question in 12:37 seems to be that the Messiah is indeed the Son of David but that this expression of his identity is insufficient by itself. The Messiah is more than simply an heir to David's throne, since he is also David's Lord. Any view of the Messiah that does not take his unique authority as Lord into consideration is insufficient. Ἤκουεν, 3rd sg. impf. act. indic. of ἀκούω, "hear, listen to" (on the impf. to portray the reactions of people, see 1:21); αὐτοῦ, gen. dir. obj.; ἡδέως, adv. mng. "gladly, eagerly, with delight."

FOR FURTHER STUDY

29. Jesus as Lord

Bousset, Wilhelm. *Kyrios Christos: A History of the Belief in Christ from the Beginnings of Christianity to Irenaeus.* 2nd ed. Waco, TX: Baylor University Press, 2013.

Broadhead, Edwin K. "Lord." Pages 135–44 in *Naming Jesus: Titular Christology in the Gospel of Mark.* JSNTSup 175. Sheffield, UK: Sheffield Academic Press, 1999.

Hahn, Ferdinand. "Kyrios." Pages 68–135 in *The Titles of Jesus in Christology: Their History in Early Christianity.* New York: World Publishing, 1969.

Head, Peter M. "Christology and Titles: Jesus as Teacher and Lord." Pages 148–73 in *Christology and the Synoptic Problem: An Argument for Markan Priority.* SNTSMS 94. Cambridge: Cambridge University Press, 1997.

Hurtado, Larry W. *Lord Jesus Christ: Devotion to Jesus in Earliest Christianity.* Grand Rapids: Eerdmans, 2003.

Johansson, Daniel. "*Kyrios* in the Gospel of Mark." *JSNT* 33 (2010): 101–24.

Longenecker, Richard N. "Lordship and Attendant Features." Pages 120–47 in *The Christology of Early Jewish Christianity.* Grand Rapids: Baker, 1970.

Vermes, Geza. "Jesus the Lord." Pages 103–28 in *Jesus the Jew: A Historian's Reading of the Gospels.* Philadelphia: Fortress, 1981.

*Williams, Joel F. "The Characterization of Jesus as Lord in Mark's Gospel." Pages 107–26 in *Character Studies and the Gospel of Mark.* Edited by Christopher W. Skinner and Matthew Ryan Hauge. LNTS 483. London: Bloomsbury T&T Clark, 2014.

(vi) Critique of the Behavior of the Scribes (12:38–40)

12:38 In 12:38–40, Jesus criticizes the behavior of the scribes. They love the public recognition that comes from their role as teachers of the law, but in spite of their outward show of religious activity, they are exploiting the poor and vulnerable, the very people they should be serving. Ἐν, "in the course of" (temp., BDAG 330a; cf. 4:2); αὐτοῦ, subj. gen.; on the impf. with ἔλεγεν, see 1:21; 2:16; βλέπετε, 2nd pl. pres. act. impv. of βλέπω, "beware of, watch out for" (mng. when used with ἀπό [see BDAG 179c; Decker 1:212; cf. 8:15]). The ptc. θελόντων (gen. pl. masc. of pres. act. ptc. of θέλω, "like, take pleasure in" [BDAG 448b]; adj. ptc.), as a form of the vb. θέλω, can be followed either by an inf. or by an acc. dir. obj. (BDAG 448b–c; Decker 2:138). In a somewhat awkward cstr., θελόντων is first followed by an inf. and then by three acc. dir. objects, with all four items being linked by καί. As a result, the list of what the scribes desire includes four par. items, par. in the sense that they are comparable examples of self-promoting behavior, not in the sense that they match grammatically. Στολαῖς, dat. pl. fem. of στολή, -ῆς, ἡ, "long flowing robe"; περιπατεῖν, pres. act. inf. of περιπατέω, "walk around"; complementary inf.; ἀσπασμούς, acc. pl. masc. of ἀσπασμός, -οῦ, ὁ, "greeting"; ἀγοραῖς, dat. pl. fem. of ἀγορά, -ᾶς, ἡ, "marketplace."

12:39 Πρωτοκαθεδρίας, acc. pl. fem. of πρωτοκαθεδρία, -ας, ἡ, "best, seat, seat of honor." The most important seats in the synagogue, which were reserved for respected guests and learned teachers, were on a bench, facing the congregation, in front of the chest that contained the Scriptures (Cranfield 384; Evans 278; cf. t. Meg. 3.21). Πρωτοκλισίας, acc. pl. fem. of πρωτοκλισία, -ας, ἡ, "place of honor at a meal"; δείπνοις, dat. pl. neut. of δεῖπνον, -ου, τό, "banquet, dinner celebration." At the time of Jesus, the seating arrangement at banquets was a matter of significant social concern, with the most honored places reserved for the most honored guests (cf. Luke 14:7–11; 1QS 6:8–9; b. Ber. 46b).

12:40 The grammatical structure in v. 40 shifts abruptly with the use of two nom. participles (οἱ κατεσθίοντες and προσευχόμενοι). The nom. participles likely stand in appos. to the gen. cstr. τῶν γραμματέων τῶν θελόντων and therefore continue to describe the scribes, who enjoy the prestige associated with their position (R 413, 458; cf. France 491). The shift in case is explainable in light of the distance between the nom. participles and the preceding gen. cstr. (T 317; cf. Strauss 557). Therefore, the sentence that began with "beware of the scribes" in v. 38 continues through v. 40a, and then v. 40b, which begins with οὗτοι, constitutes a new sentence (cf. e.g., NASB; ESV; see the par. but less grammatically awkward sentence in Luke 20:46–47). Κατεσθίοντες, nom. pl. masc. of pres. act. ptc. of κατεσθίω, "devour" (on κατά as a prep. prefix, see 1:36); subst. ptc. in appos. to τῶν γραμματέων; προφάσει, dat. sg. fem. of πρόφασις, -εως, ἡ, "pretense, appearance's sake"; dat. of manner; μακρός, "for a long time" (neut. acc. pl. adj. used as an adv. [cf. BDAG 613a; Taylor 495]); προσευχόμενοι, nom. pl. masc. of pres. mid. ptc. of dep. προσεύχομαι, "pray"; also subst. ptc. in appos. to τῶν γραμματέων; λήμψονται, 3rd pl. fut. mid. indic. of λαμβάνω, "receive" (dep. in fut.); περισσότερον, acc. sg. neut. of περισσότερος, -α, -ον, "greater, more severe" (comp. form of περισσός); attrib. adj.

(vii) Commendation of Sacrificial Devotion (12:41–44)

12:41 Within 11:33–12:44, a section on Jesus's conflict with the religious leaders, Mark presents two individuals who receive Jesus's approval, the wise scribe and the poor widow. Like these two individuals, those who lead God's people must have a commitment to love God and others wholeheartedly and must have a willingness to live with sacrificial devotion. Καθίσας, nom. sg. masc. of aor. act. ptc. of καθίζω, "sit down"; temp. adv. ptc. antecedent; κατέναντι, "opposite" (adv. functioning as a prep. with a gen. obj.); both γαζοφυλακίου [gen. sg. neut.] and later in the verse γαζοφυλάκιον [acc. sg. neut.] are from γαζοφυλάκιον, -ου, τό, "offering box, receptacle, treasury." According to the Mishnah (m. Sheqalim 6.5), there were thirteen "Shofar-chests" (trumpet-shaped receptacles) located in the temple, into which people could cast money. The trumpet-shaped opening for these offering boxes helps to make sense of the repeated reference in this passage to throwing in gifts (Decker 2:140–41). Ἐθεώρει, 3rd sg. impf. act. indic. of θεωρέω, "observe, watch" (impf. for background information [see 1:21; cf. ἔβαλλον later in 12:41]); βάλλει, on the. pres. in indir. discourse, see 2:1; χαλκόν, acc. sg. masc. of χαλκός, -οῦ, ὁ, "money"; ἔβαλλον, 3rd pl. impf. act. indic. of βάλλω, "throw in, put in"; πολλά, subst. adj., "large amounts" (lit: "many things").

12:42 Ἐλθοῦσα, nom. sg. fem. of aor. act. ptc. of ἔρχομαι, "come"; temp. adv. ptc. antecedent; ἔβαλεν, 3rd sg. aor. act. indic. of βάλλω, "throw, put"; λεπτά, acc. pl. neut. of λεπτός, -ά, -όν, "small, thin" (the adj. was used as a subst. with the neut. for a "small copper coin," BDAG 592d). A λεπτόν was the least valuable coin in circulation at that time (MM 374). As Mark points out, two λεπτά were equal to a quadrans (on ὅ ἐστιν, see 3:17; κοδράντης, nom. sg. masc. of κοδράντης, -ου, ὁ, quadrans, penny), the smallest Roman coin, which in turn was worth one-sixty-fourth of a denarius (EDNT 2:349–50). Therefore, the value of each λεπτόν was quite small in comparison to a denarius, a coin that served as a standard daily wage for a manual laborer (cf. Matt 20:2).

12:43 Προσκαλεσάμενος, nom. sg. masc. of aor. mid. ptc. of προσκαλέω, "summon, call to oneself" (mng. with mid.); temp. adv. ptc. antecedent; on ἀμήν, see 3:28; πλεῖον, neut. comp. form of πολύς used as a subst. adj.; πάντων, gen. of comp.; ἔβαλεν, 3rd sg. aor. act. indic. of βάλλω, "throw in, put in"; βαλλόντων, gen. pl. masc. of pres. act. ptc. of βάλλω, "throw, put"; adj. ptc.; γαζοφυλάκιον, acc. sg. neut. of γαζοφυλάκιον, -ου, τό, "offering box, receptacle, treasury." Jesus, who was watching the scene from the perspective of what God values, was able to understand the relative worth of the widow's gift in comparison to the gifts of all the other contributors. She gave more, and even if no one else at the scene noticed, Jesus did.

12:44 Περισσεύοντος, gen. sg. neut. of pres. act. ptc. of περισσεύω, "abound, be available in abundance" (BDAG 805b); subst. ptc.; αὐτοῖς, dat. of interest (advantage); ἔβαλον, 3rd pl. aor. act. indic. of βάλλω, "throw in, put in" (a constative aor. may summarize multiple occurrences [see Fanning 167–68, 258–59]); ὑστερήσεως, gen. sg. fem. of ὑστέρησις, -εως, ἡ, "need, lack, poverty"; πάντα ὅσα, "all that" (see 11:24); εἶχεν, 3rd sg. impf. act. indic. of ἔχω, "have"; ἔβαλεν, 3rd sg. aor. act. indic. of βάλλω, "throw in, put in." This poor widow gave her whole life, i.e., the full extent of all the resources that she had to live on (βίον, acc. sg. masc. of βίος, -ου, ὁ, life, means of subsistence, resources needed to live (BDAG 177b; LN 57.18); acc. in appos. to πάντα.

HOMILETICAL SUGGESTIONS

What Does God Expect from Those Who Lead His People (12:13–44)?

1. A lesson from the wise scribe: God expects a wholehearted love for him and a selfless love toward others. (12:28–34)
2. A lesson from the poor widow: God expects a sacrificial devotion on behalf of his work. (12:41–44)

(c) [Transition] Departure out of the Temple and Prediction of Its Destruction: The Eschatological Discourse (13:1–37)

Jesus's eschatological discourse in ch. 13 is similar to his parables discourse in ch. 4 in that it serves as a transitional passage. Ch. 13 is a fitting end to the section on Jesus's conflict with the religious leaders in the temple, because it starts with Jesus predicting the destruction of the temple and shows how this destruction should be understood within the framework of the events at the end of the present age. Ch. 13 is also important for making sense of the account of Jesus's death and resurrection in chs. 14–16. In the eschatological discourse, Jesus predicts the coming of false Christs who perform signs and wonders for the purpose of leading others astray (13:5–6, 22). The following passion narrative reveals the way of the true Christ, which is the way of the cross. Jesus's life and destiny set the pattern for his own followers, who must be willing to suffer for his name (13:9–13). Yet the eschatological discourse also makes clear that the cross is not the end, since Jesus will be vindicated (13:26; cf. 14:62), as will his followers (13:13, 27).

(i) The Prediction of the Temple's Destruction (13:1–4)

13:1 Ἐκπορευομένου, gen. sg. masc. of pres. mid. ptc. of dep. ἐκπορεύομαι, "go out"; gen. abs., temp. adv. ptc. contemp. (on the use and misuse of gen. abs. participles in Mark, see 1:32 and 5:2 [cf. 13:3]; on the repetition of a prep. following a compound vb., see 1:21); λέγει, historical pres. (see 1:12, 30); μαθητῶν, partitive gen.; διδάσκαλε, voc.; on ἴδε, see 1:2 (the objects to be observed following the particle ἴδε are in the nom. case [nom. of exclamation, Wallace 59–60; cf. 3:34; 16:6]); both ποταποί (nom. pl. masc.) and ποταπαί (nom. pl. fem.) are from ποταπός, -ή, -όν, "what great, what wonderful"; οἰκοδομαί, nom. pl. fem. of οἰκοδομή, -ῆς, ἡ, "building." Although ποταπός normally functions as an interr. adj. ("of what sort?"), sometimes it serves to introduce an exclamation ("What! what great!"; BDAG 856b–c; Decker 2:144; cf. 1 John 3:1).

13:2 Οἰκοδομάς, acc. pl. fem. of οἰκοδομή, -ῆς, ἡ, "building"; ἀφεθῇ, 3rd sg. aor. pass. subjunc. of ἀφίημι, "leave"; καταλυθῇ, 3rd sg. aor. pass. subjunc. of καταλύω, "throw down." The use of οὐ μή with the aor. subjunc. (ἀφεθῇ) serves as an emph. denial of a future possibility, here the possibility that the temple will remain standing. The addition of a rel. clause that also includes οὐ μή with an aor. subjunc. (καταλυθῇ) makes Jesus's prediction of the temple's destruction doubly emph. (France 496; on οὐ μή for emph. neg., see 9:1; for further examples in Jesus's eschatological discourse, see 13:19, 30, 31).

13:3 After Jesus's emph. statement about the temple's coming destruction, four of Jesus's disciples approach him with their questions and concerns. Καθημένου, gen. sg. masc. of pres. mid. ptc. of dep. κάθημαι, "sit"; gen. abs., temp. adv. ptc. contemp.; on the use of εἰς for ἐν, here mng. "on," see 13:9; ἐλαιῶν, gen. pl. fem. of ἐλαία, -ας, ἡ, "olive" (τὸ ὄρος τῶν ἐλαιῶν, "the Mount of Olives"); κατέναντι, "opposite" (adv. functioning as a prep. that takes a gen. obj.); ἐπηρώτα, 3rd sg. impf. act. indic. of ἐπερωτάω, "ask" (on ἐπερωτάω in the impf., see 4:1; on a sg. vb. with a compound subj., see 12:33); κατ' ἰδίαν, idiomatic phrase mng. "privately" (BDAG 467c; T 18).

13:4 Εἰπόν, 2nd sg. aor. act. impv. of λέγω, "say, tell" (a 1st aor. ending [without the -σ-] on a 2nd aor. stem [see 8:5]); πότε, interr. adv. mng. "when?"; ἔσται, 3rd sg. fut. mid. indic. of εἰμί, "be" (dep. in fut.; sg. vb. with a neut. pl. subj. [see 3:11]); on the mng. of σημεῖον in Mark, see 8:11; μέλλη, 3rd sg. pres. act. subjunc. of μέλλω, "be about to" (also sg. vb. with a neut. pl. subj.); subjunc. in indef. temp. clause; συντελεῖσθαι, pres. pass. inf. of συντελέω, "carry out, fulfill, accomplish"; complementary inf. In light of the portrayal of the disciples in the broader narrative of Mark's Gospel, it seems unlikely that the disciples' words in 13:4 should be understood as a simple request for information, free from self-concern. The broader narrative encourages us to anticipate that their questions grow out of their misunderstanding and self-interest and that Jesus will need to correct them (for a similar corrective view, see Neil D. Nelson Jr., "'This Generation' in Matt 24:34: A Literary Critical Perspective," *JETS* 38 [1995]: 370–73). Interpreting the disciples as misguided at the beginning of ch. 13 helps explain why Jesus's teaching does not seem to offer a straightforward answer to the disciples' questions about the temple. Instead, Jesus corrects his disciples by telling them not what they want to know but what they need to know concerning the future in order to live properly in the present: that disasters and persecutions are not signs of the end but characteristic difficulties in the present age (13:5–13); that the intensified tribulation at the end of the age will arrive so suddenly and take place so rapidly that there will be no time for careful preparation (13:14–23); and that the coming of the Son of Man offers hope and vindication for his chosen ones (13:24–27). In addition, Mark attaches a series of Jesus's parables and sayings to the end of the discourse that emphasize the need to be ready for the master's coming (13:28–37).

(ii) The Beginning of Woes (13:5–13)

13:5 Ἤρξατο, 3rd sg. aor. mid. indic. of ἄρχω, "begin" (mng. with mid.; on ἄρχομαι, see 1:45); λέγειν, pres. act. inf. of λέγω, "say"; complementary inf.; βλέπετε, 2nd pl. pres. act. impv. of βλέπω, "watch out, beware" (BDAG 179c); μή, "that . . . not, lest" (functioning as a conj.; BDAG 646b); πλανήσῃ, 3rd sg. aor. act. subjunc. of πλανάω, "mislead, deceive" (Wallace 477 labels the mood as "subjunc. with vbs. of fearing,

etc."). The use of βλέπετε in 13:5 is the first in a series of impv. forms in Jesus's discourse, most of which are pres. tense (fifteen pres. imperatives out of nineteen total;
there is also one indir. command that uses ἵνα plus the pres. subjunc. [13:34]; see
13:15 on the three aor. impv. forms in vv. 15–16 [the aor. impv. μάθετε in 13:28, a
general precept, is exceptional and perhaps ingr. in function; cf. Fanning 368]). Since
the pres. impv. normally expresses a general precept for a broad audience (see 1:15),
the consistent use of the pres. impv. forms in Jesus's discourse in ch. 13 conveys that
his commands and prohibitions are relevant not just to the four disciples but to all of
his followers (cf. 13:37 where this point is made directly).

13:6 Ἐλεύσονται, 3rd pl. fut. mid. indic. of dep. ἔρχομαι, "come"; λέγοντες, nom. pl.
masc. of pres. act. ptc. of λέγω, "say"; adv. ptc. of means (cf. 1:40; 5:35); ὅτι, introduces dir. discourse; πλανήσουσιν, 3rd pl. fut. act. indic. of πλανάω, "mislead, deceive."
The phrase "in my name" (ἐπὶ τῷ ὀνόματί μου) may indicate only that the deceivers
claim to represent Jesus and act with his authority (cf. the use of ἐπὶ τῷ ὀνόματί μου in
9:39), but the following quotation of their words seem to be asserting more than that.
Their words, ἐγώ εἰμι, are a normal Gk. idiom for "I am he" or "I am the one" (Strauss
572). When the deceivers say, "I am he," they are apparently laying claim to Jesus's
name or identity as the Messiah. They are "false Christs" (cf. 13:21–22).

13:7 Ἀκούσητε, 2nd pl. aor. act. subjunc. of ἀκούω, "hear about, learn about"; subjunc.
in indef. temp. clause; both πολέμους (acc. pl. masc.) and πολέμων (gen. pl. masc.; obj.
gen.) are from πόλεμος, -ου, ὁ, "war"; ἀκοάς, acc. pl. fem. of ἀκοή, -ῆς, ἡ, "rumor";
θροεῖσθε, 2nd pl. pres. pass. impv. of θροέω, "be disturbed, be alarmed" (mng. with
pass.; in 2 Thess 2:2 the pass. form of θροέω stands par. to σαλευθῆναι . . . ἀπὸ τοῦ
νοός "to be shaken and thereby lose your calmness of mind" [BDAG 680b]); δεῖ, 3rd
sg. pres. act. indic. of δεῖ, "it is necessary, one must"; γενέσθαι, aor. mid. inf. of dep.
γίνομαι, "come about, happen"; subst. use of the inf., subj. of δεῖ; τέλος, nom. subj. of
an implied ἐστιν. In the context of ch. 13, "the end" refers to the time of intensified
tribulation that will take place just before the coming of the Son of Man, the final
event that draws this present age to a close (13:14–27). According to 13:7–8, wars and
natural disasters are normal for this present evil age and do not signal the soon arrival
of the end.

13:8 Ἐγερθήσεται, 3rd sg. fut. pass. indic. of ἐγείρω, "rise up against, rise up in arms
against, rise up to make war against" (mng. with pass. followed by ἐπί [BDAG 272b;
LN 55.2]); ἔσονται, 3rd pl. fut. mid. indic. of εἰμί, "be" (dep. in fut.); σεισμοί, nom. pl.
masc. of σεισμός, -οῦ, ὁ, "earthquake"; κατὰ τόπους, "in various places, in place after
place" (distributive use of κατά, indicating that events are divided among a number of
individual locations [BDAG 511c; cf. Harris 155–57; Wallace 377]; for temp. examples of the distributive use, see 14:49; 15:6); λιμοί, nom. pl. masc. or fem. of λιμός,
-οῦ, ὁ or ἡ, "famine"; ὠδίνων, gen. pl. fem. of ὠδίν, -ῖνος, ἡ, "birth pain"; partitive gen.

13:9 Βλέπετε, 2nd pl. pres. act. impv. of βλέπω, "look to, watch out for" (BDAG
179c); ἑαυτούς, "yourselves" (the pl. forms of the 3rd pers. refl. pron. ἑαυτοῦ function
also as the 1st and 2nd pl. forms [Z §209]; cf. 9:50; 14:7). The command to watch out

for yourselves is made more emphatic by directly expressing the nom. pers. pron. ὑμεῖς as the subj. of βλέπετε (a nom. pers. pron. with an impv. is rare in Mark; out of more than 140 instances of 2nd pers. impv. forms in Mark, the nom. pers. pron. appears only in 6:37; 13:9, 23, 29 [cf. ὑμεῖς αὐτοί with the δεῦτε in 6:31]; on nom. pers. pronouns, see Wallace 321–23). Παραδώσουσιν, 3rd pl. fut. act. indic. of παραδίδωμι, "hand over" (on indef. pl. vbs., see 1:22). Through the repeated use of παραδίδωμι, Mark's Gospel creates three par. stories: the arrest of John the Baptist as the forerunner to Jesus (1:14), the condemnation of Jesus himself (e.g., 9:31; 10:33; 14:41; 15:1, 10, 15), and the persecution faced by Jesus's followers (13:9, 11–12). Συνέδρια, acc. pl. neut. of συνέδριον, -ου, τό, "council." The prep. εἰς in the phrase εἰς συναγωγάς expresses a set location ("in") and therefore serves as an example of the use of εἰς where ἐν would be expected (on εἰς for ἐν, see BDF §205; R 592–93; Z §99; Wallace 359; Harris 84–86; cf. BDAG 289b). Mark 13 has a number of such examples, including in 13:3, 9, 16, and perhaps in 13:13 (see also 1:9, 39; 5:14 [twice], 34; 6:8; 10:10; 14:9; on εἰς for ἐν in Mark, see C. H. Turner, "Marcan Usage: Notes, Critical and Exegetical, on the Second Gospel," *JTS* 26 [1924–25]: 14–20). Δαρήσεσθε, 2nd pl. fut. pass. indic. of δέρω, "beat"; ἐπί, "before, in the presence of" (in the context of official proceedings [BDAG 363d; R 603]); ἡγεμόνων, gen. pl. masc. of ἡγεμών, -όνος, ὁ, "governor"; σταθήσεσθε, 2nd pl. fut. pass. indic. of ἵστημι, "stand trial, appear in court" (fut. act. intrans. mng. with fut. pass. form [BDAG 482c; BDF §97]); μαρτύριον, acc. sg. neut. of μαρτύριον, -ου, τό, "testimony"; αὐτοῖς, "against them" (dat. of interest [disadvantage]; Wallace 144; cf. KMP 124–25; *TDNT* 4:503; Lane 459, 461 [see the discussion at 1:44]).

13:10 In the midst of his description of future persecution (13:9, 11–13), Jesus interrupts his own line of thought and sets forth the one great task to be accomplished by his followers in the present age: the gospel must be proclaimed to all the nations. Εἰς, "to" or "in" (after vbs. of saying, teaching, proclaiming; BDAG 289c); ἔθνη, "nations, groups of people" (cf. BDAG 276c–d; see also Rev 5:9; 7:9; 11:9; 14:6, where ἔθνος "nation" appears as a par. term with "tribe," "language," and "people"; πρῶτος, "first" (neut. form used as an adv. of time; BDAG 893b). The use of the word "first" indicates a temporal relationship in which the proclamation of the gospel to the nations must take place before some other event. That event is likely the coming of the Son of Man (13:26), since at that point the angels will gather the elect from the ends of the earth (13:27). Δεῖ, 3rd sg. pres. act. indic. of δεῖ, "it is necessary, one must"; κηρυχθῆναι, aor. pass. inf. of κηρύσσω, "proclaim, preach"; subst. use of the inf., subj. of δεῖ; εὐαγγέλιον, acc. of reference or respect (on εὐαγγέλιον, see 1:1).

13:11 Ἄγωσιν, 3rd pl. pres. act. subjunc. of ἄγω, "lead away, arrest, take into custody" (BDAG 16c; LN 15.165); subjunc. in indef. temp. clause (on indef. pl. vbs., see 1:22). The ptc. παραδιδόντες (nom. pl. masc. of pres. act. ptc. of παραδίδωμι, "hand over") may either be a temp. adv. ptc. expressing contemp. time ("as they are in the process of handing you over") or perhaps more likely an adv. ptc. of result and therefore subsequent to the main vb. ("and so hand you over"; cf. 9:10). Προμεριμνᾶτε, 2nd pl. pres. act. impv. of προμεριμνάω, "be anxious about beforehand, worry about beforehand"; λαλήσητε, 2nd pl. aor. act. subjunc. of λαλέω, "speak, say"; delib. subjunc. in an indir.

question (Taylor 508; on the retention of the subjunc. mood in indir. discourse, see Z §348). The indef. rel. pron. (ὃ ἐάν) functions as a pendent acc. (cf. Wallace 198; Turner, *Style* 21), i.e., it appears at the beginning of the clause as though it were going to be the dir. obj. of the following vb. (λαλεῖτε) but then is left "hanging" syntactically because it is replaced by a resumptive pron. (τοῦτο), which is the actual dir. obj. (cf. the use of the pendent nom. in 7:20; 13:13). Δοθῇ, 3rd sg. aor. pass. subjunc. of δίδωμι, "give"; subjunc. in indef. rel. cause; λαλεῖτε, 2nd pl. pres. act. impv. of λαλέω, "speak, say"; λαλοῦντες, nom. pl. masc. of pres. act. ptc. of λαλέω, "speak"; subst. ptc., pred. nom.

13:12 Παραδώσει, 3rd sg. fut. act. indic. of παραδίδωμι, "hand over"; ἐπαναστήσονται, 3rd pl. fut. mid. indic. of ἐπανίστημι, "rise up, rise up in rebellion" (dep. in fut.; on the mng. of ἐπανίστημι, see BDAG 359a; LN 39.34); ἐπί (with acc.): "against" (BDAG 366a; on the repetition of the prep. after a compound vb., see 1:21); γονεῖς, acc. pl. masc. of γονεύς, -έως, ὁ, "parents" (mng. with pl.; BDAG 205a); θανατώσουσιν, 3rd pl. fut. act. indic. of θανατόω, "have someone put to death, put to death."

13:13 Ἔσεσθε, 2nd pl. fut. mid. indic. of εἰμί, "be" (dep. in fut.); μισούμενοι, nom. pl. masc. of pres. pass. ptc. of μισέω, "hate"; periph. ptc. The use of the fut. indic. of εἰμί with a pres. periph. ptc. is not common in the NT, with clear examples being limited to Matt 10:22; 24:9; Mark 13:13, 25; Luke 1:20; 5:10; 21:17, 24; 22:69; Acts 6:4 (only in ms. D); 1 Cor 14:9 (Fanning 317–19; Wallace 567, 648–49). In a fut. periph. cstr., the form of εἰμί shows the future expectation of the action, while the pres. tense ptc. communicates the aspect, portraying the action as in process (cf. Decker 2:152, 160–61). The fut. periph. cstr. in 13:13 has the added factor of using the ptc. in the pass. voice, creating a stative sense, so that the verse portrays a future ongoing state of hatred against believers (cf. Fanning 318). The subst. ptc. ὁ ὑπομείνας (nom. sg. masc. of aor. act. ptc. of ὑπομένω, "endure"), as a pendent nom., comes at the beginning of the sentence presumably as the subj. of the main vb., but then it is replaced later by a resumptive pron. (οὗτος), which functions as the actual subj. (Marcus 2:883–84; Decker 2:152; Wallace 51–52; cf. 7:20). Σωθήσεται, 3rd sg. fut. pass. indic. of σῴζω, "save." Salvation in the context of 13:13 seems to convey the nuance of vindication, deliverance from accusation and shame (Lane 460, 464; cf. the similar use of the related noun σωτηρία in LXX Job 13:16 and Phil 1:19, both verses in which someone who has been obedient to God expects to be delivered from false accusations and unjust opposition).

FOR FURTHER STUDY

30. Mission to the Gentiles in Mark

Bennema, Cornelis. "Gentile Characters and the Motif of Proclamation in the Gospel of Mark." Pages 215–31 in *Character Studies and the Gospel of Mark*. Edited by Christopher W. Skinner and Matthew Ryan Hauge. LNTS 483. London: Bloomsbury T&T Clark, 2014.

Bird, Michael F. *Jesus and the Origins of the Gentile Mission*. LNTS 331. London: T&T Clark, 2006.

Garland, David E. "Mission in Mark." Pages 455–71 in *A Theology of Mark's Gospel: Good News about Jesus the Messiah, the Son of God*. Grand Rapids: Zondervan, 2015.

Hahn, Ferdinand. *Mission in the New Testament*. SBT 47. Naperville, IL: Alec R. Allenson, 1965.

Iverson, Kelly R. *Gentiles in the Gospel of Mark: "Even the Dogs under the Table Eat the Children's Crumbs."* LNTS 339. London: T&T Clark, 2007.

Jeremias, Joachim. *Jesus' Promise to the Nations*. SBT 24. Naperville, IL: Alec R. Allenson, 1958.

Köstenberger, Andreas J., and Peter T. O'Brien. "Mark." Pages 73–86 in *Salvation to the Ends of the Earth: A Biblical Theology of Mission*. NSBT. Downers Grove, IL: InterVarsity, 2001.

Schnabel, Eckhard J. *Early Christian Mission*. 2 vols. Downers Grove, IL: InterVarsity, 2002.

Senior, Donald, and Carroll Stuhlmueller. *The Biblical Foundations for Mission*. Maryknoll, NY: Orbis, 1983.

*Williams, Joel F. "Mission in Mark." Pages 137–51 in *Mission in the New Testament: An Evangelical Approach*. Edited by William J. Larkin Jr. and Joel F. Williams. Maryknoll, NY: Orbis, 1998.

HOMILETICAL SUGGESTIONS

What Will the Present Age Be Like? (13:5–13)

1. The great trauma of the present age (which will not signal the end)
   a. Deception (13:5–6)
   b. War (13:7–8a)
   c. Natural disasters (13:8b)
   d. Persecution (13:9, 11–12)
   e. Hatred (13:13)
2. The great task of the present age (which must happen before the end)
   a. The mission: The proclamation of the gospel to all nations in the midst of a hostile world.
   b. The message of the mission: the gospel
   c. The method of the mission: proclamation
   d. The scope of the mission: all the nations
   e. The context of the mission: a hostile world

(iii) The Days of the Tribulation (13:14–23)

13:14 In contrast (δέ) to what he has been teaching until this point, Jesus directs his disciples' attention to a particular event that will initiate a time of great tribulation at the very end of the age just before the coming of the Son of Man. Jesus's reference to an event that signals the beginning of the end—the abomination of desolation—points to the central tension in the eschatological discourse as a whole. The discourse begins with Jesus correcting his disciples' desire for a sign and ends with Jesus encouraging his disciples simply to remain faithful, since no one knows the time of the end. Then in the middle of the discourse, Jesus seems to introduce a sign that will signal the time of intense suffering at the end of the age. Perhaps the best way to resolve the tension is by recognizing that the abomination of desolation will appear so suddenly and lead so swiftly to the difficult events of the end that it does not function as a sign at all, if by a sign we mean some event that allows Jesus's followers to prepare for a time of suffering and hopefully by preparing for it to be able to avoid it (Hooker 300–302). Once again, there is nothing to be done except to be prepared at all times by serving faithfully with endurance.

Ἴδητε, 2nd pl. aor. act. subjunc. of ὁράω, "see"; subjunc. in an indef. temp. clause; βδέλυγμα, acc. sg. neut. of βδέλυγμα, -ατος, τό, "abomination"; ἐρημώσεως, gen. sg. fem. of ἐρήμωσις, -εως, ἡ, "desolation" (likely a gen. of product, an abomination that produces a desolated place [Strauss 578]). The whole phrase "abomination of desolation" derives from the book of Daniel (cf. Matt 24:15), which apparently uses references to this abomination to predict the setting up of idolatrous worship at the temple site so that it is left deserted by God's people (Dan 9:27; 11:31; 12:11; cf. Matt 24:15; on the use of Daniel's words by Jesus to point to a future eschatological event, see Taylor 511–12; Evans 318–20; Edwards 398–99). Ἑστηκότα, acc. sg. masc. of pf. act. ptc. of ἵστημι, "stand" (pres. intrans. mng. with pf.; BDAG 482d–483a); δεῖ, 3rd sg. pres. act. indic. of δεῖ, "it is proper, one must, one ought." As a masc. ptc., ἑστηκότα does not directly modify the neut. noun βδέλυγμα ("abomination") as an adj. ptc., but rather it functions as a subst. ptc. in appos. to βδέλυγμα. Therefore, it is not the abomination that is standing, but rather the abomination is a man who is standing where he should not be. Customarily, the impers. vb. δεῖ is accompanied by an acc. of ref. and an inf. that functions as the subj. of the vb. (cf. BDAG 214b; Wallace 600), both of which are implied rather than stated in this instance. Therefore, the phrase ὅπου οὐ δεῖ implies "where it is not proper (for him to stand)," i.e., "where he must not stand." Ἀναγινώσκων, nom. sg. masc. of pres. act. ptc. of ἀναγινώσκω, "read"; subst. ptc.; νοείτω, 3rd sg. pres. act. impv. of νοέω, "understand, consider carefully, take special note of" (BDAG 675a; LN 30.3). Mark's parenthetical narrative aside (ὁ ἀναγινώσκων νοείτω) assumes a social context in which a reader publicly read a text aloud to a gathered assembly (Col 4:16; 1 Thess 5:27; Rev 1:3), which was the normal practice at the time of Mark's Gospel. Mark's note is an indication to the reader that this is a place in his work that calls for careful attention and study, as well as perhaps additional explanation to the listeners (see Yarbro Collins 597–98, 608). On the art. with a prep. phrase (οἱ ἐν τῇ Ἰουδαίᾳ) to make it function like a noun, see 1:36 (the same cstr. appears in 13:15 and 13:16); φευγέτωσαν, 3rd pl. pres. act. impv. of φεύγω, "flee."

13:15 Δώματος, gen. sg. neut. of δῶμα, -ατος, τό, "roof, housetop"; καταβάτω, 3rd sg. aor. act. impv. of καταβαίνω, "come down, go down"; εἰσελθάτω, 3rd sg. aor. act. impv. of εἰσέρχομαι, "go into, enter"; ἆραι, aor. act. inf. of αἴρω, "take away, take along"; inf. of purpose. Most of the imperatives in Jesus's eschatological discourse use the pres. tense, since they give general commands to a broad audience (see 13:5). When Jesus shifts to concrete illustrations, the imperatives switch to the aor., since the normal pattern is to use the aor. for specific commands in particular circumstances (see 1:25; 2:11). The commands in vv. 15–16 are unusual in that prohibitions using the aor. tense normally employ μή with the aor. subjunc., not—as here—μή with the aor. impv. (Wallace 469, 487, 723). Instances of μή with the aor. impv. seem to be restricted to eight examples in the NT, all in the teaching of Jesus in the Synoptic Gospels and all with 3rd person commands (Matt 6:3; 24:17, 18; Mark 13:15 [twice], 16; Luke 17:31 [twice]; Wallace 487, 723; KMP 210 [note also that seven of the eight examples overlap, since Matt 24:17–18 and Luke 17:31 are par. to Mark 13:15–16]).

13:16 On εἰς for ἐν; see 13:9; ἐπιστρεψάτω, 3rd sg. aor. act. impv. of ἐπιστρέφω, "return." Normally in Mark, ὀπίσω functions as a prep. that takes a gen. obj. (1:7, 17, 20; 8:33, 34), but in the phrase εἰς τὰ ὀπίσω, ὀπίσω is functioning as an adv., which—since it follows the art.—is being used as a noun (cf. R 645). Ἆραι, aor. act. inf. of αἴρω, "take away, take along"; inf. of purpose. Why is there a need for an immediate and urgent flight? The closest par. in the OT to Jesus's command to flee immediately to the mountains appears in Gen 19:16–17, where Lot and his family were compelled to flee for their lives to the mountains to escape the divine judgment that was about to fall (cf. Luke 17:28–32). What creates the need for flight is the imminent judgment of God against defiant human rebellion.

13:17 Both vv. 17 and 18 highlight certain hindrances that could make the situation more difficult and therefore more dangerous for those who are seeking to flee. On οὐαί, see 14:21; γαστρί, dat. sg. fem. of γαστήρ, -τρός, ἡ, "womb"; ἐχούσαις, dat. pl. fem. of pres. act. ptc. of ἔχω, "have" (with ἐν γαστρὶ ἔχειν used idiomatically for "to be pregnant" [BDAG 190b, 420c; Spicq 1:294]); subst. ptc.; dat. of interest (disadvantage); θηλαζούσαις, dat. pl. fem. of pres. act. ptc. of θηλάζω, "breast-feed an infant, nurse" (BDAG 455a); also subst. ptc. and dat. of interest (disadvantage).

13:18 Προσεύχεσθε, 2nd pl. pres. mid. impv. of dep. προσεύχομαι, "pray"; γένηται, 3rd sg. aor. mid. subjunc. of dep. γίνομαι, "come to be, take place, happen"; subjunc. in a dir. obj. ἵνα clause to express the content of a prayer (see 5:10); χειμῶνος, gen. sg. masc. of χειμών, -ῶνος, ὁ, "winter"; gen. of time (T 235; Porter, *Idioms* 96).

13:19 According to vv. 19–22, the end of the age will be a time of intensified suffering as well as intensified deception. Ἔσονται, 3rd pl. fut. mid. indic. of εἰμί, "be" (dep. in fut.). The rel. clause that further clarifies the nature of the coming tribulation (which begins with οἵα) is complicated to translate due to Sem. influence (Z §§201–2; R 722; Moule 176; BDF §297). Since in Heb. and Aram. the rel. pron. is indecl. and without gender, another pers. pron. is often added to indicate the case, number, and gender of the rel. pron. (see 7:25; cf. 1:7). This grammatical pattern creates an unnecessary redundancy for both Gk. and Eng. In this verse, the rel. clause begins not with a rel. pron. but with a rel. adj. (οἵα, nom. sg. fem. of οἷος, -α, -ον, "of what sort as") and then follows with a redundant adj. (τοιαύτη, "of such a kind as, such as"). In Eng., it is probably best to eliminate the redundancy and just translate the adj. τοιαύτη (cf. BDAG 701d, 1009d–1010a). Γέγονεν, 3rd sg. pf. act. indic. of γίνομαι, "come to be, take place, happen"; κτίσεως, gen. sg. fem. of κτίσις, -εως, ἡ, "creation, world"; gen. of appos.; ἔκτισεν, 3rd sg. aor. act. indic. of κτίζω, "create." The art. τοῦ causes the adv. νῦν to function as a noun and therefore as the obj. of the prep. ἕως (BDAG 681c; R 547–48; cf. Wallace 231–32). In Eng., it is necessary either to eliminate the art. ("until now") or to translate the adv. as a noun phrase ("until the present time"). Γένηται, 3rd sg. aor. mid. subjunc. of dep. γίνομαι, "come to be, take place, happen"; emph. neg. subjunc. (see 13:2).

13:20 In 13:20, the aor. tense is used to depict future events. This use of the aor. tense may be classified as a proleptic aor. or more narrowly as an aor. of divine decree—portraying an event as determined by God in the past and therefore certain but not yet worked out on earth until the future (cf. Fanning 269–74, esp. 274; France 527). The verse begins with a 2nd class contrary-to-fact cond. clause, as indicated both by the use of μή with the indic. in the cond. and by the presence of ἄν in the conclusion (see Porter, *Idioms* 256; cf. BDF §428). Typically, the aor. indic. in both halves of a 2nd class cond. sentence indicates that the cond. is presented as not true in the past, with the result that the conclusion is also not true in the past (Wallace 695). If the Lord had not shortened the days (ἐκολόβωσεν, 3rd sg. aor. act. indic. of κολοβόω, "shorten, cut short"), no one would have been saved (ἐσώθη, 3rd sg. aor. pass. indic. of σώζω, "save, save from physical death" [BDAG 982b–c]). The phrase πᾶσα σάρξ, "all flesh," is equivalent to "every person" or "everyone" (BDAG 915d; cf. BDF §275). When negated by οὐκ, the phrase becomes equivalent to "no person" or "no one" or, in Gk., οὐδείς (BDAG 915d; R 752; on the Sem. background, see T 196; Z §446). Ἐκλεκτούς, acc. pl. masc. of ἐκλεκτός, -ή, -όν, "chosen, elect"; subst. adj.; ἐξελέξατο, 3rd sg. aor. mid. indic. of ἐκλέγομαι, "choose for oneself, select for oneself."

13:21 Εἴπῃ, 3rd sg. aor. act. subjunc. of λέγω, "say"; subjunc. in a 3rd class cond. clause; on ἴδε, see 1:2; on the freq. omission of the 3rd pers. sg. form ἐστίν in exclamations, see BDF §127 (omitting "is" in such expressions is less common in Eng.). The prohibition "do not believe" (μή plus πιστεύετε [2nd pl. pres. act. impv. of πιστεύω, "believe"]) implies but does not state a dir. obj. Translations offer one of two options:

   1. "Do not believe it," i.e., what is being claimed (e.g., NIV; NRSV; ESV).
   *2. "Do not believe him," i.e., anyone making such a claim (e.g., NASB; NET; cf. KJV).

The difference is perhaps negligible, but the closest par. in Mark's Gospel (in 11:31) uses αὐτῷ (which in context likely means "him") as the dir. obj. after οὐκ ἐπιστεύσατε, with "him" referring to John the Baptist.

13:22 Ἐγερθήσονται, 3rd pl. fut. pass. indic. of ἐγείρω, "appear" (act. intrans. mng. with pass. when used with reference to prophets; BDAG 272b); ψευδόχριστοι, nom. pl. masc. of ψευδόχριστος, -ου, ὁ, "false messiah"; ψευδοπροφῆται, nom. pl. masc. of ψευδοπροφήτης, -ου, ὁ, "false prophet"; δώσουσιν, 3rd pl. fut. act. indic. of δίδωμι, "produce, cause to appear, give" (BDAG 242c; cf. Acts 2:19); τέρατα, acc. pl. neut. of τέρας, -ατος, τό, "wonder, omen, portent"; ἀποπλανᾶν, pres. act. inf. of ἀποπλανάω, "mislead"; inf. of purpose; ἐκλεκτούς, acc. pl. masc. of ἐκλεκτός, -ή, -όν, "chosen, elect"; subst. adj. Normally the aor. tense is used with an inf. of purpose in Mark and not the pres. tense, as is the case with ἀποπλανᾶν (see 1:24; 3:15). In addition, while this is the only example of πρὸς τό plus an inf. in Mark, within the NT as a whole an aor. inf. more often follows πρὸς τό than a pres. inf. (cf. R 891; eight out of the twelve examples are aor.; moreover, the use of the pres. inf. δεῖν in Luke 18:1 and Acts 26:9 and the pres. inf. δύνασθαι in Eph 6:11 may be lexically determined and so less significant). Therefore, the use of the pres. tense with ἀποπλανᾶν is unusual and likely intended to emphasize the ongoing danger of deception for the elect (prog. pres.). The added 1st class cond. clause εἰ δυνατόν reflects the perspective of the deceivers; they are making every effort to see if it is possible to mislead the elect, and they are hoping that indeed it is.

13:23 Jesus finishes his predictions concerning the intensified difficulties at the end of the age by repeating his command to watch out. Βλέπετε, 2nd pl. pres. act. impv. of βλέπω, "watch out, beware" (BDAG 179c; on ὑμεῖς with the impv., see 13:9); προείρηκα, 1st sg. pf. act. indic. of προλέγω, "tell beforehand, warn."

(iv) The Coming of the Son of Man (13:24–27)

13:24 Two prep. phrases at the beginning of v. 24 tie the coming of the Son of Man to the time of the tribulation without any delay. The events that Jesus will predict next take place "in those days" (ἐν ἐκείναις ταῖς ἡμέραις), i.e., the days of tribulation that immediately follow the abomination of desolation (see the references to "those days" in 13:17, 19). In addition, they take place "after that tribulation" (μετὰ τὴν θλῖψιν ἐκείνην), i.e., at the end of the great suffering that belongs to those days. Σκοτισθήσεται, 3rd sg. fut. pass. indic. of σκοτίζω, "become dark, be darkened" (mng. with pass.); σελήνη, nom. sg. fem. of σελήνη, -ης, ἡ, "moon"; δώσει, 3rd sg. fut. act. indic. of δίδωμι, "give, produce" (BDAG 242c); φέγγος, acc. sg. neut. of φέγγος, -ους, τό, "light, radiance."

13:25 Ἀστέρες, nom. pl. masc. of ἀστήρ, -έρος, ὁ, "star"; ἔσονται, 3rd pl. fut. mid. indic. of εἰμί, "be" (dep. in fut.); πίπτοντες, nom. pl. masc. of pres. act. ptc. of πίπτω, "fall"; periph. ptc. As noted concerning the fut. periph. cstr. in 13:13, the fut. tense of εἰμί points to the time of the action, while the pres. tense of the ptc. portrays the action as in process. The fut. periph. cstr. in 13:25 differs from the one in 13:13 in that the voice of the ptc. is act. rather than pass. Therefore, unlike the cstr. in 13:13 that conveys a fut. ongoing state, the fut. periph. ptc. in 13:25 vividly portrays the falling of the stars as an action in progress in the future (cf. Fanning 318). In light of the par. in v. 25, the reference to "the powers" probably serves as a poetic synonym for the stars (cf. France 532). The 2nd use of the art. αἱ indicates that the prep. phrase is functioning adj. to modify δυνάμεις (cf. 6:11; 11:2, 25; 15:43). Σαλευθήσονται, 3rd pl. fut. pass. indic. of σαλεύω, "shake, cause to totter."

13:26 Ὄψονται, 3rd pl. fut. mid. indic. of ὁράω, "see" (dep. in fut.). A common grammatical feature in Mark is the use of indef. 3rd pers. pl. vbs., indef. in the sense that no subj. is stated or implied beyond the general sense of "people" (see 1:22). In the context of Jesus's eschatological discourse, the "they" who will see the coming of the Son of Man is a broader group than the "you" whom Jesus has been addressing throughout the discourse or the "elect" mentioned in the following verse (cf. also 14:62 where the coming of the Son of Man will be visible to Jesus's opponents). Ἐρχόμενον, acc. sg. masc. of pres. mid. ptc. of dep. ἔρχομαι, "come"; supplementary (complementary) ptc. (on ἐν with a form of ἔρχομαι, see 5:27); νεφέλαις, dat. pl. fem. of νεφέλη, -ης, ἡ, "cloud."

Jesus's words about the Son of Man in 13:26 allude to Dan 7:13–14, where one like a son of man is coming with the clouds of heaven to receive from the Ancient of Days an eternal kingdom (on "the Son of Man," see 2:10; 8:31). This allusion to Daniel 7 helps explain the consistent pattern in Mark's Gospel in which every reference to the Son of Man includes the art. (either ὁ υἱὸς τοῦ ἀνθρώπου or τὸν υἱὸν τοῦ ἀνθρώπου). The use of an art. not only with υἱός but also with the gen. ἀνθρώπου is the normal Gk. idiom, since, with gen. phrases in Gk., the head noun and the gen. noun usually both have an art. or both lack an art. (on Apollonius' Canon, see Wallace 239–40; KMP 161–62). Therefore, there is no special significance to the art. before the gen. ἀνθρώπου; the significant point is simply that the phrase as a whole is def. rather than indef. (see C. F. D. Moule, "Neglected Features in the Problem of 'the Son of Man,'" in *Essays in New Testament Interpretation* [Cambridge: Cambridge University Press, 1982], 82–83; C. F. D. Moule, "The 'Son of Man': Some of the Facts," *NTS* 41 [1995]: 277). Grammatically, the best explanation for the use of the art. in the phrase "the Son of Man" is that the art. points to a figure that is well-known, i.e., the figure in Daniel 7 (Wallace 240; cf. 225; Moule, "Neglected Feature," 77; Moule, "Some of the Facts," 277–78). By using the title "the Son of Man" for himself, Jesus portrays himself as the representative for God's people who will come to receive an eternal kingdom and rule over all nations and people, so that all the kingdoms under heaven might be given over to the people of God (Dan 7:13–14, 27).

13:27 Ἀποστελεῖ, 3rd sg. fut. act. indic. of ἀποστέλλω, "send"; ἐπισυνάξει, 3rd sg. fut. act. indic. of ἐπισυνάγω, "gather together"; ἐκλεκτούς, acc. pl. masc. of ἐκλεκτός, -ή, -όν, "chosen, elect"; ἐκ τῶν τεσσάρων ἀνέμων, "from the four winds" (i.e., from all directions; Decker 2:162; cf. BDAG 77b); ἕως, used as a prep. taking a gen. obj.; ἄκρου, gen. sg. neut. of ἄκρον, -ου, τό, "extreme limit, end." Elsewhere ἄκρον is used for the very top of a lofty mountain (LXX Isa 28:4) or for the very tip of a finger (Luke 16:24). The angels gather together the elect from the very farthest limits of heaven and earth.

HOMILETICAL SUGGESTIONS

What Will the End of the Age Be Like? (13:14–27)

1. The final hardships (13:14–23)
    a. Intensified rebellion (13:14)
    b. Intensified suffering (13:15–20)
    c. Intensified deception (13:21–23)
2. The final hope (13:24–27)
    a. Jesus's coming will be powerful.

b. Jesus's coming will be visible.

c. Jesus's coming will be rescuing.

(v) Warnings to Be Ready (13:28–37)

13:28 At the end of the eschatological discourse, Mark appends a series of largely independent parables and sayings, linking them together through a catchword pattern (cf. Taylor 519–20; Hooker 320; Brooks 216; see 9:38 and 11:23 concerning the same organizational pattern elsewhere in Mark). Therefore, 13:5–27 offers Jesus's immediate answer to the disciples' questions in 13:4, but then Mark attaches parables and sayings from Jesus that connect back to that initial answer and with one another through catchwords (see, e.g., how ὅταν ἴδητε in 13:29 links back to ὅταν . . . ἴδητε in 13:14; ταῦτα . . . γένηται in 13:30 back to ταῦτα γινόμενα in 13:29; and παρελεύσονται in 13:31 back to παρέλθῃ in 13:30). In light of this catchword pattern, it is unlikely that 13:28–37 should be read as a sustained and unified argument or as a direct answer to the questions posed by the disciples back in 13:4. Instead, the parables and sayings in 13:28–37 should be understood individually as part of Jesus's overall teaching on the future.

Συκῆς, gen. sg. fem. of συκῆ, -ῆς, ἡ, "fig tree"; μάθετε, 2nd pl. aor. act. impv. μανθάνω, "learn" (on the aor. impv. μάθετε, see 13:5). The indef. temp. conj. ὅταν conveys contingency and the adv. ἤδη anticipates completion, so that together they express "as soon as" (cf. Decker 2:163). Κλάδος, nom. sg. masc. of κλάδος, -ου, ὁ, "branch"; ἁπαλός, nom. sg. masc. of ἁπαλός, -ή, -όν, "tender"; pred. adj.; γένηται, 3rd sg. aor. mid. subjunc. of dep. γίνομαι, "become"; subjunc. in an indef. temp. clause; ἐκφύῃ, 3rd sg. pres. act. subjunc. of ἐκφύω, "put forth, cause to grow"; φύλλα, acc. pl. neut. of φύλλον, -ου, τό, "leaf." The vb. ἐκφύῃ serves as an example of how the accent can make a difference in mng. (R 232; BDAG 312b–c). If the vb. is accented as ἐκφύῃ, it is a pres. act. subjunc. form with a trans. mng., and φύλλα functions as the neut. acc. dir. obj.—the fig tree puts forth leaves (cf., e.g., NA[28]; UBS[5]). If the vb. is accented as ἐκφυῇ, it is a 2nd aor. pass. subjunc. form with an intrans. mng., and φύλλα functions as a neut. nom. pl. subj. with a sg. vb.—the leaves sprout (cf. e.g., NIV; NLT). Although the difference in mng. is probably insignificant, the benefit in accenting ἐκφύῃ as a pres. act. subjunc. is that it does not unnecessarily force a change in the subj. and allows ὁ κλάδος to serve as the subj. of both γένηται and ἐκφύῃ (Swete 314; Cranfield 407). Θέρος, nom. sg. neut. of θέρος, -ους, τό, "summer."

13:29 Ἴδητε, 2nd pl. aor. act. subjunc. of ὁράω, "see"; subjunc. in an indef. temp. clause; γινόμενα, acc. pl. neut. of pres. mid. ptc. of dep. γίνομαι, "come to be, take place, happen"; supplementary (complementary) ptc.; γινώσκετε, 2nd pl. pres. act. impv. of γινώσκω, "know." The vb. in the main clause, γινώσκετε, can be either indic. (NIV; NRSV; ESV) or impv. (NASB; NET; CSB). The extended teaching in 13:28–37 both begins and ends with a parable, with the parable of the fig tree at the beginning and the parable of the master's return at the end. Both parables conclude with the lesson to be learned—expressed in the final parable with γρηγορεῖτε οὖν (13:35), which functions more transparently as an impv. Therefore, the lesson for the initial parable is also likely a command. The nom. pers. pron. ὑμεῖς, which is grammatically unnecessary in light of the ending of γινώσκετε, highlights the subj. in a way that draws attention to the command and emphasizes its importance (cf. 13:9, 23). Since Eng. normally states the subj. "you" with an indic. vb. but not with an impv. vb., it may be wise to omit translating ὑμεῖς in order to make it clear that "know" in this context is an impv. (cf. CSB). Ἐπί with the dat.: "at" (expressing immediate proximity; BDAG 363d); on the pl. of θύρα with a sg. sense in fixed idioms, see T 27 (cf. Jas 5:9).

13:30 On ἀμὴν λέγω ὑμῖν, see 3:28; παρέλθῃ, 3rd sg. aor. act. subjunc. of παρέρχομαι, "pass away"; emph. neg. subjunc. (on the emph. neg. subjunc., see 9:1; 13:2). The phrase "this generation" (ἡ γενεὰ αὕτη) potentially has both a moral and a temporal connotation (cf. *NIDNTT* 2:36; David K. Lowery, "Matthew," in *The Bible Knowledge Key Word Study: The Gospels*, ed. Darrell L. Bock [Colorado Springs: Victor, 2002], 98, 100; Susan M. Rieske, "What Is the Meaning of 'This Generation' in Matthew 23:36," *BSac* 165 [2008]: 209–26), but in Mark's Gospel the moral aspect of the phrase is certainly primary—"this generation" conveys the idea of "this evil generation" (for more on "this generation," see 8:12). In Mark's Gospel, "this generation" is a pejorative label, a metaphorical expression used to refer to a sinful and unbelieving class of people who are destined for the judgment of God (for the same point with regard to Matthew's Gospel, see Nelson, "'This Generation' in Matt 24:34," 369–85). In 13:30, the vb. παρέρχομαι conveys the idea of passing away, coming to an end, or perishing (*TDNT* 2:682). This (evil) generation, the class of people who stubbornly refuse to believe and who therefore rebel against God, will continue on until the end of the age and only then will come to an end. Most often, μέχρι (which can take the spelling μέχρις when the next word begins with a vowel [BDAG 644b]) functions as a prep. with an obj. in the gen. case, but it can also serve as a conj. mng. "until" (Eph 4:13). In a similar way, μέχρις οὗ can function like a conj. mng. "until" (Mark 13:30; Gal 4:19; cf. BDAG 644c), although the phrase is probably an abbreviation for μέχρις τοῦ χρόνου ᾧ ("until the time in which") and therefore μέχρις in 13:30 is still technically acting as a prep. (Harris 248). Γένηται, 3rd sg. aor. mid. subjunc. of dep. γίνομαι, "come to be, take place, happen"; subjunc. in an indef. temp. clause (sg. vb. with neut. pl. subj. [see 3:11]).

13:31 Παρελεύσονται, 3rd pl. fut. mid. indic. of dep. παρέρχομαι, "pass away." The normal pattern in Mark for expressing emph. neg. is οὐ μή plus an aor. subjunc. vb. (see 9:1), but twice in Mark the pattern changes to οὐ μή plus a fut. indic. vb. (13:31; 14:31). Both the cstr. with the aor. subjunc. and the cstr. with the fut. indic. have the same force, a decisive denial that a particular event will take place in the future (ZG 153; Wallace 468).

13:32 In the context of the eschatological discourse as a whole, the phrase "that day or hour" seems to refer to the time of the culminating event at the end of the age, the coming of the Son of Man. Indeed, this is the one event described in the eschatological discourse in which the angels, Jesus as the Son, and the Father actively participate—the Son of Man will come with the holy angels in the glory of the Father (13:26–27; cf. 8:38). No one knows (οἶδεν, 3rd sg. pf. act. indic. of οἶδα, "know"; on οἶδα, see 1:24) when the Son of Man will come, not even the angels in heaven nor the Son but only the Father (for οὐδεὶς . . . οὐδὲ . . . οὐδέ as "no one . . . not even . . . nor," cf. BDAG 735a; on εἰ μή as "but only," see Z §470; Turner, *Style* 13, 92).

13:33 For the fourth time now in the eschatological discourse, Jesus commands his followers to "watch out" (see 13:5, 9, 23, 33). Βλέπετε, 2nd pl. pres. act. impv. of βλέπω, "watch out, beware" (BDAG 179c); ἀγρυπνεῖτε, 2nd pl. pres. act. impv. of ἀγρυπνέω, "stay alert, be alert." A significant number of mss. add another command with the words καὶ προσεύχεσθε ("and pray"). However, the words are probably not orig., since it is easier to account for their addition by copyists who were familiar with Jesus's commands in 14:38 to "watch and pray" than to explain their omission in mss. such as B and D (Metzger 95; Brooks 218; Stein 626). Οἴδατε, 2nd pl. pf. act. indic. of οἶδα, "know"; πότε, "when" (interr. adv. introducing an indir. question [BDAG 856c; R 1176–77]).

13:34 At times in Mark, ὡς can follow a form of εἰμί and introduce an entire clause that functions as a pred. adj. (6:34; 12:25; cf. BDAG 1104c). In 13:34, the form of εἰμί is implied rather than stated (ὡς, "it is like"). Ἀπόδημος, nom. sg. masc. of ἀπόδημος, -ον, "away on a journey"; ἀφείς, nom. sg. masc. of aor. act. ptc. of ἀφίημι, "leave, depart from"; adj. ptc. (without an art. to modify an anar. noun); δούς, nom. sg. masc. of aor. act. ptc. of δίδωμι, "give"; adj. ptc.; ἔργον, "assigned task, specific work assignment"(LN 42.42; cf. NIV). The noun ἔργον stands in appos. to ἐξουσίαν, clarifying the nature of the authority given to the slaves ("who gave to his slaves authority, to each one his assigned task"). Θυρωρῷ, dat. sg. masc. of θυρωρός, -οῦ, ὁ, "doorkeeper"; ἐνετείλατο, 3rd sg. aor. mid. indic. of dep. ἐντέλλομαι, "command"; γρηγορῇ, 3rd sg. pres. act. subjunc. of γρηγορέω, "keep watch, stay alert"; subjunc. in a dir. obj. ἵνα clause (equivalent to an inf. of indir. discourse [see 5:10]).

13:35 Γρηγορεῖτε, 2nd pl. pres. act. impv. of γρηγορέω, "keep watch, stay alert." The vb. γρηγορέω was newly formed in the Hellenistic period, built from ἐγρήγορα, the pf. tense form of ἐγείρω, thus conveying in part the state of wakefulness (BDAG 207d; R 65, 148, 351; BDF §73; during the same period the vb. στήκω was formed from ἕστηκα, the pf. form of ἵστημι [3:31; 11:25]). Yet the vb. γρηγορέω came to denote more than simply staying awake, emphasizing also the need to remain alert, vigilant, or watchful (Decker 2:168). Οἴδατε, 2nd pl. pf. act. indic. of οἶδα, "know"; πότε, introduces an indir. question (see 13:33); ἔρχεται, 3rd sg. pres. mid. indic. of dep. ἔρχομαι, "come"; futuristic pres. (see Wallace 535–36; KMP 262–63); ἤ . . . ἤ, "whether . . . or"; ὀψέ, adv. mng. "in the evening"; μεσονύκτιον, acc. sg. neut. of μεσονύκτιον, -ου, τό, "midnight" (an acc. of time that is functioning like a dat. of time to indicate a temporal point: "at midnight" [cf. BDAG 634c; R 469–71]); ἀλεκτοροφωνίας, gen. sg. fem. of ἀλεκτοροφωνία, -ας, ἡ, "crowing of a rooster, cockcrow" (a gen. of time that is also functioning like a dat. of time: "at cockcrow" [cf. BDAG 41d; BDF §186; R 471; T 235]); πρωΐ, adv. mng. "early in the morning."

13:36 In 13:36, μή functions as a conj. that introduces a neg. purpose clause with a subjunc. vb. ("lest, so that . . . not" [BDAG 646b; ZG 153; Decker 2:169]). As a subordinating conj., μή depends on the impv. γρηγορεῖτε in the previous verse and explains why believers must continue to keep watch—so that, if the master of the house comes suddenly, he might not find them sleeping. Ἐλθών, nom. sg. masc. of aor. act. ptc. of ἔρχομαι, "come"; cond. adv. ptc. (cf. NIV; Decker 2:169); ἐξαίφνης, adv. mng. "suddenly, unexpectedly"; εὕρῃ, 3rd sg. aor. act. subjunc. of εὑρίσκω, "find"; καθεύδοντας, acc. pl. masc. of pres. act. ptc. of καθεύδω, "sleep"; adj. ptc. functioning as a complement in a dbl. acc. obj. complement cstr. (cf. Decker 2:169).

13:37 Since the rel. pron. ὅ does not have an antecedent, it can be translated as "what," so that the entire rel. clause ("what I say to you") can function as the dir. obj. of the 2nd λέγω in the verse (see 2:24). Γρηγορεῖτε, 2nd pl. pres. act. impv. of γρηγορέω, "keep watch, stay alert."

FOR FURTHER STUDY

31. The Eschatological Discourse in Mark

Adams, Edward. "The Coming of the Son of Man in Mark's Gospel." *TynBul* 56.2 (2005): 39–61.

Allison, Dale C. "Jesus and the Victory of Apocalyptic." Pages 126–41 in *Jesus and the Restoration of Israel: A Critical Assessment of N. T. Wright's* Jesus and the Victory of God. Edited by Carey C. Newman. Downers Grove, IL: IVP Academic, 1999.

Beasley-Murray, George R. *Jesus and the Last Days: The Interpretation of the Olivet Discourse*. Peabody, MA: Hendrickson, 1993.

France, R. T. "The Reference of Mark 13:24–27." Pages 227–39 in *Jesus and the Old Testament: His Application of Old Testament Passages to Himself and His Mission*. London: Tyndale, 1971.

Geddert, Timothy J. *Watchwords: Mark 13 in Markan Eschatology*. JSNTSup 26. Sheffield, UK: Sheffield Academic Press, 1989.

Hartman, Lars. *Prophecy Interpreted: The Formation of Some Jewish Apocalyptic Texts and of the Eschatological Discourse Mark 13 Par.* ConBNT 1. Lund: Gleerup, 1966.

Juel, Donald H. "Watching and Weariness: The So-Called Markan Apocalypse." Pages 77–88 in *A Master of Surprise: Mark Interpreted*. Minneapolis: Fortress, 1994.

Köstenberger, Andreas J., Alexander E. Stewart, and Apollo Makara. *Jesus and the Future: Understanding What He Taught about the End Times*. Bellingham, WA: Lexham Press, 2017.

Marxsen, Willi. "Mark 13." Pages 151–206 in *Mark the Evangelist: Studies on the Redaction History of the Gospel*. Nashville: Abingdon, 1969.

*Stein, Robert H. *Jesus, the Temple and the Coming Son of Man: A Commentary on Mark 13*. Downers Grove, IL: IVP Academic, 2014.

Wright, N. T. "Stories of the Kingdom (3): Judgment and Vindication." Pages 320–68 in *Jesus and the Victory of God*. Minneapolis: Fortress, 1996.

Yarbro Collins, Adela. "Mark 13: An Apocalyptic Discourse." Pages 73–91 in *The Beginning of the Gospel: Probings of Mark in Context*. Minneapolis: Fortress, 1992.

———. "The Apocalyptic Rhetoric of Mark 13 in Historical Context." *BR* 41 (1996): 5–36.

HOMILETICAL SUGGESTIONS

Four Warnings to Watch Out (13:5–37)

1. Watch out! Be faithful in the midst of deception (because false teaching is part of the present age). (13:5)
2. Watch out! Be faithful in the midst of persecution (because opposition is part of the present age). (13:9)
3. Watch out! Be prepared for increased deception and persecution (because even greater suffering may come suddenly, and we do not know when). (13:23)
4. Watch out! Be prepared for the coming of Jesus (because Jesus may come suddenly and we do not know when). (13:33)

Two Parables: Ready to Be Ready (13:28–37)

1. The parable of the fig tree: Always be ready, because the end will come with a swift conclusion. (13:28–29)
2. The parable of the master's return: Always be ready, because Jesus could come at any time. (13:33–37)

C. JESUS'S DEATH AND RESURRECTION IN JERUSALEM (14:1–16:8)

The passion narrative—the account of Jesus's suffering, death, and resurrection—does not have a clear, unifying setting. All of the events take place in and around Jerusalem, but the city itself is hardly mentioned (see only 15:41). Instead of making Jerusalem a clear defining setting for the events in chs. 14–16, Mark uses a series of settings: in Bethany, at the home of Simon the leper (14:3); a large upstairs room (14:15); the Mount of Olives (14:26); Gethsemane (14:32); the home of the high priest (14:53–54); the palace (15:16); Golgatha, the Place of the Skull (15:22); and the tomb (15:46; 16:2). In a sense, all of these settings move Jesus toward the cross or away from it after his death.

In comparison to the rest of Mark's Gospel, the passion narrative is less episodic and reads more like a smoothly connected narrative with each event leading naturally into the next. The passion narrative, therefore, is a series of interconnected events: the anointing at Bethany intertwined with the plot to betray Jesus (14:1–11); Jesus's last supper with his disciples (14:12–25); Jesus's prayer and arrest in Gethsemane (14:26–52); Jesus's trial before the Sanhedrin, intertwined with the description of Peter's denials (14:53–72); Jesus's trial before Pilate, followed by the soldiers' mocking of Jesus (15:1–20); the crucifixion and burial (15:21–47), and finally Jesus's resurrection and the discovery of the empty tomb (16:1–8). These changing events take place in rough correspondence with changes in specific settings.

The passion narrative brings resolution to the two prominent plotlines in Mark's Gospel. Mark's portrayal of the disciples shifts in some new directions in ch. 14. First, Mark splits off the story line of Judas from that of the rest of the disciples. Judas turns into a traitor, handing Jesus over to the religious leaders for money (14:10–11, 43–46). Second, Mark shows the rest of the disciples moving from misunderstanding to failure through their flight at the time of Jesus's arrest (14:50) and through Peter's denials (14:66–72). The narrative concerning the disciples ends with Peter weeping. Although the disciples are referred to later, they never again appear in the remaining narrative. Their story is left off at the point where it illustrates the disastrous results of failing to count the cost of devotion to Jesus.

The resolution of the plotline with regard to the religious leaders creates an ironic ending. In Gethsemane, Jesus bows to the will of the Father; he will give his life for others (14:35–40; cf. 10:45). Then most of the passion narrative details how the religious leaders go about fulfilling their desire to destroy Jesus (14:1–2; cf. 3:6; 11:18). The result is a deeply ironic story in which the religious leaders help to fulfill the will of the Father through their own malicious schemes. This irony is clear in the series of mocking scenes in which Jesus is ridiculed (14:65; 15:16–20, 29–32). For those who reject Jesus, it is preposterous that he could be a prophet or the king of Israel or the Messiah who saves. In a sense, the resurrection is God's answer to the religious leaders. They were wrong about Jesus's identity and about their own ability to destroy him, because God has overcome the death of his Messiah with resurrected life.

1. Anointing at Bethany and Betrayal Plot (14:1–11)

14:1 Mark holds together in a single passage the plot to kill Jesus and the account of Jesus's anointing in Bethany (on Mark's sandwich technique, see 3:22), in this way highlighting both the devotion of the woman who anoints Jesus and the treachery of the religious leaders and Judas. Ἦν, 3rd sg. impf. act. indic. of εἰμί, "be" (sg. vb. with compound subj. [see 12:33]). At times, in light of some temporal indication in the context, an impf. tense (such as ἦν) can be used to point to an action that is about to take place (cf. ἐπέφωσκεν in Luke 23:54; see BDF §323, where this use of the impf. is regarded as analogous to a futuristic pres. [cf. Swete 319; Cranfield 413]). The word πάσχα can refer to the Passover festival (as here in 14:1), the Passover lamb (14:12), or the Passover meal (14:12, 14, 16; BDAG 784c–d). Ἄζυμα, nom. pl. neut. of ἄζυμος, -ον, "unleavened" (although the subst. use of the adj. with the neut. pl. indicates "the Festival of Unleavened Bread" [BDAG 23a]; names of feasts and other days of celebration often appear in the pl. [R 408; T 26–27; Taylor 528; cf. 6:21]); ἐζήτουν, 3rd pl. impf. act. indic. of ζητέω, "seek" (impf. for background information [see 1:21]; cf. ἔλεγον in 14:2); κρατήσαντες, nom. pl. masc. of aor. act. ptc. of κρατέω, "seize, arrest"; attendant circumstance ptc.; ἐν, "by" (manner; see Z §117; cf. 9:1); δόλῳ, dat. sg. masc. of δόλος, -ου, ὁ, "deceit, stealth, cunning"; ἀποκτείνωσιν, 3rd pl. pres. or aor. act. subjunc. of ἀποκτείνω, "kill, put to death" (on the retention of the delib. subjunc. in an indir. question, cf. Z §348; BDAG 901c; see 9:6).

14:2 The subj. of ἔλεγον (3rd pl. impf. act. indic. of λέγω, "say") is not directly stated in the context. However, Mark's Gospel frequently uses indef. pl. vbs., where the unexpressed subj. of the vb. is simply the general idea of "some people" (see 1:22; cf. ἔλεγον as an indef. pl. vb. in 3:21). Some indef. group of people—perhaps a subgroup of the chief priests and scribes or a group of advisors to the religious leaders—were giving their counsel about what should or should not be done with Jesus (cf. Z §§3, 5; C. H. Turner, "Marcan Usage: Notes, Critical and Exegetical, on the Second Gospel," *JTS* 25 [1924]: 384–85). Ἐν, "during" (temp.); ἑορτῇ, dat. sg. fem. of ἑορτή, -ῆς, ἡ, "festival." The verbless clause μὴ ἐν τῇ ἑορτῇ apparently assumes a form of κρατέω, based on the preceding verse, likely an aor. subjunc. form expressing prohibition in light of the use of the neg. μή (BDF §481; Decker 2:171). Μήποτε, "lest, in order that . . . not" (conj. indicating a negated purpose; BDAG 648c–d). When used as a conj., μήποτε most often introduces a clause with an aor. subjunc. vb. (cf. 4:12), but it can also use a fut. indic. vb. with no clear difference in mng. (cf. esp. Matt 7:6, which uses both). Ἔσται, 3rd sg. fut. mid. indic. of εἰμί, "be" (dep. in fut.; impers. use of εἰμί [Decker 2:171]); θόρυβος, nom. sg. masc. of θόρυβος, -ου, ὁ, "riot, uproar, turmoil"; λαοῦ, subj. gen.

14:3 Ὄντος, gen. sg. masc. of pres. act. ptc. of εἰμί, "be"; gen. abs., temp. adv. ptc. contemp.; λεπροῦ, gen. sg. masc. of λεπρός, -οῦ, ὁ, "leper, person with a bad skin disease" (λεπρός is technically an adj. that normally functions as a subst., BDAG 592c–d); κατακειμένου, gen. sg. masc. of pres. mid. ptc. of dep. κατάκειμαι, "recline for a meal, recline at the table, dine"; temp. adv. ptc. contemp.; ἦλθεν, 3rd sg. aor. act. indic. of ἔρχομαι, "come"; ἔχουσα, nom. sg. fem. of pres. act. ptc. of ἔχω, "have"; adj. ptc. (without an art. to modify an anar. noun). At times, a ptc. form of ἔχω conveys the same sense as the prep. "with," since both can introduce what is in someone's possession (R 1127; T 154). Ἀλάβαστρον, acc. sg. fem. of ἀλάβαστρος, -ου, ἡ, "alabaster jar, jar made of alabaster stone, jar made of valuable stone" (LN 6.131; both uses of ἀλάβαστρον in 14:3 are likely 2nd decl. fem. forms [cf. NA²⁸]; on the gender of ἀλάβαστρος, see BDAG 40d; BDF §49); μύρου, gen. sg. neut. of μύρον, -ου, τό, "perfume, ointment." The four gen. words following ἀλάβαστρον (μύρου νάρδου πιστικῆς πολυτελοῦς) all modify a preceding word in some way. The alabaster jar contains perfume (μύρου, gen. of content), while the perfume is made out of nard (νάρδου, gen. sg. fem. of νάρδος, -ου, ἡ, "nard, oil of nard, a sweet-smelling oil called nard" [cf. LN 6.210]; gen. of material). The following two gen. words are both adjectives, both apparently fem., and therefore both modifying νάρδου—"pure and very expensive nard" (πιστικῆς, gen. sg. fem. of πιστικός, -ή, -όν, "genuine, pure" [on the mng. of πιστικός, see Spicq 3:108–9, where he argues that it derives from πιστός]; πολυτελοῦς, gen. fem. sg. of πολυτελής, -ές, "very expensive, very costly"). The SBLGNT—probably correctly—makes a grammatical break after πολυτελοῦς, indicating the start of a new thought with συντρίψασα (cf. France 552). Συντρίψασα, nom. sg. fem. of aor. act. ptc. of συντρίβω, "break, break open"; temp. adv. ptc. antecedent; κατέχεεν, 3rd sg. aor. act. indic. of καταχέω, "pour out on, pour down over" (καταχέω takes a gen. dir. obj. in light of the prep. prefix κατά [R 511–12; BDF §181; cf. BDAG 529d–530a]).

14:4 Ἦσαν, 3rd pl. impf. act. indic. of εἰμί, "be"; ἀγανακτοῦντες, nom. pl. masc. of pres. act. ptc. of ἀγανακτέω, "express one's indignation, express one's displeasure"; periph. ptc. In Mark, an impf. periph. cstr. can leave the impression that the action was continuing on for some time (see 1:22), in this case communicating at the very least that the complaint went on long enough to create noticeable trouble for the woman and to call for a necessary rebuke from Jesus (14:6). On ἑαυτούς as an equivalent to ἀλλήλους, see 1:27; εἰς τί, "why?" (BDAG 290d; see also 15:34); ἀπώλεια, nom. sg. fem. of ἀπώλεια, -ας, ἡ, waste (i.e., a destructive act that demonstrates a complete disregard for the value of something; cf. LN 65.14); μύρου, gen. sg. neut. of μύρον, -ου, τό, "perfume, ointment"; γέγονεν, 3rd sg. pf. act. indic. of γίνομαι, "come to be, take place, happen."

14:5 Ἠδύνατο, 3rd sg. impf. mid. indic. of dep. δύναμαι, "be able to, can"; μύρον, nom. sg. neut. of μύρον, -ου, τό, "perfume, ointment"; πραθῆναι, aor. pass. inf. of πιπράσκω, "sell"; complementary inf.; ἐπάνω, adv. mng. "more than" (cf. BDAG 359b–c); δηναρίων, gen. pl. neut. of δηνάριον, -ου, τό, "denarius"; τριακοσίων, gen. pl. neut. of τριακόσιοι, -αι, -α, "three hundred." The phrase δηναρίων τριακοσίων is functioning as a gen. of price (Wallace 122; KMP 103; Swete 323). Although ἐπάνω often serves as an improper prep. followed by the gen., in this verse ἐπάνω is simply an adv. modifying the phrase δηναρίων τριακοσίων, which is also adv. ("for more than three hundred denarii" [R 511, 674; Harris 246; Cranfield 416]). Δοθῆναι, aor. pass. inf. of δίδωμι, "give"; complementary inf.; ἐνεβριμῶντο, 3rd pl. impf. mid. indic. of dep. ἐμβριμάομαι, "scold, denounce harshly" (LN 33.421; BDAG 322a–b; on ἐμβριμάομαι, see 1:43; impf. used to portray an action in a vivid way as in progress [see 1:21]); αὐτῇ, dat. dir. obj.

14:6 Ἄφετε, 2nd pl. aor. act. impv. of ἀφίημι, "let be, leave alone"; τί, "why?" (see 2:7); κόπους, acc. pl. masc. of κόπος, -ου, ὁ, "difficulty, trouble"; παρέχετε, from παρέχω, "cause, make happen" (κόπους παρέχειν, "to cause trouble, bother" [see BDAG 558d]); αὐτῇ, dat. of interest (disadvantage); ἠργάσατο, 3rd sg. aor. mid. indic. of dep. ἐργάζομαι, "do, accomplish, carry out" (BDAG 389c). The prep. phrase ἐν ἐμοί serves as an example of a place where ἐν with the dat. stands in for the simple dat. to convey a dat. of interest expressing advantage (T 264).

14:7 Ἑαυτῶν, "you" (on ἑαυτῶν as the 2nd pers. pl. refl. pron., see 13:9; on the translation of the refl. pron. as a pers. pron. after μετά, see 8:14); θέλητε, 2nd pl. pres. act. subjunc. of θέλω, "want, wish"; subjunc. in an indef. temp. clause; δύνασθε, 2nd pl. pres. mid. indic. of dep. δύναμαι, "be able to, can"; αὐτοῖς, dat. of interest (advantage); εὖ, adv. mng. "well"; ποιῆσαι, aor. act. inf. of ποιέω, "do"; complementary inf. (the phrase εὖ ποιῆσαι means "to do good, to show kindness" [BDAG 401d]). One type of futuristic pres. is similar to the gnomic pres. in that it states a general truth in a proverbial way. However, in contrast to the gnomic pres., this kind of futuristic pres. tense focuses attention on the outworking of the general principle within a fut. setting (Fanning 224–25); i.e., both instances of ἔχετε in v. 7 use the pres. tense but point to the fut., i.e., to fut. opportunities to care for the poor and to the fut. absence of Jesus (see Z §278; cf. 3:29; 2 Cor 5:1).

14:8 When a form of ἔχω is followed by an inf., the resulting translation is often "can, be able to, be in one's power to" (BDAG 421a–b; ZG 154). In v. 8, the vb. ἔσχεν implies but does not state the complementary inf. ποιῆσαι (BDAG 421b; Cranfield 417): "what [on ὅ as "what," see 2:24] she was able to do [ἔσχεν, 3rd sg. aor. act. indic. of ἔχω, "can, be able to"], she did" (ἐποίησεν, 3rd sg. aor. act. indic. of ποιέω, "do"). Technically, προέλαβεν (3rd sg. aor. act. indic. of προλαμβάνω, "anticipate, do something beforehand") is the main vb., and the following inf. (μυρίσαι, aor. act. inf. of μυρίζω, "anoint") functions subst. as the dir. obj. of the vb. However, in this case, the main vb. actually functions more like an adv., and the main verbal idea is transferred to the following inf. (R 551; T 226–27): "she anointed beforehand." Εἰς, "for" (purpose); ἐνταφιασμόν, acc. sg. masc. of ἐνταφιασμός, -οῦ, ὁ, "burial, preparation for burial."

14:9 On ἀμὴν δὲ λέγω ὑμῖν, see 3:28; ὅπου ἐάν, "wherever" (see 9:18); κηρυχθῇ, 3rd sg. aor. pass. subjunc. of κηρύσσω, "proclaim, preach"; subjunc. in an indef. rel. clause; εἰς, "in" (εἰς used for ἐν; cf. ZG 154; see 13:9); καί, adjunctive; ὅ, "what" (see 2:24); ἐποίησεν, 3rd sg. aor. act. indic. of ποιέω, "do"; λαληθήσεται, 3rd sg. fut. pass. indic. of λαλέω, "tell, proclaim, report" (cf. BDAG 582d); μνημόσυνον, acc. sg. neut. of μνημόσυνον, -ου, τό, "memory" (on εἰς μνημόσυνόν τινος as "in memory of someone," using an obj. gen., see BDAG 290d, 655d).

14:10 The purpose for the art. ὁ is to make clear that the adj. εἷς is functioning as a noun, that is, as a subst. adj. (which is followed by the partitive gen. τῶν δώδεκα), with the result that ὁ εἷς stands in appos. to Ἰούδας Ἰσκαριώθ and further clarifies the identity of Judas (Decker 2:178–79; for a similar grammatical use of the art. with εἰς in the early papyri, see MM 187). Ἀπῆλθεν, 3rd sg. aor. act. indic. of ἀπέρχομαι, "depart, go"; παραδοῖ, 3rd sg. aor. act. subjunc. of παραδίδωμι, "hand over"; subjunc. in a purpose ἵνα clause (on subjunc. forms for δίδωμι and its compounds, see 8:37; on the significance of παραδίδωμι, see 3:19).

14:11 On οἱ δέ, see 1:45; ἀκούσαντες, nom. pl. masc. of aor. act. ptc. of ἀκούω, "hear"; temp. adv. ptc. antecedent; ἐχάρησαν, 3rd pl. aor. pass. indic. of χαίρω, "rejoice, be glad" (dep. in aor.); ἐπηγγείλαντο, 3rd pl. aor. mid. indic. of dep. ἐπαγγέλλομαι, "promise"; ἀργύριον, acc. sg. neut. of ἀργύριον, -ου, τό, "money, silver money"; δοῦναι, aor. act. inf. of δίδωμι, give; inf. of indir. discourse (R 1036); ἐζήτει, 3rd sg. impf. act. indic. of ζητέω, "seek, look for"; εὐκαίρως, adv. mng. "conveniently, at an opportune time"; παραδοῖ, 3rd sg. aor. act. subjunc. of παραδίδωμι, "hand over"; delib. subjunc. Mark structures his statement about Judas at the end of 14:11 according to the same pattern he used in describing the plot of the religious leaders in 14:1: an impf. form of ζητέω followed by πῶς and a delib. subjunc. In both instances, Mark uses the impf. tense to provide background information (see 1:21), so that the continuing narrative stands under the shadow of the treacherous plan shared by the religious leaders and Judas to have Jesus arrested quietly and away from the crowd.

FOR FURTHER STUDY

32. The Passion Narrative in Mark

Best, Ernest. *The Temptation and the Passion: The Markan Soteriology.* 2nd ed. SNTSMS 2. Cambridge: Cambridge University Press, 1990.

Broadhead, Edwin K. *Prophet, Son, Messiah: Narrative Form and Function in Mark 14–16.* JSNTSup 97. Sheffield, UK: Sheffield Academic Press, 1994.

*Brown, Raymond E. *The Death of the Messiah, from Gethsemane to the Grave: A Commentary on the Passion Narratives in the Four Gospels.* 2 vols. ABRL. New York: Doubleday, 1994.

Kelber, Werner H., ed. *The Passion in Mark: Studies on Mark 14–16.* Philadelphia: Fortress, 1976.

Matera, Frank J. *The Kingship of Jesus: Composition and Theology in Mark 15.* SBLDS 66. Chico, CA: Scholars Press, 1982.

Nickelsburg, George W. E. "The Genre and Function of the Mark Passion Narrative." *HTR* 73 (1980): 153–84.

Senior, Donald. *The Passion of Jesus in the Gospel of Mark.* Collegeville, MN: Liturgical Press, 1984.

Van Oyen, Geert, and Tom Shepherd, eds. *The Trial and Death of Jesus: Essays on the Passion Narrative in Mark.* Leuven, BE: Peeters, 2006.

Williams, Joel F. "Foreshadowing, Echoes, and the Blasphemy at the Cross (Mark 15:29)." *JBL* 132 (2013): 913–33.

Yarbro Collins, Adela. "The Passion Narrative of Mark." Pages 92–118 in *The Beginning of the Gospel: Probings of Mark in Context.* Minneapolis: Fortress, 1992.

———. "From Noble Death to Crucified Messiah." *NTS* 40 (1994): 481–503.

HOMILETICAL SUGGESTIONS

An Extravagant Gift to Jesus (14:3–9)

1. What do we learn about Jesus?
   a. Jesus knows his destiny as the Messiah.
   b. Jesus knows the uniqueness of this moment in God's eternal plan.
   c. Jesus knows the deeper significance of our gifts to him.
2. What do we learn about following Jesus?
   a. We wisely give ourselves sacrificially to Jesus (because he is worthy).
   b. We wisely ignore others' opinions when we give ourselves sacrificially to Jesus (because his opinion matters most).

2. The Last Supper (14:12–25)

14:12 A significant motif in 14:12–16 and throughout ch. 14 is that Jesus is able to see what the future holds; therefore, he is taking the way of the cross, fully aware of what will happen to him. Τῇ πρώτῃ ἡμέρᾳ, "on the first day" (dat. of time [Wallace 157; KMP 130; cf. R 522]); ἀζύμων, gen. pl. neut. of ἄζυμος, -ον, "Festival of Unleavened Bread" (see 14:1); partitive gen.; τὸ πάσχα, "the Passover lamb" (see 14:1; BDAG 784d); ἔθυον, 3rd pl. impf. act. indic. of θύω, "slaughter sacrificially, sacrifice" (on indef. pl. vbs., see 1:22; customary impf. [Strauss 619; cf. NIV: "when it was customary to sacrifice"]); λέγουσιν, historical pres. (on such vbs., see 1:12; other examples include λέγουσιν in v. 12, ἀποστέλλει and λέγει in v. 13, and ἔρχεται in v. 17); ἀπελθόντες, nom. pl. masc. of aor. act. ptc. of ἀπέρχομαι, "depart, go"; attendant circumstance ptc.; ἑτοιμάσωμεν, 1st pl. aor. act. subjunc. of ἑτοιμάζω, "prepare, make preparations"; subjunc. after an implied complementary ἵνα. Whenever Mark uses a 2nd pers. form of θέλω in a question and follows it with a 1st person subjunc. vb., he implies but does not state the conj. ἵνα between the form of θέλω and the subjunc. vb. (see 10:36). This implied complementary ἵνα clause is equivalent in mng. to a complementary inf. (see Wallace 476) and is best translated that way in Eng. ("to make preparations"). As an attendant circumstance ptc., ἀπελθόντες conveys an action that is coordinate to the one expressed by ἑτοιμάσωμεν, taking on the same grammatical function as that subjunc. vb. ("to go and to make preparations"). Φάγῃς, 2nd sg. aor. act. subjunc. of ἐσθίω, "eat"; subjunc. in a purpose ἵνα clause; τὸ πάσχα, "the Passover meal" (see 14:1; cf. the same mng. in 14:14, 16).

14:13 Μαθητῶν, partitive gen.; ὑπάγετε, 2nd pl. pres. act. impv. of ὑπάγω, "go, depart" (on the pres. impv. of ὑπάγω, see 1:25; 2:11); ἀπαντήσει, 3rd sg. fut. act. indic. of ἀπαντάω, "meet"; ὑμῖν, dat. dir. obj.; κεράμιον, acc. sg. neut. of κεράμιον, -ου, τό, "earthenware vessel, jar"; ὕδατος, gen. of content (R 499); βαστάζων, nom. sg. masc. of pres. act. ptc. of βαστάζω, "carry, bear"; adj. ptc. (without an art., since it is modifying an anar. noun); ἀκολουθήσατε, 2nd pl. aor. act. impv. of ἀκολουθέω, "follow" (on the aor. impv. ἀκολουθήσατε as a specific command, see Fanning 345–46; cf. the other remaining commands in Jesus's instructions to his two disciples, which are aor. impv.

forms and specific commands [εἴπατε in v. 14 and ἑτοιμάσατε in v. 15]); αὐτῷ, dat. dir. obj.

14:14 Εἰσέλθῃ, 3rd sg. aor. act. subjunc. of εἰσέρχομαι, "go into, enter"; subjunc. in an indef. rel. clause; εἴπατε, 2nd pl. aor. act. impv. of λέγω, "say, tell"; οἰκοδεσπότῃ, dat. sg. masc. of οἰκοδεσπότης, -ου, ὁ, "master of the house, owner of the house"; ὅτι, introduces dir. discourse; κατάλυμα, nom. sg. neut. of κατάλυμα, -ατος, τό, "guest room." The vb. καταλύω, which is related to the noun κατάλυμα (see R 151), sometimes means "to halt on a journey to find lodging" (Luke 9:12; 19:7; cf. BDAG 522a–b). In an analogous way, the noun κατάλυμα refers to a guest room, a place where a traveler can find rest and lodging (cf. 1 Sam 1:18 LXX; Jer 14:8 LXX; Let. Arist. 181), and in this case a room where Jesus and his disciples can share a meal. Φάγω, 1st sg. aor. act. subjunc. of ἐσθίω, "eat"; delib. subjunc. (R 955, 960, 969).

14:15 Δείξει, 3rd sg. fut. act. indic. of δείκνυμι, "show"; ἀνάγαιον, acc. sg. neut. of ἀνάγαιον, -ου, τό, "a room upstairs, an upper room." The noun ἀνάγαιον, formed from ἀνά and γῆ, refers to a room on the level above the ground floor, i.e., an upstairs room (ZG 155; LN 7.27; BDAG 59c; Bruce 436). Three modifiers follow ἀνάγαιον, describing the room as large (μέγα), furnished (ἐστρωμένον, acc. sg. neut. of pf. pass. ptc. of στρωννύω, "furnish" [the word στρωννύω offers no guidance for how elaborate or how simple the furnishings for the meal might have been; cf. Cranfield 422]; an adj. ptc. without an art. modifying an anar. noun), and ready for use (ἕτοιμον, acc. sg. neut. of ἕτοιμος, -η, -ον, "ready, ready for use"). Ἑτοιμάσατε, 2nd pl. aor. act. impv. of ἑτοιμάζω, "prepare, make preparations"; ἡμῖν, dat. of interest (advantage).

14:16 Ἐξῆλθον, 3rd pl. aor. act. indic. of ἐξέρχομαι, "go out, leave"; ἦλθον, 3rd pl. aor. act. indic. of ἔρχομαι, "come, go"; εὗρον, 3rd pl. aor. act. indic. of εὑρίσκω, "find" (εὗρον assumes but does not state a dir. obj. [Wallace 409], but in Eng. it is necessary to supply one: "everything"). Gk. and Eng. have two different ways to express an action that takes place before another past event. Eng. uses the pluperf. (e.g., "had said"), while Gk. simply uses an impf. or aor. vb. (e.g., εἶπεν) and allows the context to show that the action preceded some other event (see 5:8). Ἡτοίμασαν, 3rd pl. aor. act. indic. of ἑτοιμάζω, "prepare, make preparations for."

14:17 In 14:17–21, Mark once again emphasizes Jesus's predictive power by describing how Jesus prophesied at the Passover meal that one of his own disciples would betray him and hand him over to the ruling authorities. Ὀψίας, gen. sg. fem. of ὀψία, -ας, ἡ, "evening"; γενομένης, gen. sg. fem. of aor. mid. ptc. of dep. γίνομαι, "come to be, come" (BDAG 197c); gen. abs., temp. adv. ptc. antecedent; ἔρχεται, 3rd sg. pres. mid. indic. of dep. ἔρχομαι, "come, arrive."

14:18 Ἀνακειμένων, gen. pl. masc. of pres. mid. ptc. of dep. ἀνάκειμαι, "recline for dinner, be at the table" (cf. LN 17.23); ἐσθιόντων, gen. pl. masc. of pres. act. ptc. of ἐσθίω, "eat." Both ἀνακειμένων and ἐσθιόντων are gen. abs. participles and temp. adv. participles expressing contemp. time. On ἀμήν, see 3:28; ἐξ ὑμῶν, partitive (see Z §80); παραδώσει, 3rd sg. fut. act. indic. of παραδίδωμι, "hand over" (on παραδίδωμι, see 1:14; 3:19); ἐσθίων, nom. sg. masc. of pres. act. ptc. of ἐσθίω, "eat"; subst. ptc. in appos. to εἷς.

14:19 Ἤρξαντο, 3rd pl. aor. mid. indic. of ἄρχω, "begin" (mng. with mid.; on ἄρχομαι, see 1:45); λυπεῖσθαι, pres. pass. inf. of λυπέω, "grieve, be sad, be distressed" (mng. with pass.); complementary inf.; λέγειν, pres. act. inf. of λέγω, "say"; complementary inf. The phrase εἷς κατὰ εἷς is an idiomatic expression that conveys a distributive idea, emphasizing each and every individual in the group: "one by one" or "one after the other" (BDAG 293b). The nom. case after the prep. κατά stands out as unusual; normally the acc. case follows κατά when it conveys a distributive idea (ἕνα rather than εἷς). However, in this idiomatic expression, the numeral εἷς is apparently being used as an indecl. form (Decker 2:185; cf. Z §10). The question from each of the disciples is only briefly stated ("I am not the one, am I?" [μήτι ἐγώ;]). No vb. appears in the question, but a form of εἰμί seems to be implied. When the interr. particle μήτι introduces a question, the question expects a neg. answer (BDAG 649c). Therefore, each disciple (which would presumably have included Judas) expected Jesus to answer no.

14:20 On ὁ δέ, see 1:45; τῶν δώδεκα, partitive gen. In Mark, the ptc. ἐμβαπτόμενος (nom. sg. masc. of pres. mid. ptc. of ἐμβάπτω, "dip"; subst. ptc., nom. in appos. to εἷς) is in the mid. voice (cf. the act. form of the ptc. ἐμβάψας in the par. in Matt 26:23, and the act. forms βάψω and βάψας [both from βάπτω rather than ἐμβάπτω] in a similar context in John 13:26). It is difficult to see any significant difference in mng. between the mid. form in Mark 14:20 and the act. forms in the other Gospels, although perhaps the mid. form calls slightly more attention to the subj. of the action (see Moule 24; cf. Swete 333: "the middle marks the act as that of Judas himself"). Since both the act. and the mid. forms of ἐμβάπτω function transitively, a dir. obj. is necessarily assumed even when not specifically stated, and in Eng. is it probably best to supply one (cf. BDAG 321b). In a Passover meal, the customary pattern would have involved dipping unleavened bread and bitter herbs into a bowl (τρύβλιον, acc. sg. neut. of τρύβλιον, -ου, τό, "bowl, dish") containing the haroseth sauce, a mixture of dried fruits, spices, and wine or vinegar (Swete 333; Brooks 228; Strauss 621). With this picture in mind, "bread" can serve as an appropriate dir. obj. for the ptc. ἐμβαπτόμενος (cf. NIV; NRSV; CSB; ESV).

14:21 Γέγραπται, 3rd sg. pf. pass. indic. of γράφω, "write"; intensive pf. (see 1:2); ὑπάγει, futuristic pres. (in this instance, the action is already happening in the pres. but will continue on and reach its completion in the fut. [see Fanning 221–23; Wallace 537; cf. 10:33; 16:7]). In Mark, μέν and δέ do not appear freq. as paired conjunctions (only in 12:5; 14:21, 38; although μέν is paired with καί in 4:4–5 and with ἀλλά in 9:12–13). In the few times that μέν and δέ stand together as a pair in Mark, they draw attention to a contrast within a saying of Jesus (cf. Cranfield 424). Since "woe" is no longer a commonly used Eng. word, perhaps another way to express the pronouncement of intense suffering conveyed by οὐαί is "how disastrous it will be" (cf. LN 22.9). This announcement of disaster may be either a lament (i.e., an expression of pity [13:17]) or a threat of judgment (i.e., an expression of condemnation [14:21]; *EDNT*

2:540; cf. Matt 18:7, which illustrates both definitions). Ἀνθρώπῳ, dat. of interest (disadvantage); παραδίδοται, 3rd sg. pres. pass. indic. of παραδίδωμι, "hand over"; futuristic pres. (similar to ὑπάγει earlier in 14:21). Jesus warns his betrayer of fut. judgment through a 2nd class contrary-to-fact cond. sentence. If that man had not been born (ἐγεννήθη, 3rd sg. aor. pass. indic. of γεννάω, "be born" [mng. with pass.]), it would have been better for him (on the positive adj. καλόν for a comp. idea, see Wallace 297; Turner, *Style* 22 [cf. 9:42, 43, 45, 47]; αὐτῷ, dat. of interest [advantage]; the vb. ἦν is omitted but assumed in the conclusion of the cond. sentence [cf. the par. in Matt 26:24 where ἦν is included]). Mark 14:21 does not follow the normal pattern for 2nd class contrary-to-fact cond. sentences, since it omits the particle ἄν in the conclusion (Porter, *Idioms* 256, 259–60; for similar examples, see BDF §360; T 91–92; Z §319; cf. 9:42). One other unusual feature of the cond. sentence in v. 21 is that in the cond. the neg. οὐκ appears rather than μή as would be normal for 2nd class cond. clauses (Mark 14:21 and the par. in Matt 26:24 are the only exceptions in the NT [see R 1016, 1169; BDF §428; T 284; Burton §469; Moule 149]).

14:22 In 14:22–25, Jesus reinterprets two particular elements in the Passover meal, the bread and the cup of wine, showing that for him they have a deeper significance and point ahead to his coming death. Ἐσθιόντων, gen. pl. masc. of pres. act. ptc. of ἐσθίω, "eat"; gen. abs. ptc.; temp. adv. ptc. contemp.; αὐτῶν, gen. subj. of ἐσθιόντων (referring presumably to Jesus and his disciples [cf. αὐτῶν with ἐσθιόντων in 14:18]). Λαβών (nom. sg. masc. of aor. act. ptc. of λαμβάνω, "take, receive") and εὐλογήσας (nom. sg. masc. of aor. act. ptc. εὐλογέω, "bless, give thanks, praise"), are both temp. adv. participles expressing antecedent time. The dir. obj. of λαβών, "bread" (ἄρτον), is also the implied dir. obj. for two of the following vbs. (ἔκλασεν and ἔδωκεν) and for the impv. (λάβετε) in Jesus's saying. The dir. obj. of εὐλογήσας is left unexpressed, but the blessing is likely directed toward God based on the context of the Passover meal and the par. with "giving thanks" (εὐχαριστήσας) in v. 23 (cf. Stein 650; Strauss 624; see 6:41): "after he took bread and blessed (God for it)." Ἔκλασεν, 3rd sg. aor. act. indic. of κλάω, break; ἔδωκεν, 3rd sg. aor. act. indic. of δίδωμι, "give"; λάβετε, 2nd pl. aor. act. impv. of λαμβάνω, "take, receive." The antecedent of the pron. τοῦτο is ἄρτον, even though τοῦτο is neut. and ἄρτον is masc. Instead of agreeing with its antecedent, τοῦτο is made to agree with the neut. pred. nom. σῶμα (cf. BDF §132).

14:23 Λαβών (nom. sg. masc. of aor. act. ptc. of λαμβάνω, "take, receive") and εὐχαριστήσας (nom. sg. masc. of aor. act. ptc. of εὐχαριστέω, "give thanks") are both temp. adv. participles expressing antecedent time. Ἔδωκεν, 3rd sg. aor. act. indic. of δίδωμι, "give"; ἔπιον, 3rd pl. aor. act. indic. of πίνω, "drink"; πάντες, "they all" (modifies the implied subj. of ἔπιον).

14:24 As in v. 22, τοῦτο is likely neut. because it agrees with the neut. pred. nom., this time αἷμα, rather than because it agrees with its neut. antecedent ποτήριον. Διαθήκης, gen. of purpose (see Decker 2:190); ἐκχυννόμενον, nom. sg. neut. of pres. pass. ptc. of ἐκχύννω (alternate spelling of ἐκχέω; see BDF §§73, 101), "pour out, shed"; adj. ptc. A pres. ptc. can express a futuristic sense, as seems to be the case with ἐκχυννόμενον, since it points ahead to the shedding of Jesus's blood through his death on the cross (on ἐκχυννόμενον as a futuristic pres., see Z §§282–83; Fanning 412–13; Taylor 546; Cranfield 427). The use of πολλῶν in 14:24 is probably not intended to communicate that Jesus gave himself for many as opposed to all. Instead the point of using "many" is to say that Jesus shed his blood for all, who are in fact many (see the discussion at 10:45).

14:25 On ἀμήν, see 3:28; οὐκέτι οὐ μή, "will certainly no longer, will never again" (three negatives in a row strengthen Jesus's statement about what will not happen in the future [see 1:44], but in Eng. it is necessary to translate them in such a way that they do not cancel one another out); πίω, 1st sg. aor. act. subjunc. of πίνω, "drink"; emph. neg. subjunc.; γενήματος, gen. sg. neut. of γένημα, -ατος, τό, "product, fruit" (on the distinction between γενήμα and γεννήμα, see R 213; *TDNT* 1:685; MM 123–24); ἀμπέλου, gen. sg. fem. of ἄμπελος, -ου, ἡ, "vine, grapevine"; subj. gen.; ἕως, "until" (used as a prep. taking a gen. obj.); ὅταν, "when" (introducing a clause that is epex. to the noun ἡμέρας, further explaining the time reference of "that day" [Decker 2:192; cf. BDF §394; 1 John 5:2]); πίνω, 1st sg. pres. act. subjunc. of πίνω, "drink"; subjunc. in an indef. temp. clause. The adj. καινόν appears somewhat unexpectedly after the vb. πίνω, since it does not have a noun in the context to modify. However, neut. acc. adjectives, both sg. and pl., can be used adv. (on the use of an adj. as an adv. acc., see R 488, 659; Wallace 200–201; Porter, *Idioms* 121–22), and that seems to be the function of καινόν in this context ("in a new way"). Other examples of neut. acc. adjectives used adv. in Mark include: ἔννυχα (1:35), ἔσχατον (12:6, 22), λοιπόν (14:41), μακρά (12:40), μικρόν (14:35), μόνον (5:36; 6:8), ὀλίγον (1:19; 6:31), περισσότερον (7:36), πολύ (12:27), πολλά (1:45; 3:12; 5:10, 23, 38, 43; 6:20, 23; 9:26), πρῶτον (3:27; 4:28; 7:27; 9:11, 12; 13:10), and τρίτον (14:41).

FOR FURTHER STUDY

33. The Last Supper in Mark

Bahr, Gordon J. "The Seder of Passover and the Eucharistic Words." *NovT* 12 (1970): 181–202.

Jeremias, Joachim. *The Eucharistic Words of Jesus*. Philadelphia: Fortress, 1977.

Köstenberger, Andreas J. "Was the Last Supper a Passover Meal?" Pages 6–30 in *The Lord's Supper: Remembering and Proclaiming Christ until He Comes*. Edited by Thomas R. Schreiner and Matthew R. Crawford. NAC Studies in Bible and Theology 10. Nashville: B&H Academic, 2010.

Marcus, Joel. "Passover and Last Supper Revisited." *NTS* 59 (2013): 303–24.

Marshall, I. Howard. *Last Supper and Lord's Supper*. Grand Rapids: Eerdmans, 1980.

————. "The Last Supper." Pages 481–588 in *Key Events in the Life of the Historical Jesus: A Collaborative Explanation of Context and Coherence*. Edited by Darrell L. Bock and Robert L. Webb. WUNT 1/247. Tübingen: Mohr Siebeck, 2009.

McKnight, Scot. "Part Four: Jesus and the Last Supper." Pages 241–334 in *Jesus and His Death: Historiography, the Historical Jesus, and Atonement Theory*. Waco, TX: Baylor University Press, 2005.

Pennington, Jonathan T. "The Lord's Last Supper in the Fourfold Witness of the Gospels."
Pages 31–67 in *The Lord's Supper: Remembering and Proclaiming Christ until He
Comes*. Edited by Thomas R. Schreiner and Matthew R. Crawford. NAC Studies in
Bible and Theology 10. Nashville: B&H Academic, 2010.
*Pitre, Brant. *Jesus and the Last Supper*. Grand Rapids: Eerdmans, 2015.
Robbins, Vernon K. "Last Meal: Preparation, Betrayal, and Absence (Mark 14:12–25)."
Pages 21–40 in *The Passion in Mark: Studies on Mark 14–16*. Edited by Werner H.
Kelber. Philadelphia: Fortress, 1976.

HOMILETICAL SUGGESTIONS

The Significance of the Supper (14:22–25)

1. Jesus's body, broken for us so that we might be made whole (14:22)
2. Jesus's blood, poured out for us so that we might enter a new covenant (14:23–24)
3. Jesus's prediction, spoken for us so that we might find hope in the coming kingdom (14:25)

3. Prayer and Arrest at Gethsemane (14:26–52)

14:26 Mark 14:26 both draws to a close the celebration of the Passover meal with the singing of a hymn (ὑμνήσαντες, nom. pl. masc. of aor. act. ptc. of ὑμνέω, "sing a hymn"; temp. adv. ptc. antecedent) and leads to a new setting and consequently to a new section. Ἐξῆλθον, 3rd pl. aor. act. indic. of ἐξέρχομαι, "go out"; ἐλαιῶν, gen. pl. fem. of ἐλαία, -ας, ἡ, "olive" (τὸ ὄρος τῶν ἐλαιῶν, "the Mount of Olives"). With the shift in setting in v. 26, the narrative moves into a new section, one that includes: Jesus's prediction of his disciples' coming failure (14:27–31), his prayer at Gethsemane (14:32–42), and his betrayal and arrest (14:43–52).

14:27 Λέγει, historical pres. (see 1:12, 30). Mark regularly conveys the sense of an ongoing conversation through the use of the historical pres. with a form of λέγω (see also 14:30) or with an impf. tense form of λέγω (see 14:31; cf. ἐλάλει in v. 31). Ὅτι (1st use): introduces dir. discourse; σκανδαλισθήσεσθε, 2nd pl. fut. pass. indic. of σκανδαλίζω, "let oneself be led into sin, fall away" (mng. with pass. [BDAG 926a]; on σκανδαλίζω, see 9:43); ὅτι (2nd use): introduces a causal clause; γέγραπται, 3rd sg. pf. pass. indic. of γράφω, "write" (on γέγραπται, see 1:2); πατάξω, 1st sg. fut. act. indic. of πατάσσω, "strike, strike down"; ποιμένα, acc. sg. masc. of ποιμήν, -ένος, ὁ, "shepherd"; διασκορπισθήσονται, 3rd pl. fut. pass. indic. of διασκορπίζω, "scatter, disperse."

14:28 Ἐγερθῆναι, aor. pass. inf. of ἐγείρω, "raise"; inf. of antecedent time; με, acc. subj. of inf. The cstr. μετὰ τό with the inf. occurs twice in Mark (1:14; 14:28) and twelve other times in the NT (not counting Mark 16:19 in the longer ending; see Matt 26:32; Luke 12:5; 22:20; Acts 1:3; 7:4; 10:41; 15:13; 19:21; 20:1; 1 Cor 11:25; Heb 10:15, 26). All these examples use the aor. tense with the inf., except for Heb 10:15, which uses the pf. tense. The summary viewpoint of the aor. tense is an appropriate choice for depicting an action that precedes the action of the main vb., and in this way the cstr.

of μετά τό with an aor. inf. is similar to a temp. adv. ptc. expressing antecedent time, which also normally takes the aor. tense in Mark (cf. Campbell, *VANIV* 18, 110–12; R 1074). The aor. tense of the inf. itself does not convey the time of the action, which is determined instead by contextual factors like the use of the prep. μετά and the time of the action for the main vb. (cf. Porter, *VA* 388). For the present v., that means the action in the inf. takes place sometime before the fut. action in the main vb. (προάξω, 1st sg. fut. act. indic. of προάγω, "go before, go ahead of").

14:29 Ἔφη, 3rd sg. impf. or aor. act. indic. of φημί, "say"; σκανδαλισθήσονται, 3rd pl. fut. pass. indic. of σκανδαλίζω, "let oneself be led into sin, fall away" (mng. with pass.; BDAG 926a). The words εἰ καί function together as a concessive conj. ("even though, although"; Wallace 663; BDF §457), but the ensuing concessive clause still remains a subspecies of the 1st class cond. clause (BDF §374). Therefore, Peter, at least for the sake of argument, assumes that all the other disciples will fall away (cf. Wallace 690). When ἀλλά introduces a conclusion after a cond. clause, it serves as a marker of emph. contrast and can be translated as "certainly" or "at least" (LN 91.11; BDF §448).

14:30 On ἀμὴν λέγω σοι, see 3:28 (this is the last of thirteen times in Mark that Jesus begins a statement in this way and the only time that he directs this introductory formula to an individual rather than to a group). The nom. form of the pers. pron. σύ, which is unnecessary given the ending of the vb. ἀπαρνήσῃ, emphasizes the subj. and draws attention to Peter and his failure (on nom. pers. pronouns, see Wallace 321–23; also, for the sake of emph., σύ appears right at the beginning of the clause, while the related vb. ἀπαρνήσῃ does not appear until the end). Πρὶν ἤ, "before" (a temp. conj. often followed by an inf. [BDAG 863d]); δίς, adv. mng. "twice" (on the text-critical problem related to the omission of δίς in v. 30, see 14:68); ἀλέκτορα, acc. sg. masc. of ἀλέκτωρ, -ορος, ὁ, "rooster"; acc. subj. of the inf.; φωνῆσαι, aor. act. inf. of φωνέω, "crow" (BDAG 1071a); inf. of subsequent time; τρίς, adv. mng. "three times"; ἀπαρνήσῃ, 2nd sg. fut. mid. indic. of dep. ἀπαρνέομαι, "deny." The cstr. πρίν or πρὶν ἤ with the inf. occurs eleven times in the NT, eight times without ἤ (Matt 26:34, 75; Mark 14:72; Luke 22:61; John 4:49; 8:58; 14:29; Acts 2:20) and three times with ἤ (Matt 1:8; Mark 14:30; Acts 7:2). In addition, πρὶν ἤ appears twice in the NT without an inf. (with a subjunc. vb. [Luke 2:26] and with opt. vbs. [Acts 25:16]). All the examples in the NT of the cstr. πρίν or πρὶν ἤ with the inf. use the aor., with the summary viewpoint of the aor. tense functioning as an appropriate depiction for an action that takes place after the main verbal focus of the sentence (cf. Campbell, *VANIV* 110–12). The aor. tense of the inf. does not indicate the time of the action, which is determined by other contextual factors, such as the conj. πρίν or πρὶν ἤ and the time of the main vb. (cf. Porter, *VA* 388). In the present v., the action expressed by the inf. φωνῆσαι occurs after the fut. main vb. ἀπαρνήσῃ and is therefore also fut. in time.

14:31 On ὁ δέ, see 1:45; ἐκπερισσῶς, adv. mng. "emphatically, vehemently"; ἐλάλει, 3rd sg. impf. act. indic. of λαλέω, "speak"; ἐάν, "even if" (which seems appropriate in light of the extreme nature of the cond. [see Taylor 550]); δέῃ, 3rd sg. pres. act. subjunc. of δεῖ, "it is necessary, one must"; subjunc. in a 3rd class cond. clause; με, acc.

of reference or respect; συναποθανεῖν, aor. act. inf. of συναποθνήσκω, "die with"; subst. use of the inf., subj. of δέῃ; σοι, dat. of association (cf. R 528–29); ἀπαρνήσομαι, 1st sg. fut. mid. indic. of dep. ἀπαρνέομαι, "deny" (on the fut. indic. with οὐ μή, see 13:31); ὡσαύτως, adv. mng. "likewise, in the same way, similarly"; καί, adjunctive.

14:32 With Jesus's arrival at a place called Gethsemane, a unique scene within Mark's Gospel begins, one in which Jesus wavers before the messianic task but then ultimately submits himself to the Father's plan. The use of ἔρχονται (3rd pl. pres. mid. indic. of dep. ἔρχομαι, "come") fits a common pattern in Mark in which a historical pres. vb. of motion opens a new scene and initiates a string of such vbs. (λέγει in v. 32, παραλαμβάνει in v. 33, and λέγει in v. 34 [see 1:12]). Later in the scene, Mark also uses a string of historical pres. vbs. when Jesus returns from his solitary place of prayer to check on his disciples, both for the first time (ἔρχεται, εὑρίσκει, and λέγει in v. 37) and for the third time (ἔρχεται and λέγει in v. 41). This clustering of historical pres. vbs. within the passage, along with the use of the impf. tense to describe Jesus's dramatic act of prayer to the Father in 14:35–36 (ἔπιπτεν, προσηύχετο, and ἔλεγεν; on the impf., see 1:21), provides a particularly vivid description of the events in Gethsemane, showing the action as it unfolds. Χωρίον, acc. sg. neut. of χωρίον, -ου, τό, "place"; καθίσατε, 2nd pl. aor. act. impv. of καθίζω, "sit, sit down"; ἕως, "while" (BDAG 423c; LN 67.139; R 976; Cranfield 430; on ἕως as a conj., see 6:10); προσεύξωμαι, 1st sg. aor. mid. subjunc. of dep. προσεύχομαι, "pray"; subjunc. in an indef. temp. clause.

14:33 Ἤρξατο, 3rd sg. aor. mid. indic. of ἄρχω, "begin" (mng. with mid.; on ἄρχομαι, see 1:45); ἐκθαμβεῖσθαι, pres. pass. inf. of ἐκθαμβέω, "be deeply distressed, be overwhelmed" (mng. with pass.); complementary inf. The vb. ἐκθαμβέω, which in the NT occurs only in Mark (9:15; 14:33; 16:5, 6), intensifies the related vb. θαμβέω, another word that within the NT only appears in Mark (1:27; 10:24, 32). Both vbs. can indicate an emotional response of amazement or distress toward an unusual event that has just happened or in anticipation of some difficulty that is soon to arrive (cf. BDAG 303a, 442c). Mark further emphasizes the distress of Jesus's emotional state by adding another strong term (ἀδημονεῖν, pres. act. inf. of ἀδημονέω, "be troubled, be anxious"; complementary inf.; cf. France 582).

14:34 Περίλυπος, nom. sg. fem. of περίλυπος, -ον, "deeply grieved, overwhelmingly sorrowful" (the prep. prefix περι- in this instance intensifies the adj., functioning like other adjectives such as περιαλγής "extremely painful," περίπικρος "very bitter," and περιχαρής "exceedingly glad"); ἕως, "until, to the point of" (used as a prep. taking a gen. obj.); μείνατε, 2nd pl. aor. act. impv. of μένω, "remain, stay"; γρηγορεῖτε, 2nd pl. pres. act. impv. of γρηγορέω, "watch, be on the alert." The shift in tense from aor. (μείνατε) to pres. (γρηγορεῖτε) is likely significant. Specific commands to the disciples, such as "sit here" (καθίσατε in v. 32) or "remain here" (μείνατε in v. 34; cf. Fanning 334), use aor. impv. forms (see 1:25; 2:11; cf. also Jesus's specific requests using παρένεγκε in v. 36 and παρέλθῃ in v. 35 [Fanning 384]). Commands to the disciples in this passage that call for constancy and vigilance take the pres. tense, commands such as "watch" (γρηγορεῖτε in vv. 34, 38) and "pray" (προσεύχεσθε in v. 38), emphasizing the prog. nature of the demanded action in keeping with the aspect of the pres. tense (cf. Fanning 364–65).

14:35 Προελθών, nom. sg. masc. of aor. act. ptc. of προέρχομαι, "go forward, go on"; temp. adv. ptc. antecedent; μικρόν, "for a short distance" (neut. acc. adj. used adv.; see 14:25; cf. BDAG 651a). At this point, Mark moves the story line forward using impf. vbs., portraying the depth of Jesus's emotion in a vivid way by showing the dramatic scene in progress as it unfolds (see 1:21; cf. Swete 343). Ἔπιπτεν, 3rd sg. impf. act. indic. of πίπτω, "fall"; ἐπί, "to, toward" (indicating motion; see Harris 137; BDAG 364a); προσηύχετο, 3rd sg. impf. mid. indic. of dep. προσεύχομαι, "pray" (see also the impf. vb. ἔλεγεν in v. 36); παρέλθῃ, 3rd sg. aor. act. subjunc. of παρέρχομαι, "pass"; subjunc. in a dir. obj. ἵνα clause to express the content of a prayer (see 5:10). The 1st class cond. (εἰ δυνατόν ἐστιν) assumes in this context that it was indeed possible for the Father to grant Jesus's request, since as the next verse points out all things are possible for him.

14:36 The prayer in v. 36 begins with an address to αββα, an Aram. word immediately translated into Gk. as ὁ πατήρ (a nom. with an art. in place of the voc. [cf. T 34; Z §34; BDF §147]; on Aram. words, see 7:34). At the time of Jesus, the Aram. word αββα belonged to the familiar language of the family, and, although it was certainly used by children, it was not a childish expression. Adults would also use αββα, since it was the appropriate and adult way to address one's father (James Barr, "'Abbā' Isn't 'Daddy,'" *JTS* 39 [1988]: 28–47). Therefore, αββα is a family word that communicates a close relationship with God, as with one's Father. Σοι, dat. of interest (advantage); παρένεγκε, 2nd sg. aor. act. impv. of παραφέρω, "take, remove"; on "cup" (ποτήριον) as a metaphor for the judgment of God, esp. in the OT, see Ps 11:6; 75:8; Isa 51:17, 22; Jer 25:15–17; 49:12; Lam 4:21–22; Ezek 23:31–35; Hab 2:16; Zech 12:2 (cf. Pss. Sol. 8:13–14; Rev 14:10; 16:19); τί, "what" (the interr. pron. τί is used for the rel. pron. ὅ [R 737; Z §221; BDF §298]).

14:37 Ἔρχεται, 3rd sg. pres. mid. indic. of dep. ἔρχομαι, "come, go"; καθεύδοντας, acc. pl. masc. of pres. act. ptc. of καθεύδω, "sleep"; supplementary (complementary) ptc. (the same vb. appears later in the verse [καθεύδεις]). Jesus directs his questions specifically to Peter, the one who most vehemently protested against Jesus's prediction of his coming failure (14:29, 31), but he addresses him as "Simon," his old name (cf. 3:16; Σίμων, nom. for voc., since there is no separate voc. form for 3rd decl. nasal stem nouns [MH 134]). Jesus's second question begins with οὐκ, indicating that an affirmative answer is expected (BDF §§427, 440; BDAG 734a): "You were able [ἴσχυσας, 2nd sg. aor. act. indic. of ἰσχύω, "be able to, have power to"] to watch [γρηγορῆσαι, aor. act. inf. of γρηγορέω, "watch, be on the alert"; complementary inf.] for one hour [ὥραν, acc. for extent of time], weren't you?"

14:38 By using pl. impv. forms, Jesus shifts his attention from Peter alone to all three disciples together. Γρηγορεῖτε, 2nd pl. pres. act. impv. of γρηγορέω, "watch, be on the alert"; προσεύχεσθε, 2nd pl. pres. mid. impv. of dep. προσεύχομαι, "pray"; ἔλθητε, 2nd pl. aor. act. subjunc. of ἔρχομαι, "come"; subjunc. in a dir. obj. ἵνα clause; πειρασμόν, acc. sg. masc. of πειρασμός, -οῦ, ὁ, "temptation, testing." The ἵνα clause likely gives the content of the prayer rather than the purpose for why the disciples should watch and pray, since in the immediately preceding context, in v. 35, a ἵνα clause following a form of προσεύχομαι clearly gives the content of the prayer (cf. 13:18). Πρόθυμον, nom. sg. neut. of πρόθυμος, -ον, "willing, eager."

14:39 Ἀπελθών, nom. sg. masc. of aor. act. ptc. of ἀπέρχομαι, "depart, go away"; temp. adv. ptc. antecedent; προσηύξατο, 3rd sg. aor. mid. indic. of dep. προσεύχομαι, "pray"; τὸν αὐτὸν λόγον, "the same prayer" (on αὐτός as an identifying adj. mng. "same," see BDAG 153d; Wallace 349–50; cf. KMP 392; on λόγος as what someone says and therefore in the context of 14:39 as "prayer," see BDAG 599b); εἰπών, nom. sg. masc. of aor. act. ptc. of λέγω, "say"; redundant ptc.

14:40 Ἐλθών, nom. sg. masc. of aor. act. ptc. of ἔρχομαι, "come, go"; temp. adv. ptc. antecedent; εὗρεν, 3rd sg. aor. act. indic. of εὑρίσκω, "find"; καθεύδοντας, acc. pl. masc. of pres. act. ptc. of καθεύδω, "sleep"; supplementary (complementary) ptc.; ἦσαν, 3rd pl. impf. act. indic. of εἰμί, "be"; καταβαρυνόμενοι, nom. pl. masc. of pres. pass. ptc. of καταβαρύνω, "be very heavy" (mng. with pass.); periph. ptc. (on the intensifying function of the prep. prefix κατα-, see 1:36). By stating that the disciples did not know (ᾔδεισαν, 3rd pl. pluperf. act. indic. of οἶδα, "know"; on the pluperf. of οἶδα, see 1:24) what they should answer him (ἀποκριθῶσιν, 3rd pl. aor. pass. subjunc. of dep. ἀποκρίνομαι, "answer"; delib. subjunc.; on the subjunc. in indir. questions, see 9:6), Mark implies that Jesus once again challenged their behavior with rebuking questions.

14:41 Ἔρχεται, 3rd sg. pres. mid. indic. of dep. ἔρχομαι, "come, go"; τρίτον, "for the third time" (neut. acc. adj. used adv.). While it is possible that Jesus's words, καθεύδετε τὸ λοιπὸν καὶ ἀναπαύεσθε, are a statement of surprise ("You are still sleeping and resting!") or an ironic command ("Sleep on and on and rest!"), they are best taken as a question ("Are you still sleeping and resting?"; καθεύδετε from καθεύδω, "sleep"; λοιπόν, "still, on and on, for the remaining time" [neut. acc. adj. used adv.; on the adv. acc., see 14:25; cf. BDAG 602d, R 486–87; BDF §§160, 451]; ἀναπαύεσθε, 2nd pl. pres. mid. indic. of ἀναπαύω, "rest" [mng. with mid.]). The consistent pattern in the passage is that Jesus returns from prayer to find his disciples sleeping, and then he asks them rebuking questions.

A number of suggestions have been made for how to translate ἀπέχει, "one of the puzzling words in Mk.'s vocabulary" (Bruce 440). However, two options stand out as most likely, since they both account for ἀπέχει being intrans. in 14:41:

1. "It is enough!" With this option, ἀπέχει is understood as an indef. vb., one without a clearly stated or implied subj., and as a one-word statement. Most Eng. translations take this option. BDAG 102d regards the context as a strong determining factor in support of this translation, even though the evidence for this as a possible mng. for ἀπέχω in other literature is minimal and comparatively late.

*2. "Is it far away?" With this option, ἀπέχει is understood as a one-word question, and the implied subj. of the vb. ("the hour") comes from the answer to the question that immediately follows. The following words also indicate that the answer to the question is a negative one: "Is the hour far away? No, the hour has come" (ἦλθεν, 3rd sg. aor. act. indic. of ἔρχομαι, "come"; consummative aor.).

In support of the second option is the fact that "to be far away" is a significantly more common mng. for the vb., esp. in the LXX (e.g., Gen 44:4; Deut 12:21; Ps 103:12 [102:12 LXX]; Prov 15:29; 22:5; Isa 54:14; 55:9; Ezek 8:6; 11:15; 22:5; Joel 3:8 [4:8 LXX]; cf. MM 57–58). In addition, ἀπέχω appears one other time in Mark (7:6), in a quotation of Isa 29:13: "This people honors me with their lips, but their heart *is far* from me" (emphasis added). In light of this lexical data, ἀπέχει is probably another rebuking question from Jesus in which he chides his disciples for acting as if the moment of crisis is still far away, when in fact it is not (see Evans 416–17; cf. Marcus 2:980–81; Strauss 636; for a long list of other possible options, see Cranfield 435–36). On ἰδού, see 1:2; παραδίδοται, 3rd sg. pres. pass. indic. of παραδίδωμι, hand over, deliver up (on παραδίδωμι, see 1:14); futuristic pres. (see 9:31).

14:42 Ἐγείρεσθε, 2nd pl. pres. pass. impv. of ἐγείρω, get up, stand up (mng. with pass. impv., BDAG 272b–c); ἄγωμεν, 1st pl. pres. act. subjunc. of ἄγω, "go" (BDAG 17a); hort. subjunc. Both ἐγείρεσθε and ἄγωμεν are vbs. of motion that idiomatically use the pres. tense in specific commands (see 2:11). Παραδιδούς, nom. sg. masc. of pres. act. ptc. of παραδίδωμι, "hand over"; subst. ptc.; ἤγγικεν, 3rd sg. pf. act. indic. of ἐγγίζω, come near, approach.

14:43 Λαλοῦντος, gen. sg. masc. of pres. act ptc. of λαλέω, "speak"; gen. abs., temp. adv. ptc. contemp.; παραγίνεται, 3rd sg. pres. mid. indic. of dep. παραγίνομαι, "come, arrive"; historical pres. (focusing on the arrival of new participants in scene [see 1:12]); sg. vb. with a compound subj. (see 12:33); ξύλων, gen. pl. neut. of ξύλον, -ου, τό, "club, heavy stick," LN 6.31.

14:44 Δεδώκει, 3rd sg. pluperf. act. indic. of δίδωμι, "give." The pluperf. tense occurs only seven times in Mark. The three pluperf. forms of οἶδα (1:34; 9:6; 14:40), along with the one pluperf. form of εἴωθα (10:1), simply convey a past stative mng. without any implication of a prior action that produced the state (see 1:24; cf. Fanning 308; Wallace 586). The remaining three uses of the pluperf. occur in explanatory clauses that break into the narration of events and fill in background information, clauses introduced by δέ (14:44), the rel. pron. οἵτινες (15:7), or γάρ (15:10). In addition, the pluperf. periph. cstr. appears six times in Mark (always using ἦν plus a pf. pass. ptc.), also in explanatory clauses offering background information (see 1:33). In these instances, the clauses begin with καί (1:6, 33; 15:26), γάρ (6:52), δέ (15:7), or the rel. pron. ὅ (15:46). In all these examples of the pluperf. in explanatory clauses, incl. the one in 14:44, the past state of events serves as a background for the foreground narrative (Fanning 306–7; cf. Decker 2:209). Παραδιδούς, nom. sg. masc. of pres. act. ptc. of παραδίδωμι, "hand over"; subst. ptc.; σύσσημον, acc. sg. neut. of σύσσημον, -ου, τό, "signal, sign"; λέγων, nom. sg. masc. of pres. act. ptc. of λέγω, "say"; adv. ptc. of means; φιλήσω, 1st sg. aor. act. subjunc. of φιλέω, "kiss" (BDAG 1056d–57a); subjunc. in indef. rel. clause; κρατήσατε, 2nd pl. aor. act. impv. of κρατέω, "seize, arrest"; ἀπάγετε, 2nd pl. pres. act. impv. of ἀπάγω, "lead away" (on complicating factors with regard to the pres. impv. with compound forms of ἄγω, see Fanning 343, 346–47); ἀσφαλῶς, adv. mng. "under tight security, under close guard, securely."

14:45 Ἐλθών, nom. sg. masc. of aor. act. ptc. of ἔρχομαι, "come"; temp. adv. ptc. antecedent; προσελθών, nom. sg. masc. of aor. act. ptc. of προσέρχομαι, "approach, go to"; temp. adv. ptc. antecedent; αὐτῷ, dat. dir. obj. Judas's use of ῥαββί ("master, teacher, rabbi"), a form of address expressing honor toward a greatly respected leader or teacher, serves to heighten the insincerity and deceitfulness of Judas's actions (on ῥαββί, see 9:5). Κατεφίλησεν, 3rd sg. aor. act. indic. of καταφιλέω, "kiss."

14:46 On οἱ δέ, see 1:45; ἐπέβαλον, 3rd pl. aor. act. indic. of ἐπιβάλλω, "lay on, put on" (ἐπιβάλλω can take two objects, one in the acc. [χεῖρας] and one in the dat. [αὐτῷ]); on the art. as a poss. pron. (e.g., with τὰς χεῖρας), see R 684, 769–70; Wallace 215–16. The expression "to lay hands on someone" can often assume that the action is being done with physical force and violence (cf. BDAG 367d; e.g., Esth 6:2; Luke 20:19; 21:12; John 7:44; Acts 4:3; 5:18; 12:1; 21:27; Jos. *J.W.* 2.18.7 §491; MM 235). Ἐκράτησαν, 3rd pl. aor. act. indic. of κρατέω, "seize, arrest."

14:47 Since εἷς and τις can overlap in mng. (R 675), some Gk. mss omitted τις (‭א‬, A, L, 579, 700), while one omitted εἷς, shortening all of εἷς δέ τις τῶν παρεστηκότων down to καί τις (D). When used together, the two words mean "a certain one" (BDAG 293a) and seem to increase the focus on just one individual (cf. Luke 22:50; John 11:49). Παρεστηκότων, gen. pl. masc. of pf. act. ptc. of παρίστημι, "be present, stand near" (pf. expresses a pres. tense intrans. mng.; BDAG 778c–d); subst. ptc., partitive gen.; σπασάμενος, nom. sg. masc. of aor. mid. ptc. of σπάω, "draw, pull out" (mng. with mid.); temp. adv. ptc. antecedent; ἔπαισεν, 3rd sg. aor. act. indic. of παίω, "strike"; ἀφεῖλεν, 3rd sg. aor. act. indic. of ἀφαιρέω, "take away, cut off"; ὠτάριον, acc. sg. neut. of ὠτάριον, -ου, τό, "ear" (on being careful not to overinterpret diminutives in Mark, such as ὠτάριον, see 3:9).

14:48 Ἀποκριθείς, nom. sg. masc. of aor. pass. ptc. of dep. ἀποκρίνομαι, "answer"; redundant ptc.; ἐπί, "against" (cf. 3:24–26; 13:12); λῃστήν, acc. sg. masc. of λῃστής, -οῦ, ὁ, "robber, violent criminal." The noun λῃστής refers to someone who steals through threats or acts of violence (see 11:17). After Jesus's demonstration in the temple (11:17), Jesus characterized the chief priests as robbers (λῃστῶν), and now they arrest Jesus as though instead he were a dangerous robber. This par. is important for understanding the mng. of λῃστής in the present context. To interpret λῃστής in 14:48 as "revolutionary" or "insurrectionist" (cf. NIV; NLT) obscures the ironic par. between Jesus's charge against the temple leaders in 11:17 and their treatment of him according to 14:48. Ἐξήλθατε, 2nd pl. aor. act. indic. of ἐξέρχομαι, "come out"; ξύλων, gen. pl. neut. of ξύλον, -ου, τό, "club, heavy stick"; συλλαβεῖν, aor. act. inf. of συλλαμβάνω, "capture, apprehend, arrest"; inf. of purpose.

14:49 Καθ᾽ ἡμέραν, "daily, day by day" (BDAG 512a). The distributive use of κατά points to the division of an event into parts, indicating in this instance that the event took place on a number of days (on the distributive use of κατά, see Harris 155–57; Wallace 377; cf. 13:8; 15:6). Ἤμην, 1st sg. impf. mid. indic. of εἰμί, "be" (dep. in 1st sg. impf.); πρός, "with" (used with a form of εἰμί to convey not motion but a position with others [Harris 191; Moule 52; Wallace 359]); διδάσκων, nom. sg. masc. of pres. act. ptc. of διδάσκω, "teach"; temp. adv. ptc. contemp.; καί, "and yet" (contrastive; cf. 12:12); ἐκρατήσατε, 2nd pl. aor. act. indic. of κρατέω, "seize, arrest." The expression ἀλλ᾽ ἵνα in this context is likely elliptical (R 1187; BDF §448), so that it is necessary to supply the implied clause between ἀλλ᾽ and ἵνα (cf. NASB; NET): "but this has happened in order that the Scriptures might be fulfilled" (πληρωθῶσιν, 3rd pl. aor. pass. subjunc. of πληρόω, "fulfill"; subjunc. in a purpose ἵνα clause).

14:50 Ἀφέντες, nom. pl. masc. of aor. act. ptc. of ἀφίημι, "leave, desert"; temp. adv. ptc. antecedent; ἔφυγον, 3rd pl. aor. act. indic. of φεύγω, "flee, run away." Although the subj. of ἔφυγον is left unspecified, it is clear from the flow of the narrative that those who have fled are the disciples, fulfilling Jesus's prediction that they would fall away (14:27). Earlier the disciples left everything (ἀφέντες [1:18, 20]; ἀφήκαμεν [10:28]) to follow Jesus, but now they leave (ἀφέντες [14:50]) Jesus to save their lives.

14:51 Νεανίσκος, nom. sg. masc. of νεανίσκος, -ου, ὁ, "young man"; τις, "a certain" (when used as an adj.; τις can also be translated in this context simply as an indef. pron., i.e., "a/an" [cf. BDAG 1008c; Wallace 347]); συνηκολούθει, 3rd sg. impf. act. indic. of συνακολουθέω, "follow"; αὐτῷ, dat. dir. obj. Both the impf. tense with συνηκολούθει and the historical pres. with κρατοῦσιν later in the v. 51 portray the dramatic scene in a vivid way, showing the action as it unfolds (see 1:12, 21). Περιβεβλημένος, nom. sg. masc. of pf. mid. ptc. of περιβάλλω, "wear, put something on oneself" (mng. with mid.; BDAG 799c); adj. ptc. without an art. to modify an anar. noun; σινδόνα, acc. sg. fem. of σινδών, -όνος, ἡ, "linen garment, linen cloak"; γυμνοῦ, gen. sg. neut. of γυμνός, -ή, -όν, "naked" (although the adj. is used subst. here for "naked body" [BDAG 208c]).

Unfortunately, many Eng. translations add words that mistakenly portray the young man's manner of dress as oddly out of the ordinary (on the description of the young man's clothing in the historical context of ancient Greco-Roman garments in general, see esp. Erin Vearncombe, "Cloaks, Conflict, and Mark 14:51–52," *CBQ* 75 [2013]: 683–703). They do so by adding that the young man wore "nothing but" (NASB; NIV; NRSV; ESV) or "only" (NET; GNB; NLT) a linen garment, words not found in the Gk. text. In addition, certain translations of σινδόνα and περιβεβλημένος have the potential to portray the young man's manner of dress as unusual in unnecessary ways. The word σινδών was used for fine linen cloth (MM 575; cf. 15:46), but also for anything made out of such cloth, incl. clothing or garments (LSJ 1600). Various terms, incl. σινδών, could take the place of the more freq. used ἱμάτιον ("garment, cloak" [which appears twelve times in Mark]), in the case of σινδών to emphasize that the piece of clothing was made out of expensive material rather than out of wool (Vearncombe, "Cloaks," 684–93; cf. Taylor 562; Cranfield 438–39). Therefore, "linen garment" (NIV) is a more appropriate translation for σινδόνα within a description of what someone is wearing than "linen cloth" (CSB; ESV; NET; NKJV; NRSV) or "linen sheet" (NASB). Moreover, περιβεβλημένος is a typical expression for describing what someone is wearing (cf. περιβεβλημένον in 16:5), and to translate it, e.g., as "thrown around" (NKJV) miscommunicates, conveying that the young man had somehow clothed himself in a hurried manner. What is unexpected is that Mark needlessly goes out of his way to describe the young man as wearing his clothing over his naked body, perhaps simply as a way to prepare for the young man's humiliating flight in the next verse. The adj. γυμνός is a broad term, ranging from an indication that someone is completely bare to an indication that someone is just not fully clothed, depending on the context (*TDNT* 1:773–74; *EDNT* 1:265; cf. John 21:7). An individual could be considered γυμνός when found only in an undergarment or only with an inner tunic on and not an outer cloak as well (Vearncombe, "Cloaks," 691–92, 702; cf. MM 133).

14:52 On ὁ δέ, see 1:45; καταλιπών, nom. sg. masc. of aor. act. ptc. of καταλείπω, "leave behind"; temp. adv. ptc. antecedent; σινδόνα, acc. sg. fem. of σινδών, -όνος, ἡ, "linen garment, linen cloak"; γυμνός, nom. sg. masc. of γυμνός, -ή, -όν, "naked"; ἔφυγεν, 3rd sg. aor. act. indic. of φεύγω, "flee, run away." When the young man runs away naked, it suggests that he was so overpowered and beaten in an attack or attempted arrest that he was barely able to escape with his life (on "fleeing naked" as an idiomatic expression for a brutal and humiliating defeat, see Amos 2:16; 2 Macc 11:12; Acts 19:16). Mark 14:51–52 offers yet another example of failure, a picture of a "would-be" disciple, dressed in an expensive garment and therefore perhaps unfamiliar with sacrifice, who chose to follow Jesus even after his arrest but was unprepared for the cost. He was badly beaten and ran off in shame.

HOMILETICAL SUGGESTIONS

Two Contrasting Scenes (4:35–41; 14:26–42): Asleep in the Storm and Alone in the Garden

1. What do we learn about Jesus?
    a. The rest of faith: Jesus completely trusted the Father's plan even in the midst of difficulties. (4:37–38)
    b. The wrestle of faith: Jesus completely submitted to the Father's plan even in the midst of a desire for another way. (14:33–36)
2. What do we learn about following Jesus?
    a. Faith instead of fear: Fear is an enemy of our trust in God's plan. (4:40–41)
    b. Prayer instead of pride: Pride is an enemy of our trust in God's strength. (14:29, 31, 37)

4. Trial before the Sanhedrin and Denials by Peter (14:53–72)

14:53 The setting changes and a new unit begins in v. 53, when the arresting party leads Jesus to the residence of the high priest. Ἀπήγαγον, 3rd pl. aor. act. indic. of ἀπάγω, "lead away"; συνέρχονται, 3rd pl. pres. mid. indic. of dep. συνέρχομαι, "come together, assemble, gather"; historical pres. (introducing new participants in a scene [see 1:12]). Although Mark begins in v. 53 with a focus on Jesus and the start of his trial, he shifts his attention to Peter in the following verse, where Peter makes his way into the courtyard of the high priest. Then in 14:55–65, Mark narrates the trial of Jesus before the Sanhedrin, followed by the account of Peter's denials in 14:66–72. This intertwining of Jesus's story and Peter's story encourages a comp. between the faithfulness of Jesus and the failure of Peter.

14:54 Ἀπὸ μακρόθεν, "from far away, from a distance" (see 5:6); ἠκολούθησεν, 3rd sg. aor. act. indic. of ἀκολουθέω, "follow"; αὐτῷ, dat. dir. obj.; ἕως ἔσω, "right into" (BDAG 423d; ἕως is used here as a prep. ["until"] with the adv. of place ἔσω functioning subst. as the obj. of the prep. ["the inside"]; the following prep. phrase, εἰς τὴν αὐλήν, specifies the location "right into the courtyard" [Decker 2:217]); αὐλήν, acc. sg. fem. of αὐλή, -ῆς, ἡ, "courtyard"; ἦν, 3rd sg. impf. act. indic. of εἰμί, "be"; συγκαθήμενος, nom. sg. masc. of pres. mid. ptc. of dep. συγκάθημαι, "sit with"; periph. ptc.; ὑπηρετῶν, gen. pl. masc. of ὑπηρέτης, -ου, ὁ, "servant, officer," TDNT 8:540; θερμαινόμενος, nom. sg. masc. of pres. mid. ptc. of θερμαίνω, "warm oneself" (mng. with mid.); periph. ptc.; dir. mid. (R 807; Z §232; Wallace 417; KMP 195). The use of the periph. impf. with "was sitting with" and "was warming himself" leaves the impression that these actions continued on for a significant period of time (see 1:22). Πρός, "near, at" (when used without expressing motion [R 625]). Φῶς can mean "fire," an object that gives light (BDAG 1073c; LN 2.5), and it is perhaps used in this context to communicate that Peter was clearly visible by the light of the fire (Decker 2:217; cf. Cranfield 441).

14:55 Συνέδριον, nom. sg. neut. of συνέδριον, -ου, τό, Sanhedrin; ἐζήτουν, 3rd pl. impf. act. indic. of ζητέω, "seek, look for"; θανατῶσαι, aor. act. inf. of θανατόω, "put to death, hand someone over to be killed"; inf. of purpose; καί, "and yet" (contrastive); ηὕρισκον, 3rd pl. impf. act. indic. of εὑρίσκω, "find." As elsewhere, Mark uses impf. vbs. when providing background information for the main story line (ἐζήτουν and ηὕρισκον in v. 55, ἐψευδομαρτύρουν in vv. 56–57 [see 1:21]). In this passage, Mark uses the various attempts at false testimony against Jesus as background to prepare the way for the heart of the passage, which begins with the high priest's direct questions to Jesus.

14:56 In v. 56, Mark gives the reason (γάρ) why the ruling council was not able to find the evidence it needed to condemn Jesus—because of the inconsistency of the false testimony against him. Ἐψευδομαρτύρουν, 3rd pl. impf. act. indic. of ψευδομαρτυρέω, bear false witness, give false testimony; καί, "and yet" (contrastive); ἴσαι, nom. pl. fem. of ἴσος, -η, -ον, "consistent, equal"; ἦσαν, 3rd pl. impf. act. indic. of εἰμί, "be."

14:57 Mark offers a specific example of false testimony in vv. 57–59 by focusing on the words of just some individuals (τινες), a smaller group among the many false witnesses. Ἀναστάντες, nom. pl. masc. of aor. act. ptc. of ἀνίστημι, "stand up, rise"; temp. adv. ptc. antecedent; ἐψευδομαρτύρουν, 3rd pl. impf. act. indic. of ψευδομαρτυρέω, "bear false witness, give false testimony"; λέγοντες, nom. pl. masc. of pres. act. ptc. of λέγω, "say"; redundant ptc.

14:58–59 Ὅτι, introduces dir. discourse; ἠκούσαμεν, 1st pl. aor. act. indic. of ἀκούω, "hear"; αὐτοῦ, gen. dir. obj.; λέγοντος, gen. sg. masc. of pres. act. ptc. of λέγω, "say"; supplementary (complementary) ptc.; once again ὅτι introduces dir. discourse; καταλύσω, 1st sg. fut. act. indic. of καταλύω, "destroy"; χειροποίητον, acc. sg. masc. of χειροποίητος, -ον, "made with human hands"; διά, "within" (temp. sense for the period of time within which something takes place [see BDF §223; T 267; Z §115]); ἀχειροποίητον, acc. sg. masc. of ἀχειροποίητος, -ον, "not made with human hands"; οἰκοδομήσω, 1st sg. fut. act. indic. of οἰκοδομέω, "build." Since the ending of a vb. already indicates the subj., nom. pers. pronouns such as ἡμεῖς and ἐγώ are grammatically unnecessary and may appear for the sake of emph. (cf. BDF §277). In this way, the accusers lay stress upon themselves and their own contribution to the trial, while they also highlight the self-exalting nature of Jesus's claim to be able to destroy the temple. Καί, "and yet" (contrastive); ἴση, nom. sg. fem. of ἴσος, -η, -ον, "consistent, equal"; ἦν, 3rd sg. impf. act. indic. of εἰμί, "be"; αὐτῶν, subj. gen.

14:60 Ἀναστάς, nom. sg. masc. of aor. act. ptc. of ἀνίστημι, "stand up, rise"; temp. adv. ptc. antecedent (the use of εἰς with ἀναστάς implies motion in this context: "he stood up and moved into the midst of the assembly" [Moule 68; Harris 85]; cf. 3:3); ἐπηρώτησεν, 3rd sg. aor. act. indic. of ἐπερωτάω, "ask"; λέγων, nom. sg. masc. of pres. act. ptc. of λέγω, "say"; redundant ptc. The high priest's words in v. 60 are best understood as two questions, with τί functioning as an interr. pron. rather than as a rel. pron. (T 49; Cranfield 442). Since the first question begins with οὐκ, the expected answer is an affirmative one (see 4:21, 38), resulting in a question that perhaps expresses a tone of indignation or exasperation or at least confusion on the part of the high priest (R 917; Decker 2:221): "You really are answering nothing, aren't you?" (ἀποκρίνῃ, 2nd sg. pres. mid. indic. of dep. ἀποκρίνομαι, "answer"). The second question in v. 60 seems to be more like a demand, insisting that Jesus should respond to his accusers: "What are these men testifying against you?" (καταμαρτυροῦσιν, from καταμαρτυρέω, "testify against, bear witness against"; καταμαρτυρέω can take two objects, one in the acc. and one in the gen. [BDAG 522b]).

14:61 On ὁ δέ, see 1:45; ἐσιώπα, 3rd sg. impf. act. indic. of σιωπάω, "remain silent, be silent"; ἀπεκρίνατο, 3rd sg. aor. mid. indic. of dep. ἀποκρίνομαι, "answer" (on dbl. negatives to strengthen a statement, see 1:44). Mark's Gospel uses the aor. mid. of ἀποκρίνομαι just this one time, here in 14:61, while the aor. pass. of ἀποκρίνομαι appears twenty-seven times in Mark. Interestingly, the balance is the exact opposite in the non-literary Koine papyri, where the aor. mid. predominates over the aor. pass. Although aor. mid. forms of ἀποκρίνομαι occur more frequently in the papyri, they appear almost exclusively in legal reports (MM 64; cf. Decker 2:222). In this way, ἀπεκρίνατο, as an aor. mid., is appropriate to the legal context of the trial scene in Mark. Ἐπηρώτα, 3rd sg. impf. act. indic. of ἐπερωτάω, "ask" (on ἐπερωτάω, see 4:10); λέγει, historical pres. (see 1:12, 30); εὐλογητοῦ, gen. sg. masc. of εὐλογητός, -ή, -όν, "blessed"; subst. adj.

14:62 After having remained silent up to this point, Jesus now answers the high priest's question about his identity directly. With the words ἐγώ εἰμι ("I am"), Jesus identifies himself openly with the titles in the high priest's question, that he is the Christ and the Son of God (on these two titles, see 1:1). However, he also further clarifies what these titles mean for him by using words drawn from Ps 110:1 and Dan 7:13–14, passages that portray the Messiah as exalted to a position of authority over his enemies and as receiving from God an eternal dominion over all the nations. Ὄψεσθε, 2nd pl. fut. mid. indic. of ὁράω, "see" (dep. in fut.; note that ὄψεσθε is pl. and therefore addressed to more than just the high priest); ἐκ δεξιῶν, "at the right hand" (see 10:37); καθήμενον, acc. sg. masc. of pres. mid. ptc. of dep. κάθημαι, "sit"; supplementary (complementary) ptc.; ἐρχόμενον, acc. sg. masc. of pres. mid. ptc. of dep. ἔρχομαι, "come"; supplementary (complementary) ptc.; νεφελῶν, gen. pl. fem. of νεφέλη, -ης, ἡ, "cloud." The fact that the high priest and the members of the ruling council will see Jesus's messianic exaltation and coming as the Son of Man means that he will be vindicated in their eyes and that they will necessarily acknowledge his authority over them.

14:63 Διαρρήξας, nom. sg. masc. of aor. act. ptc. of διαρρήγνυμι, "tear"; temp. adv. ptc. antecedent; χιτῶνας, acc. pl. masc. of χιτών, -ῶνος, ὁ, "clothes" (mng. with pl. [BDAG 1085b; LN 6.162]; the pl. χιτῶνας for "clothes" is similar to the pl. ἱμάτια or ἱματίων for "clothes" in 5:28, 30; 9:3; 15:20, 24); on the neut. form τί being used adv. for "why," see 2:7 (an adj. use such as "what need" [cf. NASB; NKJV; ESV] would demand the fem. form τίνα [cf. Heb 7:11]); μαρτύρων, obj. gen. Although the tearing of one's clothes was often solely an expression of uncontrolled grief (e.g., Gen 37:34; Josh 7:6; 2 Sam 1:11; 2 Kgs 19:1; Job 1:20; Jer 41:5; Jdt 14:19; Acts 14:14), it eventually became in the context of a courtroom scene a dramatic gesture to declare a judgment of blasphemy (m. Sanhedrin 7:5).

14:64 Ἠκούσατε, 2nd pl. aor. act. indic. of ἀκούω, "hear"; βλασφημίας, gen. sg. fem. of βλασφημία, -ας, ἡ, "blasphemy"; gen. dir. obj. (on βλασφημία, see 2:7). The general rule for ἀκούω is that the vb. uses a gen. obj. for the person being heard (e.g., 9:7) and an acc. obj. for the thing being heard (e.g., 4:16, 18). However, at times NT writers waver between the acc. and the gen. for the thing being heard (BDF §173; T 233; cf. the acc. βλασφημίαν in Matt 26:65). Φαίνεται, 3rd sg. pres. pass. indic. of φαίνω, "appear, seem" (act. intrans. mng. with pass. form [BDAG 1047c; MM 663]). The pass. form of φαίνω, when used with an act. and intrans. sense, typically occurs in a context where a decision is being made. As a result, the high priest's question is essentially "What is your decision?" (BDAG 1047c; cf. NRSV; ESV; CSB). On οἱ δέ, see 1:45; κατέκριναν, 3rd pl. aor. act. indic. of κατακρίνω, "condemn, pronounce (a sentence)"; αὐτόν, acc. subj. of inf.; ἔνοχον, acc. sg. masc. of ἔνοχος, -ον, "guilty, deserving" (BDAG 338d); pred. acc.; εἶναι, pres. act. inf. of εἰμί, "be"; inf. of indir. discourse (R 1036; Decker 2:225); θανάτου, obj. gen. (on the death penalty for blasphemy, see Lev 24:16). On the interplay of factors that likely led to the charge of blasphemy against Jesus, see esp. Darrell L. Bock, *Blasphemy and Exaltation in Judaism: The Charge against Jesus in Mark 14:53–65*, repr. ed. [Grand Rapids: Baker, 2000]).

14:65 Ἤρξαντο, 3rd pl. aor. mid. indic. of ἄρχω, "begin" (mng. with mid.; on ἄρχομαι, see 1:45); ἐμπτύειν, pres. act. inf. of ἐμπτύω, "spit on"; complementary inf.; αὐτῷ, dat. dir. obj.; περικαλύπτειν, pres. act. inf. of περικαλύπτω, "cover, conceal"; complementary inf.; κολαφίζειν, pres. act. inf. of κολαφίζω, "beat, strike with the fist"; complementary inf.; λέγειν, pres. act. inf. of λέγω, "say"; complementary inf.; προφήτευσον, 2nd sg. aor. act. impv. of προφητεύω, "prophesy, reveal"; ὑπηρέται, nom. pl. masc. of ὑπηρέτης, -ου, ὁ, "servant, officer" (*TDNT* 8:540); ῥαπίσμασιν, dat. pl. neut. of ῥάπισμα, -ατος, τό, "blow, slap in the face"; dat. of manner (Wallace 162; KMP 132; cf. R 530); ἔλαβον, 3rd pl. aor. act. indic. of λαμβάνω, "take, receive." The idea of "receiving someone with blows," a likely Lat. idiom (Moule 192; BDF §5; Turner, *Style* 29), would be better expressed in a different way in Eng., using a second finite vb. rather than a dat. of manner: "The servants took him and beat him" (cf. LN 19.4).

14:66 Back in 14:54, the narrative sequence concerning Peter ended abruptly with him in the courtyard of the high priest, warming himself by the fire, but now, beginning in 14:66 after Jesus's trial, the spotlight is back on Peter. Ὄντος, gen. sg. masc. of pres. act. ptc. of εἰμί, "be"; gen. abs., temp. adv. ptc. contemp.; κάτω, adv. mng. "below"; αὐλῇ, dat. sg. fem. of αὐλή, -ῆς, ἡ, "courtyard"; ἔρχεται, 3rd sg. pres. mid. indic. of dep. ἔρχομαι, "come" by; historical pres. (starting a new scene [see 1:12]); παιδισκῶν, gen. pl. fem. of παιδίσκη, -ης, ἡ, "female slave"; partitive gen. (on "one" [μία] followed by the gen., see 5:22; on not over-interpreting the diminutives in Mark, see 3:9). Although the noun παιδίσκη may have at one time meant "young woman" or "girl," it came to be consistently used for a "female slave" (BDAG 749d; MM 74; cf. e.g., Exod 21:20–21 LXX; Eccl 2:7 LXX; Acts 16:16; Gal 4:22).

14:67 Ἰδοῦσα, nom. sg. fem. of aor. act. ptc. of ὁράω, "see"; temp. adv. ptc. antecedent; θερμαινόμενον, acc. sg. masc. of pres. mid. ptc. of θερμαίνω, "warm oneself" (mng. with mid.); dir. mid. (see 14:54); supplementary (complementary) ptc.; ἐμβλέψασα, nom. sg. fem. of aor. act. ptc. of ἐμβλέπω, "look at directly, look at intently" (BDAG 321d); temp. adv. ptc. antecedent; αὐτῷ, dat. dir. obj. The participles ἰδοῦσα and ἐμβλέψασα can be synonymous, but since ἐμβλέψασα follows so quickly and otherwise unnecessarily after ἰδοῦσα, it seems to indicate not just another glance but rather a more intensive action on the part of the female slave, a careful and direct look at Peter (Decker 2:227–28; Strauss 663). Λέγει, historical pres. (see 1:12, 30); καί, adjunctive; ἦσθα, 2nd sg. impf. act. indic. of εἰμί, "be" (ἦσθα was an old pf. form that came to be used as an impf. and at times as a replacement for ἦς [MH 203]); Ἰησοῦ, gen. in simple appos. to Ναζαρηνοῦ.

14:68 On ὁ δέ, see 1:45 (the same use of the art. appears in 14:70–71); ἠρνήσατο, 3rd sg. aor. mid. indic. of dep. ἀρνέομαι, "deny, disown, repudiate." Since the vb. ἀρνέομαι is trans., it assumes a dir. obj. even when one is not stated, as in 14:68 and 14:70. Although most Eng. translations supply "it" as the dir. obj., conveying that Peter was rejecting the truth of the slave's statement, the implied dir. obj. could just as easily be "him"—Peter was denying or disowning Jesus (cf. Cranfield 446; BDAG 132d). Indeed, in 14:30 Jesus predicted that Peter would deny him, using ἀπαρνέομαι—a compound form of ἀρνέομαι—and the pers. pron. με as the dir. obj. Λέγων, nom. sg. masc. of pres. act. ptc. of λέγω, "say"; redundant ptc.; οἶδα, 1st sg. pf. act. indic. of οἶδα, "know" (on οἶδα, see 1:24); ἐπίσταμαι, 1st sg. pres. mid. indic. of dep. ἐπίσταμαι, "understand"; ἐξῆλθεν, 3rd sg. aor. act. indic. of ἐξέρχομαι, "go out"; προαύλιον, acc. sg. neut. of προαύλιον, -ου, τό, "gateway, forecourt."

The words at the end of v. 68, "and a rooster crowed," constitute a significant text-critical problem (ἀλέκτωρ, nom. sg. masc. of ἀλέκτωρ, -ορος, ὁ, "rooster"; ἐφώνησεν, 3rd sg. aor. act. indic. of φωνέω, "crow" [BDAG 1071a]). A number of important Gk. mss. omit the words καὶ ἀλέκτωρ ἐφώνησεν (א, B, L, W, Ψ, 579, and 892). What makes the text-critical problem even more difficult is that it connects with textual problems that appear elsewhere in Mark, since Mark's Gospel—in contrast to the other three Gospels—seems to indicate that a rooster crowed twice, once after Peter's first denial and a second time after his third denial (see 14:30, 72). The most common explanation for the various textual problems is that all the references indicating a second rooster crow are orig. to Mark's account and that all the omissions arose as a way to harmonize Mark's Gospel with the par. accounts in Matthew, Luke, and John (e.g., Metzger 96–98; France 573, 618; Yarbro Collins 658, 697–98). In this way, Mark's Gospel orig. portrayed Peter as receiving a warning shot, an initial crowing of the rooster just after his first denial, so that Peter's continuing repudiation of Jesus is all the more egregious. For another possible solution, one that regards the shorter readings that indicate a single rooster crow as orig., see John W. Wenham, "How Many Cock-Crowings? The Problem of Harmonistic Text-Variants," NTS 25 (1978–79): 523–25.

14:69 Παιδίσκη, nom. sg. fem. of παιδίσκη, -ης, ἡ, "female slave"; ἰδοῦσα, nom. sg. fem. of aor. act. ptc. of ὁράω, "see, look at"; temp. adv. ptc. antecedent; ἤρξατο, 3rd sg. aor. mid. indic. of ἄρχω, "begin" (mng. with mid.; on ἄρχομαι, see 1:45 [cf. 14:71]); λέγειν, pres. act. inf. of λέγω, "say"; complementary inf.; παρεστῶσιν, dat. pl. masc. of pf. act. ptc. of παρίστημι, "be present, stand nearby" (pres. tense intrans. use with pf., BDAG 778c–d); subst. ptc.; ὅτι, introduces dir. discourse. The prep. ἐκ can have a partitive sense (Moule 72; Wallace 371), but with that sense in v. 69 it also implies a pred. nom. on which the prep. phrase then depends: "one of them" (see also 14:70). In this way, the female slave identified Peter not just as someone who had been with Jesus as in v. 67 but as someone who actually belonged to the group of his followers.

14:70 Ἠρνεῖτο, 3rd sg. impf. mid. indic. of dep. ἀρνέομαι, "deny, disown, repudiate" (on the impf. to portray a dramatic action in progress as it unfolds, see 1:21). The third and last challenge to Peter came not from the female slave but from the bystanders (παρεστῶτες, nom. pl. masc. of pf. act. ptc. of παρίστημι, "be present, stand nearby" [pres. tense intrans. use with pf., BDAG 778c–d]; subst. ptc.), who point to Peter's status as a Galilean as evidence that he is indeed also one of Jesus's followers (ἀληθῶς, adv. mng. "in truth, certainly"; καί, adjunctive). How the bystanders knew that Peter was a Galilean Mark does not say, but the most likely explanation would be his accent, a point that Matthew states directly (Matt 26:73; cf. Evans 466; France 622; Strauss 664).

14:71 Ἤρξατο, 3rd sg. aor. mid. indic. of ἄρχω, "begin" (mng. with mid.); ἀναθεματίζειν, pres. act. inf. of ἀναθεματίζω, "curse, put oneself under a curse"; complementary inf. To put someone—incl. possibly oneself—under a curse meant to assign that individual to harm and destruction under divine wrath (cf. *TDNT* 1:354). Since ἀναθεματίζω is a trans. vb., the object of the curse is normally expressed, but that is not the case in 14:71. In all likelihood, Peter was pronouncing a potential curse on himself as a way of supporting the truth of his claims (BDAG 63c; *EDNT* 1:81 [implied dir. obj.: ἑαυτόν]; cf. Acts 23:12, 14, 21; 1 Sam 20:13; 2 Sam 3:9; 1 Kgs 19:2; 20:10; 1 En. 6:4–7). Ὀμνύναι, pres. act. inf. of ὄμνυμι (alternate spelling of ὀμνύω, [BDAG 705d]), "swear, take an oath"; complementary inf.; ὅτι, introduces dir. discourse; οἶδα, 1st sg. pf. act. indic. of οἶδα, "know"; λέγετε, "talk about, speak of" (when used with an acc. noun or pron.; cf. John 6:71; 8:27; 1 Cor 10:29 [see Taylor 575; Cranfield 448]).

14:72 Δευτέρου, gen. sg. neut. of δεύτερος, -α, -ον, "second" (the prep. phrase ἐκ δευτέρου is functioning adv. and is equivalent to the neut. acc. adj. form δεύτερον used as an adv.: "a second time, for the second time" [BDAG 221a; cf. R 550]); on the text-critical problem related to ἐκ δευτέρου, see 14:68; ἀλέκτωρ, nom. sg. masc. of ἀλέκτωρ, -ορος, ὁ, "rooster"; ἐφώνησεν, 3rd sg. aor. act. indic. of φωνέω, "crow" (BDAG 1071a); ἀνεμνήσθη, 3rd sg. aor. pass. indic. of ἀναμιμνήσκω, "be reminded of, remember" (mng. with pass.); ὡς, "that, which" (on ὡς as practically equivalent to a rel. pron. in this context, see BDAG 1104a; T 137); εἶπεν, "had spoken" (on the aor. for prior past action, see 5:8); ὅτι, introduces dir. discourse; πρίν, a temp. conj. mng. "before," often followed by an inf. (see 14:30); ἀλέκτορα, acc. sg. masc. of ἀλέκτωρ, -ορος, ὁ, "rooster"; acc. subj. of inf.; φωνῆσαι, aor. act. inf. of φωνέω, "crow"; inf. of subsequent time; δίς, adv. mng. "twice"; on the text-critical problem related to δίς, see 14:68; τρίς, adv. mng. "three times"; ἀπαρνήσῃ, 2nd sg. fut. mid. indic. of dep. ἀπαρνέομαι, "deny."

The ptc. ἐπιβαλών stands as "one of the unsolved enigmas" of Mark's vocabulary (Swete 366). The vb. ἐπιβάλλω appears elsewhere in Mark's Gospel in ways that fit within the boundaries of its common uses (4:37: "throw [themselves] on"; 11:7: "put on"; 14:46: "lay [hands] on"). Yet none of the more common uses for ἐπιβάλλω fits the context of 14:72. One possibility, perhaps the most likely, is that Mark was using ἐπιβάλλω as a synonym for the related compound vb. συμβάλλω, which can mean "reflect on, give careful thought to, ponder" (e.g., Luke 2:19, "Mary held all these sayings in her memory and reflected on them [συμβάλλουσα] in her heart"; cf. LN 30.7). The resulting translation would then be: "And after he thought deeply about this, he wept" (ἐπιβαλών, nom. sg. masc. of aor. act. ptc. of ἐπιβάλλω, "reflect on, think about seriously, think about deeply" [LN 30.7; cf. LSJ 624]; temp. adv. ptc. antecedent; ἔκλαιεν, 3rd sg. impf. act. indic. of κλαίω, "weep" [on the impf. to portray a dramatic action in progress as it unfolds, see 1:21]).

FOR FURTHER STUDY

34. Jesus's Trial in Mark

Bammel, E. "The Trial before Pilate." Pages 415–51 in *Jesus and the Politics of His Day*. Edited by Ernst Bammel and C. F. D. Moule. Cambridge: Cambridge University Press, 1984.

Bammel, Ernst, ed. *The Trial of Jesus: Cambridge Studies in Honour of C. F. D. Moule*. SBT 13. Naperville, IL: Alec R. Allenson, 1970.

Blinzler, Josef. *The Trial of Jesus: The Jewish and Roman Proceedings against Jesus Christ Described and Assessed from the Oldest Accounts*. Westminster, MD: Neuman, 1959.

*Bock, Darrell L. *Blasphemy and Exultation in Judaism: The Charge against Jesus in Mark 14:53–65*. Repr, ed. Grand Rapids: Baker, 2000.

Catchpole, David R. *The Trial of Jesus: A Study in the Gospels and Jewish Historiography from 1770 to the Present Day*. Leiden: Brill, 1971.

Chapman, David W., and Eckhard J. Schnabel. *The Trial and Crucifixion of Jesus: Texts and Commentary*. WUNT 1/344. Tübingen: Mohr Siebeck, 2015.

Donahue, John R. *Are You the Christ? The Trial Narrative in the Gospel of Mark*. SBLDS 10. Missoula, MT: Society of Biblical Literature, 1973.

Juel, Donald. *Messiah and Temple: The Trial of Jesus in the Gospel of Mark*. SBLDS 31. Missoula, MT: Scholars Press, 1977.

Marcus, Joel. "Mark 14:61: 'Are You the Messiah-Son-of-God?'" *NovT* 31 (1989): 125–41.

Perrin, Norman. "The High Priest's Question and Jesus' Answer (Mark 14:61–62)." Pages 80–95 in *The Passion in Mark: Studies on Mark 14–16*. Edited by Werner H. Kelber. Philadelphia: Fortress, 1976.

Winter, Paul. *On the Trial of Jesus*. 2nd ed. Revised and edited by T. A. Burkill and Geza Vermes. Berlin: de Gruyter, 1974.

Yarbro Collins, Adela. "The Charge of Blasphemy in Mark 14.64." *JSNT* 26 (2004): 379–401.

HOMILETICAL SUGGESTIONS

The Trial of Jesus and the Trial of Peter (14:53–72)

1. What do we learn about Jesus?
   a. He spoke the truth about his identity.
   b. He spoke the truth about his future glory.
   c. He spoke the truth without consideration for the consequences.
2. What do we learn about discipleship faithfulness and failure?
   a. The cost of discipleship faithfulness is real.
   b. The heartbreak of discipleship failure is more devastating.

The Portrait of Jesus according to Mark 14

1. Jesus knows what the future holds.

    a. He understood the circumstances that his disciples would face (e.g., 14:12–16, 27–31).

    b. He understood the destiny that he himself would face (e.g., 14:8, 22–25, 27).

2. Jesus followed the Father's will, even though he knew what the future would hold.

3. Believers do not always know what the future holds.

4. Believers can seek the Father's will, even though they do not know what the future holds.

5. Trial before Pilate and Mocking by Soldiers (15:1–20)

15:1 Ch. 15 points to a shift in setting with the religious leaders making a plan to hand Jesus over to the Roman governor on a political charge—that he claimed to be the King of the Jews—and to ask for his execution. Πρωΐ, adv. mng. "early in the morning"; συμβούλιον, acc. sg. neut. of συμβούλιον, -ου, τό, "plan." Although συμβούλιον can refer to an official council meeting (ESV: "held a consultation"), Mark earlier used συμβούλιον instead for a "plan" (i.e., a decision made by a group for how to proceed) in the only other time the word appears in his Gospel (3:6), and that is probably the sense in 15:1 as well (NET: "after forming a plan"; cf. BDAG 957b). Ποιήσαντες, nom. pl. masc. of aor. act. ptc. of ποιέω, "make, form"; temp. adv. ptc. antecedent; καί (3rd use): "that is" (see ZG 160; Z §455 [i.e., the Sanhedrin is not another group but is constituted by the chief priests, elders, and scribes]); συνέδριον, nom. sg. neut. of συνέδριον, -ου, τό, Sanhedrin; δήσαντες, nom. pl. masc. of aor. act. ptc. of δέω, "bind"; temp. adv. ptc. antecedent; ἀπήνεγκαν, 3rd pl. aor. act. indic. of ἀποφέρω, "lead away"; παρέδωκαν, 3rd pl. aor. act. indic. of παραδίδωμι, "hand over" (on παραδίδωμι, see 1:14; 3:19).

15:2 Ἐπηρώτησεν, 3rd sg. aor. act. indic. of ἐπερωτάω, "ask"; βασιλεύς, pred. nom.; Ἰουδαίων, gen. of subordination. Jesus's answer to Pilate's question is noncommittal, neither a direct affirmation nor a direct denial (on ὁ δέ, see 1:45; ἀποκριθείς, nom. sg. masc. of aor. pass. ptc. of dep. ἀποκρίνομαι, "answer"; redundant ptc.; λέγει, historical pres. [see 1:30]). His answer ("you say") seems to convey something like: "That is your way of speaking; I would not express myself with quite those same words" (see Margaret Thrall, *Greek Particles in the New Testament: Linguistics and Exegetical Studies*, NTTS 3 [Leiden: Brill, 1962], 75–77; Thrall regards σὺ λέγεις in Mark 15:2, σὺ λέγεις ὅτι βασιλεύς εἰμι in John 18:37, and ὑμεῖς λέγετε in Luke 22:70 as intentionally ambiguous, but she understands σὺ εἶπας in Matt 26:25, 64, with the aor. rather than the pres. tense, as directly affirmative: "You have made the decisive statement," implying also "and you are right."). At the very least, Jesus's answer in the present v. is ambiguous enough that Pilate saw no need to condemn him immediately as an insurrectionist and later apparently was willing to release him (cf. Hooker 367–68; Brooks 250).

15:3 Κατηγόρουν, 3rd pl. impf. act. indic. of κατηγορέω, "accuse" (impf. used for background information; see 1:21). The vb. κατηγορέω can take two objects, one in the gen. (αὐτοῦ) for the person being accused (cf. 3:2) and one in the acc. (πολλά) for what the person is being accused of (Decker 2:236–37; cf. BDAG 533b; R 511). Although the neut. acc. pl. form πολλά (from πολύς) functions freq. as an intensifying adv. in Mark (see 1:45; 3:12; 5:10, 23, 38, 43; 6:20, 23; 9:26), in 15:3 πολλά is best understood as the acc. dir. obj. of κατηγόρουν, based on the normal case usage with κατηγορέω (Decker 2:237) and based on the corresponding use of πόσα ("how many things") as the acc. dir. obj. of κατηγοροῦσιν in 15:4 (ZG 160; Cranfield 49; cf. NIV: "The chief priests accused him of many things").

15:4 Ἐπηρώτα, 3rd sg. impf. act. indic. of ἐπερωτάω, "ask" (on ἐπερωτάω, see 4:10); λέγων, nom. sg. masc. of pres. act. ptc. of λέγω, "say"; redundant ptc. Since Pilate's question begins with οὐκ, the expected answer is affirmative (see 4:21, 38; cf. the similar question from the high priest in 14:60). Wording the question in this way seems to express some confusion or perhaps frustration on the part of Pilate: "You really plan to answer nothing, don't you?" (ἀποκρίνῃ, 2nd sg. pres. mid. indic. of dep. ἀποκρίνομαι, "answer"). With his following words, Pilate apparently intended to pressure Jesus into responding to the charges made against him: "Look at how many things they are accusing you of" (on ἴδε, see 1:2; πόσα, interr. pron. introducing an indir. question [R 292]; κατηγοροῦσιν, from κατηγορέω, "accuse"; κατηγορέω takes a gen. obj. [σου] and an acc. obj. [πόσα]; see 15:3).

15:5 On how dbl. negatives strengthen a statement, see 1:44; ἀπεκρίθη, 3rd sg. aor. pass. indic. of dep. ἀποκρίνομαι, "answer"; θαυμάζειν, pres. act. inf. of θαυμάζω, "wonder, marvel, be astonished"; inf. of result; Πιλᾶτον, acc. subj. of inf. From this point on in Mark's narrative, Jesus goes almost completely silent. His only remaining words are in his cry from the cross, questioning why God has forsaken him.

15:6 In v. 6, Mark begins to provide background information to explain Pilate's release of a prisoner, with the prisoner potentially being Jesus (on the impf. for background information, see 1:21; cf. the impf. in 15:10). However, the impf. vb. ἀπέλυεν is used additionally for a customary action, given the distributive use of κατά at the beginning of the verse (Fanning 173–74, 246; cf. Decker 2:238–39). The distributive use of κατά indicates the division of an event into a series of parts and therefore the repetition of a particular action on a number of occasions (see 14:49). At each celebration of the festival (ἑορτήν, acc. sg. fem. of ἑορτή, -ῆς, ἡ, "festival, feast"; on κατά in 15:6, see R 608; BDAG 512b), Pilate was customarily releasing one prisoner whom the people requested (ἀπέλυεν, 3rd sg. impf. act. indic. of ἀπολύω, "release, set free"; δέσμιον, acc. sg. masc. of δέσμιος, -ου, ὁ, "prisoner"; παρῃτοῦντο, 3rd pl. impf. mid. indic. of dep. παραιτέομαι, "ask for, request").

15:7 In 15:7, Mark continues to provide background information but shifts to pluperf. forms (on the pluperf. indic. and the pluperf. periph. cstr. for background information, see 14:44; cf. the pluperf. in 15:10). The background information in v. 7 has to do with a man named Barabbas (λεγόμενος, nom. sg. masc. of pres. pass. ptc. of λέγω, "call, name" [BDAG 590b]; subst. ptc.; Βαραββᾶς, pred. nom. after a pass. form functioning as an equative vb. [cf. Wallace 40]). Barabbas is an Aram. patronymic, a name derived from the name of one's father. It would not be necessary to know Aram. to discern the significance of the name, since Mark's Gospel itself provides sufficient information to make sense of it (Marcus 2:1028; see 10:46, which defines the Aram. name "Bartimaeus" as "son of Timaeus," and 14:36, which translates "Abba" as "father"). "Barabbas" means "son of the father" (note also that it takes 1st decl. masc. endings [for general rules on the decl. of Sem. names, see MH 143]). The contrast between Barabbas and Jesus, the true and faithful Son of Abba, only increases the irony of the scene. Barabbas had been imprisoned with certain rebels (ἦν, 3rd sg. impf. act. indic. of εἰμί, "be"; στασιαστῶν, gen. pl. masc. of στασιαστής, -οῦ, ὁ, "rebel, revolutionary, insurrectionist"; δεδεμένος, nom. sg. masc. of pf. pass. ptc. of δέω, "bind, imprison"; pluperf. periph. ptc. cstr.). The rel. pron. οἵτινες, which in this context is equivalent to the simple rel. pron. οἵ (BDAG 730a; cf. R 727; Z §216), points back to στασιαστῶν as its antecedent. Therefore, Mark indicates that it was the rebels who had committed murder in the insurrection without directly implicating Barabbas in that crime (στάσει, dat. sg. fem. of στάσις, -εως, ἡ, "uprising, revolt, rebellion, insurrection"; φόνον, acc. sg. masc. of φόνος, -ου, ὁ, "murder"; πεποιήκεισαν, 3rd pl. pluperf. act. indic. of ποιέω, commit).

15:8 Having covered the necessary background information in vv. 6–7, Mark returns to the main sequence of events in v. 8. Ἀναβάς, nom. sg. masc. of aor. act. ptc. of ἀναβαίνω, "go up, come up"; temp. adv. ptc. antecedent; ἤρξατο, 3rd sg. aor. mid. indic. of ἄρχω, "begin" (mng. with mid.; on ἄρχομαι, see 1:45); αἰτεῖσθαι, pres. mid. inf. of αἰτέω, ask (mng. with mid.); complementary inf. (on the use of the mid. of αἰτέω within the context of business dealings and contracts, see 6:24). The inf. αἰτεῖσθαι assumes both a request and someone to receive that request. Mark does not state either directly but rather allows the following subord. clause to supply the necessary information for filling in the missing words: "The crowd began to ask (Pilate to do) just as he was customarily doing for them" (ἐποίει, 3rd sg. impf. act. indic. of ποιέω, "do" [because it refers back to the customary impf. ἀπέλυεν in v. 6, ἐποίει is also a customary impf.]; αὐτοῖς, dat. of interest [advantage]).

15:9 Ἀπεκρίθη, 3rd sg. aor. pass. indic. of dep. ἀποκρίνομαι, "answer"; λέγων, nom. sg. masc. of pres. act. ptc. of λέγω, "say"; redundant ptc.; ἀπολύσω, 1st sg. aor. act. subjunc. of ἀπολύω, "release, set free"; subjunc. after an implied complementary ἵνα. Whenever Mark uses a 2nd pers. form of θέλω in a question and follows it with a 1st pers. subjunc., he implies but does not state a complementary ἵνα before the subjunc. vb. (see the discussion at 10:36; cf. also 10:51; 14:12; 15:12). The implied complementary ἵνα along with the subjunc. ἀπολύσω is functionally equivalent to a complementary inf. and should be translated that way ("do you want me to release"). The same grammatical structure will appear again in Pilate's next question in 15:12.

15:10 In v. 10, Mark explains the reason why (γάρ) Pilate asked the crowd concerning the release of Jesus—because he knew (ἐγίνωσκεν, 3rd sg. impf. act. indic. of γινώσκω,

"know") that the chief priests had handed him over on account of envy (φθόνον, acc.
sg. masc. of φθόνος, -ου, ὁ, "envy, jealousy"; παραδεδώκεισαν, 3rd pl. pluperf. act.
indic. of παραδίδωμι, "hand over").

15:11 The vb. ἀνασείω is a synonym of σείω, which can mean lit. "to shake," as in,
e.g., the shaking of an earthquake (cf. Matt 27:51; Heb 12:26), or fig. "to stir up," as
in inciting a crowd to create a disturbance (cf. Matt 21:10; BDAG 71b, 918c–d). The
two occurrences of ἀνασείω in the NT (Mark 15:11; Luke 23:5) both follow the fig.
use, here in 15:11 for stirring up the crowd to ask for the release of Barabbas instead of
Jesus (ἀνέσεισαν, 3rd pl. aor. act. indic. of ἀνασείω, "shake up, stir up, incite"; ἀπολύσῃ,
3rd sg. aor. act. subjunc. of ἀπολύω, "release, set free"; subjunc. in a purpose ἵνα
clause). The subord. clause ἵνα μᾶλλον τὸν Βαραββᾶν ἀπολύσῃ αὐτοῖς is a compressed
way to say "in order that they might ask him to release Barabbas to them instead" (cf.
Cranfield 451).

15:12 Ἀποκριθείς, nom. sg. masc. of aor. pass. ptc. of dep. ἀποκρίνομαι, "answer";
redundant ptc.; on the impf. with λέγω, see 2:16; ποιήσω, 1st sg. aor. act. subjunc. of
ποιέω, "do" with (when ποιέω means "do with," it can take a dbl. acc. of the person
[implied antecedent of ὅν] and the thing [τί]; cf. BDAG 841a; R 484); subjunc. after an
implied complementary ἵνα (on the translation of ποιήσω as a complementary inf., see
15:9); ὅν, "the one whom" (rel. pron. without an antecedent, which should be supplied
in Eng. [cf. 3:13]); when λέγω means "call," it can take a dbl. acc. with an obj. (ὅν)
and a complement (βασιλέα, BDAG 590b; cf. 10:18; 12:37). Just as earlier in v. 9, so
now also in v. 12 αὐτοῖς refers to the people of the crowd, with the implication being
that throughout this section (15:6–15) Pilate's conversation is back and forth with the
crowd and not directly with the chief priests.

15:13 On οἱ δέ, see 1:45 (cf. also 15:14); ἔκραξαν, 3rd pl. aor. act. indic. of κράζω, "cry
out, shout"; σταύρωσον, 2nd sg. aor. act. impv. of σταυρόω, "crucify." The use of πάλιν
in v. 13 presents some difficulty for interpretation, since this is the first outcry from the
crowd directly mentioned by Mark (see BDAG 753a for a list of possible solutions).
Although some versions solve the problem by translating πάλιν as "back" (e.g., NET:
"they shouted back"; cf. NASB; NRSV; NLT), πάλιν normally means "back" with vbs.
of motion (e.g., 2:1; 11:3, 27; 14:40) and "again" with vbs. of speaking (e.g., 10:1, 24;
14:61, 69, 70; 15:12). It is perhaps better to translate πάλιν as "again," thereby indicating that the crowd had indeed already cried out to Pilate, presumably in v. 11, when
the chief priests stirred up the people to demand the release of Barabbas (cf. Decker
2:243–44).

15:14 The conj. γάρ shows that the point of the question is to find the reason for the
crowd's previous demand. When used in a question in this way, Eng. idiom calls for
γάρ to be translated as an initial separate question (BDAG 189c; ZG 161): "Why?
What evil did he do?" (ἐποίησεν, 3rd sg. aor. act. indic. of ποιέω, "do"). The crowd
does not answer the question directly but simply restates the previous demand more
insistently (περισσῶς, adv. mng. "even more, all the more"; ἔκραξαν, 3rd pl. aor. act.
indic. of κράζω, "cry out"; σταύρωσον, 2nd sg. aor. act. impv. of σταυρόω, "crucify").

15:15 Βουλόμενος, nom. sg. masc. of pres. mid. ptc. of dep. βούλομαι, "wish, want, plan"; adv. ptc. of cause; ὄχλῳ, dat. of interest (advantage); ποιῆσαι, aor. act. inf. of ποιέω, "make"; complementary inf. The phrase τῷ ὄχλῳ τὸ ἱκανὸν ποιῆσαι (lit: "to do that which is sufficient for the crowd") involves a Lat. idiom mng. "to satisfy the crowd" or "to please the crowd" (LN 25.96; BDF §5; Moule 192). Ἀπέλυσεν, 3rd sg. aor. act. indic. of ἀπολύω, "release, set free"; παρέδωκεν, 3rd sg. aor. act. indic. of παραδίδωμι, "hand over" (on παραδίδωμι, see 1:14; 3:19); φραγελλώσας, nom. sg. masc. of aor. act. ptc. of φραγελλόω, "scourge, flog, have someone scourged"; temp. adv. ptc. antecedent; causative act. (cf. Wallace 412; Marcus 2:1031); σταυρωθῇ, 3rd sg. aor. pass. subjunc. of σταυρόω, "crucify"; subjunc. in a purpose ἵνα clause. By using the ptc. φραγελλώσας, Mark makes reference to the common Roman practice of tying a condemned prisoner to a post and scourging him with a whip as a prelude to crucifixion (cf. Philo, *Flaccus* 72; Jos., *J.W.* 2.14.9 §306; 2.14.9 §308; 5.11.1 §449). The whip (φραγέλλιον; Lat.: flagellum) consisted of leather straps with pieces of bone and bits of metal embedded in the straps. In contrast to the Jewish practice, which allowed only thirty-nine lashes, the Roman custom put no such limitation on the number of strokes. In many cases, the beating itself was so severe that it was fatal (*TDNT* 4:515–19).

15:16 Ἀπήγαγον, 3rd pl. aor. act. indic. of ἀπάγω, "lead away." Normally, ἔσω, which occurs only nine times in the NT, serves as an adv. mng. "inside," but here it functions as a prep. mng. "into" with a gen. obj. (R 642–43; Moule 85; Harris 246). Συγκαλοῦσιν, from συγκαλέω, "call together, summon"; historical pres. Beginning with συγκαλοῦσιν, Mark clusters together a whole series of historical pres. vbs., both in the mocking scene in vv. 16–20 and in the following crucifixion scene. To this cluster of historical pres. vbs. in the mocking scene (συγκαλοῦσιν in v. 16; ἐνδιδύσκουσιν and περιτιθέασιν in v. 17; ἐξάγουσιν in v. 20), Mark inserts several impf. vbs. in v. 19 as well (ἔτυπτον, ἐνέπτυον, and προσεκύνουν). The result is a series of dramatic events portrayed in a vivid way, as though the action has slowed down so that the audience can watch it as it unfolds in the narrative (on historical pres. vbs. [see 1:12]; on impf. vbs. [see 1:21]). Σπεῖραν, acc. sg. fem. of σπεῖρα, -ης, ἡ, "cohort." The noun σπεῖρα typically functions as a reference to a Roman cohort, a company of soldiers that was one-tenth of a legion or around 600 solders, although the number could vary (BDAG 936; cf. Jos., *J.W.* 3.4.2 §67). It is difficult to know if Mark intended to use σπεῖρα as a precise military term or to employ it more loosely for all the soldiers who were available at the governor's residence at that time. However, Mark's choice of words—"the whole cohort"—leaves the impression that a large number of soldiers joined in the subsequent mocking of Jesus with the full participation of all those who were present.

15:17 The soldiers mock Jesus by pretending to dress him with royal attire and to pay homage to him as a king, but their cruel actions communicate that they believe him to be a powerless fool. Yet for Mark's audience, Jesus is in truth the messianic king, just not the kind of king that the soldiers would have expected, a ruler who would willingly give his life for his people. Ἐνδιδύσκουσιν, from ἐνδιδύσκω, "dress with, put on" (ἐνδιδύσκουσιν takes a dbl. acc. with an obj. of the pers. [αὐτόν] and an obj. of the thing [πορφύραν]; see 15:20); πορφύραν, acc. sg. fem. of πορφύρα, -ας, ἡ, "purple cloak, purple clothing"; περιτιθέασιν, 3rd pl. pres. act. indic. of περιτίθημι, "place on" (περιτίθημι often takes a dat. obj. [αὐτῷ] indicating on whom or what an acc. obj. is placed [here an implied αὐτόν pointing forward to στέφανον]; cf. 15:36); πλέξαντες, nom. pl. masc. of aor. act. ptc. of πλέκω, "weave together, twist together"; temp. adv. ptc. antecedent; ἀκάνθινον, acc. sg. masc. of ἀκάνθινος, -η, -ον, "thorny, made of thorn branches"; στέφανον, acc. sg. masc. of στέφανος, -ου, ὁ, "crown, wreath."

15:18 Ἤρξαντο, 3rd pl. aor. mid. indic. of ἄρχω, "begin" (mng. with mid.; on ἄρχομαι, see 1:45); ἀσπάζεσθαι, pres. mid. inf. of dep. ἀσπάζομαι, "greet, welcome, acclaim"; complementary inf.; χαῖρε, 2nd sg. pres. act. impv. of χαίρω, "hail, greetings" (mng. with impv., cf. BDAG 1075b). The impv. χαῖρε served as a common and formalized expression of greeting, one that implied a wish that the person so greeted would have reasons to rejoice (cf. LN 33.22). Βασιλεῦ, voc. (MH 142).

15:19 Ἔτυπτον, 3rd pl. impf. act. indic. of τύπτω, "strike, beat"; καλάμῳ, dat. sg. masc. of κάλαμος, -ου, ὁ, "reed, staff"; dat. of means/ instr.; ἐνέπτυον, 3rd pl. impf. act. indic. of ἐμπτύω, "spit on"; αὐτῷ, dat. dir. obj.; τιθέντες, nom. pl. masc. of pres. act. ptc. of τίθημι, "place, bend"; temp. adv. ptc. contemp.; γόνατα, acc. pl. neut. of γόνυ, -ατος, τό, "knee." The ptc. clause τιθέντες τὰ γόνατα (probably a Lat. idiom [BDF §5; Moule 192; Turner, *Style* 29]) lit. means "placing the knees (on the ground)," but it can be translated into Eng. as "kneeling down," in this way absorbing the reference to "the knees" into the verbal phrase itself (cf. BDAG 1003d; LN 8.47; 17.19). Προσεκύνουν, 3rd pl. impf. act. indic. of προσκυνέω, "prostrate oneself before, pay homage to, worship"; αὐτῷ, dat. dir. obj.

15:20 Ἐνέπαιξαν, 3rd pl. aor. act. indic. of ἐμπαίζω, "mock, ridicule" (on the aor. for prior past action ["had mocked"], see 3:10; 5:8; αὐτῷ, dat. dir. obj. Mark's use of the vb. ἐμπαίζω to summarize the soldiers' actions recalls the use of the same vb. in 10:34, where Jesus predicted that, after being handed over to the Gentiles, they would mock him. In fact, Mark records three scenes in which Jesus is mocked, at the end of his hearing before the Sanhedrin, where he is rejected as a false prophet (14:65); at the end of his trial before Pilate, where he is mocked as a false king (15:16–20); and at the crucifixion, where he is ridiculed as a false messiah who cannot save (15:29–32). Ἐξέδυσαν, 3rd pl. aor. act. indic. of ἐκδύω, "take off"; πορφύραν, acc. sg. fem. of πορφύρα, -ας, ἡ, "purple cloak, purple clothing"; ἐνέδυσαν, 3rd pl. aor. act. indic. of ἐνδύω, "put on, clothe"). In Gk., vbs. related to clothing can take a dbl. acc. (cf. R 483; Moule 33; Wallace 181–82). Therefore, ἐξέδυσαν has an acc. for the pers. affected (αὐτόν) and another for the clothing removed (πορφύραν). Likewise, ἐνέδυσαν takes both an acc. for the pers. clothed (αὐτόν) and another for the clothing put on him (ἱμάτια). Ἐξάγουσιν, from ἐξάγω, "lead out, bring out"; σταυρώσωσιν, 3rd pl. aor. act. subjunc. of σταυρόω, "crucify"; subjunc. in a purpose ἵνα clause.

FOR FURTHER STUDY

35. Crucifixion

Chapman, David W. *Ancient Jewish and Christian Perceptions of Crucifixion*. WUNT 2/244. Tübingen: Mohr Siebeck, 2008.

Chapman, David W., and Eckhard J. Schnabel. *The Trial and Crucifixion of Jesus: Texts and Commentary*. WUNT 1/344. Tübingen: Mohr Siebeck, 2015.

Cook, John Granger. *Crucifixion in the Mediterranean World*. WUNT 1/327. Tübingen: Mohr Siebeck, 2014. Reprint edition.

Edwards, William D., Wesley J. Gabel, and Floyd E. Hosmer. "On the Physical Death of Jesus Christ." *Journal of the American Medical Association* 255 (1986): 1455–63.

Fitzmyer, Joseph A. "Crucifixion in Ancient Palestine, Qumran Literature, and the New Testament." *CBQ* 40 (1978): 493–513.

*Hengel, Martin. *Crucifixion in the Ancient World and the Folly of the Message of the Cross*. Philadelphia: Fortress, 1977.

Maslen, Matthew W., and Piers D. Mitchell. "Medical Theories on the Cause of Death in Crucifixion." *Journal of the Royal Society of Medicine* 99 (2006): 185–88.

Miller, Johnny V. "The Time of the Crucifixion." *JETS* 26 (1983): 157–66.

Samuelsson, Gunnar. *Crucifixion in Antiquity: An Inquiry into the Background and Significance of the New Testament Terminology of Crucifixion*. 2nd ed. WUNT 2/310. Tübingen: Mohr Siebeck, 2013.

Tzaferis, Vassilios. "Crucifixion: The Archaeological Evidence." *Biblical Archaeology Review* 11.1 (1985): 44–53.

HOMILETICAL SUGGESTIONS

Three Mocking Scenes: The Foolishness of Rejecting Jesus

1. The mocking scene at the trial: Jesus is a true prophet. (14:65)
2. The mocking scene at the palace: Jesus is the true king. (15:16–20)
3. The mocking scene at the cross: Jesus is the true Messiah who is able to save. (15:29–32)

6. Crucifixion and Burial (15:21–47)

15:21 As in the previous verses (see 15:16), Mark clusters together a number of historical pres. vbs. in the crucifixion scene (see ἀγγαρεύουσιν in v. 21, φέρουσιν in v. 22, σταυροῦσιν and διαμερίζονται in v. 24, and σταυροῦσιν in v. 27). This repeated use of the historical pres. serves to slow down the narrative, vividly portraying past actions as though they were taking place in the present, right before our eyes (see 1:12). In addition, Mark clusters together a number of impf. vbs. in the crucifixion scene (ἐδίδουν in v. 23, ἐβλασφήμουν in v. 29, ἔλεγον in v. 31, ὠνείδιζον in v. 32, ἔλεγον in v. 35, and ἐπότιζεν in v. 36), further slowing down the action and calling on the audience to watch the action in progress as it unfolds in the past (see 1:21). The pace of the narrative decreases dramatically, and the events at the cross progress in a way that demands careful attention and thought.

Ἀγγαρεύουσιν, from ἀγγαρεύω, "force, compel, press into service"; παράγοντα, acc. sg. masc. of pres. act. ptc. of παράγω, "pass by"; subst. ptc.; Σίμωνα, acc. in simple appos. to παράγοντα; ἐρχόμενον, acc. sg. masc. of pres. mid. ptc. of dep. ἔρχομαι, "come"; adj. ptc. without an art. because it is modifying the indef. subst. ptc. παράγοντα; πατέρα, acc. in simple appos. to Σίμωνα; Ἀλεξάνδρου and Ῥούφου, gen. of relationship. Mark's wording for Simon taking up his cross (ἄρῃ τὸν σταυρὸν αὐτοῦ [15:21]; ἄρῃ, 3rd sg. aor. act. subjunc. of αἴρω, "take up"; subjunc. in a complementary ἵνα clause) echoes the command that Jesus gave to anyone who wanted to follow him—he must take up his cross (ἀράτω τὸν σταυρὸν αὐτοῦ [8:34]; Cranfield 455; Hooker 372). While the phrase is essentially the same, the referent of αὐτοῦ has changed to Jesus himself, and the task of taking up the cross falls not to one of Jesus's followers but to someone who just happened to be passing by.

15:22 On φέρω in the sense of "bring" or "lead," see BDAG 1051d; France 641 (cf. 7:32; 8:22; 9:17–20; 11:2, 7); τὸν Γολγοθᾶν τόπον, lit. "the Golgotha place" (on Aram. words, see 7:34). In a grammatically awkward way, Mark places the acc. fem. proper noun Γολγοθᾶν in a 1st attrib. adj. position between the art. and τόπον, apparently forcing Γολγοθᾶν to function as an adj. even though it is not an adj. and cannot therefore agree in gender with τόπον (Decker 2:250). By understanding Γολγοθᾶν to be functioning as an adj., it is possible to make better sense of Mark's subsequent translation. The name Γολγοθᾶ derives from an Aram. word that by itself only means "skull" (BDAG 204d). Yet the whole phrase τὸν Γολγοθᾶν τόπον would mean "Place of the Skull," just as Mark stated in his translation (μεθερμηνευόμενον, nom. sg. neut. of pres. pass. ptc. of μεθερμηνεύω, translate; periph. ptc. [see 5:41]; κρανίου, gen. sg. neut. of κρανίον, -ου, τό, "skull").

15:23 Although unspecified, the subj. of ἐδίδουν in context would be the soldiers (i.e., the same as the subj. of ἐξάγουσιν in 15:20, ἀγγαρεύουσιν in 15:21, and φέρουσιν in 15:22). Ἐδίδουν, 3rd pl. impf. act. indic. of δίδωμι, "give, offer"; ἐσμυρνισμένον, acc. sg. masc. of pf. pass. ptc. of σμυρνίζω, "flavor with myrrh, mix with myrrh"; adj. ptc. without an art. modifying an anar. noun. Since wine mixed with myrrh was considered a delicacy (*TDNT* 7:458–59; cf. Pliny the Elder, *Natural History* 14.15 §92), the soldiers were in effect offering Jesus a drink of expensive wine or at least pretending to do so. The purpose for this action was probably not to relieve Jesus's suffering or to quench his thirst but rather to continue mocking him, as if offering a fine wine to the king (Evans 500–501; Strauss 690). Ὅς δέ, "but this one" or "but he" (on ὅς as a dem. pron., see R 695; BDAG 727d; MM 459); ἔλαβεν, 3rd sg. aor. act. indic. of λαμβάνω, "take, receive" (since λαμβάνω is typically trans., a dir. obj. for ἔλαβεν is implied).

15:24 Mark provides no details about the nature of Jesus's crucifixion or the physical suffering that it entailed. He only briefly states, "And they crucified him" (σταυροῦσιν, historical pres.). In Mark's narrative, the emph. falls more on Jesus's pain at being forsaken by God (15:34). Mark describes the division of Jesus's clothing in language that recalls Ps 22:18. Διαμερίζονται, 3rd pl. pres. mid. indic. of διαμερίζω, "divide among one another" (mng. with mid. [cf. BDAG 233d]); βάλλοντες, nom. pl. masc. of pres.

act. ptc. of βάλλω, "throw, cast"; adv. ptc. of means; κλῆρον, acc. sg. masc. of κλῆρος, -ου, ὁ, "lot" (Eng. idiom calls for the pl. in "casting lots," whereas Gk. can use either the sg. [e.g., Matt 27:35; Mark 15:24] or the pl. [e.g., Luke 23:34]); ἄρῃ, 3rd sg. aor. act. subjunc. of αἴρω, "take away"; delib. subjunc. The clause τίς τί ἄρῃ ("who should take what") is an indir. question that constitutes a dbl. interr. (R 737, 916, 1044, 1176; BDF §298; Decker 2:252), in this case blending together two delib. questions: "Who should take?" (τίς ἄρῃ;) and "What should he take?" (τί ἄρῃ;). Mark's allusion to Psalm 22 in this verse does not stand alone, since there are a number of allusions to the lament psalms in Mark's crucifixion scene (see esp. the use of Ps 22:7–8 in Mark 15:29, Ps 22:1 in Mark 15:34, and Ps 69:21 in Mark 15:36).

15:25 Ἦν, 3rd sg. impf. act. indic. of εἰμί, "be"; ὥρα, pred. nom. (ὥρα, which normally lacks the art. when used with an ordinal numeral [e.g., τρίτη], is still def. [R 793; T 178–79; Wallace 248]). Mark's freq. use of the coordinating conj. καί (see 1:5) means that he uses it here in a place where a subordinating temp. conj. such as ὅτε might otherwise be expected (R 1183; Moule 172; Z §§454–55). Ἐσταύρωσαν, 3rd pl. aor. act. indic. of σταυρόω, "crucify." By referring to the third hour in 15:25, the sixth hour in 15:33, and the ninth hour in 15:33–34—a precise pattern with three-hour intervals—Mark leaves the impression that all the events surrounding Jesus's death took place on schedule, according to a divinely ordered plan (cf. Hooker 373; Marcus 2:1043).

15:26 A public notice, likely attached to the cross (cf. Matt 27:37; John 19:19), announced the crime for which Jesus was being executed. Ἦν, 3rd sg. impf. act. indic. of εἰμί, "be"; ἐπιγραφή, nom. sg. fem. of ἐπιγραφή, -ῆς, ἡ, "inscription, written notice"; αἰτίας, gen. sg. fem. of αἰτία, -ας, ἡ, "charge"; obj. gen.; αὐτοῦ, obj. gen. (i.e., "they brought a charge against him"); ἐπιγεγραμμένη, nom. sg. fem. of pf. pass. ptc. of ἐπιγράφω, "write, inscribe, place (an inscription) over" (BDAG 370a); periph. ptc. (on the pluperf. periph. cstr., see 1:33; 14:44).

15:27 Λῃστάς, acc. pl. masc. of λῃστής, -οῦ, ὁ, "robber" (on λῃστής, see 11:17); ἕνα ... καὶ ἕνα, acc. in simple appos. to λῃστάς; ἐκ, "at, on" (expressing a position next to someone [see 10:37]); εὐωνύμων, gen. pl. neut. of εὐώνυμος, -ον, "left" (on the pl. with δεξιῶν and εὐωνύμων where Eng. would use the sg., see R 408; BDF §141). The language concerning "one at his right and one at his left" echoes the wording found in 10:37, 40, i.e., in Jesus's conversation with James and John (see the discussion at 10:38).

A number of important early mss. of Mark's Gospel do not include the words in 15:28: καὶ ἐπληρώθη ἡ γραφὴ ἡ λέγουσα, Καὶ μετὰ ἀνόμων ἐλογίσθη ("And the Scripture was fulfilled that says, 'And he was counted with the lawless'"). In fact, the earliest and best representatives of Alexandrian and Western mss. are among those that lack the words in v. 28 (א, A, B, C, D, Ψ). The words also do not easily fit within Mark's style, since he almost never elsewhere directly quotes from the OT to indicate the fulfillment of Scripture, and the verse can easily be explained as a later scribal addition derived from Luke 22:37 (Metzger 99; Strauss 693). Most recent translations skip straight from Mark 15:27 to 15:29 and do not include v. 28 (NKJV is an exception, as is NASB, which includes v. 28 but puts it in brackets to indicate that it is not in the earliest mss.).

15:29–30 Παραπορευόμενοι, nom. pl. masc. of pres. mid. ptc. of dep. παραπορεύομαι, "pass by"; subst. ptc.; ἐβλασφήμουν, 3rd pl. impf. act. indic. of βλασφημέω, "blaspheme." Mark's Gospel includes an alternating pattern of accusations concerning blasphemy. Those who oppose Jesus accuse him of blasphemy, while Jesus—or Mark himself—characterize the words of these opponents in the same way (2:6–7; 3:28–29; 14:63–64; 15:29–32). Unfortunately, most translations obscure this final step in the pattern by failing to translate ἐβλασφήμουν as "blasphemed" (see NKJV for an exception). Yet, for Mark, to suggest that God would send a Messiah who would choose to save himself rather than others was blasphemous, arrogantly dishonoring to God and to his work in the world (see Joel F. Williams, "Foreshadowing, Echoes, and the Blasphemy at the Cross [Mark 15:29]," *JBL* 132 [2013]: 913–33). Κινοῦντες, nom. pl. masc. of pres. act. ptc. of κινέω, "shake." To shake one's head conveyed scorn or contempt toward someone, esp. toward a person who was suffering in misery (cf. BDAG 545a; LN 16.2; see 2 Kgs 19:21; Job 16:4; Ps 22:7; Jer 18:16; Lam 2:15; Sir 12:18; 13:7 [cf. Ps 108:25 LXX, which uses σαλεύω instead of κινέω]). Λέγοντες, nom. pl. masc. of pres. act. ptc. of λέγω, "say" (since κινοῦντες and λέγοντες are joined together by καί, the use of the ptc. should be the same with both, likely here adv. ptc. of means [cf. Decker 2:254]). The mockers in Mark 15:29 begin their words with οὐά, an exclamation that conveys ridicule (LN 33.411) or scornful wonder (BDAG 734b; cf. MM 464). It is difficult to find a corresponding expression in Eng., since in Eng. ridicule is communicated more often through the use of insulting names or mocking laughter (e.g., CSB: "Ha!"). One possibility is to remove the exclamation and translate λέγοντες as "saying with ridicule," so that the following words are not taken at face value but are understood as being stated with a sarcastic and derisive tone. Both καταλύων (nom. sg. masc. of pres. act. ptc. of καταλύω, destroy) and οἰκοδομῶν (nom. sg. masc. of pres. act. ptc. of οἰκοδομέω, "build") are perhaps best explained as adj. participles modifying the implied subj. of the impv. σῶσον in v. 30 (e.g., NIV: "You who are going to destroy the temple and build it in three days"). Σῶσον, 2nd sg. aor. act. impv. of σῴζω, "save"; καταβάς, nom. sg. masc. of aor. act. ptc. of καταβαίνω, "come down"; adv. ptc. of means.

15:31 Καί, adjunctive; ἐμπαίζοντες, nom. pl. masc. of pres. act. ptc. of ἐμπαίζω, "mock, ridicule"; temp. adv. ptc. contemp.; πρὸς ἀλλήλους, "to one another" or "among themselves" (when used with vbs. of speaking [BDAG 874b]); ἔσωσεν, 3rd sg. aor. act. indic. of σῴζω, "save"; δύναται, 3rd sg. pres. mid. indic. of dep. δύναμαι, "be able to, can"; σῶσαι, aor. act. inf. of σῴζω, "save"; complementary inf. Jesus rescued others through his healing work (cf. σῴζω in 3:4; 5:23, 28, 34; 6:56; 10:52), but now he is unable to rescue himself from his suffering on the cross. The irony in the context of Mark's Gospel is, of course, that Jesus is able to save others in a deeper way, in a way that ultimately includes eternal life in the kingdom of God (cf. σῴζω in 10:26 with the related expressions concerning salvation in 10:17, 23–25, 30), and he is able to do so precisely because he refused to save and serve himself.

15:32 Βασιλεύς, nom. in simple appos. to Χριστός; Ἰσραήλ, gen. of subordination (Wallace 103); καταβάτω, 3rd sg. aor. act. impv. of καταβαίνω, "come down." If Jesus were to come down from the cross, the religious leaders claim that they would see and believe (ἴδωμεν, 1st pl. aor. act. subjunc. of ὁράω, "see"; πιστεύσωμεν, 1st pl. aor. act. subjunc. of πιστεύω, "believe"; for both vbs., subjunc. in a purpose ἵνα clause [Decker 2:256]). In the context of Mark's narrative, the irony is that if Jesus had not gone the way of the cross, their faith would have been useless. At the end of v. 32, Mark portrays Jesus as completely rejected at the cross, even by those who were crucified with him (συνεσταυρωμένοι, nom. pl. masc. of pf. pass. ptc. of συσταυρόω, "crucify with"; subst. ptc.; ὠνείδιζον, 3rd pl. impf. act. indic. of ὀνειδίζω, "heap insults on, revile so as to bring shame," BDAG 710c).

15:33 Γενομένης, gen. sg. fem. of aor. mid. ptc. of dep. γίνομαι, "come, arrive" (BDAG 197c); gen. abs.; temp. adv. ptc. antecedent; ἕκτης, gen. sg. fem. of ἕκτος, -η, -ον, "sixth" (on ὥρα with an ordinal numeral as def., see 15:25); ἐγένετο, 3rd sg. aor. mid. indic. of dep. γίνομαι, "come, arise, develop" (BDAG 197b); on γῆ as mng. "region, territory, land," see LN 1.79 (cf. Strauss 701); ἕως, used as a prep. taking a gen. obj.; ἐνάτης, gen. sg. fem. of ἔνατος, -η, -ον, "ninth." Back in 13:24, Jesus predicted that the sun would be darkened (σκοτισθήσεται), symbolizing the eschatological judgment at the end of the age (cf. Isa 13:9–10; 24:23; Joel 2:10; 3:15; Amos 5:18–20; 8:9; Zeph 1:14–15). In the same way, the darkness (σκότος) at the time of the crucifixion functions as a symbolic expression of God's judgment, both as experienced by the Messiah at that moment and as previewing the coming judgment at the end of the age.

15:34 Various factors cause this v. to stand out prominently in the context of Mark's crucifixion account. This is the first time that Jesus's name is directly mentioned in the crucifixion scene. The last time Jesus's name appeared in the narrative was back in 15:15, when Pilate handed Jesus over to be crucified. In addition, the last time Jesus spoke was also back at his trial before Pilate (15:2). From that point on, Jesus has nothing else to say to anyone for the rest of Mark's Gospel, except for this one question to God in v. 34. Ἐνάτῃ, dat. sg. fem. of ἔνατος, -η, -ον, "ninth"; ὥρα, dat. of time (the art. τῇ is anaphoric, since otherwise ὥρα with an ordinal numeral would not take an art., T 178–79); ἐβόησεν, 3rd sg. aor. act. indic. of βοάω, "cry out, shout"; φωνῇ, dat. of means. The vb. βοάω generally indicates a cry marked by strong emotion, often a pleading call for help from someone who is in distress or anguish (a use esp. common in the LXX; see, e.g., Num 12:13; 1 Kgdms 12:10; 2 Kgdms 22:7; Neh 9:4; Isa 58:9; Hab 1:2; 1 Macc 3:50; cf. BDAG 180a; MM 113). Mark also emphasizes Jesus's cry about being forsaken by God, by first quoting it in Aram. and then translating it into Gk. (on the Aram., see Douglas J. Moo, *The Old Testament in the Gospel Passion Narratives* [Sheffield, UK: Almond, 1983], 264–68; on ὅ ἐστιν as a set phrase, see 3:17; μεθερμηνευόμενον, nom. sg. neut. of pres. pass. ptc. of μεθερμηνεύω, "translate"; on μεθερμηνευόμενον as a periph. ptc., see 5:41; θεός, nom. for voc.; εἰς τί, "why?" [BDAG 290d; see also 14:4]; ἐγκατέλιπες, 2nd sg. aor. act. indic. of ἐγκαταλείπω, "forsake, abandon").

15:35 Παρεστηκότων, gen. pl. masc. of pf. act. ptc. of παρίστημι, "be present, stand nearby" (pres. tense intrans. use with pf. [BDAG 778c–d; ZG 163]); subst. ptc. and partitive gen.; ἀκούσαντες, nom. pl. masc. of aor. act. ptc. of ἀκούω, "hear"; temp. adv. ptc. antecedent. Certain bystanders, who thought that Jesus was crying out to Elijah for help, called on others to see the situation as they saw it (ἴδε, "look, behold" [on ἴδε, see 1:2]). According to the next verse, one individual decided to act on their inordinate misunderstanding and to use it as an opportunity to mock Jesus further.

15:36 Δραμών, nom. sg. masc. of aor. act. ptc. of τρέχω, "run"; γεμίσας, nom. sg. masc. of aor. act. ptc. of γεμίζω, "fill"; σπόγγον, acc. sg. masc. of σπόγγος, -ου, ὁ, "sponge"; ὄξους, gen. sg. neut. of ὄξος, -ους, τό, "sour wine, wine vinegar"; gen. of content. Sour wine (ὄξος) was not of the same quality as regular wine (οἶνος), but it was less expensive and therefore common among people at the lower economic levels of society as a useful drink for quenching thirst (BDAG 715b). Περιθείς, nom. sg. masc. of aor. act. ptc. of περιτίθημι, "put on"; καλάμῳ, dat. sg. masc. of κάλαμος, -ου, ὁ, "stick, reed, staff"; dat. dir. obj. (περιτίθημι often takes a dat. obj. indicating on whom or what an acc. obj. is placed, which in this context is an implied αὐτόν [cf. 15:17]); the three participles—δραμών, γεμίσας, and περιθείς—each function as a temp. adv. ptc. expressing antecedent time; ἐπότιζεν, 3rd sg. impf. act. indic. of ποτίζω, "give to drink, offer a drink"; λέγων, nom. sg. masc. of pres. act. ptc. of λέγω, "say"; temp. adv. ptc. contemp. It is possible to translate ἄφετε ἴδωμεν as two commands or only as one:

1. As two commands: "Leave him alone! Let's see . . ." (NET; cf. NIV).
*2. As one command: "Let's see . . ." (CSB; cf. NASB).

A 2nd pers., sg. or pl., impv. form of ἀφίημι can serve to introduce a hort. subjunc. and identify it as such (BDAG 157b; BDF §364; MM 97; R 430, 931–32). A similar example in the sg. occurs with ἄφες ἐκβάλω in Matt 7:4 and Luke 6:42 where ἄφες signals that the next word ἐκβάλω is a hort. subjunc., so that the two words should be taken together as "let me take it out." In the same way, ἄφετε (2nd pl. aor. act. impv. of ἀφίημι, "let") and ἴδωμεν (1st pl. aor. act. subjunc. of ὁράω, "see"; hort. subjunc.) are best translated in combination with one another as "let us see" (Cranfield 459). Εἰ, "whether" (when introducing an indir. question [see 10:2]); ἔρχεται, 3rd sg. pres. mid. indic. of dep. ἔρχομαι, "come"; futuristic pres.; καθελεῖν, aor. act. inf. of καθαιρέω, "take down"; purpose inf.

15:37 In the present v., Mark seems to resume where he left off in v. 34, i.e., before he interrupted the narrative sequence in vv. 35–36 to describe the reaction of the bystanders. Therefore, the ptc. clause ἀφεὶς φωνὴν μεγάλην (ἀφείς, nom. sg. masc. of aor. act. ptc. of ἀφίημι, "utter, give up" [BDAG 156c]; temp. adv. ptc. antecedent) is likely a back reference to Jesus's cry in v. 34 rather than a second cry (Marcus 2:1056; cf. the similarity in language between φωνῇ μεγάλῃ and φωνὴν μεγάλην). Mark used a similar dbl. reference in vv. 24, 25 to Jesus's crucifixion (καὶ σταυροῦσιν αὐτόν in v. 24 with καὶ ἐσταύρωσαν αὐτόν in v. 25; in this instance a description of the division of Jesus's clothes interrupts the narrative flow before the second reference to Jesus's crucifixion resumes the story). The implication is that Jesus only speaks once from the cross in

Mark's Gospel, with an anguished question directed toward God concerning his aban-
donment. Ἐξέπνευσεν, 3rd sg. aor. act. indic. of ἐκπνέω, "expire, breathe one's last"
(fig. expression for "die," BDAG 308d; LN 23.103).

15:38 Καταπέτασμα, nom. sg. neut. of καταπέτασμα, -ατος, τό, "curtain, veil"; ἐσχίσθη,
3rd sg. aor. pass. indic. of σχίζω, "tear"; ἄνωθεν, adv. mng. "from above" (the prep.
ἀπό serves to strengthen the -θεν suffix; therefore, ἀπ᾽ ἄνωθεν as whole means "from
above"; cf. ἀπὸ μακρόθεν in 5:6; see Taylor 597); κάτω, adv. mng. "downwards, down"
(adv. functioning as a subst. and as the obj. of the prep. ἕως, "until the bottom"; cf. ἕως
τοῦ νῦν in 13:19; the entire phrase ἀπ᾽ ἄνωθεν ἕως κάτω can be translated "from top to
bottom" [BDAG 92b, 535c]). In the LXX, καταπέτασμα is used both for the curtain at
the entrance into the holy place (e.g., Exod 26:37) and for the curtain that separated
the most holy place (or Holy of Holies) from the holy place (e.g., Exod 26:33). In
addition, in Josephus's description of the temple, καταπέτασμα refers to both the outer
curtain (*J.W.* 5.5.4 §212) and the inner one (*J.W.* 5.5.5 §219). Therefore, it would be
impossible just based on the usage of the word καταπέτασμα itself to determine which
curtain Mark had in mind. The vb. σχίζω only appears twice in Mark, both times for
acts of God, for the tearing of the heavens at Jesus's baptism (1:10) and for the tearing
of the temple's curtain at Jesus's death (15:38).

15:39 Ἰδών, nom. sg. masc. of aor. act. ptc. of ὁράω, "see"; temp. adv. ptc. antecedent;
κεντυρίων, nom. sg. masc. of κεντυρίων, -ωνος, ὁ, "centurion" (an officer in the Roman
army who presided over a division of about 100 men [BDAG 299a; *EDNT* 1:405] and
in this context probably the officer in charge of the detachment of soldiers carrying out
the crucifixion [Strauss 705]); παρεστηκώς, nom. sg. masc. of pf. act. ptc. of παρίστημι,
"be present, stand nearby" (pres. tense intrans. use with pf., BDAG 778c–d); adj. ptc.;
ἐναντίας, gen. sg. fem. of ἐναντίος, -α, -ον, "opposite" (but the entire prep. phrase ἐξ
ἐναντίας also means "opposite" [BDAG 296b, 331a]); ἐξέπνευσεν, 3rd sg. aor. act.
indic. of ἐκπνέω, "expire, breathe one's last"; ἀληθῶς, adv. mng. "in truth, truly"; ἦν,
3rd sg. impf. act. indic. of εἰμί, "be." There are only two times in Mark's Gospel when
a human character—outside of Jesus himself—declares the identity of Jesus, when
Peter confesses him to be the Christ in 8:29 and when the centurion confesses him to
be υἱὸς θεοῦ in 15:39. Together these two confessions correspond to Mark's own initial
identification of Jesus in 1:1 (Ἰησοῦ Χριστοῦ υἱοῦ θεοῦ).

The pred. nom. υἱὸς θεοῦ in 15:39 fits with both Apollonius's Canon and Colwell's
construction. According to Apollonius's Canon, in a gen. phrase with two nouns the
head noun and the gen. noun normally either both have or both lack the art. (e.g., ὁ υἱὸς
τοῦ θεοῦ [3:11] or υἱὸς θεοῦ [15:39]; Moule 114–15; T 179–80; Wallace 239–40; KMP
161). The vast majority of such phrases in Mark's Gospel follow Apollonius's Canon,
with the only fairly common exception involving the use of an anar. proper name as
the gen. noun when the head noun has an art. (e.g., 1:29–30 [an exception not always
followed, cf., e.g., 6:3]; for others, see Sanford D. Hull, "Exceptions to Apollonius'
Canon in the New Testament: A Grammatical Study," *TJ* 7 [1986]: 3–16). Perhaps
one other pertinent exception involves υἱὲ τοῦ θεοῦ in 5:7, where the head noun is voc.
and therefore cannot take an art. (see also 15:18). One implication of Apollonius's

Canon is that, with a noun phrase such as υἱὸς θεοῦ, both nouns or either noun could be def. even though they lack an art., depending on the context (cf. R 780; Wallace 245, 250–52; KMP 161–62). In addition, as an anar. pred. nom. that precedes the equative vb., υἱὸς θεοῦ also fits the pattern of Colwell's construction. A few other instances of Colwell's construction appear in Mark's Gospel (e.g., 2:28; 3:35; 11:32; 12:35), with the example from 12:35 (ὁ Χριστὸς υἱὸς Δαυίδ ἐστιν) serving as the closest par. to 15:39. Colwell's rule states that def. pred. nouns that precede the vb. usually lack the art. (see E. C. Colwell, "A Definite Rule for the Use of the Article in the Greek New Testament," *JBL* 52 [1933]: 12–21). One implication of Colwell's rule is that a pred. nom. that fits Colwell's construction (i.e., it is anar. and precedes the equative vb.) may be def. and can be translated that way even though it lacks the art., once again depending on the context (cf. Colwell 20). The context of Mark's Gospel as a whole certainly suggests that υἱὸς θεοῦ in the centurion's confession should be regarded as a def. expression, since it is def. elsewhere in Mark (e.g., 3:11; 14:62) and since God's own perspective is that Jesus is "the Son" (1:11; 9:7). Because the consistent pattern in Mark's Gospel is to present Jesus as "the Son of God," it is unlikely that Mark would use the centurion's confession at a high point toward the end of his Gospel to introduce a different concept using the words υἱὸς θεοῦ (for a similar argument, see Philip G. Davis, "Mark's Christological Paradox," *JSNT* 35 [1989]: 3–18, esp. 11–12).

15:40 At the very end of the crucifixion scene, Mark introduces certain women followers of Jesus, while noting three from the group in particular who will have an important role in the final part of the narrative as witnesses to the death, burial, and resurrection of Jesus. Ἦσαν, 3rd pl. impf. act. indic. of εἰμί, "be"; 1st and 2nd use of καί, adjunctive; μακρόθεν, adv. used in combination with the prep. ἀπό so that the whole phrase means "from far away, from a distance" (see 5:6); θεωροῦσαι, nom. pl. fem. of pres. act. ptc. of θεωρέω, "look on, watch, observe"; periph. ptc. In this context, the impf. periph. cstr. portrays the action as in progress, while also leaving the impression that the women were watching for an extended period of time (see 1:22). Ἰακώβου and Ἰωσῆτος, gen. of relationship; μικροῦ, may indicate that James was younger in age or shorter in stature (BDAG 651a; LN 67.116, 81.13).

15:41 Ἦν, 3rd sg. impf. act. indic. of εἰμί, "be"; ἠκολούθουν, 3rd pl. impf. act. indic. of ἀκολουθέω, "follow"; διηκόνουν, 3rd pl. impf. act. indic. of διακονέω, "serve, render assistance to, provide for" (both ἀκολουθέω and διακονέω take a dat. dir. obj.; impf. for background information [see 1:21]). Through the use of ἠκολούθουν and διηκόνουν, Mark portrays these three women as living according to the teaching of Jesus, since they took on the task of following him (cf. ἀκολουθείτω in 8:34) and lived a life of service (cf. διάκονος in 9:35 and 10:43). Συναναβᾶσαι, nom. pl. fem. of aor. act. ptc. of συναναβαίνω, "go up with, come up with"; adj. ptc.; αὐτῷ, dat. of association (cf. R 529).

15:42 According to Deut 21:22–23, the body of an executed criminal that was hanging on a tree must be taken down and buried. To leave the corpse hanging all night would defile the land that God had given to his people (cf. Jos., *J.W.* 4.5.2 §317). Since it was already evening, the burial of Jesus was a pressing matter in order to maintain obedience to the Mosaic law (ὀψίας, gen. sg. fem. of ὀψία, -ας, ἡ, "evening" [on ὀψία as a broad temporal reference that could include the late afternoon, see 6:47 and Marcus 2:1070]; γενομένης, gen. sg. fem. of aor. mid. ptc. of dep. γίνομαι, "come to be, come" [BDAG 197c]; gen. abs.; temp. adv. ptc. antecedent). A further complicating factor was that it was the day of preparation (ἦν, 3rd sg. impf. act. indic. of εἰμί, "be"; παρασκευή, nom. sg. fem. of παρασκευή, -ῆς, ἡ, "day of preparation" [BDAG 771b; NIDNTT 3:408]), i.e., the day before the Sabbath, which would begin at sunset (on ὅ ἐστιν as a set phrase, see 3:17; προσάββατον, nom. sg. neut. of προσάββατον, -ου, τό, the day before the Sabbath).

15:43 Ἐλθών, nom. sg. masc. of aor. act. ptc. of ἔρχομαι, "come"; temp. adv. ptc. antecedent; εὐσχήμων, nom. sg. masc. of εὐσχήμων, -ον, "prominent, respected"; βουλευτής, nom. sg. masc. of βουλευτής, -οῦ, ὁ, "member of the council"; καί (1st use): adjunctive; αὐτός, intensive pron.; ἦν, 3rd sg. impf. act. indic. of εἰμί, "be"; προσδεχόμενος, nom. sg. masc. of pres. mid. ptc. of dep. προσδέχομαι, "wait for, look forward to"; periph. ptc. In this context, the impf. periph. cstr. stresses the customary nature of the action, that waiting expectantly for the kingdom of God was a consistent pattern for Joseph (see 1:22). Τολμήσας, nom. sg. masc. of aor. act. ptc. of τολμάω, "act with courage, summon up one's courage"; adv. ptc. of manner (Taylor 600); εἰσῆλθεν, 3rd sg. aor. act. indic. of εἰσέρχομαι, "enter, go"; ἠτήσατο, 3rd sg. aor. mid. indic. of αἰτέω, "ask for" (mng. with mid.; on the mid. voice with αἰτέω within legal or contractual contexts, see 6:24).

15:44 Ἐθαύμασεν, 3rd sg. aor. act. indic. of θαυμάζω, "marvel, be surprised, be astonished." At times, εἰ occurs in much the same sense as ὅτι ("that") when following a vb. or vb. phrase that expresses an emotion such as astonishment or indignation (Acts 26:8; 1 John 3:13; see Burton §277; R 965, 1024; Z §404; Cranfield 462). Τέθνηκεν, 3rd sg. pf. act. indic. of θνῄσκω, "die" (in Gk. the pf. tense in the orig. thought is retained in indir. discourse, while in Eng. it is moved back in time [see Wallace 457; Z §346; cf. 5:29]). Προσκαλεσάμενος, nom. sg. masc. of aor. mid. ptc. of προσκαλέω, "summon, call to oneself" (mng. with mid.); temp. adv. ptc. antecedent; κεντυρίωνα, acc. sg. masc. of κεντυρίων, -ωνος, ὁ, "centurion"; ἐπηρώτησεν, 3rd sg. aor. act. indic. of ἐπερωτάω, "ask"; εἰ, "whether" (after a vb. of asking to introduce an indir. question [see 10:2]); πάλαι, adv. mng. "already, some time ago"; ἀπέθανεν, 3rd sg. aor. act. indic. of ἀποθνῄσκω, "die" (on the aor. in indir. discourse, see 5:16). The adv. πάλαι is similar to ἤδη in that it can mean "already," but it seems to envision a somewhat longer time span than that suggested by ἤδη (BDAG 751b–c; LN 67.22). The point seems to be that Pilate wanted to know if Jesus had indeed died so quickly and if it had happened long enough ago to confirm that he was really dead.

15:45 Γνούς, nom. sg. masc. of aor. act. ptc. of γινώσκω, "learn, find out, ascertain" (BDAG 200a–b); temp. adv. ptc. antecedent; κεντυρίωνος, gen. sg. masc. of κεντυρίων, -ωνος, ὁ, "centurion"; ἐδωρήσατο, 3rd sg. aor. mid. indic. of dep. δωρέομαι, "grant, present"; πτῶμα, acc. sg. neut. of πτῶμα, -ατος, τό, "corpse, dead body." The art. τῷ serves to clarify that the indecl. name Ἰωσήφ is in the dat. case as the indir. obj. (on the art. with indecl. nouns, see R 760; BDF §260; Wallace 240–41). Mark does not typically use an art. with indecl. names, allowing the context to show the case (see, e.g., 1:9; 2:26; 3:22; 6:53; 10:46–48; 11:10; 12:26, 35; 15:32). Mark shifts from the word σῶμα in 15:43 to πτῶμα in 15:45. The only other time πτῶμα occurs in Mark's Gospel is in 6:29 where the disciples of John the Baptist came to take his dead body in order to place it in a tomb. Now, however, Jesus's own disciples are absent from the scene.

15:46 Ἀγοράσας, nom. sg. masc. of aor. act. ptc. of ἀγοράζω, "buy, purchase"; temp. adv. ptc. antecedent; σινδόνα, acc. sg. fem. of σινδών, -όνος, ἡ, "linen cloth"; καθελών, nom. sg. masc. of aor. act. ptc. of καθαιρέω, "take down"; temp. adv. ptc. antecedent; ἐνείλησεν, 3rd sg. aor. act. indic. of ἐνειλέω, "wrap up in"; ἔθηκεν, 3rd sg. aor. act. indic. of τίθημι, "lay, place" (see the note on the pl. form ἔθηκαν in 16:6). By using the masc. pron. αὐτόν, Mark indicates that the antecedent is not πτῶμα in v. 45 or σῶμα in v. 43, both of which are neut., but rather Ἰησοῦ in v. 43. Ἦν, 3rd sg. impf. act. indic. of εἰμί, "be"; λελατομημένον, nom. sg. neut. of pf. pass. ptc. of λατομέω, "hew, cut (out of a rock)"; periph. ptc. (on the pluperf. periph. cstr. for background information, see 1:33; 14:44); πέτρας, gen. sg. fem. of πέτρα, -ας, ἡ, "rock"; προσεκύλισεν, 3rd sg. aor. act. indic. of προσκυλίω, "roll."

15:47 On the use of the fem. art. ἡ followed by a gen. of relationship (Ἰωσῆτος) to imply "the mother," see R 501, 767; T 168; cf. Wallace 83, 235–36 (see also the similar use for ἡ in 16:1); ἐθεώρουν, 3rd pl. impf. act. indic. of θεωρέω, "watch, observe"; ποῦ, introduces an indir. question (Decker 2:270); τέθειται, 3rd sg. pf. pass. indic. of τίθημι, "lay, place" (on the pf. tense in indir. discourse, see 5:29; 15:44). As he freq. does, Mark uses an impf. vb. (here ἐθεώρουν) when providing background information that is important for the continuing narrative (see 1:21). What the women observe in ch. 15—the death and burial of Jesus—prepares the way for what they discover in ch. 16—the empty tomb.

FOR FURTHER STUDY

36. Jesus as the Son of God

Bateman IV, Herbert W. "Defining the Titles 'Christ' and 'Son of God' in Mark's Narrative Presentation of Jesus." *JETS* 50 (2007): 537–59.

Broadhead, Edwin K. "Son of God." Pages 116–23 in *Naming Jesus: Titular Christology in the Gospel of Mark*. JSNTSup 175. Sheffield, UK: Sheffield Academic Press, 1999.

Carson, D. A. *Jesus the Son of God: A Christological Title Often Overlooked, Sometimes Misunderstood, and Currently Disputed*. Wheaton, IL: Crossway, 2012.

Gamel, Brian K. *Mark 15:39 as a Markan Theology of Revelation: The Centurion's Confession as Apocalyptic Unveiling*. LNTS 574. London: Bloomsbury T&T Clark, 2017.

Gurtner, Daniel M. "The Rending of the Veil and Markan Christology: 'Unveiling' the ΥΙΟΣ ΘΕΟΥ (Mark 15:38–49)." *BibInt* 15 (2007): 292–306.

Hahn, Ferdinand. "Son of God." Pages 279–346 in *The Titles of Jesus in Christology: Their History in Early Christianity*. New York: World Publishing, 1969.

Hengel, Martin. *The Son of God: The Origin of Christology and the History of Jewish-Hellenistic Religion*. Philadelphia: Fortress, 1976.

Kingsbury, Jack Dean. "The Christology of Mark: The Davidic Messiah-King, the Son of God." Pages 47–155 in *The Christology of Mark's Gospel*. Philadelphia: Fortress, 1983.

Marcus, Joel. "Mark 14:61: 'Are You the Messiah-Son-of-God?'" *NovT* 31 (1989): 125–41.

*Yarbro Collins, Adela. "Mark and His Readers: The Son of God among Jews." *HTR* 92 (1999): 393–408.

*———. "Mark and His Readers: The Son of God among Greeks and Romans." *HTR* 93 (2000): 85–100.

Yarbro Collins, Adela, and John J. Collins. *King and Messiah as Son of God: Divine, Human, and Angelic Messianic Figures in Biblical and Related Literature*. Grand Rapids: Eerdmans, 2008.

HOMILETICAL SUGGESTIONS

The Identity of Jesus according to Mark 15

1. Jesus is the perfect king.
   a. He was not the kind of king people expected.
   b. He was the kind of king people needed.
2. Jesus is the perfect lamenter.
   a. Jesus gave himself to the full experience of our pain.
   b. Jesus stood as our representative to bring our lament to God.
   c. God was moved to compassion toward Jesus and toward all those whom he represented.

7. Resurrection (16:1–8)

The end of Mark's Gospel presents a number of interpretive problems, not the least of which is a significant text-critical problem that becomes obvious at 16:8 (for a detailed presentation of both the external and internal evidence, see James Keith Elliott, "The Text and Language of the Endings to Mark's Gospel," *TZ* [1971]: 255–62; Metzger 102–6). The issue, as is well known, is that Mark's Gospel ends in different ways in the ms. tradition: (1) The ending at 16:8 is attested by ℵ and B (the two oldest mss. of Mark's Gospel), as well as by 304 and a number of early version mss. (cf. Metzger 102). Eusebius in the early 4th cen. (in *Quaestiones ad Mariunum*) and Jerome in the early 5th cen. (in *Epistola* 120) both indicated that Mark's Gospel ended in this way in almost all of the mss. known to them. (2) One ms., the Old Latin ms. k, includes only the so-called shorter ending after 16:8, namely, a brief report of Jesus commissioning his disciples to proclaim the message of salvation throughout the world. The so-called shorter ending, which has no real claim to authenticity due to the lack of ms. evidence, is important because it serves as a further witness for the circulation of Mark's Gospel without 16:9–20. (3) The vast majority of mss. conclude with the so-called longer ending (16:9–20), although some of the mss. also contain scribal notes or symbols indicating doubt as to the authenticity of these verses (see, e.g., family 1). (4) Several witnesses (e.g., L, Ψ, 083, 099, and 579) contain the shorter ending followed by the longer ending.

The overwhelming consensus among NT scholars is that the actual writing of Mark the evangelist himself ends with 16:8 (cf. Stein 727: "The 'shorter' and 'longer' endings' of Mark are acknowledged by almost all scholars to be later additions to Mark's Gospel"). This consensus rests on several factors: the omission of 16:9–20 from the earliest mss. of Mark, the awkward transition between 16:8 and 16:9, and the distinctive vocabulary and unique uses of words in 16:9–20 when compared with the rest of Mark's Gospel (on the distinctive linguistic features of 16:9–20, see Elliott, "Text and Language," 258–62; on the likelihood that, in light of the awkward transition at v. 9, the longer ending was actually an excerpt taken from another document rather than an intentionally composed ending for Mark's Gospel, see Metzger 105; Cranfield 472). Yet this general agreement raises an important question: How should the rather abrupt ending at 16:8 with the fearful silence of the women be explained? No consensus exists on the answer to this question. Proposals include: (1) that Mark orig. wrote more after 16:8 but the final part of the ending was somehow lost; (2) that Mark was for some reason unable to finish writing his Gospel; and (3) that Mark intended to end his Gospel at 16:8—Mark ended with the fearful silence of the women because that was exactly where he wanted his audience to stop and think. Of these proposals, the last one seems to be the least speculative. Before we propose a lost ending or a different but never-written one, it seems prudent to think deeply about how the ending at 16:8 might make sense within the context of Mark's narrative (for more on the ending of Mark's Gospel and its interpretation, see Joel F. Williams, "Literary Approaches to the End of Mark's Gospel," *JETS* 42 [1999]: 21–35).

16:1 Although interpretive problems related to the ending of Mark's Gospel call for careful attention, it is important not to overlook Mark's main point of 16:1–8, which is that Jesus is alive, having been raised from the dead. Διαγενομένου, gen. sg. neut. of aor. mid. ptc. of dep. διαγίνομαι, "pass, be over"; gen. abs.; temp. adv. ptc. antecedent; on the art. with ἡ τοῦ Ἰακώβου, see 15:47; ἠγόρασαν, 3rd pl. aor. act. indic. of ἀγοράζω, "buy, purchase"; ἀρώματα, acc. pl. neut. of ἄρωμα, -ατος, τό, "fragrant spice"; ἐλθοῦσαι, nom. pl. fem. of aor. act. ptc. of ἔρχομαι, "go, come"; attendant circumstance ptc. (Wallace 644; Decker 2:271); ἀλείψωσιν, 3rd pl. aor. act. subjunc. of ἀλείφω, "anoint"; subjunc. in a purpose ἵνα clause. Anointing a body with fragrant spices or perfumes as part of the burial process was an act of devotion intended to honor the dead by offsetting the odor of decomposition (cf. Lane 585).

16:2 Mark uses temp. references at the beginning and end of v. 2 to show that the women came to the tomb as soon as possible on Sunday morning but also at a time when the darkness of night was passing and the circumstances at the tomb were visible. Λίαν, adv. mng. "very, exceedingly"; πρωΐ, adv. mng. "early, early in the morning"; μιᾷ, dat. of time (BDF §200; on the cardinal number ["one"] for the ordinal ["first"], see R 671–72; T 187; Z §154; an implied ἡμέρᾳ explains the use of the fem. form μιᾷ

[Decker 2:271]; on the pl. of σάββατον as "week," see BDAG 910a); ἔρχονται, 3rd pl. pres. mid. indic. of dep. ἔρχομαι, "go, come"; historical pres. (expressing a shift in location [see 1:12]); on ἐπί for movement leading to or close to something, see BDAG 364c; ἀνατείλαντος, gen. sg. masc. of aor. act. ptc. of ἀνατέλλω, "rise, dawn"; gen. abs.; temp. adv. ptc. antecedent (on the aor. with a temp. adv. ptc., see 1:5). Normally in Mark, a gen. abs. ptc. precedes the main vb., but here (and in 4:35) it follows the vb. (BDF §423; T 322).

16:3 Ἑαυτάς, "one another" (see 1:27); ἀποκυλίσει, 3rd sg. fut. act indic. of ἀποκυλίω, "roll away"; ἡμῖν, dat. of interest (advantage); μνημείου, partitive gen. When the women ask their question about who will roll away the stone for them, it does not necessarily betray a foolish lack of planning on their part. Instead, their words may have been intended not as a real question but as a rhetorical one, an expression of their grief over their misfortune and their painful awareness that they had no one to help them (Marcus 2:1079–80).

16:4 Ἀναβλέψασαι, nom. pl. fem. of aor. act. ptc. of ἀναβλέπω, "look up"; temp. adv. ptc. antecedent. At times, Mark uses a historical pres. vb. to describe a particularly dramatic event in a vivid way (see 1:12), and that seems to be the case with θεωροῦσιν, which portrays the action as though we are noticing the open tomb at the same time as the women (cf. Fanning 233). Ἀποκεκύλισται, 3rd sg. pf. pass. indic. of ἀποκυλίω, "roll away" (on the pf. tense in indir. discourse, see 5:29; 15:44). Mark sometimes uses γάρ to introduce a narrative aside, a brief explanation rather than a direct reason for a preceding statement (γάρ, "now" [cf. BDAG 189d]; see 1:16). Here the explanation—that the stone was extremely large (ἦν, 3rd sg. impf. act. indic. of εἰμί, "be"; σφόδρα, adv. mng. "extremely, very")—seems more immediately relevant as a clarification for why the women were concerned about the stone in the first place back in v. 3. However, Mark waits until after the women recognize that it has already been moved in v. 4 to introduce the clarification, apparently to emphasize the significance of what just took place (Hooker 384).

16:5 Εἰσελθοῦσαι, nom. pl. fem. of aor. act. ptc. of εἰσέρχομαι, "go into, enter"; temp. adv. ptc. antecedent; εἶδον, 3rd pl. aor. act. indic. of ὁράω, "see"; νεανίσκον, acc. sg. masc. of νεανίσκος, -ου, ὁ, "young man." Mark uses "young man" as a way to refer to an angel (Evans 535–36; France 678–79), evidently to narrate the scene from the perspective of the women—that was how he appeared to the women (cf. the similar use of νεανίσκος in Jos., Ant. 5.6.2 §213; 5.8.3 §279 and of the synonym νεανίας [also "young man"] in 2 Macc 3:26, 33; Jos., Ant. 5.8.2 §277). Καθήμενον, acc. sg. masc. of pres. mid. ptc. of dep. κάθημαι, "sit"; supplementary (complementary) ptc.; on the pl. with δεξιοῖς where Eng. uses the sg., see R 408; BDF §141; περιβεβλημένον, acc. sg. masc. of pf. mid. ptc. of περιβάλλω, "wear, put something on oneself" (mng. with mid., BDAG 799c); adj. ptc. without an art. to modify an anar. noun; στολήν, acc. sg. fem. of στολή, -ῆς, ἡ, "long, flowing robe"; λευκήν, acc. sg. fem. of λευκός, -ή, -όν, "white"; ἐξεθαμβήθησαν, 3rd pl. aor. pass. indic. of ἐκθαμβέω, "be overwhelmed, be alarmed" (mng. with pass.).

16:6 On ὁ δέ, see 1:45; λέγει, historical pres. (see 1:12, 30); ἐκθαμβεῖσθε, 2nd pl. pres. pass. impv. of ἐκθαμβέω, "be overwhelmed, be alarmed" (mng. with pass.; pres. tense prohibition used for a specific command likely to call for the stop of an action already in progress [cf. Fanning 335–37, 364–65]); ἐσταυρωμένον, acc. sg. masc. of pf. pass. ptc. of σταυρόω, "crucify"; adj. ptc.; ἠγέρθη, 3rd sg. aor. pass. indic. of ἐγείρω, "raise"; consummative aor. Although a pass. form of ἐγείρω can express an act. intrans. mng. ("he has risen"; cf. 2:12; 4:27; 13:8, 22; 14:42), it seems to be used with a pass. mng. in Mark when referring to the resurrection from the dead, thereby drawing some attention to resurrection as an act of God ("he has been raised"; cf. 6:14, 16; 12:26; 14:28; 16:6; see Cranfield 466; Hooker 385). Ἴδε, "look, behold" (see 1:2); τόπος, nom. of exclamation (Wallace 59–60; cf. 3:34; 13:1); ἔθηκαν, 3rd pl. aor. act. indic. of τίθημι, "lay, place" (the pl. with ἔθηκαν makes clear what was not directly stated in 15:46 but perhaps should have been obvious, that Joseph of Arimathea had help in burying Jesus). The resurrection of Jesus is the reason why it is no longer the time for fearful alarm. He was condemned to death and crucified as a messianic pretender, but the resurrection is God's vindication of Jesus—he is indeed the Christ, the King of Israel (15:26, 31–32). The resurrection is also God's acknowledgment and acceptance of Jesus's service on behalf of his people. He served them by doing what they could not do for themselves (10:45), taking the cup of God's judgment (14:36), and bearing the pain of being forsaken by God (15:34).

16:7 Ὑπάγετε, 2nd pl. pres. act. impv. of ὑπάγω, "go, depart" (on the pres. impv. of ὑπάγω, see 2:11); εἴπατε, 2nd pl. aor. act. impv. of λέγω, "say, tell"; ὅτι, introduces dir. discourse; προάγει, from προάγω, "go before, go ahead of" (προάγει is a type of futuristic pres., i.e., the action, which is already happening, will reach its completion in the fut. [see Fanning 221–23; Wallace 537; cf. 10:33; 14:21]); ὄψεσθε, 2nd pl. fut. mid. indic. of ὁράω, "see" (dep. in fut.). The purpose for the predicted meeting between Jesus and his disciples in Galilee is apparently to restore the disciples' relationship with Jesus after their failure and to prepare them once again to be his followers as "fishers of people" (1:16–20). This promise of restoration is implied in Jesus's words in 14:27–28. There, Jesus's prediction of a meeting in Galilee after the resurrection (14:28) stands in direct contrast to his immediately preceding prediction concerning the failure and scattering of the disciples (14:27). Therefore, the predicted meeting in Galilee is a time for the shepherd to gather together his scattered sheep, a time for Jesus to regroup and restore his failed disciples. This promised meeting would undoubtedly take place because the promise is based on the word of Jesus.

16:8 Ἐξελθοῦσαι, nom. pl. fem. of aor. act. ptc. of ἐξέρχομαι, "come out, go out"; temp. adv. ptc. antecedent; ἔφυγον, 3rd pl. aor. act. indic. of φεύγω, "flee"; εἶχεν, 3rd sg. impf. act. indic. of ἔχω, "hold, seize, grip" (BDAG 420d–21a; εἶχεν is a sg. vb. with a compound subj. [see 12:33]); τρόμος, nom. sg. masc. of τρόμος, -ου, ὁ, "trembling"; ἔκστασις, nom. sg. fem. of ἔκστασις, -εως, ἡ, "amazement, astonishment"; οὐδενὶ οὐδέν, dbl. neg. used to strengthen a statement (see 1:44); ἐφοβοῦντο, 3rd pl. impf. pass. indic. of φοβέομαι, "fear, be afraid" (for other places in Mark where φοβέομαι is used abs., i.e., without a dir. obj. or modifying clause, see 5:15, 33, 36; 6:50; 10:32). At times, Mark uses impf. vbs. for particularly dramatic actions to portray them vividly as though they were in progress (see 1:21), which seems to be the purpose for Mark's use of the impf. in v. 8 with εἶχεν and ἐφοβοῦντο, both of which point to particularly striking responses on the part of the women.

Interpreters sometimes offer various opinions on the question: "Is it possible for a book to end with the conj. γάρ as the last word?" From a grammatical standpoint the answer is straightforward: "if a sentence can end with γάρ, a book can end with such a sentence" (P. W. van der Horst, "Can a Book End with ΓΑΡ? A Note on Mark XVI. 88," *JTS* 23 [1972]: 122)—and without question, a sentence can end with γάρ. Since γάρ is a postpos. conj., it never comes first in a clause, appearing normally as the second word in the clause (R 424; BDF §475; γάρ occasionally comes third in Mark [e.g., 1:38; 9:34; 13:33]). In a two-word sentence containing this conj., γάρ necessarily ends the sentence. One relevant example appears in Gen 18:15 LXX, which gives the reason for Sarah's dishonesty with a two-word sentence: ἐφοβήθη γάρ "for she was afraid" (for other examples, see BDAG 189a–b; for a more extensive study of sentences ending with γάρ and the role that genre may or may not have played in their use, see Kelly R. Iverson, "A Further Word on Final Γάρ [Mark 16:8]," *CBQ* 68 [2006]: 79–94). Moreover, Mark is not opposed to using brief γάρ clauses. Although no other two-word γάρ clauses appear in Mark's Gospel, three-word (1:16; 9:6; 11:18) and four-word (1:38; 3:21; 5:42; 9:49; 14:70; 15:14; 16:4) γάρ clauses do. Two of such examples are in fact similar in vocabulary to the last sentence in 16:8: ἔκφοβοι γάρ ἐγένοντο ("for they became very much afraid"; 9:6) and ἐφοβοῦντο γάρ αὐτόν ("for they were afraid of him"; 11:18; of course, Mark can also use short clauses with other conjunctions; see, e.g., καὶ ἐφοβήθησαν in 5:15). In terms of grammar, nothing stands in the way of regarding the last brief γάρ clause in 16:8 as the intended ending of Mark's Gospel.

If Mark's Gospel did orig. end with the women fleeing in fearful silence, what is the significance of that ending? Perhaps the key to any adequate solution to this challenging exegetical problem involves finding a careful balance between the certainty of the promise conveyed in 16:7 and the apparent disobedience of the women in 16:8 (see Andrew T. Lincoln, "The Promise and the Failure: Mark 16:7, 8," *JBL* 108 [1989]: 283–300; cf. Williams, "Literary Approaches," 33–35). It is difficult to take the response of the women at the tomb in 16:8 as anything other than a failure on their part, at least an initial failure. The flight (ἔφυγον) of the women from the tomb recalls the cowardly desertion (ἔφυγον) of the disciples at the arrest of Jesus (14:50; cf. also ἔφυγεν in 14:52). The angel commanded the women to stop being alarmed, since the resurrection of Jesus gives them every reason for hope, but the level of emotion for the women only increases, and a trembling alarm takes hold of them. It is true that the silence of the women was likely not unending, but since it immediately follows the young man's command to go and tell, this silence reads like an initial response of disobedience, all the more so because it arises out of fear (cf. 4:40–41; 6:50; 9:32; 10:32). Does the disobedient silence of the women in 16:8 negate the implied promise of restoration in 16:7? No, the promise of restoration for the disciples holds true, because it is based on the words of Jesus (14:27–28) and because it is necessary to account for the post-resurrection ministry of the disciples (10:35–40; 13:9–13). Mark's Gospel never describes how the immediate silence of the women is overcome, but the truth of the promised restoration remains certain. Does the certainty of the promise in 16:7 negate the significance of the women's disobedience in 16:8? No, their reaction stands as an important warning that fear and failure are continuing possibilities for followers of Jesus even after the resurrection. Therefore, Mark's Gospel ends with both an encouragement and a warning: Jesus has the power to forgive; his followers have the potential to fail.

FOR FURTHER STUDY

37. The Ending of Mark's Gospel

Black, David Alan, ed. *Perspectives on the Ending of Mark: 4 Views*. Nashville: B&H Academic, 2008.

Boomershine, Thomas E. "Mark 16:8 and the Apostolic Commission." *JBL* 100 (1981): 225–39.

Boomershine, Thomas E., and Gilbert L. Bartholomew, "The Narrative Technique of Mark 16:8." *JBL* 100 (1981): 213–23.

Catchpole, David. "The Fearful Silence of the Women at the Tomb: A Study in Markan Theology." *JTSA* 18 (1977): 3–10.

Croy, N. Clayton. *The Mutilation of Mark's Gospel*. Nashville: Abingdon, 2003.

Elliott, James Keith. "The Text and Language of the Endings to Mark's Gospel." *TZ* 27 (1971): 255–62.

Farmer, William R. *The Last Twelve Verses of Mark*. SNTSMS 25. Cambridge: Cambridge University Press, 1974.

Gaventa, Beverly Roberts, and Patrick D. Miller, eds. *The Ending of Mark and the Ends of God: Essays in Memory of Donald Harrisville Juel*. Louisville: Westminster John Knox, 2005.

Iverson, Kelly R. "A Further Word on Final Γάρ (Mark 16:8)." *CBQ* 68 (2006): 79–94.

Knox, Wilfred Lawrence. "The Ending of St. Mark's Gospel." *HTR* 35 (1942): 13–23.

Lincoln, Andrew T. "The Promise and the Failure: Mark 16:7, 8." *JBL* 108 (1989): 283–300.

Magness, J. Lee. *Sense and Absence: Structure and Suspension in the Ending of Mark's Gospel*. Semeia Studies. Atlanta: Scholars Press, 1986.

Osborne, Grant R. *The Resurrection Narratives: A Redactional Study*. Grand Rapids: Baker, 1984.

Peterson, Norman R. "When Is the End Not the End? Literary Reflections on the Ending of Mark's Narrative." *Int* 34 (1980): 151–66.

Stein, Robert H. "The Ending of Mark." *BBR* 18 (2008): 79–98.

van der Horst, P. W. "Can a Book End with ΓΑΡ? A Note on Mark XVI. 8." *JTS* 23 (1972): 121–24.

*Williams, Joel F. "Literary Approaches to the End of Mark's Gospel." *JETS* 42 (1999): 21–35.

HOMILETICAL SUGGESTIONS

He Is Risen Indeed (16:1–8)

1. The truth of the resurrection
   a. The announcement of the angel
   b. The evidence of the empty tomb
   c. The eyewitness of the women
   d. The fulfillment of Jesus's promise
2. The significance of the resurrection
   a. The cup: The resurrection proves that Jesus indeed bore the judgment for our sins. (14:36)
   b. The charge: The resurrection proves that Jesus actually is the messianic king. (15:26)
   c. The cry: The resurrection proves that the followers of Jesus will never be forsaken by God. (15:34)

Exegetical Outline

I. Jesus as the Powerful Messiah (1:1–8:26)
   A. The Beginning of Jesus's Ministry: Preparation in the Wilderness
      (1:1–13)
      1. Opening (1:1)
      2. John the Baptist's Preaching in the Wilderness (1:2–4)
      3. John the Baptist's Baptizing Ministry in the Jordan (1:5–8)
      4. Jesus's Baptism in the Jordan (1:9–11)
      5. Jesus's Temptation in the Wilderness (1:12–13)
   B. Jesus's Initial Ministry in Galilee (1:14–3:35)
      1. Summary and Initial Response (1:14–45)
         (a) [Transition] Summary of Jesus's Preaching in Galilee (1:14–15)
         (b) Calling of Disciples: The Inner Circle (1:16–20)
         (c) One Day in Capernaum (1:21–39)
         (d) Healing of the Leper (1:40–45)
      2. Controversy with Religious Leaders (2:1–3:6)
         (a) Conflict over Healing and Forgiving Sin (2:1–12)
         (b) Conflict over Eating with Sinners (2:13–17)
         (c) Conflict over Fasting (2:18–22)
         (d) Conflict over Eating on the Sabbath (2:23–28)
         (e) Conflict over Healing on the Sabbath (3:1–6)
      3. Summary and Initial Decision (3:7–35)
         (a) Summary of Jesus's Healing in Galilee (3:7–12)
         (b) Calling of Disciples: The Twelve (3:13–19)
         (c) Rejection by Jesus's Family and by the Scribes (3:20–30)
         (d) Jesus's True Family (3:31–35)
   C. Jesus's Ministry on and around the Sea of Galilee (4:1–8:26)
      1. Cycle 1: Calming of the Sea (4:1–5:20)
         (a) [Transition] Jesus's Ministry to the Crowd: The Parables
             Discourse (4:1–34)
             (i)   The Parable of the Soils (4:1–20)
             (ii) Encouragements to Listen (4:21–25)
             (iii) The Parable of the Seed Growing by Itself (4:26–29)

      (iv) The Parable of the Mustard Seed (4:30–32)

      (v) Summary of Jesus's Teaching through Parables (4:33–34)

    (b) First Boat Scene: Stilling of the Storm (4:35–41)

    (c) Healing of the Gerasene Demoniac (5:1–20)

  2. Interval: Faith and Unbelief (5:21–6:29)

    (a) The Faith of the Hemorrhaging Woman and Jairus (5:21–43)

    (b) Unbelief at Nazareth (6:1–6)

    (c) Mission of the Disciples and the Unbelief of Herod (6:7–29)

  3. Cycle 2: Walking on the Sea (6:30–56)

    (a) Jesus's Ministry to the Crowd: Feeding of the Five Thousand (6:30–44)

    (b) Second Boat Scene: Walking on the Water (6:45–52)

    (c) Healing at Gennesaret (6:53–56)

  4. Interval: Matters of the Heart (7:1–37)

    (a) Dispute over Tradition (7:1–23)

    (b) Healing of a Gentile Woman's Daughter (7:24–30)

    (c) Healing of a Gentile Who Is Deaf (7:31–37)

  5. Cycle 3: Conversation on the Sea (8:1–26)

    (a) Jesus's Ministry to the Crowd: Feeding of the Four Thousand (8:1–9)

    (b) Test from the Pharisees (8:10–13)

    (c) Third Boat Scene: Warning about Leaven (8:14–21)

    (d) [Transition] Healing of the Blind Man of Bethsaida (8:22–26)

II. Jesus as the Suffering Son of God (8:27–16:8)

  A. Jesus's Ministry on the Way to Jerusalem (8:27–10:52)

    1. Cycle 1: Prediction and Response (8:27–38)

      (a) First Passion Prediction (8:27–31)

      (b) Misunderstanding by the Disciples: Rebuke of Peter (8:32–33)

      (c) Jesus's Instructions on Discipleship: Taking Up the Cross (8:34–38)

    2. Interval: What Followers of Jesus Can Expect (9:1–29)

      (a) The Transfiguration (9:1–8)

      (b) Teaching on Elijah (9:9–13)

      (c) Healing of the Possessed Boy (9:14–29)

    3. Cycle 2: Prediction and Response (9:30–50)

      (a) Second Passion Prediction (9:30–32)

      (b) Misunderstanding by the Disciples: Debate about the Greatest (9:33–34)

      (c) Jesus's Instructions on Discipleship: Learning to Be Last (9:35–50)

    4. Interval: What Jesus Expects of His Followers (10:1–31)

      (a) Teaching on Divorce (10:1–12)

      (b) Children and the Kingdom (10:13–16)

      (c) The Rich Man (10:17–31)

    5. Cycle 3: Prediction and Response (10:32–45)

      (a) Third Passion Prediction (10:32–34)

      (b) Misunderstanding by the Disciples: Request of James and John (10:35–41)

      (c) Jesus's Instructions on Discipleship: Learning to Be a Servant (10:42–45)

      (d) [Transition] Healing of Blind Bartimaeus (10:46–52)

B. Jesus's Ministry at the Temple (11:1–13:37)

    1. First Trip to the Temple (11:1–11)

      (a) Travel to the Temple: The Triumphal Entry (11:1–10)

      (b) Observation of the Temple and Departure to Bethany (11:11)

    2. Second Trip to the Temple (11:12–19)

      (a) Travel to the Temple: Cursing of the Fig Tree (11:12–14)

      (b) Cleansing of the Temple (11:15–18)

      (c) Departure out of the City (11:19)

    3. Third Trip to the Temple (11:20–13:37)

      (a) Travel to the Temple: Cursed Fig Tree and the Prayer of Faith (11:20–26)

      (b) Teaching in the Temple (11:27–12:44)

         (i)   Question and Parable about Jesus's Authority (11:27–12:12)

         (ii) Question about Taxes (12:13–17)

         (iii) Question about the Resurrection (12:18–27)

         (iv) Question about the Greatest Commandment (12:28–34)

         (v) Critique of the Teaching of the Scribes (12:35–37)

         (vi) Critique of the Behavior of the Scribes (12:38–40)

         (vii) Commendation of Sacrificial Devotion (12:41–44)

      (c) [Transition] Departure out of the Temple and Prediction of Its Destruction: The Eschatological Discourse (13:1–37)

         (i)   The Prediction of the Temple's Destruction (13:1–4)

         (ii) The Beginning of Woes (13:5–13)

         (iii) The Days of the Tribulation (13:14–23)

         (iv) The Coming of the Son of Man (13:24–27)

         (v) Warnings to Be Ready (13:28–37)

C. Jesus's Death on the Cross and Resurrection in Jerusalem (14:1–16:8)

    1. Anointing at Bethany and Betrayal Plot (14:1–11)

    2. The Last Supper (14:12–25)

    3. Prayer and Arrest at Gethsemane (14:26–52)

    4. Trial before the Sanhedrin and Denials by Peter (14:53–72)

    5. Trial before Pilate and Mocking by Soldiers (15:1–20)

    6. Crucifixion and Burial (15:21–47)

    7. Resurrection (16:1–8)

Grammar Index

Scripture Index